Central and Eastern Europe, 1944–1993

This major comparative analysis of the state socialist experim
Central and Eastern Europe is based on a complex examin
political and economic history. Ivan Berend, with an insight d
through personal experience, follows a consistent *longue*
comparative approach, which connects the remote past with
in a unique way. The communist modernization attempt, ext   ly
ruthless in its first period and oppressive right up to its collapse,   t in
the broad framework of a semi-successful modernization of the region in
the previous century.

Berend links the internal social basis of the communist regimes
(especially broad in the Balkans) to the relative economic–social
backwardness of the region. The temporary success of the socialist
experiment generated a catch-up process, societal security, and consequently, transient legitimization for the regimes. Their subsequent
erosion and collapse, based on technological-structural changes and a
structural crisis, are also presented in their economic, social, and political
complexity, including social and generational changes, the role of
"moral virus" of the opposition, the regimes' inability to adjust, and the
repeated use of the nationalist card. In Berend's view, the post-communist
transformation is closely connected to long-term historical processes
and the countries' repeated efforts to come to terms with their peripheral
position in relation to Europe.

This book is distinguished by its unique complexity of time, region,
and theme. It covers the history of Central and Eastern Europe from the
birth of state socialism to its collapse, and the subsequent movement
toward parliamentary, market systems. Berend's method is consistently
thematic (not, as is usual, country-by-country), and his analysis
encompasses economic, social, political, and cultural issues. It is a major
contribution to the economic history of the twentieth century.

Cambridge Studies in Modern Economic History

Cambridge Studies in Modern Economic History is a major new initiative in economic history publishing, and a flagship series for Cambridge University Press in an area of scholarly activity in which it has long been active. Books in this series will primarily be concerned with the history of economic performance, output and productivity, assessing the characteristics, causes and consequences of economic growth (and stagnation) in the western world. This range of enquiry, rather than any one methodological or analytic approach, will be the defining characteristic of volumes in the series.

The first titles in the series are

1 *Central and Eastern Europe, 1944–1993: Detour from the periphery to the periphery*
IVAN BEREND
ISBN 0 521 55066 1

2 *Spanish Agriculture: The Long Siesta, 1765–1965*
JAMES SIMPSON
ISBN 0 521 49630 6

Central and Eastern Europe, 1944–1993

Detour from the periphery to the periphery

Ivan T. Berend

University of California, Los Angeles

CAMBRIDGE
UNIVERSITY PRESS

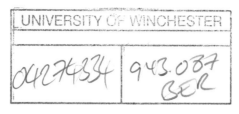

CAMBRIDGE UNIVERSITY PRESS
Cambridge, New York, Melbourne, Madrid, Cape Town, Singapore,
São Paulo, Delhi, Dubai, Tokyo

Cambridge University Press
The Edinburgh Building, Cambridge CB2 8RU, UK

Published in the United States of America by Cambridge University Press, New York

www.cambridge.org
Information on this title: www.cambridge.org/9780521550666

First published 1996
Reprinted 1998, 2001, 2004, 2005

A catalogue record for this publication is available from the British Library

Library of Congress Cataloguing in Publication data
Berend, T. Iván (Tibor Iván) 1930–
    Central and Eastern Europe, 1944–1993: detour from the periphery
to the periphery / Ivan T. Berend
        p.   cm. – (Cambridge studies in modern economic history: 1)
    Includes bibliographical references (p.).
    ISBN 0-521-55066-1
    1. Communism – Europe, Eastern – History.   2. Europe, Eastern –
History – 20th century.   3. Europe, Eastern – Politics and
government – 20th century.   I. Title.   II. Series.
    HX240.7.A6B47   1995
    335.43′0947–dc20   95-5926 CIP

ISBN 978-0-521-55066-6 Hardback
ISBN 978-0-521-66352-6 Paperback

Transferred to digital printing 2010

For Kati

The Communist regimes executed tens of thousands, imprisoned hundreds of thousands, staged show-trials, and practiced mass intimidation ... Communism will be remembered largely as the twentieth century's most extraordinary political and intellectual aberration.

(Zbigniev Brzezinski, *The Grand Failure*, 1989)

Several severe social and human problems of Europe and the world are rooted in the aberrations of capitalism. Communism was a reaction to reckless capitalism. The change of the latter was due, in a great deal, to the ideas of socialism.

(Pope John-Paul II, Statement in *La Stampa*, 1993)

Marx's systematic theory never had any validity ... Capitalism proved to be entirely immune to the revolutionary appeals of Marxism ... The defects of a pseudo-scientific theory turned into state dogma needed to be addressed without qualifications.

(Richard Pipes, Contention. *Debates in Society, Culture, and Science*, Fall 1991)

The Bolshevik model ... was essentially a model for modernizing backward agrarian economies ... I have to remind you of the incredible sufferings it imposed on the peoples ... And yet ... up to a point it worked better than anything else since ... 1918. For most of the common citizens of the more backward countries in the region ... it was probably the best period in their history.

(Eric Hobsbawm, The New Threat to History, *New York Review of Books*, 1993)

The best we can say is always partial and incomplete ... Only by entertaining multiple and mutually limiting points of view, building up a composite picture, can we approach the real richness of the world.

(Niels Bohr)

Contents

Preface

Central and Eastern European socialism is now a closed chapter of history. Its nearly half century long existence initiated a library of literature. It was described as totalitarian, its post-Stalinist stage post-totalitarian regime a mere enlargement of the "evil Soviet empire," which imposed her regime on the area, and built a bloc with special economic (Comecon) and military (Warsaw Pact) systems.

A series of studies has been published documenting the rebellions against "real" socialism maintaining that the regime never gained legitimization, that its performance reflected a consistently low efficiency, and that ultimately even its own elite lost confidence in its ability to adjust to a transforming world and to modernize. When the Soviet Union became unable to maintain its control, the regime's elite gave up without resistance and the system collapsed with unexpected speed.

A vast literature on the other hand, documented unprecedented economic growth and a successful struggle against traditional backwardness and rigid social hierarchy. Authors of the region repeated Monsieur Pangloss's words on a "best of possible worlds."

Fears and/or hopes were expressed on a permanent enlargement of world socialism from one country with roughly 200,000 inhabitants (1917) to twenty-six countries on four continents with nearly 1.7 billion people (1986), which would gradually catch up with the Western world and bring about a convergence of competing capitalism and socialism in a bi-polar world system. A leading economist and giant intellect, the Austrian–American Joseph Schumpeter, predicted in 1928 that "a socialist form of society will inevitably emerge from an equally inevitable decomposition of capitalist society." What will contribute toward the decline of capitalism, Schumpeter states, will not be economic failures, but "its very success undermines the social institutions which protect it, and 'inevitably' creates conditions in which it will not be able to live and which strongly point to socialism as the heir apparent" (Schumpeter, 1976, pp. 61, 409).

Thousands of sound and overpoliticized analyses were published.

Biased Cold War interpretations confronted each other. The early 1990s opened a unique window of opportunity to revisit this closed chapter of history. First of all, the Cold War with its unavoidable political biases, is over. The first few years of transition with all of their successes and failures will help to provide a better understanding of long-term historical trends and regional potentials. A great amount of new sources and knowledge are at hand, and a much better historical perspective has emerged.

I am personally strongly motivated to revisit the last half-century drama of Central and Eastern Europe. The region and period in question are part of my personal life. The story of my book begins in 1944. In this year I "celebrated" my fourteenth birthday in a Hungarian prison. A major part of the story ends in 1989 when I headed two committees: one worked out the first Three Year Plan of marketization and privatization for Hungary, and the other one "rehabilitated" the 1956 uprising. During the exciting but difficult years between 1989 and 1993, I was a member of the Hungarian International Blue Ribbon Commission, advising on transformation.

I witnessed three revolutions – after 1945, in 1956, and in 1989 – and having seen the deformation of the first, and the defeat of the second, I was able to contribute to the third, which was a unique reform-revolution.

Fascism and Stalinism, reforms and their collapse, belief, disappointment, and renewed belief, all belong to my personal experience. The chapter of history reviewed here was opened and closed during my lifetime. It was sometimes quite unbearable and frightening, but always extremely interesting. I attempt to present it *sine studio partium*.

The history of Central and Eastern European socialism is only a part of a centuries-long process. Its origin and characteristics are not understandable without the *longue durée* of the region's history.

The communist experiment was part of a twentieth-century rebellion of the unsuccessful peripheries, which were humiliated by economic backwardness and the increasing gap which separated them from the advanced Western core. They suffered from social ills in their hierarchical societies, as well as from mass poverty, autocratic political regimes and foreign domination. The "dual-revolution" of the late eighteenth and early nineteenth centuries had no roots in this area and was unable to elevate these peripheral nations to the exclusive club of the rich, industrialized nations, with their well-functioning market automatism and nation-states with stable parliamentary democracies.

The failure of nineteenth-century industrialization and parliamentary democracies was rooted in earlier centuries and preceding failures. Far away from the emerging modern Atlantic trade, and missing the Western "primitive" capital accumulation, as well as the gradual loosening of feudal structures and the subsequent agricultural revolution and proto-industrialization, Central and Eastern Europe found itself on the food delivering periphery of the Western core of a rising world system. Declining to an earlier stage of serfdom, the region did not experience the rise of absolutist states, homogenizing different ethnic, linguistic, and religious groups and forming nations and nation-states out of multi-ethnic societies; instead, this "unfinished part of Europe" (Jászi, 1961) lost its independence, and all the countries of the region were absorbed by the Ottoman, Habsburg, and Russian multi-national empires between the fifteenth and eighteenth centuries.

Were all these striking differences between the two parts of Europe a consequence of tragic historical "accidents" of foreign occupations that effectively detached this area from the West, as generations of historians of the region suggested? Or did some precursors of Central and Eastern Europe's decline exist earlier when "imported" feudal structures were much weaker and more sketchy? Were the "genuine peculiarities" of the ninth to thirteenth-century Central and Eastern Europe ultimately rooted in the fact that it adopted Christian-feudal culture a half a millennium later than did the "West" in the Carolingian empire? These questions were brilliantly analyzed by Jenö Szücs, who recalled that the border between Western Europe and Central and Eastern Europe was, mysteriously, the same River Elbe-Saale line at the time of the death of Charlemagne in 815 as in 1945, when the American and Soviet armies met there (Szücs, 1985).

The enigmatic destiny of the region, however, was broken in certain periods when its peoples, at least those of its Western rim, successfully adopted Western institutions and followed an "imitative" development. In doing so, they "joined" the rest of Europe and became more or less equal parts of it, as was the case between the tenth and fifteenth centuries, and as was attempted during the half century before World War I.

A struggle for a national awakening, the creation of a standardized national language and culture, and the quest for establishing a nation-state out of the "Kultur-nation" (Meinecke, 1922) characterized the entire nineteenth century in Central and Eastern Europe. A "Westernizing" intellectual elite advocated the values of the Enlightenment, the French Revolution, and liberalism. A political and economic elite "imported" everything from the Code Napoleon and modern property rights to agricultural technology, capital, and free market principles. Railroads, certainly the most characteristic symbols of nineteenth-century modernization, not only helped create a national market by providing a country-wide transportation network, but also physically linked the region to Europe, and became the most important vehicle of an export-led industrialization attempt.

The modernization drive, based on Western principles, was unable to achieve the aspired-to goal. The gap did not narrow (Western Europe achieved a 75 percent per capita increase of its GNP, whereas Hungary and Poland managed only slightly more than 60 percent, and Bulgaria and Serbia roughly 30 percent), and Central and Eastern Europe remained the poor agricultural and peasant part of the continent. The per capita industrial production of the region varied between one-third and two-thirds of the European average, and was surpassed by the Western countries by between a half and two and a half times (Bairock, 1976).

Moreover, after repeated political crises and uprisings, the struggle for independence was suppressed, and with the exception of the Balkans, which had been liberated from Ottoman rule, the map of the region remained as it was drawn in Vienna in 1815. The region continued to be on Europe's periphery at the dawn of the twentieth century (Berend and Ránki, 1982).

This repeated failure and embarrassment, augmented by the destruction and disappointment of World War I, generated the desperate twentieth-century rebellions that engulfed the region. A frustrated Central and Eastern Europe aggressively turned against the West.

Belated national revolutions led to the (re)establishment of independent states. Historical justice was granted to several oppressed peoples who realized their right to self-determination; others, however, were not provided the same opportunity. Minorities revolted throughout the region and continuously challenged the existing status quo.

Hatred against former oppressors inflamed the area, and new centralizing forces developed against minorities and neighbors, indeed against anybody who was not "one of us." Old national exclusiveness and more recent passions of revenge, a plethora of oversensitive national emotions, mobilized entire nations against one another.

The logic of a continuous national struggle shifted several genuine national movements toward right-wing extremism. A Völkisch "national socialism" advanced xenophobia as a leading political trend and transformed social-political dissatisfaction into an "anti-Semitic revolution." The Hungarian "Irredenta" and Slovak and Croat separatism linked their national movements to the fascist and nazi powers, who challenged Versailles and sought to redraw the map of Europe. The Romanian "Poporanismul" and its successor, Zelea-Codreanu's "Legion," set out to realize its "mission" and subordinate human rights to the supreme interest of the nation, both as a community and as an eternal entity. A mythical supreme national interest was defined by charismatic leaders, dangerous visionaries, and demagogues who mobilized the masses.

The right-wing revolt rejected Western values and institutions and replaced them with an authoritarian, interventionist state promoting an isolationist protectionism that equated national independence with economic self-sufficiency. Political pluralism was rejected on behalf of national or racial unity. A violent discrimination (leading to elimination) was implemented against "Volksfremde" elements, i.e., those who were "alien to the nation," using the German Völkisch term on ethnic and religious minorities. It went hand in hand with an exalted national agitation to safeguard and unite "Staatsfremde" fellow Sudetan Germans, Transylvanian Hungarians, "Bulgarian Macedonians," and those who lived as minorities in "alien" neighboring countries.

Dissatisfied nations were ready to join those who demanded and promised a "new European order," who declared a war of the "proletarian nations" against the "bourgeois nations," as Enrico Corradini suggested (in 1910) and Mussolini co-opted, and who were ready "to lead the oppressed nations," as Moeller van den Broek phrased the "German mission" in his *The Third Reich* which was published at the time of Hitler's first and unsuccessful coup attempt (Moeller van den Brock, 1931).

All these extreme ideas were embraced by political movements in interwar Central and Eastern Europe, and were fueled by unfair peace treaties that generated hatred and fear of decline in the countries on the periphery of Europe, postwar economic chaos, and most particularly the desperation of the thirties – the years of an unprecedented Great Depression.

A political alliance and economic agreements formed a nazi-led bloc of small authoritarian states, which institutionalized anti-Semitism, followed import substitution, introduced strong state intervention, and prepared for a new war which led to a massacre and destruction which was unprecedented in the history of the region (Berend and Dorchardt, 1986).

At this historical juncture, a communist rebellion, another form of revolt of the periphery, became dominant in Central and Eastern Europe. It was both strongly different from and strikingly similar to the nationalist and right-wing revolts. It represented an even more steadfast anti-Western revolution that rejected capitalism and all of its political and economic institutions. Its emergence coincided with that of the others in the most desperate countries of the region by the end of World War I.

The communist ideology represented an early twentieth-century peripheral version of nineteenth-century Marxism. Marxism and the workers' movement split at that time into two opposing trends: a Western social democratic "reformism" and an Eastern revolutionary Bolshevism.

The Marxist concept of socialism denied the possibility of a proletarian revolution in backward countries, maintaining that it could do nothing but equalize poverty and reproduce old conflicts. As Marx and Engels stressed in their *German Ideology*, this type of poor, peripheral "local communism" was bound to perish. Only in the advanced countries of the West was it possible to realize the international revolution they envisioned, in effect by expropriating the expropriators at their high level of economic development and creating a just and prosperous, egalitarian, and genuinely democratic society (based on collective ownership and direct people's representation) (Marx, 1970).

Working in an ever-changing environment, within Western social democracy the various transformations in society were recognized: the emergence of a middle class and the gradual disappearance of nineteenth-century class society. Also recognized was the possibility of parliamentary struggle based on a democratic mass party and, instead of revolution, reform based on the transformation of capitalism into an "organized welfare" society.

Capitalism in the European periphery, however, preserved its nineteenth-century characteristics with its backward economies, polarized societies, and authoritarian regimes. This became the cradle of Bolshevism. Humiliation led to the first revolutionary attempts to "introduce" communism in Russia, Hungary, Slovakia, Bulgaria, and Bavaria after World War I. All, except Russia, were immediately suppressed.

The Russian revolution, however, after an idealistic first stage when it sought to be only an initiator of a world revolution, turned toward the realization of socialism in a single backward peasant country. The Stalinist Soviet Union founded a regime which combined a ruthless, forced economic modernization model with vestiges of an egalitarian Utopia. It was able to attract religious believers and generate the support of masses who saw it as the only hope of coping with socio-economic ills.

The Great Depression and the climax of parliamentary democracies in Europe, the unprecedented tragedy and destruction of World War II, together with a victoriously emerging Soviet super power made the communist ideas of rejecting capitalism and the parliamentary system a predominate force. It became a blueprint for regimes that attracted desperate peoples. The promise of rapid growth, modernization, and catching up with the West, were attractive prospects as the utopian prophecies of a just society.

Little remained, however, of the genuine Marxist vision, and the system which was imposed or adopted in Central and Eastern Europe was strongly laden with traditional Russian despotism and influenced by the region's peripheral standing. To quote Plato, "a plant ... which grows and matures into all virtue, but, if sown and planted in an alien soil, becomes the most noxious of all weeds" (Plato, 1897, p. 318) – state socialism became a rather different plant than the one assumed to grow in the affluent Western soil as Marx had predicted.

Communist ideas, nevertheless, still represented eternal aspirations that had pervaded human history from its beginnings. One should not forget that Plato's ideal "Republic" was already a negation of the "two evils: wealth . . . and poverty" (ibid., p. 245). The Platonian elite should not have "any property beyond what is absolutely necessary; neither should they have a private house." The lack of private property and the difference between "meum and tuum" revealed an ideology that stressed common goals and a society in which "all tend towards a common end" (ibid., pp. 242, 288–9, 290–1).

Similar ideas were embodied in the miraculous island of Thomas More's *Utopia* in the early sixteenth century. The moneyless, collective society did not know private property. There was a rotation of people between towns and countryside, and everybody worked in the field for two years. Every ten years people exchanged houses; moreover, "their clothing . . . is the same everywhere throughout the island . . . " and they "take their meals in common." The sick are cured in public hospitals. "Children under the age of five sit together in the nursery." "[S]ince they share everything equally, it follows that no one can ever be reduced to poverty . . . the whole island is like a single family" (More, 1975, pp. 50, 57–8, 61).

The same dreams have prevailed in human history throughout the centuries. They especially flourished during the eighteenth century. Jean-Jacques Rousseau repeated the condemnation of private ownership: "The first person who, having enclosed a plot of land, took it into his head to say this is mine and found people simple enough to believe him, was the true founder of civil society. What crimes, wars, murders, what miseries and horrors would the human race have been spared, had someone pulled up the stakes or filled in the ditch and cried out to his fellow men: 'Do not listen to this impostor. You are lost if you forget that the fruits of the earth belong to all and the earth to no one!'" (Rousseau, 1983, p. 140).

Private ownership, as he stated in his *Social Contract*, made even the law unjust, since "laws are always useful to those who have possessions and harmful to those who have nothing." The just society, according to the moral giant of the Enlightenment, requires a "social state . . . [in which] all have something and none of them has too much" (ibid., p. 29).

The dream of a free, egalitarian society became a scientific theory with Marx and the banner of a mass movement in the nineteenth century. It was transformed into a practical experiment in the twentieth century.

The result was a mixture of oppressive, dictatorial Kafkaesque state socialism, which neglected human rights and personal freedom, and a long-lasting state of euphoria accompanied by the introduction of a premature welfare system. The regime which attempted to brainwash its citizens and bloodily suppressed their rebellions at the same time created an unprecedented security for the lower layers of society. It was equally paradoxical that the regime, with its stressed internationalist ideology, suppressed open xenophobia and nationalism, yet this policy was orchestrated by an expansionist Soviet Union in order to assure its domination.

Indeed, Central and Eastern Europe's postwar history embodied the most ironical paradoxes: it was at the same time liberated *and* oppressed, euphoric *and* desperate, obediently subservient *and* most heroically and militantly rebellious. Its promise of a breakthrough ended with a break down.

The effort to escape from the traditional peripheral position via central planning and forced industrialization, though not unsuccessful until the mid 1970s, did ultimately fail. The modernization, built on an early twentieth-century technological-structural pattern, led to rapid industrialization but was genuinely unable to meet the technological demands of the post-World War II world economy, and lost its transitory economic advantages by the mid 1970s. The challenge of the structural crisis undermined the regime's economy, which began to decline. The transitory legitimacy achieved by most of the governments of the region during the 1960s–70s, by modernizing their countries, running nationalist courses and raising consumerism and living standards, was eliminated by the failures of the 1980s. Opposition in some of the countries and a social-democratized reform-from-within trend in others were significantly strengthened, and state socialism collapsed without significant resistance.

Central and Eastern Europe, after a century of revolts against peripheral backwardness; after several, though different types of, revolutions and four decades of desperate experiment, in the end always ended up where it had started. After its long detour, Central and Eastern Europe was still languishing on the periphery of Europe.

After several decades of rejecting Western values, a peaceful but still dramatic revolution in the last decade of this century destroyed all beliefs in the old regime, and with equal fervor turned back to Western values and passionately sought to integrate them into its newly emerging community.

Central and Eastern Europe is still facing the same unsolved historical problems that existed before its stormy revolutionary attempts: unfinished nation-building, the building of a modern democracy and civil society, and economic modernization are on the agenda.

The first years of transformation are the scenes of the first free elections, the establishment of multi-party parliamentary systems. The tremendous efforts and impressive successes of marketization and privatization, the adoption of Western constitutions, property rights, and stock exchanges are inseparably mixed with the failures of the new, this time *laissez faire*, utopia. The euphoria of freedom is mixed with a frightening loss of security, growing poverty and exploding xenophobia, and nationalist fundamentalism.

The caravan of Central and Eastern Europe is marching again. The declared goal is to "arrive" in Europe. Will this new experiment succeed? Or will the peoples of the region continue their detour and end up again on the periphery of Europe? The ultimate answers will be given in the twenty-first century. The historian cannot predict the future but, *in statu nascendi*, is able to analyze the imminent trends of history.

The goal of this book is to present a complex analysis of post-World War II Central and East European history integrated into a broader framework; to connect history with the transformation of the present and the perspectives of the future. A strongly comparative approach will offer compensation for the lack of detailed information on the individual countries. A highly structural treatment attempts to highlight the striking incongruity of the history of postwar Central and Eastern Europe. The difficult interplay of ideological, economic, social and political, internal and external factors are the focus of the analysis.

The discourse, covering originally seven (now twelve) countries between Germany and Russia, always deals with the entire region rather than a country by country approach. It represents a continuous implicit, and often explicit, debate with stereotypes, and attempts to add its own voice to the multi-voice chorus of interpretations.

Acknowledgments

I have been fortunate in the interest and care which this book has received from Cambridge University Press – the publisher of four of my books during the last one-and-a-half decades – and personally from publishing director Mr Richard Fisher, as well as from Professor Barry Supple, a good old friend, and an editor of the series.

This book could not have been accomplished without the quiet, ideal working conditions, stimulating intellectual atmosphere and outstanding library collection at the University of California in Los Angles. I should like to express my special gratitude to UCLA – I had joined the faculty in 1990 – and, for having granted sufficient research assistance, to its Academic Senate and the Center for German and European Studies at Berkeley.

I also profited from the scholarly debates with a great number of colleagues at various conferences at which I participated and presented papers or organized sessions on the topic during these years at Yale, Minnesota, Berkeley, and the Congress of the International Economic History Association in Milan and its preparatory meeting, arranged by the Südosteuropa-Gesellschaft in Munich.

Mr Robert Levy, my outstanding graduate student and research assistant, gave me a valuable helping hand in revising the English of my manuscript, the first book I was audacious enough to write in that language.

I gained the greatest help and most thorough assistance from my wife Kati who read and discussed each chapter, assisted in library work and encouraged my taking the (adventurous) step in writing this book, for the first time in my life, on a word processor.

Los Angeles, April 8, 1995
Ivan T. Berend

Part I

Out from Europe: the introduction of state socialism, the Stalinist decades, and revolts against them

In the period between the world wars the Eastern European peripheries, where modernization began to falter in the nineteenth century and Western values came under criticism in the twentieth, instituted anti–parliamentary dictatorships. The regimes' attempts at protectionist, import–substituting industrialization proved unsuccessful. The course chosen by the region in the interwar period culminated in nazi occupation, a reign of terror by collaborationist fascist governments, and the unprecedented tragic devastations of World War II.

Even after the war the region was unable to return to "normalcy." As a consequence of internal social forces or external Soviet force (and as often as not a combination of the two) and the increasingly tense atmosphere of the Cold War and a divided Europe, governments in the continent's central and southeastern regions shifted from the extreme right to the extreme left. Was the result a new dictatorship of modernization? Was it yet another attempt at breaking loose from the periphery?

Hoping to exploit the attraction of the Soviet model of industrialization and planned economy for underdeveloped agrarian countries, Central and Eastern Europe launched a program of enforced industrialization and dismantled the former hierarchy of social caste in the consistent framework of Stalinist socialism's closed society and ruthless dictatorship. The Soviet bloc, its institutions, ideology, and cultural politics hermetically sealed off from the West, thus used a state socialist, anti-humanist model to combat its historical backwardness. It withdrew from Europe in order to catch up with and surpass it.

1 Communist seizure of power, 1944–8

Disrupted historical continuity

Fascism and nazism, which appeared in the interwar period, became dominant in Central and Eastern Europe during the tragic years of World War II. It occurred either through nazi-German occupation or with the takeover of domestic nazi-fascist groupings. In most cases these two factors did not exclude but complemented each other. Independent countries (Poland, Czechoslovakia, Yugoslavia, and Albania) were annexed and ruled by a nazi (or partly Mussolini's) administration, others became allies of Hitler (such as Hungary, Romania, and Bulgaria), or were created by him (as "independent" allied Slovakia and Croatia), bringing to power long existing internal nazi-fascist parties.

The peoples of the region reacted in various ways. Heroic, self-sacrificing partisan warfare (especially in Yugoslavia and Albania) and dramatic uprisings (in Poland and Czechoslovakia), passive resistance as well as passive collaboration (in most of the countries), active cooperation in the annihilation of Jews (in Slovakia, Croatia, Hungary, Romania, and Poland) – these phenomena were present at the same time in each country.

The military aftermath of the war in 1944 and early 1945, as a result of the victorious advance of the Allied forces, including the Red Army in Central and Eastern Europe, led to a bloody and spectacular collapse of fascism. The decline and breakdown of Axis-regimes in Yugoslavia and Albania were brought about, or at least assisted, by the actions of internal partisan armies during the general course of the war. In other cases the process was accelerated by coups (Romania), which removed the local fascist government and resulted in a conversion to the Allied side, or brought about entirely by foreign troops (Bulgaria, Czechoslovakia and Hungary).

The domination of German nazism and the collaborating internal governments was eliminated. Members of fascist administrations, armies, and police forces physically disappeared: most fled to the West, quite a few were killed during the war, while high-ranking military personnel and politicians were executed as war criminals. Thus not only the most notorious Hungarian nazis, such as Szálasi, Baky, and Endre, were tried and hanged, but, among others, Imrédy and Bárdossy, former prime ministers, who had introduced the anti-Jewish laws and issued the declaration of war. In Hungary, altogether 189 war criminals were executed and 27,000 sentenced from the almost 60,000 people who were investigated and tried.

In Bulgaria, 2,138 generals, high ranking officers and former cabinet members were executed, and an additional 3,500 were imprisoned. The state apparatus and public servants were also purged. In Hungary, three-member committees investigated the political activities of public employees and dismissed 60,000 people from their positions. Beside right-wing elements, thousands were dismissed owing to personal revenge and virulent competition among rival political parties.

A highly emotional atmosphere of vengeance characterized postwar Europe. Arrests and punishment sometimes went beyond the legal framework. The intransigent harshness of de-nazification and castigation of collaborators was a reaction to the war. The historical moment was determined by emotions generated by the unspeakable horror and inhumanity of nazism. An additional factor, communist ambitions to eliminate totally elements of the *ancien régime* in order to clear the ground for a later introduction of socialism, also contributed.

The old regimes were buried under the ruins of war and fascism. Political continuity was shattered. The restoration of prewar regimes or governments was impossible everywhere, except Czechoslovakia, and the internal political vacuum was filled by new forces.

Discontinuity became an overwhelming characteristic of postwar Central and Eastern Europe. Not only political regimes were changed but borders as well. Poland was shifted to the West: she lost roughly 70,000 square miles of her prewar territory to Russia and was compensated by 40,000 square miles from Germany. Former East Poland became West Ukraine, former East Prussia was transformed into West Poland. The wartime Hungarian borders shrunk back to the prewar standard. Hungary had to give back the Northern and Eastern territories regained by the first and second Vienna decisions. Romania acquired Northern Transylvania from Hungary but lost Bessarabia to the Soviet Union. Yugoslavia was enlarged by former Italian territories on the Adriatic sea.

Beside territorial changes, tens of millions of people were annihilated or forced to move. Nations were literally decimated. Large groups of minorities disappeared. The bloodiest massacre in history savagely struck Central and Eastern Europe. More than five-sixths of the unthinkable death-toll of the war was paid by Russia, Germany, and the smaller countries that fell in between, the latter having lost roughly 10 million people. Poland represented one of the most tragic cases with 3 million deaths, more than 10 percent of her population. Yugoslavia, according to highly contradictory and debated figures, lost between 0.7–1.7 million lives. The larger figure, reported by Tito's postwar administration, also represented about 10 percent of the population. Romania, Hungary, and Czechoslovakia, with 0.5, 0.5, and 0.2 million deaths respectively, also suffered a great deal.

The Holocaust of the Jews was unparalleled in history. The Jewish minority in Poland fell from 3 million to 600,000 and half of Hungarian and Romanian Jews were eradicated. Jewish communities, which represented roughly 10, 5, and 5 percent of Poland's, Romania's and Hungary's population respectively, declined in all cases to 2–3 percent. Those who survived, altogether roughly 1.5 million people, proceeded to escape from their homeland, especially after the shock of postwar pogroms in Kielce (Poland) and Kúnmadaras (Hungary). Occurring a few months after the Holocaust, this contributed to the emigration of more than half of surviving Jewry. Those who remained represented only 1 percent of the population.

The second largest single minority, the Germans, were forced to leave after the war. Because of the great powers' agreement and the philosophy of "collective responsibility," Germans (those who declared themselves to be "Volks-Deutsch" and had joined the nazi "Volksbund," but in reality a greater number) were expelled. Half a million Germans fled, followed by nearly 2.2 million expatriates from Czechoslovakia. Another 2 million Germans had to leave former East Prussia, now Western Poland. The majority of the 8 to 9 million Germans who lived in that territory before the war escaped with the retreating Wermacht. Sudetenland in Czechoslovakia and East Prussia, now incorporated into Poland, were virtually "cleansed" ethnically after the war. Hundreds of thousands of Saxons and Schwabians were transported from Hungary (200,000) and Romania to Germany.

Nearly 100,000 Hungarians were labelled as fascists and expelled from Czechoslovakia (ironically from Southern Slovakia, which was a part of "independent" fascist Slovakia).

As a result of the redrawn map, approximately 2 million Poles moved from former Eastern Poland, now absorbed by the Soviet Union, to the newly annexed Western Poland (and roughly 2.5 million Poles joined them from overpopulated central regions). In Western Poland, emptied by fleeing or expelled Germans, 4.5 million new settlers found established homes after the war. This was also the case in the deserted western borderland of Czechoslovakia, where nearly 2 million Czechs and

Slovaks moved from the overpopulated inner regions. In other words, at least 10–15 million people began a new life in a new place, or even in a new country. Lack of continuity was thus also characterized by mass migration, unparalleled in the history of the region.

The war devastated a great part of the national wealth, produced by generations. Physical havoc played an additional role in breaking continuity. Poland, Yugoslavia, and Hungary were among the most devastated countries after the war. Half of their railroad capacity was destroyed, and 75 percent of Polish and 36 percent of Hungarian bridges were ruined. Yugoslavia lost half of her deep-sea vessels, all of her motor cars, and even 40 percent of her peasant carts. One of the most devastated cities of Europe was Warsaw, where 85 percent of the buildings were ruined or damaged. Budapest was in ruins as well, with 27 percent of its buildings severely damaged or destroyed and all of its famous Danube bridges blown up. The infrastructure of most of these countries had thus fallen back by seventy years.

Animal stock suffered the most. Cattle, horses, and pigs were confiscated, stolen, and slaughtered, amounting to a 50–80 percent loss for all three countries. In Poland, as much as 25 percent of its forests was mowed down. Bombing and the ground war destroyed 25–35 percent of the industrial capacity of the countries mentioned above. Czechoslovakia, Romania, and Bulgaria deteriorated much less.

As a result of serious bottlenecks caused by demolition, a great part of the existing capacities remained ineffective. A severe shortage of energy and transportation crippled most of those industries left intact. While industrial capacity diminished by 25 percent, the actual decline of output reached 85 percent in Hungary during the spring and summer of 1945. A devastating hyper-inflation, a world record of 12 percent price increases per hour (!) in the late spring of 1946, pushed the country back to the age of trade in kind.

Mass-graves, refugees, ruins, chaos, poverty, and humiliation characterized Central and Eastern Europe at the war's end. Continuity was disrupted. The end of the interwar course, and the emergence of a new era, however, promised also a discontinuity of misery, national hatred, nazi-fascist influence, genocide and war. Postwar desperation was thus mixed with enthusiasm for a new opening. A spring air brought fresh hope to the people who wanted to believe that something new may emerge from the ruins of the old world.

The broken continuity opened the gates to newly arising internal political forces and external powers. The destiny of Central and Eastern Europe was to be determined by them.

Great power interference: the seeds of a Cold War sown in Poland and Greece

The victorious great powers wanted to guarantee international security and avoid new wars. Roosevelt found security in both American economic and military strength, unparalleled in history, as well as in international cooperation. In Teheran he spoke of an international order supervised by "four policemen," America, Russia, Great Britain, and China. The basis of international understanding to him was American–Russian cooperation.

Stalin also wanted the wartime alliance to remain alive. It was especially important to him because of severe war devastation and losses in the Soviet Union, and the increased economic gap between his country and the United States. In the meantime he also wanted to build up a security zone around his Western border, and did not want to tolerate hostile governments next to him.

Churchill preferred a clear division of spheres of interest, based on agreements. He wanted to rebuild the great power position of Britain as a leading Mediterranean power and as a senior partner of the United States in Europe.

These goals, in spite of several points of common interest, began to confront each other. The first central issue of conflict was the Polish question. Stalin did not hesitate to begin building up the requested security zone. In the summit meetings of the Big Three, his allies accepted his arguments and agreed to shift Poland toward the West, granting former Eastern Poland (up to the post-World War I so called Curzon-line) to Russia, and compensating Poland with former East German territories. Stalin, however, wanted a "friendly" government in Poland as well. It led to a break with the Polish government-in-exile in London.

In July and August 1941 two Soviet–Polish agreements were signed, the same as were made with Czechoslovakia. Polish prisoners of war were released, and General Wladyislaw Anders organized a Polish army under the operational command of the Red Army. There was, however, permanent conflict with the Soviets, and ultimately the Anders army left the Soviet Union for the Middle East in July 1942, and went under British command. Permanent controversy and refusal to meet Stalin's territorial demands by the Polish government-in-exile caused further tensions. The Katyn affair, the German discovery of the mass graves of Polish officers massacred by the Soviets,[1] sharpened the conflict and led

---

[1] The Politburo of the Bolshevik Party ordered the massacre of 27,000 Polish officers, prisoners of war in Russian camps since 1939. About 5,000 of them were killed and buried in mass graves in Katyn and later found by the German army, which occupied the area. Hitler disclosed details of his discovery, and accused the Soviets of staging the massacre. Stalin denied the charge, and angrily denounced a "Nazi provocation." The Polish government-in-exile, however, believed the allegation of Soviet culpability, which was proved by top secret archival documents only in the fall of 1992.

to a turning point: Stalin broke off diplomatic relations with the exiled Polish government.

At the beginning of 1943 Stalin initiated the organization of a new Polish army, led by Colonel Berling, with the participation of Soviet officers of Polish origin (or name). A Polish Committee of National Liberation was founded in Lublin in July 1944. This parallel army and government was formed and directed by Stalin and led by Polish communists. The civil administration in liberated Poland was handed over to the Lublin Committee, which declared itself the provisional government of Poland in December 1944.

The Lublin Committee and its military units initiated a ruthless attack, in cooperation with the Red Army, against the exiled London government's partisan Home Army. Therefore, even before the end of World War II, one of the anti-fascist great powers turned against a former ally, a heroic anti-Hitler resistance movement, and annihilated it. The liberation of Poland was combined with an exported "civil war" against the national, anti-German (but also non- or even anti-communist) Polish Home Army.

The scene of the first "battle" of this Soviet orchestrated "civil war" was in Warsaw, where the Red Army, which had already reached the capital and remained in the Praga district on the other side of the Vistula river, passively watched while the nazi military machine bloodily slaughtered the Warsaw uprising. The uprising became a litmus-test in measuring confronting interests. "Operation Tempest," as it was named, was more "a struggle for political power in liberated Poland . . . than a fight against the Germans" (Kimball, 1984, p. 260).

True, General Bor-Komarowski, head of the underground and uprising, refused, against British advice, to inform the Soviet government about the planned action. Moreover, the Polish Home Army was alarmed by the unique Russian advance of 450 miles during the summer-offensive in July, 1944, and attempted to liberate the country. On August 1, General Bor-Komarowski began the attack. Stalin, having seen the anti-Soviet motivations behind it, reacted angrily, and called the uprising a "reckless and terrible adventure" (Kimball, 1984, p. 281).

The silent Soviet assistance to the German massacre of 200,000 in the leveling of Warsaw was later "explained" by the Soviets as a consequence of their lines of communication and supplies being stretched to the breaking point. In reality, a Polish civil war had begun. Clashes commenced between the two anti-nazi troops, the communists, and the national non-communists, with the active participation of Soviet combat units, and the killing and arrest of legendary resistance fighters became a tragic epilogue in the history of World War II Poland. A most infamous episode in this drama took place when sixteen leaders of the Polish non-communist resistance army were invited to the Soviet headquarters in Warsaw to "coordinate the Polish actions with that of the Soviet Army" against the Germans in January 1945. All were arrested and thirteen of them were imprisoned for anti-Soviet actions.

An almost permanent debate has emerged about the future Polish provisional government. Stalin explicitly expressed in December 1944 that "the problem of Poland is inseparable from the problem of security of the Soviet Union" (Kimball, 1984, p. 476).

The acceptance of the communist Lublin Committee as the authentic Polish government was Stalin's basic aim at this stage, but it was confronted with the strongest Western resistance. It generated an open conflict between Stalin and Roosevelt. "I see no prospect," Roosevelt stated, for "transferring . . . recognition from the Government in London to the Lublin Committee in its present form" (Kimball, 1984, pp. 482–3). His last words, however, offered a compromise: the Lublin Committee was acceptable, not "in its present form," but in an enlarged form with the participation of Mikolajczik's London men. Churchill and Roosevelt pushed Mikolajczik to cooperate with the Soviets. The only compromise accepted by Stalin, because of British and American demands, was to guarantee a vice-premiership for Mikolajczik, the head of the exiled government in London, and to form portfolios for his colleagues.

Why did Roosevelt and Churchill make all these compromises? Was it because the Red Army was strongly needed against nazi Germany and Japan to save British and American lives? Was it also because Roosevelt believed, as he said to Edward Stettinius, that the Soviet Union "had the power in Eastern Europe," and therefore accepted Soviet control in the area? Or did they view "wartime arrangements as temporary, subject to revision at a postwar peace conference" (Kimball, 1984, pp. 481–2)? Ultimately both Churchill and Roosevelt were definitely convinced that internationally controlled free elections after the war would solve everything, a principle which was accepted in Yalta and endorsed by Stalin. It seemed to be satisfactory to the Western leaders, since this could assure further Soviet military cooperation, including the use of Soviet troops against Japan, which was vital to them.

But Stalin, cunningly enough, accepted the short-run security concessions while confident of being able to transform them into long-term dominance. Long, repeated bargaining decided the fate of Central and Eastern Europe. The policy to accept Soviet security interests, at the war's end, was characteristic of Western opinion at large. John Lukacs, historian of the Cold War, aptly stated: "never . . . was the power and prestige of Russia greater than in 1945 ... admiration for Russia was a tremendous force" (Lukacs, 1961, pp. 18, 49).

This atmosphere was reflected by the conservative British *The Times*, which proclaimed in an editorial in the fall of 1944:

what Russia seeks on her Western frontier is her own security. Great Britain has traditionally opposed any intervention by the Great Powers in the Low Countries or the Suez Canal area, and United States has done the same in Central America – areas that these two great powers have always properly considered vital to their own security. It would therefore be inconsistent to ask Russia today to give up a wholly identical right to security. (Fontaine, 1968–9, p. 217)

The communist-led five-party coalition in Poland in the end represented only a facade masking Soviet domination and an actual communist takeover. (Mikolajczyk, 1948)

In other cases Stalin did not rush to exploit the opportunity for Soviet military advance, and intended to remain within the framework agreed at the summits. He was also ready to make compromises. The time for this arrived in the fall of 1944.

Churchill, who advocated a most rapid Western military advance and the liberation of as much European territory as possible, was forced to give up his dreams; in May 1944 he realized that American and British troops would not reach Budapest and the Balkans. The communist-led Yugoslav, Albanian, and Greek partisans already controlled most of the rural areas of their countries. Churchill saw the guarantee of security in a traditional division of spheres of interest between Britain and Russia in the European theater. With the military successes of the Western allies in early fall strengthening his position, he initiated a bilateral meeting in Moscow. Between October 9 and 17, Churchill, Eden, Stalin, and Molotov participated in an unusually long, intimate, and pragmatic Anglo-Soviet talk. On the very first evening, in a tête-à-tête meeting with Stalin, when Roosevelt's observer, Averell Harriman (Harriman, 1975), was not present, Churchill felt that, as he described in his book:

the moment was apt for business so I said, "Let us settle about our affairs in the Balkans.... So far as Britain and Russia are concerned, how would it do for you to have 90 percent predominance in Romania, for us to have 90 percent of the say in Greece and so fifty-fifty about Yugoslavia?" ... I wrote out on a half-sheet of paper:

Romania	
Russia	90 percent
The others	10 percent
Greece	
Great Britain	90 percent

(in accord with USA)

Russia	10 percent
Yugoslavia	50–50 percent
Hungary	50–50 percent
Bulgaria	
Russia	75 percent
The others	25 percent

I pushed this across to Stalin . . . There was a light pause. Then he took his blue pencil and made a large tick upon it. . . . It was all settled in no more time than it takes to sit down. (Churchill, 1948–53, pp. 227–8)

The next day Eden and Molotov sat down for real bargaining over the exact percentages. Molotov made proposals and Eden made counter-offers. Agreement was finally reached: the Soviets gained 80 percent in Hungary and Bulgaria, 90 percent in Romania, and 60 percent in Yugoslavia. For a 90 percent British influence in Greece, Churchill and Eden were ready to sacrifice Central and Eastern Europe.

During their discussion, "Stalin agreed with Churchill's insistence that 'Britain must be the leading Mediterranean power', [while requesting] that they gain unrestricted access to the Mediterranean from the Black Sea" (Kimball, 1984, p. 351).

Churchill was satisfied and cabled to Roosevelt from Moscow: "Arrangements made about the Balkans are, I am sure, the best that are possible. . . . We should now be able to save Greece." Although the Polish question was pushed aside at this time, Churchil reported to Roosevelt that "Stalin made it clear that [he] . . . wants Poland, Czecho and Hungary to form a realm of . . . pro-Russian states" (Kimball, 1984, p. 359). This was a "fair bargain," and all the cards were put on to the table.

The meeting was a great success for Churchill. He thought he could save the most important British interests. But it was an even greater triumph for Stalin, whose security interests in the neighboring European areas were accepted by the Western allies, as he assumed they would be.

The seeds of later misunderstandings, however, were sown. In Stalin's mind this was a serious agreement on the postwar share of interests, while the American President viewed it as a preparatory and temporary agreement. Churchill, meanwhile, believed that he got a free hand in Athens, since during their meeting British troops had arrived in the Greek capital.

The Yugoslav and Albanian communist successes were almost repeated in Greece. Having been occupied by the Germans, the country was liberated by the communist-led Greek National Liberation Front (EAM), established in September 1941. From its scattered military units, a

People's Liberation Army (ELAS), a kind of "private" militia of the Communist Party, was organized in April 1942. The intransigent anti-nazi partisan struggle, as in the two neighboring Balkan countries, culminated in a civil war: ELAS troops fought against the much weaker royalist partisan units of Zervas, who enjoyed British support. By October 1944 the communist partisan army controlled most of the country (Kousoulas, 1965). At this point, however, British intervention halted and reversed the process. "I ... think that we should make preparation ... to have in readiness a British force." Churchill wrote to Roosevelt in August 1944, "which could be sent when the time is ripe" (Kimball, 1984, p. 279).

Roosevelt agreed: "I have no objection to your making preparations to have in readiness a sufficient British force to preserve order in Greece when the German Forces evacuate that country" (p. 297).

British troops were sent to Greece on October 4 and arrived in Athens on the 14th. In the meantime Churchill got a free hand even from Stalin. The road for action was cleared. Churchill urged brutal intervention: "having paid the price we have to Russia, for freedom of action in Greece, we should not hesitate to use British troops. I fully expect a clash with EAM" (Carlton, 1981, p. 248). The British Commander in Chief, General Scobie, ordered the disarmament of the communist guerilla troops. ELAS leaders refused and organized a great protest demonstration in Athens. Shots were fired,[2] and a thirty-three day battle began.

Churchill dictated a cable to Scobie. As one of his aides wrote in his diary: "He was in a bloodthirsty mood, and did not take kindly to suggestions that we should avoid bloodshed if possible" (Carlton, 1981, p. 249).

"We have to hold and dominate Athens," he cabled to General Scobie, "... with bloodshed if necessary.... Do not hesitate to act as if you were in a conquered city where a local rebellion is in progress." He later wrote in his memoirs: "It is no use doing things like this by halves" (Churchill, 1948–53, pp. 288–9).

The order was executed. British air and ground forces attacked and destroyed ELAS. "If our forces had not been on the spot," stated Churchill, "the whole of Greece would now be in the hands of a communist-run EAM Government" (Kimball, 1984, pp. 452, 455). "Without British intervention", added Seton-Watson, "the anti-communist forces would have been as helpless as were ... [those] in Yugoslavia and Albania" (Seton-Watson, 1961, p. 321).

---

[2] According to Fontaine, "Who fired the first shot, the Communists or the royalist police? ... Probably no one will ever know." (1968–9, p. 216.) According to Seton-Watson the demonstrators broke through the police line and panicked police opened fire (1952, p. 319).

The massacre of the former anti-nazi allies, as had occurred in Poland, was carried out before the end of the anti-nazi war. Churchill certainly did not want to risk British interests and influence, and decided to keep his Balkan bridgehead by all means possible and block the road of potential Soviet expansion in Greece, a path toward the Middle East.

The British press, however, and even the House of Commons, were indignant. The State Department released a public statement on December 5 rather critical of British actions, in terms of interference "from outside" in "liberated territories." But, in reality, the Allied powers overlooked the incident. Roosevelt cabled to Churchill: "[I] am necessarily responsive to the state of public feeling. It is for this reason that it has not been possible for this Government to take a stand with you in the present course of events in Greece" (Kimball, 1984, p. 456).

Churchill, of course, had aimed for and would have preferred to support a democratic system based on the free elections of March 1946. That effort, however, failed. The British command reorganized the Greek army and gendarmerie, and the first part of the civil war, in which the Greek extreme right-wing was directly aided by British military intervention, ended with a right-wing victory. In the end, after a renewed civil war (when the communist army was completely defeated) and years of bloody repression, and with certain democratic episodes, a cruel, right-wing military dictatorship ruled the country for a long period (Tossiza, 1978). The communist take over, nevertheless, was successfully avoided. "Churchill was the first to admit," commented Alain Fontaine, "that Stalin did fulfill his pledges with respect to Greece. . . . Without lifting a finger he allowed the British to massacre the ELAS partisans, who were led by Greek Communists" (Fontaine, 1968, p. 215). Stalin definitely expected the same generous response from his allies concerning the countries in his sphere of interests.

British and Soviet geopolitical interests were thus realized by exporting civil war to Greece and Poland. Central and Eastern Europe had become a playground for great power politics.

Genuine communist take over in Yugoslavia and Albania

Domestic forces, nevertheless, played a definite role, too. As was the case throughout liberated Europe, new political camps, especially communist-led anti-nazi resistance movements, gained momentum when new regimes were established in internal power vacuum. Even in Western countries, such as France or Italy, the communist parties secured a place in the newly formed postwar coalitions. The more successful an internal anti-nazi resistance movement was in contributing to the liberation of a given country, the more determined role it played in creating a postwar government. Hence one cannot deny the potential of self-determination, though it was indeed limited by great power politics.

In two exceptional cases domestic partisan warfare led to self-liberation, followed by the formation of new regimes under the direction of the former resistance movements, which institutionalized themselves as postwar governments. Great power arrangements formed only the framework of the internally hammered political transformation in these cases.

The pattern, from resistance to power, was the form of communist takeovers in Yugoslavia and Albania. After the German occupation of Yugoslavia in 1941, strong resistance emerged and led to the formation of partisan armies. A favorable geographical and geopolitical environment, dense wooded mountains, far away from the main roads of warfare, offered shelter for partisans. Scattered partisan groups were gradually consolidated into organized armies. One of them was led by an energetic secretary general of the Yugoslav Communist Party, Josip Broz, whose pseudonym, Tito, acquired a legendary meaning in the European resistance, and who from 1943 on successfully formed a regular army controlling huge territories. The anti-German resistance also led to sharp controversy and bitter clashes between the partisan armies of Tito and of General Mihailović, the Minister of War in the Yugoslav government-in-exile. Since Tito built up a much stronger army that became very efficient in anti-German battles, and because the British military mission revealed Mihailović's contact with the Italians, Tito, especially after May 1943, received the recognition of the Allied powers.

Tito's strong and ever growing partisan army of 300,000–400,000 troops, successful in combat and enjoying the cooperation and assistance of the Allied powers, soon became the dominant force in the country. The anti-German partisan war gradually became linked to a Yugoslav civil war. Tito's partisans, fighting against nazi occupiers, evidently fought against the collaborating Serbian local administration, the Croatian Ustashi, and even the rival Chetnik troops of the exiled government. The latter (weak, antagonized by Serb–Croat conflicts, burdened by Mihailović's cooperation with fascist Italy, and humiliated by the British abandonment of Mihailović) was actually "dethroned" by Tito, who formed his own provisional government, the National Committee of Liberation, under his presidency in November 1943. The Premier of the government-in-exile, Ivan Subašić, went to Yugoslavia to sign an agreement with Tito in December 1944, and joined his government as Minister of Foreign Affairs. A Regency was formed to replace King Peter until a legal decision could be made. The conservative Yugoslav forces surrendered (Authy, 1974).

Profiting from the victorious advance of the Red Army and the conse-
quent weakening of the occupying nazi forces, Tito's army liberated the
rural areas of the country by the summer of 1944, and freed the whole
country by May 1945.

The struggle on both sides was exceptionally ruthless and cruel. The
partisans, tortured and executed on the spot throughout the war, were
eager for revenge: when an intact Ustashi army escaped to the West and
surrendered to Western Allies at the end of the war, they were handed
over to Tito's army, and were brutally massacred. The enemy, due to the
logic of partisan warfare, had to be annihilated in the bloodiest war ever to
decimate the Yugoslav people.

The partisan-controlled government, first in liberated enclaves and
then throughout the whole country, led to a spontaneous formation of a
people's committee system, which surfaced as a new local power. Tito's
National Liberation Front emerged as a central government (enthusiastically supported by local people's committees) with all the power and
prestige to run the country. It was a unique combination of revolutionary
people's representation and a monolithic central power without opposition.
Those politicians who returned from Western emigration could not influence the process and soon resigned. An early election in November 1945,
which was held without competing opposition, led to a 96 percent victory
for Tito, an unchallengeable national hero with an enormous international
reputation.

"Partisan warfare" in peace continued to eliminate all potential opposition. A strange mixture of the just punishment of eliminating domestic
nazi collaborators, personal revenge, and an intolerant campaign against
non-communist politicians who were executed with ruthless Stalinist
methods led to the drastic liquidation of all kinds of opponents. The
wartime rival Mihailović was captured, tried, and executed in July 1946.
In addition, Jovanović, the left-wing peasant leader, Gaži and Jančiković,
the Croat peasant politicians, Trifunović and Furlan, the Radical Party
leaders, were all tried and imprisoned in 1947. An accusation of active or
even "passive collaboration" was enough to get rid of enemies, who probably
did no more than continue their business under German occupation.
Most of private business was expropriated on that basis. From a most
successful anti-nazi resistance, there emerged a monolithic communist
regime.

The pattern was rather similar in Albania. The small mountainous
Balkan country, occupied by Mussolini, was liberated by communist-led
partisan warfare. King Zogu and his entire state apparatus and governing
elite disappeared. The iron-handed communist teacher and excellent
organizer, Enver Hoxha, built up a partisan army and launched a systematic

attack against the occupiers. Here too, the resistance struggle was inseparably linked to a struggle against native collaborators and conservative
opponents, and thus simultaneously evolved into a civil war. The defeat
of Italy provided an opportunity for Hoxha's partisans to take over their
remote country, far away from the major scenes of the war. Unlike Tito,
Hoxha did not even allow the repatriation of former politicians from
Western emigration. Following in the steps of Tito, he also reorganized
his communist-led liberation movement and founded the Democratic
Front. In an early election in December 1945, without allowing the
participation of any kind of opposition, Hoxha's Front garnered 93 percent
of the votes and established a monolithic communist regime in Albania.

The Yugoslav and Albanian road (which was almost repeated by Greece)
represented a genuine revolutionary seizure of power. Victorious communist-led partisan warfare created the possibility of gaining power and
led to the introduction of the Soviet model of modernization, an attractive
one for backward countries after its historical triumph of World War II.

Genuine democratic coalitions: the Czechoslovak and Hungarian cases

The defeat of nazism strengthened left-wing political trends all over the
region. Communists became stronger than ever before. It was partly a
consequence of their uncompromising anti-nazism, courage and sacrifices
in struggle, which, in a way, legitimized these "rootless internationalists."
But, at the same time, these genuine democratic social revolutionary mass
movements, which flooded Central and Eastern Europe after the collapse
of conservative *anciens régimes*, aimed to destroy the former rigid class
hierarchy and dominating big estates. They desired a more just society
which emancipated the masses and was ready to combine democracy with
radical social reforms, and this created an adequate ground for their
advance. The communists could most easily sail the rough waves of
radical–plebeian–revolutionary public spirit and expectations.

Certain lower layers of society were ready to follow radical slogans:
young radical workers, who were attracted for a while to right-wing
radicalism, now also turned to left-wing extremism; some minorities
longed for equal rights and an eradication of majority nationalism. A
great many Jews, survivors of the Holocaust, sought security against
populist-nazi anti-semitism. All these different groups found a kind of
hope in communist programs. Moreover, communist positions were
fortified by the increasing role and influence of the Soviet Union, which
emerged from the war as a great power.

The first postwar elections in Czechoslovakia assured a relative majority for the Communist Party, the only one in the region which remained legal and had been a mass party before World War II. In the other countries the communists emerged from decades of illegality, emigration, and prisons. Most of them were running for parliamentary representation for the first time in their history. The former opposition parties generally, but most particularly the peasant parties, gained much ground as well.

A genuine revolutionary communist takeover, as in Yugoslavia or Albania, however, was unthinkable. The bulk of the population was apprehensive, frightened by the possibility of a communist acquisition of power. Communist rule meant Soviet domination. The Soviet Union, even at the height of her postwar international prestige, was hardly popular among the masses of these countries. Atrocities, rapes, and thefts suffered at the hands of arriving Soviet troops; anxiety regarding communist revenge; and fear of imminent collectivization, together with the impact of decades-long right-wing propaganda, all guaranteed a majority for anti-communist parties. The middle classes, the small-scale proprietors, and the bulk of the peasants all opposed communist power. In some cases traditional anti-Russian sentiment, centuries-long historical antagonism, especially in Poland and Hungary (where Russia was the suppressor of their eighteenth- and nineteenth-century fight for national independence), significantly contributed to anti-communism. Traditional prejudice and popular anti-Semitism also played a certain role. Communism, in some countries, was successfully equated with Jewry and labelled as "Judeo-Bolshevism."

The strengthened communist parties, therefore, could not count on a genuine revolutionary or peaceful electoral victory in Central and Eastern Europe. The basic trend all over the region was the formation of coalitions which incorporated different trends and parties. The spectrum was fairly large: on the one hand, the prewar regime was restored in Czechoslovakia; on the other, the former (partly illegal) opposition of the prewar regime, which never gained power, took over in Hungary. Czechoslovakia was the only country of the region where the restoration of a prewar democratic republic, and thus continuity, was possible. The London based government-in-exile and President Beneš were able to gain the recognition of the Soviet Union in July 1941, and agreed with Stalin to organize a Czechoslovak military unit under the operational control of the Red Army. Beneš signed mutual assistance treaties with the Soviet Union in December 1943 and in 1944, which assured to the exiled government control over the civil administration in liberated Czechoslovak territories. Beneš moved to Moscow in March 1945, and his government, based in Kosice and headed by Zdenek Fierlinger, declared its program.

Most of the traditional parties were reorganized (except the Slovak People's Party and the formerly leading Peasant Party, both banned because of their right-wing orientation during the occupation). Even though Czechoslovakia was, in most part, liberated by the Soviet Army, while Western Bohemia (to Plzen) was liberated by the Americans, both armies were recalled before the end of 1945. The prewar regime was restored and a genuine coalition was formed. The first postwar free elections of May 1946, already without the presence of foreign troops, reflected a definite shift to the left. The Communist Party had grown to become the single strongest party in the parliament with 38 percent of the votes, followed by the Czech National Socialist Party (18 percent), the People's Party (16 percent), and others.

The balance of power was guaranteed by the presidency of Eduard Beneš, an institution in continuity himself, and the premiership of Klement Gottwald, head of the communists. The key position of minister of foreign affairs was granted to the son of the founding father of the republic, Jan Masaryk. Though newly formed Czechoslovakia became more radical and plebeian than ever before, it was still a continuation of the former republic.

In Hungary, a plebeian radicalization was markedly stronger. Both the former ruling government parties and the extreme right-wing organizations were compromised and dissipated from the political arena. Power automatically went over to the former opposition, which had never succeeded in running the country during the Horthy era. At the very beginning, parallel to the advancing Soviet troops, liberated villages and townships spontaneously formed self-governing people's "National Committees." A kind of revolutionary self-government, dominated by previously oppressed democratic and left-wing groups, was established. They welcomed the Red Army as a double liberator from both German oppressors and the regime. At the end of 1944 a provisional parliament and government was formed, made up of representatives of the former opposition parties, including the Communist Party.

A revolutionary, spontaneously started land reform parcelled out the big estates, which dominated the countryside and comprised roughly 40 percent of the land. De-nazification and a radical purge of former state and public offices initiated a change of guard. Soviet-backed communists acquired great power in all newly formed institutions.

The first free elections in November 1945, however, halted this process and consolidated a more balanced, genuine coalition. The absolute majority (57 percent) was given to the Smallholders Party, a democratic peasant opposition party in the 1930s. In the new situation, however, the Smallholders attracted the votes of those urban and non-peasant voters who were frightened by a communist takeover. The Communist Party, on the other hand, did not receive more than 17 percent of the votes. Roughly the same percentage was given to the Social Democratic Party, while the radical, left-wing Peasant Party won 9 percent. These three parties, with more than 40 percent of votes, formed a so-called "left-wing block," which was assisted from outside by the strong, communist-led trade unions. The head of the Smallholders, Zoltán Tildy, after the proclamation of the Hungarian Republic (February 1946), became its first president. The other leader of the party, Ferenc Nagy, headed a genuine coalition government. Certain key positions, however, most importantly the ministry of interior, the police force, and the secret police, were granted to the communists owing to direct Soviet intervention. The communists' power was stronger than the percentage of votes they received.

After the liberation, similar genuine coalitions were formed in Romania and Bulgaria. In Romania, even a kind of continuity was assured by King Michael, who remained at his post and appointed a coalition government headed by General Sănătescu, and consisted of four members both of the National Peasant Party and the National Liberal Party, the two traditional governing parties in interwar Romania. The shift toward the left was expressed by the participation of the socialists (with three portfolios) and the communists (with one minister in the cabinet).

In Bulgaria, the traditional democratic Agrarian Union and its leader, Dr. G.M. Dimitrov, played a leading role in a genuine coalition with all the left-wing parties, including the communists.

Various political parties with rather different programs and aims participated and competed with each other in free elections. They formed real coalitions, based upon common short-run goals and interests, in an atmosphere of a kind of national emergency, and in most cases in the presence of the Red Army and a Soviet-led Allied Control Commission. The coalition of former ruling and/or opposition parties was democratic and more radical than any prewar government in the region. Democratization was linked with fundamental social reforms.

The common platform of postwar Central and Eastern European coalition governments was strict anti-fascism, from legislation to purges and punishment of nazi murderers and collaborators.

The coalition governments, furthermore, wanted to create an institutional, legal basis for democracy. Parliamentary and electoral reforms were introduced and new constitutions were adopted with established legal principles; human rights were secured by new legislation.

The postwar governments included left-wing forces as well, which wanted to combine the introduction of democracy with rudimentary social reforms. One of the key elements was a severe land reform. Parcelling out Czechoslovak, Polish and Hungarian big estates, which occupied 20 to 40 percent of the land of these countries, started immediately after the war. The Hungarian provisional government declared the law on land reform in March 1945 and redistributed the land among more than 642,000 families. (Estates above 100 and 200 cadastre "hold" [140 and 280 acres], big estates and peasant holdings respectively, were parcelled out.) Radicalism characterized the Polish reform of September 1944: estates over 100 hectares were handed over to more than 1 million families. (483,000 farms from the newly created 788,000 located on the former German territories.) Czechoslovakia distributed German and Hungarian landed estates in three stages (June 1945, July 1947 and March 1948), then all the estates above 50 hectares. Altogether, 14 percent of the land was given to 350,000 families. Big estates in the Balkan countries were insignificant, and thus land reforms in Bulgaria, Yugoslavia and Romania touched only 2 to 8.5 percent of the land respectively. Estates larger than 50 hectares practically disappeared in the region.

The Church was strictly separated from the state. In most of the countries, important social policy and welfare measures were initiated. Old age pensions, health insurance and the improvement of working conditions became generalized. Equal rights and equal wages for women were guaranteed. Still existing feudal ranks and titles such as count and baron were deleted. Education was extended to children of peasant and workers' families. The coalition governments sought to build a popular, Jacobin democracy.

In foreign policy, they aimed at creating a secure international position: friendship with neighboring countries and an equal, correct alliance with both the Western democracies and the Soviet Union.

The democratic coalition governments in Central and Eastern Europe suffered from permanent pressure on the part of the controlling Soviet authorities. The Allied Control Commissions and Soviet troops in the former enemy countries (Romania, Bulgaria, and Hungary) provided the legal means for Stalin, with the acquiescence of the other Allied powers, to intervene to assure Soviet "security interests." In practice, this possibility was granted to the Soviet Union in Poland, too.

Stalin, who strongly desired to maintain the war-alliance, ordered the communist parties to remain moderate. He wanted to avoid open conflicts with his allies. Stalin was cautious enough not to provoke Western powers. The Soviet Union suffered the most devastating war destruction, paid the heaviest death-toll and deteriorated in a severe postwar economic decline. The 27 million deaths, a devastated Ukraine, an industrial capacity cut by 42 percent and a harsh famine in the country was in striking contrast with the considerable strength acquired by the United States, which doubled her industrial production and GNP during the war. The difference in industrial potential which existed between the United States and the Soviet Union before the war quadrupled. The military capability of the United States, with its monopoly of the Bomb, sharply increased. "Truman expressed his pride," wrote the historian of postwar international relations, "saying that America could tell itself that it had come out of this war the most powerful nation on earth and perhaps the most powerful nation in all history" (Fontaine, 1968–9 p. 267).

This is why Stalin did not rush to exploit the opportunity of an immediate expansion. He opposed Tito's rush to introduce the Soviet system in Yugoslavia. (Tito did not accept Stalin's ukaz, and this actually led to the first conflict between them.)

Mátyás Rákosi in Hungary obediently followed Stalin's orders and accused the older communist generation of 1919 of being "leftist adventurers" for urging the party to take advantage of the presence of the Red Army and introduce socialism. Following Stalin's tactics, the Hungarian communists encouraged private entrepreneurs to open their businesses. At the first national party conference of May 1945, the strongly emphasized leitmotif of communist policy was coalition, reconstruction, private enterprise, and moderation.

On the other hand, Stalin, panicked by an imagined possibility of a Western attack, and monomaniacal and paranoid enough to see an enemy in every ally, concentrated on building up a controlled buffer-zone under his unquestioned domination along the Western border of the Soviet Union. Accepting the importance of genuine coalitions in Central and Eastern Europe, on the one hand, he secretly began to prepare for his later dominance, on the other. Soviet military commanders of the Allied Control Commissions – in several cases leading associates of Stalin, such as Kliment Voroshilov in Hungary – strongly asserted Soviet security interests and the requirement of constant de-nazification, and did not hesitate to use open pressure to assure communist control of key power positions, such as the secret police, the security organs, the ministries of interiors, or the like. They achieved this with equal effect in Czechoslovakia and Hungary. Indeed, intervention became an everyday practice, and assured important power positions for the communists, irrelevant of their electoral success or failure (Hammond, 1982).

The "bogus coalition" of the "people's democracies"

The political situation, nevertheless, was deficient for Stalin, who asserted that the Soviet Union had a vital strategic interest in Central and

Eastern Europe. Thus, in these cases, he did not tolerate the domination of potentially anti-Soviet, anti-communist political forces.

Hugh Seton-Watson speaks about three stages of the communist seizure of power, beginning with a genuine coalition and followed by a "bogus" coalition, which led to monolithic communist power (Seton-Watson, 1961, pp. 169–71). The first stage, a genuine democratic coalition, never existed in Poland; after a very short period of limited pluralism in which the peasant party played a strong role, Poland dropped immediately into the second stage, the bogus coalition.

The Polish pattern was soon followed in Romania and Bulgaria, where Stalin attained the upper hand through his deal with Churchill. A few months after his compromise in Greece, Stalin sought to cash Churchill's check. The Soviet Union forced Romania and Bulgaria to oust all independent-minded coalition partners and replace them with left-wing fellow travelers or simply obedient collaborators.

This transition in Romania occurred in the most spectacular way. During the period of the short-lived real coalition between August 1944 and March 1945, strong tension and bloody political and ethnic confrontations were evident. Conservative-nationalist Maniu (National Peasant Party) guardsmen unleashed anti-Hungarian pogroms. Battles erupted in Moldavia as well. A communist mass demonstration took place at the Palace Square on February 24, 1945, in which the communists led attacks against public offices, triggering a violent anti-communist backlash.

The political crisis reached its climax at the end of February 1945. At this point, Stalin did not hesitate to intervene openly. The Soviet troops, present in the country, occupied the headquarters of the Romanian army and disarmed the Romanian troops. Meanwhile, the Soviet deputy minister of foreign affairs, Vishinsky, arrived in Bucharest and demanded the appointment of a new premier, Petru Groza, head of the Ploughman's Front, an ally of the communists. King Michael acceded to the Soviet ultimatum, and, on March 6, 1945, the National Democratic Front of the communists, socialists, Tătărăscu's liberals, and the Ploughman formed a "bogus" coalition (Giurescu, 1971). "I realize," wrote Eden to Churchill after the March "incident" in Bucharest, "that if we invoke the Yalta Declaration in respect of Roumania, we may expect the Russians to do the same in regard to Greece or elsewhere" (Fontaine, 1968–9, p. 254).

Roughly the same thing happened in Bulgaria. Strong Soviet pressure led to the resignation of Dr. Dimitrov, the leader of the Agrarian Union. The partner parties of the coalition were taken over by fellow travelers, loyal to the communists. Real independent groups were thus pushed aside, and the genuine coalition ended. The Soviet type "elections" of November 1945, held without opposition, led to the victory of the "bogus," communist-led coalition. Genuine coalitions survived the final year of the war only in Czechoslovakia and Hungary.

After the November elections in 1945, the absolute majority of the Smallholder's Party was tactfully counterbalanced by the left-wing block. The cunning communist leader Mátyás Rákosi successfully combined the mobilization of radical masses, assistance from the Soviet Union, and heavy reliance on the secret police to mastermind his "salami tactics," in which the majority Smallholders were gradually sliced into smaller and smaller parts. The communists and the left-wing block demanded the expulsion of various steadfast politicians based on false accusations and the fabricated "anti-republic conspiracy" case. An "unmasked conspiracy" was exploited in order to weaken the leadership of the Smallholders centering on Secretary General Béla Kovács. When the parliament refused to give a green light for proceedings against Kovács, the Soviets directly intervened: appealing to their "security interests," they arrested and deported Kovács to the Gulags in February 1947. Others were expelled from the party as a result of a combination of communist political pressure, blackmail, and arrests. Three leading expelled Smallholder politicians, Sulyok, Pfeiffer, and Barankovics, formed independent opposition parties.

The final blow fell in May 1947. Prime Minister Ferenc Nagy left the country on May 14 to visit Switzerland. On May 28, at an extraordinary meeting of the government chaired by Rákosi, the communist deputy prime minister, a Soviet bill of indictment on the Béla Kovács affair was presented with Kovács's "damning testimony" on Nagy. The government called on him to resign and return. The manipulated timing offered an easy solution: Nagy signed a letter of resignation but never returned to Hungary.

The genuine Smallholder's Party was destroyed and taken over by second-rate fellow travelers. Lajos Dinnyés became prime minister; István Dobi, a former left-wing peasant politician, linked the party to the left-wing block. The "sliced" Smallholder's Party was no longer an obstacle. The elections of August 1947 (still a free one in spite of a scandalous falsification of a few tens of thousands of added communist votes), led to the victory of the government coalition: the communists gained no more than 22 percent, but with the Social Democratic Party (17 percent), Peasant Party, and the surrendered remnants of the "Gleichschalted" Smallholders, the coalition received roughly 60 percent of the votes. The newly formed opposition parties won 40 percent and remained for a short time in the parliament until they were eliminated (Balogh, 1985).

Communist-led coalitions, declared to be Peoples' Democracies, were a cautiously prepared transition toward Soviet-type state socialism. In most cases the Peoples' Democracies carried out major nationalizations. As early as January 1946, all industrial firms employing more than fifty workers were nationalized in Poland. Former German property was completely expropriated, and certain sectors, such as mining, energy, sugar, textile, printing, and flour-mills, were nationalized regardless of size. In Hungary, after an early nationalization of coal mines, followed by the complete state control (actual nationalization) of the four biggest iron-steel and engineering firms "for the period of war reparations," the ten biggest banks (and their industrial shares) were nationalized in the fall of 1946. The bulk of Hungarian industry, with 57 percent of its employees, was actually taken over by the state.

Similar steps were taken in Czechoslovakia, where the communists were strong enough in the coalition to initiate them. In October 1945 the parliament passed a law of nationalization: all banks, mines, the bulk of the iron, steel, and chemical industries, and all firms that employed more than 400 employees were expropriated.

In 1947 all of these countries introduced two- and three-year reconstruction plans (planning, except in Yugoslavia, was not the Soviet-type, but more of a radical form of state intervention), partly by reintroducing war-economy measures (Kaser, 1987). Needless to say, state intervention and nationalization became rather widespread in quite a few European countries. Great Britain nationalized her coal mines soon after the war. Huge state sectors were built up in France, Italy, and Austria.

War-devastated Central and Eastern Europe, suffering from severe shortages of food, energy, raw materials, and transportation capacities, and in some cases obliged to pay war reparations (both Hungary and Romania paid $300 million, and Bulgaria $65 million), could not survive without state rationing, distribution, and control. (War compensation itself absorbed 15–17 percent of the national income in the immediate postwar year, but still represented a 7–10 percent burden up to 1947.) State intervention was thus necessary owing to the postwar economic crisis. Hungary ended a most horrifying hyper-inflation and carried out a successful financial stabilization without foreign help in August 1946 on a production level which amounted to only half of the prewar one. Without strict state control of prices, wages, credit, and production, the relative stabilization of the currency would have been impossible. Reconstruction of the infrastructure and war compensation deliveries also belonged to the responsibilities of the state.

The government, therefore, became the most important buyer in a hardly existing market. Seventy-five percent of the income of industrial firms originated from state orders in 1946–7 in Hungary. Because of a lack of sufficient sources, the state supplied and regulated the financial market as well. On top of this, financial stabilization was already realized by a special kind of planning by 1946. As a result of hyper-inflation, financial stabilization could not automatically reconstruct price and wage structures; all these had to be planned by the state (Berend and Ránki, 1985).

If the active role of the state in economic planning emerged from postwar necessities, the situation was further exploited in the years of the "bogus" coalition, in order to strengthen the state vis-à-vis the private economy and reinforce the role of the Communist Party, which practically ran the government and monopolized state power. Communist parties took advantage of economic scarcity and skillfully used state intervention, which was indeed necessary, in order to intensify their own influence and power and also to prepare the transition toward a Soviet-type economy.

The Peoples' Democracy was thus a camouflaged transition toward a communist takeover and the Sovietization of Central and Eastern Europe (Brzezinski, 1961). But at the same time it was an arena for a rise of the peasant and worker masses and the beginning of a genuine, indigenous modernization attempt as well. A plebeian left-wing revolutionary upswing characterized most of these countries. These mass movements served as a natural basis for different kinds of left-wing peasant, socialist, and communist parties. They attacked the old social hierarchy, the still existing remnants of former "noble societies" and, in several cases, the strong dominance of the Church, which had been the biggest landlord in these countries; these movements quickly implemented the separation of Church and state, and the secularization of education. The control of large monopolies, and state intervention in general, in order to rebuild and modernize the country, were among their political demands. It was a great wave of emancipation of the masses, formerly excluded from politics. For the first time in the region, mass peasant and worker parties became part of the power structure and of government.

The communist parties, however, participating in this revolutionary struggle, and even playing a positive leading role in it, in the meantime started to manipulate and exploit the genuine mass movements for their hidden ambitions. While circulating popular, democratic slogans, they prepared for a seizure of power and the introduction of a Soviet-type regime.

The bogus coalition of the Peoples' Democracies was planned for a longer transition. As Ernö Gerö, the deputy leader of the Hungarian Communist Party, suggested at the time at an internal Party Active, the communists could not count on a complete takeover for at least ten to fifteen years. Stalin, at that time, obviously believed in the possibility of the maintenance of the war alliance and wanted to keep only one of his feet in the door. The communist-dominated regimes, without an open adoption of monolithic Soviet communism, became subservient allies of the Soviet Union.

The rise of the Cold War and the "year of the turning point": the introduction of state socialism

International relations gradually changed and arrived at a dramatic turning point in 1947–8. The wartime alliance was gradually replaced with confrontation, and in that year the break became manifest. Stalin's drive to rule Central and Eastern Europe by strengthening his communist allies was strongly motivated by his fear of a preventive Western attack. He suspiciously counted unfriendly Western steps and sought to be better prepared. On the other hand, the Western allies rightly recognized Stalin's semi-hidden expansionism as an imminent danger that should be prevented. Mutual suspicion generated desperate measures on both sides: the Cold War was in the making.

The origins of the emerging confrontation have been heatedly debated ever since its appearance. The most widespread view in the Western world is that it was Stalin's aggressive expansionism which generated a Western reaction. As John Lukacs put it: "Hitler . . . was alone responsible for the outbreak of the Second World War; Stalin . . . was the principal architect of the iron curtain and the cold war" (Lukacs, 1961, p. 65).

The Soviets, on the other hand, blamed the American administration for an anti-Soviet conspiracy, and described the Russian stand as that of self-defense. Since the Soviet Union lost the Cold War, recent interpretations seem to confirm the victor's view.

The history of the Cold War was a mixture of political and ideological antagonism, misunderstanding, suspicion, fear, and panic, and hasty reactions to all of these. Most of all, the Cold War was a consequence of interrelated, self-generating chain reactions. The Churchill–Stalin pact and the Yalta debates might have led Stalin to the conclusion that, to a certain extent, he had the upper hand in the neighboring countries and his security interests were accepted. As an old Machiavellian, he certainly was convinced that he could go a bit further if his intentions remained hidden.

Stalin must have also thought that he had been walking on a beaten path since great power interference was a common practice. The British and the Russians had jointly interfered in Persia, the British had interfered in Egypt and Iraq, the Americans in France (in the controversies between Darlan, Girand, and de Gaulle) and in Italy (in the controversies between Badoglio and the opposition).

Cordell Hull recalled the American doctrine of military intervention in other American countries in certain circumstances (Act of Chapultepec) and noted: "Once we had agreed to this new position on intervention Russia had more excuse to intervene in neighboring states, and we had less reason to oppose her doing so" (Deutscher, 1967, p. 517)".

Stalin definitely believed that his Western partners might accept a division of spheres of influence, with his interests in the East and theirs in Western Europe (Suny, 1987). Roosevelt and Churchill agreed at Roosevelt's home in Hyde Park, New York, a few weeks before Churchill's trip to Moscow, that they did not want to see a communist government in Italy. Churchill did not hesitate to seek Stalin's acceptance and cooperation in order to achieve this aim, and "Stalin tacitly agreed to use his influence to restrain the Italian communists" (Carlton, 1981, p. 244). Stalin interpreted his wartime talks with the Western allies to mean that he would have a predominant influence in Eastern Europe in exchange for American and British influence in Western Europe.

Isaac Deutscher was convinced that

Stalin was eager to show that he was keeping his hands off the spheres of British and American influence ... In Western Europe, especially in France and Italy, the Communist parties had ... gained enormous prestige and authority ... It was undoubtedly under his inspiration that the French and Italian Communist parties behaved with extraordinary, selfless moderation. (Deutscher, 1967, p. 518)

Stalin did not comment on the joint American–British action in Belgium either, which created a critical situation in Brussels in November 1944. Members of the Belgian resistance, first of all the communists, socialists, and Flemish nationalists, refused to turn in their arms to Allied military authorities. The Greek incident was not repeated in Belgium, and Stalin quietly accepted both actions.

In Central and Eastern Europe, however, he sought to strengthen his positions. Establishing his sphere of interest was certainly also inspired by Stalin's suspicion concerning the foundation of a world-wide network of American air-bases. As Henry Wallace, the former vice-president under Roosevelt and member of the Truman administration, pointed out in a confidential letter to President Truman of July 23, 1946: "to develop a security zone in Eastern Europe ... [is] small change from the point of view of military power as compared with our air bases in Greenland, Okinawa and many other places thousands of miles from our shores." Wallace added that "to the Russians all of the defense and security measures of the Western powers seem to have an aggressive intent ... going far beyond the requirements of defense" (Bronstein, 1968, pp. 240–2). The already cited historian aptly stated that "a new and world-wide American expansion was beginning between 1945 and 1947, and whether it was generated or only accelerated by Stalin's actions" was not important (Fontaine, 1968–9).

Stalin, who was suddenly dropped into the middle of great power world politics, simply continued his old routine based on domestic political tactics and began to break agreements, going further inch by inch. After the inauguration of Truman, Averell Harriman, the experienced American ambassador, suddenly arrived in Washington to see the new president: "one of the reasons that made me rush back to Washington," he explained to Truman, "was the fear that you did not understand . . . that Stalin is breaking his agreements" (Truman, 1955–6, p. 5). Harriman warned Truman that a "barbarian invasion of Europe" might occur.

Stalin's calculations, on the other hand, may have been strongly influenced by his fear of a possible American attack. Did he have real or only imagined reasons for that? Stalin carefully watched the movements of his Western allies. In February 1945 he was informed about "Operation Sunrise," a secret Anglo-American and German meeting in Bern." Obergruppenfuehrer Karl Wolff, the commander of German SS forces in Italy, initiated secret discussions regarding a German surrender, and Allen Dulles immediately began negotiating. Even if the Soviets were informed, Molotov was told by Harriman that they could not attend the discussions. Since there were a lot of hints that Germany would be ready to surrender to the Western allies and join the alliance against the Soviet Union, Molotov was shocked and responded: "it is not a question of . . . misunderstanding – it is something worse" (Kimball, 1984, p. 586). Stalin sent a nervous and angry message to Roosevelt blaming him for not telling the truth in saying "that there have been no negotiations yet" (ibid., p. 610).

A further major blow, the death of President Roosevelt, contributed to undermine Stalin's confidence in his Western allies. Churchill had cabled to Roosevelt on October 18, 1944 that Stalin, during their Moscow meeting, "several times . . . emphasized his earnest desire for your return at the election and of the advantage to Russia and to the world which that would be" (Kimball, 1984, p. 359). Roosevelt was an ally, and certainly the only ally, that Stalin had confidence in. The succession to the presidency of Harry Truman, a rather different character, certainly contributed to Stalin's increasing suspicions and fear. Truman warned Molotov in a stoic matter-of-fact manner immediately at their first meeting, and spoke of "seriously shaken confidence." When Molotov indignantly answered "I have never been talked to like that in my life," Truman did not hesitate to remark "Carry out your agreements and you will not get talked to like that" (Truman, 1955–6, p. 82). Averell Harriman, who was present at the Truman meeting, was greatly surprised by the shift in attitude.

It was not, however, only a different tone; the situation dramatically changed as well. The most important changes occurred after the successful

American landing and advance in Europe. Roosevelt, who was later blamed for his "soft" attitude toward Stalin, had sent on April 6, 1945 his agreement to Churchill's letter to Stalin with a very characteristic explanation: "I am pleased with your very clear strong message to Stalin ...Our armies will in a very few days be in a position that will permit us to become 'tougher' than has heretofore appeared advantageous to the war effort" (Kimball, 1984, p. 617).

If an improved military position had already generated Roosevelt's idea to get tougher with the Russians, Truman had much stronger reason to do so a few months later. The turning point, no doubt, was the Bomb, a weapon with the greatest psychological effect, and "a weapon with the greatest potential political impact" (Lukacs, 1961, p. 63).[3]

On July 16, 1945, the first atomic fusion bomb was exploded at the Alamogordo Air Base in New Mexico. General Leslie Groves was certainly mistaken when he wrote in his enthusiastic report of the test: "The light from the explosion was seen clearly ... at points generally to about 180 miles away. The sound was heard [from] the same distance" (Bronstein, 1968, pp. 38–9). Indeed, it could be seen and heard much further than that! The very next day the Potsdam Summit was opened. "At Potsdam," noted Truman in December 1945, "we were ... almost forced to agree to Russian occupation of Eastern Poland ... At the time we were anxious for Russian entry into the Japanese War. Of course we found later that we didn't need Russia there ... I do not think we should play compromise any longer ... I'm tired of babying the Soviets" (Truman, 1955–6, pp. 551–2).

Upon acquiring the monopoly of the atomic bomb, American strength was confirmed. "[W]hat did these thousands of peerless soldiers [of Stalin] count against a few bombs that could bring their government to its knees? At no point was Truman tempted to use America's atomic monopoly to force Russia. But this monopoly provided him with an 'umbrella' under which he could, without too many risks, pursue his policy" (Fontaine, 1968–9, p. 267).

The monopoly of the atom bomb changed American policy, which suddenly shifted from wartime collaboration to confrontation with the USSR (Nitze, 1989). From this perspective, the bomb, even though it had tremendous military importance, shortened the war and certainly, in a paradoxical way, saved hundred of thousands of lives. The physicist and

---

[3] Secretary Stimson wrote: "In March 1945 our Air Force launched its first great incendiary raid on the Tokyo area. In this raid more damage was done and more casualties were inflicted than was the case at Hiroshima ... Similar successive raids burned out a great part of the urban area of Japan, but the Japanese fought on. On August 6 one B-29 dropped a single atomic bomb on Hiroshima. Three days later a second bomb was dropped on Nagasaki and the war was over" (Bronstein, 1968, pp. 38–9).

Nobel-laureate P.M.S. Blackett's famous maxim was still true as well: "The dropping of the atomic bombs was not so much the last military act of the Second World War, as the first major operation of the cold diplomatic war."

The Cold War "process," of course, had begun much earlier. One of its most visible elements was Stalin's aggressive actions in Poland. From this point of view, everything that happened later, including Churchill's bloody intervention in Greece and Truman's "tough" policy based on the monopoly of the Bomb, was only a Western reaction to this.

Actually, it was the point of departure of a uniquely frank and long discussion (five meetings!) between Harry Hopkins, one of Roosevelt's closest foreign-policy advisors, and Stalin, who received Hopkins, as Charles Bohlen reported in a memo, as a special envoy of the new President on May 26, 1945. Hopkins explained that the American public had become seriously disturbed by Russia's actions, and "it would be very difficult for President Truman to carry forward President Roosevelt's policy." The reason for this was "centered in our inability to carry into effect the Yalta Agreement on Poland." Stalin replied that he "desired to have a friendly Poland but that Great Britain wanted to revive the system of cordon sanitaire on the Soviet borders." At the second meeting Stalin described that Soviet governmental circles "felt a certain alarm in regard to the attitude of the United States government. It was their impression that the American attitude towards the Soviet Union had perceptibly cooled once it became obvious that Germany was defeated, and . . . the Russians were no longer needed." Stalin then listed all the wrongs they endured, among them the humiliating and brutal "manner in which Lend Lease had been curtailed . . . If the refusal to continue Lend Lease was designed as pressure on the Russians in order to soften them up, then it was a fundamental mistake."

Concerning the Polish question, Stalin stressed again that "in the course of twenty-five years the Germans had twice invaded Russia via Poland . . . Germany had been able to do this because Poland had been regarded as a part of the cordon sanitaire . . . and that previous European policy had been that Polish governments must be hostile to Russia . . . It is therefore in Russia's vital interest that Poland should be both strong and friendly." In diplomatic language, Stalin also wanted to be remembered for his agreement with Churchill, and remarked "that Soviet action in Poland had been more successful than British action in Greece, and at no time had they been compelled to undertake the measures which they had done in Greece" (Bronstein, 1968, pp. 169–74).

At this time, needless to say, the Bomb was not yet on Stalin's list. A few weeks later, however, this became Issue Number One. Keeping the issue of atomic energy and the monopoly of the Bomb a secret had not been Truman's decision, but had actually been decided in Hyde Park, at Roosevelt's home during his meeting with Churchill in September 1944. Truman, who didn't know about the A-bomb, was informed of its existence by Secretary Stimson only on April 12, 1945, after his first cabinet meeting. A few days later, Stimson discussed the broader aspects of the subject with Truman. He underlined that the "question of sharing it with other nations and, if so shared, upon what terms, becomes a primary question of our foreign relations" (Bronstein, 1968, p. 4).

Seven Chicago scientists who worked on the preparation of the bomb presented a report to the Secretary of War on June 12, in which they suggested that "Russia . . . may be deeply shocked" by America using the Bomb. "If an international agreement is not concluded immediately . . . this will mean a flying start toward an unlimited armaments race" (Bulletin, 1946). Stimson suggested an immediate agreement and the invitation of the Soviets "into a partnership upon a basis of cooperation and trust . . . a satisfactory international arrangement respecting the control of this new force . . . For if we fail to approach them now . . . having this weapon . . . their suspicions and their distrust of our purposes and motives will increase." The Secretary of War suggested that "the Russians and the British would agree with us that in no event will they or we use a bomb as an instrument of war unless all three Governments agree to that use." (Bronstein, 1968, pp. 221–3). The cabinet debated Stimson's memorandum in mid-September, but the majority and President Truman rejected the recommendation.

Another liberal attempt met the same fate in the summer of 1946. Henry A. Wallace, the former one-term Vice-President and now Secretary of Commerce in the Truman cabinet, who supported Stimson's suggestion, tried to convince Truman to change his policy toward the Soviet Union in a confidential letter on July 23, 1946. "[W]e are preparing ourselves to win the war which we regard as inevitable." Stalin's policy, according to Wallace, was understandable: "I think we would react as the Russians appear to have done . . . [to equalize] our bargaining position . . . The Russians will redouble their efforts to manufacture bombs, and they may also decide to expand their 'security zone' in a serious way" (*New York Times*, 1946).

Since Truman ignored the suggestion, Wallace began a public attack. On September 20 Truman announced: "I have asked Mr. Wallace to resign from the Cabinet. It had become clear that between his view on foreign policy and those of the administration . . . there was a fundamental conflict" (Bronstein, 1968, p. 247).

The policy of cooperation was defeated, the liberals were dismissed and the "get tough with Russia" policy gained new momentum. Secretary of State Byrnes delivered a speech in Stuttgart denouncing Soviet policy and offering American assistance to Germany: "The American people want to return the government of Germany to the German people. The American people want to help the German people to win their way back to an honorable place among the free and peace-loving nations of the world" (ibid., p. 238).

Roosevelt argued for disarmament and the de-industrialization of Germany. He used strikingly strong language: "We have got to be tough with Germany and I mean the German people, not just the Nazis. You either have to castrate the German people or you have got to treat them in such a manner so they can't just go on reproducing people who want to continue in the way they have in the past." In his Quebec meeting with Churchill, Roosevelt invited Secretary Morgenthau to present a ruthless plan for destroying Germany's industrial economy "to push back the Germans to their primeval agrarian origins and to start all over again." Churchill even suggested an addendum to the statement: conversion of "Germany into a country primarily agricultural and *pastoral* in its character" (Kimball, 1984, p. 317).

This attitude was replaced by Byrnes' Stuttgart declaration offering a helping hand to the former enemy and openly denouncing a former ally. Was this the devilish logic of history at work? Or perhaps it was the most prosaic realization of the "lunatic" prediction of General de Gaulle to Colonel Passy, the chief of his Deuxième Bureau, on the very night of Pearl Harbor in 1941: "Now the war has been definitely won. And the future will have two stages: the first will be the salvation of Germany by the Allies; as for the second, I am afraid, that will be a major war between the Russians and the Americans" (Dewavrin, 1947, p. 236). If de Gaulle could have this vision in 1941, would not Stalin have developed the very same suspicion after having been informed in Potsdam of the existence of the American bomb and having experienced the change in American attitude?

His genuine aggressiveness and expansionism was reinforced by a monomaniacal anxiety over his endangered security. He saw a kind of security in building a buffer zone between his potential enemies and the Soviet Union. It was a return to the traditional Russian military doctrine, which had already been used against Napoleon and was implemented twice during World War I, when territory offered the possibility of withdrawal, and against surviving German offensives. The Brest–Litowsk compromise led to the loss of huge territories, but Stalin did everything to regain them from 1939 on. He realized how much the large size of his country had contributed to his victory. To acquire further territories, in his eyes, became more important in 1945–6 than ever before.

On the other hand, the victorious Western great powers learned another lesson from World War II. The "appeasement policy" of Chamberlain had not satiated but actually increased the appetite of the aggressor. Hence the only sensible and rational policy was one of strength and firm resistance.

Misunderstanding and suspicion complemented each other. One cannot know what would have happened had a stable policy of Allied cooperation survived Hiroshima. Was it a naive dream that trust would generate trust, as Stimson argued? The questions above are not answerable anymore. This alternative was lost in the sea of unrealized possibilities. With so many others, cooperation became one of Hiroshima's countless victims.

A self-generating Cold War rapidly emerged. Fear produced fear, aggressiveness led to aggressiveness. Churchill, the most stable wartime partner of the Soviets, cabled his dramatic vision to Truman on May 12: "An iron curtain is drawn down upon their front . . . the whole of the region east of the line Lubeck–Trieste–Corfu will soon be completely in . . . [Soviet] hands. To this must be added the further enormous area . . . which will, I suppose, in a few weeks be occupied, when the Americans retreat, by the Russian power" (Fontaine, 1968–9, p. 243).

The fear of Russian occupation of the European continent (a paranoia equivalent to Stalin's monomania?) was formulated for the first time. Churchill expressed his fear in a more explicit way in a conversation with Joseph Davis, the special envoy of the President, on May 26–7: "The present lines . . . of the British and US Armies should be maintained, lest Communism should dominate and control all of Western Europe" (Bronstein, 1968, p. 177).

Less than a year later, on March 5, 1946, Churchill accepted the invitation of the remote Westminster College in Fulton, Missouri, Truman's alma mater, and delivered his dramatic message:

Nobody knows what Soviet Russia and its Communist international organization intends to do . . . or what are the limits, if any, to their expansive . . . tendencies . . . From Stettin to Trieste an iron curtain has descended across the Continent. [Behind that] the Communist parties . . . are seeking everywhere to obtain totalitarian control . . . throughout the world, Communist fifth columns are established and work in complete unity . . . [which] constitute a growing challenge and peril to Christian civilization . . . Our . . . dangers . . . will not be removed by . . . a policy of appeasement . . . the old doctrine of a balance of power is unsound. (Churchill, 1974, pp. 7290–2)

What motivated Churchill's almost hysterical declaration of a policy of military strength and confrontation in the place of cooperation? His suspicion and old hatred against an expansionist new communist super power? The lesson of the appeasement policy that he condemned and did not want to let happen again? His effort to strengthen or rebuild Britain's European great power position based upon his strongly advertised concept of the unity of the English-speaking nations against a communist evil? Probably all of these.

A week later, Stalin, in an interview, answered in the same tone: "I do not know whether he and his friends will succeed in organizing a new armed campaign against Eastern Europe after the Second World War; but if they do succeed ... it may confidently be said that they will be thrashed just as they were 26 years ago" (Fontaine, 1968–9, pp. 267–77).

The Fulton speech was not the start of the Cold War but made it manifest. Afterwards, both parties soon switched into the fifth gear. A day after the Fulton speech the Truman administration sent a warning to the Soviet government urging the withdrawal of Soviet troops from Iran; instead they started to move toward Teheran. The United States stood firm and, two weeks later, Stalin acceded to the demand and promised a retreat within two months.

In August 1946, Soviet troop movements were reported along the Turkish border to establish a permanent Soviet base in the Dardanelles. The famous American battleship *Missouri* and the giant aircraft carrier *Franklin Roosevelt* appeared at Istanbul. Stalin backed down.

After these incidents, a new chapter in the Greek civil war was opened. The British informed Washington of their plans to withdraw their 40,000 troops from the country, their presence there having become a heavy burden that they did not wish to carry anymore. But without the British presence, the royalist government was clearly threatened with collapse. Truman stepped in. On March 11, 1947 he declared to Congress that the United States had to "support free peoples who are resisting attempted subjugation by armed minorities or by outside pressures." Truman suggested economic and financial aid to assure "economic stability and orderly political process ... The seeds of totalitarian regimes are nurtured by misery and want. They reach their full growth when the hope of a people for a better life has died. We must keep that hope alive" (Truman, 1955–6, p. 106).

The "Truman doctrine" was introduced. It was a declaration of an anti-communist crusade or, as Senator Edwin Johnson called it, "a declaration of war against Russia." Truman began to realize the concept of the "containment policy," formulated by George Kennan.[4]

[4] George Kennan, analyzing the Russian attitude, declared: "At bottom of Kremlin's neurotic view of world affairs is traditional and instinctive Russian sense of insecurity ... Soviet power, unlike that of Hitlerite Germany, is neither schematic nor adventuristic ... It does not take unnecessary risks ... it is highly sensitive to logic of force. For this reason

General Patton, the *enfant terrible* of the American military machine (still in the fall of 1947), warned the world to prepare for the "inevitable Third World War," and stated that "he could reach [Moscow] in thirty days." (Fontaine, 1968–9, p. 299). Patton was forced to retire. In a few months General Lucius Clay sent a secret message to Washington from Berlin expressing his feeling that the war "may come with dramatic suddenness" (Bronstein, 1968, p. 269). The atmosphere of panic and war hysteria was already in the air.

The "declaration of war" and the warning for the preparation of an inevitable Third World War occurred at the same time on the other side of the iron curtain as well. Top delegates of eight European communist parties gathered in the castle of Szklarska Poreba in Poland in October 1947 to establish the Cominform, which was founded "to coordinate the activities of the Communist Parties." Zhdanov, the chief ideologue of Stalin, delivering the opening speech, repeated Churchill's idea in another way: two camps had been set up in the world, "the imperialist and anti-democratic camp, on the one hand, and the anti-imperialist and democratic camp, on the other." The latter, headed by the Soviet Union, was to resist the threat of new wars and "imperialist expansion" (Stokes, 1991, pp. 40–2).

The open confrontation became an everyday routine. When Secretary of State George Marshall announced his plan to help the world to "return to normal economic health" in his speech at Harvard University on June 5, 1947, and the United States offered 13 billion dollars for this aim, the Soviets indignantly refused it as "political pressure with the help of dollars" and interference in the internal affairs of other countries" (*Pravda*, 1947). The Central and Eastern European countries and Finland were forced to act accordingly.[5]

The Big Three could no longer agree on the solution to the German question. The American, British, then French occupation zones were united; a "Bi-zonia" then "Tri-zonia" were established. When the Western powers introduced a new currency in their merged occupation zones in West Germany on June 23, 1948, the Soviet Army closed all routes to the Western zones of Berlin in retaliation, provoking the sharpest

it can easily withdraw – and usually does – when strong resistance is encountered at any point." (The full text of the George Kennan cable of February 22, 1946 in: *Truman*, pp. 202, 210.)

[5] Stalin had received the invitation to join, hesitated for a few weeks, even sent Molotov (with a delegation of eighty-nine people!) to Paris, then decided to answer in an aggressive way. Molotov with his men left Paris at 4.00 a.m. on July 3, 1947 and attacked the Plan as an attempt to divide Europe. Allan Dulles, in a recently discovered manuscript, however, also flatly stated that the Plan was "not a philanthropic enterprise ... But ... the only peaceful cause now open to us which may answer the communist challenge" (Dulles, 1993, p. 116).

postwar crisis. The fear of a new war swept over Europe. A top communist leader said in a later interview that they had received information from Stalin in the spring of 1948 that "World War III is inevitable in three to four years."[6] Ana Pauker, the Minister of Foreign Affairs of Romania, said basically the same to family members in the late 1950s.[7]

Up to this time, one could not exclude the possibility of an alternative to Russian domination of Central and Eastern Europe. "The pattern exists in the case of Finland. It is surely the case that the Western powers would have tolerated Russian influence over the countries of Eastern Europe comparable to that exercised over Finland, and regarded it as the legitimate outcome of Russia's anxieties for her own security" (Luard, 1964, pp. 59–60).[8]

The same author cited certain interpretations of the fact that Communist control of Central and Eastern Europe reached its final stage only in 1947–8: "The intensification of Communist control over Eastern Europe was the consequence rather than the cause of the breakdowns of relations with the West . . . [T]here may be some truth in this view" (ibid., p. 52). It is certainly more accurate to say that the Sovietization of the unfortunate region was both a cause and a consequence of the collapse of the wartime alliance and its replacement with mutual suspicion, distrust, misunderstanding, and hostility. Four decades of Cold War followed.

Stalin changed his tactics and decided to speed up the open Sovietization of Central and Eastern Europe. In "the year of the turning point," 1947–8, the communist take over was completed. The most dramatic and thrilling change occurred in Czechoslovakia, the only country of the region where a genuine coalition and democracy still survived. In February 1948 a deep political crisis was provoked. Domestic communist forces, using their legal role in the government, mobilized the Factory Councils and the Farmers' Union and, with a kind of coup d'etat, took over the police. As a response, non-communist members of the government resigned (Svitak, 1990). "The current crisis of power," stated Gottwald at a meeting in the National Theater on February 22, "is nothing more than a general attempt by the reactionary forces to turn back the development achieved up to now" (Gottwald, 1981, p. 433). Communist crowds occupied the streets, and President Beneš had no other alternative

---

[6] Author's interview made in 1960 with Ernö Gerö, Number 2 in the Hungarian hierarchy in the Stalinist period.

[7] This fact was discovered by Robert Levy, who interviewed Tatiana Brătescu, the daughter of Ana Pauker, in December, 1990.

[8] The author also stresses the alternative to the German solution. The pattern in this case is Austria. "The occupation of Austria, its division into zones and the further division of the capital, lying within the Russian zone, exactly paralleled the occupation of Germany. But there the similarity ceased" (Luard, 1964, p. 39).

but to appoint a communist-led People's Front government.[9] The minister of foreign affairs, Jan Masaryk, a symbol of Czechoslovak democracy who decided to remain in his post, was found dead in the grounds of a courtyard of his ministry in March.

A Soviet type "election" in May 1948, without the participation of any kind of opposition, resulted in an 86 percent victory for the communists. President Beneš resigned in June and died a few months later. Czechoslovak democracy died with him. The inauguration of the new president, Klement Gottwald, head of the Communist Party, was the inauguration of dictatorial state socialism in Czechoslovakia.

The transition from "bogus" coalition to a monolithic state socialist system was perfected all over Central and Eastern Europe in a few months. Two major steps characterized the elimination of coalitions. The allied coalition partners were pushed out and the social democratic parties absorbed. Both actions were executed in a cruel manner. Nikola Petkov, the leader of the Agrarians in Bulgaria, was arrested in June 1947 on fabricated charges of conspiracy; he was tried, condemned and executed in September. The opposition socialist leader Lulchev was arrested in the summer and sentenced to fifteen years imprisonment in November 1948. In Romania, in June 1947, Mihalache and Maniu, National Peasant Party leaders, were arrested and given life sentences. Titel Petrescu, the opposition socialist leader who refused fusion with the communists, was arrested in May 1948. King Michael was forced to abdicate at the end of 1947, but allowed to leave the country. In Poland the peasant leader, Mikolajczik, having been informed of plans for his arrest (two political trials presented "evidence" against him), secretly left the country. Most of the Hungarian opposition leaders, Imre Kovács, Béla Sulyok, Zoltán Pfeiffer, and Károly Peyer, also escaped. Cardinal József Mindszenty was arrested and imprisoned.

Throughout Central and Eastern Europe in 1947–8, all non-communist political parties were annihilated. Social democratic parties shared the same fate, but were liquidated in a different way. Several non-collaborating socialist leaders were promptly expelled from the parties. In Poland quite a few did not return from exile (e.g., Arciszewski), or were arrested by the Soviets (e.g., Puzak). In Hungary Károly Peyer, followed by the independent-minded centrists Antal Bán and Anna Kéthly, were expelled. The parties were taken over by either left-wing communist sympathizers

---

[9] Gustav Husák, on the occasion of the 25th anniversary of the "triumphant February revolution," as the communist coup was officially named, stated: "When the bourgeoisie attempted to carry out their counterrevolutionary reversal in February, millions of . . . members of the working class answered the call of the Party . . . The powerful force of the people . . . pushed through a decisive revolutionary and constitutional resolution . . ." (Husák, 1977, p. 139).

and/or ambitious second-rate party officials (a Cyrankiewicz in Poland or a Fierlinger in Czechoslovakia) who were ready to merge with the communist parties. Social democracy was eliminated by fusion. It happened in a uniform way in 1948: in February in Romania, in June in Hungary and Czechoslovakia, in August in Bulgaria, and in December in Poland.

Very many politicians, former coalition or opposition members who were ready to collaborate, were given low governmental posts in order to demonstrate the existence of a "broad peoples' front." Very many quietly disappeared from political life; quite a few became victims of later purges.

Obtacles no longer existed. André Malraux's aphorism, each failed communism generates its fascism and each failed fascism leads to its communism, had materialized in this part of Europe. The communist seizure of power was concluded in 1947–8.

2 The closed society in Stalinist state socialism after 1948

In the late 1940s and early 1950s, the Central and Eastern European countries obediently copied the Stalinist regime. They all declared the dictatorship of the proletariat and introduced the monolithic party–state political structures. This system, which was "introduced" according to a blueprint, was transplanted from the pages of textbooks into institutional and social reality. The system was constructed on a stringent ideological basis of "Marxism–Leninism" and its Soviet enforcement.

The ideological foundations

From mid nineteenth-century Marxist principles, via turn of the century Leninism, to Stalin's ideological canonization of Soviet practice, a simplified but consistent ideological system was constituted. A brief summary of its conceptual make-up might help to illuminate the aims and characteristics of the foundation of the regime.

The point of departure was the Marxian notion of the development of social formations, which saw mankind as marching from ancient, primitive communism, through the stages of class societies (slavery, feudalism, capitalism), toward an ideal advanced communist society. The engine of progress is the development of the force of production, namely technology and human knowledge. In the first stage of each social formation, the mode of production creates an encouraging environment and impetus for the rapid progress of the force of production, but each social formation reaches its zenith and after that point becomes an obstacle for its further advance.

In class societies, the struggle of the oppressed classes against the ruling class undermines and destroys the obsolete social formation and creates a new one, which again assures subsequent progress. The history of mankind is a history of class struggle. Capitalism, progressive and constructive at its first stage, provided a tremendous impetus to economic development, but at its higher stage, fulfilled its historical mission and became an obstacle for further development of productive forces. To sweep away all hindering social and institutional barriers, the "basic contradiction of capitalism," a highly socialized production versus entirely private expropriation, would have to be solved.

The social force which alone was destined to carry out the order of history is the industrial proletariat. This most progressive class was created by capitalism, but now become its grave-digger. Fighting for its own interests, the proletariat is realizing its historical mission and is serving the interests of the majority of the society.

This struggle reached its final stage in the age of imperialism, a concept heavily debated around the turn of the century by Karl Kautsky, Rosa Luxemburg, Nikolai Bukharin, and Lenin. While Kautsky argued that imperialism is a "policy" of the bourgeoisie which may be changed through the organized struggle of the workers, the latter three agreed that imperialism is the last and closing phase of capitalism, the epoch of proletarian revolution.

At that time "Marxian Marxism" split into two diverging trends, a Western social democratism and an Eastern Bolshevism. Social democratic Marxism followed a peaceful reform policy based on a democratic mass movement and parliamentary struggle, while Bolshevism initiated the split and prepared for violent revolution.

This new age, argued Lenin, requires a new type of revolutionary vanguard party, which will "revolutionarize" society, prepare and organize the revolution, and be the leading architect of a new society. Lenin rejected the genuine Marxian concept that revolution would come in the most advanced countries, which would act together (Marx, 1970), insisting that the proletarian revolution would not happen in the core of rich countries with their corrupted workers–aristocracy and reformist socialist parties, but on the fragile and weak fringe of the imperialist world system. Russia alone, Lenin declared, might start the process.

World War I and the Bolshevik revolution constituted the opening act. In the backward peripheries a "permanent revolution," originally a concept of Trotsky, emerged out of the realization of a missing bourgeois revolution, through the laying down of the foundations of socialism, followed by the accomplishment of the first stages of socialism leading toward a communist society.

This process was accompanied by the continuing decline of capitalism. As a consequence of unavoidable wars and major crises, originating from imperialist capitalism, more and more countries and regions would break from the capitalistic world system.

All this led to a permanent sharpening of the class struggle within and between countries after the proletarian revolution. In the international arena, according to Stalin, war was unavoidable because of the increasing aggressiveness of world imperialism. The clash between the two camps would lead to a further spreading of socialism until the final collapse of capitalism.

The revolutionary proletariat destroys the bourgeois state, expropriates private property, and mobilizes the alliance of the poor peasantry, with the latter voluntarily joining collective farms and constructing a new, socialist form of collective ownership in the place of private farming. This idea, invented by Kautsky and adopted by the old Friedrich Engels, became a theoretical pillar of Leninist peasant policy, and was then translated by Stalin into the practice of forced collectivization. In initiating a cultural revolution, the proletariat constructed its own intelligentsia. By organizing its own dictatorship, a dictatorship of the majority of the society, the proletariat erected a just and equal society where the big lie of capitalist "democracy" and "equality" was replaced by concrete and genuine material democracy of social-state ownership and the most direct democratic people's representation. Marx predicted a permanent increase of the proletariat – since capitalism polarizes the middle strata of the society – and thus dictatorship would represent the democracy of the majority by taking over the bourgeois state.

After the Paris Commune, Marx changed his mind, and, instead of taking over the bourgeois state, he suggested the introduction of the new, "Paris Commune" type of direct people's representation. (It served later as a basis for Lenin suggesting a Soviet [council] form, born of the 1905 Russian revolution, as a form of worker's self-organization and representation, which was reproduced after the revolution of February 1917.)

As Marx and Engels' *Communist Manifesto* already predicted, socialism, based on collective ownership, would replace the market economy with planning, and thus re-establish a harmony between the mode of production and the force of production, which opens unlimited prospects and the highest possible growth rate. Planned economies do not know economic crises and destroy all barriers to technological development. They also offer a more just redistribution.

The egalitarian principle of distribution was laid down by Marx, who maintained that the proletariat would realize a just and equal distribution of income. This would occur in the first stage (socialism), due to the principle of "from each according to his ability, to each according to his work," as well as in the final, advanced stage (communism), based on "from each according to his ability, to each according to his needs." Marx believed in direct distribution instead of using money, as did the Bolsheviks, after their revolution (Marx, 1966).

The dream and ultimate goal of socialism and communism was a just and equal society, without private ownership and with an equal distribution of wealth. Communist ideas, noted the Italian philosopher Norberto Bobbio, in writing about the defeat of the communist Utopia, "are present in the history of human thinking since Plato. Aristotle, although criticizing Plato, also added that all men think justice be a kind of equality" (Bobbio, 1990, 1994).

Stalin's only genuine contribution to communist ideology was the thesis that Russia could only start the communist revolution, but, in contrast with Lenin's and Trotsky's views, could also "build up socialism in one country." He summarized the theory of "Leninism," the Bolshevik version of Marxism and the Russian experience, in a simplified text book manner in his "Short History" of the Bolshevik party. The works of Stalin became akin to communist bibles (Stalin, 1947).

All the key principles of "building socialism" were rigorously sanctioned. The regulations of collective farms, the wage system, the detailed limitations of small-scale private activity or so-called personal property, were ideologically determined.

Ideology played a central role in the building of state socialism. It served, first of all, as a pattern to be realized, as well as a religious doctrine and thus a basis for legitimizing contemporary actions for a desired future.

Political structures: the state-party in the center

At the center of the newly built political regime stood the Communist Party, which became the unquestionable monopolist of power: a state-party (Tomaszewski, 1989). From an illegal and elitist organization, these parties became huge mass organizations in the postwar years. After having seized power, the system was run by the party. All major decisions were made, all major institutions were directed and controlled, and all major personal appointments were initiated by the party.

Whether government, legislature, or court, or whether central or local state organizations, all played only a formal executive role, and were responsible for the realization of central decisions made by the party. Communist state-parties actually constructed an organizational structure that was appropriate for this task: they had secretaries and departments which were responsible for certain fields, such as the economy, health, education, army, or foreign relations. The party was both a legislative and executive institution. Official state organizations had no independent role or autonomy, and merely "translated" party decisions to state actions (Skilling, 1966).

A five-year economic plan, for example, was conceptualized and developed by a department of the Central Committee, headed by one of the secretaries of the Central Committee, and then was accepted and formed as a resolution that was compulsory for the party and state organizations. Afterwards the government's planning offices worked out the detailed plan, the parliaments enacted them as laws, and the various ministries "broke down" the plan for sectors and firms and controlled their execution (Kaser, 1970).

A uniform system, with minor differences in certain details, was equally characteristic of the entire region. The communist state-parties had a hierarchy, modelled from the Stalinist Bolshevik organization. The highest authority was the head of the party, in most cases the secretary general (in Czechoslovakia the president), a kind of mini-Stalin or semi-god. The top leaders, in several cases, were well-known heroes of the labor movement and the anti-nazi resistance: Yugoslavia's Tito and Albania's Enver Hoxha were legendary partisan leaders. Bulgaria's Georgi Dimitrov was a celebrated hero of the Leipzig Reichstag-trial in 1933 who defeated his accusers before the nazi-court. Hungary's Mátyás Rákosi was a people's commissar of the 1919 Hungarian Council's Republic and then a prisoner in Horthy's prisons for sixteen years, and Georghe Gheorghiu-Dej spent more than a decade in prison in Romania.

Others, such as Klement Gottwald of Czechoslovakia, Boleslaw Bierut of Poland, or Vlko Chervenkov of Bulgaria (after the death of Dimitrov), became heads of their parties after having spent many years in Russia and working up the party bureaucracy, but could not claim a heroic background. All the "number ones" were declared to be "the best pupils of Stalin" and the same local "cult of personality" developed around them as had around Stalin. They were all wise and calm, had an unlimited knowledge and working capability, and were infallible experts of both economic and artistic issues. A statement, speech or article of a secretary general revealed the direction for the country, and became a text to study and cite.

Two secretary generals: Tito and Gottwald

To introduce a most genuine hero-type of communist leader, the best example is certainly Josip Broz Tito, a living legend at the age of fifty-three, when he became the head of liberated communist Yugoslavia.

Tito was born in a small village of Kumrovec in a mixed Croatian–Slovenian peasant family of fifteen children. He was poorly educated because he had to work on the fields by the age of eight. His first independent decision was, at the age of fifteen, to move to Sisak to train as a mechanic, and work from 6 a.m. to 6 p.m. At the age of eighteen, a young, independent worker, he joined the Metal Workers' Union and in two years became a member of the Social Democratic Party.

As a non-commissioned officer of the Austro-Hungarian army, he found himself at the Russian front in 1915. Severely wounded in his left side by a two yards-long Circassian lance, he was placed in the ward for the dying in a prisoner of war hospital near Kazan, but survived to join the International Red Guard immediately after the Bolshevik Revolution, and joined the Communist Party in January 1919.

After a few years of living a poor worker's life in Yugoslavia during the first half of the 1920s, he began to live the life of a professional revolutionary. Changing his job according to his party and union tasks, Tito was occasionally imprisoned and emerged as a hero of a trial in the stormy year of 1928. Having spent five years in prison and a few years of Comintern work, Tito became the secretary general of the Yugoslav Communist Party in 1937 and an organizer of the resistance movement after the nazi occupation.

He soon built up a large, well-organized army, fought for quite a long time without outside assistance, defeated the Chetnik attacks and several German offensives, miraculously escaped numerous German traps, and won the unquestioned recognition of the Big Three in Teheran. Enthusiastically elected as President and Marshal already in November 1943, Tito became the internationally celebrated liberator of Yugoslavia.

This background itself was more than appropriate to establish a formidable reputation both inside the country and internationally. Tito was, however, much more than a "regular" communist hero. He was "a man for all seasons," a proper gentleman living a full life. Coming from a village of 200 inhabitants, he became a world citizen who lived in Vienna, Prague, Budapest, and Munich as a young worker, spent half a decade in war- and revolution-ridden Russia from St. Petersburg to Siberia, resided at the Hotel Luxor on Gorki Street in Moscow during the dramatic thirties as an employee of the Comintern, and worked in an office in Paris recruiting volunteers for the Spanish civil war.

Having been trained as a locksmith (the tip of his index finger on his left hand was caught in a machine), Tito was an uneducated man, but he was fluent in German and Russian, spoke some French, and even managed to learn English in his sixties. He was also a dedicated sportsman, having trained as a skier in the winter of 1913–14, attained second place in the Monarchy's all-army fencing championship in Budapest on the eve of the war, and joined a mountain climbing club in 1934. In 1940 he translated the *History of the Bolshevik Party*. Occasionally, he also played the piano.

As his one time comrade Milovan Djilas characterized him: "he seemed to know something about everything ... his skill was considerable in general technical matters ... no machine or mechanical process was alien to him. ... He was familiar with agriculture and farm production" (Djilas, 1980, pp. 8–9). But Tito was first and foremost a glittering political genius: stabile, decisive, and self-confident enough to swim against the stream; a charismatic leader who revolted against Royal

Yugoslavia and struggled against Hitler. Although having been a former Comintern employee in Moscow and a selected party leader of the Comintern, he made his own decisions and did not consult with Stalin. When it became unavoidable, he did not hesitate to follow his own road and risk an open confrontation with the Soviet Union. He was also a successful military leader without a real military education. He was always willing and ready to learn.

Tito, unlike quite a few communist leaders, was a flesh and blood man with "an unconquerable will to live," using Djilas' words. He was a man "passionate in everything – food and drink, love and hate, decision-making," a man, who "laughed wholeheartedly at a well-told joke, sometimes to the point of tears . . . his body heaving with amusement" (Djilas, 1980, pp. 15, 119, 121). Unlike all the other fellow communist leaders, Tito was extravagant. He had four wives, always much younger than himself (twelve years younger in the first and thirty in the fourth case), and always striking beauties. He married two of them, while the two others remained common-law wives.

In addition, he also had a strong attraction to elegance and luxury, which was even more unorthodox and visible. As a symbolic and characteristic action, from the honorarium of the translation of the *History of the Bolshevik Party*, Tito bought a diamond ring in 1940(!) "He was always clean-shaven, neat, and organized," remembers his comrade in arms during the war years, "as if invulnerable to the conditions of war. Everything that was his . . . had to be superior" (Djilas, 1980, p. 22).

He loved and was not afraid to live in palaces: in 1941, when his partisans seized control of Užice, he occupied the finest building of the city. A few days after the liberation of Belgrade, he went to see the Royal Palace, ordered its restoration and rushed to move in before the war ended. In power, he was a notorious collector of powerful cars and yachts, had palaces all over the country, loved well-tailored suits and uniforms.

Tito was not an imitator but a competitor of Stalin. "Yugoslavia," noted Djilas, "was too small for Tito" (Djilas, 1980, p. 69), a man larger than life. "It is small wonder," wrote his British biographer, "that this extraordinary man, who has lived through enough experience for several full lives, should have become a legend in his own lifetime" (Auty, 1974, p. 345).

A man Tito met in Moscow in the mid thirties while working in the Comintern, a man elected to the Presidium of the Executive Committee of that organization in 1935, the year Tito arrived in Moscow, was the Czechoslovak communist Klement Gottwald. They lived for a while in the same building. Up to that point, the lives of these two men represented a twin story.

Gottwald, only four years younger than Tito, was born in a poor farm-worker's family in Dedice, a small Moravian village. From the rural environment of the same Austro-Hungarian Monarchy, he became an apprentice in Vienna at the age of twelve, then, as a carpenter, joined the Social Democratic youth organization in 1912. Like Tito, Gottwald also became a soldier in the Monarchy's army during the war.

The parallels of the life stories of the two secretary generals began to part in the 1920s, when Gottwald's spectacular party career began. From the left-wing of social democracy, he soon joined the communists and was already working as editor of party newspapers in the early twenties. With a political career of a communist politician possible and legal in democratic Czechoslovakia, this talented worker was on his way. At the age of twenty-nine he was elected as a member of the Central Committee and the Politburo. Out of conviction, he became an advocate of the Bolshevization of the Czechoslovak Communist Party, a Stalinist trend of the twenties in the international communist movement, and sought the confidence of Stalin. In 1928, he was elected as a member of the Executive Committee of the Communist International, and established very close connections with the Soviet party. This became the basis for his further successes.

An ardent revolutionary, he played a major role in the internal battles of the party to establish a proper Stalinist line, which led him to the post of secretary general of the Czechoslovak Communist Party by 1929. In the same year, he became a representative in the parliament. Obediently following the Stalinist doctrine he attacked the social democrats in his first speech in the House in December 1929: "We call you social fascist, and you say this is calling names. An ass could say the same . . . if you called him an ass . . . or a murderer, if you called him so. . . . It isn't calling anyone names . . . it is an expression of a real fact . . . you and your parties have nothing in common with the workers. You . . . belong to the single bourgeois family, the family of fascists!" (Gottwald, 1954, pp. 15–16).

A few years later, after having changed the official line of the Comintern and announcing the new program of Popular Front policy, Gottwald declared at the seventh congress of the Czechoslovak Communist Party: "we at our Congress today, set the working class, set our Party, the task of achieving a united popular front at all costs" (ibid., pp. 60–1).

If Tito's attitude was always the independent, courageous one of an initiator, Gottwald always followed a cautious road, emulating Stalin and the Comintern. He never wanted to be a forerunner, and never wanted to stand out. Gottwald was totally satisfied with the role of executing decisions.

If Tito did not make compromises in his private life, Gottwald's was a painful compromise: he married the waitress of a small Slovakian tavern he met in the late twenties and with whom he had an illegitimate daughter. His wife, who became fat, confused "difficult" words such as "conservation" and "conversation." In the evenings, however, he sought refuge with one or two bottles of red wine and often became drunk and fell asleep in his armchair.

"Klema," as he was called by friends and close comrades until he was called "Comrade President" owing to a Politburo decision, had several good qualities. "He had a fantastic memory. He remembered everything that caught his interest . . . also, he had extraordinary common sense, a Czech type of common sense, down to earth, realistic, and not carried away with wishful thinking. . . . He behaved," noted Eugen Loebl, "like a man who owns a farm and is interested in its management" (Loebl, 1976, p. 17).

He used his dictatorial power in a paternalistic way. He, however, more resembled an employee rather than a boss, and hardly ever rushed to be the first to carry out orders. Though initially displaying some reluctance and, at times, indignation, in the end he rarely resisted the dominant trends, and considered himself safe in this position.

During the great Soviet purges, Gottwald, like a mere parrot, dutifully repeated Stalin's accusations: "The trial showed," he emphasized before party officials in February 1937, "that Trotsky had negotiated a pact against the Soviet Union with Hitler's Germany and . . . had been preparing to restore capitalism. . . . [T]his shameful end of Trotsky and Trotskysm . . . [was] absolutely logical" (ibid., pp. 73, 77).

Constantly adapting to ever changing Soviet lines was "absolutely logical" to Gottwald, especially after the many years spent as an immigrant in Moscow. He learned to adjust and forget his own views. Gottwald did not rush to "unmask" Tito by copying Soviet show trials, and delayed the invitation of Soviet "advisors," but in the end sacrificed his best comrades, including the man he absolutely believed in, Rudolf Slansky, and arranged the bloodiest purge of Central and Eastern Europe.

Eugen Loebl, in his book, *My Mind on Trial*, described a most telling episode from 1949. One of Gottwald's closest aids, Geminder, arrived back from Moscow, with a clear message of Stalin's dissatisfaction. Gottwald became angry. In his presidential apartment that night, and having sipped the second bottle of wine, he turned to Loebl and cried: "Stalin, that son of a bitch who does he think he is, that he can treat me like his messenger boy? . . . I am Klement Gottwald! And Czechoslovakia will be Gottwald's Czechoslovakia, not Stalin's . . . Listen . . . always talk friendship with the Soviet Union, but *do* what is good for us" (ibid. pp. 22–3).

Soon afterwards, Loebl was arrested and became Prisoner 1437, one of the victims of the Slansky trial. Gottwald followed his own advice in the opposite manner: he talked about what was good for Czechoslovakia and did what Stalin ordered.

Following Stalin's mad initiative and seeking to save himself by executing his orders, Gottwald "discovered" the "anti-state conspiracy," the "new channel by which treachery and espionage penetrated into the Communist Party . . . Zionism" – as he addressed in a conference of the party in December 1952 (Loebl, 1979, p. 230).

Klement Gottwald, a genuine revolutionary worker, thus became a prototype of the obedient and subservient party clerk. As his life was linked with Stalin's, Gottwald, symbolically enough, died with him as well. Catching pneumonia at Stalin's funeral, he died nine days after his master.

Party hierarchy and discipline

Independent of their past and background, communist leaders of Central and Eastern Europe followed the footsteps of Stalin. On this basis, they were the most powerful masters of their countries.

The party leadership was a rather well-structured organization of decision making. The highest authority was formally given to the party congress, held every fourth or fifth year. Between two congresses, the same authority was given to the Central Committee (80 to 150 members), elected by the congress. The Central Committees, however, had a one to three day session two or three times a year. In the meantime the secretary general ran the entire apparatus with the elected secretaries (responsible for foreign affairs, economy, culture, security, party organization, etc.). Under his leadership the secretaries formed the Secretariat of the Central Committee (eight to ten members). The decisions, made at this level, were based on the work of a huge, ministerial-type apparatus. The Central Committee machine was the real government of the given countries. Its departments were set up according to the requirements of state affairs. The departments prepared the government's resolutions, but also controlled its execution, thus the state apparatus. All major long-term decisions were made by the Politburo (ten to fifteen members), elected by the plenum of the Central Committee and was in some cases called the presidium of the Central Committee, which was the leading body of the party and acted on behalf of the Central Committee between its rare sessions. Party congresses and the sessions of the Central Committee became rather formal yet festive. Real power was concentrated in the hands of small, exclusive bodies, such as the Politburo, the Secretariat, and their professional apparatus.

The hierarchy of the state-party was reproduced at the local level. Each

Table 2.1. *Growth of Communist Party Membership Between 1945 and 1949 (in millions)*

	Poland	Czechoslovakia	Hungary	Yugoslavia	Bulgaria	Romania
1945	0.24	0.71	0.15	0.14	0.03	0.22
1949	1.37	2.31	1.20	0.78	0.50	0.94

Notes: The figures for 1945: in Poland, December; in Czechoslovakia, August; in Hungary, May; in Yugoslavia, December; in Bulgaria, September; in Romania, September. The 1949 figures: in Poland, December 1948; in Czechoslovakia, May; in Hungary, March; in Yugoslavia, November 1952; in Bulgaria, June 1948; in Romania, September 1948.
Source: Brzezinski, 1961, p. 86.

administrative unit of the state (republic, county, town, and even their sub-units, such as district or village), each ministry, including its separate departments, each firm and even its workshops, each university and its departments, all had their party organizations. Party and executive committees, headed by the party secretary and a small leading body, and a network of party organizations, existed inside each institution. The members had regular plenary meetings, but they were organized into small groups and party cells, according to the organization pattern of their institution. The state-party played the same role at the local level as it did nationally. They controlled and determined the activity of each firm, office, or school.

The state-party was not only a center of decision making but also a mass organization. From former illegal elite parties, the Central and Eastern European communist parties began to expand immediately after the war. This process gained momentum after power had been seized. Beside workers, left-wing intellectuals, and enthusiastic young people, more and more careerists joined, those who wanted to keep their positions and those who sought advantages and advancement.

A membership of one to two million meant that in certain cases every fourth or fifth man and woman from the active population were members of the party.

The huge army of freshly recruited communists were strictly organized and disciplined. The Bolshevik principle of "democratic centralism" was rigidly adopted. According to this rule, different views or debates were possible only before a decision was made, but afterwards there was no place for doubt or contention, and working for the realization of all party policies was compulsory.

The unity of the party was paramount, and forming a "faction" or questioning a resolution was considered equal to treason. The paramilitary discipline of the highly centralized illegal communist parties, however, was not easy to introduce or maintain in augmented mass parties. After attaining power, the parties initiated ruthless purges to cleanse their ranks and assure their "vanguard" character and iron discipline. The mass purges ended with heavy expulsions: roughly 370,000 party members were expelled from the Communist Party in Poland, as many as 550,000 in Czechoslovakia, 200,000 both in Hungary and Romania, and 90,000 in Bulgaria. Thus, every fourth member was expelled from the vanguard, for being hostile, alien, petty-bourgeois, a right-wing social democrat, or immature. Expulsion had serious and sometimes existential consequences. The mass state-parties thus became very disciplined, and were in the hands of the central leadership.

Most of the non-party members were recruited and organized by a set of official mass organizations. The communist youth organization, and for the youngest (elementary school) generation, the "Pioneer" organization, were virtually compulsory to join. There were loosely built women's "movements" and "patriotic" or people's front organizations. The broadest mass organizations were the trade unions, with a huge professional bureaucracy and playing partly the role of a state office, responsible for health care, distributing certain social aids, and assuring places in the huge network of the union (Pravda and Ruble, 1986).

All the mass organizations were under the guidance and control of the party. They served as "transmissions" between the party and certain layers of the population, and were responsible for popularizing the party's program and mobilizing members for its realization. They were "preparatory schools" from which the party could select and recruit their most loyal activists. The huge army of mass organizations was subordinated to and centrally directed by the party.

Legal framework, structure and characteristics of party-state

The merging of the party and the state was consistently realized. At the top level it was guaranteed by a personal union of the head of the party and of the state. The secretaries general of the communist parties became prime ministers or presidents, and formed their governments to serve as executive state organs of the party. The foundation of party-states was legalized by newly enacted constitutions. Yugoslavia and Albania introduced their "people's democratic" constitutions as early as 1946. Bulgaria followed in 1947, Romania and Czechoslovakia in 1948. These early constitutions, however, reflected a transitory stage. The first "genuine" state socialist constitutions, modeled after the 1936 Soviet constitution, were introduced after the "year of the turning point," between 1949 and 1952 in Hungary, Poland, and Romania.

As a basic characteristic, the Central and Eastern European countries institutionalized the "dictatorship of the proletariat," the "leading role of the Communist Party," and Marxist–Leninist ideology. One of the clearest expressions of these principles was formulated in the Albanian constitution: "The Socialist People's Republic of Albania is a state of the dictatorship of the proletariat"(I/2); "The Albanian Labor Party is the vanguard of the proletariat and the sole leading force of the state and society"(I/3). The Romanian constitution flatly declared that the "Romanian Communist Party expresses and serves the vital interests and efforts of the people ... [and] leads all the mass- and social organizations and activity of the state organs" (II/26).

The legal constitutional foundations of state socialism incorporated the principle of "socialist ownership." The Czechoslovak constitution describes two basic forms of socialist ownership: state ownership and cooperative ownership (I/8). Small-scale private ownership was granted (I/9), but "expropriation of labor" was prohibited. The Albanian constitution accepted "personal ownership," but limited its sphere to family houses, consumer durables, etc., which were prohibited to be used "against the interests of society"; hence, the use of "personal property" for generating income was generally prohibited (I/23). The Bulgarian constitution stated that "state ownership is the highest form of socialist ownership" and "the different forms of collective ownerships gradually ... will be transformed into a unified people's ownership" (II/15). All the constitutions declared the socialist principle of distribution, using Marx's terminology: "from each according to his ability, to each according to his work."

An important part of these constitutions declared protection for all human rights, including freedom of speech, assembly, press, research and publications. All these formal rights were, in several cases, *expressis verbis* subordinated to public, social or political interests. In the Romanian case, the constitution formulated: "The freedom of speech and press, the freedom of gatherings and demonstrations may not be used against the socialist order" (II/29). In Albania, from the 1960s on, the constitution also maintained: "The State does not recognize any kind of religion" (I/37), and "the foundation of religious organizations" was prohibited (II/55). The legal limitations, however, were much less important than the lack of practical realization of constitutional human rights.

The situation was rather different concerning basic social rights, which were not only guaranteed but mostly realized as well: the right to work, to free public health care, free education, etc. The Albanian constitution refered to the "right to work, which is guaranteed by the state" (II/44), and "paid vacations before and after having delivered a baby," and warranted that the "state is running kindergardens"(II/48).

Because of the constitutionally assured leading role of the communist party, the principle of a divided legislative, executive power, and the independence of the courts were canceled, and all these spheres of power were united in the hands of the party. The parliaments, formally the highest legislative bodies, lost their real importance. Their role became reduced to reformulating party resolutions to state laws. The Polish constitution proclaimed that the "Sejm [parliament] has sessions at least twice a year" (III/22) (Kovács, 1985), an edict found in all other constitutions. It was the same in Romania, while the Bulgarian constitution mentioned three sessions. In Hungary two or three sessions were formulated. Since one session generally took two or three days and everything was unanimously accepted, the sessions of the parliament became a demonstration of unity. They expressed the acceptance of the whole population, whose representatives sat in the parliament and were elected by the entire nation.

"Elections," however, were also festive occasions, organized mass demonstrations like a May Day parade. The candidates were carefully chosen, formally by the People's Front, actually by party organs, and there was only one candidate to one seat. In every fourth, and then fifth year, all citizens were actually compelled to vote for the candidate. To stay away was considered suspicious, and "agitators" would appear at one's home. The uncontrolled results were always spectacular: roughly 96–97 percent participation, with 98.3–98.8 percent voting in the affirmative.

During their few work days, parliaments could not fulfill even their formal legislative task. The rights and responsibilities of the assembly between its two sessions were given to a collective State or "Presidential" council, which had the right to enact law-decrees (or statutory rules). The Bulgarian constitution claimed that the "State-council . . . is the highest organ of the Parliament and assures the unity of legislative and executive activities" (V/90). The State-council had the right not only to enact laws (V/93), but even to declare war and appoint the chief of staff and members of the government (V/94). As a most extreme case, the Bulgarian constitution asserted that the State-council may delegate its rights (i.e., the rights of the parliament) to the president of the State-council (V/96), who usually was the secretary general of the party. Moreover, governments in most cases governed by decree.

Like the legislature, the courts were also absorbed by the monolithic party-state. Formally they belonged to the Ministry of Justice, which appointed the judges. In major cases even the sentence was decided by corresponding party organs. With the exception of political show trials, party and state officials were never tried for criminal offenses. Instead, they were often quietly removed or placed in another post, in order to maintain the prestige of the party. The decision was in the hands of party organizations.

One of the strongest pillars of the party-state was the institution of the *nomenclatura*. The power of appointment of state and company officials at each level, from ministries to firms, from universities and agricultural cooperatives to state offices, was put in the hands of the corresponding party organ: at the top level, the power was given to the Central Committee of the party; at medium and lower levels, it was allotted to the city and county committees. Personnel policy was thus stringently centralized. The state-party ruled and controlled each and every sphere of society, the economy, and culture.

The structures described above were unmistakably characteristic of the "closed society" of state socialism, often called totalitarian. The term "totalitarian regime" became popular as a historical and political category after World War II. The pioneering works of Karl Popper (1950) and Hannah Arendt (1951) described its characteristics and analyzed its origins. A totalitarian regime must not be confused with a dictatorship. The difference between the two is not the harshness of dictatorship, for they are two completely different types of government. A totalitarian regime is a much more consistent tyranny, since it determines every aspect of life from the political, to the economic, to the cultural; from public to private, from the way of thinking to the way of expression, in an entirely state-owned and state-run society.

Although totalitarianism is an appropriate concept to characterize certain structural features of Stalinist state socialism, it is also misleading. First, the concept of totalitarianism equates nazism with communism. No doubt, it helps to understand their striking structural similarities, but it fails to distinguish or rather confuses substantial differences between them. Unlike the inhuman, elitist-racist, and extremely exclusive nationalist nazi ideology, which originated from a desperate nineteenth-century anti-humanist and anti-Enlightenment Völkisch extremism, communist ideology is rooted in two thousand years of Western values. From the aspect of the history of human ideas, Norberto Bobbio stressed, fascism and communism cannot be compared. The basic idea of public ownership and egalitarian distribution, right or wrong, was represented by philosophers, politically minded writers and even theologists for hundreds and hundreds of years. The first attempt, rightly or wrongly, to actualize the Utopia shared by Plato, Thomas More, and Rousseau (who all condemned inequality, originating in private ownership), was historically significant (Bobbio, 1990, 1994).

Besides basic ideological differences, state socialism, unlike nazism, also had a democratic, revolutionary background in the nineteenth century social democratic movement. Although their paths diverged in the twentieth century, a common origin and legacy had an impact on the communist movement as well. The communists were among the most uncompromising champions of resistance to nazism, and fought together with democrats against nazism all over Europe.

The communist parties, although having degenerated into ruthless, bloody Stalinist dictatorships, still retained a connection with the workers and the lower, oppressed layers of society, and realized a drastic and forced social modernization to elevate the lower classes and a great part of backward societies. Communist parties and state socialist regimes thus preserved important elements from their democratic and revolutionary heritage.

The concept of totalitarianism is, furthermore, confusing from a second major aspect as well. Although the Stalinist regime sought to rule and control the whole society and every sphere of life, the centralized apparatus and bureaucratic hierarchy also had to work in the opposite direction, transmitting the requirements and needs of the people, their dissatisfactions and resistance. Even the disciplined mass party was not merely a weapon in the hands of a dictatorial central power, but became an instrument for realizing local and group interests.

Thus the monolithic party, in a paradoxical way, was itself an institution of a fragmentary pluralism. The highly centralized and autocratically led party still cannot be equated with a simple instrument for the dictates of the high-ranking party elite. The latter had to mobilize the whole mass party, its local organizations in towns, villages, firms, and institutions. The Politburo, for example, would not be able to realize the party's "right" concerning the *nomenclatura*, except at the top national level. At local levels, the local party organizations played a determinant role. True, they had to follow the given "party line" and carry out instructions from the centre. The reality, however, was never as simple as that. Party organizations always represented and expressed "group" interests, and was even able to satisfy them.

Party organizations offered the possibility of building local pressure groups for pursuing the interests of certain social groupings. These pressure groups often paved the way for an organized mediocrity in their struggle against "elitism," professional excellence, and status in the interests of the "mean" and the lower layers of society. A natural selection (with definite exceptions) led to the rise of a talented core that occupied the leading positions of the administration, business and education. At universities the best scholars were usually appointed as professors. In a firm's research laboratory the best researcher would gain higher status and privileges. In a workshop the best engineers, foremen, and skilled workers earned the best reputations. Those who were non-competitive and could not achieve status and privilege through merit were able to counterbalance the power and influence of the former groups by using the party organizations to organize themselves as rival pressure groups based on political influence. The executive committee of a local party organization, at the factory, institution or university level, gave the upper hand to professionally second-rate people. It became a kind of unwritten rule (with exceptions) that poorly qualified engineers, professionally unsuccessful faculty members, and poorly skilled workers dominated the party committees of the firms, universities, and institutions.

Party organs, therefore, not only transmitted the orders of the higher command, but enforced and safeguarded the interests of the mean. The revolution of state socialism was, in a way, the revolution of mediocrity. They could satisfy their interests, through appointments and elevations, using the *nomenclatura* in their hands. They were able to successfully struggle against "elitism" and "bourgeois expertise" to assure equal, but in practice predominant, preference for political loyalty, social origins, or revolutionary vigilance.

A great many "average people" in the party were not humiliated by being subordinated to the hierarchy because their real power and influence, and their real interests, lay in attaining influence and advantages at the local level. The party-state was in reality not as totalitarian as could theoretically be assumed from its structures and articulated goals. This, of course, did not lead to the "democratization" of the system, but it definitely enlarged mass participation, as well as certain elements of undesigned, rather partial and fragmented pluralism. It did not secure privileges for all simple party members, but created an institutional framework for safeguarding local self-interest.

The legal system of terror and beyond

All these facts do not deny that there was an unthinkable centralization of power, which caused the strong dependency of the populace (Staar, 1988). Legalized by a new legislation, including a new criminal code, laws prohibited and punished anti-state and anti-party activities by hostile, illegal organizations. A remark or a joke in a company or a public place might cause an immediate arrest. According to the Czechoslovak criminal code (I/100), incitement in the presence of at least two others against the socialist system or alliance was subject to three years in prison. In Yugoslavia (X/118) "hostile propaganda," either written, spoken, or even drawn, including rumors, which "falsely" characterized the situation of the country's social-political state, could be punished by twelve years imprisonment. In Romania even failing to report hostile propaganda or conspiracy (I/170) was enough for a two to seven year sentence; spouses and close relatives were no exceptions. The XIX/127 paragraph of the Polish criminal code declared that "weakening of people's power, generating dissatisfaction and unrest and the disturbance of the people's economy by damaging machinery or buildings," may be penalized with five years in prison, but in very serious cases even with capital punishment.

Diversion or sabotage were punishable by death or fifteen to twenty years in prison in Romania (X/115), and from three years to death in Yugoslavia. Draconian laws defended newly created public property. The IV/224 paragraph of the Romanian criminal code sanctioned, according to the seriousness of the case, prison sentences of fifteen to twenty years, three to twelve years, and six months to four years for stealing, and even the use of the death penalty. In Yugoslavia, if the damage was over 10,000 dinars, sentences could be ten years (XIX/258).

The planned economy was underpinned with similarly rigorous laws. The deviation from central plans without acceptable reason was punished, depending on the seriousness, with three to fifteen years' imprisonment. Any harm to the compulsory delivery system in agriculture led to police intervention, purge, confiscation, and imprisonment. Most private business was declared to be illegal. Strict restrictions limited the possibility of producing for the market. The number of animals to be kept in a peasant household was proscribed, and illegally slaughtering a pig was condemned. Police atrocities and legal procedures became everyday phenomena. The II/117 and 118 paragraphs of the Czechoslovak criminal code, which called for the punishment of three to eight years for "illegal" private business, including the employment of too many people, was mandated. The same crime was punished in Yugoslavia (XIX/226;226/b) with imprisonment from three months to eight years.

The labor code introduced similarly austere regulations. Workers were not allowed to leave their firms without the company's approval. If employees changed jobs without such approval, they lost all pension and health care privileges. The Romanian criminal code (IX/325) punished begging with up to three years in jail, while "hanging around" (IX/327), meaning a person of active age without a job and permanent accommodation, might result in a sentence of up to three years. These type of laws regulated every aspect of the citizens' life, including that of marriage. Paragraph IX/304 of the Romanian criminal code, certainly unparalleled in Europe, punished sex outside the marriage with six months' imprisonment.

Indirect evidence, and the accused's own testimony, was considered legal evidence against him or her in court. Legal terrorization, however, was complemented by unlimited and uncontrolled illegal terrorization by the police, and especially by the secret police, who could arrest, torture and even kill anyone without retribution. Legal limitations on keeping people in jail without trial did not exist. The police had the right to intern anyone for many years without legal procedures being taken.

The fear of a ringing bell or a stopping car in the earliest morning hours, the horror of the disappearance of countless people, terrorized the entire society. High-ranking party officials, celebrated managers of state companies, private peasants, or industrial workers could all equally become victims of lawlessness, and hundreds of thousands actually did.

Purges against "nationalist deviations": Gomulka and Patraşcanu

The most spectacular cases that shocked the Central and Eastern European societies were the major purges and show trials of the highest party leadership, which claimed some of the most prominent leaders, including secretaries general, top Politburo members, heroes of the Spanish civil war and the resistance movements. The first and mildest wave of purges of this type began in 1948. The first prominent victims were Wladislaw Gomulka, the Secretary General of the Polish Communist Party, and Lucreţiu Patraşcanu, a leading Romanian communist and Minister of Justice.

The head of the Polish communist party was criticized by his own Politburo because of his speech delivered at the session of the Central Committee on March 3, 1948. The Politburo declared in a statement that the attitude of the Secretary General "represents a serious move in favor of the nationalist-bourgeois and reformistic traditions," and criticized Gomulka because he "did not review with the Politburo the ideological content of his speech" (Gomulka, 1987, pp. 15–16). At the August meeting of the Central Committee, then in December at the Unification Congress of the communist and social democratic parties, Gomulka was accused of underestimating the role of the Soviet Union and following a nationalist road. His concept of pursuing a "Polish road to socialism" was severely criticized, and his position opposing the creation of the Cominform and the collectivization of the countryside was subject to harsh attack.

Gomulka was first removed and replaced by Boleslaw Bierut, a former émigré, who carried out Stalin's idea to form the Lublin Committee at the end of the war (Rachowicz, 1977). Gomulka was then expelled from the party and arrested (in 1951), but was never tried and executed.

Patraşcanu, who belonged to the wing of Romanian communists that remained in the country, and was imprisoned a number of times, was also accused of being a bourgeois nationalist, of being intolerant of the minorities and of underestimating the enemy's forces. Patraşcanu was expelled from the party and imprisoned. Surprisingly enough, he was executed in April 1954, at a time when some of the purges were already condemned in other countries. Patraşcanu's execution, therefore, certainly did not belong to the "regular" process of the purges, but was a "safety measure" by Gheorghiu-Dej to get rid of a potential competitor (Frunza, 1990).

The first major purges did not have the character of the Stalinist purges of the 1930s with show trials, prefabricated confessions, and executions. Both the above cases, however, were rather important. Both victims belonged to the "home-communists" and were accused of nationalist deviations. Their removal was part of the process of eliminating any kind of nationalistic road or potentially independent line from Moscow, and demonstrated the strong determination of Stalin to create a bloc which obediently duplicated the Soviet model. Stalin could easily find enthusiastic domestic help. Top-level purges offered excellent possibilities to exterminate rivals and solve power struggles. The real reason, however, is not explicable on a domestic basis or by internal motivations. Early purges in Central and Eastern Europe were part of the Sovietization of the region – initiated, conceptualized, and planned by the Soviet secret police, and only carried out by a small group of unconditionally loyal, frightened, and ambitious local party and secret police officials. The first Soviet-type purges soon followed in Hungary, Bulgaria, and Albania.

To "unmask Tito": show-trials of Rajk, Kostov and Xoxe

In the building of a Soviet bloc, a uniform, obedient, allied "Socialist camp" designed according to the Soviet pattern, Tito became a major obstacle. Tito's independent actions posed a problem for Stalin beginning in November 1943, when he declared the formation of his government. Stalin was scared of the Allied reaction and angrily declared: "it is a stab in the back of the Soviet Union" (Authy, 1974, p. 271). He also lamented about the red stars on the caps of the partisans and explained to Djilas that stars were not necessary because they might irritate the Western allies.

Stalin started to attack and to remove Tito (Vucinich, 1982). The affair was highlighted in the spring of 1948. Two letters from the Bolshevik Party to the Yugoslavs criticized certain mistakes and deviations by the Yugoslav Communist Party. Behind the scenes, Stalin tried to recruit loyal followers in the Yugoslav leadership who were ready to turn against Tito and accept the Soviet line. Tito's ambition, self-confidence, and reputation of mythic proportions made him a competitor to Stalin. When Tito initiated a kind of unification with Albania, it did not irritate Stalin. He even gave his blessing to this step, cynically formulating his message to Tito: "We have no special interest in Albania." Stalin later explained to Djilas in early January 1948 that "We agree to Yugoslavia swallowing Albania!" Djilas adds: "At this he gathered together the fingers of his right hand and, bringing them to his mouth, he made a motion as if to swallow them" (Djilas, 1962, p. 143).

But the formation of a Balkan confederation, incorporating Bulgaria and Romania, and even initiating steps toward Hungary, was simply too much. Tito's Yugoslavia attempted to act as a kind of second socialist center. The realization of these plans went against Stalin's aim of rapid Sovietization of the region. An independent South-Eastern European confederation under Yugoslav leadership would be a potential rival and a serious barrier to the realization of Stalin's concept. After the speeding-up of confederation plans in 1947–8, when Dimitrov joined Tito and made a statement in Bucharest on the unavoidable development of a customs union and a confederation of the Peoples' Democracies, a surprising Soviet attack openly clarified Stalin's opposition: "The Editorial Board of *Pravda*," it was stated on January 28, 1948, "maintains that the problem of these countries is not this cooked-up federation, confederation or customs union, but the defense and strengthening of their independence and sovereignty by mobilizing and organizing the internal people's democratic forces" (*Pravda*, 1948).

Tito and Dimitrov were invited to Moscow. Tito did not go but sent Kardelj, Djilas, and Bakarić in his place. The humiliating conversations were superbly described by Djilas: In February 1948, in Stalin's Kremlin office, twelve angry or humiliated men were seated around the table. The Soviet delegation was headed by Stalin and included Molotov, Zhdanov, Suslov, and others; the Bulgarian delegation was headed by Dimitrov and the Yugoslav by Kardelj. Molotov began by announcing that "serious differences had appeared between the Soviet Government on the one hand and the Yugoslav and Bulgarian Governments on the other hand, which is 'impermissible' . . . Yugoslavia and Bulgaria had signed a treaty of alliance not only without the knowledge of but contrary to the views of the Soviet Government." When Dimitrov tried to explain and justify his steps, "Stalin kept interrupting without letting him finish . . . 'You chatter, like women from the housetops, whatever occurs to you . . . You wanted to shine with originality! It was completely wrong, for such a federation is inconceivable . . . ,' shouted Stalin. I glanced sidelong at Dimitrov. His ears were red, and big red blotches cropped up on his face," Djilas recalled. When Kardelj answered to one of Stalin's accusations,

Stalin cried: "It's not so! You don't consult at all. That is not your mistake, but your policy – yes, your policy!" (Djilas, 1962, pp. 175–6, 180, 185).

Stalin was sure that an obedient and dependent Dimitrov would fall into line, and thought that it would be "enough to move his small finger" and Tito would disappear. But he failed. The Cominform was thus mobilized and used to launch harsh attacks. Those Yugoslav high-ranking communists who remained loyal to Stalin, however, were not strong enough to carry out the planned replacement of Tito. He and his closest ruling circle unquestionably dominated the situation. Hebrang, Zhujević, and others could not remove Tito, and Tito ruthlessly ousted them. His party killed and imprisoned Cominform loyalists, and thousands more escaped to neighboring countries. Tito was excommunicated by Stalin but remained the head of an independent Yugoslavia.

The danger of Titoism (later called National Communism) independent from the Soviet Union, and the threat of an independent alliance of the Central and Eastern European countries, had to be exterminated. Massive purges and spectacular show trials were needed to "unmask" Tito, destroy all potential links with him, and attempt to assure a homogeneous, Sovietized bloc with frightened, terrorized, and obedient local communist leaders. In July 1948, Andrei Zhdanov "revealed" at the Bucharest session of the Cominform that the Soviet Union "had proof in [its] possession about Tito's conspiratorial attempts to subvert the Peoples' Democracies in the service of the imperialist espionage agencies" (Hodos, 1987, p. 35).

It was a clear announcement of the preparation of future purges. Rákosi, the subservient Hungarian communist leader, was an ideal collaborator to be utilized. He was invited to Moscow in the early summer of 1948 for consultations. The stage was soon set.

On a Sunday in August 1948, Rákosi invited four members of his Politburo to his home. As one of them, János Kádár, later revealed, "Farkas reported on an intelligence report . . . – from a 'reliable agent in Switzerland' – according to which Rajk was suspected of being an agent for the American espionage organization." László Rajk, thirty-nine years old, a hero of the Spanish civil war and a leader of the illegal Hungarian Communist Party, a member of the Politburo and Minister of the Interior, an uncompromising Stalinist and the "strong man" of the party in the struggle for power, was selected as the main actor of a model trial. Careful preparation began. A special branch was formed under General Gábor Péter, head of the secret police, with his two closest aides, Colonels Szücs and Décsi. They "translated" the Soviet guidelines to fit the Hungarian environment. They worked together with General Fyodor Byelkin, head of the Soviet Security Service for southeastern Europe, who sent two top MVD agents, Generals Likhachov and Makarov, and a whole group of (forty) Soviet "advisors" to Budapest.

The final preparations were concluded when Noel Field arrived in Prague. He was the chosen "agent of the American espionage organization, who smuggled his spies into top ranks of the Communist parties." A Harvard graduate and an American communist, who, as the European director of the Unitarian Service Committee in Switzerland during the war, helped (mostly communist) refugees to promote anti-nazi underground movements, Field was lured from Geneva to Prague by the Czechoslovak secret police on the direct orders of General Byelkin. Field arrived on May 5, 1949. On the same day Colonel Szücs arrived from Budapest as well. Field was arrested and taken to Budapest. On May 18, Tibor Szönyi, head of the Cadres Department of the Central Committee, a former émigré in Vienna and then in Zurich, where he had close contact with Noel Field, was arrested. Rajk followed twelve days later.

The cautiously selected "traitors" and precisely planned procedures assured the success of this nefarious case. Rajk was forced to confess that he was an agent of Horthy's secret police and sent to Spain as a provocateur. His task, after the war, was to infiltrate the party leadership, where he worked for Allen Dulles and Tito. He had a direct connection with Ranković, the head of Tito's secret police, and prepared a plot to kill Rákosi, Farkas, and Gerö and take over the country. The Rajk trial had to prove that Tito was a traitor, an American agent who sought to undermine socialism and separate the Peoples' Democracies from the Soviet Union.

The Rajk case had several secondary aims and messages. It also had to illustrate Stalin's thesis: the class struggle becomes increasingly intense as the enemy is implanted into the party, even among its high-ranking officials, thus making "revolutionary vigilance" especially important, particularly in the case of intellectuals and those who have lived in the West. All the actors were chosen according to this principle: workers and peasants were not among the accused, as it was proudly stated already in the very first communiqué on the arrests. There were no "Muscovites" among them either. Quite a few, however, were from those who lived in Western exile during the war years, or worked in the illegal home movement. Many were of Jewish origin.

The show trial also had to prove that nationalist or other deviations from the party line almost automatically lead to the enemy camp and treason. To squash any doubts, those who lamented or questioned anything had to share the fate of the accused. György Aczél, the secretary of the Baranya-county party-organization, who rushed to Budapest to declare that an arrested friend of his was not guilty, and that he was "ready to put his arm into fire" for him, was arrested and incorporated into the case. This instance was to prove that there is only one loyalty: loyalty to the party.

The victims were endlessly tortured both psychologically and physically. The accused had to write and rewrite their curricula vitae, which were reinterpreted by the interrogators. Harmless contacts became criminal events, real or assumed mistakes became a service to the enemy, all with the intent of generating a kind of self-doubt and uncertainty. Interrogations sometimes went on and on for thirty-six hours by rotating interrogators. Brutal beatings and humiliating torment began immediately. Victims were forced to crawl naked on the floor while brutally beaten. Their teeth were kicked out. Others were hung for hours, their testicles lashed.

Quite a few were beaten to the point of insanity and even death. Endre Havas, a former member of the French resistance movement and a defendant of the Rajk case, and Alexander Kowalski, a former parachuted Polish partisan, lost their minds during the brutal tortures. The former was subsequently beaten to death in his cell, while the latter died in an insane asylum. István Ries, the Hungarian Minister of Justice, and Waclaw Dobrzynski, a general of the Polish secret police, were both beaten to death. Some, such as Milan Reiman and Vlasta Vesela in Prague, escaped by suicide.

The arsenal of torment was endless. One of the survivors later revealed that "sixteen hours a day he had to . . . march up and down his cell, not sitting down even for meals. . . . Even sleep was denied – the short six hours were interrupted by banging on the door every ten minutes, at which he had to leap to his feet and present his report" (Slingova, 1968, p. 79). This went on and on for weeks. Arrested and tortured by their own comrades, deathly tired, confused, and without hope, these people after a few months became psychologically and physically broken human wrecks. "There comes a point," described one of the victims, "where you can stand the interrogations and the torture no longer, and you say to yourself: I want everything to come to an end even at the price of my life. Better death than to go on like this – and this was basically the secret of all 'confessions'" (Goldstucker, 1979, p. 65).[1]

Some, such as Rajk, however, in the most brutal part of his calvary, resisted accepting the accusations. At this point, the methods were abruptly changed. High-ranking comrades, followed by General Byelkin himself, personally convinced Rajk that he had to undertake the role designed for him as a service to the world communist movement. Stalin

---

Goldstucker's first sentence to his interrogator helps to understand the psychological confusion: "You have me at a great disadvantage, because had I been arrested by the enemy, I would resist – but here is my own Party doing it to me. This breaks my resolve" (p. 63).

and the party knew that he was innocent, he was told, but the accusations against Tito were true and the movement needed his sacrifice to unmask Tito. After the trial he would be taken away with his family and allowed to live with a different name. (A similar thing happened to one of the survivors of the Rajk affair, George Hodos, who described his case in his book.)[2]

Beating and brutality were stopped. They received good food and books to read. This dramatic change, together with the former cruelties that could come back again at any time, definitely worked. Most of the victims, faithful and disciplined religious communists, were victims not only of a brutal cynical power, but of their own beliefs and desires to follow the party line. Both murderers and victims served the same god and believed in the same goals. (One of the victims of the Prague purges, L. Frejka, wrote a letter hours before his execution to Gottwald, explaining that he confessed to everything because "I tried to the utmost to fulfill my duty toward the working people and the Communist Party" [Slingova, 1968, p. 94].)

We learned from the authentic descriptions of survivors that preparations for a trial began after several months of struggle, when the defendants were already broken. They had to learn and memorize their confessions and answers to the judge's questions word by word. They learned all the acts and dialogues of face to face interrogations and practiced their parts with their interrogators (Szász, 1979). Rehearsals were staged, and sometimes the defendants were even told that this was already the real trial with live radio broadcasts and the participation of foreign journalists, who were actually plain-clothes secret policemen. The victims never knew whether it was or was not the actual trial.

All in all, former revolutionary heroes, who bravely resisted Gestapo tortures and behaved heroically in Horthy's prisons, now obediently parroted the most horrible, fabricated accusations, and confessed to imaginary crimes, including their role as Gestapo spies. They accepted capital punishment and quite a few, including Rajk himself, cried under

---

[2] Lieutenant Ervin Faludi, an interrogator whom he knew from a local party organization told him in February 1950: "'only your statement is missing. If we don't do it now, you will be tried anyhow, and thirteen witnesses will prove your guilt. You will never leave the prison alive.' Then he sent the silent typist out of the room. 'Listen well Hodos,' he continued, and reverted to the familiar thou form of address, I know you were a devoted member of the party. You must understand that we have to reinterpret your statements, politicize the mistakes . . . If you collaborate, we will know that you are not an enemy.' He and I would write the final protocol together and I would receive a short prison sentence: three years. He could assure me of that even before the trial . . . For the first six weeks, I would live in a villa, my wife could visit me . . . I would work under an assumed name for one of the provincial newspapers until it would be possible to return to Budapest . . . I collaborated. I signed" (Hodos, 1987, pp. 70–1).

the gallows: "Long live Stalin and the Party!" There were a few exceptions. Traicho Kostov, the main actor of the Bulgarian anti-Titoist trial, after giving up resistance, signing his confession, and obediently following all instructions during his open and broadcasted trial, suddenly took advantage of the possibility of repudiating his entire confession and, with his final words, stated: "I consider it as a duty to my conscience to declare before this court and through it to Bulgarian public opinion, that I was never in the service of British intelligence, never participated in the conspiratorial and criminal plans of Tito" (Slingova, 1968, p. 22).

There were some who did not give up resistance at all. Colonel Géza Vietoris, an illegal communist printer, and later one of the founders of the political police, "with his body torn and bleeding . . . signed a confession that he was a police informer and a go-between for Rajk and the fascist police. Then he asked for a cigarette; when he finished it, he retracted the confession. For weeks, the cycle was repeated: torture, confession, retraction. . . . He was sent without trial to a concentration camp" (Hodos, 1987, pp. 69–70).

The Kafkaesque trial, staged in September 1949, achieved its goal: all of the defendants "revealed" their treason in the service of Tito and Dulles. "The joint plan of the American imperialists and Tito," declared Szönyi, "was not recently hatched. . . . These plans are the offspring of the marriage into which Tito entered with the imperialists back in 1944." Another victim, General Pálffy, disclosed at the trial that his Yugoslav counterparts "enumerated to me the countries involved in the plot to create a Balkan federation, made up of Hungary, Bulgaria, and Albania, with Yugoslavia as a leading power." Lazar Brankov, former head of the Yugoslav military mission to Hungary, who left Yugoslavia after the split with Stalin, and who represented the "Yugoslav connection" in the trial, disclosed that Ranković told him "that Yugoslavia should become a central, leading state in the Balkans and in Central Europe and should organize a bloc which would become a federation of bourgeois democratic republics with an orientation toward the West" (Hodos, 1987, pp. 59–63).

Rákosi, delivered a speech on September 30 at the Party Activ of Budapest. He underlined that Rajk confessed that "at the same time as the murder of Hungarian communist leaders and the intervention of Tito's army, they were to organize revolts in the People's Democracies . . . we have to understand that on our southern borders an adventurist gang, capable of anything, is ready to jump and act. . . . One of the lessons to learn is that we have to strengthen our army even more" (Rákosi, 1949).

The verdict was declared on September 24, 1949, and Rajk and four other defendants were executed a few days later. A series of secret trials followed: between 1949 and 1951, more than thirty follow-up trials dealt with 141 defendants. Fifteen were executed, eleven received life sentences, and dozens were sentenced to long prison terms.

Similar show trials were arranged in neighboring Bulgaria and Albania, two countries which closely and enthusiastically collaborated in the preparation of a Balkan confederation. In Bulgaria, the closest ally of Tito in its preparation was Georgi Dimitrov, the best-known champion of the anti-Hitler struggle, and the celebrated secretary general of the Comintern in Moscow. Dimitrov was thus an inappropriate traitor and leading actor of a Bulgarian show trial. He actually silently disappeared from Sofia in January 1949 at the age of sixty-three. A short communiqué reported his illness and his undergoing medical treatment in Moscow in April. His death was reported in July 1949 (Isusov, 1990).

The search for a suitable leading actor began in May 1948. Traicho Kostov, one of the founders of the Bulgarian Communist Party, a hero who was crippled at police headquarters in the 1920s (he jumped from a fourth floor window to avoid giving information about his comrades during endless torture), was chosen instead.

The number-two man in the party, Kostov, disappeared from public view at the end of 1948. His trial was staged in December 1949, where he was accused of treason and having been a police informer during the war and an agent of the British and American espionage agencies and Tito since 1944. Most of the script was borrowed from the Rajk case, since the same team of Soviet advisors conceptualized the purge; only the names, dates and places were "translated." After discarding his final repudiation of his confession in a letter to the presidium of the National Assembly, which he now claimed was made as "a result of extremely excited nerves," Kostov was hanged on December 16, 1949. Roughly 200 victims were tried and sentenced, and half of the Central Committee of the Bulgarian party was removed.

Albania, which went further in cooperating with Tito, and even prepared to merge its economy and army with Yugoslavia, made a dramatic reversal after the Cominform resolution and began accusing Tito of having tried to incorporate Albania as the seventh republic of Yugoslavia. The genuine and real protagonist of this union, a member of the Politburo, Minister of the Interior, and head of the secret police, became a natural victim of Albania's anti-Tito action.

Following Stalin's instructions and with the direct help of Soviet "advisors," the reckoning this time did not follow the accustomed tribal, vendetta-type show down, but was dressed in the form of a trial, where, behind closed doors, "Koci Xoxe and his gang," the "Titoist subversion center," were forced to confess to their "treacherous activity" in the service of Tito and the British Intelligence Service. Xoxe admitted that he was recruited by the monarchist police as an informer in the 1930s, and had worked with Tito's men since 1943 in order, "that after seizing power in both countries, Xoxe should steer the policy of the Albanian party in the direction to absorb Albania into Yugoslavia" (Hodos, 1987, p. 11). They had prepared the murder of Hoxha and the overthrow of the Albanian government to create an anti-Soviet bastion in the Balkans. Xoxe was hanged in July.

Permanent purges. The Slansky trial and the anti-Zionist card

The major trials of 1949, orchestrated by Stalin and Beria, had the special mission of hammering together a homogeneous, united, and uniform Soviet bloc, while destroying all kinds of independent lines, different roads, and potentially competitive smaller groupings.

In each country, however, purges began to take on an independent life. According to Zbignùw Brzezinski, "the purges were closely related to the new phase of development. . . . Power, in brief, corrupts, and a totalitarian system lacks the competitive qualities of democratic party struggle to minimize the corruption. The method of resolving dilemmas was the purge" (Brzezinski, 1961, p. 91). Purges, of course, had a much broader importance than that. They offered a mechanism to eliminate potential deviations or personal enemies. They became a regular form of power struggle in a rigid and centralized political structure. They served to prevent doubts and criticism as well as create an atmosphere of terror. Purges thus belonged to the logic and requirements of Stalinist systems.

No doubt, the Kostov trial was strongly intermixed with the rivalry over succession in Bulgaria and with the emergence of Vlko Chervenkov to the vacated post of Dimitrov. In Romania the purges, more evident than in any other country, were part of the struggle for power. For Gheorghe Gheorghiu-Dej, secretary general of the Romanian Communist Party, purges were the weapons in his struggle for unquestioned rule. Within the Romanian party elite, three rival groups competed against each other. The "prison (or Grivița) group" headed by Gheorghiu-Dej; the "Moscow bureau" or "troika" represented by Ana Pauker, Vasile Luca, and Teohari Georgescu; and the illegal home leadership of Foriş, Koffler, and Patraşcanu.

From the latter group Foriş Patraşcanu and Koffler were killed by Dej. Dej's power, however, was not crowned since the powerful "troika" acted in a rather sovereign way, opposed several steps of Dej, and continued along independent lines on certain issues.[3] They had direct

Soviet connections and monopolized the secret police. In the first years Dej would feel, and not without reason, that he was more of a figurehead of the party rather than its real overlord. In 1952 the possibility arrived to seize power. The high-tide of purges, let alone Stalin and Beria's messages, encouraged his actions. At the Central Committee session Dej attacked the troika. They were severely criticized for right-wing deviations, in Pauker's case, for opposing collectivization, while Luca was accused of sabotaging the development of heavy industry. Rumors spread regarding Pauker's supposed contacts with foreign intelligence via Israel (where her father and brother had moved to) and Swiss bank accounts. All three were dismissed from their posts, while Luca (who was a Hungarian) was tried and sentenced to death in October 1954 (thus, after the death of Stalin), which was reduced to life imprisonment. Luca in fact died in prison. The others' lives were saved (Pauker was imprisoned for a short time and released after the death of Stalin) but disappeared from public life.

Romania was the only country in the region where purges, though initiated by Stalin, did not serve direct Soviet interests. Gheorghiu-Dej outsmarted Stalin and Beria and exterminated all his rivals. Moreover, in December 1961, he successfully manoeuvred against calls for de-Stalinization by declaring the purges he carried out in 1952 to be the earliest examples of de-Stalinization. "Once Pauker, Luca and Georgescu were expelled from the party, the dead hand of Stalinism was lifted." Pretending to forget all the accusations of right-wing, anti-Leninist deviations, he now re-appointed his victims as left-wing Stalinists. "We de-Stalinized during Stalin's time, in our country there are no grave injustices to be forgiven, no one has to be rehabilitated posthumously" (Hodos, 1987, p. 106).

A nightmare of permanent purges characterized the early fifties in Hungary, where, after the Rajk trial, they became an everyday phenomenon. In 1950 most of the former leading social democrats who contributed to the purge and filled important posts were arrested. Arpád Szakasits, president of the party after the fusion, György Marosán, István Ries, Imre Vajda, and many others were imprisoned.

In 1951 a new group of home communists followed, among many others János Kádár, deputy secretary-general and Minister of the Interior, and Gyula Kállai, Minister of Foreign Affairs.

Towards the end of 1952, the staging of a new major purge, the Hungarian "anti-Zionist" case, was already under preparation. Based on

---

[3] Robert Levy discovered, for example, Ana Pauker's independent line regarding Jewish emigration. In the early fifties, Romania was the only Soviet bloc country where mass Jewish emigration to Israel was allowed.

the Soviet pattern, the chief executors of former purges were from time to time exterminated. After the Rajk case, Colonel Szücs, the deputy head of the AVH and one of the main architects of the Rajk trial, was arrested together with his brother and forced to share the fate of his former victims. Both were brutally tortured and killed in boiling oil. Then, General Gábor Péter, head of the secret police and manager of all previous purges, was selected as one of the main defendants of an "anti-Zionist" trial. Some medical doctors were already arrested to duplicate the Soviet "Doctor's Plot," which was arranged at the same time. This purge, nevertheless, never materialized because of the death of Stalin. His successors immediately closed the Soviet "anti-Zionist" case, and rehabilitated its victims. (General Péter, however, remained in jail and was blamed by Rákosi for all the constructed purges and unlawfulness when investigations and rehabilitations became unavoidable.)

Himself a Jew, Rákosi definitely wanted to produce a spectacular "anti-Zionist" trial to prove his uncompromising and unquestionable loyalty. He also wanted to pretend and demonstrate to the Hungarian population that he was not Jewish.[4]

The real anti-Jewish show trial, however, was not organized in Budapest but in Prague. In the spring of 1949 the anti-Tito campaign reached Prague as well. Fourteen communist functionaries, among them "Spaniards" and the so-called Field group, were arrested and sentenced. Another group, the "Londoners," was also examined but uniquely found to be not guilty. A Sveikian preparation of a major purge led nowhere. Backed by the Soviets, Rákosi wrote an angry letter to Gottwald urging the arrest of those whose names were planned to be mentioned in the Rajk trial in September. As expected, President Gottwald invited Soviet advisors to help the Czechoslovak security organs. In October, Generals Makarov and Likhachov left Budapest, where they supervised the Rajk case, and arrived in Prague. Several arrests in the following months revealed an end of the former hesitancy, and in 1950–1 the process was escalated (Kaplan, 1986). Slovak communists, among them Gustav Husák, Vladimir Clementis, the Minister of Foreign Affairs, Otto Šling, party secretary of the Brno organization, Marie Švermova, member of the Politburo, Karel Švab, the chief of the secret police and Bedrich Reicin, head of military intelligence, were among the victims (Kaplan, 1978).

In spite of the broad range of the purge, two important developments

---

[4] A veteran communist, Arpád Haas, who told his story to the author, returned to Hungary from the Soviet-zone of Austria and visited Rákosi in his office to offer his services in the economic sphere. Rákosi flatly rejected his volunteering with the explanation: "You have to understand that it is impossible because you, comrade Haas, are Jewish." The surprised veteran responded: "But, you, comrade Rákosi, you are also Jewish." Rákosi's answer was even more surprising to Mr Haas: "No, I am not!"

slowed down the procedure. No adequate central figure, such as a Rajk or a Kostov, was found and because of the delay, another belated anti-Tito show trial lost its political importance for Stalin. In the spring of 1951 Beria instructed the Soviet "advisors" to change the concept of the planned trial and, instead of focusing on Tito, prepare to unmask a Jewish–Zionist plot. Interrogations from that time on were directed against the secretary general of the party, Rudolf Slansky, and designed to collect incriminating "evidence" against him. Even Gottwald was informed only in August. In November 1951, Stalin demanded Slansky's arrest as the head of a Zionist-imperialist anti-party conspiracy. Eleven Jewish defendants were selected for the main trial. The methods to break the defendants were dramatically effective. Slansky resisted for quite a long time against the accusation of being a Zionist conspirator. His attempted suicides failed.

His gradual collapse was carefully followed by his "interrogators," partly through a planted cell mate who reported Slansky's reaction to each interrogation and torment (Kaplan, 1990). The victims in the end confessed to all the unbelievable fabricated charges. Slansky agreed, among other accusations, that in the economic plans he "slowed down the development of heavy industry" (Report, 1952a). Ludvik Frejka added: "Slansky told us . . . to preserve the pre-war structure of the economy and the dependence of Czechoslovakia on the West . . . [by keeping] an extremely high percentage [60 percent] of foreign trade with the West" (Report, 1952b). On November 27, 1952, eleven death sentences were pronounced. Six days later the victims were hanged.

The murderous message of the Prague trial was nothing less than that Stalinist communism had opened a new front and begun a new campaign: anti-Semitism. The indictment underlined, for example, that the notorious American spies, Hermann and Noel Field, "in the selection of refugee agents . . . followed two criteria. First, they must belong to the political left, and second, they should be Jews." All the defendants were called by their original Jewish–German names (André Simone, for example, was referred to as Otto Katz), and the conclusion was directly formulated: "Slansky, Geminder, and the other plotters supported the subversive activities of Zionism, the trusted agent of the imperialists." "For the American imperialists the Zionist organizations offered an advanced base in their fight against the people's democracies and the Soviet Union." Israel was also directly targeted: "The government of Ben Gurion, the lackey of American imperialism, transformed Israel into an American possession and . . . a deployment zone against the USSR" (Hodos, 1987, pp. 84–5).

In the early fifties, a major anti-Jewish purge cleansed the Polish army.

Fourteen high-ranking officers of the general staff's intelligence section, all of them Jewish, were arrested and "charged with forming a spy ring within the army in the service of the imperialist powers" (Hodos, 1987, p. 149). General Waclaw Komar, a "Spaniard" and chief of the military intelligence department, was selected as the head of the conspiracy.

What was the goal of the series of "anti-Zionist" cases, of the strong political campaign which unleashed anti-Semitism? Was it a last, mad, sclerotic effort of Stalin to channel strong popular discontent with his terror system into an anti-Semitic reservoir? Was it a legitimizing attempt by playing the anti-Semitic card? Jews as scapegoats were often sacrificed in Central and Eastern Europe. The harsh atrocities of forced collectivization in the countryside, the failures and serious negative side effects of forced accumulation and industrialization in the towns, sacrificing the living standards and causing overall shortages, generated mass dissatisfaction (Muller, 1982). Cruel dictatorship and terror were not enough and might even have been counterproductive in handling emerging crises. Stalin, however, had a last trump-card to play: the strong overrepresentation of Jews in the communist leadership (Muller, 1982). In Hungary Mátyás Rákosi and the other two leading members of the Muscovite "troika" Gerö, and Farkas, the chief ideologue, Révai, and the head of the AVH, General Péter, were all Jewish. The case was rather similar in Poland, where, with the exception of Bierut, the secretary general, most of the key positions of the party were filled with Jews: Jakub Berman and Radkiewicz, responsible for security, Hilary Minc for economic affairs, Roman Zambrowski for state administration, and the leading figures of the secret police and intelligence such as Romkowski, Swiatlo, Piasecki, Fejgin, and others (Toranska, 1987). To a lesser extent, the same phenomenon was visible in Czechoslovakia and Romania as well.

Jews joined the communist movement in Central and Eastern Europe in relatively great numbers. As a minority and highly urbanized community, they reacted in a rather sensitive way to the backwardness, poverty, deep social conflict, and harsh national antagonisms that characterized the region, and searched for solutions. Quite a few emigrated or joined Zionist movements, but many assimilated Jews opted to join the deeply international and anti-nationalist communist movement (Horowitz, 1986). Moreover, during the interwar years, the violent political anti-Semitism of the Slovak Hlinka-guard, the Romanian Iron Guard, the Hungarian Arrow Cross, and all the other fascist–nazi movements strengthened the attractiveness of communism. During the horrors of the war and the Holocaust, the main antagonist of Hitler, the hope and liberator of the region, and the savior of the remnants of Jewish communities, was the Soviet Union. A high percentage of surviving

Jewish intellectuals, workers, employees, and even small proprietors joined postwar communist parties.

Jewish overrepresentation, therefore, became a durable fact in the communist movement of the region, and enabled Stalin to build a base for recruiting loyal followers before and after the seizure of power. In the early 1950s, however, this overrepresentation became an obstacle, and contributed to undermining legitimizing efforts. On the other hand, it also offered a clear opportunity for Stalin and Beria. The extermination of a Jewish-imperialist enemy in these countries, where anti-Semitism was deeply rooted, could help legitimize the regimes. Sacrificing Jewish communists was intended to prove that all the existing troubles, errors, and crimes were not a consequence of imported Soviet communism, but of Jewish leadership. Stalin was ready to use this weapon a few years after the European Jewish Holocaust. (After his death in March 1953, even his closest associates and most loyal henchmen halted the anti-Jewish campaign.) The bloody waves of permanent purges with hundreds and thousands of victims, however, were only the tip of the iceberg.

"The underwater body of the iceberg": mass terror

The show trials represented the horror of the Stalinist dictatorship. In quantitative terms, however, they represented only a tiny part of its unlawful terror. Taking the Czechoslovak example, the Slansky trial and all the accompanying cases in the country, which represented the bloodiest purge in the region, claimed 278 victims. In contrast, 547 priests were sentenced between 1949 and 1955; 1,493 white-collar employees were imprisoned in 1953–4 alone. During the ruthless collectivization drive of the early fifties, nearly 80,000 peasants were cited at some court proceedings.

Altogether the victims of political trials after February 1948, including the verdicts of local courts, numbered 83,000 people, and the average sentence was nine to ten years. The number of those tried and sentenced for economic crimes totalled twice that number. The total number of death sentences (between 1948 and 1953) was 232, and 178 of them were executed.

There were, of course, several other forms of political harassment. A register made in the middle of 1949 consisted of 130,000 names. More than 24,000 men had to serve in special "labor battalions." The number of victims who were sent to forced labor camps was roughly 100,000.

Several tens of thousands of families lost their economic livelihood. After February 1948 more than 3,500 ministerial employees, almost 3,300 other public administration officers, altogether 28,000 state and public employees, 17,000 army officers, and about 25,000 clerical and white-collar employees of the economic sphere, trade unions, and other labor organizations were dismissed from their jobs for political reasons. Two-thirds of them could not find any other work but a manual worker's job. Out of 247,000 shopkeepers, only 6,500 could preserve their economic existence between 1948 and 1958. Additionally, 200,000 small-scale handicraft workshop workers disappeared (Kaplan, 1986).

A hysterical search for enemies and a pathological wave of denunciations (a popular form of taking revenge) unleashed a kind of "legal" man-hunt in Hungary. In the early 1950s prosecuting attorneys examined 1,017,698 cases, which means that practically every third family of the country had some trouble with the police and the state. It is true that "only" half of the examined (511,270 persons) were actually charged. For political reasons nearly 30,000 people were sentenced, but the number of all the condemned reached almost 400,000. Another 30,000–40,000 people were interned without trial, including those who were relocated from the big cities and were forced to work in camps because of their bourgeois or aristocratic origins, or their having been members of the high-ranking officer corps and state administration in the Horthy regime. The number of well-to-do peasants who were registered on a nationwide "kulak-list" and consequently proscribed was 70,000 (Zinner, 1991).

Families who lost their livelihood were of a more or less equal number. About 75,000 former high-ranking officials of the prewar state administration and officer corps, entrepreneurs, and landowners, and more than 300,000 shopkeepers and artisans, had to find a new, and in most cases a blue-collar, existence.

The body of the iceberg was very thick. Every third or every fourth family of the state socialist countries was confronted with the regime's "law" and police, and came to grief from them.

Ownership and institutional structure of command economy

Stalinist socialism was, however, not just a ruthless dictatorial regime. The party-state sought to own and directly dictate not only the political administrative military apparatus, but the economy as well.

Building up the system consequently meant the making of a state-economy. Major nationalizations were already carried out by some peoples' democracies in 1945–6. When sovietization began its full drive from mid 1947 on, some countries needed to implement only final measures, while others had to start from the beginning. In the former Allied countries, Yugoslavia, Poland, Czechoslovakia, and Albania, the bulk of industry was nationalized by 1946: the percentage share of state ownership in Albania's infant industries at the end of 1946 was 89 percent. In Yugoslavia and Poland, 82 percent and 80 percent respectively of gross industrial output was produced by state-owned companies in 1947, and 80 percent of industrial workers were employed by state companies in Czechoslovakia at that time. On the other hand, Romania, Bulgaria, and Hungary had a state participation of 11 percent, 16 percent, and 45 percent respectively in 1947.

In 1947–9 the process was completed. In Czechoslovakia, on April 28, 1948, all industrial enterprises which employed more than fifty people, and all wholesale and foreign trade companies, were nationalized. At the end of 1948 virtually no private firms with more than twenty employees survived. Out of the 383,000 private small-scale handicraft, service or retail shops, only 47,000 existed in 1956, with hardly more than 5 percent of the formerly employed and self-employed. In Poland, where the private employment limit of fifty persons was already enacted in January 1946, a further extermination of small-scale private enterprises was carried out, and the share of the state-owned firms reached 97 percent of national industrial output. A "battle for trade" was launched that resulted in a 95 percent role for state in wholesale trade, and 80 percent of total turnover in trade in 1948. In Yugoslavia, the most radical nationalization expropriated all industrial, banking, wholesale, and foreign trade companies by the end of 1946. The surviving 30 percent of small-scale local industry was nationalized by 1948.

In the former enemy countries, the bulk of nationalization was realized in the late 1940s. In Bulgaria, on December 23, 1947, the nationalization act expanded the state sector of industry to a share of 95 percent in one stroke; the nationalization of the banks soon followed. In Romania, a general nationalization on June 11, 1948 expropriated all firms employing more than 100 people, and by 1950 the share of the state sector in industry reached over 92 percent. Hungarian piecemeal nationalization was crowned with an overall nationalization of industrial firms employing more than 100 people in March 1948, and another decree in December 1949 completed the process by expropriating all firms with ten or more employees and all units without consideration of employment in certain areas, such as printing, pharmacies, etc.

The national economies of Central and Eastern Europe were reorganized according to the Soviet pattern in 1948–9. The new banking system was based on the National Banks, which took on a central role, having been granted a monopoly of short-term lending in addition to the former monopoly on issuing bank notes. The so-called single account system provided for all enterprises' payments and receipts to go through the

National Bank. Around the National Banks were established specialized banks, such as a central Investment Bank handling long-term investments financed by the state budget; a Foreign Trade Bank which centralized all foreign exchange matters; and a nationwide Savings Bank network which acted primarily as a citizens' savings and credit bank. The highly centralized banking system was directed by the Ministry of Finance.

The institutional framework of state-owned industry also had to be created. Independent national companies were formed, but closely integrated with the state organization of industry. This was headed by the Ministry of Industry, which consequently could not direct thousands of firms. Therefore, a network of four to seven industrial ministries were founded, the so-called industrial branch ministries (such as ministry of mining, engineering, or food processing), which were responsible for certain sectors. Various sub-divisions, industrial directorates, and horizontally organized industrial centers were also established. The former ones were basically administrative organs, kind of departments of the ministry, while the others exercised direct control of production, material procurement, and "marketing." This organizational-administrative framework was often modified, reorganized, and also differed from country to country in many and even important details, but the basis of industrial organization followed this pattern. The institutions of control being established were well-suited to the needs of a strong and comprehensively planned economy, the essence of a socialist economic system.

Central planning

Planning was not unknown in Central and Eastern Europe before the war. The so-called Central Industrial Area in Poland in the mid 1930s and the "Györ Program," a five-year armament plan in Hungary initiated in 1938, clearly represented certain planning efforts to cope with industrial backwardness in connection with war preparation. Planning became much more important during the postwar years, when comprehensive two- to three-year reconstruction plans directed the economies from 1947 on. Soviet-type central planning was, however, inaugurated only in Yugoslavia. This was the only country of the region where, by January 1, 1947 on, a Five Year Plan copied both the methods and the objectives of the first Soviet Five Year Plan. The model was soon followed elsewhere: in 1949 Czechoslovakia and Bulgaria, in 1950 Poland and Hungary, and in 1951 Romania and Albania initiated similar plans.

After the political decisions, central plans were worked out by large planning offices. (In the fifties 1,200 staff members worked at the Polish

Planning Commission, while 700 worked at the Hungarian, and 500 at the Romanian, planning commissions). Production was, according to detailed plans, worked out for every year and every company, and plans were based on an extraordinarily great number of indicators. The plans gave precise prescriptions as to how much the companies were allowed for investment and spending, how much they could use of goods, raw materials, energy, and manpower, and what they were to produce, including a strictly defined assortment of products, specifying the quality, quantity, and cost of production. On the basis of these production plans, the planning office prepared the material plans, which were used by the relevant ministries and branches of the planning office to order the yearly and quarterly distribution of materials.

The chain of directives regulating production, material supply, investment, etc. was broken down by years and even quarters, as well as by ministries and enterprises, so that each directive became more of a strict, personally addressed order (Kornai, 1992, pp. 110–30).

The most centralized and hierarchical planning, however, could not neglect the participation of the firms. If plans were entirely unrealistic and the firms could not fulfill them, it was a disaster for the authorities as well (the measure of their success was the fulfillment of the plan, too). This led to a kind of bargain. Central planners required cooperation, while firm managers sought concessions. Higher investments were promised by the one side, while higher plan-targets were accepted by the other. In most cases this bargaining was entirely informal based on personal connections, but in some cases, such as Czechoslovakia's "protiplan" (counter-plan) of the early fifties and the planning from below", based on central guidelines, in Poland, it embodied institutionalized forms (Soós, 1986).

The aim was to carry out central decisions and minimize "accidental" elements as much as possible in economic life. To this end markets, market prices, and money were forced out of the economic arena. Trade was mostly replaced by central state distribution. In the early fifties, price reforms were introduced which replaced market prices with fixed prices, determined and controlled by central authorities. It also did away with the direct connection between the price level and the fluctuation of consumer (retail) and producer (wholesale) prices. Investment goods were to be sold at cost or even below, with substantial state subsidies. The cost price, therefore, bore no fixed relation to the sale price. Producer (or factory) prices in the state sector were considered as mere technicalities, the technical means of balancing the books. The prices of basic materials were thus kept down, without regard even for the growing cost of production. Prices did not reflect real relative costs.

Ending the influence of market effects made companies practically independent of the cost and quality of their products. Marketability, cost, quality, or the technological standards of their goods played no part in company's standing. Because of the lack of market forces, the company interest in fulfilling central directives was reinforced by the system of bonuses and wages. It was, however, impossible for a company to keep to the letter of such a comprehensive system (with hundreds of compulsory plan indicators). Companies concentrated their resources on fulfilling those plan indicators that were the most important and most rewarding for them. For years the bonus regulations motivated companies to achieve targets by fulfilling and overfulfilling the so-called global production plan index. This plan index was the primary criterion for bonuses for a long time, and, of course, was not merely coincidental. It was motivated by the main objectives of economic policy: a maximum growth rate for preferred industrial branches. If the global production plan index was fulfilled or overfulfilled, the managerial staff earned a large bonus, sometimes as much as one third to a half of their annual salary, and at a progressively increasing rate. Underfulfillment had major consequences, not only denying a bonus, but different kinds of punishments.

All the other plan indicators were also compulsory: a 100 percent product-mix was prescribed for the Polish firms under the Ministry of Light Industry, and 94 percent for plants that belonged to the Ministry of Food Industry in the 1950s. Imposed assorted requirements were expressed by dozens of indicators. It was, however, impossible to link a bonus to each of the indicators. Thus many other economic considerations, such as quality, product range, and the cost of production, were subordinated. Consequently, it often happened, as in the case of the Debrecen Clothing Factory or the Csepel Truck Factory in Hungary, that the firms fulfilled the global production plan by 127 percent and 107 percent, but underfulfilled (55 percent and 65 percent respectively) the plan indicators of product-mix in 1951. Since fulfilling global production plans was easier without real consideration of quality, quality usually declined (Kornai, 1959).

Strict central control and harsh punishments served as an "incentive" to fulfill all the compulsory indicators. This led to an overbureaucratization of the economy. As substitutes for a lack of market incentives, more and more regulations were introduced in an effort to eliminate the undesirable side effects of central planning. More precise information and the maximum possible central interference was thought necessary in order to carry all the central directives. Planning offices and controlling ministries collected both daily and ten-day production indicators from the companies. In certain periods the retailing companies had to report on the daily turnover of sugar, fat, oil, flour, bread, and meat. All the reports were processed and necessary central interventions made. Thus, more and more detailed regulations and orders inundated the companies. In the first half of 1951, every coal mine received 1,025 ministerial and other regulations or general orders in Hungary. The enormous information hunger of the system and the flood of intervening regulations brought with it a phenomenal expansion of bureaucracy. Because of the extremely hierarchical and centralized character of the planning and administrative system, much more information was demanded than was actually used. According to a rough estimate of Kaser and Zielinski concerning the Central and Eastern European countries, "only one fifth of data submitted were, in fact, used for planning purposes" (Kaser and Zielinski, 1970, p. 28).

The ultimate sanction for the enforcement of compulsory plan indicators, and thus the guarantor of central planning, was harsh reprisal. "Strict measures must be taken to make the plan effective," remarked Ernö Gerö, the overlord of the Hungarian economy in the early fifties. "Those breaking it must receive not only disciplinary punishment but, in more serious cases ... must be brought to trial" (Gerö, 1952, p. 10). The criminal codes of the countries, as already illustrated, offered a "legal" safeguard for the plan; thus central planning in its classic Stalinist form was based on terror and fear.

Two special fields required peculiar institutions in central planning: foreign trade and agriculture. Compulsory indicators did not work in either sector – in the former, because it was connected with other countries, including those with market economies; in the latter, because it was not state-owned, and indeed was comprised during the first years of hundreds of thousands of small peasant farms.

Consequently, the state sought to counterbalance all the accidental elements in foreign trade that were impossible to plan for. To achieve this, foreign trade prices were hermetically isolated from domestic prices. In the case of exports, producing companies delivered their products, ordered by the plan, to foreign trade companies, which paid the domestic producer's price for them. Foreign trade companies then sold the product sometimes for a much lower, or in some cases higher, price than that paid to the domestic producer. The difference, however, was bridged by the state's price levelling fund. The same happened in the case of imports. Imported goods were sold to domestic firms at the internal producer's price, and the price differences, again, were levelled by the state fund.

Foreign trade with capitalist countries, however, was undesirable from both the economic and political standpoint. Instead, trade was restructured and directed to the Soviet Union and to other socialist countries. The regional agreement system of the Council of Mutual Economic Aid (CMEA) offered a new framework from 1949 onwards, and soon it was adjusted to the special requirements of centrally planned economies. A changeover to fixed prices took place during the Korean War, and price fluctuations, strongly disadvantageous for planning, were eliminated. From then on (up to 1957), the rigid price system of the CMEA became totally independent of world market price fluctuations and price ratios, thus eliminating the spontaneous effects of the market (Kaser, 1965; Ausch, 1972).

Planning in agriculture had a different, and independent mechanism. In spite of plan directives, planning was based on two pillars: the compulsory delivery system and the compulsory sowing plans. The latter prescribed the main crops and the amount of land allocated to them. The nationwide figures, calculated by the planning offices, were broken down to regions, counties, villages, and farms by territorial, local administrative authorities. The most effective institution, however, was the delivery system, which prescribed the responsibility of the peasants to the state (based on the value and quality of land per unit) in exact quantities, irrespective of the given quantity of crop. Since it was assured by law and force, compulsory delivery was not a market activity. Prices were fixed at an unrealistically low level around the cost of production. (It served to channel agricultural incomes into the state's accumulation fund.)

The strictly centralized system of planning was, as Oscar Lange, the Polish economist and venerated scholar of the political economy of "market socialism" suggested, "*sui generis* a war economy" (Lange, 1958). It provided the highest possible capital accumulation, because of total price, wage and income controls. The relatively poor, mostly agricultural countries of Poland, Hungary, Romania and Bulgaria, with traditionally low rates of capital accumulation (about 6 percent of their gross national product in the interwar decades), thus achieved surprisingly high accumulation levels of 22–30 percent in the first half of the 1950s. By annihilating the market, the countries of Central and Eastern Europe entered a period of "primitive accumulation." The planning mechanism, moreover, enabled them to concentrate resources and development on centrally chosen projects, to an extent unknown before. Thus it seemed to be a promising system for rapid industrialization, with a uniquely high rate of industrial investment and growth.

But the unavoidable price of these advantages stemming from the war-like character of the system was the neglect of up-to-date technology, and the cost of production and competitiveness, which resulted in wasteful investment and production processes. Frozen stocks of unfinished investment projects, huge piles of unsaleable products, the wasting of materials, energy, and labor, all the consequences of a lack of market incentives and entrepreneurial interests, ultimately shot holes in the system, holes through which a great part of the national product disappeared. According to the author's calculations, about one-fifth of the potential growth of the national income was lost in this manner in Hungary between 1949 and 1953.

Forced, import-substituting industrialization

Central planning and the war-type economic institutions of the command economy, in spite of all their drawbacks, nevertheless served the central strategic goal of forced industrialization. All other considerations were subordinated to this aim. This was the essence of the Soviet-type modernization model, which offered a breakthrough for non-industrialized countries.

An absolute preference for the most rapid growth was reinforced by military considerations in the isolated Soviet Union, especially from the early 1930s on.

The origins of the Soviet model and the central aim of war preparation determined both the speed and structure of industrialization. It followed a turn-of-the-century technological-structural pattern of the advanced West, and was thus based on the development of the iron and steel industries and traditional engineering. The industrialization strategy, embodied in the first Five Year Plan of the Soviet Union, was canonized as a socialist principle. The countries of Central and Eastern Europe were forced to copy the Soviet model. Terrorized by the purges and by the expulsion of victims such as Gomulka, frightened by the excommunication of Tito and by the executions of the Hungarian, Bulgarian, and Albanian "Titoists," all obediently imitated the first Soviet Five Year Plan in their own plans, which were enforced from the late forties throughout the region.

The most visible characteristic of the industrialization plans of the early fifties was their speed. Investment plans became more and more ambitious. The first draft of the Hungarian Five Year Plan, in the fall of 1948, sought to guarantee investments of 27.6 billion forints. "Our basic aim in this five year period in general," declared one of the chief planners "is not to create brand new industrial and agricultural projects, but . . . to eliminate bottlenecks" (Berend, 1964, p. 74). In April 1949 the investment program was increased to 35 billion forints, in December to 50.9 billion, and then in February 1951 to 85 billion forints, which was more than three times higher than the first version. Annual investment jumped from 4.25 to 17 billion forints from 1948 to 1951. In Czechoslovakia, 60 billion krowns were invested in the Two Year Plan. In the first variant of the Five Year Plan, 336 billion was earmarked for investment, but it was increased to 558 billion. The average annual investment in the Five Year Plans of Bulgaria, Poland, and Romania was also two to four times higher than previous reconstruction plans at the end of the forties, which already represented a higher investment level than prewar ones. With huge investment injections (in Poland 1,287 new factories were planned to be built during the Six Year Plan), an industrial great leap forward, a two to three times increase in industrial production in half a decade, was aspired to (Bauer, 1981).

The planned index of growth in national income for five years in Hungary was raised from 63 percent to 130 percent, and the annual industrial growth rate from 13 percent to 26 percent. The plan channelled more than half of investments into industry, and about 90 percent of it was concentrated in the so-called heavy industrial sectors. Increased production of basic materials received special emphasis. Two-thirds of the total industrial investment was earmarked for the development of mining and metallurgy. The index of metallurgical investment reflected an extraordinary escalation: with 1950 equal to 100, the investment index in 1951 was 264; in 1952, 463; and in 1953, 489. This trend was universal in the region. In Bulgaria industrial investment represented 43 percent of all ventures, almost 84 percent of which was channelled into the heavy industries. In Romania the percentage share of industrial investment reached more than 53 percent, of which 83 percent went to heavy industries. Industrialization was thus equated with the development of the heavy industries, most particularly mining, metallurgy, and engineering.

As Stalin's industrialization drive in the thirties was strongly determined by war preparations, the same was true for Central and Eastern Europe in the early fifties. The manifestation of the Cold War, and especially the outbreak of the Korean War at the beginning of the first economic plans, led to hectic war preparations. This was the very motive for the successive upward revisions of the plans. From secret archival sources it has been revealed that the Hungarian Five Year Plan allocated half of the increased expenditures to military purposes. Moreover, these disbursements of the plan were concentrated into the first three years. Consequently outlays for civilian and military purposes in 1950 were about equal.

Defense considerations affected the structural policy of industrialization as well. This was the very reason why special preference was given to the production of strategic materials and to efforts in achieving self-sufficiency.

Cost of production, profitability, and even technological standards, were neglected. "Investment is always determined by political interests," stated an internal party report in 1951, "with economic indicators taking second place" (Berend, 1964, p. 95).

Industrial consumer goods production, agriculture, and services were neglected. In huge industrial investment projects, consumer good industries were allocated 2–4 percent of investments, agriculture 10–14 percent and infrastructure, including trade and transportation, about 30–36 percent. In contrast to the extremely high growth rates of investment goods production, which ranged between 23 and 28 percent in Romania, Bulgaria, Poland and Hungary, consumer goods industries had only an 8–10 percent growth rate, while agriculture mostly stagnated and suffered severe shortages of supply. Shortages soon generated the reintroduction of wartime rationing (Kornai, 1971, p. 219). "In the middle of 1951," noted Professor Jezierski regarding the Polish situation, "supply in both agricultural and industrial consumer goods deteriorated and serious shortage appeared, and rationing, which was abolished, on January 1, 1949, was again implemented" (Jezierski, 1971, p. 219). In Hungary this occurred at the beginning of 1951.

Forced industrialization led to immense social tensions and to economic chaos. An increasing hunger for energy and raw materials was never satisfied. The instability of energy supplies became an everyday phenomenon and resulted in restrictions on firms' and the population's consumption. Because of the feverish pace, the overabundance of new and overly ambitious projects, and a lack of proper preparation, a great and ever-increasing number of the investment projects were left unfinished. One-quarter of Polish investment projects remained unfinished during the Six Year Plan, as were many of the more than 11,000 construction projects in Bulgaria.

Almost none of the megalomaniac first Five Year Plans were fulfilled in Central and Eastern Europe. In 1953–4, all were revised and moderated. There was no war to justify a policy which turned out to be highly irrational and, from many points of view, counterproductive. Mátyás Rákosi explained the reason for the failure of economic plans to a rehabilitated survivor of the Rajk trial, in his office in the mid fifties: "We prepared for the war and all of the sudden the peace collapsed around our ears."[5]

The arduous economic endeavor was closely connected with a drive for self-sufficiency. Its roots were multifarious. The Soviet modernization

GyÖrgy Aczél, former secretary of the party organization of Baranya county, a victim of the Rajk case, described his conversation with Rákosi after his release from prison in an interview with the author in 1978.

model itself embodied an import-substituting concept *par excellence.* This characteristic was strengthened by defense considerations in the growing hostility of the Cold War. Stalin proclaimed the existence of two independent, capitalist, and socialist, world markets. As a pragmatic consequence, the Council of Mutual Economic Aid (CMEA) was established in January 1949. It well served the planned economies. A regional system which used fixed prices, eliminated hard currency from foreign trade, and guaranteed regional self-sufficiency with a maximum separation from the world market, was the only way to realize the challenging socialist economic strategy.

CMEA, however, was also a weapon of Soviet domination. The rigidly bilateral character of the agreement assured such dominance in trade with the dependent countries. All former trade began to collapse after 1945, and most of all after 1948. Practically all of the countries of the region increased their trade in the CMEA framework from a previous 10 to 20 to a 60 percent to 75 percent share. About half this ratio was Soviet trade in the Central and Eastern European countries.

In spite of this fact, regional self-sufficiency in the CMEA framework and Soviet trade connections created a "pull effect" and helped the region's emulous industrialization plans. The Soviet Union assured the delivery of huge amounts of raw materials and energy and opened her vast markets to the second-rate, non-compatible engineering products and industrial consumer goods that would not have been saleable on Western markets, but, in most cases, still represented a higher standard than domestic products in the Soviet Union. For the new industries of the Central and Eastern European countries, this became a major factor, a sort of "hot house" for industrialization, which offered a safe shelter against a demanding and, for the weaker industries, devastating world market. On the other hand, these advantages killed the technological inspiration of the competitive milieu of the world market and fostered a building up of obsolete production lines. Soviet and CMEA trade, as did import-substitution itself, gave only a quantitative impetus in an outdated structure, and with an adopted antiquated technology.

The most negative effect of this isolationist "Socialist World-market" was its contribution to the realization of the autarkic orientation, which would not have been possible in international frameworks. Trade with capitalist market economies was given only a marginal importance. It was used in case of an emergency, if certain materials, machines, spare parts or goods were not available from socialist sources. Central and Eastern Europe made a tremendous effort to replace imported goods with domestic products. Hence, planning and forced industrialization in the isolationist CMEA framework created a closed economy, appropriate to the system.

A closed society, barbed-wire fences and dictated art

As an organic element of and a logical supplement to the Stalinist system, state-socialist structures necessitated the absolute isolation of the countries from external influences and connections. Building up a consistent regime thus meant total insulation. After 1947–8 the countries of Central and Eastern Europe were rigidly closed. Indeed, after 1949 all the borders, including the ones with each other, were hermetically shut. Traveling abroad was prohibited. Citizens could not get a passport. A Pole could not visit Czechoslovakia and Hungarians were unable to see their close relatives in Romania. The Western borders were heavily guarded and strongly fortified. Churchill certainly could not foresee that his famous imagined "iron curtain" was quite literally realized. Mine fields, barbed wire fences, and watch-towers encompassed the countries like prisons. Even a few mile strip along the border, the so-called "border-zone," was closed and strictly controlled, and special permission was needed to enter. An attempt to escape was more than hazardous, and many who took that risk lost their lives and even more were imprisoned for years.

Besides being physically closed, the countries of the region behind the barbed-wire fences and mine fields formed a closed society. Instead of public well-being and interest based on individual freedom of decision and action, instead of harmony born out of freedom, the great liberal French and British concept at the turn of the nineteenth-century, a collectivist ideal prevailed. Public interest and well-being were not to be realized by individual decisions, harmonized by the "invisible hand" of the free market, but only by a sternly visible state, the divine representation and agent of the public good. The state, on behalf of the community, is responsible for all individuals and decides their fate. No one can be very rich, but no one can be impoverished either. A secure and equal existence is assured to the whole community. Harmony and well-being was to be achieved by state control and regulations.

State socialist regimes ideologically differentiated among three layers of interests: personal, group, and society as a whole. This represented a hierarchy where personal interest was at the bottom of the list, while society, represented by the state, was at the top. The "lower" layers had to be subordinated to the "higher." The individual had to sacrifice his or her own interest to the higher stake of a community, a collective, firm, or cooperative, but even the latter had to serve the whole society, which was equated with the state. To realize "group interest," meaning the interest of a collective farm or a state-owned firm, at the cost of the state was not only a moral, but a legal crime as well.

In a closed society, as Karl Popper formulated, "the tribe is everything and the individual nothing." The open society is an abstract entity of independent individuals, who make their own decisions, do not accept taboos and are critical of existing institutions. The closed society, in contrast, is a united "organism," "tribal," and collectivist, whose life is regulated by unquestioned "magical taboos" and institutions, which are "sacrosanct-taboos" (Popper, 1950, pp. 169–70, 185, 468).

While collectivism in some countries of the region, such as Russia and the Balkans, was deeply rooted in egalitarian village communities that organized collective work and survived up to the twentieth century, this was not the case for the more successfully modernized Central European countries. After the horrors of the war, occupation, and, in some cases, resistance, strong collective experiences permeated these societies. Collective suffering, collective responsibility, the need for collective efforts to reconstruct ruined countries, however, all laid the groundwork for the introduction of collectivism. Enthusiastic young people were ready to sacrifice their summer vacations and week-ends to go to the big construction works of Nowa Huta or Dunapentele, and enjoyed the invigorating experience of collective work, of being a part of a huge collective.

However, a forced and compulsory collectivism was also imposed on these societies. Collective vacations and organized free time, as well as collective folk dancing and singing folk songs, were positive manifestations of these attempts. Forced collectivism, on the other hand, embodied a peevish intolerance against otherness. A generated xenophobia outlawed Western music and modern dances as "decadent" and imposed uniform collective experiences. The local communities, a class, a department of an office, or even a university, especially party cells, organized collective life which aspired to indoctrinate individuals. One of the most important institutions of this sort was what was essentially a secularized "communist confession," the compulsory practice of self-criticism. It was a kind of open confession in a community meeting when the "confessor" (priest) was the community itself. Not only public activities but even private life was a subject of open debate. Individuals were very often humiliated, ruthless pressure was put upon people to change their habits, rid themselves of selfish "petty bourgeois attitudes," and subordinate themselves to the community.

"Magical taboos" and "sacrosanct institutions" were unquestionable. Marxism–Leninism became a secularized religion, a collection of truths, with ready-made answers. All existing and newly created institutions served indoctrination through its teaching. Schools, textbooks, indeed a whole network of ideological retraining, targeted both new and older generations. Seminars were organized in offices and work places, and even university professors had to participate in basic courses on Marxism–Leninism and lectures on the Short History of the Bolshevik Party. "Newspaper half-hours" became a regular institution before the work day to brainwash the populace: even on everyday events, domestic or international, one had to have a uniform view, centrally formulated and directed. Personal and especially different opinions were not tolerated and were easily stamped as "hostile."

Party propaganda did not stop at the doorsteps of families. Beside all the official and traditional means, "home-propaganda" was organized by local party organizations. A pair of "agitators" regularly visited homes and families to talk about everyday life, explain current events, and interpret international trends. If they encountered a hostile reception or strongly critical attitude they had to report their experiences; thus propaganda and repression had points of close contact, and in fact overlapped.

The most important means of brainwashing was the total control and central manipulation of information and communication. In order to actualize a proper central direction and promote the view of "declining capitalism" and the permanent success of "establishing socialism," it was essential to control all media and orchestrate nationwide propaganda, which was uniform from schools to newspapers, radio broadcasting to public speeches, mass rallies to art-products, and to exclude all information from outside the country. Foreign broadcasts were permanently jammed. Western newspapers and books were prohibited. Censorship banned all kinds of "hostile ideology" including poems and writings reflecting a "pessimistic mood." Personal correspondences were censored and often confiscated. Certain branches of science and scholarship, such as modern gene-biology, psychology, computer studies, or sociology, were claimed to be "bourgeois sciences" and outlawed. Party-state propaganda, functioning in a vacuum of all other information, tended to penetrate every aspect of life, and set out to prove the "Big Lie": it insisted that living standards were increasing, while they sharply declined, that Soviet agriculture was the most modern in the world, and Western capitalism was on the brink of collapse. Everything which could carry information other than the official avenues was strictly controlled, and, indeed, entirely subordinated to the goal of the "education of the population." The direction of literature, music, or the fine arts, acquired a blunt political-ideological importance, and became an inseparable element of the closed society.

Crusade for a uniform socialist realism

As in the case of political-institutional structures, a blueprint was also ready-made and adoptable for cultural policy. In the Soviet Union the ruthless campaign of the 1930s purged the entire art field, and introduced a compulsory educational, "understandable," and optimistic propaganda-art, the so-called socialist realism. Modernism was criticized as rootless, cosmopolitan, and mere formalism, and the short-lived deliberate early marriage between revolutionary avant-garde art and the Bolshevik revolution was replaced by a conservative-populist art dictatorship of the party-state. Art became an inseparable part of "agit prop" activity.

A new and devastating purification campaign of Stalin and Zhdanov was launched in the Soviet Union between 1946 and 1948, in the years when the new socialist regimes emerged. They immediately adopted the Soviet art policy and used the speeches of Zhdanov, the resolutions of the Soviet party, and the example of the already *gleichschalt*-ed Soviet art as a guide.

Soviet art policy of these years determined Central and Eastern European art from the late forties on. In 1946 the Central Committee of the Bolshevik Party banned the periodical *Leningrad* and reorganized *Zvezda*. Zhdanov, in his introductory speech, brutally attacked the poet Akhmatova, "the representative of the reactionary, barren of ideas, literary gutter," whose poems were published in *Leningrad*. Akhmatova's poetry expresses the "aristocratic-bourgeois trend of literature," its themes are "individualist and narrow," based on her "unimportant personal experiences and private life." "What is most important for her is the motive of love and eroticism, linked with the motives of sorrow, damnation, longing, death and mysticism. . . . The atmosphere of loneliness and desperation is incompatible with Soviet literature. . . . These poems . . . may infect the awareness of our youth" (Zhdanov, 1952, pp. 90–3, 99, 101). Zhdanov declared that literature, as Lenin stated, must be "party-literature" that counterbalances bourgeois morality and spirit, and accused literary functionaries in the editorial boards and in the Writers Union of being apolitical.

Two years later, in 1948, Zhdanov's attack was launched against "formalist music," "alien to Soviet art." "The Union of Composers is in the hands of a group. I am speaking about comrade Shostakovich, Prokofiev, Hachaturian, Popov, Kabalevski and Shebalin. . . . Exactly these comrades may be reckoned as leading figures of the trend of formalist music. . . . This trend, behind the shield of faked-innovations, rejected classical traditions, rejected the popular character of music. . . . The people," declared Zhdanov, "do not want music they cannot understand."

When the first new postwar opera, Muradieli's *Great Friendship*, was performed, after a decade-long break that had been caused by earlier ruthless attacks against modern music, an immediate new campaign was propelled: the entire Central Committee went to see the opera, whereupon a meeting was organized with musical experts at the Central Committee. "The hopes of the Central Committee failed," Zhdanov declared. "There is not one single melody in this opera worth remembering." There are "noisy improvisations" and "shocking impact." "Sometimes one recalls the noise of construction work." The composer, "striving to obtain originality," replaces genuine lezginka-music of the mountain people of the Caucasus with "his own music." Moreover, though the story of the opera featured the northern Caucasus in the period when Soviet power was established in the region, it "drastically falsifies history" by presenting the Georgians and Osets as enemies of the Russians, and neglects to build on the folk music of the area (Zhdanov, 1952, pp. 41–4, 54, 56, 67).

Brutal party interventions were copied all over Central and Eastern Europe, where little local Zhdanovs expelled writers and artists from literary and artistic life and imposed the uniform strait-jacket of "socialist realism" on every artist. One of the local purifiers, the Hungarian József Révai, member of the Politburo and responsible for the "Bolshevization" of Hungarian art, subserviently repeated Zhdanov's argument: "We have to struggle against capitalist ideology in people's consciousness, in morals and habits. . . . We have to use all possible means to re-educate our people in a socialist spirit: schools, propaganda, art, literature, movies and all forms of popular cultural activities have to serve this aim" (Révai, 1952, p. 6). The Party led a campaign for "the party-mindedness and agit propist character" of literature (ibid., p. 18).

Following the Zhdanovist pattern, a permanent purge to carry out the propagandist mission of "socialist realism" ensued. In literature, the most infamous attack was instigated by Révai against Tibor Déry's *Felelet* (Answer), a novel on the interwar life of the Hungarian workers and their political movements. The sharpest criticism was directed against the "falsification" of the labor movement of the thirties, since the novel "described the life of the workers, presenting the communist party only in its periphery . . . and the every day life of the workers is going on without the presence of communists." The central communist heroine of the novel, a student named Júlia Nagy, was "preoccupied with her private problems and love affairs," and had a schism with the party because of her love with a burgher. "I am not saying that a communist may or has to fall in love only with another communist . . . [B]ut in the case of a true communist, these two emotions, the devotion to the party and personal love, may not run parallel." The class struggle appears as a moral problem. Révai condemned Déry's preference for "so-called historical reality" rather than "stressing the historically progressive elements of life, even if they are present only in their embryonic form," which would thus mean that it is inaccurate to portray the communist party only in its "at that time [marginal] position" without "taking into account its role in forming the future." It pays to cite Révai's brutally frank concluding remarks: "In the debate on *Felelet*, Déry declared that 'the writer tries to defend his right to write about topics he wants to write about.' In our world, however, the writer does not have this 'right.' . . . The tastes and views of the writer might oppose the views and interests of the people, the state and the party. It is not the people and the state who have to adjust to the tastes and views of the writer, but the writer who has . . . to identify himself with the interests of building socialism" (ibid., pp. 119–21, 125, 130, 142).

In some countries of the region, the regime not only regulated and directed the writers, but established special educational institutions for them: in Romania, copying the pattern of the Soviet Gorki-school, a one-year school was founded for "writer's training."

"Death humor" in poetry, "rotten, stuffy sexuality," "*Weltschmerz*" were all targets of harsh criticism. In a speech at the conference of the Association of Theater and Movie Artists in October 1951, Révai clearly formulated the political, agit prop requirements regarding movies and theater performances: "The new hero . . . never fails in his struggle against the old social forces. The negative heroes, representing the declining old society, are not tragic figures but are despicable even in their demise. In the new socialist dramas Fortinbras does not appear at the end, but is the main hero from the very beginning to the end." On the same occasion, Révai also underlined that "laughing is also a weapon in the class struggle" (ibid., p. 78).

In April 1951, "bourgeois modernist," "cosmopolitan functionalist" modern architecture was harshly attacked. This cultural policy encompassed classical works as well. As was the case with Kafka in Czechoslovakia, Imre Madách's classical nineteenth-century national drama, *Az ember tragédiája* (The tragedy of mankind), was banned because of its "pessimism," and Béla Bartók's *Csodálatos mandarin* (The miraculous mandarin) was ordered off the stage because of its "formalism" and "lack of attractiveness to captivate a new audience."

The Soviet-initiated cultural policy was largely uniform all over Central and Eastern Europe, and socialist-realist literature, cinema, theater, music, architecture, and fine arts were strikingly similar throughout the region (Aaman, 1992). This adopted socialist realism had three main components. The first was the ideal and practice of Soviet art, which was seen as an inseparable element of socialism. The second was partly connected to the cultural traditions of the communist and, in a way, labor movement in general. The third element, with the broadest popular basis, was a sort of populist peasant cultural tradition. The three, though they confronted each other from several points of view, still had a great number of points in common, such as the rejection of Western culture and a strong attraction to collectivism.

One of the most appealing and popular cultural activities was the folk dance and chorus movement. In 1949–50 there were 776 choirs in Hungary, and in 1952–3 their number was 2,596. This "healthy" popular art was destined to replace "decadent" Western dance and jazz music. The difference between popular and high culture was to be eliminated, in order to create music or paintings that are "understandable for all." To indoctrinate and "conquer" the youth was particularly inspired. "A part of the youth has a wrong habit of entertainment," remarked the official communist youth daily in 1952. "They are copying bourgeois customs, their chatting is aimless and empty. . . . If we are unable to give new content to their leisure-time, we would leave the ground to the enemy, which tries to mislead the youth via their amusements as well. . . . Entertainment is a weapon of the class struggle" (Losonczi, 1974, p. 225).

The cultural policy and, as a part of it, art policy were elements of a uniform system, and differences among the countries hardly existed. The main principles of socialist-realist fine arts in the different countries were identical. In Poland the principles were declared in 1949 in the meeting of the Association of Polish Artists in Nieborow, which subsequently became an official doctrine. As the president of the Association, Wlodzimierz Sokorski, defined them, the requirements of socialist-realist fine arts were a total rejection of "formalism" and a return to the experience of realistic trends of previous centuries. It is a collective art which expresses national characteristics and follows the Soviet example. "Socialist-realism includes the organization of reality as well [sic!], the selection of values and the exclusion of circumstance" (Sokorski, 1952, p. 6).

The overlord of the Czechoslovak art policy, Václav Kopecky, formulated the rejection of modernism at the 9th Congress of the communist party in the following way: "Socialist-realism does not tolerate any kind of anti-art trends, any sort of low-level art. . . . Socialist-realism does not allow ugliness, objectivity without emotions. . . . Socialist-realism opposes everything which is deformed . . . or lack of forms" (Kopecki, 1950, p. 2).

At the 5th Congress of the Bulgarian Communist Party, party chief Vlko Chervenkov himself formulated the main principles: "We must permanently struggle against modernism and formalism, against those basic trends of West European bourgeois fine arts, and strengthen the realistic trend of Bulgarian art" (Belmustakov, 1951, p. 54).

The party-state immediately created a new organizational network for art: all artistic groupings were abolished, and artists had to be members of the official association, which was a semi-state organization. In several cases, such as in Poland, Czechoslovakia, and Bulgaria, the associations had members and candidate members. Moreover, the members received a monthly "salary", but had to present a certain number of works, evaluated by an official state-jury, which were exhibited and sold. The right to organize exhibitions was "nationalized" and became the monopoly of (as it was called in Poland) the Central Bureau of Fine Arts Exhibitions. Also, as in the Polish case, all training was concentrated into the National Institute of Fine Arts. To demonstrate compulsory examples to be followed, nation wide exhibitions, such as the First National Exhibition of Fine Arts, were organized. All artists were ordered to "present their draft paintings in advance to a jury, which would analyze and evaluate them from ideological and artistic points of view." In early 1950, a three-day conference was held to openly debate the drafts, and artists, "members of the party, began to criticize each other's works and practised self-criticism in order to rid themselves of shortcomings of their works" (Fenyö, 1950, p. 121). The Polish party leader Boleslaw Bierut was not interested in arts, except architecture, which was the focus of his emotional interest. He wanted to personally see almost every blueprint of important buildings, and he developed the idea that new socialist constructions may not be intermingled with "capitalist buildings;" thus entire neighborhoods of new buildings would have to be rearranged as well.

The First National Exhibition was a breakthrough of Polish socialist-realism. More than 3,000 works were submitted, from which 388 works of 271 artists were selected and exhibited. Official statistics registered 2 million visitors. The most preferred topics of the paintings were the reconstruction and electrification of the country, and work heroes, portraits of Stakhanovist "shock" workers. Surprisingly few portraits of Secretary General Boleslaw Bierut or even Stalin were exhibited. In Czechoslovakia, however, the cult of party chief Klement Gottwald abounded in such exhibitions. In Romania, the portraits of Stalin and the typical Soviet-type genre paintings, such as Anastasiu's "Ilich's lamps will illuminate us" and Angheluta's "We are learning from the masters of Soviet sport," dominated the exhibitions. The leader, Gheorghe Gheorghiu-Dej, became one of the favorite topics of sculptures and paintings from 1952–3 on (Stefan Szönyi painted a work that was meant to be emulated, "Comrade Gheorghiu-Dej working on the electrification plan of the country," in 1953.) "At the First Hungarian Art Exhibition [in] 1950, genre paintings were exhibited in their greatest numbers. . . . The renewed genre-painting reflects the life and the happiness of the liberated people and their new relation to work. . . . The new painting has a story and has a hero" (Szegi, 1950, pp. 321–30).

Huge statues of Stalin appeared in the squares and streets of every city. The most monumental Stalin statue was erected in Prague, on top of a hill towering above the city. In Budapest, a new square was built for the ritual annual parades and official demonstrations, and the Stalin Statue, "modest in its greatness and great in its modesty, as the great Stalin himself," as József Révai formulated in his speech at the dedication ceremony, stood in the middle of the square. Hundreds and thousands of Lenin statues were planted all over Central and Eastern Europe, standing steadily, with a stretched out right-arm, pointing out the road to follow.

Historical tableaus on famous episodes of the labor movement and idealized party history became more frequent in Poland in 1951–2, when the Polish hero of the Bolshevik revolution, Felix Dzierzyński,the founder of the "fist of the revolution," the Cheka, became the topic of a special exhibition. He was the theme of the huge, representative painting of Polish socialist-realism, "Dzierzyński, the leader of the Warsaw uprising in 1905," the work of an eight-member art collective, the preferred method of producing gigantic, collective socialist-realist works. In Czechoslovakia the main representative work of socialist realism, "The Czechoslovak people greet comrade Stalin," was produced by a painter's troika.

At the third Polish National Exhibition in 1952, the landscape painting, appeared. As minister of culture Stefan Dybowski argued: "Our country is in a revolutionary transformation. A new landscape is in the making on a daily basis. Gigantic buildings are towering in socialism. . . . Instead of an aging capitalistic landscape, which, in a sentimental way, neglected civilization, we are creating a new landscape" (Dybowski, 1953).

The "soc-realization" of art was accompanied by a permanent attack against modernists, who were condemned for "formalism." The world famous Romanian avant-garde painter, Maxy, who remained in Romania and tried to adjust to the new trend, and indeed became the director of the National Museum, was accused of being a "hidden" formalist. Gheorghiu-Dej warned that "foreign influences are easily hiding in the fields of ideology, literature, arts and sciences." The vigilant ideological watchdog translated this message: "Certain artists, for example Grigorescu, declared that they had changed and had stopped being formalists. Moreover, the painter Maxy, not only in statements but even in his paintings, made certain concessions to realism and attempted to show a complete break with his past. But the works of an artist manifest the reality clearer than his statements" (*Szabad Müvészet*, 1952, p. 322).

The leading Czech communist avant-garde painter, Karel Teige, was bluntly accused of being a "lackey of Wall Street imperialism" and ostracized, as was Lajos Kassák, the internationally renowned left-wing Hungarian constructivist. In Poland, the fellow-traveler artistic group of "Autodidacts," the first allies of official socialist-realism, was soon harshly denounced for a lack of compulsory optimism, and "neobarbarism." A similar campaign was launched against the so-called "partisan art" in Yugoslavia and Bulgaria, which was first recognized as a pioneer of socialist art. These genuine revolutionary trends, however, could not fit into the narrow framework of socialist-realism. Official art policy made an alliance with representatives of conservative academism and post-impressionist colorists. Quite often the leading artists of the 1930s, when the pathetic monumentalist-fascist novecento of Mussolini's Italy became the leading official trend in most of these countries, became the spokesmen of soc-real, which was much closer to them than to the old avant-garde communist and left-wing artists of the region. As a symbolic example, it pays to note that the most exemplary Lenin statue in Budapest was made by Pál Páczay, one of the most talented representatives of the "School of Rome," the Hungarian art-trend of the 1930s that openly emulated Mussolini's Italy. In Poland the same Wladislaw Skocilas who organized the first Soviet art exhibition in Poland in the early fifties, also founded the *Blok Zawodowy Artystów Plastików*, the official artist organization of the authoritarian Pilsudski regime, in 1934.

The conservative national schools of painting in interwar Slovakia, Romania, and Bulgaria could easily adjust to the new requirements of socialist realism. The representatives of this school played the leading role of the Slovak *Tvar* Association, the agent of the official trend by 1949. The conservative academism originated from the Munich-school, represented by Ivanov, Stanchev and Panajotov in interwar Bulgaria, and became the natural basis for postwar socialist-realism in the country.

As was the case in several dictatorial regimes with a centrally directed and compulsorily optimistic, heroic, and didactic art-trend, the goals of the authorities were backed by conservative artists who were marginalized by rapidly changing "isms" by the turn of the century on, who had continued to follow the old nineteenth-century school and were thus rendered obsolete and quickly by-passed, but who were now given government sanction to take over the art establishment once again. Their "rehabilitation" went hand in hand with a deliberate return to nineteenth-century romantic and national realism.

Of course, artists still produced some excellent paintings and sculptures, despite the party-state control and the institutionalized dictatorship of the arts. The monopolized and strictly commanded film industry produced some films of exceptional value. There were novels and poems of great merit, published by strictly supervised editorial boards. It is not my aim to describe the literary and artistic life of the period, and I will also not attempt to explain the reasons for the emergence of outstanding works. One must not forget, however, the often overlooked fact that a great number of previously oppressed talents emerged from the peasantry and workers, and that a newly educated young and enthusiastic intelligentsia had risen with new experiences of the bitter, bloody episode of the war, the disappointment and humiliation of the thirties, and the sincere experience of liberation. All these, in spite of the strict prescriptions, compulsory blueprints, and permanent interventions, still provided possibilities to prominent talents to produce high quality art. That was, of course, the exception. As a rule, however, art in Central and Eastern Europe became a subordinated weapon of party-state propaganda, an effective tool for influencing and brainwashing the population, for strengthening the fraudulent lies of official propaganda.

Behind the "Iron Curtain" not only was a different political system, economic structure, and social order established, but art-trends and entertainment, knowledge of the world, concepts of history and interpretation of facts all became different from that in the West. The countries of Central and Eastern Europe plummeted into a strictly controlled and permanently brutalized meticulous quarantine.

3 Reforms, revolutions, and the loosening bloc, the 1950s and 1960s

Stalinist Central and Eastern European socialism, in a few years after its introduction, declined into a deep crisis. The reasons for this were an overly expensive military build-up and an irrational and extremely rapid industrialization drive accompanied by declining standards of living. The turbulent and ruthless collectivization effort in the countryside, with its devastating impact on food supplies, led to deep desperation. The severe shortage of food, housing, and practically every kind of consumer good, which coincided with unrelenting propaganda boasting of untold successes, undermined the system's credibility. The paranoid terror and search for enemies permeated the entire society with fear. The overpoliticization of every sphere of life, including culture, art, and even the private domain of everyday life, alienated the people. A hypocritical "internationalism" assured the interest of an expansionist, interventionist Soviet Union, which dictated to and dominated her vassals. In a Kafkaesque Central and Eastern Europe, everything cried for a change.

The struggle against Stalinism and for reform began almost immediately with the introduction of Soviet socialism and a bloc-policy in the region, and the different variations, at distinctive stages, accompanied its existence until its collapse. In the region as a whole, there was continuity of struggle. The first revolt against Stalinism and Soviet domination emerged in Yugoslavia as early as 1948, when a "disobedient" Tito was excommunicated from the socialist camp. The Soviet–Yugoslav confrontation had a dual importance: it led to the formation of an independent, national road toward socialism, which was coupled with comprehensive, pioneering reforms that offered an alternative to Soviet state socialism. The Yugoslav revolt gained decisive momentum in the 1950s, but arrived at new stages in the 1960s.

In the midst of this process, and in close interrelationship with it, the death of Stalin in the spring of 1953 generated a "thaw," a liberalization, and certain moderate reforms and policy changes, guided by the new Soviet leadership and dictated to others as well. The controversial years of 1953–6, the Soviet-led de-Stalinization, became a period of genuine eruption of popular dissatisfaction and moral crisis within the elite, and of even mass movements in some countries. These years led to the major revolutions of 1956, peaceful in Poland and most violent Hungary. The "thaw" and the watershed of 1956 opened a new chapter in the history of state socialism: the emergence of a reformed, and more liberal moderate post-Stalinist era.

After the loosening of previous strict uniformity and extreme central-ization of power in the hands of the Soviet leadership on a "bloc level," some countries of the region (Albania and partly Romania), beside the already independent Yugoslavia, turned to independent national roads. Paradoxically, however, in successfully rebelling against the monolithic Soviet empire-building, Albania and Romania resisted Soviet de-Stalinization and sought to preserve their orthodox Stalinism. The rising "national Stalinism," however, contributed to the erosion of a united Soviet bloc and indirectly helped foster the spread of liberal reforms in some other countries of the region, consequently contributing to the erosion of state socialism itself. The Prague Spring in Czechoslovakia in 1968, and the introduction of the Hungarian economic reforms by the mid 1960s, were accompanied by a recurring crisis in Poland. The reform from within and from above was deeply rooted in post-Stalinism and gained its strongest momentum in Hungary.

The unbroken chain of (different types of) revolts and reforms thus characterized the history of Central and Eastern European socialism during this period. The countries of the region, however, did not revolt in unison. The crises, reforms, and rebellions had almost always a different center. Some of the countries enjoyed decades of peaceful stability or were frozen into ruthless dictatorships, silently and without real opposition.

The destiny of state socialism was determined by some decisive and renowned revolts. Their milestones, marking the turning points of postwar Central and Eastern European history, are the dramatic years of 1948 (the Yugoslav revolt and emergence of national communism, combined with major reforms), 1953 (the "thaw" of liberalization), 1956 (the crucial turning-point of the Polish and Hungarian revolutions, followed by the Albanian and Romanian revolts against Soviet de-Stalinization and domination), and 1968 (the Prague Spring, and the Hungarian reform breakthrough).

These years and events, retrospectively and historically, were stepping stones toward a general crisis and the revolts and new reform breakthroughs of the 1980s, primarily in Poland and Hungary, which led to the "*Annus of Mirabilis*" 1989.

1948: the emergence of a Yugoslav model

The first critical blow that hit Stalinism was the opening of Yugoslavia's separate road. Its origin was Stalin's attempt to discipline, and then destroy, Tito. After the Soviet "criticism" of Yugoslav policy, the infamous decisions of the Cominform in 1948 excommunicated Yugoslavia from the communist world movement. "The Information Bureau considers," stated the resolution, "that nationalist elements, which previously existed in a disguised form, managed . . . to reach a dominant position in the leadership of the Communist Party of Yugoslavia, and . . . has taken the road to nationalism" (Stokes, 1991, p. 64).

The first reaction, the 5th Congress of the Yugoslav Communist Party in July 1948, sought to prove that the Soviet condemnations were not true. The party, trying to answer Stalin's criticisms, initiated a collectivization drive in the countryside. In the fall of that year, the Yugoslav delegation consistently voted with the Soviet Union at the United Nations, and Stalin's portraits were carried together with the pictures of Marx, Lenin, and Tito during the ritual May Day parade, even in 1949. The break, however, was soon completed: the arranged show trials of Rajk, Kostov, and Xoxe, followed by the Cominform's resolution in 1949, "unmasked" Tito and his leadership as a "gang of traitors, police informers and imperialist agents" who had infiltrated the party.

Yugoslavia had to try to find her own independent way. It gradually developed from 1948 to 1953 on. Instead of trying to defend themselves, by the winter of 1949–50 they had launched an ideological counterattack, accusing the Soviet Union "of revisionism, characterized by chauvinistic imperialism in its foreign policy and by bureaucratic despotism in its domestic structure" (Rothschild, 1989, p. 141). Yugoslav communism, which first adopted the Soviet model, began to depart from it and its "deformations." A series of reforms and political and institutional changes gradually built an alternative, independent model of state socialism (*Yugoslavia's Way*, 1958). The first country, though just a small part of the monolithic rock mass of the Soviet bloc, had broken away. Tito masterfully designed the policy of non-alignment and built up a respected, independent international position. From the late fifties, with the collaboration of Nasser and Nehru, Tito became the chief architect of the movement that had the cooperation of the "Third World" countries. Yugoslavia organized the first conference of the non-aligned nations in Belgrade in 1961 with twenty-three participating nations.

The main internal characteristics of the new model expressed the will to democratize the system and to replace Soviet-type bureaucratic state domination. Political rigor and pressure were eased. The compulsory socialist-realism was abandoned and freedom of artistic expression assured. Borders were opened for tourism and Western products, which became available in the shops. Though freedom had strict limitations, and certain taboos, such as the one-party system and the leading role of the Communist Party, remained unquestionable, Yugoslavia, from the early fifties on, differed quite markedly from other state socialist countries.

The essence of change, however, was manifest in the most conspicuous way in three central fields. The first among them was the introduction of self-management, a genuine attempt to replace state bureaucracy with, as it was later formulated by the party program, the "direct power of the working people." Self-management was institutionalized by "Workers' Councils," the "democratic economic-political organs of social self-management through which direct producers independently manage enterprises . . . on behalf of the . . . community. . . . The state," maintained the party program, "is not at all the main instrument of socialist construction" (*Yugoslavia's Way*, 1958). As Milovan Djilas later described it, the idea emerged in the spring of 1950 from re-reading Marx and his idea on the future society as a "free association of producers." The practical realization was developed by Edvard Kardelj, the chief ideologue of "Titoism," who linked self-management with the workers' councils, which had previously played a formal role as powerless consultative bodies for management. Tito recognized the great potential of self-management and declared that it "would be the beginning of democracy, something that socialism had not yet achieved," and "a radical departure from Stalinism" (Stokes, 1991, p. 96).

The law, which was passed on June 26, 1950, handed over management of all economic enterprises to the workers. The institution was extended to the area of services, including schools, hospitals, and the civil service. The Workers' Councils, which were elected every other year, gained considerable power. In a certain state-regulated framework (taxation, investment and wage regulations), they made decisions on the conditions of work, investments and income distribution, production, and marketing. Their role was significantly strengthened by abolishing central price regulations and control of foreign trade (Tyson, 1980).

The institution developed as a consistent political system, and the new 1953 constitution introduced a bicameral structure, with the second chamber designated as the Council of Producers. Representation for the different branches was assured by their contribution to the national income. The 1974 constitution created a consistent system of self-management. The Yugoslav constitution, certainly the world's longest, provided detailed and strongly ideological regulations on more than 120 pages and in 406 points, declaring that "the workers and other working people had a social contract . . . regulating their relations and . . . interests . . . in a self-managerial way" (Kovács, 1985, p. 239).

The reform profoundly limited the role of the state bureaucracy and decentralized a formerly overcentralized regime. Central planning gradually lost its importance, and the Yugoslav economy, though basically non-private, gradually became market-oriented with free market prices and a labor market. Suddenly increasing unemployment was counterbalanced by allowing Yugoslav guest-workers to go to Western Europe. Decentralization, however, did not stop at this stage. The federal structure of the Yugoslav state, which was more a formality than a reality, was gradually reinforced in a significant way. The federal government was abolished with the exception of Foreign Affairs, Defense, and Interior Affairs. The legislative independence of the republics was strongly increased and the party itself was reorganized and decentralized as the League of Communists of Yugoslavia in November 1952. The republics and the republics' communist parties became more and more independent. The reforms were from time to time institutionalized by the new constitutions of 1953, 1963, and 1974 (Pasic, 1987).

An additional major element of the Yugoslav reforms was the return to private farming. It was announced in a decree on March 30, 1953, which allowed a stepping away from the cooperative farms. By the end of the year, more than three quarters of the cooperatives were dissolved. This decisive step was coupled with the abolition of the compulsory delivery system. The main pillar of central planning in agriculture was thus destroyed, and a stable taxation was introduced. A part of the mostly small-scale private economy was reestablished. Yugoslavia made major steps toward a new socialist model, which was more democratic and market-oriented, more liberal, and less state controlled.

The party, however, at least under Tito, preserved its leading role and, mobilizing its more than one million members, successfully manipulated the new institutions, including the workers' councils and the system of self-management, which tended more to be ideological myth rather than the reality of people's direct power. When Milovan Djilas openly challenged Leninism and the vanguard role of the party and argued for the liquidation of its apparatus, he was eventually expelled from the party, and even imprisoned. When national conflict, either from the Croatian or Serbian side, endangered federal interests, Tito did not hesitate to purge the republics, including the state and local council apparatus, as well as the company managements. Institutions, formally under self-managerial control, obediently followed the orders from the center, clearly showing the formality of the one party system. "De-stateization" and democratization, although a permanent process which made important achievements, had strong limitations in Tito's "national communism."

The "thaw": 1953–6

On March 5, 1953 a few years after Tito's revolt, Stalin died. He was buried next to Lenin, and spontaneous mourning followed. An exalted crowd crushed to death hundreds of people to get a last chance to see him. The death of a mythic semi-god, as he had been presented, became the source of a crisis.

The revision of his policy began immediately. His closest and most obedient aids, his hand-picked heirs, declared a "New Course." The *primus inter pares* in the "collective leadership," prime minister Georgi Malenkov, in his speech on August 8, 1953, declared the important new principles, among them the possibility of "peaceful coexistence of the two systems." Regarding the most important domestic policy issues, Malenkov focused on the "measures to further increase the well-being of the population." The content of the "New Course" was accomplished by a new agricultural policy, which aimed at radically improving the food supply, as well as strictly limiting the drive to industrialization.

The principle of "collective leadership" was declared. Stalin's posts, which were inherited by Malenkov, who became first secretary of the party and prime minister, were soon separated. Malenkov kept the premiership, while the party was directed by Nikita Khrushchev, who became first secretary only in September. In the first months, Lavrenti Beria, the head of the secret police, joined the leading troika as minister of the interior and deputy prime minister. The "collective leadership," however, did not remain for long.

The first short chapter of the struggle for absolute power was ended in July 1953, when Beria was arrested and executed as a traitor. The second chapter was not very much longer: in February 1955, Malenkov was removed from the premiership. Although that post was given to Marshal Bulganin, it was taken over by Nikita Khrushchev, thereby ending the power struggle with the restoration of absolute power.

Nevertheless, after Stalin's death the principle of collective leadership and later the accusation of the Stalinist "cult of personality" both became inseparable parts of the "New Course," which generated a cautious de-Stalinization process. International tensions, East–West confrontation, and domestic political extremism and terror were all equally challenged, and the ice of the Cold War and frozen Stalinism began to melt. As Soviet writer Ilya Erenburg remarked, the spring of 1953 set in with a political "thaw."

Malenkov's "thaw," based paradoxically on Stalin's empire-building traditions, was designed for Central and Eastern Europe as a whole. The Soviet leadership realized that the irrational war preparations, extreme industrialization and forced collectivization, caused tremendous economic-political tensions in the region. The situation became too explosive, and they decided to intervene.

The new Soviet directives were imposed on East Germany, which declared its new course on June 9, 1953, first among the "Peoples' Democracies." A delegation of the Hungarian party, headed by Mátyás Rákosi, was invited to Moscow, on June 13–14. At the meeting, the Soviet Politburo harshly criticized the severe failures of Rákosi's policies, and demanded an immediate change. They stated that a clique of four, Rákosi, Gerö, Farkas and Révai, monopolized power and made all the decisions, used extreme terror and had an economic policy that led to a decline in living standards. As a consequence, "the regime is threatened by a people's uprising!" – stated most of the Soviet leaders, remembers András Hegedüs, a member of the Hungarian delegation. When Rákosi tried to debate the issue and mentioned Soviet intentions, Beria replied: "Rákosi should already know that we can break everybody's backbone!" (Hegedüs, 1988, pp. 200, 202).

Malenkov proposed that Rákosi must be replaced by Imre Nagy as prime minister, but should remain first secretary of the party. "Since prime minister Malenkov stood higher in the Soviet hierarchy than Khrushchev, who already led the party apparatus as secretary of the Central Committee, we assumed," Hegedüs remarked, recalling the view of the Hungarian delegation, "that because of Soviet intentions, Imre Nagy will be the 'first man'" (Hegedüs, 1988, p. 202).

The Central Committee of the Hungarian party gathered less than two weeks later, and made its resolution at a plenary session on June 27–8. The Rákosi clique was personally accused of responsibility for deformations, and the resolution ended with a clear anti-Semitic remark: the personal policy of the Rákosi-quadriga "lifted only very few cadres of Hungarian origin [i.e., non-Jewish] to top positions" (Balogh, 1986, p. 501). The criticism of the Stalinist past was much deeper, and the changes announced were much stronger, because of Imre Nagy's impressive and steady contribution to the debate.

Imre Nagy

The New Course, designed and ordered by the Soviet party, gained great momentum in Hungary, since this was the only country in the region where the reform attempt had a charismatic leader, Prime Minister Imre Nagy. Nagy was selected by Malenkov to achieve the new political will in Hungary. According to certain unproven assumptions, Malenkov knew Nagy quite well, because Nagy had worked as a personal secretary to Malenkov during some of his years in Moscow (1930–44). Information purposely "leaked" by Rákosi, as well as certain KGB documents that came to light decades later in 1989, revealed that Nagy reported to the KGB using a pseudonym.

After the war Nagy became Minister of Agriculture in the first provisional government, and the architect of the radical land reform. In May, he became a prominent member of the Politburo. However, being an expert in agriculture and having worked in the thirties at the Institute of Agriculture in Moscow, Nagy had his own ideas, similar to Bukharin's, regarding agricultural and economic policy, and advocated an independent Hungarian road. He confronted the Rákosi leadership at the end of 1947, opposing collectivization and the anti-kulak policy, and was removed from the Politburo in early 1948. Nagy then became a professor of agricultural economics at the Budapest University of Economics. He was not arrested; and his disgrace did not last long. Coinciding with the emergence of Malenkov in Stalin's last years, he moved back into the Central Committee apparatus, became a member of the cabinet, and, from early 1951, a member of the Politburo again.

Unlike most other party leaders who were ordered to change the official party line and who reluctantly obeyed, Nagy wholeheartedly advocated the policy of change. Nagy remained a kind of naive politician. A man who never loved power, with a genuinely mediative character and strong academic interests, he achieved a historical role, and identified himself with it. A man who learned to subordinate himself as an enthusiastic young revolutionary, coming from a Hungarian peasant–railroad worker background and joining the Russian revolution and the Communist Party as a prisoner of war, and then learning to adjust during his fifteen-year stay in Stalinist Russia, he was ready to accept the party line and partake in self-criticism. He did it in the late forties when he was crushed by Rákosi, and he remained obedient in the early fifties after his quiet rehabilitation.

In 1953 the role was provided to him, and, again, he accepted and followed Soviet advice. He was ready to deliver moderate, public speeches to demonstrate party unity (with Rákosi!). From that time on, however, Imre Nagy emerged as a sovereign representative of a communist enlightenment movement, a forerunner of democratic, national, reform-communism.

At the age of fifty-seven, he took on the difficult historical role of a savior of his country. He did not want to adjust any longer; he did not subordinate himself and his mission to party discipline. He started his journey, consistently and faithfully. He realized that Imre Nagy the politician and reform leader was much larger than Imre Nagy the citizen. He embodied a mission and became a symbol, a center to which reformer-revolutionaries gathered, and he remained faithful to his assignment, subordinating himself to this goal.

Nagy began his march for democratic socialism, an independent road to prosperity, and suffered expulsion and humiliation, but he became the leader of a revolution, and, in his last year, an uncompromising hero for freedom. His ideas and goals placed him in a role which led to prison and the gallows. He could have avoided it, and he even offered his services to those who overthrew him, but in the end he refused a life-saving compromise. All this happened in a few short years. . . . It is only the summer of 1953.

The New Course all over

The population of the country was informed of the New Course by the government program of Imre Nagy, announced by him on July 4 in parliament. Nagy promulgated a radical reduction in industrial investment, slowing down the pace of industrialization, which went together with "the steady improvement of the living standards. . . . The government considers as one of its most important tasks to increase substantially the investments in agriculture . . . in order to bring about the earliest and biggest possible boom in production." In one of the most promising parts of his program, Nagy declared that "the Government . . . will make it possible for cooperative farm members . . . to withdraw from the cooperative." Moreover, it will permit the winding down of cooperative farms. The program criticized excessive state ownership and reintroduced private enterprise, mostly in retail trade and crafts. Nagy's government went much further than most of the "new coursers": it condemned "coercive measures" against the church and religion and declared tolerance; an immediate amnesty was announced, internment camps and police-courts were abolished; and compulsorily "resettled class enemies" gained back their right "to choose their residence in compliance with legal provisions applying to all citizens." "The consolidation of legality is one of the most urgent tasks of the government" (Daniels, 1962, pp. 212–14).

The program was immediately inaugurated. The whole country was revitalized and suddenly awakened from its depressing nightmare. Since the Soviet leadership was convinced that Rákosi was the best guarantee for realizing their power interests, the Stalinist nucleus of the Hungarian party leadership remained in power and sabotaged radical changes. A split and confrontation inside the party was unavoidable. The Stalinists gathered around Rákosi while Nagy became the center of an emerging reform wing, which achieved a breakthrough in October 1954. At the plenum of the Central Committee, Nagy criticized harshly the Stalinist resistance against the New Course reform and won the agreement of the majority. The leading journalists of the party daily, *Szabad Nép*, openly revolted against the Rákosi group and demanded the independence of the media, while attacking conservative resistance and the slow rehabilitation of victims. The affair precipitated the awakening and revolt of the party-intelligentsia.

On October 23–4 a new Peoples' Front organization was founded, initiated by Nagy and headed by his son-in-law. It sought to pluralize the political structure, and Nagy argued for personal membership instead of member organizations. He insisted that the Front "has to safeguard the realization of our great national goals . . . and will control the accomplishment of law, justice and benevolence in all spheres of governmental activity and social life" (Balogh *et al.*, 1985, p. 382). Imre Nagy's People's Front was a sort of new party formation set against the political monopoly of the existing party.

The October breakthrough in 1954 mobilized the party intellectuals, especially the young, enthusiastic generations, and transformed their naive beliefs into a more sober attempt at change. The Writers' Union became the yeast of a new political fermentation. A reform-communist wing emerged, and a bitter confrontation characterized the years between 1953 and 1956.

György Péter, the head of the Statistical Office, published his powerful concept of market-oriented economic reform in the fall of 1954. János Kornai's work on the overcentralization of the economic system was debated in the late summer of 1956. A reforming economic policy was in the making. The conservative Stalinist wing, however, launched a devastating counterattack. A new resolution of the Central Committee in March 1955 accused Nagy and the reformists of "right-wing" deviation. The preference for industrialization was restored, together with a new spurt of collectivization and anti-kulak actions. The Stalinist line gained the upper hand. A victorious Rákosi took his revenge: a few weeks after Georgi Malenkov was defeated and lost the premiership in the Soviet Union in February 1955, Imre Nagy lost his first battle against Rákosi, was removed from the premiership in April, and was expelled from the party.

The Pyrrhic victory of Hungarian Stalinism, however, could not stop the process of a strengthening opposition-from-within. Dissatisfaction increased, and the collapse of promising reforms and the fall of an honest and popular political leader sharpened the confrontation and led to a deeper crisis.

Although the dynamism of the Hungarian process was not universal in Central and Eastern Europe, the new policy was decreed throughout the area and certain changes began. The "New Course" was declared in

Poland on July 21, in Romania on August 22, in Bulgaria on September 9, and in Czechoslovakia on September 15. In most cases, such as Romania, self-criticism was rather mild and moderate: "besides the achievements, there were serious mistakes in our economic policy," stated Gheorge Gheorghiu-Dej. "First of all we exaggerated the pace of industrialization . . . and the living standards of the workers did not increase adequately, compared with the general development of the national economy" (Gheorghiu-Dej, 1953). This tone was rather understandable since Dej, like other party leaders in the region, had been the head of the party in the most extreme Stalinist years, and now became the commander of the "New Course" as well. He was ready to announce the slowing down of the industrialization and collectivization drive and to increase agricultural production and living standards. Following the Soviet pattern of introducing "collective leadership," he resigned from one of his top positions and, like Malenkov, kept the premiership. Gheorghiu-Dej, however, did not want a real analysis and drastic change. Moreover, with his exceptional instinct for power, he soon had second thoughts about dividing personal power: in the fall of 1955, he took back the post of first secretary of the party and, against Soviet orders, once again concentrated party and government power in his own hands.

Indeed, Gheorghiu-Dej had no intention of tolerating a dangerous potential rival, a would-be successor during this period when the errors of the fifties were being criticized. Lucreţiu Patraşcanu, the "national communist" victim of the first wave of Stalinist purges in Romania, who was arrested in 1948 and, though not tried, was kept in jail, was sentenced to death on April 14, 1954 and executed, a year after the death of Stalin, when rehabilitation of the victims had become a major issue in Hungary.

Vlko Chervenkov, the despot of Bulgaria since the death of Dimitrov in 1949, was also rather mild in his criticism of the early fifties. He stressed that "the results of industrialization, achieved during the first five year plan, make it now possible to develop the production of consumer goods in a maximal pace and rapidly improve the material and cultural conditions of the population" (Chervenkov, 1959, p. 35). He also announced a very partial and limited amnesty and initiated a "collective leadership," resigning as secretary general of the party, while keeping the premiership. A small group of intellectuals, especially the Writers' Union and its journal *Plamuk*, became an organ of strident criticism. Emil Manov, Todor Genov and other writers, most of them party members, led the rebellion, which was ruthlessly suppressed after 1956. Nevertheless Chervenkov did not survive. Retaining the premiership turned out to be a miscalculation: the new party chief, Todor Zhivkov, removed Chervenkov a year after the fall of Malenkov, in April 1956.

"Investments and economic successes created the prerequisites and opportunity," argued Viliam Široký quite similarly in Czechoslovakia in 1953, "to take special attention to slow down the increase of investments into the heavy industries and increase the consumption of the population and assure the rise of their standard of living" (Široký, 1953, p. 586). That was the essence of the announcement of the New Course in Czechoslovakia, Poland, and Albania as well.

With the exception of Hungary, the "New Course" throughout the region remained moderate. In the political arena, accusations regarding the lack of collective leadership and the separation of state and party command, accompanied by a more liberal political line, constrained progress. Those who had the best power instincts, such as Enver Hohxa or Boleslaw Bierut, remained party chiefs and resigned as prime ministers. In Czechoslovakia the Stalinist Klement Gottwald made his last service to his party by clearing the way for personnel changes: he became ill at the burial of Stalin on a frosty March day in Moscow, and died of pneumonia nine days later. A collective leadership took over: Antonin Zapotocky as president of the state, Viliam Široký as prime minister, and Antonin Novotny as first secretary of the party. It is small wonder that in a few years Novotny seized power, taking over the presidency as well as replacing Zapotocký.

The centrally initiated "thaw," although aiming only to correct and not radically change the policy line, and to ease accumulating tensions, was both led and sabotaged by former Stalinist party chiefs, who were responsible for the criticized errors (and crimes) of the troublesome fifties. However, at the same time, it unleashed new forces of revolt. Besides the Hungarian national reform-communism, bitter popular dissatisfaction and unrest erupted quite quickly.

On June 16, 1953, a week after the declaration introducing the New Course in East Germany, construction workers demonstrated against changes in working conditions in East Berlin, and on the next day an uprising erupted in the capital and in other cities. The masses attacked state and party offices, and the first popular revolt against the regime was suppressed by Soviet tanks. Similarly, a so-called monetary reform on May 30 in Czechoslovakia, which sought to curb inflation, generated strikes in Plzen, and this rare open protest swept over the country. There were strikes in Prague and in Strakonice. The corrective New Course reform from above immediately led to open unrest and revolt from below.

The "thaw," reluctant, over cautious and unable to produce real change, was, however, of significance in breaking the iron logic and consistency of Stalinism. The turn toward "legality" and against the violation of legal norms, and the curbing of unlimited police terror, essentially reduced fear, thus breaking the ultimate guarantee of dictatorial regimes. The condemnation of "past mistakes" and even crimes revealed the buried truth and broke the "Big Lie" supporting a "superior, just and essentially most democratic system," the pillars of Stalinist propaganda. A rather partial liberalization hit the massive isolating walls of a comprehensively closed society, and opened the doors to let in information and contact from the outside world.

Its consistency broken, the regime became much more vulnerable. Revolts against dictatorships rarely erupt at the peak of oppression. Revolution comes when half-hearted liberalization moderates terror and seeks to create a more acceptable era. This happened in the mid fifties in Central and Eastern Europe.

1956: one and a half revolutions

The genie, freed from the closed bottle of Stalinism in 1953, refused to go back in. There was very little progress made with the reforms. Central and Eastern Europe, began to depart from strict, consistent Stalinism. After the proclamation of the New Course, a few major international events formed the milestones of a genuine transformation.

A departure from international confrontation was signaled on July 27, 1953 by the truce signed in Korea; on July 21 the four great powers agreed to end the war in Indochina. The world turned back from the brink of a Third World War. The great powers returned to the conference table: in Berlin the ministers of foreign affairs had a promising meeting in early 1954, on the German and Austrian questions among others. Within a year, on May 15 in Vienna, the foreign ministers signed the agreement on Austria. The Soviet Union, without territorial compensation, withdrew her troops, and Austria became independent and neutral.

On May 27, 1955, the Soviet delegation, led by First Secretary Khrushchev and Prime Minister Bulganin, went to their Canossa: in an official visit to Tito's Yugoslavia, they recognized Yugoslavia as a socialist state and normalized relations; moreover, the joint declaration stressed the "mutual respect for ... different forms of socialist development" (Brzezinski, 1961, pp. 174–5).

The process of rapprochement was completed by the dissolution of the Cominform (April 1956) – a symbol and institution of uniformity – which excommunicated Tito. In June 1956, Tito returned Khrushchev's gesture and visited Moscow, and on that occasion Pravda published an article by Kardelj, the chief ideologue of Titoism.

The acknowledgment of the national Yugoslav road to socialism has had tremendous importance in the emerging diversity. Tito's, up to that time, isolated and condemned road now became an alternative to Soviet-type socialism. The national road or "national communism," free from the strait-jacket of the Soviet pattern, seeking to address national goals and characteristics, became a powerful temptation for the neighboring countries, which gradually rebuilt their contact with Yugoslavia. The rapprochement between Yugoslavia and the Soviet Union gave an enormous impetus to emerging "national communism" in Poland and Hungary in the coming months, and quite soon in Albania and Romania as well.

Progress, which began with the New Course in March 1953, had gained new impetus at the 20th Congress of the Soviet Communist Party in February 1956. Khrushchev, struggling to consolidate his power against his rivals, made a sharp turn against Stalinism, mostly equating it with the "cult of personality" and violation of "socialist legality." His speech at the secret session of the congress unmasked Stalin's ruthless terror, including some of the purges, and rejected the Stalinist theory of the intensifying class struggle after the communist seizure of power both internally and in the international arena, which makes war unavoidable. Instead, Khrushchev emphasized the possibility of the peaceful coexistence of capitalism and socialism, and the potential of a non-revolutionary road toward power for the proletariat. He also acknowledged the "different roads of transition to socialism," and characterized the connections among socialist countries as "relations of fully equal rights" (Brzezinski, 1961, pp. 179–80).

The 20th Congress had a tremendous impact on Central and Eastern Europe. The decade-long history of Stalinism in these countries, the system's sacrosanct principles and the celebrated leaders who realized them, were now all undermined. The attack against Stalinism assaulted the Central and Eastern European regimes. Poland and Hungary sank into a peculiarly deep crisis. The march of history in these countries proceeded at top speed toward a revolt and revolution. In 1956 the process became unstoppable.

The Polish October

Poland's New Course had a slow start and a cautious advance from 1953–6. The adoption of the New Course was delayed and more restrained than elsewhere (Brzezinski, 1961, p. 236). History, however, took a sharp turn in early 1956. First of all, the 20th party congress urged reform. Boleslaw Bierut, the Stalinist leader who led the Polish party delegation to the congress in February, fell ill and died in Moscow of a heart disorder on March 12, 1956. As Gottwald succumbed to Stalin's death, Bierut, symbolically, was carried off by the harsh de-Stalinization drive of the 20th Congress.

The revolt of the party-intelligentsia gained momentum. The process actually began at the time of the New Course. The defection of Lieutenant-Colonel Swiatlo, a leading officer in the infamous Polish secret police at the end of 1953, opened the Pandora's box containing the most horrible secrets of the fifties. Both the Stalinist crimes and the direct Soviet command of the secret police were methodically documented and broadcast, contributing to the moral-political crisis. The party's Politburo was "isolated" and severely attacked, and the session of the Central Committee in January 1955 became a plenum of severe criticism and revolt against the past and the leadership. "The first major shift ..." remarked Zbigniev Brzezinski, "thus occurred *within* the party apparatus and Central Committee at the end of 1954 and at the beginning of 1955. Undisputed leadership of the Politburo was for the first time challenged and tenuous links established between the restless elements in the party and the discontented populace" (Brzezinski, 1961, p. 238).

Intellectuals' discussion clubs began to mushroom from the spring of 1955 on: within a year there were more than two hundred clubs in Poland. *Nowa Kultura*, the organ of the Polish Writers' Union, published the poem of Adam Wazyk in August 1955, with the famous lines: "I will never believe, my dear, that a lion is a little lamb; I will never believe, my dear, that a little lamb is a lion. ... We make demands on this earth; for which we did not throw dice; for which a million perished in battle; for a clear truth; for the bread of freedom; for burning reason; for burning reason" (Zinner, 1956, pp. 44, 48).

The writers and the intelligentsia sensitively expressed the mood of the country, and their revolt inside the party (Wazyk's seditious poem ended with the following two lines: "We demanded these every day; We demanded through the Party") had a strong basis, since in 1956 almost 40 percent of party members in Poland were intellectuals. Their percentage in the decisive Warsaw area was nearly 65 percent.

The intellectual landslide continued unabated and strengthened from February–March 1956 on. A new factor of the revolt of the party intelligentsia was the Cominform statement, in February 1956, on the "groundless" liquidation of the Communist Party of Poland in 1938, actually the murder of the whole prewar party leadership in Soviet emigration at that time.

The intellectual revolt culminated at the 19th session of the Council of Culture and Art, which expressed the thirst for truth and the condemnation of lies. Antoni Slonimski disclosed the reason for the Polish misfortune: Soviet domination. He rejected the official explanation of the deformations:

"first of all," stated Slonimski, "it is not the cult of personality . . . but the system which permits the individual to conduct such dangerous activities. Only a true democratization . . . a restoration of public opinion, and the return . . . to rational and unfettered thought can save us from Caesarism" (Zinner, 1956, pp. 49, 54). Slonimski, however, believed in a socialist renaissance, as did a great number of the rebelling intellectuals.

The revolt of the intelligentsia and the party and the slow de-Stalinization, which led to the quiet release of Gomulka from prison at the end of 1954 (he was still accused of nationalist deviation but not of treason), and led to the removal in May 1956 of Jakub Berman, the number two man in the Stalinist hierarchy, chief ideologue and the leader responsible for security matters, was suddenly reinforced by the violent revolt of the workers.

On June 28, 1956 the workers of the Cegielski factory and other firms of Poznan took on to the streets. The demonstration turned into a bloody riot. The workers' dissatisfaction was rooted in changes in the working conditions and the elimination of progressive piecework rates, which diminished the income of three quarters of the workers. Desperate demonstrators began to attack public buildings and police barracks, and a two-day battle with the armed forces left fifty-three dead and more than three hundred people wounded (Trojanowicz, 1981). The government reaction was firm. Premier Cyrankiewicz, who arrived at the scene, stated that the Poznan event was "an armed uprising against the people's rule . . . [and] murderous provocateurs have taken advantage of . . . dissatisfaction. . . . Every provocateur," he added, ". . . who will dare raise his hand against the people's rule may be sure that . . . the authorities will chop off his hand" (Zinner, 1956, pp. 131, 133, 135).

More than three hundred persons were arrested. "We cannot idly bypass attempts that are aimed at weakening the international ties of the socialist camp under the slogan of so-called national peculiarities," warned Soviet Prime Minister Bulganin, who arrived in Warsaw on July 21. "We cannot pass by in silence the attempts which aim at undermining the power of the people's democratic state under the guise of 'spreading democracy'" (*Pravda*, 1956).

The workers' uprising and its bloody repression, however, led to a turning point in the process of political fermentation. At the end of July, the 7th plenum of the Central Committee of the Polish party became a scene of the most heated debate and resulted in a split in the party leadership. The resolution of the plenum formulated "that the tragic events in Poznan, which caused a deep shock throughout the . . . nation, cast a new light upon the political and social situation of the country" (Zinner, 1956, pp. 146–7).

The conservative, pro-Soviet, so-called Natolinist faction of the leadership, which did not want real changes, suggested a limit to the number of leaders of Jewish origin, the release of Cardinal Wyszynski and a compromise with the church, the inclusion of Gomulka into the Politburo, and a 50 percent wage increase. A reformist group advocated further institutional reforms toward a social democratic trend, and sought to strengthen personal freedoms, liberalism, legality, and economic reforms to revitalize the bankrupt economy. In the late summer of 1957, an advisory economic council, headed by Oscar Lange, the long-time advocate of market-socialism, worked out a reform to build in a market into the planned economy.

But neither the demagogic measures suggested by the conservatives, nor the more moderate reform resolution of the 7th plenum, offered any real solution. The economic reform, stipulated in the resolution of the Central Committee, was extremely limited. It included a decrease in the number of compulsory plan indicators to curb bureaucratic over centralization, abolishing the compulsory delivery of milk, but keeping the whole delivery system alive. It allowed "loyal kulaks" to join cooperative farms, and called for the liberalization of small-scale, cottage industries. All the other major decisions were postponed.

Polish society was hungry for change and would not tolerate hesitation any longer. In some of the Warsaw factories, workers' councils were founded. The communist youth organization's weekly, *Po Prostu*, became an organ of an independent and democratic transformation, and openly criticized Soviet-type collectivization. All the hopes and demands were connected to the question of Gomulka's role. The realization of his "Polish road to socialism" became a myth and a symbol of national independence, and a hope for democratization.

Wladyslaw Gomulka, the charismatic key figure of the Polish revolution in 1956, was fifty-one years old. Born to a peasant-worker's family in the mining town of Krosno in 1905, himself a worker who became a blacksmith apprentice at the age of fourteen and joined the trade unions two years later, Gomulka became a communist in 1925. During a labor riot in Lodz, he was wounded and arrested in 1932. In 1936 he was sentenced to seven years' imprisonment for his underground activities, but was released when the German attack began in September 1939, and participated in the defense of Warsaw. During the dramatic war years, he participated in armed actions against the German occupants, throwing hand grenades into the Cafe Club and the Central Station. After the reorganization of the Communist Party of Poland he became the secretary of the Warsaw organization in December 1942, and then secretary-general of the party in November 1943.

Gomulka's formal education ended at age fourteen, but he was self-educated in the way of old-style socialist workers, and had a very strong character. He was a profound thinker who made his own decisions and did not like concessions. Gomulka was an uncompromising communist who could harmonize his religious Marxist–Leninist belief with a similarly devout patriotism. He was ready to serve his party, but as a politician he remained fair, frank, and sensitive to human justice and was always loyal to his friends. He easily lost his patience in debates because he was convinced he was right. In the crucial turning point of 1948–9, Gomulka refused to adjust to the compulsory Soviet line and opposed the rapid sovietization of Poland. As head of his party he advocated gradualism and opposed collectivization. Consequently, he was condemned. During the expulsion proceedings Gomulka rejected the forced self-criticism and defended his concept of a "Polish road to socialism" (Gibney, 1959, p. 54). In Miedzeszyn prison, he remained unbending and insisted on his innocence. An open trial remained out of the question. After three years of imprisonment, on Christmas Eve, 1954, Gomulka became the antithesis of compromised Stalinists.

His party membership was reestablished in early August 1956. The party functionaries learned from an official letter that "the resolution of the Plenum of the Central Committee of the 3rd of November 1949 which referred to unsubstantiated and unfair objections raised against Wladyslaw Gomulka . . . [was anulled, and his] party member status was restored" (Gomulka, 1987, pp. 86, 88).

Party intellectuals demanded "the widely anticipated return of comrade Gomulka to active political life," as the resolution of the party organization of the Polish Writers' Union openly declared in September 1956. The resolution added: "Confidence of the whole nation in the party is lacking . . . we ask comrade Gomulka, a man whose unwavering attitude inspired the confidence of the nation, to present his opinion concerning the basic problems of our lives and ways of building socialism in Poland" (Gomulka, 1987, pp. 98–9).

In mid October a short communiqué on the session of the Politburo stated that "Comrade Gomulka took part in the meeting." The press reported the resignation of Hilary Minc, the third member of the leading Stalinist troika, responsible for economic policy. This step was connected to an agreement between a demoralized, split, and desperate party leadership and Gomulka, concluded at the weekend of October 13–15. Gomulka's inclusion in the leadership could not happen on the basis of the Natolin group's conservative concept. He remained steadfast and robustly stuck to his platform, which required a severe condemnation of the past, and a removal of the Stalinist old guard (Raina, 1969).

In the crucial summer and fall of 1956, Gomulka became the key figure in Polish history. His past and his views gave him considerable significance. "As a symbol, Gomulka offered something to everyone," explained Zbigniew Brzezinski. "He was a former victim of Stalinism and its recognized opponent. . . . To the anti-Communists, he was the leader of a movement toward independence; to the revisionists, toward a democratic socialism. To the concerned Communists, he was the savior of the crumbling Communist rule" (Brzezinski, 1961, p. 334).

The frightened Stalinists and the Soviet leadership, however, wanted to block Gomulka's road back to power. Some conservative Politburo members of the Natolin group sent an urgent message to Moscow, triggering the prepared anti-Soviet move. On October 17, the Soviet ambassador presented an invitation for consultations in Moscow, but the Politburo declined. The Soviet Army at its Western base in Legnica was mobilized and prepared to move toward Warsaw.

The desperate Natolinists presented a list of 700 party reformists and intellectuals, including Gomulka, to the Bezpieka, the state security ministry, for arrest. A demoralized secret police refused. The incident became public and the pro-Gomulka party committee of Warsaw mobilized armed workers. The 50,000 strong elite security army of the secret police also joined in and protected the headquarters of the Central Committee, the radio, and other public offices, since Prime Minister Cyrankiewicz appointed General Waclaw Komar, a newly rehabilitated victim of Stalinism and a strong supporter of Gomulka, as head of that elite security army in the summer of that year. The Stalinist resistance bequeathed a rather theatrical heroic character to the incident and to its main actors (Syrop, 1957).

In an agitated atmosphere the 8th plenum of the Central Committee was opened on October 19, 1956. About the same time a Soviet airplane, with Khrushchev, Molotov, Kaganovich, and Mikoyan on board, approached Warsaw airport. The unexpected top-ranking delegation arriving without invitation sought to impose the consultation refused by the Polish party two days earlier. Soviet army units began to move from Wroclaw toward Warsaw. The control tower of the airport at first did not allow the plane to land. The Central Committee, meanwhile, with an unusual agenda, rushed to coopt to its ranks Wladislaw Gomulka and his three closest comrades in arms. First Secretary Ochab, in an even more unusual move, announced that the Politburo suggest the reelection of the secretary-general of the party, with its candidate to the post being Gomulka. Then the session was suspended and a Polish Politburo delegation, which included Gomulka, hurried to the airport. An angry Khrushchev, humiliated by the delayed landing and insulted by the

Polish reluctance, shouted "traitors" to his hosts. "We shed our blood for this country and now you want to sell out to the Americans and the Zionists!" (Gibney, 1959, p. 11).

There was a tense and highly emotional debate in the Belvedere Palace. Khrushchev indignantly accused the Poles of not giving information on the situation and of the planned personnel changes, and demanded a guarantee that a pro-Soviet majority would be retained in the Politburo. Ochab announced that they would not negotiate if the Soviet troops continued their march toward Warsaw. Khrushchev ordered Marshal Konev to stop. The Soviet first secretary, however, did not "leave any doubts about his alternative. If opposed, the Russians would use all the force they had." "When Khrushchev finished, Gomulka made the Polish reply. 'Now I shall speak' he said, 'not here, but over the radio to the Polish nation, and I shall tell them the whole truth about what has been happening here'" (Gibney, 1959, p. 12).

Soviet ambassador Ponomarenko informed his superiors of the preparations in Warsaw: in the sixteen huge industrial complexes in the suburbs of the capital, workers' committees had formed an improvised militia which remained on duty, ready to alert their units to march into the city. General Komar's secret police army surrounded the city, ready for action against the Soviet garrisons.

At the end of the long, tense negotiations in the early morning hours of October 20, the Russians were convinced that Gomulka was the only man who could save the situation. Khrushchev had accepted the principle of the national road toward socialism in a joint statement with Tito quite recently. He also accepted Gomulka's requirements on internal independence, a rearrangement of the relationship with the church, and a halt to collectivization. At 6 o'clock in the morning, the Soviet delegation left Warsaw. In a few hours, Gomulka delivered a long speech at the resumed session of the Central Committee and announced his program.

In his powerful speech, Gomulka stated that "the working class recently gave a painful lesson to the Party leadership and the government . . . the Poznan workers shouted in a powerful voice: Enough! This cannot go on any longer! Turn back from the false road" (Zinner, 1956, pp. 206–7).

Gomulka's judgment on the Stalinist past was harsh, and emphasized the unequal relations with the Soviet Union, as well as the major mistakes of industrialization and the false road of forced collectivization. "Each country should have full independence, and the rights . . . to a sovereign government in an independent country. . . . This is how it should be and . . . this is how it is beginning to be." His analysis and program went far beyond the economic reforms of the New Course and was closely connected to a profound democratization. The parliament, Gomulka stated, must be "the supreme organ of state powers," and the "elevation of the role of the Sejm" will have "the greatest importance in our democratization program." "The elections," he added, "will be carried out on the basis of the new electoral law which allows the people to elect and not only to vote" (Zinner, 1956, pp. 227, 236–7).

The resolution of the Central Committee, which was based on Gomulka's program, also called for the establishment of "workers' self-government as an organ of workers' participation in the management . . . [including] the right to participate directly in the appointment and dismissal of the director of the enterprise." The resolution declared the possibility of "dissolution of cooperatives" (Zinner, 1956, pp. 245, 253).

Gomulka's Polish 'October revolution' of 1956, as the Poznan revolt and its aftermath, Gomulka's rise to power, was often called, succeeded. A few hours after having been elected first-secretary of the party, he received a telephone call from Moscow. Khrushchev warmly offered his congratulations and invited him for an official visit. After Tito's Yugoslavia, Poland now also embarked on the road to national communism. Its importance was even greater since it happened in a country where, unlike Yugoslavia, socialism was imposed by Stalin, and Soviet domination was assured by the massive presence of the Soviet army (Rykowski and Wladyka, 1989). In a few days, as a solidarity demonstration with the workers of Poznan, the Hungarian uprising began.

"The October Revolution in Poland," as an enthusiastic contemporary reporter (and later an analytical political scientist) declared, "was more lasting . . . [and] more deadly to Communism. Where the Hungarian revolt failed, the Polish half-succeeded" (Gibney, 1959, p. xii).[1] In reality, the Polish October had its strict limitations. It was less a revolution of half successes, than a successful half revolution. In the revolutionary situation, when Stalinist state socialism morally collapsed, the Polish October represented a bold, heroic revolt, which, however, remained in the framework of a compromise. It became victorious before it erupted, because of its limitations. It was recognized by the Soviet Union because it was limited.

Gomulka became not only a guarantor of change, but also of continuity. He destroyed Stalinism but replaced it with a post-Stalinist structure. Without an essential transformation of the party-state structures, he made major concessions to the population. He rejected humiliating

---

[1] His view was shared by Brzezinski in his outstanding book. Comparing the Polish and the Hungarian events, he stated on the Polish October that 'its significance for the Communist states was, in many ways, greater than that of the Hungarian revolution abruptly crushed by Soviet arms'. Brzezinski, 1961, p. 236.

subservient dependence on the Soviet Union, but ensured that Poland would remain in the Soviet bloc. "The Polish People's Republic," as expressed by Norman Davies, "ceased to be a puppet state, and became a client state." The Polish party, he added, "never gained the strength or the confidence to advance beyond the compromises" (Davies, 1986, p. 11). It should be added, however, that such was Central and Eastern European reality. Any kind of further movement (violent as in Hungary three days after the victory of the Polish October, or peaceful as in Czechoslovakia twelve years later) generated a furious Soviet reaction and was ruthlessly suppressed.

The result of the compromise of the Polish October was not a viable democratic, efficient socialism in an independent Poland, which was what had been sought by Gomulka, but, in contrast to the intention of the reformers, a weakening of the system, destroying its consistency and undermining its stability. Norman Davies spoke about "three specific features of the Polish order" under Gomulka: "an independent Catholic Church, a free peasantry, and a curious brand of bogus political pluralism" (Davies, 1986, p. 11). Interestingly enough, none of the changes had an economic impact.

Collectivization was canceled and never re-started, and the peasant farms were reestablished and occupied 80 percent of the Polish countryside. This created a unique, huge private sector of the economy and was designed to achieve agricultural prosperity. But in reality, the Poles were unable to achieve such a goal, since they settled for the worst possible compromise between an independent policy and the Soviet system. Private farming was combined with the well-known Soviet policy of fixed, low agricultural prices and high prices for industrial goods, especially those consumed by the peasantry (agricultural machinery, artificial fertilizers, etc.). The agriculture-based state accumulation, which served a basically unchanged industrialization policy, killed not only the required incentives but curbed investments for production. The Polish peasantry, as a report from the 1970s clearly showed, were "disappointed and lost their confidence and do not believe in the promises of stability and continuity of the agricultural policy . . . Farmers cannot buy land from the state reserve, only old machinary is available to buy, there are very little fertilizer and construction materials" (Kuczynski, 1981, p. 51).

In the end, Polish agriculture became one of the worst in Central and Eastern Europe, unable either to produce sufficient quantities for highly needed exports or to supply the population. Some Western analyses, such as Andrzej Korbonski's, later suggested that the lack of collectivization caused more serious troubles in Poland, and that carrying out

collectivization would improve the situation (Korbonski, 1965). Bread riots became a regular occurrence in Poland. Ironically, one of them led to the removal of Gomulka himself.

The halting of collectivization, however, had major political importance. Nearly half of the population remained mostly free, strongly independent from the state, and outside the state-socialist organizations. This factor contributed to a pluralization and freedom of Polish society to a degree unparalleled in other countries of the region.

The compromise with the Catholic Church, which was institutionalized in an agreement signed in December 1956, created the only fully independent church in the region. In an almost entirely (96 percent) Catholic country, where the church historically was equated with the Polish nation (against German protestantism and Russian Greek Ortho-doxy), an independent church became the basic institution of pluralism. The church had an exceptional integrity and reputation, its outstanding leader, Cardinal Stefan Wyszynski, primate of Poland for a third of a century, and who was released from prison when Gomulka took over, became a substantial partner in the stabilization process. The moral and political independence of the church powerfully counterbalanced and defeated the ideological-political efforts of the party-state. Polish state socialism, in spite of major concessions and Gomulka's tremendous popularity at that time, never gained even a transitory legitimacy.

The third element of the compromise, the proposed democratization, institutionally did not bring much more than a faked "multi-party system," with obedient satellite parties that received a role no larger than that of the traditional "transmission" organizations of the one-party structure. The role of the Sejm, in spite of Gomulka's promises, in the end remained among the festive formalities of the party-state. Democrat-ization as a policy instrument, however, without major institutional changes, created a much higher degree of personal freedom, freedom of speech, art and publication, than in the other Central and Eastern European countries. Poland, after October 1956, was not a closed society any longer. A sort of civil society began to develop with accepted elements of pluralism and a sophisticated opposition that emerged from the late sixties on. The result in the short run was a mostly unfettered but inefficient Poland. In the long run, it was the erosion and the collapse of the system.

The Hungarian October

Rákosi's victory over Nagy in the spring of 1955 proved to be rather counterproductive. The full restoration of the Stalinist regime was impossible. A strong group of party intellectuals and the young generation, which survived the horrors of nazism, occupation, and war, and enthusiastically joined the party in the postwar years with the hope of an entire moral and social renewal, felt that they had been cheated.

Raymond Aron touched the heart of the matter when he observed: "The Hungarian intellectuals . . . like Imre Nagy and his friends, were party members . . . [and they] were ashamed of themselves. . . . [F]rom a moral point of view, however, they were victims of the regime just like the rest of the population" (Aron, 1966, p. 20). The blinkers fell from their eyes and their unquestioning faith was replaced by moral indignation and hatred. They learned the truth and understood the alternatives, and now angrily rejected self-delusion and continued lies. The Hungarian Stalinist leadership formally regained power, but could no longer use it as previously. This was especially so after the 20th party congress in the Soviet Union. Imre Nagy was expelled from the party, the greatest victory for Rákosi; but within three months, he had to face the extremely repugnant and explosive issue of rehabilitating his own victims.

After the 20th Congress László Rajk and his co-defendants had to be fully rehabilitated. On March 27, 1956, Rákosi, in a party-aktiv, declared that the trial and execution of Rajk was entirely groundless, and that the victims were to be rehabilitated. Using the classical Stalinist method, however, he accused "the hostile, false provocation" of General Gábor Péter, the sinister chief of the secret police ("and his gang") who was already in prison. In less then two months, however, Rákosi had to go further and recognize his own personal responsibility.

In these tormented months, Imre Nagy became the catalyst for the birth of a party opposition. A meditative character, sitting at his desk, he tried to analyze the historical situation in a small number of studies. Nagy clarified his concept in a polemic with Rákosi. In "The Five Basic Principles of International Relations," in his "Ethics and Morals in Hungarian Public Life," and in "A Few Timely Questions," he developed a consistent anti-Rákosi program. Condemning repressive "Bonapartism," he spoke on "the degeneration of power . . . endangering the fate of socialism and the democratic basis of our social system. Power is increasingly being torn away from the people and turned sharply against them." What emerged, continued Nagy, was "a Party dictatorship . . . [that] relies on a personal dictatorship" (Nagy, 1957, p. 50).

In the place of the "political amok-runner" leadership, he advocated the concept of democratic socialism. In January 1956, Nagy surmised, this was already inseparable from national independence. It was a *sine qua non* of building democratic socialism. The minority dictatorship of Bonapartism, he argued, was "lacking mass support." Therefore Rákosi's Stalinist despotism "cannot stand on its own feet. . . . They not only voluntarily accept" humiliating Soviet domination, but "cling to it, because this is the only solid support to insure their power. ... The people cannot be free if the nation is not independent, if it does not possess complete sovereignty" (Nagy, 1957, pp. 30–1).

The peaceful coexistence of countries with different systems offers a possibility of "neutrality or active coexistence" and "cooperation against the policies of the power groups." Nagy did not exclude the possibility of an Austrian-type neutrality for Hungary, and concluded: "It is the sovereign right of the Hungarian people to decide in which form they believe the most advantageous international status will be assured" (Nagy, 1957, p. 33). Many students of the topic were astonished at the striking contradictions of Nagy's views: he preserved his true Leninism and confidence in the system, and did not realize the unbridgeable conflict between it and his ideal of an independent, democratic national communism.[2] This naiveté, however, characterized the greatest part of the rebelling party intelligentsia, as well as the generations which had experienced the bitter lessons of Central and Eastern European history in the first half of the century and longed for a just, new society and friendship with previously hostile nations. For them, the problem was Stalinist degeneration of the system, and the solution was to return "to true Marxism–Leninism." It certainly was an unavoidable stage of a long march.

A defeated Nagy, a victim of Rákosi and the embodiment of the struggle against Stalinism, became a national hero and a symbol. A strong group of "reform-communists," dominated by Géza Losonczy, Ferenc Donáth, Miklós Vásárhelyi, and Sándor Haraszti, gradually formed a parallel political center around him. On the occasion of his sixtieth birthday, Nagy's home became a place of pilgrimage, a pilgrimage that expressed a sort of national unity behind him.

The triumphant Rákosi group was unable to reestablish its monolithic rule. An important mobilizing institution of the emerging pluralism was the Petöfi Circle, founded by the communist youth organization (DISz) in March 1956 as an open discussion forum. Gábor Táncos and its organizers virtually joined the Nagy group. Between March and October 1956 a series of debates were held in crowded auditoriums on economic policy, the situation of major social science disciplines such as history and philosophy, the educational system, technological development, the state of agriculture, and on other burning issues. The climax of the debates was the June session on the press and information, attended by 6,000 people.

---

[2] The "Publisher's Note" in Imre Nagy's book *On Communism* mentioned "the tragic irony ... of Nagy's position," which "reveals the insoluble contradictions besetting Communist dogma and practice." (Nagy, 1957, p. vi) Bill Lomax remarked: "Nagy, while still believing in the ideals, refused to see any contradiction between them and the system through which he sought to achieve them." (Lomax, 1976, p. 54.)

The reform-communist writer Tibor Déry desperately attacked Révai, the Stalinist cultural dictator of the fifties. There was a standing ovation when Géza Losonczy demanded the return of Imre Nagy to the political leadership. This was a mass rally of the opposition and an open attack against the Stalinist leadership. The "open rebellion . . . of the Petöfi Circle," concluded Michael Polanyi, "was the actual beginning of the Hungarian Revolution, which broke out violently in October" (Polanyi, 1969, p. 24).

The other institution of rebellion was the Writers' Union. In the November 10, 1955 session of the Union, a great many of reform-communist writers openly revolted against the Rákosi group. The vitriolic attacks of Tibor Déry, Zoltán Zelk, Tamás Aczél, and others outspokenly rejected the "March Resolution" of the Central Committee, Rákosi's victory over Nagy. Initiated by thirty writers and signed by many others, including the leading figures of the Nagy group, a memorandum was sent to the Central Committee in early November demanding the return to the "June policy" of 1953. At the end of March 1956, the Union voted against the party-state candidate and independently elected its secretary general.

The Union's weekly, *Irodalmi Ujság*, became a regular forum for the party-opposition. Tibor Tardos condemned, in a self-critical way, his previous blind faith: "whenever I heard complaints, I found an explanation; I said it was an exception, an exaggeration . . . We even discarded respect for human life . . . sacrificing it to faith" (Tardos, 1956). Gyula Háy emotionally protested against "wrong and harmful resolutions passed without opposition, thoughtless servility . . . the persecution of criticism, the whitewashing of liars . . . the crushing of rights and law." He concluded with a passionate appeal: "The time has come for us to be converted to the truth, the over-all, unconditional, profound truth which serves the people and the Party" (Háy, 1956).

Rákosi and his group reacted in a traditionally Stalinist way. In December, a Central Committee resolution condemned the organized "right-wing opportunism" of certain literary circles and the attempts to organize an opposition faction within the party" (*Irodalmi Ujság*, 1955). On June 30, 1956, after his satisfactory visit to Moscow, Rákosi went much further. A new resolution of the Central Committee declared: "The open opposition against the Party and People's Democracy is mainly organized by a certain group which has formed around Imre Nagy." The resolution also "decisively condemns the anti-Party manifestations that took place in the Petöfi Circle . . . [where] certain speakers . . . have gone so far as to deny the leading role of the Party and the working class, and advocated bourgeois and counter-revolutionary views" (Resolution,

1956a). The minister of the interior provisionally suspended the work of the Petöfi Circle and, on July 12, according to widespread rumors, as George Pálóczi-Horváth in the 'Epilogue' of Imre Nagy's book later reported, Rákosi decided on the liquidation of the center of opposition and presented a plan for settling the "Nagy conspiracy." "He had a list of four hundred people whose arrest he demanded. The first name on the list was that of Imre Nagy." He suggested banning the Writers' Union and its weekly as well (Nagy, 1957, p. 298).[3]

In his *Unexpected Revolution* Paul Kecskeméti argued that "up to the actual outbreak of the revolution the stirring of opposition and agitation for reform had very much the character of an internal family affair within the party itself" (Kecskeméti, 1961, pp. 1–2). Bill Lomax had certainly been right in reflecting this view, considering the "evidence of far greater mass dissent. . . . Even the elite revolt of the writers can itself be seen as giving expression and voice to this popular discontent . . . The crisis of elite legitimacy was not so much cause as expression of the lack of popular legitimacy" (Lomax, 1984, p. 74).

This was the main reason that in the summer of 1956 Rákosi no longer had the power to destroy the opposition. On July 17, Anastas Mikoyan arrived in Budapest. "I and Rákosi unsuspectingly went to the airport to meet him," recalled then Prime Minister András Hegedüs, in his "self-biographical analysis." "Driving back, all three of us were sitting in the back seat. . . . We had almost arrived . . . when Mikoyan suddenly turned to Rákosi and said: 'We thought in the Presidium of the Party that you, comrade Rákosi, considering your poor state of health, should resign.'" Rákosi, noticing that it certainly was a mistaken and politically counterproductive idea, did not protest but remarked: "If the comrades are thinking that way I do not and should not have any objection" (Hegedüs, 1988, p. 266). On the next day the Central Committee received Rákosi's resignation letter and his personal explanation, and, at his own request, relieved him of the post of first secretary and member of the Politburo for "health reasons."

The Soviet leadership, however, was in no mood for risk-taking, and thus demanded the appointment of "their man" Ernö Gerö, who was equally responsible for the Stalinist period, and hardly one to lead a moral rejuvenation. But, in the summer of 1956, Khrushchev and his colleagues were yet unwilling to accept Imre Nagy, who was accused of right-wing deviations; and the resolution was formulated with the personal contribution of Suslov. They did not have confidence in János Kádár either, the favorite of the Hungarian party apparatus. He was, first of all, a

---

[3] Certainly on this basis, Brzezinski wrote about this assumed episode as a fact, as a Central Committee meeting on July 12 when the Committee refused to accept Rákosi's plan.

"home-communist" and a victim of the purges recently released from prison.

At a session of the Central Committee where Ernö Gerö declared that the Party "turned over a new, clean leaf," a resolution was adopted that repeated the discredited old goals and slogans, such as "the basis of the development of the entire national economy . . . is heavy industry." It also declared that the "Central Committee is firmly resolved . . . to implement the policy of the socialist transformation of agriculture" (Resolution, 1956b). The proposal of the second Five Year Plan, which was accepted at the session, was based on the same Stalinist principles as the first Five Year Plan, which had failed and led to catastrophe. It represented only a more moderate version of the same concept. The program of democratization was based on the empty and irrelevant concept that "the cult of personality . . . does not spring from the essential characteristics of the socialist system" (Resolution, 1956b). The politically minded public was already convinced of the opposite. Discredited politicians thus offered a discounted program. A last opportunity for peaceful renewal was omitted.

On October 6, a cool fall day, hundreds of thousands of silent people pilgrimaged in the stormy wind to the Kerepesi-cemetery, a national pantheon, where the executed victims of the Rajk show trial were reburied. "People," wrote the *Szabad Nép* next day, "remember the dark practices of tyranny, lawlessness, slander, and defrauding of the people . . . " (*Szabad Nép*, 1956). The air was filled with unbearable tension, but there was no explosion yet.

Within a week, on October 13, the dailies published the news of the arrest of General Mihály Farkas, one of the leading executors of the purges. On the same day, the Politburo adopted the resolution of Imre Nagy's reinstatement to the party. Within another week, the Hungarian media reported in detail Gomulka's rise to power. At the same time, the university students of the South Hungarian town Szeged, followed by those in Budapest, reestablished the postwar student organization (MEFESz), and deserted the monolithic communist youth organization.

On October 22 the universities of Budapest, Szeged, Miskolc, Pécs, and Sopron became the scenes of endless emotional meetings. The fourteen-point proclamation demanding democratic socialism, formulated by the Petöfi Circle, was accepted at the Karl Marx University of Economics, and then reformulated and radicalized at the meeting of the Technical School of Budapest. The revolt against the compulsory study of the Russian language was soon linked with the demand for the departure of the Soviet army. On the next day solidarity demonstrations were also decided on and proclaimed. The meetings continued far into the night.

In the early morning hours of October 23, a special train carrying a Hungarian party and a government delegation, headed by Gerö, returned from Yugoslavia to the Keleti sftation. The nervous political leaders drove directly to party headquarters to immediately convene a meeting of the Politburo. They decided to ban the demonstrations. But, after they met with various delegations, the confused Politburo members changed their mind. After further debate, however, they banned them again, and then changed course yet again. The morally discredited party leadership collapsed. The agitated students spent the whole morning at the universities and were informed of the contradictory and changing decisions. At 3 p.m. an estimated 50,000 students began their silent march to the Petöfi statue, then to the statue of Josef Bem, the Polish freedom fighter and hero of the Hungarian 1848 Revolution.

The multitude grew to 150,000–200,000, and they enjoyed the sympathy of the population which packed the sidewalks. In the Bem square students began to cut out the Soviet-type coat-of-arms from the Hungarian tricolors. The crowd slowly moved toward the parliament and, refusing to hear anybody else, demanded to hear Imre Nagy. It was already dark when Nagy briefly addressed them from one of the balconies. In the meantime other large groups gathered in front of the headquarters of the party daily and the national radio. They insisted on broadcasting their demands, but were refused. The crowd began to attack the building, which was guarded by a unit of the security troops. At 8 p.m. Ernö Gerö addressed the people on the radio and condemned the mob and the nationalist demonstration. His speech added fuel to the flames. Meanwhile the first shooting began on the narrow Bródy Sándor street, in front of the radio building.

A spontaneous, elemental, genuine people's uprising erupted. Symbolically, among the first actions, the huge Stalin statue, towering above the parade square, was hurled down from its base (it was also quite symbolic that his bronze boots remained), hauled toward the downtown area, and cut up into pieces. Stalinism was destroyed.

During the first hours of the uprising, a scared and uncertain party leadership, aware of their complete isolation, asked the Soviet army units stationed in the country to restore order and crush the "counter-revolutionary gangs" of "fascist reactionary elements." An overwrought emergency session of the Central Committee, after deliberating the entire night, urgently elected Imre Nagy to the Politburo and appointed him prime minister in the early morning hours of October 24. Gerö, however, remained at his post.

Because of the immediate Soviet military intervention, the anti-Stalinist popular uprising became, on the very first day, a desperate fight for independence. The police force and a part of the army joined the uprising; the larger part of the army passively waited in their garrisons and the government worried about using them. Besides the Soviet army, only the security forces and certain border guard units confronted the irregular but enthusiastic insurgents. A curfew and summary jurisdiction, which were immediately introduced, followed by the first proclamation of Prime Minister Imre Nagy on October 24 promising the realization of the "Hungarian road to democratic socialism," no longer had any effect: the uprising had risen to become a Hungarian–Soviet war.

The next day, security units opened fire on the crowds of peaceful demonstrators in front of the parliament building. Dozens of dead were left on the pavement. The armed struggle gained new impetus. At major junctions of the city strong armed insurgent centers emerged. The streets of the inner districts of the city were covered with destroyed and newly built barricades, burned out Soviet tanks and armored vehicles, burned bodies of Soviet soldiers, and hundreds and hundreds of young people, insurgents who had fallen in the fight. Several buildings were destroyed by the canons of heavy Soviet tanks, seeking to regain control of the city and blindly spraying machine-gun fire in every direction. In these days, when the capital became a battle field, the workers, who remained silent in the very first days, began to take over firms and organize workers' councils.

In the morning hours of October 25, Mikoyan and Suslov arrived in Budapest; Serov, the KGB chief, was already there. In an emergency Politburo session Mikoyan suggested the replacement of Gerö by János Kádár as first secretary of the party. The armed fight went on and remained unstoppable. Both the Politburo and the government were reorganized. A reform-communist majority was first established, followed by steps to form a coalition government. Zoltán Tildy, the previously imprisoned former president and head of the Smallholders Party, and Béla Kovács, the former secretary-general of the Smallholders Party who had just returned from a Soviet prison where he had been interned for nine years, were coopted into Nagy's cabinet. The government, however, was not recognized by the freedom fighters.

The real turning point, however, occurred on October 28. Imre Nagy, himself confused and undecided, during the first days of the revolution, trapped by the *fait accompli* of Soviet intervention and the marriage with a still Stalinist party leadership of Gerö, soon arrived at a consistent concept and policy. His closest aides, especially Géza Losonczy and Ferenc Donáth, were now all central figures in a dramatic political transformation, and played a principal role in Nagy's decisive steps. In his radio statement on October 28, he condemned the former depictions of the uprising as counter-revolutionary. Indeed, he now spoke of "a great national and democratic movement . . . unifying all our people . . . [and] aims at guaranteeing our national freedom, independence . . . on the way of democracy . . . the only foundation for socialism in our country. This great movement exploded because of the grave crimes committed during the past historic period" (Zinner, 1956, p. 429). Nagy also announced his agreement with the Soviet authorities on the immediate withdrawal of the Soviet army from Budapest, and the beginning of negotiations on a complete withdrawal of all Soviet troops from the country. He announced the dissolution of the hated state security organs and the reestablishment of old national symbols and holidays. On the very same day the party's Central Committee transferred its mandate to a six-member presidium, dominated by the Nagy group, which began the reorganization of the party. The discredited former leaders left the country by Soviet military planes to Moscow.

The now recognized victorious revolution still continued. Workers' councils and Revolutionary Committees were founded nationwide. New and more radical political demands were adopted. The power of the government was rather formal and strongly questioned. At the beginning destroying Stalinism and introducing a true, human, democratic, and independent Hungarian socialism was what dominated the political arena. But anti-communism rapidly gained momentum and the restoration of a genuine postwar democratic coalition now became the goal. Different conservative and even right-wing sympathies also appeared. It was a definite political shift to sweep away any sort of socialism. Old and new political organizations and groupings were formed.

In two days Nagy declared the return to a multi-party system. "In the interest of the further democratization of the country's life," he said in his proclamation on behalf of the government and the presidium of the party, "the Cabinet abolishes the one-party system and places the country's government on the basis of democratic cooperation between the coalition parties, reborn in 1945" (Zinner, 1956, p. 454). On the same day János Kádár announced full agreement with the introduction of the multi-party system, and stated that the party will start "to some extent from scratch," but under "clearer conditions." On October 31, the Smallholders Party, the Hungarian Independence Party, the Social Democratic Party and the Petöfi Party announced their reestablishment, followed on the next day by two Catholic parties and many others. On that very day János Kádár declared the abolition of the Hungarian Workers Party, which had "degenerated to a medium of despotism and national slavery through the blind and criminal policy of Hungarian . . . Stalinism. . . . In a glorious uprising, our people have shaken off the Rákosi regime" (Zinner, 1956, p. 464). He declared the foundation of a new party, the Hungarian Socialist Workers Party.

Kádár also warned of the danger of an "open counter-revolution" and the reemergence of "the old gentry world." He was not alone. Anna Kéthly, the uncompromising democrat freed from prison, and president of the reemerging Social Democratic Party, declared that the nation's "bitterness may be utilized by the counter-revolution for its own sake" (Kethly, 1956). On the next day, November 2, the same warning of the danger of a counter-revolution was anticipated in an article written by the prestigious populist writer, László Németh: "The danger is . . . in the short run, that the nation . . . following the initiators of revenge, might commit something which is beyond redemption any longer. In the longer run: people running towards new positions to regain their old glitter . . . transform the revolution to a counter-revolution . . . to something similar to the political course of 1920" (Németh, 1956).

These warnings were partly due to the extent of the violence: the searching for enemies, the hanging of recognized secret police agents in the streets, the storming of the Köztársaság Square headquarters of the Budapest committee of the Communist Party, and the lynching of several communists and soldiers during the last days of October. Several representatives of the interwar Horthy regime also thought that their time had arrived. Former landowners appeared in the countryside. These developments led to firm statements from credible and prestigious leaders of the revolution. Anna Kéthly announced that "the firms, the mines and the land have to remain in the hands of the people" (Kéthly, 1956). Béla Kovács stated that "nobody would dream about the old regime. The world of the counts, bankers and capitalists collapsed for ever . . ." (Kovács, 1956), and József Dudás, one of the (later executed) military leaders of the insurgents, declared: "We do not give back the land, we will fight as hard against any kind of bourgeois restoration as we defeated Rákosi and Gerö" (Dudás, 1956).

In the euphoria of the victory, at the end of the first week, the revolution arrived at a new stage, and a new struggle for power began. In the midst of the celebration of the unbelievable military victory over the Soviet army units, which had withdrawn from Budapest, reports arrived that new Soviet troops were arriving in the country and moving toward the capital. On November 1 and 2, Soviet tanks surrounded Hungarian airports and occupied railroads and stations. The government sent urgent notes to the Soviet embassy and government.

On that very day Nagy proclaimed that his government, "giving expression to the undivided will of the Hungarian millions, declares the neutrality" of the country "without joining any power blocs" (Zinner, 1956, pp. 463–4). He turned to Dag Hammarskjold, secretary-general of the United Nations, and asked the United Nations to guarantee Hungary's neutrality.

The Hungarian revolution reached its climax. The Stalinist regime was destroyed, and the multi-party parliamentary system was restored together with the freedom and sovereignty of the country, which declared its leaving the Soviet bloc. All this occurred as a result of a heroic, uncompromising armed revolt, and a mass revolution that lasted less than two weeks (Lomax, 1980).

The Hungarian 1956 was a unique case in the history of Central and Eastern European anti-communism. It started as a demand for radical reform to create a democratic, humane, and efficient socialist system, initiated and led by reform communists. The popular uprising automatically became an openly anti-Soviet struggle for independence, encompassing a week of desperate war against the powerful Soviet army – the only such war in post-World War II Central and Eastern European history. In addition, these events displayed an unparalleled dynamism. The Nagy government, which was repeatedly re-organized but still unable to stabilize power, was rapidly pushed to shifting from national reform-communism to an acceptance of the multi-party system, as well as a declaration of neutrality. The Hungarian revolution went full steam ahead to its logical conclusion.

Indeed, only a second Soviet military intervention of November 4, 1956 was ultimately able to crush the revolution and reestablish state socialism in Hungary. It was followed by brutal repression, a new exodus of about 200,000 people from the defeated country, and the imprisonment and execution of thousands. Bill Lomax suggests that "the total number executed, either under Martial Law or after court convictions, was very probably in excess of 2,000" (Lomax, 1984). Reliable sources mentioned nearly 400, including the trial and execution of Imre Nagy.

The destiny of the Hungarian revolution, on the one hand, clearly revealed the sober realism and self-limitation of the Polish half revolution. On the other, as Milovan Djilas observed in the darkest days of repression in 1957, "the wound which the Hungarian Revolution inflicted on Communism can never be completely healed . . . Yugoslav Communism, separating itself from Moscow, initiated the crisis of Soviet imperialism . . . Hungary means the beginning of the end of Communism generally" (Djilas, 1984, pp. 92–3).

Emerging independence of new national Stalinist countries – the bloc in a deepening crisis

The one and a half revolution in October 1956 and its massive aftermath launched a tremendous blow to the uniform and united Soviet bloc. The national roads in Poland and Hungary represented both a degree of independence from the Soviet Union and a deviation from Soviet socialism. The emerging diversity challenged uniformity and weakened the consistency of the uniform pre-1956 regimes.

From this point of view, resistance against Soviet de-Stalinization in Romania and Albania during the post-1956 period, even if it was not related to the Polish or Hungarian events (on the contrary, they sought to avoid such a path) still belonged to their aftermath. Some direct connections also existed. Khrushchev, attempting to counterbalance the great international scandal and the deep crisis within the communist movement caused by the two Soviet military interventions in Hungary, withdrew Soviet troops from Romania. It was an irony of history that the Hungarians, who fought for such a development, were unable to obtain it, while the Romanians, who had not even requested it, received it as a free gift. This was, of course, a much less risky step because of Romania's geopolitical situation. She was surrounded by socialist countries with a long Soviet border, and displayed a rather stable internal state. Her leadership was steadfast and cooperative with the Soviet government regarding the Hungarian question.

The firmness of the Romanian and Albanian leadership concerning the 1956 revolts was connected to their unchanged Stalinist command. In most of the state socialist countries the Stalinist party chiefs who led the Sovietization of their countries vanished. Tito, a faithful Stalinist, cleaned his record in 1948 and became a hero of the earliest de-Stalinization. His prestige and reputation, as well as the legitimacy of his regime, became much stronger after the death of Stalin and the open apology by the new Soviet leadership.

Four prominent Stalinists disappeared from the scene between 1953 and 1956: Gottwald and Bierut died, Rákosi and Chervenkov were removed. Only two survived the "thaw" and the de-Stalinization campaign of the 20th party congress: Romania's Gheorghe Gheorghiu-Dej and Albania's Enver Hoxha. This was the case because they distanced themselves from a de-Stalinizing Soviet bloc.

Hoxha reluctantly made a few steps in line with the "New Course" and resigned from his state positions. He strictly rejected, however, any kind of de-Stalinization, including the rehabilitation of his victims and Tito. Hoxha recognized that he could not lead that process without being the first victim of it. A clear message was sent to him by the April 1956 meeting of the Tirana party organization. Two months after the 20th party congress in Moscow, Hoxha and his "cult of personality" was harshly criticized at the session. Delegates demanded reports on the purges of 1949 and called for the establishment of "party-democracy."

After dissolving the meeting Hoxha did not hesitate to expel and even arrest those who addressed the meeting. In an article published in *Pravda* on November 8, Hoxha denounced Yugoslav revisionism as the root of

Central and Eastern European rebellions, and defended Stalin as having "been right on matters concerning the vital interest of the working class . . . and on the struggle against imperialism" (Logoreci, 1977, p. 123). In 1958, on the occasion of Imre Nagy's execution in Hungary, Hoxha rushed to strengthen his anti-Tito rhetoric, stating that Nagy engaged in a conspiracy with Tito to destroy "the unity of the Socialist bloc" (Hacker, 1983, p. 618).

Rejecting de-Stalinization in order to preserve his power, Hoxha had to distance himself from the "revisionist" Soviet Union. At the end of the fifties and in the early sixties two important events provided him with a helping hand. Nikita Khrushchev's ambitious plan to revitalize an ailing Comecon suggested a centrally planned division of labor in the "Socialist Camp." According to his plan the different member countries would specialize and develop efficient mass production in certain fields, where traditions allowed it, and supply the others, while halting their former attempts toward self-sufficiency. A rational idea in the form of an imperial central command, it endangered the region's countries and would lead toward stronger economic dependency on the Soviet Union. In addition, Khrushchev suggested to Tirana that it concentrate on the extraction of raw materials and on the development of agriculture. This provided Hoxha the opportunity defend Albanian national interests. The challenge to the ambitious Albanian modernization plans was flatly rejected. As a response, Hoxha switched to a higher gear in his Stalinist collectivization and industrialization drive. From 1955 on, a ruthless anti-kulak campaign and forced collectivization resulted in the completion of the process by 1959, when, except for the poor highland areas, 83 percent of arable land was collectivized. The third Five Year Plan from 1961 on concentrated 54 percent of investments into the continuation of a comprehensive industrialization, with the aim of achieving industrial self-sufficiency.

At the same time a dramatic conflict developed between the Soviet Union and China, which became manifest in June 1960 at the Bucharest meeting of the party chiefs, where an open debate erupted: Khrushchev criticized Mao's Stalinist concept on peace and war, while China denounced the "infection of Yugoslav revisionism." Albania was the only country which rejected the indictment of China. In November 1960, at the conference of eighty-one communist and workers' parties in Moscow, the open debate continued. Hoxha harshly condemned the Soviet Union, while Khrushchev, from his position of power, attempted to use blackmail: in April the Albanian government was informed that the credit promised to finance its Five Year Plan was not available.

The Chinese–Albanian axis, which was formed between early 1960 and February 1961, rescued the Albanian economy. In December of that year, Moscow broke off diplomatic relations with Tirana. Hoxha successfully defended his Stalinist line by introducing his national Stalinism. In the following years Albania left the Comecon and the Warsaw Pact, and Hoxha depicted himself as the savior of the national independence of his country. This proved to be, at least for a certain period, a decisive basis for legitimizing his regime.

Albania's successful revolt against the Soviet Union was cautiously repeated by another Stalinist party chief, Romania's Gheorghiu-Dej. Though he could not avoid taking some initial steps corresponding to the "New Course," he rejected additional measures after the 20th party congress and the events in Poland and Hungary. Instead, from the end of 1956 on, he decided to destroy the anti-Stalinist opposition in Romania. An aggressive purge was launched, first of all against intellectuals and students, the ferment of revolts in Poland and Hungary. The Writers' Union was denounced and classic purge-proceedings were organized at the universities, culminating in mass arrests, and a series of trials between 1957 and 1960.

The historical logic for rejecting de-Stalinization in Romania was similar to the Albanian case. The *sine qua non* of preserving the Stalinist system inside the country was the confrontation with the Soviet Union. It became unavoidable as a resistance against Khrushchev's pressure for de-Stalinization and, at the same time, as a replacement of the Soviet guarantee of communist power by a sort of national, domestic legitimization: "the communist regime and the Romanian people finally found themselves authentically on common ground" (Rothschild, 1989, p. 162). Gheorghiu-Dej began to implement his "Romanian road to socialism" in the summer of 1957 "in a manner that would ensure his political survival." He began to increasingly link his regime with the Romanian nation, and "Gheorghiu-Dejism gradually became synonymous with the attainment of the historical goals of the Romanian people: a Romania for the Romanians" (Fischer-Galati, 1970, pp. 22, 24, 26).

Romanian nationalism in the twentieth century was traditionally anti-Russian, and the Romanian party cautiously exploited this in creating a new image of itself as a savior of national independence. It became important to reinterpret the whole history of the party as a permanent struggle against "alien elements" and "immigrant groups." At a Central Committee session in November–December 1961, a well-organized series of speeches, "a covert manifesto of independence," as Paul Lendvai observed, was addressed to the party (Lendvai, 1969, p. 364). Twentieth-century Romanian nationalism, however, was also strongly inimical to Romania's national minorities – most specifically, the Jews and the Hungarians. In his struggle for power, Gheorghiu-Dej, although in a rather prudent way and without many overt manifestations, skillfully exploited these nationalistic emotions when purging the Jewish Pauker and the Hungarian Luca.

Gheorghiu-Dej was a master at hitting two birds with one stone. After 1956, when he began to destroy the liberal party-opposition, the purge was directed against the sympathizers of the Hungarian revolution, which was equated with Hungarian chauvinism and anti-Romanian irredentism. It served as an excellent vehicle to limit Hungarian autonomy in Transylvania and initiate a Romanization of the region. In 1958, a second wave of purges was directed against the middle level of party old-timers, whose majority belonged to the Jewish and Hungarian minorities. This went hand in hand with the rehabilitation of prewar nationalist historians and writers. The typical early nineteenth-century romantic historicism, the concept of the Daco-Roman continuity to create a glorious national heritage, became an official credo, and the leading representatives of this concept were given leading positions at the universities and the Academy of Sciences. Former "green shirt" nationalist historians, such as Daicoviciu and Pascu, were rehabilitated and soon recruited into, and enthusiastically joined, the party (Ionescu, 1964).

As in the Albanian case, the end of the fifties and the early sixties offered new possibilities for strengthening the orthodox Stalinist–nationalist political line. Here, too, one of the opportunities was provided by Khrushchev's new Comecon plan. Soviet planners, as in the Albanian case, recommended strengthening the agricultural and consumer goods production capacity of the Romanian economy, and opposed the import-substituting industrialization line. At the end of 1961, the chief Romanian planner, Gheorghe Gaston-Marin, sharply criticized the plan of subordinating the less-developed Comecon countries to the interests of the more developed ones, and clearly expressed the Romanian party's rejection of the plan to limit the comprehensive industrialization of the country.

The development of an independent Romanian platform in the early sixties came to a head in 1964. In April the Romanian party venomously repudiated the so-called "Valev-plan," i.e. the creation of an integrated Danube region, composed of more than 40 percent of Romania, one-third of Bulgaria and a large area of the Ukraine. The Romanian statement declared that the plan would be "a liquidation of the Romanian state and the Romanian people as a nation." The party document of April 26, often called a Romanian "declaration of independence," pronounced that "there is no one single pattern" or one "single recipe," and that no one "can decide which of the other countries or parties is right or mistaken. Developing, choosing or changing the form and method of socialist development is . . . a sovereign right of each socialist state" (Hacker, 1983, p. 676).

Romania's first major political move after the declaration was a highly publicized visit of a top level delegation to Washington. Gaston-Marin led the delegation which sought to create an opening toward the United States. "Its anti-Russian nature was only thinly disguised by the Romanian leaders . . . In May Gheorghiu-Dej appeared confident that his policies would prevail" (Fischer-Galati, 1967, pp. 104–5).

The Comecon debate took place at the time of the sharpening Russo-Chinese controversy. The split in the "Socialist Camp" effectively increased the room for maneuvering. It offered a second chance for introducing an independent, Stalinist-nationalistic policy. While Chinese alliance could replace the Soviet axis for Albania, Romania followed a more cautious road. Her geopolitical situation did not allow an open break, and there was the risk of provoking a Soviet intervention. Gheorghiu-Dej attempted to mediate between the two socialist great powers, and, when that proved impossible, he tried to stay between them. The tightrope act was balanced by a risky coquetting with the United States and China. The increasing distance from the Soviet Union, and the spectacular domestic de-Russification (with the restoration of Romanian names of streets and even a change of the alphabet and the spelling of the name of the country from Romînia to România to get rid of Slavic influence) was accompanied with a hardening of the domestic political line. The accomplishment of forced collectivization, the fortified effort of industrialization, and stronger internal control and censorship were all designed to preclude the possibility of accusing the Romanian party of bourgeois deviations.

Communism was deliberately combined with nationalism and, at the height of the Romanian–Soviet debate, between 1962 and 1965, the doors of the party were opened to about 600,000 newly recruited members. The purged "old guard" was replaced partly with enthusiastic nationalist intellectuals, partly with a newly emerged technocratic elite and a white-collar lower-middle class, who were ready to join the national course.

On March 19, 1965, Gheorghiu-Dej, the master tactician, died. A rapidly developing lung cancer killed him in less than three months, and left the party in confusion. A powerful group of rivals, Apostol, Stoica, Maurer, and Drăghici, each blocked the plan of succession of the other, and thus promoted a collective leadership with the young and paltry Nicolae Ceaușescu appointed first-secretary of the party. A "troika" of party chiefs, Ceaușescu, the president of the state Chivu Stoica, and prime minister Ion Gheorghe Maurer, was accompanied by two more rather powerful personalities from Gheorghiu-Dej's period, Gheorghe Apostol, the closest aide of Dej and head of the unions, and Alexandru Drăghici, a member of Ceaușescu's generation and head of the powerful Ministry of Interior and secret police. The collective leadership strictly followed the road of the early sixties. They judiciously maintained a calculated ambiguity, sending mixed orthodox and liberal messages to the people, allowing every group to hope for the best. More intellectual freedom was allowed ("we allow [you] . . . to decide how to write, how to paint, how to compose," addressed Ceauşescu to the writers and artists in mid 1966) (Fischer, 1989, p. 89), but a noisy campaign was initiated against long hair, beards, and miniskirts.

The leitmotif of party policy remained nationalism, which Ceauşescu masterfully combined with communism. The new constitution stated that Romania was a socialist country, and the party restored the name communist to demonstrate Romania's equal status with the Soviet Union. It was the socialist nation, and not the working class, Ceauşescu declared, that would play the central role in furthering world progress. Under the nationalist banner, abortion and divorce became practically impossible in October 1966. Childless adults were forced to pay special taxes, and Romania became the only country in Europe where adultery was an official crime punishable by imprisonment. Advocating conservative family values served the ambitious goal of generating a population explosion and creating a nation of 30 million (instead of 20 million). The independent line of Romanian foreign policy remained steadfast.

Within a few years, Romania's national Stalinism reached new heights. "Compared with the 'Ceauşescu era'," Michael Shafir aptly remarked, "Dejist manipulation of national symbols, and the extensive exploitation of the national myth, appear as child's play" (Shafir, 1985).

In the spring of 1968, Ceauşescu was roused to the offensive. To establish his personal rule he denounced his former master, Gheorghiu-Dej (together with quite a few of his collaborators who remained after Dej's leadership, and thus were rivals to Ceauşescu), for Stalinist crimes and cleared the records of some of his victims, declaring them to be innocent, for example Ştefan Foriş, the former secretary-general of the party who was assassinated in his prison cell in 1946, and Lucreţiu Patraşcanu, executed in 1954. "Of course, Gheorghiu-Dej has incontestable merits . . . but no merits . . . can excuse his abuses and responsibilities in Patraşcanu's assassination, as well as many illegal acts committed against party and government officials," declared Ceauşescu in April 1968. "Alexandru Drăghici played a leading part [among] the people responsible for the abuses," added Ceauşescu, discrediting one of his most dangerous rivals. "It was in all domains of activity that Drăghici pushed the secret police to act as the supreme leading agency, above the party" (Ceauşescu, 1969, pp. 192–3).

This was of triple benefit to Ceauşescu: first, he appeared as a liberal de-Stalinizer, the champion of truth and legality; secondly, he destroyed the myth and central role of his predecessor in Romanian party history, and thus cleared the road for creating his own legend as the revolutionary leader of postwar Romania; and, most importantly, he was able to defeat his rivals. Drăghici was removed from his posts, and the removal of Apostol and Stoica was also planned for. Dej's old "barons" were marginalized. Maurer was tolerated for a while, but new stars emerged, protegés and vassals of Ceauşescu, such as Virgin Trofin, Niculescu-Mizil, and Ion Iliescu. The Ceauşescu era was launched. He was vigilant enough not to allow even his appointees to remain too long in leading positions, and from time to time removed them in order to prevent them from establishing too much power.

In the meantime, his offensive began: in March Ceauşescu refused to sign a joint Warsaw Pact agreement on the nuclear non-proliferation treaty, the first Warsaw Pact document which was not unanimously accepted. During these same weeks, in a deepening "Czechoslovak-crisis" and an orchestrated Soviet threat of the Prague Spring, Ceauşescu had separate talks with Tito and Dubček. In July, when the Warsaw meeting of the Warsaw Pact countries issued an ultimatum and threatened Prague, Ceauşescu delivered a series of speeches offering his total support ("we have full confidence in the Communist Party of Czechoslovakia") and rushed to Prague to sign a Treaty of Friendship and Cooperation. At the session of the Central Committee in June, Ceauşescu announced his determination to improve the situation in agriculture and that there would be "better living standards for all working people" (Ceauşescu, 1969, pp. 270–1). On August 11 Ceauşescu delivered a speech in the mining center of Jiu Valley to inform his people that he rejected the Soviet proposal and pressure to introduce central Comecon planning: "We want to point out once more that the . . . statements which advocate turning CMEA into a supra statal agency and developing a uniform plan [for the bloc] . . . do not meet the needs . . . of each national economy . . . [and] would widen differences." Expressing his national line, he added: "Romania will further expand cooperation with all countries, regardless of their social and economic order" (Ceauşescu, 1969, pp. 351–2).

On August 21, 1968, the day of the Soviet coordinated invasion of Czechoslovakia, Romania remained the only country of the Warsaw Pact which refused to participate and condemned the invasion. On that very day, Ceauşescu spoke in Bucharest's Palace Square, and an agitated, enthusiastic crowd fully agreed with its courageous leader and responded emotionally, sometimes with a seemingly endless ovation, when he stated that the invasion by the five countries was "a major mistake and a grave threat to peace . . . and to socialism throughout the world [and] a shameful moment in the history of the revolutionary movement . . . It is inconceivable for a socialist state . . . to infringe on the freedom and independence of other states. There is no justification whatsoever . . . [for] military intervention in the affairs of a fraternal socialist country. Each party and nation choose their own roads of building socialism" (Ceauşescu, 1969, pp. 351–2). A genuine national enthusiasm reached new heights. "Patriotic guards" were organized, and mass training of guerilla warfare was initiated for the defense of the homeland. Ceauşescu also made minor gestures of democratization. At a rally in the University Plaza, Bucharest, on the occasion of the beginning of the academic year, he stated: "It is necessary that a greater number of agencies be drawn into the decision-making process. . . . A law has been passed for the setting up of academic senates and councils. . . . These agencies must enjoy a broad autonomy . . . Undergraduates will be represented in the academic senates." In December 1968, Ceauşescu proudly reported a great economic leap forward during his years in power: "As you know, in 1966–8 the rate of industrial growth has been 12.3 percent . . . nearly half a million workplaces have been created in non-agricultural areas . . . over 155,000 apartments have been commissioned, which has made it possible for over 500,000 persons to move into new houses" (Ceauşescu, 1969, pp. 770–2).

Ceauşescu became a veritable national hero, an authentic advocate of Romanian national interests. His personal popularity and his regime's legitimacy was established. President Charles de Gaulle rushed to Romania to restore traditional French–Romanian contacts and encourage the independent line of Ceauşescu. At the occasion of de Gaulle's visit, Ceauşescu, at an enthusiastic mass rally, announced his new, independent German policy: "We believe that recognizing the two German states and subsequently developing normal relations with them would contribute to eliminating the remains of World War II. . . . At the same time," he added, "troops should be withdrawn from the territories of other states" (Ceauşescu, 1969, pp. 224–5).

In the following year, for the first time in history, an American president, Richard Nixon, visited Romania. In 1970 and 1971, Ceauşescu was received in Washington with much respect and splendor. His triumphant Western recognition, the honorary degrees and badges of honor that were bestowed upon him in the subsequent years in the Western democracies, enhanced his internal reputation as well. The Romanians became proud of him and his independent regime. They were proud to be Romanian. Any opposition to Ceauşescu began to be seen as an attack on, and betrayal of, the nation.

A series of studies have analyzed how and why Ceauşescu used nationalism for his personal aims. Very few, however, realized that communist nationalism was not only a maneuver of certain communist regimes, but was also the result of strong historical inertia, a continuation of an extreme Central and Eastern European nationalism, born in the peculiar historical environment of the region in the nineteenth and twentieth centuries. It is difficult to decide whether communism played out the national card, or whether nationalism turned toward communism, or at the very least utilized it for its own goals. Katherine Verdery belongs to the very few who stressed: "I see the national ideology that became a hallmark of Ceaușescu's Romania as having several sources, only one of which was its purposeful instrumentalization by the Party. To a considerable extent, I argue, the Party was forced onto the terrain of national values (not unwillingly) under pressure from others, especially intellectuals, whom it could fully engage in no other manner" (Verdery, 1991, pp. 121–2).

On that very basis, the fifty-year-old Nicolae Ceaușescu began to build up his extreme Stalinist-nationalistic despotism based on his unquestioned personal power and strengthened by open nepotism, elevating his wife to second in command, and his son, brother, and thirty-six members of his family to leading posts. The oriental cult of the "Age of Ceaușescu" was certainly not reached in other countries of Europe (Fischer, 1989). His ruthless dictatorship did not allow an opposition to rise against the terror of the almighty *Securitate*. The forced Rumanization of a multi-national country, where the last prewar statistics counted 30 percent of the population belonging to national minorities, primarily Hungarians and Germans, was based on his notion of an undivided Romanian nation in Romania (Fleischman, 1989). To achieve this, he literally sold the country's Germans and Jews to West Germany and Israel respectively. Hungarian autonomy was entirely abolished, and a deliberate settlement policy created a Romanian majority in cities in the Hungarian populated territory of Transylvania. This trend culminated in a maniacal plan of "systematization" of settlements during the eighties, when thousands of villages were destroyed and the rural population forced to move into newly built townships. In a paradoxical way, Romanian nationalism was also served by the most extreme Stalinist industrialization, unique in Central and Eastern Europe in the late sixties and seventies. Ceaușescu persistently closed off and isolated his country. A country proud of her bold leader and enthusiastically following his nationalist policies became a playground of a monomaniac, paranoid dictator.

Nicolae Ceaușescu, the third son of a peasant family in the most backward province of Oltania, where a great many of the villages were simply an assortment of mud huts partially cut into the earth, a man who finished his education at the elementary school level and became a shoemaker's apprentice at the age of eleven in Bucharest, reinforced the symbolic formalities of royalty throughout his rule. Ceaușescu was a short man with a nervous, sharp glance, who monotonously read his five to six hour long speeches, hardly looking up from the text that he tightly clutched in his hands, a man with a seemingly strong inferiority complex for which he overcompensated through his despotic power and lavish life style, characterized by elegant castles and residences all over the country with gold water-taps, by travelling in caravans of Mercedes Benzes and personal helicopters, and by possessing a "sample-man" whose function was to prevent him from being poisoned. By 1974, Ceauşescu occupied all the highest posts of the country, and became the everyday topic of the news and poetry, the great *conducător* who ordered the leveling and rebuilding of the center of the capital to realize his vision of grandeur, a typical case of architectural megalomania.

The young revolutionary of the late thirties, the modest third-rate party organizer of the late forties and fifties, the charismatic national leader of the late sixties, hidden behind royal formalities and preserved by excessive terror, long recognized, praised, and privileged by the Western powers, Ceauşescu temporarily legitimized both his Stalinist rule with his extreme nationalism (internally and for the West), as well as his independent nationalism (externally, for the Soviet Union) with his orthodox Stalinism.

The Albanian and Romanian nationalist regimes, though Stalinist, launched a strong blow to the power monopoly of the Soviet Union and contributed to the relaxing of its controls. They thus indirectly helped foster the development of a more independent national road, which was in some cases connected to major reform efforts. Such a development occurred in Czechoslovakia.

Socialism with a (smashed) human face: Czechoslovakia 1968

A decade after the Polish and Hungarian October 1956, a new national reform-communism emerged to create a democratic model of socialism. The reform could not break through easily in Czechoslovakia. The phony "New Course" did not initiate real reforms between 1953 and 1956. After the death of Gottwald, the party remained in the hands of the discredited Gottwald team. The strong rivals agreed to elect a compromise candidate as party chief, Antonin Novotný, who was inconsequential enough not to be dangerous.

Novotný, who completed his education at the elementary stage (foreign words were written in the text of his speeches phonetically to avoid his mispronouncing them), and who played a minor role in the party, was elevated into the leading bodies after the fall of Slánsky. He was not a rival to the popular head of state, Antonin Zapotocky, and became a part of a collective leadership. Czechoslovak Stalinism continued, and although the accusations of Titoism and Zionism against Slánsky were withdrawn, he was not rehabilitated. Moreover, the liquidation of the Slánsky group was now praised as the first stroke against Stalinism.

The Czechoslovak party leadership strongly supported the Soviet policy against the Polish and Hungarian October. After 1956 the regime became even more conservative. In 1960 Novotný declared that socialism had been achieved and that the country was now marching toward communism, and the constitution and the name of the country was changed accordingly. Up to this point the Czechoslovak political game was rather similar to its Romanian counterpart. Novotný, who could have consolidated his power, however, was too weak to follow an independent line. In 1962 a more thorough critique of the fifties and the rehabilitation of the victims of the show trials began. In the next year the remaining three members of the Gottwald leadership were removed.

After a decade of consolidating his power, however, Novotný had to face a devastating crisis. In 1963 the country's economy collapsed. Besides the well-known and typical decline in agriculture, rapid industrial growth ceased and the gross national product declined in 1962–3. A Stalinist industrialization policy and centralized, bureaucratic planning (which brought about rapid industrialization in backward peasant countries, without consideration of cost, and technological and quality requirements) was clearly disastrous in the highly industrialized, advanced Czechoslovakia. The economic disaster was unparalleled at that time in Central and Eastern Europe and required drastic measures. A group of economists influenced by the Polish and Hungarian reform economics, Karel Kouba, Otakar Turek, Josef Goldmann, and, most importantly, Ota Šik, a Central Committee member, author of *Plan and Market Under Socialism* (1967), and the head of the Academy Institute of Economics, urged radical reforms (Šik, 1968). Some members of the Novotny leadership, such as Cernik and Strougal, supported the idea, which was accepted by Novotný as well (Soska, 1966).

In December 1963 the Central Committee discussed the issue and Šik vehemently argued for reforming central planning. An expert committee was appointed under the leadership of Šik to analyze the system of planning and management and offer suggestions. In September 1964 the Central Committee had already accepted the principles of a market-oriented economic reform. In June 1966 the reform program was sanctioned by the 13th party congress. In 1967 central planning was replaced by a regulated planned-market economy. Firms became semi-independent and, instead of receiving compulsory plan indicators, had to operate on the market and earn a profit. The price system was partly reformed and some wholesale prices were liberalized; however, most remained fixed. Investment was financed out of firms' reserves instead of the state budget. State control and intervention remained strong. Some subsidies and strict wage regulations survived. Though a half-measure, the Ota Šik economic reform was a breakthrough.

The first year of the reform, however, was a mixed blessing. The price reform generated a 29–30 percent rise in wholesale prices and a 50 percent higher inflation rate than expected, while enterprise profits, instead of the calculated 22 percent, increased by 81 percent, almost four times higher. Re-centralization reflexes began to work. The Central Committee, in its May and September plenums, tightened wage controls and reintroduced state restrictions. This immediate retreat led Ota Šik to play "an essential part in linking the failure of the reform to the question of the lack of democracy in the party," concluded Batt (Batt, 1988, p. 201).

Two other major teams of scholars began to work from the mid sixties on, based on the initiative of the party's chief ideologue, Jiři Hendrych, who promoted preparatory proposals for major reform from the mid sixties on. An interdisciplinary team headed by Radovan Richta analyzed the development of the scientific and technological revolution and its impact, and concluded with a devastating critique of previous economic policy. The role of technology and the "human factor," the importance of "a developed system of interest," and all the neglected and subordinated factors of "socialist industrialization policy" were particularly scrutinized, since without these it would be "impossible to throw open the door to the scientific and technological revolution." Without it, however, stated Richta in his *Civilizace na rozcesti* (Civilization at the crossroads) in 1966, "the new society must unconditionally perish – regardless of . . . the best of intentions." He stressed the need for free debate and the end of the era of the "obedient specialist" (Skilling, 1976, p. 127). Radovan Richta, who two years later coined the world famous term "socialism with a human face," had, along with those in his team, made a major contribution toward the case for reform and, what was even more important, toward the mobilization of the intellectuals and the transformation of the public spirit of the country.

The same could be said about the work of the other research team, headed by Zdenek Mlynař and under the auspices of the Academy of Sciences. In the fall of 1966 the team began to analyze the development of the political system and democracy in socialist society. They planned to present a report on the "most suitable conceptual model of the political system" by 1968. Mlynař himself published powerful articles on the topic, propagating the need for reforming the existing political system. The conclusions of their analysis led to a severe critique of the Stalinist political system and the need for an alternative, where the role of the party would change to become a pluralistic, democratic structure. A concept of political reform was in the making. "The ideology of reform communism in the Communist Party of Czechoslovakia was spread in the 1960s," summarized Zdanek Mlynař (Mlynař, 1980, p. 73). It should be added that reform-communism was by far the strongest and most widespread in Czechoslovakia in those years.

After a decade of rigid Stalinism, Novotný changed his ruling team, and began to move toward reform and liberalizing his regime. Although he evidently assumed that it would strengthen his position, he nonetheless followed the oft-experienced pattern of history, and was forced to disappear with the old system. In October 1967, the Central Committee revolted against him: Alexander Dubček's intervention and severe criticism of Novotný and the party's methods of work unleashed fundamental critiques by Kriegel, Spacek, and others. On the December 19th session of the Central Committee, Ota Šik made a devastating attack on, among other things, the suppression of criticism, and called for the "resignation of Novotný as first-secretary of the party and the selection of a successor by secret vote" (Skilling, 1976, p. 169).

These were decisive weeks; the presidium was split with five on each side. The climax came in late December and early January, when Josef Smrkovsky took the lead and, after a blunt debate at the session of the Central Committee, on January 6, 1968, Novotný resigned and was replaced by Alexander Dubček, who initiated the debate in October and was the only one who could muster a majority.

This was a historic moment. Though his election was the result of a compromise, the new party chief was elected immediately, without a Soviet da in advance. In Prague, however, even the main actors in this historical drama did not properly realize the importance of the situation. True, the situation was rather confusing. Eventually, Novotný resigned as first secretary, but remained president of the state and a member of the Politburo. His friends retained their positions everywhere. On a certain occasion, he remarked to them: "Don't worry, it is all right. Dubček is a weakling, he's not up to the job, and the secretaries are spineless. Our time will come!" (Skilling, 1976, p. 95). Between January and April, indeed, not much happened. On the surface things were calm and the new leadership did not even make a dramatic political declaration. Was this due to Dubček's personal character? A peaceful man with a genuine sense of democratic methods, who never ordered but sought to convince, and who had never cherished and sought power, he felt neither competent nor prepared. He had spent nineteen years in the party apparatus and appeared predictably gray and unimportant, although in the end he was the party boss of Slovakia. His disarming, broad, and open smile was probably his strongest weapon. Dubček, however, and not without conviction, and he became the charismatic leader of a peaceful revolution, the "Prague Spring" (Shawcross, 1990). Though he had no decisive vision of the future, he believed in the possibility of "socialism with a human face," a term which historically was connected with his name, and was formidable enough to make history. His innocent convictions and his simple manner, his natural, "man of the street" behavior and instinctive refusal of the "Byzantine style" all took on a tremendous importance and became a source of strength.

Alan Levy describes a telling episode: Dubček drove to the TV studio for his inauguration speech in his old, ragged car, watched and adored by a whole nation. "Dubček believed in his ideals ... at a time when the entire nation surrendered to the need for faith." After many years of mutual distrust between the leaders and the population, Dubček "trusted people ... [a]nd they trusted him. ... [W]hat was fundamental here was ... the clear fact that this mutual faith existed. ... Dubček genuinely possessed the human and political qualities to become the symbol of the Prague Spring" (Mlynař, 1980, pp. 120–2).

Indeed, the first three "eventless" months of 1968 became the decisive preparatory stage of the Prague Spring. Besides Dubček's elevation to his historical task, he removed, in his quiet way, the entire Novotný team, including Novotný himself who was compelled to resign from the Politburo and from the presidency on the very first spring day, March 21, 1968.

The Prague Spring suddenly gained momentum. On March 30, General Ludvik Svoboda, a national hero, an officer of the Czech Legion during World War I, commander of the Czechoslovak military units fighting against Hitler during World War II, Minister of Defense in the postwar coalition government, and then a bookkeeper in a collective farm during the fifties, a man of uncompromising character, was elected as president of the country. A strong new team of enthusiastic, popular reformists, Smrkovsky, Kriegel, Spacek, and Simon, took over. Dubček found an excellent manager-type aide as prime minister in his old colleague Oldrich Černik. This was a team that trusted and complemented each other. What certainly was equally important, a new reform team took over. In the cabinet, for example, professor Jiři Hajek, the former social democrat and Minister of Foreign Affairs, and Jósef Pavel, a victim of Stalinist purges in the fifties (sentenced to twenty-five years) and a genuine democrat reform-communist, took legality and democracy seriously. To the Writers' Union was appointed Eduard Goldstücker, and to the National Radio and Television, Hejzlar and Pelikan, as theoreticians, scholars, lawyers, economic experts, historians, and philosophers who played a decisive role in preparing the reforms and changing the whole political atmosphere of the country in those days, people such as Richta, Šik, Mlynař, Hübl, Kaplan, and very many others, were placed in different posts in the party and state apparatus, in social organizations, at universities, and newly founded civic institutions. The strongest reformist team in Central and Eastern Europe took over the Czechoslovak party-state (Kusin, 1971).

By the spring, when the team was ready, the complex program of a radical transformation, the so-called Action Program, was already on the table. Ambiguous as it was when published in April 1968 (*Rudé Právo*, 1968), it still represented a first sincere attempt to present a concept of "a new political system, a new model of socialist democracy." The document, which consisted of five parts, was a comprehensive and consistent proposal, posing as a first draft of a program that would culminate in a new constitution. Although it was still not "finished," the main and most advanced concept of the Prague Spring's revolution-from-above was the "Outline of a long-term program" presented at the dramatic, illegal August 22, 1968 party congress in Vysocany, Prague, when Soviet tanks occupied the capital, and when Dubček, Černik, and the top party leaders were under arrest and taken to the Soviet Union as criminals. The best basis to summarize the leading ideas of the Prague Spring is this document, which declared:

The distorted model of Socialism was applied in this country. . . . It deformed and generalized aspects which may perhaps have suited the conditions and needs of countries on the threshold of industrialization . . . [but] did not suit the real aims of socialism. . . . [The "humanist socialism" t]hat is needed . . . is a new model of democratic socialism to replace the bureaucratic system. . . . [A] socialist society must gradually begin . . . to de-monopolize politics and to extend civic liberties and the self-determination of the individual as much as the nations. . . . Socialism requires more, not less, freedom . . . freedom of the press and of expression, of assembly, movement, travel . . . it requires more, not fewer human rights. (Pelikan, 1971, pp. 107, 111)

The realization of these ideas, according to another document of the congress on the main tasks for the immediate future, was planned partly by institutionalizing human rights and freedoms, and partly by accomplishing political pluralism. The Prague Spring was a combination of "formal (parliamentary) democracy" with direct representation from different social groups and minorities, including local self-government and workers' self-management. The combination of the parliamentary system with direct representation from social and professional groups would be institutionalized by a multi-cameral system. The parliament would include three chambers, an Industrial (elected by factories), Agricultural (elected by collective and state farms), and Service (elected by health, education, and cultural institutions), and the chambers would have special powers to send back draft bills.

The abolition of a "monopoly of power invested in a state-party center" would be accompanied by the introduction of a multi-party system. Political parties, however, would exist only on the basis of acceptance of the platform of the National Front, i.e., on the basic principle of democratic socialism. Different parties could exist within this broad framework, but outside it "no political parties, or organizations fulfilling the functions of political parties, may arise or continue." There were, however, basic ambiguities and severe inconsistencies in this planned pluralism, such as when the program sought certain assurances against the possibility of losing political hegemony to the non-communist parties. The program of democratization, however, spoke about a "ten–fifteen year" transitory period, and maintained that the "political reform ... would have to go through several stages" (Pelikan, 1971, pp. 122, 127, 132).

The Prague Spring's economic program did not radically surpass the already reinforced Ota Šik reform. It was a concept of a mixed economy, where firms were independent and "separated from the state, operating under market conditions, exposed to the pressure of economic competition." In this system, the "central economic authorities would not intervene," and the national plan was only "a general framework"; efforts would be promoted only where the "market alone would not suffice to stimulate, i.e., where priority needs are to be given to social or human consideration, as in decisions affecting the environment, culture." Regarding the structure of ownership, the program specified that most of the economy would remain in collective ownership, but the latter was no longer equated with bureaucratic state ownership. In the first place, workers' self-management (workers' councils) was now responsible for creating real collective ownership, which was intended to be complemented by cooperative ownership; moreover, the program spoke about "a whole spectrum of social ownership." Private ownership, according to this concept, would only exist in "small-scale individual businesses," mostly in the service branches (Pelikan, 1971, pp. 209–10).

In spite of its limitations and inconsistencies, the reform-plan of the Czechoslovak reform-communists was the most comprehensive and radical version of the serious "reform-from-within" attempts in Central and Eastern Europe. The most decisive achievement of Dubček's Prague Spring was the preambling of *glasnost* (a term which became known two decades later). The media published and broadcasted sharp criticism, open debates, and independent views. A self-generating process had begun. By March, the atmosphere of the country was entirely transformed. The padlocks were undone and a deluge of freedom, in both expression and publication, engulfed the country. The Prague Spring became a moment of truth. A passionate debate erupted on pluralism and democracy. Ivan Sviták, a former communist and Marxist philosopher, advocated a movement toward an open society. "We want democracy, not democratization. Democratization is a minimal program on the way to democracy" (Skilling, 1976, p. 357). He rejected the idea of "shadow parties" and demanded a total elimination of the monopoly of power through free elections, with at least two new Christian and social democratic parties. Václav Havel, playwright and chairman of the Club of Independent Writers, argued in *Literární listy* on April 4 that public opinion and the democratization of the party were not a guarantee of democracy. The only way is "a real choice . . . where the people have the possibility – from time to time – freely to select those who will govern them" (Skilling, 1976, p. 357). Petr Pithart vehemently rejected the idea of the National Front framework, because it would undermine real democracy and parliamentarism. In July *Rudé Právo* published the article of Miroslav Rumler: "Even a brief account of the problems shows that non-Marxist models of growth point out a series of new relations of paramount importance for an understanding of questions of both a general worldwide and specifically Czechoslovak nature, connected with economic growth" (Rumler, 1968).

The impact of an unlimited, free debate on the issues was clearly manifested in the fact that even the members of the Communist Party changed their views radically on pluralism and democracy: according to a poll in May, 61 percent of the party members maintained that the leading role of the party was a condition of socialist democracy; in July, only 31 percent favored a single political line, and 68 percent were for several concepts of individual parties.

The press, television, and radio depicted the horrors of the fifties and the lack of proper rehabilitation, condemning those who were responsible for the crimes and who delayed taking corrective measures. In the tempestuous debate, survivors of purges such as Smrkovsky, Löbl and Goldstücker warned against a policy of revenge and argued for tolerance. The notorious case of Jan Masaryk's death in 1948, a strictly taboo subject for two decades, became a topic of impassioned open debate: in a front page article of the party daily *Rudé Právo* on April 16, Jiři Hochman did not exclude the possibility that Masaryk was murdered.

Taboos no longer existed in Prague in the spring of 1968. A euphoria of freedom and truth dominated the country, and the population began to feel that it was now responsible for its own destiny (Skvorecky, 1968). A peaceful revolution began from below. "Once fear was gone," summarizes Zdenek Mlynař, "the democratic, humanitarian national consciousness came forward as the main protagonist in the Prague Spring, and from April to June it was unquestionably the main player on the stage" (Mlynǎr, 1980, p. 118).

The democratic mass movement began to overpass the party, which aspired to maintain a share of the power. Certain efforts and "strengthened attacks," Dubček declared at the end of May, seek "to discredit morally our whole party . . . and to question its leading role." His argument was rather naive when he stated: "The renewal of the development of socialism was initiated by the communists." This gave, argued Dubček, a moral and political basis for them to aspire to a leading role in the further development of socialism. He frankly listed the limitations of this progress. "The party does not want to revise 1948, i.e., its seizure of power, and does not intend to reevaluate its merger with the social democratic party." These limitations, however, were no longer valid and had no meaning for an elemental democratic mass movement. The Soviet leaders, on the other hand, did not believe him when he stressed: "Our ties . . . with the Soviet Union . . . [are] emotionally rooted and [constitute] sincere friendship. . . . By our actions we will show our unwavering faithfulness to proletarian internationalism" (Dubček, 1968).

The revolutionary dynamic of the Prague Spring was broken in July by the open threat of a Soviet-led military intervention (Brahm, 1970). In May 1968, Brezhnev ordered the obedient party leaders of the Warsaw Pact countries to come to Moscow and began to orchestrate a joint action to stop the Prague revolt. He found more than willing collaborators in East Germany's Walter Ulbricht and, as a gloomy irony of history, in the hero of the Polish October of 1956, Wladislaw Gomulka. They not only agreed but even pushed Brezhnev toward brutal action. The generals and extreme hard-liners of his Politburo were for military action, which actually had already been decided on that month. In late June and early July, a long military manoeuvre of the Warsaw Pact in Czechoslovakian territory quite openly manifested the threat. On July 14–15 five Warsaw Pact countries met in Warsaw and openly warned: "[W]e cannot assent to hostile forces pushing your country off the path of socialism and creating the threat that Czechoslovakia may break away from the socialist commonwealth. This is no longer only your affair." The open letter of the Warsaw Pact leaders, which was published in *Pravda* on July 18, 1968, added: It is "not only your task but ours, too, to deal a resolute rebuff to the anti-communist forces." Czechoslovakia could "count on the solidarity and general assistance of the parties of the fraternal socialist countries" in the "struggle against counter-revolution" (Skilling, 1976, p. 290).

The presidium of the Czechoslovak party rejected the charges of counter-revolution, condemned the method of making decisions without representation from the member country in question, and called for bilateral talks. Dubček and his team, however, would not defend their position by suppressing *glasnost*. Was it an uncompromising faith in truth and principles? Was it weakness and lack of political experience? Was it a miscalculation and a lack of proper understanding? Was it naiveté and a blind belief in arguments and the strength of words? Did János Kádár hit the nail on the head when, after an intimate and friendly face to face talk with Dubček in which he indirectly warned the Czech leader of the impending danger, he almost desperately asked: "Do you *really* not know the kind of people you're dealing with?" (Mlynař, 1980, p. 157).

The leaders of the Prague Spring were certainly naive and inexperienced, but most of all uncompromising men of principle. The Prague Spring, however, ended in August. It was before midnight on August 20, 1968, while the members of the presidium of the Czechoslovak party were still debating, when Prime Minister Černik was called to the telephone and learned that troops of the five Warsaw Pact countries had crossed the borders. The military invasion began (Chapman, 1968). General Dzúr, the minister of defense, was arrested in his office. Shortly after 4 a.m., Soviet tanks and armored cars surrounded the headquarters of the Communist Party. "Suddenly the doors of Dubček's office flew open and about eight soldiers . . . with machine guns rushed in, surrounded us from behind . . . their weapons at the backs of our heads." When Dubček said something, a heavily decorated Soviet colonel "roared out: "No talking! Sit quietly!"" (Mlynař, 1980, p. 179).

Dubček and the top leaders arrived in Moscow as prisoners, without shoestrings and belts. The Soviet ambassador to Prague, Chervenkö, rushed to set up a "Revolutionary Workers and Peasants Government" under the leadership of Alois Indra. The attempt failed because of president Svoboda's firm stand.

The episode was rather irregular: the prisoners taken to Moscow suddenly became the Czechoslovak party and government delegation, signed an agreement and returned to Prague. In September, the same leading team, Dubček, Svoboda, Smrkovsky, Černik and Husák signed a proclamation to the entire Czechoslovak people: "We want to continue, and will continue, in the path upon which we set out in January." Did they seriously hope they could succeed with this rope dance, expressed in the next sentence of the proclamation: "We will further strengthen the socialist social order [and] develop its democratic and humanistic character"? (Provoláni, 1968).

They did not even have the chance to try: they were gradually removed, and collaborators, partly old Soviet agents, took over. Some of them, however, were enthusiastic members of the Prague Spring's leadership, such as Gustáv Husák, who replaced Dubček in April 1969. This was a man who spent a Stalinist decade in prison, joined Dubček and even now promised the continuation of "the road of January 1968" in his first TV and radio speech on April 30, 1969. "The continuation of this policy . . . is an inescapable rule if we do not want to plunge our society into backwardness. We are going to continue and broaden this road," though "cleansed of negative phenomena . . . and we have to block the road of opposition and hostile forces" (Husák, 1979, p. 10). Two years later, at the 14th party congress in 1971, Husák publicly celebrated the removal of "right-wing opportunists and adventurers who sought to introduce anarchic market relations and transform collective ownership into group-ownership" (Husák, 1979, pp. 54, 66, 67). At the 16th party congress, in May 1981, Husák labelled the Prague Spring as a "departure from class positions . . . [which] allowed the counter-revolutionary forces . . . to attack the leading role of the Party, to attack our friendship and allience with the Soviet Union, to attack the very foundations of socialism" (Husák, 1981, p. 6).

Czechoslovakia retreated by more than a decade and introduced one of the most orthodox regimes in Central and Eastern Europe. The country lost its best intellectuals, for tens of thousands escaped to the West after the Soviet invasion and hundreds of thousands were purged from the party and from their original jobs. University professors, journalists, editors, lawyers, and artists were forced into blue-collar jobs in the era of Husák's "normalization" (Simecka, 1984). The watchword during the twenty years following was no forgiveness, no rehabilitation. The country became hermetically isolated: from a short-lived openness and freedom, a closed society was restored.

János Kádár's "Hungarian Miracle"

In the very first days of January 1968, when Alexander Dubček was elected first-secretary, Hungary introduced a major price reform: under the pseudonym of the New Economic Mechanism, the Kádár regime initiated a cautious, self-limiting reform toward a new model of a socialist economy. It tactfully shied away from political structures and the institutional framework of state socialism. As a turning point toward reform, 1968 was similar in Czechoslovakia and Hungary. Certain elements of economic reform revealed similarities, and the two countries even influenced each other in the period of preparation in the mid sixties. The Prague Spring and the Hungarian Miracle embodied, however, rather different tactics and concepts of reform. The Czechoslovak 1968 was born out of a long delayed "thaw." The Hungarian reforms, paradoxically, emerged out of the ruins of the 1956 revolution.

The Hungarian revolution could not prevail and was nipped in the bud because, after a brief hesitation, even the reform-oriented leadership of Nikita Khrushchev felt it had to be suppressed. In spite of considerable international political-diplomatic turmoil, the post-Yalta arrangements remained in full strength.

History, however, followed a surprising dialectic: if the post-1953 reforms in Hungary led to a full fledged revolution, the suppressed revolution now became a springboard for real reforms. The heroic extremism and violence of the Hungarian October had a lasting impact on post-1956 Hungary. The restored state socialist regime could not continue in the old routine and, after consolidating its power, sought a compromise with the population. Failed revolutions followed by successful compromise was a rather well-known pattern in modern Hungarian history.

Though the reform opposition suffered a severe defeat, and though two thirds of the Stalinist party apparatus and nomenclature remained untouched while only the top leadership was changed, the renamed party was quite different from its predecessor. Reformists, though disorganized and subordinated to the moderate conservative-reformer center group of the new party leader János Kádár, were still present in the party, and their ranks were regularly renewed from the new generation of party intellectuals. Kádár not only tolerated a built-in reformist opposition but, in reaction to economic and social-political tensions in the country, occasionally made alliances with the opposition and provided a "playground" for it. Kádár's heavy-built figure both overshadowed and protected the reforms. His regime created fixed internal limitations but also a unique external (Soviet) tolerance. After all, he became by far the best "proconsul" in Soviet dominated Central and Eastern Europe.

János Kádár's political high-wire act, designed to guarantee continuity (to assure Soviet approbation) and achieve real changes (to gain popular acceptance), failed in the gloomy years of mass repression. A reform committee responsible for working out a new economic system to replace centralized planning, headed by Professor István Varga, a non-partisan expert and an advocate of the market economy, which drew the participation of about 200 experts, was appointed by the Kádár government on December 10, 1956. "The original draft," wrote Varga in a letter to cabinet minister Apró in the Summer of 1957, "was built on the idea that the system of compulsory plan directives . . . would be abolished and the implementation of the plan would be ensured within the system of economic incentives" (Berend, 1990, p. 49). The comprehensive reform proposals were a compromise between planning and the market. The first plan with a market-socialist "economic mechanism," was presented to the government in the early summer of 1957. It was rejected and central planning was preserved. While the first decrees of the Presidential Council legalized the workers' councils on November 24, 1956, recognizing this basic institution of the revolution, within a year they were eradicated.

After years of bloody repression and prevailing conservativism, and after consolidating its power, from the early mid 1960s on the Kádár regime turned toward cautious reforms. The tragedy of 1956 both inspired and justified a more independent internal policy on the part of the government, which distanced itself from the Soviet pattern. On the basis of an unchanged party-state political structure, and with the aim of pacifying a hostile population and seeking a compromise with it, a marked liberalization began. A pragmatic Kádár gave up the basic principle of the closed society and did not attempt to interfere in the private lives of the populace. By de-politicizing Hungarian society, the government was seeking only passive tolerance, not active participation. Kádár's popular biblical slogan, "who is not against us, is with us," promulgated in 1962, was supported by the granting of greater freedom. The freedom of travel was accompanied by expanded freedom of religion and tolerance toward the Western arts. It was paternalistically provided by the almighty party state, but the boundaries were pushed further back. Political satirists regularly caricatured the regime, and the public gratefully laughed. Several safety valves helped to release tension. Those who were released from prison and internment gradually found their place in the depoliticized and consolidated regime as professionals, experts, writers, and intellectuals. They emerged in the technocratic elite, though only in its second to third levels. During the 1970–80s several of them became respectable and recognized, well-to-do citizens, decorated with government titles and medals. Many who had emigrated in 1956 and later visited the country were shocked by the difference. Under the unchanged monolithic structures a sort of pluralism emerged between officialdom and civic life. Next to Gomulka's Poland, where the success of the half-revolution established the highest possible plurality and relative freedom, the success of the failed revolution led to similar achievements in Hungary.

The Hungarian October, however, had a much stronger and more important aftermath as well. Unlike in Poland, a structural reform of the economic system, the gradual introduction of a unique market-socialism, and, on that basis, the development of a "socialist consumer society" (or "Goulash-Communism") began.

After the failed early reform attempts, only one major reform measure of November 1956 survived: the abolition of compulsory delivery system and the compulsory sowing plan. The Imre Nagy government declared the abolition of that system, which destroyed the basic pillars of the command economy in agriculture. Instead of administrative orders and force, the relationship between the peasantry and the state was based on the market. The state had to buy products from the peasantry, and, since delivery was not compulsory, it now had to pay a more realistic market price for them.

The strong reform-wing, led by Lajos Fehér and representing the policies (without mentioning his name) of Imre Nagy, achieved only a short-lived victory with the party's declaration of a new agricultural policy in the early summer of 1957, which practically rejected Soviet-type collectivization and the exploitation of agriculture. One and half years later a cautious Kádár obediently followed the Soviet initiative to achieve collectivization. This was, however, only a partial success for the conservatives. The reform-wing was able to introduce a new model of collective farms, which embodied a sort of compromise between collective and private farming. Unlike the kolkhoz-type of collective farm, several elements of family farming were built into the system: crop-sharing inside the cooperative and market-oriented private plots, which concentrated about half of the Hungarian animal stock in private hands, represented a special combination of collective and private farming. Market prices for agricultural products were gradually restored and the typical Soviet-type price scissors essentially narrowed, assuring efficient incentives for agriculture. In a fully collectivized agricultural system, 12 percent of arable land was earmarked for mini-private plots, in cooperation with the collective big estates (for example, fodder was produced by the collective, which supplied the member families, who used it in the animal husbandry of the private plot), from which one-third of agricultural output was produced. Additionally, from the mid sixties on, agricultural enterprises were also encouraged by allowing industrial side activities. Food processing, construction, and service shops were founded and assured full year round activity and extra income for the cooperatives. As a result, Hungary developed a flourishing agricultural sector with a high level of productivity and output. Food shortages and queuing for meat disappeared in the mid sixties and supplies became abundant. Agriculture became one of the most important export sectors of the Hungarian economy.

The forces of the "reform-from-within" gradually gained ground. When the sources of extensive industrialization, primarily the unlimited labor source, dried up, and the slightly moderated economic regime had to face a disequilibrium in the balance of trade and payments, Hungary turned back to reforms. On December 10, 1964, the party's Central

Committee decided on the preparation of a major reform, and, within a year, the concept of a market-oriented reform, presented by Rezsö Nyers, a former social democrat and the leading figure of the reformers, was accepted. Compulsory plan indicators, the essence of the Soviet-type economy, were abolished. Instead, profit interest was introduced, based on a vital price reform, which allowed free market prices for about 50 percent of consumer goods and, after a gradual increase, 65 percent of factory prices. Fixed prices, however, still played an important role regarding energy and raw materials, staple products of mass consumption, and services, which all remained subsidized. The mixed price system assured the control of inflation and curbed negative social side effects (unemployment and decline), but its slow pace strongly limited the effectiveness of reform as well. State regulations, which controlled and limited the independent firms' activities, counterbalanced the impact of the profit motivation and slowed down a rise in unemployment, but they also hindered efficiency. The most important limitation of the reform was the lack of a labor and capital market, which strongly restricted the effectiveness of the products market. Institutional reforms were also postponed. Large, oversupplied state-owned monopoly companies were not pushed to compete by the market and could exploit their monopoly position. Banking remained the same: the only creditor was the National Bank, and commercial banks did not yet exist (Nyers, 1968).

Though a cautious half measure, the Hungarian economic reforms contributed to liberating the economy from its unbearable bureaucratic yoke and crippling overcentralization. Distribution was gradually replaced by marketing. Investment no longer relied on centrally made decisions, nor was it financed from the state budget, but rather was determined by the firm's ability to accumulate. (Firms were deprived of about half of their profits by taxation, while the remaining profits served mostly for investment and profit sharing.)

Needless to say, the reforms had to be very discreet so that they would not irritate conservative critics. The Soviet leadership suspiciously watched Hungarian developments. The advantage of preparing similar reforms in Hungary and Czechoslovakia completely vanished after the Warsaw Pact invasion and the crushing of the Prague Spring; these events happened in the very year of the reform breakthrough in Hungary.

Consequently, political pressure and open criticism accompanied the reform. Its architects decided on cautious gradualism and sought to wait a few years before initiating a second stage. This stage was to be introduced in the seventies with further institutional changes, with a reform of the banking system, the introduction of new taxation and a further development of marketization. However, because of the collapse of the Prague Spring and the strong conservative political backlash that followed, the second stage of the reform was not realized in the seventies, and the Hungarian reform stopped half way (Timár, 1975).

Indeed, even that was too much. *Rudé Právo* in Prague, *Neues Deutschland* in Berlin, and *Kommunist* in Moscow expressed mistrust and even open criticism. "[W]e have encountered among our friends in recent years some concern ... regarding our system of economic management," recognized the party daily *Népszabadság* in December 1973. "How can there be a planned economy if there is no compulsory plan for companies? How can the role of the state be asserted if over half the investments are in the companies' hands? These and similar questions are posed not infrequently" (Földes, 1973). The behind-the-scenes pressure was combined with a conspiracy of a group of overambitious hard-liners who formed an alliance in order to undermine the reforms. Zoltán Komócsin, the secretary of the Central Committee, became the leader of a sort of fifth column. "What was good yesterday, can become outworn by today, and changes must be made," he announced in connection with the economic reform, which was introduced a few years before. Hungary has to learn "as much as possible from the tried methods of the other socialist countries" (Komócsin, 1974).

From the mid seventies on, the anti-reform group won a majority in the leading bodies of the party. The main architects of the reform were ousted. Rezsö Nyers, Lajos Fehér, and others were removed from their leading posts. Retroactive taxation sought to curb private business and peasant "speculation" in agriculture, while the industrial side activities of the cooperatives restricted. Re-centralization strongly limited the firm's independence and strengthened informal state regulation. Sharp attacks were launced against the "petty bourgeois attitude" of consumerism and individualism, and attempts were made to restrengthen egalitarian distribution. "Incomes must be regulated. ... The sources [of] ... non-socialist tendencies must be restricted and then blocked" (Biszku, 1975), declared Béla Biszku, the other strong man of the anti-reform attack and number two in the party hierarchy.

Kádár made serious concessions to the combined external–internal anti-reform attack, which were not totally alien to his simplistic ideological commitments. Still, as a pragmatist with excellent political instincts, he skillfully maneuvered to save the main institutions of reform, which helped preserve several of its achievements and, about half a decade later, assured the continuation of the reforms.

Even in its restrained state, reform generated a kind of prosperity and a strong consumer orientation. The gradual development of a middle class with an important rise in entrepreneurship and prosperity began.

Housing, especially in the countryside, improved dramatically in the sixties and seventies. Almost three quarters of the population lived in privately owned family houses or had a holiday home. Mechanization of households, with one-third of families owning a car, with a social welfare system and secure, free health and educational systems, all resulted in a level of consumption, security, and welfare that had never existed throughout Hungarian history.

János Kádár, the most hated quisling in 1956, who never rebelled against his Soviet masters, who often professed allegiance to them, and who obediently followed the line of Soviet foreign policy, gradually became a kind of national hero and father figure, the great "chess player" and tactician who created his tolerable "Hungarian road to socialism." His achievements took on special value after the collapse of the Prague Spring, which seemed to justify the cautious gradualism and self-limiting avoidance of major political reforms. The comparison was rather advantageous to Stalinist national communism as well.

Western journals and governments often compared the Kádár regime to its neighbors, and so did the Hungarian population. Until the early 1980s Kádár's internal and external recognition was at its zenith. On the occasion of his 70th birthday in May 1982 the *Manchester Guardian* reported: "Today, János Kádár ... even in free elections, against other candidates, he would be certain to emerge the undisputed victor." The London *Observer* remarked in September 1983: "The ideas that sustained that revolt and were rejected by Kádár at that time, are precisely those that in recent years have been steadily put into operation by him. ... Kádár is now trusted and respected by most Hungarians and is as popular in the country as Tito was in Yugoslavia" (Lomax, 1984, p. 90).

János Kádár's regime became the *relative* best, and Kádár was celebrated as a master of effective compromise, a great pragmatist who masterminded the single possible *realpolitik* inside the Soviet bloc and in a bipolar world system, where Soviet domination over Central and Eastern Europe was accepted, and where this rule was at times manifested by military interventions against overly threatening deviations. Hungarian post-Stalinism became a new emerging model and a sort of alternative to Soviet-type socialism. Its full realization, however, came to naught with the Czechoslovak catastrophe of 1968.

Part II

Temporary success and terminal failure: the post-Stalinist decades–modernization, erosion, and collapse

The prospects of breaking loose from the periphery during the post-Stalinist order appeared promising. High accumulation, a rapid rate of growth, and the industrial breakthrough together with the decision to liberalize dictatorship and develop all-embracing welfare institutions and even in some instances modest consumer societies created a cohesive sense of security among the inhabitants (though certain countries complemented or replaced it with a policy of small-power nationalism). Would regimes that for the first time in the region's history had begun to close the gap with the West in terms of economic growth, social welfare, and consumption – would such regimes gain legitimacy?

A radical transformation in the world economy and its dramatic structural crisis soon put an end to the gap-closing process. In the new circumstances the genuine weakness of the import-substituting industrialization model and its insensitivity to international competition led to the erosion of previous economic and social achievements. State socialism proved incapable of adapting to the new technological and structural demands, and the region sank into a long economic – and political – crisis. Internal opposition increased, and the ruling elites lost their faith in the possibility of controlling the situation. When Soviet control ceased to be a factor, the dictatorship of modernization, identified largely with the huge demands it had placed upon the population, collapsed almost without resistance.

The separate path, the withdrawal from Europe that once promised an escape from the periphery, proved to be a dead end. The experimental flight that took off from the peripheries of Europe now landed back in the peripheries of Europe.

4   Post-Stalinist state socialism and its legitimization

"Our system is most frequently characterized as a . . . dictatorship of a bureaucracy over a society," noted Václav Havel, the outspoken dissident in the late seventies. "I am afraid that the term 'dictatorship' . . . tends to obscure rather than clarify the real nature of power in this system." In Havel's interpretation the regime differed from a classical dictatorship since it was part of an international community and possessed an effective mechanism, ideology, and some kind of revolutionary atmosphere. Moreover, it became a part of the world system in coexistence with the West. "What we have here," he continued, "is simply another form of the consumer and industrial society . . . .[T]he post-totalitarian system has been built on foundations laid by the historical encounter between dictatorship and the consumer society" (Havel, 1985, pp. 24, 27, 38).

In Havel's judgment, Central and Eastern European state socialism in the seventies was thus a special hybrid of a dictatorship and a "normal" industrial consumer society. Although reforms were cautious and limited, and revolts and revolutions were ruthlessly suppressed, they nonetheless challenged the regime, provoking unavoidable responses and gradually generating certain changes. A part of the regime's elite, which was deeply disappointed with and itself frightened by the irrationality of Stalinism, now sought, with a revitalized enthusiasm, to replace counterproductive Stalinism with a moderate and pragmatic policy to satisfy the people's interests and stabilize the regime.

As a consequence, and as a result of a permanent inner struggle between short-sighted hard-line conservatives and liberal reformers, Central and Eastern European state socialism changed and arrived at its post-Stalinist stage. The transformation, however, was rather gradual in time and uneven in space. The ambiguous New Course represented the period of transition to post-Stalinism, which became dominant after 1956.

It became impossible to return to the compromised and tragic first Stalinist decade. By the sixties, more sophisticated attempts were made to modernize the economy, increase consumption, improve living standards, and to consolidate and legitimize power. In some of the countries of the region, the regimes turned toward a sort of "enlightened absolutism" and carried out their modernization "missions" with a heavy hand, but sought to do so in a paternalistic manner by "giving" and "allowing" more to the people.

Describing post-Stalinism and its legitimization attempts, two limitations should be pointed to in advance. First of all, it is difficult to generalize about a period when Stalinist uniformity in policy, institutions, and even regarding military uniforms, began to disappear. The national roads were vastly different, the various reforms had dissimilar impacts, and de-Stalinization reached distinct levels in the different countries.

Indeed, the countries under discussion should be divided into three groups. While certain countries such as Yugoslavia, Poland, and Hungary reacted in more flexible ways, going through a number of stages of reform and drawing the furthest away from genuine Stalinism, others such as Albania and Romania remained almost frozen in a little changed "fossilized" Stalinism. Czechoslovakia, both in the early sixties and throughout the abnormal "normalization" period from the early seventies on, was basically somewhere in between these two groups, as was Bulgaria

Secondly, the transformation from Stalinism to post-Stalinism was not entirely an internal affair in these various countries. It was an aborted creature of the post-Stalin Soviet leadership, which both encouraged and limited reforms. Initiation and limitation sprang from the same sources. If de-Stalinization, which was initially imposed by the Malenkov and Khrushchev regimes, subsequently gained momentum in one of the bloc countries, it was the Soviet party and army that signaled the limitations. De-Stalinization and reforms were not allowed to go beyond a certain point, and the satellite party-states had to learn that lesson from "brotherly warnings," brutal political pressure, and, if needed, military intervention. Moreover, it was not only the top party leadership which received Soviet warnings. A large apparatus was in place that gave signals to everyone concerned.[1]

---

[1] It pays to recall a small personal experience. In 1975, a dramatic Central Committee session debated the impact of the oil crisis and what economic strategy to follow in Hungary during the next Five-Year Plan period. I was the rector of Karl Marx University of Economics in Budapest at that time, and was invited to the session as a guest and participated in the debate. When one of the members of the Central Committee argued that Hungary should turn her back on the West since the "Capitalist world market gave us a slap on the face," and urged for a new isolation in the Comecon framework, I took the floor and rejected his conclusion, arguing that the "Soviet market gave us an equal slap on the face," and noted the departure from the previous successful reform line.

On the next day I received a telephone call from the Soviet Embassy, and two officials, Musatov and Rozanov, both fluent in Hungarian, asked for an appointment and came in a few days "to talk" about my intervention and views. They were polite, they did not accuse or warn, but clearly intended to communicate that they were watching.

Additionally, in a bipolar world system, the West virtually recognized Central and Eastern Europe as a Soviet sphere of interest. There were no outside forces to turn to. The governments of the region had to reckon with this situation and search for effective compromises. They had to serve the Soviet oppressor and try to use the narrow playground that remained to them. This situation, however, was not unknown in the region. Most of the countries had suffered similar conditions in the nineteenth century as well. Poland and Hungary had had to respect unquestionable Russian and Habsburg domination respectively, which became their historical destinies after the suppression of heroic struggles for independence (in 1848–9 in Hungary, and in 1830–1 and 1863–4 in Poland). Between the 1860s and 1910s the Poles turned to the "organic work" of modernization. The Hungarians made their compromise with the bloody-handed emperor and introduced major reforms, built up a modern educational system, a dense railroad network, tripled agricultural output, and began to industrialize. Accepting foreign rule, compromising and collaborating with the oppressor (in a guaranteed world system), achieving whatever development was possible under the circumstances – this was the *Realpolitik* of the decades following the 1860s[2] as well as the 1960s in Central and Eastern Europe.

Ideological and political corrections

After the failure of Stalinist ideology, which strongly contributed to the horrors of the early fifties and the massive resistance in 1956, one of the most characteristic and visible features of post-Stalinism was an ideological correction and, in some countries, an attempt to de-ideologize the system.

Post-Stalinism actually began with an ideological purification: to restore "genuine Leninism" and eradicate mistaken Stalinist theses. The initiative was made by the 20th and 22nd Soviet party congresses. The most important "theoretical" change was the rejection of the two pillars of Stalinist ideology: the concept of the permanent sharpening of class struggle after the communist seizure of power and its extension to the international arena, as well as the theory of an unavoidable war between the imperialist and socialist worlds. These two theses had served as a justification for terror and permanent purges. This was also the theoretical basis for the class struggle in the countryside, the infamous and brutal

---

[2] József Eötvös, leading liberal reformer of mid nineteenth-century Hungary, clearly recognized this when he noted in his diary in August 1870: "Today we cannot serve the goal of national independence. The given situation of the nation ... requires us to postpone the issue of political progress and concentrate all of our efforts to develop the material and intellectual standards of our country" (Eötvös, 1978, p. 373).

'de-kulakization,' which created a civil war atmosphere in the early fifties. But it also served to justify the tremendous sacrifices imposed on the people in preparation of an unavoidable World War III.

The basic elements of the ideological foundations remained unchanged. Leninism was in its systematic, ideological form the creator of Stalinism, and the departure from the most notorious Stalinist theses strengthened a more pragmatic approach to reality. Rational economic and foreign policy considerations had not replaced the previous ideological drive, and were combined with them to make policy more reliable. Ideological consideration thus made it possible to reconsider peasant policy, economic policy, as well as foreign policy directives. Overturning the concept of a sharpening class struggle had widespread consequences in everyday life. Compulsory vigilance, the searching for enemies, and show trials disappeared. "Socialist legality" acquired a principal importance and replaced an uncontrolled, "revolutionary" police terror. Post-Stalinism was thus a kind of general moderation of the regime.

De-Stalinization, however, stopped half way in most of the countries of the region. The regime remained strongly ideological, and ideology continued to serve as a basis of judgment for "adequate" or "mistaken" policies in one or another bloc country. Stalinist hard-liners could and were always ready to use this fact in defending their interests and position, and could always rely on "brotherly international help" of fellow hard-liners in some of the other countries. Brezhnev and Suslov's Soviet Union, Ulbricht and Honecker's East Germany, Husák (1979) and Bilak's (1980) Czechoslovakia, Hoxha's (1980) Albania, and Ceauşescu's (1981) Romania remained bases for orthodox Stalinism, and often criticized attempts to create a more consistent post-Stalinist socialism in reform-oriented Poland, Yugoslavia, and Hungary. Left-over Stalinism thus had a devastating impact on all of the countries, halting the undisturbed de-Stalinization process and strengthening hard-line groups in the reforming countries. The post-Stalinist systems, themselves preserving basic elements of traditional ideology, were thus inconsistent and fragile.

The reform-oriented countries, which were unable to rid themselves of obsolete ideological baggage because of both external limitations and internal resistance, turned toward deliberate de-ideologization. In post-Stalinist Poland, Hungary, and Yugoslavia, the party gave up previous efforts to control and influence people's private lives and way of thinking. The party-state no longer attempted to brainwash the population, and instead sought to de-politicize its citizens. The party no longer required an absolute ideological-political loyalty and welcomed passive acceptance. New pragmatism had even greater importance than ideological correctness.

Since ideology was an indispensable element of the Stalinist regime and was a basic legitimizing factor, its significant weakening had far-reaching consequences. As Tocqueville recognized, the stability of a dictatorship requires conviction in an ideology. Once a dictatorship gives up this premiss, it becomes more fragile and must then change and attempt to find new legitimizing factors.

The most radical de-Stalinizing countries, Yugoslavia, Poland, and Hungary, made impressive advances in building up their post-Stalinist systems in the sixties and seventies. In the political arena, a marked liberalization tempered the regimes. Legality was strengthened and new constitutions guaranteed certain freedoms and human rights. The new Polish constitution of February 1976 declared that the police were required to get a court order before making arrests, and could not keep people in detention for more than forty-eight hours. The Yugoslav constitution of 1974 guaranteed the freedom of art and science. The Hungarian Socialist Workers' Party abolished the so-called class categorization of students, which had excluded "class alien" young people from universities, and a 1963 regulation stipulated that acceptance be based entirely on school records.

One of the most important changes was the agreement of the Polish party-state with the Roman Catholic Church in December 1956. Freedom of religion was granted, and a strong, free, and active church, with its own newspapers and publishers, and, with its role in organizing communal and social life, created the most important element of a kind of pluralism. (Szajkowski, 1983; Monticone, 1986). Hungary also renounced its hostility toward the church, and had reached agreement with the Vatican by the sixties. The free and undisturbed existence and activity of an institution that was openly anti-Marxist significantly contributed to the realization of freedom of thought and conviction.

Political consolidation was attempted by abolishing class and political discrimination. The especially hostile handling of "kulaks" was halted. Party membership was no longer a prerequisite to attain high state position, declared the Hungarian government in the sixties. Uncommitted "sins" were generally not punished. The party-state no longer required a pro-party alignment, and people could now shed all pretence of such sympathies. Although political dissidents and the intellectual and ideological opposition were carefully monitored, repressed, and punished, it was no longer the case that even active opponents of the regime were subject to torture, long imprisonment, and execution. Dissidents were sometimes imprisoned, more often dismissed from their jobs and as a rule not allowed to travel, but in most de-Stalinized countries they remained free and maintained some kind of existence. If one kept away from opposition politics and did not openly attack certain basic taboos, but visibly separated oneself from the party-state and searched for an asylum in the "second society," one did not have to fear repression.

Fear did not penetrate everyday life in post-Stalinist Yugoslavia, in Poland after 1956, or in Hungary from the mid sixties on. If, as Montesquieu clearly recognized, fear is the essence of despotism, the disappearance of, or at least a significant diminution in, fear was both a sign and an initiator of substantial changes.

International relations were also rebuilt and normalized. The countries were opened to Western tourists and visitors. Correspondence with Western friends, relatives, and colleagues in these three countries became widespread and no longer dangerous. Freedom of travel was assured for the citizens of Yugoslavia, where even work permits were issued for jobs in the West. Poland guaranteed freedom of travel from the late fifties and Hungary from the early sixties on. Major Western foundations offered grants, and citizens of de-Stalinized countries were allowed to accept them and spent longer periods at prominent universities in the United States or other countries. Western journals became available, and the broadcasts of Radio Free Europe and the Voice of America were no longer jammed. Even local news and journals provided more and more objective information on the world. Previous strict cultural and economic isolation of the closed societies was substantially reduced.

Political power was "secularized," and the party withdrew by separating the party from state leadership. The symbolic division of the previous unity of the posts of party boss and prime minister was intended to express a division of labor between party and government. The separation of legislative and executive power and the courts was not reestablished, and political power in the one-party system remained unchallenged. The supremacy of the party leadership at national and even at county and city levels remained unchanged. Direct party intervention, however, gradually weakened at lower levels. The first person in command in a state-owned firm or institution became the director, appointed by the state and not the party secretary. Moreover, the party itself was modernized, and uneducated party bureaucrats were replaced more and more by university graduates.

Yugoslavia, Poland, and gradually Hungary had thus become markedly different though the previous structures of absolute power were preserved (Rothschild, 1989). The reforms were more or less flexible reactions to genuine mass dissatisfaction, but basically remained mere policy changes within the existing political frameworks. Post-Stalinist regimes tended toward reforms, but their limitations were strictly defined. In critical situations they easily and automatically reverted to their old dictatorial practices. Freedom of travel was allowed; however, when the party-state bureaucracy deemed it politically necessary, the right to travel was immediately withdrawn from some citizens.

The permanently emphasized and celebrated "socialist legality" did not mean the abolition of party-state control over the legal system. The courts did not become independent, and the possibility of party interference survived and remained a hidden practice. A sort of indemnity for higher level party functionaries continued. It was personally and politically decided how to handle dissidents. Political considerations defined the need for arrest and the extent of punishment in political cases. Corruption and serious traffic violations (including fatal accidents) were overlooked in the case of high-ranking functionaries who, in the worst cases, were demoted to a lesser position. The subordination of law and the courts to state-party decisions endured in a basically unchanged political-institutional structure. Similarly, the more marked separation of party and state occurred without institutional guarantees, since the veto power of the party and the institution of the nomenclatura continued to exist, and the state-party preserved its overwhelming power to control appointments. In other words, all the basic elements and institutions survived Stalin and characterized the genuine post-Stalinist regimes virtually until the very end. But, except in extraordinary situations, the post-Stalinist party leadership did not attempt to use the existing weapons that were an innate part of the system's structures.

Some reforms, nevertheless, went beyond the existing structures and slightly modified them. The rejection of collectivization in agriculture and the reestablishment of free private peasant farming in Yugoslavia and Poland were of major institutional importance. These changes even had political importance since a much less controllable peasantry was created, which certainly contributed to the loosening of the party's hold on power. The system of workers' self-management in Yugoslavia, and its partial subsequent introduction in the industrial sphere in Hungary and Poland, for example, certainly broke the structural consistency of a centralized economic system and weakened the political dictatorship. The abolition of the compulsory delivery system, the ultimate "legal" basis of abusing and harassing the peasant population in the fifties, followed by the abolition of central planning in general in Yugoslavia and Hungary, and much later in Poland, represented important structural and institutional changes. Private business gained some ground and market elements broke the consistency of strict central planning and state ownership. The Polish and Yugoslav peasant farms, the Hungarian private plots, the private leasing of some state-owned shops and the small private hotels on the Yugoslav seashore and at Lake Balaton in Hungary, all represented forms of institutional changes.

Thus, compared to its previous Stalinist counterpart, the post-Stalinist system was corrected and modified, but the old structures were not destroyed.

Modernized economic policy and consumerism

Among its most important characteristics, a revised and much more pragmatic economic policy and an impressively altered strategy of favoring increased consumerism played a distinctive role in post-Stalinism. The orthodox Stalinist economic policy was substantially revised from the late fifties on. The regime continued to realize its "modernization mission," and rapid industrialization remained the nucleus of economic policy. The speed of forced industrialization, however, was slowed down in order to decrease forced capital accumulation and investments, and provide a bigger piece of the pie to the populace. Capital accumulation of 25–35 percent of the GDP in the early fifties was moderated to 20–25 percent from the sixties on. Capital formation and investments still remained high, but the consumption share of the population substantially increased. A new, central emphasis was given to a continuous increase in the standard of living.

This policy, however, permanently clashed with the still ambitious industrialization goals, especially since the system preserved its tendency to foster self-generating investment drives that often led to "over-heating" the economy. The "investment-cycles" of state socialism limited the increase in consumption and provoked frequent central interventions to ease tensions and cool down the economies. Consumption, however, sharply increased from the late fifties on, and this trend continued in the mid eighties.

Another major element of economic change was a deliberate shift from the Stalinist structural policy toward a more modern developmental trend. Overambitious industrial investments (approaching half of national investments) were decreased by, in some cases, one-third, and the previously neglected agriculture and infrastructure received more. Agricultural investments reached about 20 percent and contributed to major mechanization and chemicalization of production, which led to increased productivity and yield, and higher per capita production. Investments in services and infrastructure jumped, from the previous one-third, to half of total investments, and this accounted for better housing and better developed transportation and communications.

The structural policy of industrialization was also revised. The Stalinist industrialization pattern, based on the most extreme preferences for coal, iron, steel, and some branches of traditional engineering, and which received 75–90 percent of industrial investment during the first Five Year Plan in the various countries of the region, was essentially decreased. The previously favored production of strategic products, linked with the emphasis on war preparation, was slowed down, and a central project to develop the previously neglected chemical industry became the most favored child of post-Stalinist industrialization. A structural reorientation was also expressed by the introduction of modern engineering sectors, such as automobile production and electronic industries.

While the Stalinist industrialization pattern was based on the turn-of-the-century Western structural model of industry, the new orientation from the 1960s on attempted to draw lessons from the development trends of the advanced West (Berend, 1983).

Stalinist industrialization, furthermore, was based on an isolationist strategy and on an autarkic national economy. Of course, self-sufficiency was impossible in the relatively small Central and Eastern European countries, but a kind of "processing self-sufficiency" was attempted, whereas energy and raw material imports from the Soviet Union were assured by bilateral agreements. This concept, however, was revised in the late 1950s when Nikita Khrushchev initiated a planned division of labor among the bloc countries. The Council of Mutual Economic Aid, which provided a framework for the bilateral agreements, began to organize cooperation. The real turning point occurred in May 1956, at the Berlin session of the organization. The member countries decided on the construction of a commonly financed oil pipeline and a joint electric energy network. From the late fifties on, the central apparatus of Comecon worked on suggestions from the member countries to specialize their production and produce certain products, for the whole "Socialist common market." In engineering, the member countries agreed on the production of hundreds and thousands of products, and certain countries acquired a monopoly in the production of some products. Hungary, for example, agreed to produce 228 different types of machines, and was given the monopoly in the production for forty-eight types. Czechoslovakia and the Soviet Union became monopoly producers of certain types of trucks, Romania produced diesel locomotives for a broader Comecon market, and Bulgaria won the right to supply the member countries with certain types of computers. According to the arrangement, Hungary halted production of 3–5 ton trucks and of 5–7.5 ton special vehicles, and also stopped production of different types of agricultural machinery and freight-cars, but received a monopoly to produce buses supplying the entire Comecon. On this basis the Hungarian Ikarus Company built up a series of 12,000 buses per year and became the worlds sixth largest producer with nearly 6 percent of the world production.

Comecon's Standing Committee for the Chemical Industry initiated long-run development programs and coordination for the member countries in December 1957. On this basis all of the member countries began a rapid, coordinated investment and development program.

Although Comecon made an attempt toward modern cooperation, the program was built on bureaucratic central planning. Khrushchev in the early sixties suggested the introduction of a common Comecon plan, with a central Comecon planning office. The initiative generated, however, strong resistance because of the immense danger of direct Soviet interference into domestic economic affairs, and the proposal was dropped. In the end, multilateral agreements influenced only a marginal part (3–6 percent) of the production of some sectors, such as the engineering and chemical industries of the member countries. Still, the new projects represented a partially successful attempt at modernization. The lower rate of capital accumulation and investment, and the slower pace of economic growth, produced a more balanced development without causing a dramatic decline in other sectors of the economy nor concomitant shortages and social tensions, and led to more reliable supply and higher consumption. In the more reform-oriented countries better services and supply was brought about by a more liberal policy toward small-scale private business: "Small-scale industry is a stable element of the national economy," was the view in Poland in 1977, "it serves better the satisfaction of the population's needs in services" (Karta, 1977, p. 48).

A new consumerism became one of the key elements of post-Stalinist Central and Eastern Europe. The shortage of food disappeared in Yugoslavia and Hungary, where supply eventually became abundant, and Czechoslovakia and Bulgaria were also assured of a better supply. People became much better dressed throughout the region. The image of an almost uniform, shabbily dressed populace disappeared. Foreigners admired the elegance of Polish women in the streets of Warsaw. The import of high-quality Western consumer goods, including certain durables and even cars, the introduction of a free market in housing and construction, the appearance of private family houses meeting Western standards in the Rózsadomb district of Budapest and two or three-story homes in Polish and Hungarian villages and on the Yugoslav seashore, all revealed a conspicuous consumer orientation that made Hungary, Yugoslavia, and to a certain extent Poland, exceptional in Central and Eastern Europe. Some elements of this policy, though in a much more limited and less spectacular way, appeared in Czechoslovakia and Bulgaria as well. The possibility of creating even a limited "socialist consumer society," however, was basically excluded in most countries of the region.

The mechanization of households, practically unknown by that time, began in the early sixties: washing machines, refrigerators, television sets and other electric appliances became common in the region at a time when car ownership reached new heights in Czechoslovakia, Yugoslavia, Hungary, and Poland. Although development programs that continuously limited consumption and living standards had a preference in governmental policy, the severe shortages of consumption goods, the rationing of basic food items, and sharply declining real wages that uniformly characterized the 1950s disappeared or significantly diminished in post-Stalinist Central and Eastern Europe, with the exception of the "fossil Stalinist" states of Albania and Romania.

Social policy and the consumption of social services

Since the shortage economy was the essence of central planning and ambitious industrialization, even the consumer-oriented post-Stalinist countries had their strict limitations, and consumerism remained a poor imitation of the Western variety.

There was, however, a major field where post-Stalinist regimes became highly competitive and where consumption reached a high international standard: the consumption of social services. On an orthodox ideological basis Stalinism scored important achievements in social policy. Several major steps were made to broaden social insurance and build up a premature welfare system in the early fifties. The Stalinist dictatorship and its violent class policy, however, openly discriminated against large numbers of the population. The private peasantry, still the greatest part of the population in most of the countries, was excluded from most of the welfare measures. Discrimination affected small-scale businessmen and in certain respects even intellectuals, let alone "alien" class elements and their children. The "attentive" state thus sought to protect and assist only a minority of the population. Moreover, governmental care was drastically counterbalanced by oppression, police terror, and brutality.

Social policy, the building of a consistent social safety net and, given the economic standards of the countries, a premature welfare system became prevalent during the post-Stalinist decades. Social policy measures were nationwide and applied to all citizens. Egregious discrimination against significant layers of society disappeared.

Among the most important social services, the introduction of a general pension policy deserves to be mentioned first. A pension was a special and rare privilege in the region. Postwar legislation in the state socialist countries introduced old-age pensions, first for workers and employees of state-owned firms, and then for peasants and self-employed citizens, in effect making pensions a general right based on citizenship. In Poland the first step was made in 1946, and private handicraft self-employed workers were included in 1965. The system became complete in 1978 when independent farmers acquired the right as well. A pension was assured at the ages of sixty-five and sixty respectively for men and women after twenty-five and twenty years of work. In the mid eighties more than six million people, roughly 18 percent of the population, received a pension, and one million of them were former independent farmers.

In Czechoslovakia, a national retirement system was introduced in 1948. Peasants and members of collective farms were included in 1975, and a pension was guaranteed after twenty-five years of work and at the ages of sixty and fifty-seven for men and women respectively (additionally, the age limit for women was decreased by one year for each child). The pension was calculated on the basis of one's average salary and years in service. In the mid eighties peasant pensions were on average one third, and those of private self-employers one half, less than those of workers and employees in state-owned firms.

In Hungary, old-age pensions were introduced for workers and employees in 1950, and the system was enlarged in 1958 by including the members of cooperative farms and industrial cooperatives. Private merchants and the handicraft self-employed also acquired the right in 1962, but they received a much lower rate, and the policy was equalized for all citizens only in 1982.

A pension was granted at the ages of sixty and fifty-five for men and women respectively. In the mid eighties 22 percent of the Hungarian population was retired.

Similar retirement policies were adopted in Romania and Bulgaria, though retirement age was different and only 14 percent of the Romanian and almost 25 percent of the Bulgarian population was pensioned in the mid eighties. The latter figure was uniquely high since "old-age" pensions were granted between the ages of forty-five and sixty, depending on the job, and women retired five years earlier than men. A similar low retirement age, between fifty and sixty for men and forty-five to fifty-five for women, existed in Albania as well.

Hence, wages being genuinely low, the average pensions (mostly 50 percent to 70 percent of previous wages) assured only a rather meagre existence but undoubtedly offered some kind of basic security level for the entire population. This was even more so, given the fact that free medical insurance was also introduced into the area.

As with the retirement policy, the government gradually enrolled the entire population into a medical insurance system that became a citizen's right from the seventies on. In countries where only about a third of the population had medical insurance before World War II, and where postwar industrialization was accompanied by long-lasting neglect of the infrastructure, the expansion of medical services went hand in hand with a decline in quality. Basic services, however, were granted. Sick pay was assured, in most cases, for one year, and with certain illnesses (tuberculosis) even two, and an early disability retirement was granted if one could not go back to work.

The increased free medical services may be illustrated by three internationally comparable parameters: the number of medical doctors and hospital beds per 10,000 inhabitants, and the rate of infant mortality. In 1950, there were roughly nine to ten medical doctors per 10,000 inhabitants in the Central and Eastern European countries (with the exception of Poland, where this number was less than five). In the mid 1980s Czechoslovakia, Hungary, and Bulgaria had thirty-one to thirty-five, Poland twenty-nine, and Yugoslavia and Romania twenty doctors per 10,000 people; thus the level increased, in most cases, by three times. Additionally, in 1950, the Central and Eastern European figures represented only about half of the West German standard, whereas in the mid eighties three or four countries of the region achieved the West German level.

The number of hospital beds per 10,000 inhabitants increased from the mid sixties on, and the highest level was reached in Czechoslovakia in 1984, whose 101 hospital beds was barely behind the West German level (111 beds). Hungary, Bulgaria, and Romania followed with nearly ninety beds, whereas Poland had only seventy and Yugoslavia's level reached only half of the Czechoslovak one.

Infant mortality, an important index of health care, drastically declined: in 1950, 78–117 from each 1,000 newly born babies died in the first year of life in the region (the best and worst levels applied to Czechoslovakia and Romania respectively). By the mid 1980s, the number had declined to fifteen to twenty-three deaths, thus to one quarter to one fifth of the previous level (whereas the best and worst cases remained unchanged) (Schönfelder, 1987).

Social services had a rather broad range. Families received a fixed amount (or percentage) of child support (per child), and a contribution to meals in company cafeterias. During the seventies, Hungary pioneered the introduction of a singularly long maternity leave, granting three years leave for mothers with each newly born child, and paying a full salary for the first six months followed by a part of the salary thereafter. Maternity leave existed in one form or another in all of the countries of the region. In Yugoslavia, after paid leave, shorter working hours were guaranteed for child care. In Albania, mothers could take 180 days of maternity leave with 80 percent of their salaries.

A pre-school system was developed and, in the most socially oriented countries, it had the resources to enroll nearly the entire pre-school population between three and six years of age. The state, trade unions, and state-owned firms and institutions possessed a huge network of resorts and guaranteed one to two week vacations for a nominal fee. A person's paid vacation in Yugoslavia, for example, which was very similar to the other countries, varied, depending on the number of years of work, at between eighteen and thirty-six days. The population also enjoyed a great variety of subsidies, free or very inexpensive pharmaceutical products, heavily subsidized transport charges and rents, etc.

The post-Stalinist countries thus established a relatively high level of various social services as an important component of their welfare orientation. Hungary, which led this trend after 1956 and especially after the introduction of her economic reforms in the mid to late sixties, clearly manifested an advanced version of this policy. In 1960 she spent, for example, 6.6 percent of GDP on social insurance, but in 1983 this increased to 15.4 percent, surpassing the level of the OECD countries.

Hungary was the twentieth among the European countries regarding per capita GDP, but twelfth in social insurance spending. Hungary's 15.4 percent expenditure of her GDP for social insurance was two times higher in percentage terms than of Portugal, and surpassed the relative expenditure level of the United States (8.4 percent), Canada (12.6 percent), Great Britain (13.3 percent), and Spain and Finland (14.4 percent).

Social insurance expenditures continued to increase in Hungary during the eighties and, compared to the 3.6 percent in 1950, reached nearly one fifth of her GDP by 1990. The premature welfare system in the relatively poor countries of Central and Eastern Europe was often deformed and offered sub-standard services. Polish hospitals, especially in the eighties, could not afford to buy modern Western equipment, and even small, inexpensive appliances such as single-usage injection syringes were absent; 15–20 percent of the hospital patients got infections. In the winter of 1984–5, according to Polish reports, half of officially registered medicines were not available and half of the operations were postponed. A total banning of imports in Romania by the late seventies hindered the import of insulin and other basic medicines. "Old people were excluded from medical services," summarized Bruno Schönfelder, who conducted interviews with Romanians on the severe restrictions, "but in spite of these kinds of 'thrifty' measures ... it was normal that patients with heart-attacks were not hospitalized and two patients shared a bed" (Schönfelder, 1987, p. 115). In 1986, the periodical *Donauschwabe* described the infamous state, later publicized world-wide, of the Romanian orphanages and wards for mentally disabled children, where, in a small room of eight square meters, forty children from the ages of two to eight, were jammed on top of each other, partly dressed or naked, like small animals.

In spite of the pronounced welfare orientation of some of the post-Stalinist countries, the availability of the often free social services was not uniform. The governments were unable to properly finance a comprehensive welfare system, and the dramatic decline in services was counterbalanced by illegal payments for better care, a hospital bed, or cheap accommodations in a union-owned resort.

The research on the compromised "free" medical services and the "deliberate" fees paid for them in Hungary reveals that unofficial fees for an operation increased by five times between 1975 and 1985, and were close to an average monthly income in the mid eighties.

With all its shortcomings and distortions, however, the various welfare measures of the post-Stalinist countries assured, without discrimination, basic services for the entire population and offered at least minimal assistance. It produced a higher standard of consumption of social services than in countries with similar or even somewhat higher levels of economic development. A premature welfare system became a significant characteristic of paternalistic post-Stalinist regimes.

Evaporating "socialist–realism": liberalized cultural policy

A distinctive feature of post-Stalinism was a somewhat liberated cultural and art policy. Changes in Yugoslavia, Poland, and Hungary were dramatic. Publication of several previously banned or recently neglected works was allowed. Dostoevski, Kafka and Freud, Ionesco, Italo Calvino, and Tennessee Williams were tolerated and published. A separate literary monthly, *Nagyvilág* (Entire Word), published contemporary Western novels and literature in Hungary from the 1960s on. Theater and music life began to be transformed, and previously outlawed plays or "formalist" composers were performed. The exhibition of explicitly non-"Socialist Realist," and as non-figurative paintings now became increasingly possible. The programs of theaters, operas, and concert halls began to resemble their Western counterparts. Movie theaters and television companies often screened Western films. The "Beatles revolution" and rock music generally made a gradual breakthrough.

The liberalization of life in Hungary was rather symptomatic. After many years of denunciations of "decadent" Western music and dance, and after an unceasing effort to replace it with folk-dance movements, collective singing of folk-songs and old protest songs from the labor movement, the cultural policy changed in 1960–1. The official party daily, changing its condemning tone and ending its practice of dictating the type of music the public should hear, pragmatically acquiesced to popular demand in this regard. Within a few years, by the mid sixties, the state television channel began to organize annual music festivals based on popular vote.

The Beatles found their way to Hungary relatively easily in a single decade: they reached the height of their success in the 1960s. Rock music was adopted in Hungary in 1963 and performed openly in 1966. The 1968 music festival on Hungarian TV represented its full acceptance: all awards were given to the first Hungarian rock group, "The Illés'." Instead of trying to impose a presumably "ideologically correct" music, the regime renounced its ambitions to politicize music and adjusted itself to popular taste.

Although black lists of literary and artistic (as well as scholarly) works did not disappear even in the less repressive post-Stalinist countries, they were significantly shortened and mostly contained works considered "anti-Soviet" or explicitly "hostile" to communist ideals. Music and paintings belonged to the most de-politicized fields of the arts.

Science and art policy revealed similar features. In Hungary, Poland, and Yugoslavia, "freedom of research" was declared to be also valid for the social sciences and the humanities. In the latter fields, however, as a *contradictio in adiecto*, freedom of publication remained limited and under strict controls. Sometimes, however, even strongly critical works were allowed to be published. Sociology, psychology, genetics, computer sciences and other scholarly disciplines, previously condemned and banned as "bourgeois sciences," were formally recognized and restored to university life.

As Stalinist cultural policy had been characterized by the forced introduction of "socialist-realism," one of the most spectacular signs of change was its dismantling. In some countries socialist realism was denounced and eliminated, while in others its interpretation was so radically broadened that it was for all intents and purposes eradicated as well. In strongly de-Stalinized countries of the region, artists boldly threw off the strait-jacket of dictated art.

Yugoslavia and Poland officially declared socialist-realism a mistaken art trend and state policy, which, as was declared already at the congress of Polish artists in 1954, led to a decline in artistic works between 1949 and 1953. The "Arsenal" exhibition in Poland in 1955 was the first in Central and Eastern Europe that went beyond realism. Between 1956 and 1958 virtually any sort of censorship and state direction vanished. *Przeglad Artytyczny*, the new artistic periodical, denounced socialist-realism in its first editorial in 1957 as "decadent naturalism of a declarative, schematic art" (Wojciechowski, 1957, p. 4). Although not without renewed attacks against triumphant modernism in the sixties, Polish art became the most free and independent art in the entire region by the seventies. Abstraction, constructive non-figurative art, expressionist "deformation," surrealism, pop-art, and neo-Dada trends dominated the Polish art scene. Moreover, they continued to be dominant under the military-party regime in the eighties as well, when artists boycotted official exhibitions and exhibited in churches from 1982 on. Within a few years, in the framework of the conciliatory attempt of the Jaruzelski regime, contemporary modern art returned to its proper place. In the fall of 1986 the National Museum of Warsaw organized the first "deterrent" exhibition of the "Faces of Socialist-Realism."

In most of the other countries, particularly in Hungary and Czechoslovakia, a reformed post-socialist-realism became a sort of official trend by the mid fifties on. "Classical" socialist-realism was amalgamated with cautious post-impressionism, and twentieth-century modernism was recognized. Tivadar Csontváry and Lajos Vajda, together with the early twentieth-century Hungarian revolutionary avant-garde, were returned to their former position in museums.

Kvetoslav Chvatic attempted to prove that Czechoslovak abstract painting belonged to the progressive tradition. In that typically transitory stage of post-socialist realism in 1960, Jiři Hendrych, secretary of ideology in the Czechoslovak party, sharply attacked non-figurative art for "abandoning real life," for being "formalist and alien from life," and for not wanting to present "the beauty of the socialist life and enrich the life of the people" (Hendrych, 1960, p. 433). The Slovak party chief Jozef Lenárt, in his speech at the Central Committee of the Slovak Communist Party in May 1959, continued to speak about the role of culture and art in educating the masses "to overcome the remnants of capitalism in the masses' consciousness, and to affect and re-educate the working class on a Marxist-Leninist basis" (Lenárt, 1980, p. 47). In December 1963, however, Vladimir Koucky officially stated at the party congress that the party and government guarantee the right of free expression. The Czech surrealists and abstract artists then began to exhibit their work, and direct party control virtually faded in the late sixties.

The situation worsened decidedly after 1968, and particularly from 1972–6 when Vasil Bilak denounced "ideological diversion," rehabilitated socialist realism and insisted on "understandable" work. Gustáv Husák, in his report at the 16th party congress in May 1981, stressed the "social role of the arts . . . to reinforce in citizens an active attitude towards the ideals of socialism. . . . We support . . . artistic creativity inspired by a party-based *ésprit de corps* . . . [and] aid the creative strength of socialist realism in all of its expressive richness" (Husák, 1981, p. 39).

Czechoslovak literature was strictly controlled. The fine arts, however, were not pushed back to the fifties. A typical post-socialist-realist art prevailed with its post-impressionist, and at times expressionist, elements, and from the late seventies on even modernists could exhibit. In the eighties the neo-avant-garde again found its place in public exhibitions.

A post-socialist-realism became the characteristic art trend even in the non-reforming countries such as Romania, where the Central Committee had also denounced the previous Stalinist art trend as "simplistic, tasteless and gray naturalism," and declared a need for a modernization of socialist-realism (Lazar, 1956, p. 2). However, at the same time it warned of the "danger" of preferring artistic quality over content.

A substantial broadening of the concept of socialist-realism, however, attempted to identify socialist art with a sort of eternal grand art, and the great Romanian avant-garde sculptor Brancusi was lifted into the progressive realm of Romanian socialist-realism. The expressive style of post-impressionism was recognized, but the non-figurative, contemporary Western trends did not appear in the country. A strong central direction was preserved as a clear expression of one of the most dictatorial, quasi-Stalinist party-state systems in the region, and mandatory "representative" paintings of the "great leader," Ceauşescu, continued.

In a speech at the General Assembly of writers in 1968, Ceauşescu clearly stated that party direction and control would be continued, and that literary associations and publishers "must encourage [writers, poets and playwrights] to focus on major socialist topics and express the socialist goals and ideals. . . . Unions' leaders [have to] direct creative work and organize large-scale ideological debates among writers . . ." (Ceauşescu, 1968, pp. 26–7).

Unlike Romania, where post-socialist-realism stagnated in its first stage, or Czechoslovakia, where the post-1968 Husák era reintroduced more stringent party control, Hungary followed a rather different path. The first non-figurative exhibitions in 1957 were, indeed, succeeded by typical post-socialist-realist hybrids, but artistic freedom gradually strengthened; although authoritative, the rather tolerant art-policy of György Aczél gradually led to the incorporation of modern, contemporary art trends into the artistic life of Hungary.

Aesthetic values were recognized in post-Stalinist art policy, and rigid naturalism and Soviet-type socialist-realism were partly or entirely eliminated. Art was no longer a servant of politics and ideology, responsible for re-educating and mobilizing a new "socialist type" of people, and increasingly regained its genuine values and traditional roles.

From Central and Eastern European post-socialist-realism, a direct passage was opened in Poland, Yugoslavia, and Hungary towards Western post-modernism. A coexistence of different styles and artistic trends became characteristic from the late seventies and eighties on.

Nationalism in the post-Stalinist era

Nationalism was an additional, peculiar characteristic of the post-Stalinist era. This statement requires explanation. In the first place, nationalism was not a post-Stalinist phenomenon, since Stalinism itself was strongly nationalistic. Marxist internationalism evolved into a cynical ideological weapon in the hands of Stalin (and his successors) both for continuing the Tsarist policy of, using Lenin's term, "internal colonization," as well as achieving expansionist goals of establishing and maintaining Soviet domination of the "brotherly socialist countries."

Quite ironically, the more nationalist the Soviet Union was, the more it struggled against "nationalism": i.e., against the national aims and emotions of those nations under her domination. National roads toward socialism, therefore, were not accepted and immediately suppressed; their representatives were ruthlessly purged, or, if that failed, excommunicated and expelled from the bloc. Stalinist nationalism thus would not tolerate satellite nationalism.

Consequently, in the Stalinist era, with the exception of Tito, who ran the risk of resisting the Soviets and succeeded, the newly established state socialist regimes did not follow a nationalist line. Paradoxically enough, in those countries that successfully resisted de-Stalinization and preserved their domestic Stalinism, the party leaders, in an attempt to consolidate and stabilize their regimes, played the nationalism card. The post-Stalinist era in some countries was thus characterized by a renaissance of, in some cases, extreme nationalism. (Liberalizing reforms and nationalism were rarely applied together, the exception being Yugoslavia, which combined the two.)

Nationalism was, of course, not only a substitute for liberalizing reforms, but a deeply rooted, "natural" trend in the region. Nationalism was a strong driving force from the early nineteenth century on. It emerged earlier in the region than the nations themselves, since the idea was imported from the West and became the major instrument of nation-building in a process that continued unabated throughout the entire century. The right of self-determination, inapplicable as it was in the region, created new conflicts after the Versailles treaty that culminated in wars, civil wars, pogroms, and Holocaust during the bloody years of World War II.

Liberation from the horror and pain of the war came, paradoxically, with the beginning of Soviet domination. The former conflicts were not resolved, but rather swept under the rug. State socialism itself, in most of the countries of the region, represented a new form of subordination and national humiliation. Consequently nationalism remained a powerful force, and served as an essential "wonder weapon" to overcome reluctance and opposition and convince and mobilize people. A champion of the national cause, a guarantor of national independence, and a warrior of national grandeur easily won nationwide acceptance and could legitimize his power.

This was the case with so-called national communism in Yugoslavia, but also with "national Stalinism," a most paradoxical phenomenon of the post-Stalinist period in Albania and Romania. But attaining national goals, that is, preserving or reestablishing national independence, did not only mean curbing or resisting Soviet domination; a revitalized small-nation nationalism in Central and Eastern Europe was naturally connected with domestic national issues as well.

In Yugoslavia, where his regime was a "legitimate child" of a heroic-revolutionary partisan war, Tito, a bold, uncompromising defender of independence against a most dangerous and overpowering Stalin, continued an everyday struggle under the banner of "Yugoslavism" to keep the "Yugo" (i.e., "Southern") Slav nations together and balance internal national conflicts by both suppressing separatist endeavors and reorganizing the country on a federal basis. The permanent danger of severe internal national confrontations, the specter of Serbian "centralism" and Croatian separatism, the gloomy memory of a devastating civil war, and the temporarily successful attempt to create a new, just, multi-national Yugoslavia, all served, together with reform and consumer orientation and democratization, to validate the legitimacy of Tito's regime.

In Romania, both Gheorghiu-Dej and Ceauşescu, while maneuvering toward national independence and the liberation of the country from Soviet domination, at the same time championed the cause of national "homogenization," systematically eradicating the multi-national character of the country through the Romanianization of Transylvania. The creation of a united Romanian nation through forced assimilation, the elimination of Hungarian schools and universities, the eradication of autonomy in Transylvania, and the granting of Jewish and German emigration from the country while simultaneously imposing the highest possible population growth (by strictly banning abortion and birth control) among ethnic Romanians, all clearly classified the regime as an agent of internal national goals. Nationalism, besides anti-Soviet maneuvering, had thus an internal effect in Romania as well. All this was accompanied with extreme and efficient nationalist propaganda laden with a romanticized Romanianism.

In addition, the classical Stalinist modernization strategy, with its potential for rapid industrialization and rise in the level of education as well as cultural homogenization, gained a new momentum in the nationalist regimes. Resistance to the Soviets and oppression of national minorities, combined with a promise of a spectacular national resurgence and modernization, created a consistent policy of eliminating traditional peripheral backwardness and "catching-up."

Small-nation nationalism openly appeared during the post-Stalinist era in several countries. Beside the most spectacular Romanian and Albanian cases, some elements of nationalist policy, especially in certain critical periods, were used in many other countries as well. This was the case in Poland in 1968, when a major intellectual revolt was suppressed by unleashing open anti-Semitism. A desperate Todor Zhivkov also often played the nationalism card: in the late sixties, the Institute of History of the Bulgarian Academy of Sciences was ordered to revitalize the "Macedonian question" against Yugoslavia. "The Macedonian Problem· Historical-Political Aspects" was published in 1968. The party revised its interwar position regarding the Macedonian right to self-determination, which resulted in a resurgence in Bulgarian–Yugoslav hostility. In 1984, the government initiated a campaign of national homogenization, aiming to assimilate the vast Turkish minority in the country, which included a forced "Bulgarization" of Turkish family names and official proclamations denying the existence of a Turkish minority in the country since "so-called" Turks were actually Islamized Bulgarians.

By unleashing nationalism, the state socialist regimes sought to exploit national sensitivities and present themselves as the authentic representatives of the national interest. Some orthodox regimes which neither liberalized politically nor assured even a modicum of human rights, and which were unable to introduce consumerism, did manage, by successfully adopting nationalist policies and producing visible results in enforcing it, to at least temporarily broaden their power base, some already from the fifties on, others basically by the sixties.

Czechoslovakia represented the exception among the non-reforming countries of Central and Eastern Europe, in that it could not play the nationalist card because of her geopolitical situation and (after 1968) the strong Soviet military presence. Poland, on the other hand, though a pioneer of political liberalization, could not cope with an almost permanent economic crisis nor offer effective consumerism. But the regime, with its most delicate geopolitical situation, was unable to initiate a nationalist line as well. In periods of imminent political danger, however, both regimes played the anti-Semitic nationalist card (Checinski, 1982; Institute, 1986; Schatz, 1991).

As a consequence of the substantial reforms in the de-Stalinizing, liberalizing countries, which decisively improved the quality of life, a new atmosphere of security among the people prepared the ground for attempts at legitimizing power. Those regimes which remained frozen in at least a semi-Stalinist state sought to achieve this with nationalism.

The legitimization of state socialism

There are very well-known stereotypes regarding the legitimacy of power in state socialism. Since communist power was forcibly seized, and indeed in most cases imposed on the countries by Soviet pressure based on military presence, state socialism in the region never gained legitimacy and was preserved only by brute force. One of the most extreme observations maintained that the Central and Eastern European regimes did not even seek legitimization: "if leaders have little need to pay attention to public opinion . . . and are not vulnerable to electoral defeat, why should they be concerned at their lack of legitimacy?"

Others differentiate between legitimacy and a sort of "consolidation" (Lewis, 1984, p. 3). Although a long period of social peace and apparent cooperation did exist between the population and the regime in post-Stalinist Hungary, this was not legitimacy, suggested István Lovas and Ken Anderson: "While a transition has been made from active to passive terror," the authors stated, "social control is maintained through an enforced consensus which is predicated upon the memory, the threat, and the institutionally preserved potential for a return to terror in its active phase" (Lovas and Anderson, 1984, p. 69).

Ferenc Fehér and Ágnes Heller held a different view, and emphasized that fear no longer led to consolidation in Kádár's Hungary, but that conformism, a "collective bribery of a nation," and "group or individual corruption" did. They, however, also distinguished between *consolidation* and *legitimization*, and excluded the possibility of the latter. In their view, which is quite widespread, legitimacy by definition may only be gained through free elections in a pluralistic system; thus the regime, they maintained, was "firmly consolidated but *not* legitimized" (Lewis, 1984, pp. 69–70, 96). One can reject the view that a regime does not need, nor seek, legitimization, and is instead content on relying on terror (or the memory of it). Legitimization, nevertheless, is indispensable even for dictatorial governments because it makes command and control much easier. Legitimizing power is not a mystical procedure but a rather practical one: the regime must be able to generate an atmosphere where its laws are not questioned by a populace that feels responsible for keeping them.

As one of the most authentic experts of the question, Max Weber, suggested in his *Wirtschaft und Gesellschaft* that there are no objective single norms nor one exclusive model of legitimizing power. Legitimacy is a faith in and an acceptance of existing power. If the people have an image of the legitimacy of power, then that power is "valid." In reality, the history of state socialism was that of a permanent struggle for legitimacy, which, in most cases, was only temporarily successful.

It is a widely accepted paradigm that the only legitimate power is a freely elected one, which is based on a kind of social contract that is embodied in a set of unquestioned laws. In such a system the people obey the impersonal order and laws, and are not subordinated to an alienated power. Those who exclude the possibility of a legitimized state socialism are thinking in this paradigm (the "rational type of legitimate power," in Weberian terms), and they are entirely right to do so.

As Giovanni Sartori noted, "despite the fact that . . . a majority of the 175 countries (circa) in official existence do not qualify as even minimal democracies, the *Zeitgeist* admits one and only one legitimacy, namely, that power derives from, and is bestowed by, the people. In today's modern world there is but one 'rightful government': freely elected government" (Sartori, 1991, p. 437).

This *Zeitgeist* is, however, a rather new historical phenomenon, having originated at the time of the Enlightenment and the French Revolution, and gradually emerging during the last two centuries. Universal male suffrage was introduced only in the last third of the nineteenth century, while half of the population, all of them women, still remained "naturally" excluded until after World War I. Moreover, political systems based on free elections were consistently challenged and rejected throughout its short history and practically never realized outside the Western Core, including the Central and Eastern European periphery of the world system.

Hence, understanding the legitimization attempts of state socialism and its transitory success would not be possible without examining the peculiar Central and Eastern European historical context. In post-1848 Hungary, the victorious Franz Joseph I, who ruthlessly suppressed the Hungarian revolution and executed thirteen generals of the revolutionary Hungarian army in Arad, established legitimate power by signing the Austro-Hungarian compromise in 1867 and granting some of the rights the Hungarians demanded and were ready to die for. Moreover, during his long life, the bloody-handed emperor (whose bedroom in the Vienna Burg was decorated by paintings of his victorious battles against the

Hungarian revolution) became the beloved, jovial "father" who had unquestioned authority.

Illustrating the difference compared with the West, it pays to recall that in Hungary in the early twentieth century, a country where (noble) parliamentary traditions were one of the strongest in the entire region, only 6 percent of the population had the right to vote; and even in the 1920s during the Horthy-regime, elections were held with open ballots in the countryside and small townships.

In the Balkans, even "traditional," hereditary royal rule was introduced only in the last third of the nineteenth century, when foreign dynasties were invited to create legitimate rule (such as the Hohenzollers to the Romanian throne), or local chiefs (knazes) were consecrated to establish dynasties and "traditionalize" power (such as the Karadjordjević and Obrenović dynasties in newly liberated Serbia). In Albania, this happened only in the 1920s.

Poland in the interwar period began with a short episode of democratic constitutional power, but this was soon squashed by the *coup d'état* of Marshal Pilsudski in 1926; henceforth, political legitimization was based on Pilsudski's unquestioned charisma.

The Horthy regime, which gained power thanks to the Romanian and Czechoslovak armies' defeat of Béla Kún's Hungarian Soviet Republic, and which also dethroned the legal-traditional Habsburg dynasty (and militarily defeated King Charles IV when he attempted to regain power in 1921), went on to realize a bogus parliamentarism. After fifteen to twenty years in power, however, Horthy also evolved into a sort of "father-figure," and his regime, born of blood and the repression of his "white terror," was widely accepted and thought to be legitimate.

It pays to note that the peculiar "Royal dictatorships" in the Balkans of the 1930s represented a special type of legitimizing power. In the deep and explosive crisis, traditional inherited royal power no longer sufficed, and the king, in order to preserve and strengthen his regime, had to act as a savior of law and order; he thus had to turn toward banning parliaments and parties and introduce a centralized authoritarian rule based on the army and bureaucracy in order to avoid civil war. The bulk of the population recognized royal dictatorships as a legitimate form of power.

This brief excursion back to nineteenth- and twentieth-century Central and Eastern European history may help in understanding the complexity of the question of legitimizing power in the post-World War II period. Using the modern, "rational" paradigm, based on the contemporary *Zeitgeist*, none of the modern, late nineteenth-century and interwar Central and Eastern European regimes, with the exception of interwar Czechoslovakia with her parliamentary democracy and free elections, could be counted as legitimate. Historically speaking, however, it is hardly questionable that most of these regimes were legitimate at certain periods of their existence. How did it happen? Legitimization of the regimes in the region followed a different pattern from that of the West. Max Weber helps us to understand the difference when he historically differentiates among "three clean types of legitimate rule": beside the "rational" (modern), he also lists the "traditional" and the "charismatic" types, which represent different paradigms. If rational legitimization is based on a social contract and free elections, the more traditional societies, Weber suggests, believe in "the sanctity of age-old rules and powers. The masters are designated . . . and are obeyed because of their traditional status . . . . [T]he ruled are . . . 'subjects'" (Weber, 1978, pp. 226–7). But in "traditionalist periods," and, one should add, in the backward peripheries, if the people begin to question traditional power and revolt against it, they turn, surmises Weber, toward "charisma," which is "the great revolutionary force" (p. 245).

People may accept aggressive, violent revolutionary regimes as legitimate. In deep desperation and blind faith, explains Weber, people may recognize the power of some charismatic leader who convinced them to follow him toward Canaan, whose prophecy and promise seem to be a guarantee of success:

Charisma [is] . . . a certain quality of an individual . . . [who] is considered extraordinary and treated as endowed with supernatural . . . powers of qualities. . . . Psychologically this recognition is a matter of complete personal devotion . . . arising out of enthusiasm, or of despair and hope. (pp. 241–2)

Legitimacy in this case is maintained by the realization of "mission" and "prophecy." Charismatic legitimization requires permanent success.

All in all, there were different paradigms, and today's universally accepted rational Western parliamentary pattern was only one of them, and one which was not valid for a long time in the peripheries. In the latter areas various sorts of beliefs legitimized power. This continued in post-World War II Central and Eastern Europe. It should not be forgotten that parliamentary legitimization through free elections was highly compromised and was easy to dismiss in mid twentieth-century Europe, since nazism gained power in a properly legitimate parliamentary way. Moreover, people lost confidence in powers that they ultimately recognized as legitimate, but which could not preserve legitimacy because of their failure in the thirties and during the war.

In its postwar desperation, a devastated Central and Eastern Europe was ready to revolt against traditional power and longed for a new and promising prophecy. Stalinist socialism sought to exploit the situation and declared its mission. Marxism–Leninism embodied the prophecy and infallibility, and this was reinforced by the promise of modernization and egalitarianism as well as the painful but spectacular *tour de force* over Hitler in World War II.

The tragic failure of the fifties in Central and Eastern Europe, with their appointed "charismatic" proconsuls (a *contradictio in adjecto*) and failed prophecies, undermined the legitimization efforts of the regime. Although enthusiastic and idealistic intellectuals, inexperienced youths, and certain groups of profoundly desperate people embraced, and ambitious careerists pretended to embrace, the mission and charisma of the person and the system, the masses did not believe in, and disappointed intellectuals revolted against, the regime; broad social strata became explicitly hostile. Stalinism could not gain legitimacy in the region.

Post-Stalinist socialism, with all its reform attempts and striking rebellions, opened a new chapter in legitimizing its power. In some of the Central and Eastern European countries, of course, genuine charismatic leaders such as Yugoslavia's Tito and Albania's Hoxha continued their unchallenged rule until their deaths in the eighties. In some other countries, new charismatic figures emerged, such as Hungary's Kadár and Romania's Ceauşescu. In other countries, such as Bulgaria, Czechoslovakia, and Poland, either grey apparatchiks or technocrats took over the party leadership, and also ruled for decades up until the late eighties. (Only in Poland did permanent crises lead to frequent change: Gomulka, who emerged as a charismatic leader, lost his appeal surprisingly soon and was succeeded by typical technocrats and clerks.) Both charismatic and apparatchik leaders, however, waged a permanent struggle for legitimization. They tried to "routinize charisma" and "rationalize" (legalize) their regimes, using the Weberian terms, in order to stabilize power through legitimization. The frightening fortissimo of the violent Hungarian revolution, supported by the choir of the Berlin and Poznan uprisings and the Plzen strike, was definitely a wake-up call. The regimes could not exist without solid rational legitimization. The "New Course" and, in some reforming countries, the follow up de-Stalinization, which emphasized "legality" in the place of revolutionary terror and stressed supply-orientation and consumerism instead of a nebulous future "mission," while in most of the non-reforming, orthodox countries, a reformulated "national mission" (nationalist-Stalinism) all expressed attempts to assure legitimacy.

What actually happened in the sixties and seventies in Central and Eastern Europe was due to the traditions of the region: people began to recognize that the regime, which had been initially imposed on them, now satisfied, at least, some of their (economic) needs or (national) emotions.

In some of the cases (mostly in Hungary), Lipset's argument helps us to understand the process: a "prolonged effectiveness ... may give legitimacy to a political system" (Lipset, 1960, p. 82). In almost all the other cases, Przeworski's reasoning is more valid: "what matters for the stability of any regime is not the legitimacy ... but the presence or absence of preferable alternatives" (Przeworski, 1986, pp. 51–2). Indeed, in the bipolar world system, in which Central and Eastern Europe's place in the Soviet sphere of interest was not challenged, "preferable" alternatives may have existed, but realistic ones were totally absent.

In describing a situation that he would undoubtedly apply to post-World War II Central and Eastern Europe, Max Weber writes: "The distinction between an order derived from voluntary agreement and one which has been imposed is only relative. ... It is very common for minorities ... to impose an order which in the course of time comes to be regarded as legitimate by those who originally resisted it" (Weber, 1978, p. 37). Most of the Central and Eastern European regimes, either in their "liberalized" post-Stalinist form or with their agitated nationalism, were temporarily accepted by their respective peoples, as long as the regime worked.

Two definite exceptions should be made: Poland and Czechoslovakia. Neither of these countries could play the nationalist card because of their geopolitical situation and (in Czechoslovakia only after 1968) the strong Soviet military presence. Poland, moreover, could not cope with her almost permanent economic crisis, nor counterbalance her humiliating dependence with effective consumerism. Czechoslovakia, as the most developed and the only industrialized and democratic country before World War II, could not, as did all the other countries of the region, even temporarily profit from a state socialism that was designed for backward, non-industrialized countries, and was thus unable to produce convincing results. The Poles, as did their predecessors, revolted on almost a permanent basis. The Czechs with their Svejkian peaceful, obstructionist, recoiling tolerance, endured their fate rather quietly.

Wherever it was achieved, the fragile and temporary legitimacy in the other countries of the region rapidly eroded and then disappeared when the system declined into a deepening and terminal crisis from the late-seventies on.

5 Economic and social performance of state socialism, 1950–89

Economic transformation: industrialization on an obsolete technological basis

State socialism was a mixture of a pragmatic modernization model for backward agricultural countries to industrialize, and a utopian model for creating a more "just" society, without private ownership, and a secure society where no one may be rich but no one is left in poverty.

To realize these goals, the regime was, at certain periods, highly dictatorial, and was always strongly authoritarian, ready to sacrifice individual freedoms and redistribute incomes to create an assumed homogeneous community and assure the future national interest. The road to modernization and equality was thus paved by human suffering, humiliation, and sharp social conflicts for millions. What was social justice for the lower social layers became injustice and elimination for others.

Militant state intervention and the tremendous sacrifice imposed on the populace had, however, a profound socio-economic impact. During its four decade-long experiment, state socialism had a rather mixed record. A great many of the modernization goals were accomplished and a previously rigid, traditional society was dramatically transformed. However, lacking the socio-economic achievements which had originated in the nineteenth-century Industrial Revolution, the regime could not keep pace with contemporary "modern modernization" that emerged in the advanced world during the second half of the twentieth century. Both catching-up and a new lagging behind characterized the performance of state socialism. While the former predominated during the early period, the latter did so in the later years.

It was an experience of historical dimensions, similar to that of *Alice in Wonderland* when she was "running . . . [and] felt she could not go faster. . . . The most curious part of the thing was, [however,] that the trees and other things round [her] never changed their place at all: however fast [she] went, [she] never seemed to pass anything" (Carroll, 1976, p. 15).

In the last analysis, their successes and failures were not only *regime* specific but also *region* specific, attributable to both their peripheral location and their state socialist character.

Dramatically increased capital accumulation

The first and foremost characteristic of Central and Eastern European economic performance was the most rapid growth in its history. The main advantage of Soviet-type planning was a pattern of generating high capital accumulation in poor countries with traditionally low rates of accumulation and, based on this new "socialist primitive accumulation," to concentrate investments in an extremely one-sided way into the industrial sector of the economy.

Indeed, capital accumulation, instead of being 6–8 percent of the countries' GDP, which had characterized the interwar period, jumped to 20 percent to 35 percent from the late 1940s on. In the 1950s the growth rate of investment, in some cases, surpassed even 13 percent annually. Although extreme growth and forced accumulation were moderated by the mid fifties on, gross fixed capital investment remained very high until the 1980s, and the annual growth rate of investment for thirty years was between 9 percent and 11 percent (with the exception of Czechoslovakia, which usually had 6 percent). As poor families cannot save much from their low incomes, poor countries on the periphery of the advanced, rich core never reached such high rates of investment.

However, marked fluctuations in investments was one of the main characteristics of state socialist economies. The tendency to overheat and overinvest was manifest on both a macro- and microeconomic level, and this led to a forced slowing down in order to consolidate demand and balance consumption and investment. Consequently, in spite of the theoretical-ideological denials of the existence of economic cycles in state socialism, there was in fact an investment cycle; high investment peaks followed by sharp declines in capital input clearly characterized the four decade-long economic performance of Central and Eastern Europe. Although investment rates sharply declined from time to time, these downward trends were always followed by a new upswing. As Paul Marer calculated, the share of investment in GDP varied between 25 percent and 29 percent in 1980, and was still 21–27 percent in 1988 during the period of permanent economic crises. High accumulation and investment rates were for the first time permanently higher than in the West, thus remaining a continuous characteristic of state socialism.

According to Frederick Pryor's comparative figures, the Western world had an average 5–6 percent annual increase in fixed capital investment, which was around half that of Central and Eastern Europe between 1950 and 1980 (Pryor, 1985). Investments varied at around 20 percent of GDP in the West, and remained at a significantly lower level than that of Central and Eastern Europe in both 1980 and 1988.

The dramatic increase of capital formation served to force industrialization. In the early 1950s, more than 50 percent of investment was earmarked for industry, compared with 15–18 percent of industrial investment earlier. Although moderated in post-Stalinist decades, the preference for rapid industrial development continued until the eighties. János Kornai (based on Péter Mihályi's calculations) recently claimed that 35–48 percent of total investment went to industry during the most prosperous years of 1965–73. Moreover, the percentage share of industry in total investment remained steady between 1973 and 1983, a period of two major oil crises and a visible economic shock (Kornai, 1992, p. 175). The preference for industry served a deliberate and continuous attempt to restructure the economies of the region's countries.

The lower their initial level of industrialization was, the more state socialist countries would emphasize on industrial investment. From the mid 1960s on, Hungary represented the lowest rate of industrial investment with slightly more than one-third of investments, while Bulgaria continuously invested 42–45 percent of her resources in industry. Romania continued Stalinist-type forced industrialization, investing 48–49 percent in industry. At the same time the Western share in industrial investment – Germany and France had a stable 24–25 percent – varied between 25 percent and 30 percent in Europe.

Immense labor-input and rapid growth

A huge labor input was the other main pillar of Stalinist industrialization. Central and Eastern Europe was characterized by an "unlimited" source of labor, from the non- or partly employed agricultural population. Mass unemployment, discernible on the labor-market or disguised in rural families, was one of the most burning social problems of the countryside. Creating new jobs by increasing industrial investments was thus accompanied by drastically expanding industrial employment. In the late forties and early fifties more than 80 percent of Bulgaria's, 75 percent of Romania's, and 70 percent of Yugoslavia's population worked in agriculture. Poland and Hungary also had a rural majority of 57 percent and 53 percent respectively. The only industrialized country of the region, Czechoslovakia, still employed 40 percent of her population in agriculture (mostly in Slovakia). A relocation of occupations from low (agricultural) to high (industrial) productivity sectors became a prime mover of growth.

The pattern which was adopted was often described as a "model of extensive industrialization," meaning that the main source of expansion was labor input (in contrast to the "intensive" road which was based on technological, rather than labor, input).

From 1949–50 on, the industrialization policy was combined with brutal collectivization (or a new expropriation of the landed peasantry), which caused an exodus from the countryside. This process continued through the late sixties. In two decades 40 percent to 50 percent of the active agricultural labor force left agriculture. Consequently, by the early seventies the agricultural population had dropped to 18 percent in Czechoslovakia, 24 percent in Hungary, 32 percent in Bulgaria, and 38 percent in Poland. In Yugoslavia and Romania, the agricultural population, though sharply declining, still represented the majority, comprising 57 percent and 53 percent of the population respectively. The process of the "disappearance" of the peasantry, a continuous trend in the West from the early nineteenth century, thus now gained momentum in Central and Eastern Europe.

Labor input was enlarged by leaps and bounds. In the first decade of industrialization, the annual increase of labor input surpassed 9 percent in Yugoslavia, 8 percent in Bulgaria, and 7.4 percent in Hungary, while remaining at 4–5 percent in the other countries. Although slowed down in the sixties, labor input continued to increase by more than 5 percent in Bulgaria and 2–3 percent in the other countries, with the only exception being Romania where, in contrast to the trend of the other countries, labor input jumped from the previous 4.8 percent to 5.5 percent. Industrialization was thus fueled by massive labor input.

An increasing labor input was still possible in the seventies, and in some cases even in the eighties. The agricultural population continued to decline, and its share dropped to 10–12 percent in Czechoslovak and Hungaria, and 25 percent in Poland and Yugoslavia by the late eighties.

The consistent investment policy of industrialization worked impressively for quite a long time and led to a breakthrough: the traditionally "slow" countries of the region reached the fastest growth rates in their history, and formed the most rapidly growing region of the world from the late forties up to the mid to late seventies (Prùcha, 1977).

Instead of the 1–2 percent inter-war growth rate, official statistics triumphantly reported 6–13 percent annual growth in the first half of the 1950s. Official figures, however, were distorted, partly because the concept of national income was rather different than in the West, and partly because of propaganda lies, though Western calculations and evaluations on Central and Eastern European growth rates are only slightly different.

Table 5.1. *Per capita GNP increase, 1950–87*

Year	Czechoslovakia	Hungary	Poland	Bulgaria	Romania	Overall
1950	100	100	100	100	100	100
1987	310	307	348	485	585	369

To cite Wlodzimierz Brus's basic study in Michael Kaser's *The Economic History of Eastern Europe 1919–1975*, the corrected growth estimates (based on net material product figures) reflected much lower rates than the official ones, but still a rather high annual growth of 4–7 percent. In the second half of the sixties, growth varied between 6 and 7 percent in the northwestern part of the region, while the Balkan countries reached 8–9 percent. The early seventies did not reflect marked changes (Kaser, 1986).

Others, such as the already cited Pryor, published GDP figures for thirty years between 1950 and 1980. According to his calculations, the slowest (Hungary) and fastest (Romania) had annual growth rates of 3.6 percent and 5.8 percent respectively, with the remaining countries producing a 4–5 percent growth. According to his comparisons, the Western world had a similar 4–5 percent growth (Pryor, 1990).

One of the prominent experts on the topic, Thad P. Alton, calculated five years' average growth rates from 1950 on, and concluded that in the fifties there was a 5.2 percent and 5.1 percent growth of GNP in the first and second five years. The two halves of the sixties produced a 3.8 percent and a 3.7 percent rate and the first half of the seventies a 4.8 percent rate, followed by a slowdown in growth to 2.0 percent and 1.4 percent in the second half of the seventies and the first half of the eighties. Altogether GNP almost quadrupled (see table 5.1).

To evaluate Central and Eastern Europe's economic performance, two historical statistics deserve special attention: the Swiss economic historian Paul Bairoch's calculations from the mid seventies and the Briton Angus Maddison's figures from 1989.

Bairoch estimated and calculated Europe's economic development between 1800 and 1975, and thus presented a very broad framework to judge each country's absolute and relative advancement over time. Counting the per capita GNP (in 1960 dollar value) of the Central and Eastern European countries as the percentage of the European average, one can follow the historical performance of the region throughout different ages and historical periods (table 5.2).

Table 5.2. *Per capita GNP as a percentage of the European average*

Country	1860	1910	1938	1973
Europe	100	100	100	100
Czechoslovakia	—	98	82	117
Hungary	74	75	67	89
Poland	—	(70)	55	89
Bulgaria	68	55	63	84
Romania	64	61	51	66
Yugoslavia	71	56	50	57

Source: Bairoch, 1976.

Although some on the Western rim of the region slightly and transitorily increased their relative level in the half a century before World War I, the Central and Eastern European countries could not narrow the gap until World War II. On the contrary, the countries' relative positions declined and, by 1938, represented a lower percentage of the European average than in 1860, the year that opened a decade when economic modernization practically began in the region. The Balkans experienced a continuous relative decline throughout the entire three quarters of a century until World War II.

The long-term trend dramatically changed after World War II, and the region began to catch up and approach the average per capita GNP level of Europe. Indeed, by the mid 1970s, Czechoslovakia surpassed it, and Hungary and Poland came very close to doing so, and all of the Balkan countries made important advances. According to Bairoch's calculations, Central and Eastern Europe, for the first time in its modern nineteenth- and twentieth-century history, was able to halt its relative stagnation or decline compared with the other European countries, and narrow the gap between them and the others.

To offer another concise contrast, it pays to compare Bairoch's aggregate Western and Eastern European figures (see table 5.3).[1]

During the entire modernization period up to World War II, Central and Eastern Europe barely changed its economic position in Europe, and its per capita Gross National Product varied between 55 percent and 60 percent of the Western average. (The moderate improvement in its

[1] The geographical definition of the region is not the same in Bairoch's study and in this work. He, as most of the international organizations' statistics, included Yugoslavia in Western Europe, whereas in the Eastern figures, besides Albania, Bulgaria, Czechoslovakia, Hungary, Poland and Romania, the East German and Soviet data were also included. In spite of the regional differences, the aggregate figures reflect the leading trends and differences between the two parts of Europe (Bairoch, 1976, p. 317).

Table 5.3. *Per capita GNP (in 1960 US dollars)*

Year	Western Europe $	Western Europe index	Eastern Europe $	Eastern Europe index	Eastern Europe as % of the West
1860	384	100	214	100	56
1913	678	177	389	181	57
1938	839	218	509	238	61
1973	2,259	588	1,861	870	82

relative position in the inter-war years was generated in table 5.3 by the inclusion of the rapidly developing Soviet Union.) Although the exactness of the figures are questionable, and East–West differences cannot be fully taken into account, the postwar growth trends indicate a clear change.

Angus Maddison offers a twentieth-century world-wide comparison. He used an average "world" index of thirty-two countries, composed of sixteen advanced countries of the Organization for Economic Cooperation and Development (OECD), nine Asian, six Latin-American countries and the Soviet Union. Although this sample was only one fifth of the 160 nations of the United Nations, it represented "around four fifths of the world total in each major dimension" (Maddison, 1989, p. 13).

This comparison clearly shows that Central and Eastern Europe accomplished the fastest economic growth in its history, compared with both its own pre-World War II development, and with the growth of the contemporary, post-World War II world economy. The region was a slowly developing area in the first half of the twentieth century. Czechoslovakia and Hungary increased their GDP only by one-quarter to one-half, while Bulgaria and Yugoslavia roughly doubled their level between 1913 and 1950.

The pace of growth drastically increased during the second half of the century (between 1950 and 1987), when Czechoslovakia, Hungary, and Poland more than tripled their GDP and the Balkan countries increased their domestic product by five (Bulgaria) and six times (Romania, Yugoslavia). The periods before and after 1950 saw two entirely different growth trends in the region.

At this point, however, it should be mentioned that the two halves of the century produced two rather different growth trends all over the world. Maddison's "world" index demonstrated a 1 percent per capita growth between 1913 and 1950, compared with the 3.3 percent between 1959 and 1973 and 2.2 percent in 1973–87.

In the first half of the century, the most advanced countries achieved either a 40–50 percent increase in GDP (Britain, Germany, France,

Table 5.4. *Development of "world" (32 countries) GDP*

year	in million $	index	index
1900	1,034,956	100	35
1913	1,433,235	138	49
1950	2,951,078	285	100
1973	8,659,150	837	293
1987	13,628,455	1316	462

Belgium, Italy), or a more impressive 2–2.5 times increase (USA, Sweden, Switzerland, Japan, Denmark). In the second half of the century they accomplished a unique rate of development by increasing their GDP by 3–4 times (USA, Switzerland, Sweden, Netherlands, France, Belgium) and rocketing their growth by a 5–12 times increase (first of all Japan, but also Germany, Finland, and Austria).

The speeding up of growth after World War II was thus an international phenomenon. The best index to show this is Maddison's "world" figure of total GDP in 1980 dollar value (table 5.4).

The "world," which increased its GDP by nearly three times in a half a century between 1900 and 1950, achieved an increase of more than four and half times in the first thirty-seven years of the second half of the century. But if an extremely rapid growth became a worldwide phenomenon, it does not diminish Central and Eastern Europe's achievements. On the contrary, the region was not only able to keep up but surpass most of the other countries and regions in a period of the world's fastest economic growth.

The previously "slow" countries of state socialism attempted the impossible and sought to run twice as fast. Between 1950 and 1973, when the model appeared to work, they were able to achieve that.

Counting on a per capita basis, Maddison's "world" reached an annual 3 percent growth in its GDP and the world as a whole, taking ninety-four countries into account, had a 3.4 percent growth rate. Central and Eastern Europe, however, reached 4.2 percent. In the entire period between 1950 and 1987 the thirty-two countries' 2.5 percent and the 94 countries' 2.1 percent annual growth were surpassed by Central and Eastern Europe's 3.1 percent.

Considering all the uncertainty and possible errors in international comparisons, several corrected indexes (which substantially revised distorted and non-compatible "socialist" statistics) clearly reflect a narrowing gap between the advanced world and Central and Eastern Europe.

To evaluate its performance, it is important to compare Central and Eastern Europe's growth to other peripheral regions with a more or less similar starting level, such as Latin America and Southern Europe. Between 1950 and 1973 Central and Eastern Europe achieved much better results than both of the other peripheral regions. While Latin America had an annual per capita growth of 2.5 percent, Central and Eastern Europe had 3.9 percent. Although Mediterranean countries such as Spain and Portugal tripled, and Ireland doubled, their national product, the gap between them and Central and Eastern Europe broadened markedly to the latter's advantage at least by 20–25 percent.[2] The Spanish level declined from 66 to 64 percent of that of the Hungarian, the Portuguese dropped from 91 to 71 percent of the Bulgarian, and the Irish declined from 95 to 61 percent of the Czechoslovak level between 1950 and 1973 (Bairoch, 1976).

Reflecting a basic defect of the state socialist model from the mid 1970s on, this trend was unable to continue. The Latin American and Central and Eastern European growth rates became virtually equal between 1973 and 1989, whereas the South European countries achieved a much higher rate of growth and, after the collapse of their dictatorships and having joined the European Community, easily closed the gap and indeed surpassed Central and Eastern Europe by more than two times (217 percent) (Maddison, 1995).

In each comparison the economic success of state socialism was an impressive advancement in an era when a world made its sacrifices to the golden calf of "Economic Growth."

Structural modernization: successes and failures

"Backwardness" in the middle of the twentieth century was virtually equated with the lack of industrialization and the preservation of an agricultural economy. With the exception of Czechoslovakia, all of the countries of the region were relatively backward, with an absolute majority of their population in agriculture. In the prewar Balkans, industry played an insignificant role in the national economy. As a typical example, 55 percent of Bulgaria's GNP was produced by agriculture and less than 10 percent by industry in 1939. Even in much more developed Poland and Hungary, agriculture was the leading sector and produced 37 percent of GNP; industry's contribution was only 19 percent and 21 percent respectively in 1937–8.

---

[2] According to Angus Maddison, Mediterranean Europe (and Ireland) in 1973 modestly surpassed (by 28 percent) the per capita GDP level of Central and Eastern Europe (Maddison, 1994).

An extreme and steadfast industrialization effort in the 1950s, as the American Congress' papers revealed later (Congress, 1970), resulted in more than a 9 percent annual increase of industrial output in Hungary, Romania, Yugoslavia, and Bulgaria (the latter had a 12.7 percent rate), and the relatively "slower" Poland and Czechoslovakia also had more than 8 percent. Although the industrialization drive had slowed down somewhat by the sixties, the average annual industrial growth rate of the region in the sixties was as high as 7.6 percent per year (with more than 11 percent in Romania and Bulgaria), surpassing the Western 5.7 percent.

During the fifties and sixties these countries accomplished a breakthrough in industrialization. Industrial employment became predominant. Hungarian industrial employment, typical for the Central European region, jumped from a prewar 18 percent to 35 percent, and the industrial contribution to the GNP rose from 21 percent (1938) to 43 percent (1970). Bulgaria's industrial employment, typical for the Balkans, increased from 8 percent to 28 percent, while the industrial contribution to GNP rose from less than 10 percent to more than 40 percent during the same period.

By the late 1960s, all the countries of the region, except Albania, had become industrialized. Roughly half of the GNP was produced by industry (Czechoslovakia 61 percent, Hungary 57 percent, Poland 54 percent, Romania 52 percent, Yugoslavia 49 percent, and Bulgaria 46 percent), and only 20 percent by agriculture (Hungary, Poland, and Yugoslavia). The latter was only 12 percent in Czechoslovakia, but roughly 30 percent in Romania and Bulgaria.

Although the seventies and eighties were already characterized by a slowing down and a gradually deepening crisis, industrialization still continued. According to the United Nations statistical yearbooks, the more advanced Czechoslovakia, Poland, and Hungary doubled their industrial output between 1970 and 1988. The less industrialized Balkan countries continued by leaps and bounds: Yugoslavia increased its industrial output by 2.5 times, Bulgaria by 3 times, and Romania 5 times.

A peripheral region that was unable to follow the path of Western industrialization in the nineteenth century, which saw its relative backwardness increase in the first half of the twentieth century, and which preserved its overwhelmingly agricultural character by the mid twentieth century, Central and Eastern Europe now carried out a belated "industrial revolution."

As the most important indicator of drastic structural changes, United Nations statistics reveal that, in 1988, industry, in contrast to the 10–15 percent agricultural contribution to GDP, became the leading sector of the region's economy: in Romania, Czechoslovakia, and Bulgaria 62 percent, 61 percent, and 58 percent (respectively) of the GDP was produced by industry. In Hungary, Yugoslavia, and Poland the industrial contribution was 41 percent, 45 percent, and 48 percent respectively (*National Accounts*, 1990).

As a consequence of being a non-market economy and, at the beginning, of having a policy of self-sufficiency geared for war preperations, extreme attempts were made to develop energy and raw material production. Mining and basic industries were given absolute preference. The majority of industrial investments, between 75 percent and 92 percent, were channeled into the so-called heavy industries during the first five-year plan period. The fifties were characterized by doubling coal, iron, and steel production throughout the region.

Industrialization, however, was built on Soviet energy and raw material deliveries, since self-sufficiency, in most of the relatively small countries with limited natural resources, was out of the question. Self-sufficiency was more easily realized in the processing industries. Central planning and the lack of market incentives actually pushed each country and each firm toward self-sufficiency, in order not to be "dependent" on other non-interested countries and firms that might and did cause permanent troubles by not fulfilling or delaying deliveries, thus endangering the plan fulfillment. As a consequence, the countries of the region, which did not have a developed processing industry, sought to build up all possible branches of processing. Most of the countries lacked several branches of engineering and were characterized by the one-sided domination of food processing and consumer goods industries.

From the sixties to the eighties several new engineering branches emerged. In 1960, five countries produced roughly 53,000 trucks. In 1988, truck production for six countries reached almost 140,000. Bus production in six countries increased from fewer than 8,000 to nearly 36,000. In 1960 four of the countries produced altogether fewer than 600,000 TV sets; in 1988 all of the seven countries produced nearly 3 million sets. The Hungarian engineering industry doubled the value of production during the first Five Year Plan between 1950 and 1955, and then increased production by five times. The chemical industry, however, after more than doubling production in the first five years, owing to a Comecon decision, increased production by more than ten times by 1975. Industrialization was thus rather successful in creating new branches of industry and by increasing five to ten times the industrial output (*Industrial Statistics*, 1969, 1981, 1990).

Another significant element of traditional backwardness was also gradually overcome. Forced industrialization in the 1950s burdened agriculture heavily, since it became the primary source of capital accumulation and of labor. The price system created the "price scissors" of artificially low agricultural prices *vis-à-vis* high price levels for consumer and investment goods consumed by the peasantry. Because of the continuous exploitation of agriculture and peasantry, there was a strong net capital and labor outflow from agriculture, accompanied by brutal incidents of forced collectivization. As a consequence, net agricultural production could not surpass prewar levels for about twenty years. Counting the 1934–8 level as a basis, net production remained behind by 10–20 percent by the early fifties, and was still somewhat behind by 1956, i.e., during the entire Stalinist period.

Post-Stalinism's economic policy, however, attempted to reach an upswing in agriculture. The conclusion of collectivization around the late fifties, or the giving up of collectivization efforts (Yugoslavia and Poland), contributed to reaching this goal. The low agricultural investment levels of the early fifties were doubled in the second half of the decade. In one decade, investments, compared with 1950–4, increased by three to four times in Hungary, Bulgaria, and Czechoslovakia, five times in Poland and seven to eight times in Romania and Yugoslavia (Alton, 1990).

From the early sixties on, a complex mechanization and an increased use of chemicals in agriculture took place, with tractors, combines, and trucks replacing horse-driven ploughs and coaches, steam threshers and other old technologies in Czechoslovakia and Hungary, and also making impressive advances in the other countries of the region. The breakthrough of modern technology was well-illustrated by the fact that the use of artificial fertilizers, which had hardly existed before, reached high levels. Czechoslovakia, Hungary, and Poland used 5–12 kilograms of fertilizers (nitrogen, phosphate, and potash) per hectare of arable land during the prewar years. The quantity had risen to 200 to 300 kilograms in Poland, Hungary, and Czechoslovakia by the late eighties. (The Hungarian level jumped from the 1.3 kg. prewar level to 290 kg., the Czechoslovak level to 340 kg.) Artificial fertilizers were practically unknown – 0.2–0.6 kg. per hectare – in the Balkans before World War II. In the late 1980s, however, Yugoslavia used more than 70 kg., Albania 80–90 kg., Romania 90–100 kg., and Bulgaria 140–50 kg. per hectare (*Fertilizer Yearbook*, 1986, 1987, 1990; *Annual Fertilizer*, 1976).

Regarding agro-chemicals, the region was elevated to the level of the developed world: the usage of artificial fertilizers surpassed the world average (88 kg.); moreover, at best it matched the Japanese (336 kg.) and French (307 kg.) standard, surpassed the American (103 kg.), but remained behind the West German, Belgian, and Swiss level (400–500 kg.).

Tractors were hardly used in prewar Central and Eastern Europe:

there was only one tractor for each three thousand hectares. In Poland, Yugoslavia, and Albania, tractors were virtually unknown. In the late sixties there totaled twelve tractors per land unit in the region, which was about one-third the West European level. By the late eighties the number of tractors per land unit increased by six times in Poland, more than twenty times in Yugoslavia (fifty-eight and seventy-five tractors), and also three to four times in Albania and Romania (from three to ten or twelve tractors). Counting in tractor horsepower, the mechanization of the region's agriculture reached nearly 62 percent of the West European level: there were 2,051 and 1,268 horsepower per 1,000 hectares in Western and Eastern Europe respectively in 1982–6. Harvesting was mechanized as well: the first harvester-thresher combines appeared in the countryside in the fifties, with roughly one to two combines per 1,000 hectare land. By the mid to late eighties, however, the ratio increased to four to nine combines per land unit (*Productivity Yearbook*, 1962, 1990).

Consequently yields of wheat, corn, potatoes, and sugar-beets had basically doubled by the early seventies. In Hungary, the average yield of wheat increased from 7.9 quintals per acre in 1931–40 to 23.4 in 1976–80. The figures for corn and sugar-beets were 10.8 and 117.1 in the 1930s and 28.2 and 219.8 in the late 1970s respectively. In the best performing countries, such as Czechoslovakia, Hungary and Bulgaria, yields already surpassed the European average by 50 percent (wheat) and 20–25 percent (corn, sugar-beets) (*Productivity Yearbook*, 1949–90).

Animal stocks, after the serious decline of the war years and forced collectivization, began to rise significantly, especially pigs and poultry, and in some cases sheep as well, while cattle stock developed only moderately. Romania and Albania were exceptions, with a doubling of their cattle stock in half a century. As an average, the pig stock in the seven countries of the region trebled, but some Balkan countries such as Bulgaria, Romania, and Albania increased their stock by five to six and even ten times. Poultry production expanded by three to five times, as a consequence of the introduction of automated "poultry factories" pioneered by the Bábolna State-farm in Hungary, which imported the most advanced systems and developed them in the other countries of the region as well.

According to the United Nations Food and Agriculture Organization (FAO), agricultural output per capita had already reached nearly two-thirds the level of the United States in the second half of the sixties, and 72 percent in the first half of the eighties. The best performing country, Hungary, had practically attained the American level (98.1 percent) in the latter period.

Agriculture thus successfully overcame traditional backwardness. Although the entire period was characterized by a continuous exodus from the countryside, labor productivity increased by three to four times.

According to the FAO indexes, agricultural production increased either by 50–60 percent (Yugoslavia, Bulgaria, Poland), or nearly more than doubled (Romania, Albania, Hungary, Czechoslovakia) in postwar Central and Eastern Europe.

Some major factors of underdevelopment, however, were preserved. The structure of agricultural production remained quite traditional. In Hungary, with one of the best performing agricultural systems in the region, the extensive cultivation of field crops remained dominant. In 1938, 62 percent of arable land was given to wheat and corn, and a third of a century later the figure was still 58 percent. Field crop production represented 83 percent and 72 percent of the gross value of crop production before the war and in the late seventies respectively. In contrast, the share of market-garden, orchard, and vineyard production rose from 12 percent to 27 percent (*Productivity Yearbook*, 1990). The continuous extensive grain cultivation reflected a kind of structural rigidity in preserving traditional branches. Additionally, the cost of production remained rather high, much higher than the world's main grain producers.

As with the state socialist economy in general, agriculture was not cost sensitive. The countries of the region did not have to face world competition because most of their production was consumed on the domestic market or exported to other Comecon countries. Export to the world market was heavily subsidized because the domestic cost of production was subordinated to the need for hard currency incomes. In other words, most of the successes of the region's agriculture was achieved in isolation from and not in competition with the world agricultural market.

To accomplish nineteenth and early twentieth century economic achievements in the second half of the twentieth century, however, was not only a "delayed" fulfillment of the long missing requirements of modernization, but, in a way, was also anachronistic. Miroslav Krleža, the outstanding Yugoslav writer, expressed this basic conflict of belated modernization in a most eloquent way in his *Banquet in Blitva*. The dictator of "Blitva," the fictional country, composed of Polish, Hungarian, Croatian, and Baltic characteristics, euphorically rejoiced his country's artistic achievements in the twentieth century: "At last, here it is our Quatrocento! It was belated, but at last, it arrived!"

Central and Eastern European industrialization, which followed the old paved Western road, was, in a way, as anachronistic as an arriving Quatrocento in the age of expressionism and surrealism. While state socialist countries sought to catch up with the West by following its old path at the fastest possible pace, with the potential and hope of overtaking it, the Western world gradually turned to a new economic road. The gradual change from the old technological regime, which characterized the first postwar decades, followed by the dramatic technological explosion of the 1970s and 1980s, opened up a new chapter of industrial–technological revolution in the West.

While Central and Eastern Europe made a tremendous effort to build up iron, steel, early twentieth century engineering, and chemical industries, and industrialized on that technological basis, a new "post-industrial" society, to use Daniel Bell's term, or a "service" or "communication" society, as others described it, emerged in the West.

The change from the old technological regime began immediately after World War II. Its first milestones were the first mainframe computer with its 18,000 vacuum tubes, invented in 1946 at the University of Pennsylvania, and the transistor that was able to magnify electronic messages, invented in the Bell Laboratory in 1947. Parallel with a communication revolution in the making, and focusing around the application of computers, the service branches expanded with extraordinary speed. Car and widespread air transportation, television and an endlessly booming tourist industry speeded up the already fifty to seventy year-long process of the emergence of a broad lower middle-class, professional, clerk, and white-collar society.

The historic turning point, when the first and most advanced country reached the point when white-collar workers outnumbered blue-collar workers, occurred in the United States in 1956. As was often maintained, industrial society, the child of the Industrial Revolution, hereby ended, and a new age opened.

The transition to the new age, however, still took some time until the practical application of a set of new technologies and industries achieved a certain critical mass and could impact on every day life. After listing the early milestones on the road toward the "post-industrial" society, one should note that the new age actually opened only in the 1970s. At the beginning of this decade, the microprocessor, the "brain" of modern computers, was invented in the Silicon Valley, and this had both symbolic and practical importance. It opened the road to further and further miniaturization and an increase in capacity. Consequently the cost per bit of computer memory began to decrease by 28 percent annually from the mid seventies on. This opened the age of computerization. At that time, there were only large computers owned and used by the government, big companies, and universities. Microcomputers became popular and widely used. The developing new technology made it possible to link personal computers to large units and establish telephone connections to communicate with large computers and enter into data bases. Networks emerged, together with the newer variety of telecommunication technologies such as teleconferencing networks, cable television, and then interactive cable TV, Teletex, and Videotex, the great new inventions of the seventies. "The technical advances in microelectronics," sums up Everett Rogers, "that occurred in the 1970s and 1980s have spurred the Communication Revolution." All this was connected with an emerging new "high-technology industry ... one in which the basic technology underlying the industry changes very rapidly" (Rogers, 1986, pp. 14–15).

The most important high-technology industries, such as electronics and its sub-branch, microelectronics, centered on semiconductor chips, and their applications are the main driving force behind a new age of technology as well as biotechnology, aerospace, instrumentation, and pharmaceuticals. Modern communications and computers penetrate virtually every sphere of the economy. According to some calculations, about a quarter of the work force in the United States used computers as their primary work tool, and three-quarters of jobs were connected with computers by the mid eighties. Consequently, industrial employment continued to decrease: in 1980 only 2 percent and 22 percent of the active population worked in agriculture and blue-collar industrial jobs (respectively) in the United States.

When this new age emerged in the West in the 1970s, Central and Eastern Europe was not prepared and was unable to follow. The rigid model of modernization, although effective in industrializing backward agricultural countries and in catching up, and with an impressive growth rate on a turn of the century technological basis, was absolutely unprepared for technological reorientation. The region lagged far behind in terms of new technology. Cybernetics was rejected in the Stalinist period as a "bourgeois science" but, even in 1969, on the eve of the communication and computer age, when this ideological approach was no longer present, computers were still mostly unknown in the region. The United States was already using about 50,000 computers in that year, while the seven countries under examination had altogether about 650, compared to France, Czechoslovakia had about one-third, and Romania and Bulgaria one-twelfth, of the computers found in that country. Semiconductor technology had just appeared, and the components branch of the electronics industry was in a rather primitive condition. Computer production, which had just appeared at that time, was not compatible with Western technology.

Consequently, Central and Eastern Europe could not renew the technological bases of the old branches of industry. The technological gap broadened. As a consequence, Czechoslovakia consumed three times more fuel than France and five times more than the United States per

1,000 tons of industrial output in the sixties. Her steel consumption per unit of output was twice that of the two Western countries. To produce one ton of pig iron, Hungary and Poland used almost 40 percent more coke than Sweden. The steel input per $1,000 value of engineering products was two to four times larger than in West Germany, Austria, and Italy. Czechoslovakia reached only half of the prices of the EFTA countries' products for her exported cars or metalworking and sewing machines sold in the European Community, and hardly more than one-third for her generators, electric motors, sorting and crushing machines in the mid sixties. Hungarian machinery sold in Austria realized only 57 percent of other exporters' prices in the early sixties. Because of technological and structural obsolescence, labor productivity of the more advanced countries of the region, such as Czechoslovakia, Poland, and Hungary, was one-third to one-half of the West German level in the late sixties (Teichova, 1988).

The seventies and eighties became crisis-ridden years in Central and Eastern Europe when structural and technological renewal became impossible. The countries of the region thus continued marching, though gradually and at a slower and slower pace, still on their previous road of industrialization, developing an economy which had already become obsolete.

New competitive modern branches and export sectors based on high technology industries did not emerge, and the countries of the region could not compete on the world market where they sold food, raw materials, and unsophisticated, processed industrial products. Hence their major economic modernization achievements were accompanied and then counterbalanced by a new kind of technological and economic backwardness.

In this respect a genuine weakness of Soviet-type modernization, the subordination of services and infrastructure to industry, became a decisive obstacle to modernization in the late twentieth century. Central and Eastern Europe neglected infrastructure and services in the decades of forced industrialization. Investment into service branches was very low: it dropped from a prewar level of at least one-half of total investment to one-third by the early 1950s, and remained on a low level during the following decades. Hungary, with her reform and consumer orientation, reached a relatively higher level of 50 percent of investment in the seventies and eighties. Although the Czechoslovak and Polish figures were rather similar, the Balkan countries, especially those such as Romania and Bulgaria that continued a rather orthodox economic policy, preserved an extremely low 25–30 percent investment rate in services, and did so even later on as well (Terziiski, 1984). As a consequence, while the fixed assets of industry and agriculture increased by seven to ten times, the fixed assets of services only tripled. The annual 2–3 percent increase in services remained far behind the average growth rate. The "service" and "communication" revolutions did not arrive in the region.

Moreover, existing and long-serving infrastructure networks such as buildings, railroads, sewage, and water systems were neglected for decades and often broke down. The telephone network, which acquired an extraordinary importance in the new communication revolution, was among the neglected areas, and was considered as a sort of private luxury which only consumes scarce resources. Regarding development plans, Mátyás Rákosi remarked in the late forties: "The bourgeoisie left behind a telephone network that we do not have to develop for a century."

In 1980, when the United States, Japan, the Nordic, and Common Market countries had 79, 46, 45, and 28 telephone lines respectively per 100 inhabitants, the Central and Eastern European average was 7.4. To get a new telephone line required a 10–15 year waiting time. On top of that, a part of the existing telephone system was made up of, using Éva Ehrlich's term, "quasi-lines," often out of order and requiring hours of waiting for a dial tone (Ehrlich, 1991, p. 83).

From the late sixties on, but only for a short while, certain sectors of services and infrastructure received some preference and investment. The intensive road construction in Yugoslavia increased the length of public roads by 57 percent between 1965 and 1988. In Poland the road network grew by 24 percent. Belated and slow highway construction opened up a new period of road transportation (*Annual Bulletin of Transport*, 1961–90).

The length of railroads decreased in Hungary, Poland, and Yugoslavia by closing small lines, the "dead branches of an old tree," and road transportation dramatically increased: the quantity of delivered goods (in million ton-kilometers) increased by forty times in Poland, twenty-five times in Yugoslavia, ten and eight times in Hungary and Bulgaria respectively between 1960 and 1988. In 1980 around two-thirds of domestic deliveries (in ton-kilometers) were transported on roads in Poland, Czechoslovakia, and Hungary (*Annual Bulletin of Transport*, 1989–90).

As an element of modernization of their transportation systems, all the countries created airlines which, between the mid seventies and the late eighties, more than doubled their services (counted in so-called passenger-kilometers).

The upswing of construction works is clearly expressed by the sharp increase of cement consumption (in kilogram per inhabitants): its volume increased by four times in Hungary and Poland, and by five and nine times in Yugoslavia and Bulgaria respectively between 1955 and 1989 (*Annual Bulletin of Housing*, 1961–91).

One of the most prosperous service industries, tourism, came to the region with a ten to twenty year delay, but began to flourish in the 1970s and 1980s. It led to a 50 percent increase in tourists arriving in Yugoslavia and Czechoslovakia and a more than 70 percent increase in Hungary (while Romania and Poland suffered a decline of 20 percent and 50 percent). The 230 million guest-nights in the seven countries of the region (almost half of them in Yugoslavia) signaled the growing importance of tourism in 1987 (*European Marketing*, 1990).

In the OECD countries, a dramatic change of employment took place between 1950 and 1980: the percentage of employees in services increased from 39 percent to 59 percent, and in the eighties it already represented two-thirds to three-quarters of the population. In contrast to nineteenth century, highly polarized class societies, the rise and domination of the middle class became characteristic.

The backward countries of Latin America and Asia represented an earlier stage of the employment structure. In fifteen so-called developing countries of those regions, agricultural employment decreased from 63 percent to 45 percent and industrial employment increased from 14 percent to 21 percent between 1950 and 1980. Although service employment also increased (from 23 percent to 34 percent), it still represented only one-third of the population and thus remained at the prewar Western level.

Central and Eastern Europe's position was somewhere in between the advanced and developing world. About two-thirds of the populace of the region belonged to the blue-collar workers and farmers (or the agricultural work force of collective farms). The white-collar society, on the other hand, also increased: in Bulgaria, representing the Balkan standard, the percentage of the active population working in services, though only 10 percent in 1950, had increased to 25 percent by the mid seventies. In Hungary and especially in Czechoslovakia, service and white-collar employment reached about half of the working population.

The peripheries, without any consideration to social-political orders, the existence of markets or planned economies, followed a rather similar economic trend: they began and continued their industrialization process, and could not advance into the age of service and communication revolution. Economic modernization, with its successes and failures, generated a dramatic social transformation which eliminated most of the traditional features of the former peasant and rural societies.

Social transformation: modern societies in the making

Changing demographic trends

Before World War II, demographic trends preserved traditional, almost pre-nineteenth century features in most parts of Central and Eastern Europe. During the nineteenth century, both birth and death rates decreased in the West (to twenty-five and fifteen per 1,000), and the much faster decline of the death rates caused a rapid population growth. Central and Eastern Europe and the other peripheries, though experiencing the same population explosion, preserved their much higher birth and death rates (thirty-five to thirty-six and twenty-three to twenty-five per 1,000). Birth rates, especially in some Balkan countries, still showed this pre-industrial standard. In contrast to the seventeen to nineteen births per 1,000 inhabitants in prewar Czechoslovakia and Hungary, Poland had twenty-four, Yugoslavia twenty-seven, Romania thirty, and Albania thirty-five per 1,000. Central and Eastern Europe averaged twenty-three births per 1,000, almost the same figure as in Southern Europe, but much higher than the fewer seventeen in Northern and Western Europe. Death rates were also higher than in the West: thirteen to fifteen per 1,000 in Czechoslovakia, Hungary, Poland, and Bulgaria, eighteen to nineteen in Romania and Albania. The average figure was more than fourteen in Central and Eastern Europe, fewer than the nearly sixteen in Southern Europe, but more than the 12.6 in Northern and Western Europe.

In the half century after 1938, both birth and death rates inched closer to Western standards. Although birth rates increased by 10–15 percent during the Stalinist fifties as a consequence of forced population growth and strict anti-abortion measures, they began and continued to decline afterwards. In 1967, the average figure was fewer than eighteen per 1,000, almost the same as in the advanced West, and it went on to drop to twelve to sixteen per 1,000 throughout the region (with a difference between the lowest Hungarian figure of 11.9 and the highest Polish one of 16.1). The only exception was Albania, with her still traditional twenty-six per 1,000 births during the 1980s.

In the three decades between 1938 and 1967 when death rates in the advanced Northern and Western European world declined by 13 percent (from its generally lower level), Southern Europe showed a spectacular 42 percent and Central and Eastern Europe a 32 percent decrease. The impressive results were generated by a drastic decline of prewar infant mortality, which dropped in the region from 133 infant deaths per 1,000 population in 1938 to fifty-two in 1960 (*Demographic Yearbook*, 1950–90).

In addition to this, reduction in mortality originated from general international factors such as the postwar introduction of antibiotics and insecticides, which had a surprising impact on prewar mass diseases, such as tuberculosis, labeled "Morbus Hungaricus" in Hungary and one of the main killers in the region as a whole. Syphilis also almost disappeared and pneumonia was not life threatening any longer.

A special component in the improvement was the "advantage of backwardness," i.e., the ability to mobilize sources of improvement that already existed in the advanced West but were missing in the peripheries. The belated adoption of a broad social policy generated most of the improvements and led to a rapid catching-up.

From the 1960s on, however, a surprising and heatedly debated new upswing in death rates, a 30–50 percent increase, revealed a serious regression, though they were stabilized at the level of ten to thirteen deaths. According to United Nations statistics, the worse case was Hungary (13.4 per 1,000), where death rates almost returned to their prewar level (14.2). Bulgaria also suffered a rise and experienced a strange cycle: 13.7, 8.1, and 12 per 1,000 in 1938, 1960, and 1987 respectively.

A shocking deterioration is expressed by the index of life expectancy at the age of thirty between 1960 and 1980. Whereas the length of life increased by one to two years in the West, an opposite trend of a two to three year decline characterized Central and Eastern Europe. In one single decade between 1968 and 1977, mortality caused by cardio-vascular disease in the male age group of forty to sixty-nine jumped by a more than striking 40 percent in Bulgaria, nearly 20 percent in Poland, and 15 percent in Yugoslavia, while Japan and the United States showed a 33 percent and 25 percent decrease respectively (Vallin, 1985).

What happened in the region may be described as a successful struggle against the old mass killers, while new ones became dominant. In the place of tuberculosis, heart and circulation diseases were causing half of the deaths in some of the countries of the region. Different types of cancers became the second largest mortality factor, causing nearly a quarter of deaths. In addition, a sharply increasing rate of accidents and "unnatural" deaths, such as a mounting suicide rate, became a main factor in the mortality rate, and particularly so in Hungary. (In Hungary 13 percent of deaths were caused by non-natural causes, which became the third largest mortality factor in the late eighties.)

Paradoxically, the increasing mortality was a special and well-known consequence of a sort of "civilization advance." Better nutrition, higher consumption of meat, fat, and eggs, combined with an urban life-style, less physical work, and a much higher rate of consumption of cigarettes and alcohol all led to new diseases. In the quarter of a century after 1960, hard liquor consumption skyrocketed in the region: it increased by three and half times in Hungary and Czechoslovakia and more than doubled in Bulgaria. Poland and Hungary, where more than 40 percent of the adult population smoked (in contrast to the 25 percent in the United States) had the highest per capita cigarette consumption in the world, with more than 3,500–3,600 cigarettes per capita annually among those above the age of fifteen. This component, which was rather visible in the Western world in the first half of the twentieth century but radically suppressed after the sixties, gained ground with deadly consequences in Central and Eastern Europe after the sixties.

The "civilization disease" of a certain transitory stage of modernization, which was already overcome in the West, had only recently arrived in the East in the second half of the century. Moreover, the special historical circumstances of the region were certainly also contributing factors. The low income level, combined with a sort of consumerism and the very strong influencial effect of the Western life-style, led to desperate attempts at achieving a higher standard of living by moonlighting and working at two or three jobs. For the most part, a family could not manage without at least two salaries, which thus forced women to work while at the same time raising children and running a household.

Central and Eastern European women carried especially heavy burdens. They often rose at 5 a.m. to prepare the family for the day, took their young children to pre-school before running to their work place, stood in line for sometimes hours when shopping after their jobs, helped the children with their homework, and cooked dinner for the family before their husbands arrived home from their second jobs in the late hours. As a consequence, female mortality in the age group of forty to sixty-nine, caused by heart and circulation diseases, were three times higher in Romania than in France, two and half times higher in Hungary than in Switzerland, and almost two times higher in Yugoslavia than in Sweden in the late seventies.

It pays to note that Hungary experienced in the 1960s and 1970s a dramatic increase in suicides. Suicides per 100,000 inhabitants jumped from twenty-five in 1960 (already the highest suicide rate in the world) to almost forty-five by the mid eighties, almost twice that of the other "leading" countries.

This frightening phenomenon led to a variety of explanations, including political interpretations that attempted to provide a regime-specific key to the problem. It would be impossible, however, to make any generalizations, since suicide did not follow a similar trend in other countries of the region. In contrast, the rate was thirteen in Poland, seventeen in Bulgaria, and nineteen in Czechoslovakia. On the other hand, prosperous, democratic

European countries such as Denmark (twenty-nine), Austria (twenty-eight), Finland and Switzerland (twenty-five) had rather high rates of suicide, nearer to the striking Hungarian record. One should not expect precise, comprehensive explanations for this problem, as the reasons might be very complex, connected with traditions, local cultural circumstances, and behavior patterns (Vallin, 1985).

Besides relatively high death rates in Central and Eastern Europe, a great many births were aborted in the region: from the mid to late fifties an entirely free abortion law (combined with a lack of modern contraceptives) resulted in a record number of abortions. In the mid fifties, there were about ten to twelve reported abortions per 100 pregnancies; in 1967 the number increased to sixty, fifty, thirty-six and thirty in Hungary, Bulgaria, Czechoslovakia, and Poland respectively.

Consequently, population growth was moderate: the seven countries increased their total population from 97 million to 123 million, or by 27 percent. Behind this average, however, the different countries had rather dissimilar results, but followed a quite clear pattern. Hungary, Poland, and Czechoslovakia had a slow 7 percent to 15 percent increase, while the Balkan countries achieved an almost 50 percent population growth between 1938 and 1987.

Average life expectancy at birth followed the previous path of the West: from a prewar fifty-three to fifty-five years for men and sixty to sixty-two years for women, the average life expectancy at birth increased to sixty-five to sixty-eight years for men and seventy-four to seventy-five years for women. Thus life expectancy, as an average, though two to four years shorter than that of the West, became longer by one-fifth to one-quarter of the prewar standards in Central and Eastern Europe by the end of the 1980s (*Demographic Yearbook*, 1979–90).

Belated educational revolution

The population of the region became much better trained and educated than before. In the interwar decades the region had not yet reached the educational levels of the West at the end of the nineteenth century: illiteracy still remained a mass phenomenon. It disappeared or was mostly eliminated only in Czechoslovakia and Hungary (8 percent), while one-quarter and one-third of the population of Poland and Bulgaria respectively remained illiterate in the 1930s. This rate was reduced by nearly one-half in Yugoslavia and by 80 percent in pre-modern Albania.

Most of the countries of the region thus realized their belated nineteenth-century educational revolution after World War II by eliminating illiteracy. After the war, the educational system was rebuilt and broadened, and was offered free of charge at all levels, including higher education.

As a new preparatory institution, a pre-school system was developed, and a gradually increasing percentage of children between three and six were enrolled, connected with the rapidly increasing number of working women. In some more advanced cases, such as Czechoslovakia and Hungary, pre-schools involved almost the entire age group, while in other countries only a quarter or a third of pre-school age children.

Ten or eight years of primary school education were established in postwar Central and Eastern Europe, which assured a basic education virtually for the entire generation between six or seven to fourteen, and created a much better educated work force.

On that basis, a specialized secondary school system was founded. In prewar Central and Eastern Europe, secondary education was rather limited and elitist. In the best cases 5–10 percent of the age group were enrolled, in others (Balkans) only 1–3 percent, compared to the Western level of 60–80 percent of the age group of fourteen to eighteen. The mostly German type gymnasiums assured a very high level of comprehensive education together with a well-respected social status.

Although compulsory education ended at age sixteen, secondary education gained mass acceptance in the postwar decades as part of the belated educational revolution, and 66 percent or even 90 percent of the generation was enrolled in one type or another of the existing secondary educational institutions. The most widespread practice for more than half of the young generation, however, was to go to a vocational school which provided two to three years of modernized apprentice training for a certain required skill.[3]

Although evolving into mass education, secondary training was thus mostly vocational oriented and served the goal of training a skilled labor force, seeking to provide a narrow field of specialization. Those who

---

[3] Before the war, apprentices were trained on the job, mostly in small-scale industry, in a quite traditional guild-like way. Modern "apprentice" training was now institutionalized in a special type of narrowly specialized schools, combined with certain elements of general education. This type of school, however, was quite limited and did not offer any kind of continuation. The two other types of high schools offered a rigid specialization from the age of fourteen. The comprehensive or grammar school type of secondary education preserved its German traditions (gymnasium) and offered all-round preparation for higher education. By the 1960s on, however, the percentage of students in this type of school permanently decreased, to the advantage of the secondary technological schools. The latter offered narrow vocational specialization (granting the diploma of "technician") and guaranteed a job as accountant, nurse, foreman, laboratory technician, etc., combined with a grammar school type (although in most cases on a lower level) basic education and a possibility for higher education.

graduated at the age of seventeen to eighteen immediately began to work in one of the jobs guaranteed by the state.

The modernizing state socialist countries attempted to follow the Western revolution in higher education where, in the most advanced cases, 50–60 percent of the generation aged between nineteen and twenty-four were enrolled in higher education. The greatest increase in the East was 15–19 percent (with the exception of Romania and Albania, with less than 10 percent and 8 percent respectively), a ten to fifteen fold increase in students by the end of the eighties (*Statistical Yearbook*, UNESCO, 1973–89).

Mass higher education was thus in the making, though the percentage of enrolled students was only half or one third of the most advanced Western level. The overspecialization resulted in an ambiguous quality of non-convertible knowledge. In some ways, higher education turned its back on the requirements of a new communication age, and did not provide a sufficient base for updating former education or for re-training.

On top of this, higher education and research was deliberately separated. A huge network of research institutes was founded under the auspices of the Academy of Sciences, and the universities acted as foremost teaching institutions. As George Lukács, the noted Hungarian philosopher, once remarked, they became virtually "huge high schools." This practice of rigid separation of teaching and research, though eventually moderated, never totally disappeared in the later decades.

From the early sixties on, a majority of the students of higher education were gradually enrolled in a rapidly expanding type of lower standard specialized college (German-type "Hochschule"), which mostly offered only a higher level of specialized vocational training in accounting, foreign trade, hotel industry, construction, etc. It sought to serve the requirements of an expanding economy by training highly skilled technicians.

The Central and Eastern European educational system was characterized by a strange, upside-down hierarchy of quality: pre-schools and primary schools were on a rather high level, and the university system (with several exceptions) proved to be the least compatible with the advanced West.

A transforming society

Central and Eastern European societies preserved major elements of their previous "noble societies" up to the mid twentieth century. The dominant role of the aristocracy and gentry, in both economic and political terms, survived. The big estates occupied from 30 percent to 40 percent of the land and the former nobility still dominated the army and the state and county administration. They had a determinant role in maintaining their old value systems. One's place in society was still strongly determined by birth, and noble origins guaranteed continued status among the leading elite. Business was looked down upon as something not "gentleman-like" or as Jewish. In the meantime, a modern bourgeoisie or middle class – the white-collar workers – also emerged and dominated trade, banking, industry, and services.

The coexistence of old and new also characterized the lower strata of society. The peasantry remained the most numerous class in the overwhelmingly peasant countries. Since 40–60 percent of them were landless, a great part of the peasantry remained bounded to the large estates and continued a sort of semi-serf existence. Well-to-do, independent farmers represented only about 10 percent of the peasantry. Peasants remained traditionally excluded from the noble societies, and their social elevation was limited. A modern industrial working class also appeared, but it represented only a small layer of society.

The duality of Central and Eastern European societies also characterized the middle class. In addition to the traditional feudal gentry, a modern middle class emerged, but it remained not only limited in numbers but partly "alien" in origin. As characteristic of noble societies, where the *declassé* gentry could still maintain its status in the leading elite, and where the peasantry could not elevate itself to the rank and file of the newly formed middle class, a social vacuum was created in the middle strata of society which was filled by Germans and Jews who were strongly overrepresented in entrepreneurial, intellectual, clerical, and other white-collar occupations. The so-called dual society, which distinguished mostly the Polish and Hungarian but also the Czechoslovak and Romanian societies, represented a special mix of traditional and modern that survived until the mid twentieth century.

Most of the Balkan countries did not have their own nobility, since they were part of the Ottoman Empire for half a millennium. These societies, ruled by an Ottoman elite, remained "incomplete" without a genuine native ruling elite, and were rather homogeneous peasant societies in traditional village communities. After the liberation from Ottoman rule, however, a national elite, a sort of (using the German term) *Ersatz-klasse* or substitute class, was formed. A new military-bureaucratic elite emerged, which used state power to enrich itself through shameless corruption and abuses of power. A small native, rich peasant-merchant stratum was also elevated, and it joined the national elite.

An adequate economic and social basis for modernization was missing, and several archaic social characteristics still existed by the end of World War II.

Under state socialism, the legacies of pre-industrial society and the old rigid hierarchies were brutally and rapidly eliminated. The process of forced social restructuring began with the collapse of the old regimes and the advent of Jacobin postwar democracies. Radical land reforms parcelled out traditional big estates, which eliminated both the landed aristocracy and mass landlessness, by creating small independent peasant farms. A great part of the old ruling elite, officer corps, and state and county administration fled the countries after the war. The Holocaust and the postwar Jewish emigration of half of the Holocaust survivors, as well as the mass expulsion of Germans, decimated the old entrepreneurial strata and middle class.

The communist seizure of power gave tremendous new impetus to the process. The nationalization of industry, wholesale trade, transportation, apartment houses, and the elimination of the bulk of small-scale businesses, the handicraft industry, and family shops, virtually expropriated the entire bourgeoisie and most of the petty-bourgeoisie. The ruthless "anti-kulak" campaign of the early fifties annihilated the greatest part of the well-to-do peasantry. As a result, the entire political, economic, and administrative elite and a great part of the former middle class, altogether nearly one third of Central and Eastern European society, were uprooted, left the region, or became *declassé* and forced to earn an existence as workers and low-level clerks. In 1952, 7.5 percent of skilled workers, 11 percent of semi-skilled, and 10 percent of unskilled were *declassé* people in Czechoslovakia. The old social structure was destroyed.

The decline of the old elite precipitated rapid social mobility in the creation and rise of a new elite. In the fifties, a great number of former workers and peasants were elevated to top political, managerial, and administrative posts. The new regimes, at the time of seizing power, began to educate and train its new intelligentsia as well. Hundreds of thousands of young people from worker and peasant families were enrolled into the universities. Moreover, college admission was guaranteed to those unable to graduate from secondary schools. After a one year preparatory training, young workers entered the previously exclusive universities. During the prewar decades, only 1–2 percent of university students came from workers and peasant families in Czechoslovakia; their percentage increased to 51 percent in 1975–6. From the fifties on, all the countries of the region introduced positive discrimination, and the percentage of students of workers and peasant families increased to half of the student body.

High intergenerational mobility was now characteristic in the region. As Walter Connor noted, in Czechoslovakia, Hungary, Poland, Bulgaria, Romania, and Yugoslavia, the peasantry provided up to 10–20 percent, the workers up to 25–33 percent, of a newly formed non-manual class (Connor, 1979). Clearly expressing the general tendency for the creation of a new elite, 40 percent and 26 percent of the Hungarian administrative and intellectual elite of the early sixties had risen from workers and peasant families respectively, and only 15 percent of them had the same type of (intellectual or administrative) of family background. "Including family members, the number of rising social groupings reached about 1 million in Hungary.... The emerging and declining social groups' interchanging social positions drastically changed the societal positions and life of . . . about one quarter of the population" (Berend, 1979, p. 248).

The transformation, though spectacularly radical, still followed the well-trodden path of the old elite: the upper layers of society were traditionally linked to the state. A bureaucratic *Ersatz-klasse* and an intellectual *Bildungsbürgertum* characterized the modern elite from Germany to the Balkans. Although society was restructured with a new elite with rather different social origins, the latter became even more bureaucratic and administrative in character.

The new elite emerged in close connection with the party-state. A great number of them were party members, though party membership did not result in automatic elevation to the elite. The mass parties constituted 8–10 percent of the population in the 1980s, thus more or less comprising 15–20 percent of the active population (15.2 percent in Romania, 10.5 percent in Czechoslovakia, 8 percent in Hungary, and as an exception only 4.1 percent in Albania in 1984). At least half the party members were regular workers and peasants. Party membership, however, strongly helped one to rise in social status, and provided opportunities to receive higher positions. The elite, including the party, state, and managerial bureaucracy, enjoyed various privileges. They enjoyed certain advantages in the redistribution process. They could build a broader network of connections, enjoy special treatment in special hospitals, and have better access to goods that were missing in regular shops. In certain periods, and in some countries, they were served in special well-supplied shops. A relatively broad strata of the nomenclatura had the right to be chauffeured service cars. Milovan Djilas, a leading member of Tito's inner circle who became one of the "first" dissidents in Central and Eastern Europe, described this elite with his famous term "new class" (Djilas, 1983).

The intelligentsia (also newly created) was a part of the new elite and played a much more important role in the centralized and planned political-economic system than ever before. George Konrád and Ivan Szelenyi, two famous Hungarian dissidents, developed the concept in the mid seventies that, in state socialism, the intelligentsia will seize power and create the new ruling class (Konrád and Szelenyi, 1979).

The high mobility, however, proved to be a rather transitory phenomenon. After the changes occurred, the initial pace of mobility could not be sustained. Sociological analysis of the seventies and eighties already showed a clear tendency to reproduce the existing elite instead of continuously renewing it from below. A social rigidity reappeared that reproduced the same difficulties for workers and peasants to rise into the elite or to white-collar positions. "The transition to slower growth and a stable social structure implies," summarized Lovenduski and Woodall (1987), "that after a time only exchange mobility is possible, and that social closure frustrates the rising expectations . . ."

Social mobility, however, had more important sources than the spectacular change of guard at the pinnacle of society. During the postwar decades almost whole societies were uprooted and in a permanent state of flux. The mass exodus from the countryside as a consequence of brutal collectivization and industrialization led to the beginning of the disappearance of the peasantry. In the late sixties about a half of the offspring of peasant families became industrial workers in Czechoslovakia, Hungary, and Bulgaria, and a third or more in Poland, Romania, and Yugoslavia.

A new working class emerged: a second generation of industrial workers dominated the work force only in Czechoslovakia (60 percent of the workers came from workers' families in the mid 1970s), and formed only one quarter of the Bulgarian work force. Industrial workers were still linked to the villages. In the mid 1970s, 40 percent of Romanian workers had a peasant father and mother, 19 percent still lived in villages, and 17 percent even had some income from agricultural activity. A painful, ruthless and, during its first decade, extremely brutal forced transformation of the countryside, comparable only to the British "enclosure" in the age of "primitive accumulation," annihilated the peasant majorities of the countries.

Since the great majority of the former peasantry found a job in the rapidly increasing industrial sector, the exodus was coupled with rapid urbanization. Unlike the Western half of the continent, Central and Eastern Europe had not become urbanized by World War II. Nearly two-thirds of Poland's and Hungary's population and three-quarters of the Balkans' population lived in the countryside. The exception was Czechoslovakia, which had already become urbanized with 51 percent of the postwar population living in urban settlements. Although urbanization could not follow the rapid pace of industrialization, and a great part of the newly recruited industrial workers remained in villages and worked in rural industry or commuted to nearby industrial centers, within two decades the urban population in the relatively more developed countries of the region approached or even outnumbered those in the countryside. By 1980, nearly 60 percent of the population of Hungary and Poland lived in urban settlements of more than 10,000 citizens. In uniquely urbanized Czechoslovakia, two-thirds of the population lived in cities by the eighties. Bulgaria and Romania, previously entirely rural countries, increased their urban population to more than half of the inhabitants. Although roughly 60 percent of the population remained rural in Yugoslavia, 39 percent lived in urban settlements (*Demographic Yearbook*, 1985–90).

Urbanization developed rather spectacularly, and the capitals emerged as major European cities. Budapest and Warsaw, which had more than 1.1–1.2 million inhabitants already before World War II, increased their population by 50–100 percent. Budapest, with its 2.2 million inhabitants, concentrated more than a fifth of Hungary's population in one of the largest European metropolis centers in the late eighties. Warsaw had 1.7 million inhabitants in a marvelously rebuilt, vivid city. The strongly provincial cities of Sofia, Bucharest, and Belgrade, with their 300,000–600,000 prewar inhabitants, became big cities of 1.1, 1.9 and 1.5 million people respectively. Prague, a traditional jewel among the European cities, preserved its atmosphere and size, increasing its population from the pre-war 0.9 million to only 1.2 million by the eighties.

In addition, republican capital cities and industrial centers developed throughout the region: Zagreb (1.2 million), Skopje and Sarajevo (500,000) in Yugoslavia; Bratislava and Brno each had 400,000 inhabitants in Czechoslovakia; Poland's Lodz, Krakow, and Wroclav increased their populations by several hundred thousand to a total of between 600,000 and 900,000; Romania's Braşov, Constanţa, and Timişoara, and Bulgaria's Plovdiv and Varna, had already 300,000–400,000 inhabitants by the eighties. Albania, one of the smallest and the only rural country of Europe, still lacked any big cities. Even the capital, Tirana, had a population of only 250,000, and Shkodër, Durrës, and Vlore only about 60,000–70,000 in the eighties.

What actually happened in the region between the 1950s and 1970s (in some cases until the 1980s) was nothing other than a belated duplication of nineteenth-century Western social restructuring: besides "melting" the peasantry, a huge industrial and blue-collar worker society developed and began to predominate, comprising from 50 percent to 60 percent of the populace and concentrated in urban settlements.

As another element of social modernization, a modern lower-middle class or white-collar worker society emerged, a tendency of Western societies that began to appear from the 1870s on. Central and Eastern Europe was characterized by the weakness of these social groupings. The most developed Czechoslovakia had hardly more than 16 percent of the population employed as white-collar workers in 1950. In the early 1980s, its share comprised one-third of the population, and employees in services surpassed half of its citizens. In Bulgaria and Romania, the percentage in employment in services rose from 10–14 percent to more than 25 percent during the postwar decades. Moreover, while the first two decades of postwar transformation were characterized by the proletarization of the society, when the former self-employed became state employed workers or worker-type members of cooperative farms, the second two decades, from the mid to late sixties on, became the scene of a rising middle-class. In a broader sense, not only the white-collar workers but also a proportion of the peasant and blue-collar workers were elevated to this level, by having some private plots and private marketing activity (although to highly different degrees in the various countries), by living in mixed families, working in industry, living in villages and having some additional agricultural income, or by just doing two or more (legal or illegal) jobs. An upper strata of workers and peasants, together with white-collar workers, and, in some countries, a gradually enlarged small-scale entrepreneurial layer, certainly developed a middle-class self-consciousness, and these layers, especially in Poland and Hungary, already represented the majority of society by the seventies and eighties.

In spite of growing inequalities and social differences, the previously strictly hierarchical class societies, so strongly characteristic of pre-World War II Central and Eastern Europe, were replaced by drastically homogenized societies. Except for Poland and Yugoslavia, where 15–18 percent of the active population were independent farmers, 84–98 percent of the region's population were virtually employed, and private ownership was strictly limited to personal belongings, apartments, or family houses (*Yearbook of Labor*, 1990). Although state socialism did not create equality and re-created new inequalities and privileges, incomes did become more equal. This is well illustrated by the fact that, compared to the prewar level, the real income of the Polish white-collar worker in 1960 declined by 26 percent, while the blue-collar worker's income increased by 75 percent per employed person. As a consequence, the prewar ratio of an average white-collar worker's wage to that of a blue-collar's diminished from 2.20 to 1.12 by 1960. In the 1970s, a demagogue communist-populist "workers policy" re-emerged and enforced a new levelling of income differences. In 1973–4, blue-collar workers' salaries were increased by 18–20 percent in Hungary. In Poland, an average workers' salary was 64 percent of that of an engineer's and technician's, and it increased to 71 percent in 1974. Compared to an average clerk's salary level, the worker's salary increased from 95 percent to 103 percent. This kind of income redistribution and leveling was common for the entire region. A medical doctor in a junior position earned only 20–30 percent more than a skilled worker in Hungary, while, compared to the latter, a nurse or a high school teacher's salary was 10–30 percent lower. The average wage of the technological intelligentsia was only 1.6–1.7 times higher than blue-collar salaries in Hungary in the seventies (*Social Indication*, 1989).

Economic leveling of society was assisted by free social services such as education and health care, heavily subsidized pharmaceuticals, and other built-in subsidies for many consumer goods etc. The so-called divisible public consumption, as János Kornai compared it, consisted of 40–50 percent of increased consumption in the Central and Eastern European countries, in contrast to the 15–20 percent and, in some extreme cases, 30 percent in the market economies by the late sixties (Kornai, 1992).

Although highly paternalistic and thus politically connected with a centralized state power, and though serving to subordinate the populance, the wage policy and income regulations contributed to the homogenization of society. This was true in spite of the fact that state redistribution was far more unequal than its philosophy and propaganda claimed. Moreover, in several cases the heavily bureaucratic system worked in a rather counterproductive way and preferred strata other than those targeted. The Hungarian housing system, as Ivan Szelenyi and János Ladányi concluded, provided the largest piece of the subsidy cake (highly subsidized rents) for the intelligentsia and white-collar workers, while the entire peasantry and the greatest part of blue-collar workers, who officially were targeted, lived in their own family houses in the villages and poor industrial suburbs (Szelenyi, 1983).

The relatively poor societies still distributed the wealth (or as Winston Churchill sarcastically remarked, the poverty) more equally than ever before, with all its positive human-ethical and highly negative economic (in the long run social) consequences. It positively helped to destroy the "caste-like" walls of an old-fashioned class society, but it also refused to recognize excellence, education, higher skill, and better work. Equalization thus killed incentive and generated a destructive attitude, expressed by a popular joke of the sixties: "They pretend to pay, I pretend to work."

In social homogenization a great role was played by postwar land reforms and the collectivization of agriculture. The countryside of the region was strictly hierarchical before World War II. A "Chinese-wall" existed between the different layers of the peasantry. The landed and landless, and farmers with 2–3, 5–15, and 50 or more hectares, each represented a different "class," and intermarriages among them were almost non-existent. Landlessness was sharply curbed by land reforms.

Collectivization, in spite of its tragic social, economic, and personal consequences, resulted in a homogeneous rural society. Former landless and well-to-do peasants became equal members of collective farms, receiving their "working units" and having the same size of private plots.

Social equalization had several important non-economic factors as well. An expressive example was the transformation of the customary form of addressing. In the traditional Balkan and "noble" societies of the region, addressing was extremely hierarchical. Unlike the British and American "Mister", the French *Monsieur*, and even the German *Herr*, the Romanian *Domnul*, the Polish *Pan*, or the Hungarian *Úr* were addressed only to a member of the ruling elite or middle class, but never to those from the lower social layers. In the Hungarian language a complicated hierarchy existed even between the lower level *Úr* and higher ranking *Úr* (with different adjectives): "*Nagyságos Úr*" (addressing lower-middle-class people), "*Tekintetes Úr*" (for upper-middle class), and "*Méltóságos Úr*" (addressing the upper-class elite). On the other hand, members of the upper social echelon spoke to servants, peasants, and workers, including women from those layers, without any kind of formal addressing or by simply using "Hey, you". All this "class" language was swept away and replaced by a generally used, equal, though certainly colorless and artificial "Comrade." Speaking "downward" disappeared, and was followed by a development which, in a way, rehabilitated previous addressing, restoring a mutually and generally used *Úr* and *Pan* without discrimination and hierarchy.

Changing consumption and everyday life

Central and Eastern Europe was traditionally characterized by poor living conditions and low standards of living. Decent nutrition was a social privilege. According to a Hungarian aphorism, a peasant eats chicken only in two cases, when either he or the chicken is sick. Social status linked with good eating, and being fat represented affluence. The most important social transformation was thus a consumption explosion. It did not come quickly, since living standards sharply declined in the early fifties. From the mid fifties on, however, a rapid increase and change in the consumption of food signaled a social transformation and a rise in living standards.

In Czechoslovakia, for example, per capita meat, eggs, and sugar consumption in 1948 was lower than in 1936, and reached 28 kilograms, 95 units and 22.7 kilograms respectively. By 1989, meat and egg consumption more than tripled, while sugar consumption nearly doubled. Hungarian per capita meat and sugar consumption more than doubled between 1950 and 1989. Meat and egg consumption hardly increased in Poland, but sugar consumption nearly quadrupled, compared with 1939.

From the more prosperous sixties on, the consumption of the typical foodstuffs of poor people, such as potatoes, decreased by one quarter in Poland, one fifth in Czechoslovakia, and dropped to a half in Hungary. Consumption of cereals declined by 20 percent in Hungary and Bulgaria, 33 percent in Poland, and by about 40 percent in Yugoslavia.

Per capita meat, sugar, and egg consumption, an indication of high level nutrition, reached Western standards. The 70–90 kg. meat consumption in Central and Eastern Europe was at the same level as in West Germany, Great Britain, and Denmark (74–98 kg.) in the 1980s. The 40–46 kg. of sugar consumption of the late eighties was rather similar to the West (36–44 kg.). The annual 250 eggs consumed in West Germany was the same as the Czechoslovak and Hungarian level of the same year, but in the late eighties the latter region's standard reached 250–350 pieces. Fruit and vegetables were as often on the table in these countries as in the West. Bulgaria's per capita consumption was 223 kg., West Germany's level was 188 kg., Hungary consumed 155 kg., Denmark and the United States 122 kg. and 175 kg. respectively, Czechoslovakia s and Poland's fruit and vegetable consumption reached 128 kg. and 141 kg. respectively, the British level was 139 kg. in the 1980s (*Statisticheskoj ezhegodnik*, 1990).

In terms of food consumption, therefore, Central and Eastern Europe elevated itself to the level of the developed world. Although the poor, so-called developing world had an average of 2,350 calories daily per capita and the Latin American countries had 2,634, thus almost exactly the world average of 2,624, Central and Eastern Europe as well as the advanced Western world had 3,394 and 3,382 calories respectively (*Food Consumption*, 1981–8).

Bulgaria, Yugoslavia, and Hungary belonged to those countries of the world (together with, among others, Belgium, United States, Italy, and Holland) where overconsumption – 3,500–3,700 calories daily – was characteristic of the late seventies and early eighties, with both its advantages and serious disadvantages.

It is important to mention, however, that there were major differences in the supply and quality of products. In the state-socialist shortage economy even food supply was rather uncertain. There were permanent shortages of certain products. In Romania in the sixties, a relatively better period of supply, meat other than lamb and poultry was hardly available, and one had to go to the black-market (or "free" market) to buy beef or pork, "real meat" for certain groups of the population, and pay unrealistically high prices for it. Even in well-supplied Hungary, where queuing for meat ended in the mid sixties, veal was practically never available in shops. In all of these countries, meat was not properly prepared and was sold with a great amount of fat.

Fruit and vegetables were hardly available in the winter. Oranges and bananas, after having appeared in the sixties, most of the time were imported only before Christmas and for a short while. In some of the countries of the region such as Poland and Romania, there were permanent shortage and a continuous struggle for certain basic staples. In the seventies, a housewife in Krakow was happy to get some tomatoes on the black-market in the summer. Queuing before state shops for meat, fruit, and vegetables remained an everyday phenomenon. From the late sixties on, Hungary, Czechoslovakia, and, for a certain period, Bulgaria represented exceptions. Yugoslavia, especially the more well-to-do Slovenia and Croatia, reflected a sort of "Western oasis" of supply, with all the imported Western products making the country extremely attractive even for Czechoslovak and Hungarian tourists.

Parallel with the increased standard of living, the pattern of family expenditure changed. In the best cases of Hungary and Czechoslovakia, spending on nutrition declined from nearly one half to less than one-third of a typical family budget. Expenditures on durable goods, on the other hand, increased strikingly. A growing consumerism and a better, though always limited, supply of consumer goods characterized the period from the early sixties on. The main result of this was a breakthrough in housing, the mechanization of households, and a dramatic increase in the use of automobiles. Though official propaganda always criticized the "declining" West, central and Eastern European leaders virtually sought to follow in its footsteps and copy its changing consumption patterns.

Characteristically enough, the de-politicized consumerism of the Kádár regime in Hungary generated a political debate in the country immediately after its emergence in the early sixties. A consumer orientation or "refrigerator-socialism," as it was pejoratively called, was rejected, and the "petty-bourgeois attitude" of seeking to own summer houses and cars was strongly criticized. This debate was reproduced in the early and mid seventies, when an anti-reform campaign began. In an extremely characteristic interview in early 1973, the party-secretary of Pécs called for collective forms of leisure activities: "one can expect the individual who receives more free time from our state to use it in accordance with aims of our society ... More and more people spend ... [their free time] tilling their ... gardens ... [but] gardening isolates one from the community." The party-secretary recalled the experience of neighboring Komló, where families founded some garden "cooperative" to work together (Szentiványi, 1973).

Such attempts, however, failed. Together with a moderately increasing standard of living, the countries of the region sought to follow the attractive Western pattern of consumption. In the two decades of impressive expansion, per capita personal consumption, with rather small differences among the countries, increased by 40–50 percent in the 1960s and by another 20–50 percent in the 1970s. Construction of new dwellings gradually increased. Hungary's example clearly shows the dynamics: there were 3.3 dwellings built per 1,000 inhabitants during the early fifties, roughly 6.0 during the sixties, and 8.2 during the first half of the seventies. Using a more telling parameter, in 1950 between 228 (Poland) and 329 (Hungary) new housing units were built per 1,000 new marriages, i.e., only one-quarter to one-third of the newly emerging demand was fulfilled. In 1960, the number of new units were between 480 (Romania) and 722 (Bulgaria); thus still only one-half to three-quarters of new demand was met, and the housing situation continued to decline.

From the sixties on, however, housing conditions improved. There were, on average, 579,000 dwellings constructed in Central and Eastern Europe from 1961–5, but the number increased by 12 percent (647,000) during the second half of the decade. An upswing in the seventies is reflected by the figures of 1978 and 1980 (873,000 and 856,000), which represent a more than one-third increase compared to the late sixties. In the eighties, however, construction again strongly declined.[4] The more prosperous 1960s and 1970s thus resulted in a gradual improvement in housing. In 1960 there were 240–280 dwellings per 1,000 inhabitants in the more advanced Czechoslovakia, Hungary, and Poland. In 1985, the Czechoslovak, Hungarian, and Bulgarian level was 353–367 dwellings, while the Polish and Yugoslav was around 290, per 1,000 inhabitants. It represented an improvement compared to 1960, especially at the more advanced level, where housing, expressed in dwellings by population, improved by nearly 40 percent. The Austrian figure of 414 dwellings per 1,000 was higher by 15 percent compared to the Czechoslovak–Hungarian–Bulgarian aggregate (*Annual Bulletin of Housing*).

The overcrowding in apartments definitely diminished: there were 3.6, 3.2, and 2.8 persons per one dwelling in Hungary in 1960, 1970, and 1985 respectively. The Czechoslovak and Bulgarian figures were similar, while in Poland and Yugoslavia even in the mid eighties, on average, 3.5 persons lived in one dwelling. (The Austrian figure was 2.4 in 1985.) The average size of homes also increased. In the sixties, 60 square meters was the typical size of a Czechoslovak or Hungarian apartment. In 1985, the average size was 72 and 80 square metres in Czechoslovakia and Hungary,

---

[4] In 1985–9, it was one-quarter to one-third less than in 1980.

73 and 70 in Yugoslavia and Poland, and 65 and 58 in Bulgaria and Romania respectively. The figures partly reflect the increasing share of family homes in new housing: their share was 62 percent in Yugoslavia, 51 percent in Hungary, and 30 percent in Poland in the eighties.

Although the housing situation had markedly improved compared to prewar levels, construction could not keep up with the more rapidly rising demand, especially given the radical change in family patterns that was taking place. Prewar large families comprising three generations were split into smaller family groups, and the increased number of divorces resulted in fragmented families. The moderate increase in housing could not cover needs, and thus shortages in housing, one of the most burning social problems, were prevalent throughout the entire postwar period. New couples, in several cases, shared small one-bedroom apartments with their parents, and divorced couples had to continue living together sometimes for years. Apartments were quite often shared by two and, in some cases, even more families in the fifties and early sixties, and, though it became less common in the later period, the sharing of apartments never entirely disappeared. It was quite often the case that young couples with one or two children could not get an apartment for eight to ten years. City councils were permanently inundated with applicants who were put on endless waiting lists.

With the exception of Romania and Albania, the state in most of the countries gradually withdrew from the construction and allocation of apartments, and a free market in the construction and selling of dwellings was introduced.

Furthermore, up until the very last decade, housing was often of rather poor quality, especially in the cities. Prefabricated buildings made urban landscapes appear rather uniform and boring. The facilities in dwellings were out-dated. In the relatively more developed Hungary, only half of the dwellings had indoor plumbing in the mid seventies, and even in Budapest the number of dwellings with bathrooms increased from one-third to one-half of total dwellings between 1950 and 1975. In the middle of the period under discussion, nearly two-thirds of the dwellings in Czechoslovakia and three-quarters in Poland did not have a toilet. At the end of the eighties, however, virtually all newly built homes had indoor plumbing and bathrooms. Moreover, one-third of the Bulgarian and Yugoslav, three-quarters of the Hungarian, and 97–99 percent of the Polish and Czechoslovak newly built dwellings had central heating. Peripheral backwardness in housing conditions was thus gradually and only partly overcome by postwar advances.

Next to the improvement in nutrition, the mechanization of households certainly became the second most important characteristic of changing everyday life in the region. Refrigerators, washing machines, and TV sets were virtually non-existent in the area's households until the late fifties. In 1960, at the very beginning of the process, there were four to six refrigerators, ten to twenty televisions, and forty to sixty washing machines per 1,000 inhabitants in Hungary and Poland respectively. Czechoslovakia represented a more advanced stage; the Balkans, however, had not yet started. During the sixties and seventies televisions were found in almost all homes: there were 270–280 TVs per 1,000 people in Czechoslovakia, Hungary, and Poland in the mid eighties; thus, allowing for three to four members per family, virtually the entire population watched TV. In the Balkans, the level was lower (174–189 sets per 1,000, thus eighty to ninety sets per 100 households) but still rather advanced. In Albania, television was introduced in the late seventies and achieved roughly half the level of the other Balkan countries (*Statistical Yearbook*, 1973–89).

In the sixties and seventies, TV certainly became the most important novelty of everyday life. Entire nations sat before their sets and watched the same programs (there was one or at least two channels and, for a long time, only a few hours of broadcasting in the afternoon and evening). The movie, documentary or soccer match of the previous evening became the next day's central topic of discussion.

In the late sixties roughly every second and third household, and in the mid-eighties virtually every household, had a washing machine and refrigerator in most of the countries. The real symbol of following Western consumerism, however, was a belated start in the use of cars. In 1955 there were very few cars in the region. The dynamism of "automobilization" is impressively expressed by the examples of Poland, Yugoslavia, and Hungary (see table 5.5).

In three decades, by the late eighties, cars became widespread and Central and Eastern Europe reached the level of the poorer West European countries. In 1988, as an average of the region, there were 130 cars per 1,000 inhabitants affecting roughly every third family, which was the same level as in the South European market economies (129 cars per 1,000). Car ownership, which began in the region thirty to forty years later than in the West, attained something more than one-third of the level of the European Community (374 cars per 1,000 inhabitants) (*Annual Bulletin in Transport*, 1965–90).

With a much lower standard of living, the growing consumerism and consumption required a lot of sacrifices and hard work in these countries, where a great part of Western durable goods remained luxury items and status symbols for a long time. A Czechoslovak worker had to work 470 hours to be able to buy a TV set, while his German colleague had to work

Table 5.5. *Number of passenger cars (in 000s)*

Year	Hungary	Poland	Yugoslavia	Total	Index
1955	10	40	13	63	12
1965	99	245	188	532	100
1980	1,013	2,383	2,434	5,830	1,095
1988	1,790	4,519	3,090	9,399	17,667

only 133 hours. For a sewing machine they worked 287 and 88 hours respectively, for a transistor radio 117 and 12 hours. A popular, humorous Hungarian expression symbolized the dilemma of families in the 1970s: "*kicsi vagy kocsi,*" meaning "either a baby or a car." Most young couples did not hesitate to choose the latter. Although buyers had to wait two to five years for a new Russian *Zhiguli* or East-German *Trabant*, consumerism and modern lifestyles had arrived in the form of car ownership to Central and Eastern Europe in the second half of the twentieth century.

A third and most striking explosion of postwar consumption in the region occurred in the cultural and health services, which caused a dramatic change in lifestyles. All of these were either heavily subsidized, as in the case of books, theaters, films, and concerts, or were very cheap or even free, as with schooling and health care. Cultural consumption and health services were thus easily accessible for the masses.

Cultural activities, for one, were not subordinated to market rules, and theaters, film makers, and publishers did not have to follow market considerations. All these activities were heavily subsidized and consequently led by artistic and political (but not business) considerations. Political-ideological taboos, however, combined with strict state-party control and censorship, subjugated artistic production by excluding several non-conformist works and artistic trends. The differences in cultural policy and control among the countries of the region were rather wide and also changed over time. Ceauşescu's Romania, Husák's Czechoslovakia, and Hoxha's Albania continued strict censorship and banned critical works and Western modernism. On the other hand, cultural policy in Poland, Hungary, and Yugoslavia in the later period of post-Stalinism was much less oppressive. Central and Eastern European cultural life consequently offered a valuable "supply" of Western culture. Films attained a high artistic level in Poland, Hungary, and Czechoslovakia. Theaters performed the entire classical repertoire of European drama from Shakespeare and Molière to Chekhov and Gogol and, in some countries, a great many of the contemporary plays of Arthur Miller, Tennessee Williams, and, in the later decades, Alby, Pinter, and Beckett. The same was true for publishing: all the classics of European and American literature, as well as some contemporary writers (though selected on political considerations in most of the countries), were available. Domestic contemporary literature was strongly preferred, though critical works and writings of dissident writers were strictly excluded. In the more liberal Hungary and Poland, almost no novel or play written in this period remained unpublished. Nevertheless, self-censorship became an automatic reflex in these countries. All this led to serious cultural losses. On the other hand, the lack of commercialization in culture preserved important cultural values as well.

Reading became commonplace among a part of the population. (According to a poll in the mid-seventies, all or some members of 60 percent of the families of the most advanced northern countries of the region regularly read novels, poems, etc.) While 17.3 million copies of books and other publications appeared in Hungary in 1938, the number was 200 million publications by the late eighties. Virtually the same level of publication characterized Czechoslovakia, while Poland and Bulgaria were not far behind. Theaters, movies, and exhibitions were easily accessible and offered regular entertainment for a great part of the population.

In a paradoxical way, the fact that cultural entertainment played such a large part in everyday life was partly a consequence of the relatively poor living conditions, since these cultural activities were easily accessible to lower-income groups as well, while expensive luxury entertainment such as skiing, yachting, sailing, and tourism abroad was either impossible or available to only a small part of the population. But by the late seventies several complaints were made regarding the declining interest in culture. New leisure-time activities developed, partly connected with the increasing use of cars. Domestic and (in Yugoslavia, Poland, and Hungary) foreign tourism became accessible to the broad masses, but the consumption of culture also remained at a relatively high level, a distinct and special characteristic of the consumption pattern of the region. This was certainly the only sphere of consumption where the countries of the region achieved some advantage compared to the more advanced West.

There was a significant increase in the standard of living in the area and considerable modernization. There was, however, a high price to pay: fighting against the old backwardness, the region could not follow the newest trends in technological and structural modernization. A different kind of "backwardness" emerged which had dramatic consequences from the mid–late seventies on. After the oil crisis of 1973, a new chapter opened in the history of the region – the beginning of the collapse of state socialism.

6   Crisis and erosion of state socialism, 1973–88

What was the reason for the spectacular decline after 1973 and then the universal collapse of state socialism in Central and Eastern Europe at the end of the 1980s? What was the prelude to 1989? How did the crisis became manifest and how did the system decline into an unstoppable process of erosion?

Economic and international factors of the crisis

Emerging economic crisis

To answer these questions, one has to delve into several different layers of a rather complex historical phenomenon. The first layer may be found in the region's economic performance. If an impressive growth rate, a catching up process, and increased income in most cases provided a sort of legitimization and acceptance, the decline began when these aspects dried up. This did not happen at once, but economic trends in Central and Eastern Europe dramatically changed in about 1973.

Angus Maddison's calculations offer a broad view of the process: between 1913 and 1950, the Central and Eastern European countries comprised one of the slowest growing regions of the world. Their average 1 percent per capita GNP growth rate remained behind the growth of the advanced European "Core" countries (1.3 percent), the non-European "Core" countries (1.4 percent), Latin America (1.4 percent), and even Africa (1.2 percent); only Asia had slower growth (with its −0.1 percent).

In contrast, between 1950 and 1973, Central and Eastern Europe could boast the best performance: its unprecedented 3.9 percent average annual per capita growth surpassed the growth rate of the European and non-European "Core" (3.8 and 2.2 percent respectively), and was also better than the very rapid Asian (3.7 percent) and the less impressive Latin-American (2.5 percent) and African (1.7 percent) growth rates. According to these calculations, the region almost quadrupled its interwar rate of growth.

After 1973 this trend entirely changed. The countries of state socialism could not cope with the monumental structural crisis and lost their dynamism. According to the World Bank's figures, Hungary, which had an annual 6 percent growth rate until the late seventies, suddenly dropped to 1.6 percent and 0 percent in 1979 and 1980. Poland, strongly connected with her deep political crisis as well, had a −10.0 and −4.8 percent rate in 1981 and 1982. Yugoslavia, which previously had fluctuating but rapid growth, declined to a 1.2, 0.6, and −1.1 percent rate in 1981, 1982, and 1983 respectively (*World Tables*, 1990).

Between 1973 and 1987 the annual economic growth of the region dropped from 3.9 percent to 1.9 percent (the same rate as that of the European Core but much slower than the still tempestuously growing Asia's rate, which remained at 3.7 percent). By 1988 slow growth or stagnation was already replaced by severe decline.

These changes, dramatic and sudden as they were, could not be evaluated as mere consequences of the oil crisis or the structural crisis, which became manifest afterwards. The first stage of erosion, which at the time was not easily perceptible in every country (it was rather visible in Czechoslovakia and Hungary), emerged around the mid 1960s. The reserves of the extensive import-substituting industrialization were exhausted in this period. The "unlimited," unutilized labor force had provided the possibility of mass employment and the regrouping from lower to higher productivity branches, basically from agriculture and households to industry. The model worked (better in backward countries, while less so or not at all in the more advanced ones) until labor reserves were depleted and import substitution led to a major restructuring. (The countries of the region, of course, had to pay a very high price for their rapid growth: mistaken structural policies, careless destruction of the environment, technological backwardness, and the lack of development of modern infrastructure had tragic consequences in the later decades.) Some of the countries of the region, such as Hungary and Czechoslovakia, realized in time and in the most articulated way that their *Sturm und Drang* industrialization had reached its limits, and they had to replace "extensive" industrialization based on excessive new labor input with an "intensive" development based on increased productivity, i.e., technological development and rationalization. This argument was stressed with regard to economic reforms in these two countries in the mid sixties.

After the "extensive" sources of labor imput and new job creation dried up, a general slowing down process followed throughout Central and Eastern Europe. The Comecon countries consequently could not supply each other with all the materials and products needed, especially modern technology, which could fuel further economic growth. In other words, regional self-sufficiency decreased and the countries were forced to turn toward the world market; and, in order to pay for it, they were forced to sell their products. Consequently, inter-Comecon trade began to decrease. Poland's, Hungary's, and Romania's Comecon trade gradually dropped from 66–75 percent to 40–44 percent. There were only two countries in the region that preserved the dominance of Comecon trade until the end of the eighties, Czechoslovakia (57 percent) and Bulgaria (80 percent). As a result, trade with the free world market, which had been marginal (buying materials and products that were not readily available in the Comecon market), now became a critical part of their economic life.

This invisible transformation became a time-bomb and had dramatic consequences. The Soviet model of industrialization was based on national and regional isolation and autarky. Only in this environment could it achieve impressive growth and major structural changes. The newly industrializing countries did not have to compete with advanced adversaries in an open world market. But if they had to trade in a cut-throat world market as much as they did with the closed, non-competitive regional market, they would have to export in a competitive way, thus rendering the continuation of import substitution impossible. A great part of their production now had to cope with world market requirements. A trade reorientation required the replacement of import substitution with an export orientation.

The recognition of the need for change was a rather slow process: the first declaration on the aim to turn to export orientation was made in Hungary in October 1977. A resolution declared that "the export capacity of industry and agriculture is not in proportion to the . . . requirements . . . [and] more active participation in the international division of labor . . ." and "a marked expansion of exports" is needed (Berend, 1990, p. 241). The decision on a new economic strategy, however, remained wishful thinking.

Most of the other countries, mostly because of rigid ideological barriers, never even arrived at this stage of recognition. The second nationwide party conference in Poland declared in 1978 that economic troubles were caused by "recession and decline in the capitalist countries, and its negative impact on trade" (Krajowa, 1978). Two years later Edward Gierek reported: "Our party faced these difficult problems . . . [and] reorganized the forces and sources . . . and accomplished the goals decided by . . . the party" (Gierek, 1980, p. 104).

In a non-competitive economic environment, certain bitter attempts towards export orientation, even when tried, often failed. A most telling case was the reorientation of the Crvena Zastava automobile plant in

Kragujevac, Yugoslavia, from its import substituting production for the domestic market toward export orientation. It pays to follow the firm's story from that point on. As Michael Palairet described, after the oil shock "the authorities exerted ever increasing pressure on Zastava to boost export sales to hard currency markets. A high-cost import substituter was to be turned, by command, into an internationally competitive car maker" (Palairet, 1994, pp. 93–109).

The Zastava factory increased its capacity from a production of 400–500 cars a year in 1954–5 to 160,000 by 1972. The Fiat 600 and later the modified version of the Fiat 128 supplied the home market, and the firm became a major component producer for the same Fiat products of Poland and the Soviet Union. Using huge amounts of investments, Zastava turned to produce the Yugo 45 for export: the first Yugos left the factory in November 1980. Seeking to break into the American market, the company reached an agreement with Armand Hammer's Occidental Oil and Malcolm Brincklin, who founded the Yugo-America Inc. "The Yugo-American contract was hailed in Yugoslavia as the deal of the century." New sources were granted to the firm, which began to develop new types, the Yugo-Kabrio and the Florida. According to the ambitious plans in the framework of the Yugo-America program, 35,000 cars would be exported to the United States in 1985 and 272,000 in 1990. Though 52 percent of investments was spent abroad to import equipment, "by early 1988, Yugo sales drive was turning sour. Brincklin sold his interest in Yugo-America ... The business collapsed late in 1988. ... Zastava diverted its output to the home market ... but exchange stabilization in January 1990 caught it with hideous debts, unable to sell much abroad" (Palairet, 1994, p. 96). From almost 58,000 cars sold in the United States in 1987, sales declined to fewer than 26,000 in 1988 and 18 (!) in 1989. Quality, service, marketing, and model variety were simply not competitive, and this led to a total halt of production of Yugo-Kabrio in 1990. The government, which pushed the firm to continue exporting and paid it high amounts in subsidies, could do nothing to prevent its collapse: the loss was about $1,800 per car, totalling $240 million between 1985 and 1988, while another $400 million investment on the Florida was written off. An overall loss arising from all of Zastava's export-led ventures was around one billion dollars.

There were a few similar endeavors, though certainly nothing the size of Zastava. At the same time a few less ambitious attempts, such as the Hungarian Hungaroton's compact disc invasion of the world market, were successful.

The change of the old technological regime; structural crisis

Historically speaking, however, there was no time for hesitation. A radical restructuring in order to assure export capabilities became urgent, and further delay turned out to be suicidal. The 1973 and then 1980 Oil Crisis revealed a gradually emerging structural crisis in the world economy, which was generated by a complete change of the old technological regime. This is the basis of an understanding of the deepening crisis in Central and Eastern Europe.

The phenomenon is not unique in modern economic history. Whole "sets" of technological changes, or, as they are often called, "industrial revolutions," followed after the British Industrial Revolution, in the middle and at the end of the nineteenth century. The first, the age of the steam-engine and of textile manufacturing, followed by a revolution of the iron-steel and engineering industries (connected with the age of railroads), was rapidly followed by the second with its revolutionized chemical industry, which linked science and research with industry, and which saw new industries based on a new source of energy, electricity.

In the twentieth century, two major world wars and their aftermaths generated two additional sets of technological change, or a fourth and fifth industrial revolution. The fourth which spanned the inter-war years was characterized by the complex use of the combustion engine and by the car and aircraft industries, which entailed a managerial revolution and new ways of mass production. Also, the great breakthrough of the electro-technical industries, which were closely connected to the new war technologies, played an important role. All these went hand in hand with the building up of a new twentieth-century infrastructure of *Autobahns* and electric power stations and networks.

The fifth industrial revolution, which was closely connected to the breakdown of Central and Eastern Europe from the 1970s on, has an importance comparable only to the great turning point of the British Industrial Revolution. The gradual process, which was rooted at the end of World War II and marked by the invention of the first computer and by nuclear fusion, opened a new chapter in history.

The inventions of the postwar decades gradually transformed technology, and indeed created a new stage of civilization, the post-industrial or communication epoch. A computerized world transformed production and services, initiated a new infrastructure, and led to the introduction of robots and space technology, with new materials and new energy sources. As with textiles two hundred years before, electronics became the herald of the new age.

The Soviet-type modernization model remained light years behind the requirements of the new technological era. Moreover, the fifth industrial revolution was characterized by an entirely new industrial environment as well. It was distinguished by, to mention only the three most important emerging new characteristics, special refinement, unparalleled complexity in installation and production systems, and more complex division of labor. "Refinement," one expert suggested, "is perhaps the first comprehensible, moreover, measurable characteristic of those instruments that are transforming the world. We are assessing in microns and fractions of microns the technological parameters of the electronic circuits, whose capacities are permanently increasing. There is a permanent struggle for fractions of microns . . . [which are] characterizing the modern processing technologies, the preciseness of machine tools, and the interlocking of surfaces . . ." (Vámos, 1991, p. 3).

Central and Eastern Europe conserved its antiquated technology. It may be compared to a situation of attempting to adjust to the nineteenth-century Industrial Revolution without having railroads. A striking characteristic of the backwardness of the region from this point of view was the state of the telephone network, a prerequisite of introducing modern information technology. A telephone line in these countries was and remained a real asset, a special privilege for which many had to wait years, sometimes decades, to attain. The density of telephone lines in the region was 7.4 and 9.5 lines per 100 inhabitants in 1980 and 1987 respectively, when the figures were 26 and 34.6 per 100 people in the European market economies. Compared with the rapidly developing Southern Europe, the gap increased to 2.7 times in the eighties. The most modern new telecommunication instruments did not appear in the socialist countries until the late eighties (Ehrlich, 1991).

Another element of the new technological requirements was the tidiness of materials. The impurity of materials are measured by a hundredth or a millionth of a percent. Special alloys represent connections of critical exquisiteness to fulfill the very high specifications. All these demand the highest hygiene and cleanliness in the whole industrial environment, and a new requirement of strict limits on air-pollution in industrial firms. Central and Eastern Europe, in contrast, did not even realize (and definitely did not care about) the extent of pollution caused by its extreme, turn-of-the-century drive for industrialization. The industrial environment remained, in several cases, similar to the standards of the nineteenth century.

Complexity was the other most striking technological characteristic of the new technology. Recent electronic circuits already contain more than a million previously independent elements. A modern car or an airplane has several thousands and several tens of thousands of components respectively. Huge international systems such as telecommunications, air-transportation, or energy set-ups have an operational mechanism of immense complexity. The software of a new electronic tripping circuit may contain a few million orders, and several hundreds of thousands of different machines can operate in one computer network. Higher standards created a multitude of additional requirements. A half-sized measure, a surface twice as refined and a product twice as tidy, at times requires the fulfillment of five to ten times more factors. Several related factors that might be neglected for the production of a traditional product would have to be counterbalanced. The unparalleled complexity of the new technology characterizes the division of labor and demands more than narrow specialization. A new technological achievement is sometimes a consequence of well-organized cooperation of several hundreds or thousands of people. All the above described characteristics are closely connected with a highly developed technological civilization and the new, advanced infrastructure of the information society. Since this highly complex system is permanently transforming, it requires the maximum flexibility and adjustability (Bożyk, 1988).

In sharp contrast to the new economic requirements, a state socialist economy, characterized by a lack of market interests and adequate owner's responsibility, became rather self-sufficient in its bureaucratic ownership and managerial structures, not only on the national but on the factory level as well. Cooperation with other factories made the firms dependent, and they thus attempted to produce as many of their own parts and spare parts for their products as possible.

The fifth industrial revolution, though it emerged gradually in the postwar decades, became manifest from the early seventies on. From that time on, a severe structural crisis hit the whole world economy. This structural crisis caused economic decline, high inflation, and unemployment even in the most advanced countries. But the painful consequences were especially acute in the peripheral countries, which were unable to respond by developing new industries of their own. In other words, their old leading sectors had declined, but they could not adjust and build up new leading industries based on new technology.

The turn of the 1970s to 1980s was devastating for those countries, which could not adjust and restructure their trade and production. The consequences were surprisingly similar in Latin America and in Central and Eastern Europe. State socialism, however, created special, additional obstacles. On top of the "natural" peripheral disadvantage was their continued fidelity to post-Stalinist ideology, the notorious equation of the Soviet model with "socialism" and the rigid rejection of structural or even policy changes as "revisionism" or as attempts to restore capitalism, which caused an unbreakable barrier of rigidity. The Soviet Union controlled and – by military intervention or political pressure – blocked the road toward radical changes in East Central Europe. The rigidity of the system created and preserved a social, economic, and technological environment which collided head on with the new technological requirements.

Though the Soviet Union was able to preserve her rule over the satellite regimes and prevent their adjustment, she could not halt, and indeed significantly contributed to, the erosion of their systems.

"Destruction without creation": increasing gap and the debt-trap

The structural crisis of the 1970s and 1980s had rather different consequences in the West than in the East. Though growth slowed down or stopped in each country, there were, beneath the surface, quite different trends in each. In the West took place a sharp decline from the mid to late seventies to the early eighties. This was the shock of adjustment. In the meantime, an adjustment began which led to a new prosperity from the early or mid eighties on.

In Central and Eastern Europe, where market automatism did not exist, the government should have recognized the character of world market changes and responded accordingly. Instead of a spontaneous, instant market reaction, the response was entirely bureaucratic and rather delayed. First of all, the various governments did not recognize the changes and, at least for another half decade, continued their previous economic policy to force rapid growth according to their ideological values.

In Poland, world economic changes emerged at the same time as to the expansionist, adventurist economic policies of the Gierek administration, which attempted to overcome economic troubles by implementing a super-investment and growth project: in the first half of the seventies, investment was increased by 133 percent, and in 1975 GNP increased by 29 percent while real wages increased by almost 7 percent. Expanding the obsolete structure of the economy on such an unparalleled time scale led to real disaster. Because of the expansion of the old obsolete heavy industries, Poland, a traditional energy exporter, became a net energy importer by the end of the seventies, and declined into its most severe economic crises.

The still generally high growth rate, with the required, equally high rate of foreign trade – in the mid 1970s exports reached nearly half of the Hungarian, and between one fifth to one quarter of the Polish, Yugoslav, or Romanian GDP – exacerbated the troubles throughout the region. The antiquated technology and obsolete export structure of the previously import-substituting countries led to a permanent decline of their terms of trade. In the first five years, after the first oil shock, the countries of the region suffered a 10 percent to 20 percent decline. Deterioration, however, continued: according to the calculations of Éva Ehrlich (based on the Economic Survey of Europe), the terms of trade in the region as a whole declined by 6 percent between 1970 and 1975, 12 percent by 1980, and 19 percent by 1985. Some of the countries of the region suffered a 26–32 percent decline. In the early to mid eighties, therefore, the countries of the region had to export roughly one-fifth more (in some cases almost one-third more) than they did for the same amount of imports before 1973 (*Statistical Yearbook*, 1990).

A continuation of forced rapid growth led to an ever-increasing accumulation of trade deficits and undermined the economies. The crisis gradually accelerated and became deeper and more prolonged. Previous prosperity was followed by one and half decades of crisis with increasingly slower and slower growth, followed by stagnation and then decline. In the crucial years of 1986–9 Hungary had an annual growth rate of 0.9, Poland of 0.2, Yugoslavia of 0.5, and Romania of 0.7 percent. In contrast, in these four years the OECD countries had already reached an annual growth of 3.6 percent. The gap, which had previously narrowed between Central and Eastern Europe and the West, began to widen again: according to certain calculations the gap between the state socialist countries and the United States increased from 1:3 to 1:4 between 1980 and 1989. In this single decade, the difference compared to the European Common Market doubled.

Not only did the differing rate of growth and its evolving trends cause a growing gap. The real and major difference was that all this happened in Central and Eastern Europe without real adjustment and restructuring. The accumulating deficit, moreoever, required some kind of financial solution. The countries that wanted to maintain their growth rate (and living standards) had to turn to the international credit market. Most of the countries of the region did so from 1974 on, because they surmised that only stop-gap measures were needed to bridge the few years of transitory turmoil before economic prosperity resumed. This was certainly encouraged by the relatively cheap offer of oil-dollars in the seventies.

This short sighted policy led to a dramatic backlash. On top of the structural crisis, a crisis of indebtedness emerged as well. As a disastrous consequence of a mistaken economic expansionism, the Gierek era propped up its economy with 20 billion dollar loans. By the early 1980s Hungary, Poland, Romania, and Bulgaria had accumulated huge amounts of debt, varying from 10 to 30 billion dollars. The net value of debt in the region as a whole increased from 6 to 79 billion dollars between 1970 and

1980. Indebtedness became a self-generating process from that time on, and the 1980s led to a hopeless and devastating spiralling of debt. By 1990 Poland had accumulated 41.8, Hungary 20.3, and Bulgaria 9.8 billion dollars of net debt. On a per capita basis Hungarian indebtedness was the highest, $2,585 compared to the Polish $1,100 and the Bulgarian $1,068 debt level. At the end of the eighties her total debt was slightly two times higher than her export value, while the corresponding figures for Bulgaria and Poland were three and even five times higher respectively. At the end of the eighties, the debt service consumed 40 percent of Hungarian hard currency income, 45 percent of Polish, and 75 percent of Bulgarian.

Additionally, the international financial market "hardened" dramatically from the early eighties on. Unlimited and cheap credit was no longer available, and the rate of interest increased to a record 14–16 percent. Indebtedness, except for Hungary, bankrupted most of the countries: Poland, Yugoslavia, and Bulgaria became insolvent and asked for rescheduling. Indebtedness, furthermore, seriously hindered any adjustment, since an important 5–8 percent of the GNP was leaking out of the countries and significantly weakened their investment possibilities. Most of the new credits served the repayments for the old ones. From the more than $20 billion that made up the Hungarian debts, only about $4–5 billion was invested in the economy. The countries of the region were arrested in the indebtedness trap.

The Central and Eastern European countries made a last, bitter attempt to change the economic trend and launched an export offensive in 1980–4. Éva Ehrlich's calculated aggregate figures reflect an increase in exports of 25 percent (pushed by offering special incentives, neglecting the cost of production and efficiency, and paying export premiums and subsidies), while imports were decreased by draconian measures. Consequently the balance of trade and payments improved and the debt burden declined to $72 billion. The countries, however, exhausted their reserves. From 1984–8 the volume of exports hardly increased at all (by 8 percent), but imports accelerated by nearly 20 percent. Both essentially collapsed in the next two years, declining by 30 and 25 percent respectively; indebtedness jumped to $110 billion (Ehrlich, 1991, pp. 91–2).

Romania was the only country in the region which decided to escape from the indebtedness trap by paying back the debt: halving it by 1985 and eliminating it by 1989. It succeeded: while the net amount of Romanian debt in the mid 1980s was as much as its hard currency export income, it was only 1 percent of them in 1989. The draconian enforcement of repayment, however, devastated Romanian consumers, emptied the shelves of stores, and darkened the hardly illuminated cities and the cold, unheated homes. Electricity consumption in 1985, for example, dropped to 20 percent of the 1979 level. Since imports were drastically cut, the whole economy was ruined. Romania escaped from the indebtedness trap but fell into an even deeper poverty trap.

What happened in the region between the mid seventies and the late eighties was not a unique phenomenon at all. Latin American growth also decreased from 2.5 percent to 0.8 percent, and a huge trade deficit – in the late eighties, Mexico had an annual trade deficit of roughly $20 billion, which was equal to the entire amount of Hungarian debt – and indebtedness were characteristic as well. The total amount of debt in Brazil, Mexico, and Argentina surpassed the level of exports by three to five times, and the annual debt service consumed 50–62 percent of export incomes in the late 1980s. The Latin American performance was thus strikingly similar to its Central and Eastern European counterparts (Fishlow, 1986; Iglesias, 1985; Reisen, 1985).

It should be noted that the reaction of the two regions to the structural crisis shows a common, typically peripheral response to a dramatic international challenge. The consequences definitely reflected basic similarities.

The repercussions in Central and Eastern Europe, however, were dramatic. Since state socialism ruled the entire economy, the deepening economic crisis undermined the transitory legitimacy of the regime. Surplus income, redistributed by the state, disappeared with the vanished economic growth. The moderate but increasing standard of living stopped entirely, the premature welfare state lost its basis, and the low-level security, including full employment, became uncertain. The emerging economic disaster gradually became a comprehensive crisis of the regime.

Habermas was definitely right when he stated in his *Legitimization Crisis*, that "if government crisis management fails, it lags behind programmatic demands that it has placed on itself. The penalty for this failure is withdrawal of legitimization" (cited in Lewis, 1984). In the analysis of Domenico Nuti, the crisis of the regime originated "in the inability of the economy to change from a structure relatively well-suited to the process of extensive developments to one more in tune with the needs of intensive development" (Lewis, 1984, pp. 10–11).

Changing external conditions: the demise of the Soviet Union

The climax came in the late eighties when the external guarantor of the regime weakened and collapsed. State socialism was not only an internal regime, but was assured by one of the super powers. Therefore it was futile to question or challenge its rule, and it was futile to wait for any kind of internal explosion or foreign intervention. The over-ambitious Soviet expansionism during the time of Leonid Brezhnev, however, met its Waterloo. The role of a dominating super power in the age of the replacement of the old technological regime was undermined by the erosion and decline of the Soviet economic model and economic power.

A one to two decade-long process of a new, different sort of "thaw" emerged, when the previously unquestionable Soviet ideological, political, and military domination, and indeed Soviet power itself, began to melt. By the mid-1970s, in spite of repeated crises, there was a permanent advance of Soviet socialism, which gained a footing in Europe, Asia, Africa, and Latin America, and reached its zenith with nearly one third of the world's population and territory under the rule of monolithic communist parties.

Though the system's advance and military competitiveness still continued and reached its height in the eighties, the international political ideological environment, based on changing economic, technological, and military power, began to change drastically from the mid 1970s on. Changes in defense technology suddenly began to alter the balance of power and made it clear that the Soviet Union could not remain in the race. The expensive programs of the eighties, such as "Star Wars," ended the age when the Soviet Union was an equal military partner, ready and able to compete.

In other words, the Central and Eastern European crisis coincided with a fundamental erosion of Soviet military power, and the latter's ability to dominate the entire region. At the beginning this was not yet apparent, but it soon became clear in the economic arena, and then even more so in the international political and ideological battlefields. The Soviet Union, in short, lost the Cold War because it could no longer carry its economic burdens and keep up with revolutionary advanced technologies that permanently transformed the military and required continuous and costly modernization.

What in fact happened was characterized by several, historically speaking, accidental events. It was certainly coincidental that the decades-long Soviet drive to institutionalize the post-World War II European status quo and achieve an established and recognized balance of power led, after prolonged Western resistance, to the Helsinki negotiations and agreement in the mid 1970s. The Final Act of the Conference on Security and Cooperation in Europe was signed on August 1, 1975. It was greeted as a victory by Soviet diplomacy, but it soon turned out to be a Pyrrhic victory.

At the same time, coincidentally, the West European communist movement openly revolted against Soviet ideology, publicly rejected the

Eastern socialist model, and demonstratively identified itself with social democratic values (Urban, 1979). Enrico Berlinguer, the head of the Italian Communist Party, the strongest in the West, emphatically expressed his faith in democracy and presented a "Eurocommunist" concept at the All-European Conference of the Communist and Workers' Parties in East Berlin in June 1976. In the following year, the Spanish communist leader Santiago Carillo published his book, *Eurocommunism and the State*, which was the strongest possible in-house critique of Soviet communism.

The culmination of the two phenomena, the Helsinki process and the revelation of Eurocommunism, was coincidental. Although accidental in timing, these two events were historically connected both with each other and with the deepening crisis of Central and Eastern Europe. All of these trends were rooted in the transformation of the postwar world and the failure of state socialism to adjust to it.

The so-called Helsinki process was a genuine Soviet initiative, closely connected to a Soviet effort to ease the increasing and unbearable burden of the arms race and achieve an institutionalized détente, which would stabilize her international power position, including her dominance over Central and Eastern Europe. To accomplish this, however, the Soviet Union had to make serious compromises. As a consequence, the Helsinki agreement became a rather mixed blessing, especially because of the so-called "Basket Three." The Final Act had three main parts, or "baskets" of fields of cooperation. Basket one contained security; Basket two, economic, scientific, and environmental; Basket three human rights and humanitarian and cultural issues.

Brezhnev, no doubt, achieved the reaffirmation of the postwar status quo. The existing borders, including the separation of Germany, were also assured. Some Western critics of Helsinki maintained that the West sold out Eastern Europe (again), and that the Final Act was the "last nail in the coffin of an independent Eastern Europe." Others, however, realized "two distinct opportunities arising from the Final Act" (Tokes, 1978, p. 145).

One of these was a kind of legal guarantee for the Central and Eastern European countries to loosen the noose of Soviet domination and enlarge their independent playground. The ten principles guiding relations between participating states affirmed the national sovereignty of the signatory states and the principle of non-intervention. Half of the chapter, moreover, contained principles and measures guaranteeing their implementation. The second opportunity was created by the form of Western intervention that was most heatedly debated, and at the beginning rejected by the Soviets: Basket three, which provided a legal basis to resist state and party interference and safeguard personal and social liberties. A major Western political and ideological attack was based on Basket three issues, rightly aiming toward the weakest point of the enemy and establishing the most advantageous battlefield for the West. "Most East Europeans would concede," concluded the analyst, "that the performance of Western market economies and specifically the delivery of state benefits in welfare, education, and health services . . . leave much to be desired and would not regard the Western model as an irresistible alternative to the economic status quo in Communist Eastern Europe. Therefore, it is the question of civil liberties that has the potential to generate new tensions between the people and the regimes" (Tokes, 1978, p. 464).

Western democracies, on this very basis, successfully challenged their post-Stalinist adversaries and convincingly questioned their legitimacy. This policy became a major factor of the political and moral undermining of the system, which economically was already groggy. One of the most imminent impacts of the Helsinki process was a new and increased expectation of the population, as well as a strengthened opposition throughout the region. Though some of the state socialist countries, and especially the Soviet Union, continued their oppressive practice against dissidents, their subjugation became much more uncomfortable, now being disclosed worldwide on a legal basis of an international agreement, signed by the Eastern countries.It provided justification for permanent criticism and challenged the dictatorial practices of most of the Central and Eastern European countries. The risk of joining the opposition was definitely decreased. The more liberal the country, the more true this was. It is more than symbolic that the Czechoslovak Charter 77 movement's first manifesto of January 1977 was based on, among other things, the Helsinki agreement on social and cultural rights, which became law in the country (in March 1976) following the Helsinki accord.

Helsinki also contributed to weakening the Soviet alliance system, since it served as a legal basis for strengthening national sovereignty and making the realization of the Brezhnev doctrine more difficult. The Helsinki agreement strengthened the Yugoslav and Romanian positions against Soviet interventionism, but also generated a move toward greater autonomy in loyal countries such as Kádár's Hungary. It was often stated in Western journals that the price of domestic reforms in Hungary was a foreign policy unquestionably loyal to the Soviet line. After 1975, however, there was an elaborate (but for tactical reasons, always down-played) opening to restore the country's Western relations, and to rebuild connections with the church (Kádár visited the Pope in 1977) and with West European social democratic parties. Kádár's personal diplomacy, intensive travelling, and state visits contributed to ever-increasing Western trade and economic connections, but also to a further opening of the country. The almost provocatively improving American–Hungarian relations in the late seventies, that were literally "crowned" with the gesture of giving back the holy Hungarian crown to Hungary by the Carter administration, at a time of a resurgence of the Cold War and the nadir of Soviet–American relations, is convincing evidence in itself. The same opening characterized Gierek's Poland in the seventies. The homogeneity of the Soviet bloc was broken and became a mere semblance of its former self.

State socialist regimes, however, were challenged not only from without but also from within the international communist movement. It was a long march for some leading West European Communist parties to surrender to social democratic values. As "real socialism" lost its attractiveness and the economic expansion came to a halt, and as its failure as a modernization model and as a new type of international solidarity movement – having been revealed as a camouflage for Soviet expansionism – became clear, the West European communist parties stopped following or accepting the Soviet line and revised their basic Marxist–Leninist positions. The Western communist parties accepted as fact, for example, the emergence and dominance of the middle class in postwar Western, "post-industrial" societies, and gave up the concept of the dictatorship of the proletariat. Instead of a monolithic one party system, they accepted political pluralism, a parliamentary multi-party system, and human rights.

The social-democratization of Western communist parties led to a double revolt: a refusal to serve Soviet interests as well as a rejection of the Soviet model of socialism. It was clearly expressed by the Italian Communist Party when Enrico Berlinguer announced in June 1976: "We are fighting for a socialist society that has at its foundation the affirmation of the value of individual and collective freedoms and their guarantee, the principles of the secular, non-ideological nature of the State and its democratic organization, the plurality of political parties and the possibility of altering government majorities, the autonomy of the trade unions, religious freedom, freedom of expression, of culture and the arts and sciences" (Tokes, 1978, p. 473). A "Eurocommunist summit" of the leaders of the Italian, Spanish, and French Communist Parties met in March 1977 and articulated new common principles, such as total autonomy from the Soviet Union, domestic democratic reformism, and regional Europeanism. Eurocommunism adopted the parliamentary road to power in a pluralistic political structure, and accepted and supported private ownership within a framework of mixed economy (Antonian, 1987). This strategy was strongly Europeanist based on "priorities within the framework of an open economy and coordinated efforts to find supranational solutions to the problems raised by transnational capitalism" (Hassner, 1976, p. 62). In this approach the reality was not the "Communization of European countries, but the Europeanization of communist parties." As one of the most popular East European jokes of the late seventies formulated, paraphrasing the famous starting sentence of the Communist Manifesto: "A ghost is haunting Communism: the ghost of Europe."

If the Helsinki agreement and the increased international consciousness of Basket three strengthened the opposition, encouraged the non- or anti-communist forces, and weakened the regime's oppressive reprisals against them in Central and Eastern Europe, Eurocommunism fortified the opposition-from-within, the liberal party-intelligentsia, and the reform wings in a remarkable way. It offered a renewed left-wing democratic and humanistic platform in opposition to the rigid conservativism and hypocrisy of bureaucratic Soviet socialism. It offered a hope of ending the crisis and finding a way out.

The state socialist regimes were attacked from both sides, and lost ground because they had no real answers to their critics and, most of all, to their towering economic, social, and political difficulties, except to deny their existence. As in the boxing ring, when a fighter recognizes that his adversary is becoming weaker and launches even more devastating blows, the newly emerged Western leaders (Ronald Reagan and Margaret Thatcher) led ever stronger ideological assaults against "evil" Soviet communism and called for a virtual crusade against it. In the eighties, they convincingly promulgated neo-liberal values as the single possible key to opening the golden gate of a prosperous new future. Conservative, fundamentalist communist parties, similarly ideological and rigid, were ready to respond with confrontation, by strengthening their power positions, continuing an overambitious arms race, and even launching new military actions (such as in Afghanistan). All these, however, became more and more suicidal in the continuous economic decline. It was impossible to follow the old line for long. Indeed, the aggressive response to the world challenge was soon replaced by new efforts toward adjustment.

Another historical accident helped bring about this policy shift. After four strokes, the already partially paralyzed and strongly sclerotic Leonid Brezhnev died, and after a grotesque but symbolic intermezzo of twice appointing dying men to the post of secretary general (Andropov, then Chernienko), a new energetic leader, Mikhael Gorbachev, emerged, expressing the last attempt of revitalizing and modernizing the Soviet Union. His "new course" began with the rather superficial initiative of *uskarenie*, or increasing speed and generating dynamism, and of trying to purge the country from rotten corruption and alcoholism. Gorbachev's most impressive characteristics were, however, his ability to learn and gradually understand the depth of the problems, a flexibility to adjust, and the courage, moreover, to draw the proper conclusions. *Uskarenie*, thus, was soon replaced by *glastnost* and *perestroika*, expressing a much better and deeper understanding. The new openness and restructuring opened a new chapter in Soviet international politics as well (Dawisha, 1988). The withdrawal from Afghanistan and the rejection of the class struggle as the leading principle of foreign policy were coupled with a new, non-interventionist policy toward Central and Eastern Europe. The Brezhnev doctrine did not survive its founding father for long, and was quietly buried in the late eighties (Pravda, 1992).

The rise and the anatomy of the opposition: the "moral virus"

The erosion of state socialism in Central and Eastern Europe and the diminishing control of the Soviet Union, on this very basis, unleashed different kinds of opposition to the regime. Mass revolts and rebellious reform-communists attacked Stalinist and post-Stalinist regimes and Soviet domination from the early to mid fifties on, but a permanent "dissident" movement and political opposition with an independent theoretical platform and organization was born only after 1968.

From that time on, one can theoretically differentiate among three rudimentary patterns of opposition: a moral, intellectual passive resistance attempting to build a "second society"; an organized, and if necessary, violent mass movement, openly confronting the regime; and a radicalized "reform-from-within" movement that shifted toward "social-democratization." These trends almost never existed anywhere in a "pure" form, but in combinations of each. Their purest "prototypes," however, were linked with Czechoslovakia, Poland, and Hungary. In the changing internal and international environment of the late seventies and eighties, all three trends of opposing and seeking to transform state socialist regimes were strengthened to an impressive degree. Some of the countries began to move forward. A vertical chain of accommodating, and in a way transforming countries, Poland, Hungary, and Yugoslavia, were opposed by a horizontal chain of non-reforming, orthodox hard-line regimes from East Germany, via Czechoslovakia, and Romania to Bulgaria and Albania.

The harsh realities of "existing socialism" and the deep disappointment of young revolutionaries, especially after the sharp conflicts and confrontations of the mid fifties, led to the emergence of an intellectual critique and opposition from the 1960s on. Based on the attempt of a broad Western intellectual left, disappointed in the East European "realization of Marxian socialism," and aiming to create a new clean, pure theoretical basis for a renewal, they opposed "Marxism–Leninism" and turned back to the young Marx, to his ignored *Economic and Philosophical Manuscripts*. The rediscovery of Marx's humanist philosophy was to provide a theory of substantial criticism of state socialism (Taras, 1992).

One of the pioneering workshops and a nucleus of later opposition groupings was the *Praxis* group. Yugoslav Marxist philosophers gathered around the Zagreb periodical *Praxis* between 1964 and 1974, and developed a consistent, critical concept on the regime. They having reconstructed Marx's views maintained that no revolution in the region was yet complete since seizure of power ("political revolution") is only the first episode of a long process of social revolution.

The initial phase led to the rule of an elite and to a bureaucratic state, and a bureaucratic state ownership, thus the working class was still exploited; the monopolistic party was a typical bourgeois type of political organization, and a real participatory democracy had not been created.

Marx's human being, the "man of praxis" capable of free creative activity to transform the world and satisfy basic human needs was still blocked by the existing historical conditions in Central and Eastern Europe. As Mihailo Marković summarized this concept, the discrepancy between the individual's actual (strongly limited) possibilities and his/her potential essence led to alienation. Critical analysis was necessary to clarify the required practical steps that would open the road toward human self-realization, toward a praxis to continue and accomplish a real social revolution. The consistent critical analysis of state socialism aimed at the return to genuine Marxism and a rebuilding of socialism based on its pure interpretation. That philosophy served as a banner for massive student revolts in Belgrade, Zagreb, and Sarajevo in June 1968, which led to official repression against the *Praxis* group (Crocker, 1983).

The turning point in the political life of the region generally came in 1968. The brutal suppression of the Prague Spring extinguished the hope of several radical reformers in the reformability of existing socialism. In desperation, several turned back to "clear," "real" Marxism and shifted toward an uncompromising stand on human rights, freedom, and democracy. They cut off all connections with the establishment and from the reform-from-within position, and boldly became "dissenters," in a self-sacrificing way gradually forming their independent enclaves, often arrested, but becoming more consistent in their ideology, actions, and sense of mission.

A classic transitory form of this type of opposition were the Czechoslovak reformers, who began their movement once they were expelled after 1968–9. "The Party of the Expelled," as they called themselves, found recruits from the almost half a million former party members who were expelled for positions taken during and after the fall of the Prague Spring. "The possibilities of putting up opposition within the party by now appeared exhausted," realized a group of reformists, "thus a başis of resistance had to be found outside it." In their "Manifesto of 28 October 1970," they desperately stated that "politically we have been robbed of our rights" and reformulated a program for a pluralistic, democratic socialist system, guaranteeing freedom and human rights, with independent trade unions and judiciary (Pelikan, 1976, pp. 29, 127).

The pioneering Polish dissidents were also recruited from the rank and file of the revisionists who believed that the revolution was just beginning in October 1956. They had, however, painfully realized that for Gomulka, in whom they had placed their hopes for realizing a "pure" and democratic socialism, the revolution ended with his elevation. Gomulka went on the attack against revisionist "bourgeois democrats, for whom there was no place in Poland," at the May 1957 plenum of the Central Committee, "which was almost a betrayal of the October Plenum" (Raina, 1978, p. 59). The target was the most popular journal *Po Prostu* and the philosopher Kolakowski, a major critic of the bureaucratic party-state and an advocate of democratic socialism. Major reformers of the party leadership were pushed out, and the anti-Semitic nationalist (often called "Partisan") group, which included Generals Mieczyslaw Moczar and Grzegorz Korczynski, emerged in the party hierarchy.

A "pure" Marxist analysis of the Polish situation, drafted by two young researchers, Jacek Kuron and Karol Modzelewski, at Warsaw University in 1964, which advocated changes based on "the real" Marx, was suppressed. After their expulsion from the party, the two authors appealed to the party in an open letter of 1965, criticizing bureaucratic, alienating state ownership and monolithic party rule, and arguing for reform: "By the nature of things, the revolution that will overthrow the bureaucratic system is a proletarian revolution." They suggested the introduction of workers' self-management, and a "revolution . . . of an enormous majority of society directed against the rule of the minority . . . , which is why it does not have to be carried out by force of arms" (Raina, 1978, p. 86). In July 1965 Kuron and Modzelewski were imprisoned, and in the fall of 1966 Kolakowski was expelled from the party. The suppression of democratic reform-communism inside the party was accomplished in Poland in 1968.

These far-sighted and disappointed reform-communists became the first dissidents in Central and Eastern Europe. Their rank and file was also filled by young, disillusioned intellectuals, the "so-called 'second generation socialist intelligentsia.' The trend has been particularly noticeable in Poland, Czechoslovakia, and Hungary, where many prominent dissidents are in fact the children of former party functionaries who held high office during the Stalinist era" (Bugajski and Pollack, 1989, p. 43). This group, psychologically strongly motivated, ashamed of the blind faith of their parents, initially often turned to "pure" Marxism and even revolutionary Maoism, but later often became the hard-core of dissident groupings.

In the history of the opposition, a special chapter has to be given to the 1968 student demonstrations in Warsaw. The students originally protested the banning of *Forefather's Eve*, a patriotic and anti-Russian play of Adam Mickiewicz that had become a national classic. In January 1968 a series of demonstrations and student strikes engulfed Warsaw University. Adam Michnik and Henryk Szlajfer, the main organizers, were expelled from the university. The police brutally attacked the students in March, which culminated in a formal battle with hundreds of wounded and hundreds of arrested students. Endless protests and sit-in strikes followed at universities throughout the country.

The repression which followed reflected the total bankruptcy of ailing Polish reformism. Gomulka had already opened a demagogic anti-Semitic campaign in 1967, when he declared that "we do not want a Fifth Column to be created in our country," that "every Polish citizen should have only one fatherland – People's Poland," and that the party and government would not cause "any difficulty" for Jews "in moving to Israel if they wished to" (Bugajski and Pollack, 1989, p. 110). If this was already an overt attempt to channel mass dissatisfaction into the classic canal of Polish anti-Semitism, the real opportunity for playing the anti-Semitic card arrived with the student revolt: their leaders were simply denounced as Jews. "In reality, they express the interests of their patrons – the Zionists," declared a leaflet of Moczar's Ministry of Interior. "Michnik, Blumsztajn, Szlajfer cannot and shall not teach us the tradition of patriotism" (ibid., pp. 115, 140).[1] Indeed, within a few days reformist intellectuals, state employees, and university professors were all dismissed from their jobs; dozens of students were expelled from the universities; the departments of Economics, Philosophy, Sociology were closed; and 1,616 students had lost their right to study. But the repressive measures were mainly directed against intellectuals of Jewish descent. Andrzej Werblan, one of the most prominent party ideologues, declared that

[1] Gomulka himself at a party rally in March accused the rebels as a "reactionary minority and revisionist," and forecast that the Jews "sooner or later [will] leave this country."

"revisionism and Zionism were one and the same thing: enemies of communism," and that the problems could only be solved by correcting the "irregular ethnic composition in the central institutions" (ibid., pp. 149–51).[2] By equating the reformist revolt with Polish Jewry, which comprised no more than 0.2 percent of the population, by purging the party, universities and state apparatus of Jews and forcing the bulk of them to emigrate, the party's anti-Jewish "revolution" closed the chapter of reform-communism in Poland.

"The trends represented a 'real Marxism' . . .[that] criticized official ideology . . . [and hoped for] the emergence of a renewed, 'creative' Marxism which will be able to direct political decisions," promulgated György Bence and János Kis, two disappointed former Marxists from the second generation of the George Lukács school, and authentic Hungarian dissidents. "When the debates were closed by administrative methods around 1968, it became clear that political power is not eager to accept the advice of Marxists, and that the Marxist trends opposing official ideology . . . lost . . . the justification of their very existence. After their forced silencing . . . most of its followers, openly or silently, departed from Marxism . . . A tiny minority was isolated from official culture and deliberately marginalized itself" (Bence and Kis, 1978, p. 73).

This process was also connected with the emergence of a new international trend of conservativism, following the student revolts of 1968. Leftism and a revival of Marxism, which strongly characterized Western intellectual life of the sixties and reached its zenith in 1968, almost instantly disappeared and was replaced by a new-conservativism oposing violent intervention into historical processes. The intellectual critics of state socialism that returned to a "true Marxism" had also turned to an influential Western left before 1968. An ideological defeat and deep disappointment weakened not only the Western left, but pushed the handful of Central and Eastern European opposition groups toward a new orientation. This was the time when the two leading Hungarian dissidents, György Bence and János Kis, wrote their first basic work, a critique of Karl Marx's *Das Kapital*. A few years later they published, under the pseudonym Marc Rakovski, a new work on Soviet-type society, concluding that "the liberalization of the Soviet-type societies is impossible." They denied the possibility of creating a "market with its self-regulating mechanism" via reforms, and stressed the "absolute inner institutional limitations of democratization" (Rakovski, 1978, pp. 84–8).

In the seventies, the former "true" Marxist critics became political

---

[2] The party organization of the Ministry of Foreign Affairs and the Polish Foreign Trade Agency passed resolutions on "an unconditional purge of Zionists", and stressed that there is "no place for the agents of international imperialism and its Zionist lackeys."

opponents of the regime. An opposition movement was in the making. This trend was strongly international, and expressed solidarity and built connections with similar dissident groups in other bloc countries. They protested against the Warsaw Pact invasion of Czechoslovakia as well as oppressive measures against dissidents (Curry, 1983).

Opposition also emerged from non-communist democratic and religious groups, which gained some legal standing in the post-Stalin era, especially in Poland and Hungary. They also sought a renewal and peaceful development toward democracy based on the system's efforts of self-reforming from the late fifties on, but lost their hopes by the late sixties. The strongest Catholic organizations emerged in Poland, where Gomulka's compromise in 1956 led to the founding of *Znak* (Sign), which took over the weekly *Tygodnik Powszechny* and opened "Catholic Intellectual Clubs" (KIK). The Catholic Church had twenty publishing ventures, which put out nearly one and half million copies of eighty-nine different newspapers and periodicals. These organizations and publications played an important role in the formation of a Catholic opposition. In a unique way, until 1976 "the *Znak* movement also had five deputies in the Sejm 'who constituted the nearest thing to an opposition party in the whole of Eastern Europe'" (Bugajski and Pollack, 1989, p. 146).

The opposition movement gained momentum in the second half of the seventies, when the economic crisis erupted and the transitory advantages of the economic model eroded and disappeared. It occurred, quite by chance, when the Eastern governments signed the Helsinki agreement. Safeguarding the implementation of guaranteed rights and reporting the violations of the agreement, together with militant Western propaganda and watchfulness, offered an excellent battleground for the opposition. By the second half of the seventies, an emerging popular dissatisfaction and frustration, the rising international interest as well as an open forum for safeguarding human rights and protesting violations all comprised a fertile soil for the rise of the opposition. Everything that happened before 1976–7 belonged to a preparatory stage, and the small, isolated groups represented only a sort of proto-opposition movement. In 1976–7, two major events led to a breakthrough. The scenes were Poland and Czechoslovakia.

The political concept of the opposition, the scholarly critique of state socialism and the demand for a pluralistic, democratic society, had already been formulated and promoted by courageous independent-minded intellectuals in the sixties. Groups of intellectuals and students occasionally protested and organized lectures, debates, and at times even demonstrations in Poland. There was no violence, however, and protests remained passive at the time of the workers' riots in 1970. In June 1976, when the revolt against price increases turned into a uprising of sorts in Ursus and Radom, where agitated workers attacked the party headquarters and raised barricades, clashed with riot-police forces and suffered a number of wounded, the dissident intellectuals acted. Kuron, Michnik, and others, the sole fighters of the previous decades, wrote an open letter to the speaker of the Sejm, and fourteen of them founded the Committee for the Defense of the Workers on September 23, 1976. They appealed to the people, maintaining that economic rights were not achievable without political liberty (Kuron, 1978). The Committee organized assistance for the families of about 2,500 arrested workers in Ursus and Radom. The worldwide publicity and the contribution of the Catholic Church generated a great amount of sympathy and recognition for the Committee. Denunciations and arrests could not block the road of an emerging opposition movement. On September 29, 1977, the Committee announced that it had renamed and reshaped itself into the Social Self-Defense Committee (KOR), which intended "to oppose reprisals made for political, ideological, religious or racial reasons . . . to oppose violations of the rule of law . . . to fight for institutional guarantees of civil rights and freedoms . . . [and] to support and protect all social initiatives made in the cause of human and civil rights" (Raina, 1978, p. 344).

"Under" the official institutions of the establishment, a parallel set of private institutions began to function. A Xeroxed monthly, *Opinia* (Opinion), served as an official bulletin for the Committee. In addition, KOR also published its *Biuletyn Informacyjny* and its theoretical political journal *Krytyka*; a special publication, *Robotnik* (Worker), dealt with the problems of the Polish workers. Reports on violations of the law, political pamphlets, and scholarly and literary publications were published illegally in order to publicize true history and philosophical ideas. A literary publication, *Zapis*, offered its pages to novels of first rate writers, whose works were rejected by official publishers.

This so-called *samizdat* literature was accompanied by private performances and concerts, seminars, and exhibitions, held in private homes. A parallel network of information was created in Poland, and a "second society" was in the making. This grass-roots movement of building up a civil society, independent from official ideology and institutions, gained momentum from the late seventies on. In a "Declaration" released in January 1978, sixty-two Polish scholars announced the foundation of the Society of Scientific Courses. The name and institution was a deliberate copy of a traditional Polish organization established in 1885 in Russian Poland in order to create an independent university, free from Tsarist political and ideological interference, and to promote the development of free education and independent thought.

The "Flying University," as it was popularly called because its "classes" were held in private homes, became an important forum.

During the 1980s, after the founding of the independent trade union, Solidarity, a gradual rise of a well-structured and developed civil society characterized Poland. Dissidents already dreamed about a consistent system of a "parallel polis." When the so-called second economy began to flourish in some of the countries by the eighties, it seemed to be a realization of these dreams.

The Polish opposition movement served as a pattern for other countries. After the long, humiliating years of the Husák regime, which trampled upon basic human rights and plunged the Czechoslovak population into political apathy and reluctant collaboration, a small group of intellectuals began a peaceful revolt. A minor event, the arrest and trial of a group of young rock musicians, alarmed a few intellectuals, who saw the trial as a "confrontation of two differing . . . conceptions of life," and sought to help the young people, "who wanted no more than to be able to live within the truth, to play music they enjoyed, to sing songs . . . and to live freely in dignity. . . . " They openly confronted "the sterile puritanism" of the establishment (Havel, 1985, p. 46).

On January 1, 1977 the group formed an informal association and made its Charter 77 declaration, which enlisted valid laws and international agreements, most particularly the Helsinki agreement on civil, political, economic, and cultural rights, signed by the Czechoslovak republic on March 23, 1976, and which were now permanently curtailed and even completely eliminated (Bugajski, 1987). The Charter 77 declaration announced that it was not seeking to establish an organization. Charter 77 "has no rules, permanent bodies or formal membership . . . It does not form the basis for any oppositional activity . . . it seeks to promote the general public interest." Without a political or reform program, Charter 77 declared its readiness "to conduct a constructive dialogue with the political and state authorities, particularly by drawing attention to individual cases where human and civil rights are violated" (Havel, 1985, p. 221). The group had a rather mixed background, with signatories coming from former Prague Spring reformists (one of the spokesmen was Jiři Hajek, a former minister of foreign affairs during the Spring days), non-communist democrats (another spokesman was Václav Havel), and Catholic thinkers. Charter 77 became a major representative and a moral symbol of the Central and Eastern European opposition movements. The group developed a consistent position based on a deep critical analysis of the regime, which was brilliantly formulated by Václav Havel in his *Power of the Powerless*: The regime, which was not a regular dictatorship but a part of an international system with a consistent ideology, became "closer to ideology than it does to reality." Its "highest secular authority," as in the case of Byzantine theocracy, "is identical with the highest spiritual authority," and "theory itself, ritual itself, ideology itself, makes decisions that affect people, and not the other way around." Consequently, people "must *live within a lie*. They need not accept the lie . . . but they must behave as though they did" (Havel, 1985, pp. 25, 31, 333).

Charter 77 intellectuals firmly believed that they would be able to peacefully to undermine the main pillars of the regime if they rejected the ritual and broke the rules of the game: by openly declaring what they really thought and what life really reflected, and defended people's interests and protested openly against the oppression of human rights, they would to inspire more and more people to do the same and thus live in dignity and truth. "If the main pillar of the system is living a lie, then it is not surprising that the fundamental threat to it is living the truth. This is why it must be suppressed more severely than anything else." The Chartists were convinced that the confrontation of a handful of dissidents with the regime would be "politically hopeless." "A mini-party like the Charter would certainly not stand a chance." They thus deliberately chose to follow a non-violent, peaceful strategy. They were persuaded that "the virus of truth as it slowly spread through the tissue of the life of lies, [would] gradually caus[e] it to disintegrate." If the society would reawaken, its "final outcome [would be] political reform" (Havel, 1985, pp. 41–4). The destruction of the regime by open confrontation would be impossible. First of all, "in this situation, no attempt at revolt could ever hope to set up even a minimum of resonance in the rest of society [which is] . . . submerged in a consumer rat-race." Revolt "would also be almost technically impossible to carry off. Most probably it would be liquidated before it had a chance" to act (Havel, p. 70). What remained was the struggle through legal means, serving and spreading the truth and defending the human rights of individuals, working within the boundaries of the law, attempting to follow a strategy of "taking them at their own word" that would lead to a "social awakening" (although it might be slow, a sort of "creeping process") and induce actual changes. To realize this the "basic job of the 'dissident movements' . . . [in its] most mature stage so far, is what Václav Benda has called the development of parallel structures" (Havel, pp. 78, 81, 85).

A similar passive resistance movement existed in Hungary. It emerged in exactly the same year as its Czechoslovak counterpart (1977), and was an expression of solidarity of the Hungarian dissidents with the Charter 77 people. More than 200 people signed a petition protesting the 1979 trial of Charter 77 leaders, and sent it to János Kádár. From the early eighties on, a deteriorating domestic economic situation strengthened the positions of the opposition. "For long, the majority seemed to be right. Living conditions, substantially improved, albeit slowly; the cultural policy also became more flexible," declared three leading Hungarian dissidents in their open letter to the signataries of Charter 77 in October 1979. But, they continued, "the limitations of this development became clearer ... more and more people are dissatisfied with lesser and lesser achievements ... and do not want to sacrifice the hope of democracy for such a price" (Bence, Kis, and Kenedi, 1979, p. 138). In the changing political environment Hungarian dissidents began to publish their *samizdats*, organized their Flying University, and openly challenged taboos, such as espousing the real history of 1956, which played a central role in attacking the regime. Challenging the official concept on 1956 as a "counterrevolution" automatically questioned the legitimacy of the Kádár regime. The role of the Soviet Union and the Yalta agreement, another long-lasting taboo, was openly attacked as well. The opposition focused on issues that were "uncomfortable" for the party, and told the truth regarding long-denied but existing poverty. They even founded an organization (*Szegényeket Támogató Alap*, or Fund to Help the Poor) to organize social assistance. The Hungarian opposition thus violated the "gentlemen's agreement" between the population and government not to touch certain political questions in exchange for relatively better economic and political conditions (Hoffman, 1993).

In most of the other countries of the region, opposition movements did not exist except for isolated dissidents. Writers, artists, and social scientists, such as Romania's Paul Goma and Dorin Tudoran, Bulgaria's Zhiliu Zhelev, Yugoslavia's Milovan Djilas and Mihajlo Mihajlov, and many others, were severely harassed. Their activity was focused on issuing reports of major violations of human rights in their country, which were smuggled abroad. Yanko Yankov and Volodya Nakov were charged with this type of activity in Bulgaria in the early eighties. The very first attempt to organize a "Green" opposition and even stage demonstrations in Bulgaria occurred only at the end of the eighties. The outspoken, heroic Romanian Doinca Cornea wrote an open letter to the dictator in September 1988, which was broadcast by the Western media: "Throughout the years you have tried to make decisions by yourself in every field. ... Today ... you are responsible for the deterioration or exhaustion of the nation's most important assets ... we demand that society be reoriented ... on the basis of truth ... [and] democratic and liberal criteria" (Cornea, 1991, pp. 74–6). She was immediately put under house arrest. The regimes tried to get rid of these "anti-social" elements and avoid international repudiation, and in several cases forced dissidents to emigrate.

Dissidents and the opposition were strictly controlled, while police informers and modern wire-tapping technology were widely used. Dissidents' papers were often confiscated, their meetings recorded. The representatives of Charter 77 were arrested and tried. On October 24, 1979 Petr Uhl, Václav Benda, Jiři Dienstbier, Václav Havel, Ota Bednarova, and Dana Nemcova were convicted and imprisoned. The same treatment was given to Djilas and Mihajlov in Yugoslavia. The movement could not spread and conquer.

In some cases the opposition movements could not and did not aim to provide any kind of long-term political and economic program, and instead stressed their anti-political character. At the end of the seventies, Václav Havel emphasized that the Charter movement "had no intention of presenting an alternative political program, [since] it sees its mission as something quite different . . . " (Havel, 1988, p. 55). George Konrád, the Hungarian dissident, repeated Havel's idea in a more extreme way in his *Antipolitics*, written in 1982, when he focused on de-politicization: "A society does not become politically conscious when it shares some political philosophy, but rather when it refuses to be fooled by any of them." "We ought to depoliticize our lives . . . [s]o I would describe the democratic opposition as not a political but an antipolitical opposition" (Konrád, 1983, pp. 227, 229).

It is quite evident, however, that the accentuated antipolitical character of this movement and the rejection of organizing political parties with alternative political programs, was a sort of self-defense, an attempt to avoid harsh repression. But because of this tactical element, the intellectual opposition basically lacked a consistent alternative concept on the future, and their humanistic and democratic *Weltanschauung* was penetrated by rather mixed, idealistic, unrealistic, naive, and sometimes confused notions. Konrád tried to keep "three steps" from dirty politics when he stated: "Any intellectuals who choose to compete for central-government advisory or executive posts are already doubtful members of the intellectual aristocracy," and also rejected as inadequate political-economic systems in general: "I don't like communism . . . It doesn't follow from this that I have to like capitalism . . . since the fact of communist exploitation doesn't put a prettier face on capitalist exploitation" (Konrád, 1983, pp. 224–5, 236–7).

Havel's deep and sharp critical stand in analyzing state socialism, became entirely uncertain and confused regarding the future. Like Konrád, he was also submerged in an idealistic intellectual world, developed high norms that conflicted with reality, and thus was unable to suggest practical solutions: "The human failure that . . . [state socialism] mirrors is only one variant of the general failure of modern humanity," since "modern humanity" shows a "general inability ... to be master of its own situation." He also rejected the "more subtle and refined" manipulation of parliamentary democracies, which "can offer no fundamental opposition to the automatism of technological civilization and the industrial-consumer society, for they, too, are being dragged helplessly along by it." Havel rejected a return "to the everyday mechanisms of Western (or if you like bourgeois) democracy." In 1968, he thought the two-party system to be a good solution, but, as he later noted, has since realized "that it is just not that simple." A multi-party system and free elections themselves could not make society immune to some new form of violence. "As far as the economic life of society goes" continued Havel, "I believe in the principle of self-management ... the genuine (i.e., informal) participation of workers in economic decision-making." As an expression of his dissatisfaction in every existing system, Havel introduced the term "post-democratic system," something amorphous and indefinable, which was to symbolize an intellectual dream of an imagined faultless society (Havel, 1985, pp. 90–4).

The strength and importance of democratic opposition movements, however, were not related to its vision of the future, and not weakened by their intellectual idealism. Nor was the number of the dissidents acquired a crucial factor, either. With the exception of Poland, where the opposition movement acquired a special dimension, the reality in every country where an opposition existed reflected William Echikson's remark, that "the few dissidents who existed in 1987 Hungary found it hard to fill a private coffeehouse" (Echikson, 1992, p. 427). The number of signatories of the Charter 77 declaration in January 1977 totaled only 241, and even in 1988 there were only 2,000 dissidents in Czechoslovakia, "a ghetto of its own members," as Skilling, described it. The number of Hungarian dissident activists, according to Bugajski and Pollack, was fewer than 300.

Nevertheless, one cannot measure the political importance and impact of the opposition based on mere numbers and long-term programs, for their real strength laid in their moral and political stand. They challenged state-party control and influenced political thinking nationwide. Their lectures in youth clubs and private apartments were enlightening, their samizdats awakened intellectuals, their message spread among students and thinkers. The existence and brave representation of diverging views and alternative concepts permanently challenged official ideology and monolithic structures. Moreover, from the late seventies and eighties on, uncertain regimes, at times, allowed them a broader playground and more relative freedom. There were, of course, a lot of differences among the various countries, but Poland and Hungary definitely offered a more advantageous battleground for dissidents than other countries in the region. Moreover, as Janusz Bugajski and Maxine Pollack suggested: "Budapest upholds a thin and changeable dividing line between permissible criticism and proscribed dissent. ... Budapest usually avoids open confrontation with the 'dissent community' ... [Moreover] Hungary's dissenting intelligentsia is often referred to as the 'semi-legal' opposition" (Bugajski and Pollack, 1989, p. 128). This was exactly the political environment in which Sándor Radnóti noted: "One of the most important goals of the *samizdats* is to force back censorship and self-censoring in the non-*samizdat* publications as well," thus a further heterogenization of public life (Radnóti, 1979, p. 140).

One should not forget that the social status and recognition of the intelligentsia in Central and Eastern Europe was traditionally high since the early nineteenth century, and it was now considerably enhanced by official condemnations and the romance of persecution. The opposition also had a much higher status and was somewhat protected, since the Helsinki agreement and its follow-up conferences provided a certain shelter and at least assured worldwide publicity for the dissenters and any official retaliation against them. They had a strange kind of power, which the government could not entirely neglect, especially because of their international reputations. George Konrád noted in the early eighties that "international public opinion, reflecting the influence of international culture, can become a counterweight to the state's cultural dictatorship; it can curb the tendency of the sovereign state to become omnicompetent" (Konrád, 1983, pp. 215–16). Konrád mentioned the role of international film festivals and the Frankfurt Book Fair, whose value judgments are superior compared to those of the "state culture's high command," and the indemnity assured by a concerned "international intellectual elite." All of the leading Western journals and magazines published interviews with dissidents and reported the repression against them. Additionally, throughout this period, various Western foundations and institutions offered grants and scholarships and invited dissidents and other intellectuals to study and lecture abroad. From the early to mid eighties on, George Soros, the Hungarian born American multimillionaire and philanthrop, established a foundation that began to work in Hungary and many other countries, which guaranteed a transitory independent existence for dissidents, and provided technical assistance for publications, Xerox machines, travel funds, etc. Radio Free Europe played an extraordinary role in popularizing dissident views, and became the most important source of non-official information in the region.

This international factor undoubtedly strengthened the dissidents' position. The peaceful intellectual opposition was increasingly able to influence the future of state socialism engulfed in an ever deepening crisis.

The lost young generations, required pluralism and democracy

As a consequence and a sign of erosion, the Communist Party, which had attracted the young generation after the war, had entirely lost them by the late seventies and eighties. Indicative of this was the fact that they rejected the previously compulsory official youth organization and no longer joined the party in most of the countries. In 1970 one-quarter of the members of the Polish Communist Party were under the age of thirty; by 1985 their share declined to less than 7 percent. In the same year, similarly, their share in Hungary was 7.5 percent. Two thirds of the members of the Bulgarian Communist Party were under the age of forty, and every fourth member was younger than thirty when the party seized power. The decrease in representation of the young was already characteristic in the sixties and seventies, when the percentage of the postwar generation halved and only every tenth party member was younger than thirty by 1980. In the second half of the eighties, the most orthodox, strictly controlled countries experienced this as well. In Romania, where party membership was almost unavoidable, the share of the generation under thirty in party membership declined from 30 to 20 percent in a half a decade. As the Czechoslovak *Zivot Strany* reported at the end of the decade, "at present it is virtually impossible to talk of any interest among young people in joining the party" (*Zivot Strany*, 1989). In isolated Albania, newspapers complained of an "increasingly unruly and undisciplined young generation, which was allegedly exposed to strong foreign influences" (Mastny, 1989, p. 305).

This erosion was connected with an important generational change: a new, postwar generation reached adulthood in the 1970s. A thirty-year-old person in the late 1980s was born in the late fifties and began secondary school training in the early seventies. These generations had entirely different life experiences and expectations than their parents had had.

The prewar generations had survived the hardships of the Great Depression, and the devastation of war, and millions of families were forced to start a new life from scratch. As adults, they went through the most frightening experiences of the final years of Stalinism, and had constantly feared the sound of brakes and the door-bell ringing at dawn. On the other hand, the prewar generations, at one time or another had experienced the euphoria of liberation – liberation from the nightmare of war, from peasant misery, from villages without electricity, from one-room schools, or from the stigma of being second-class citizens. The prewar generations appreciated basic achievements such as attaining a proper diet, acquiring a secure job and a pension, having low quality but guaranteed health care, or moving into a new home where three generations no longer had to live crowded together under one roof. They experienced the excitement of having a modern bathroom, of watching the first television broadcast of their lives, and owning their first motor-car. They were grateful when finally allowed to travel abroad. They welcomed the "gifts" of post-Stalinist liberalization and the adoption of a cultural policy that maintained a certain tolerance. These people knew in their bones that things had been and could be much worse, and they were ready to make compromises to keep what they had. They accepted the limitations and cautiously avoided challenging the accepted way of life.

The postwar generations were free of the fears of their fathers. The young accepted living standards which for the old were magnificent achievements, and they therefore longed for more and for something rather different: more independence and freedom, and to be rid of such crippling mediocrity. They were attracted by the enticing Western life style: the music, freedom and affluence. They wanted to make up their own minds and, unlike their parents, very much desired to challenge the system. What appeared to be determination to the old was often reckoned as being against human nature by the young. They were not satisfied with the liberation from backward rural settlements, and lamented the severe urban housing shortages, the shoddy, pre-fabricated buildings, and their tiny drab apartments. They were not happy with an East German two-stroked *Trabant* and longed for "real" Western cars. They often suffered under uneducated bosses in their work places, where half of executive positions were occupied by unqualified political appointees. They despaired from the lack of social mobility, that characterized state socialist regimes from the seventies on, when the industrialization drive slowed down and the previous gigantic social changes were halted. They resented the fact that most positions were filled with what were now elderly people, who were appointed as top managers, generals or university professors in their twenties and early thirties after the communist seizure of power. After many decades of unlimited job opportunities, certain career-openings were now closed, and full employment no longer appeared the certainty it once was. All in all, the new postwar generations were alienated from the regime and did not accept it as something "relatively better" or as a result of some unquestionable destiny. Additionally, young intellectuals were affected by markedly different international influences and incentives during the seventies and eighties than those of their predecessors. The defeat of the 1968 student revolt closed a chapter of intellectual leftism that was replaced by conservative political trends. The young generations, which were a natural, receptive base and reserve for left-wing radicalism in postwar

Central and Eastern Europe, now became a reservoir of either non-political apathy or of active opposition.

When the communist mass movement, which is an inseparable part of the monolithic structures, declined into a passive formality, and mass support, though far from representing the majority of the populace even at its height, decreased and then disappeared, the authoritarian character of the regimes was stripped naked, and lost all justification. Ambitious national, revolutionary or modernization values and goals, or "saving" a nation from internal chaos, civil war or from a frightening external enemy, which might once have proved the need and "rationale" for using naked force, now evaporated.

From the mid seventies on, the discrediting of a communist ideology made even a soft dictatorship less and less possible. In the deepening crisis and with loss of popular support, the oppressive power became self-contained simply to keep itself alive. The strict control and repression of "undisciplined" intellectuals in order to keep them from either disclosing the truth, which was in most cases known but forbidden to be spoken, or calling for change, caused more and more domestic and international trouble for these repressive governments. The arrest of dissidents or even the dismissal of an outspoken journalist was immediately reported by the international press, and this kept the regimes permanently on the defensive. The values of the successful Western democracies, which appeared in an idealized manner, became very attractive. For intellectuals, the content of Helsinki's Basket three seemed to be sufficient even for filling the empty baskets of queuing East European housewives. Democracy, freedom, and reintegration with Europe became a sweet day dream, and intellectuals sought to achieve it either by "bridge building" between the different systems, by "democratization" and reform of the regime in pushing it closer to the West, or by destroying the regime altogether. In the given historical context it was not the economic problems themselves but the monolithic political regime that became the heart of the matter, the assumed and acknowledged reason for the decline.

Reform, openness, freedom and transformation of political structures became the leitmotif of political struggles. The historical momentum gained a great dimension in Poland and Hungary.

7　The collapse: a revolutionary symphony in four movements, 1989

Erosion finally reached its conclusion in the miraculous year of 1989. State socialism, which mastered a third of the entire world, spectacularly collapsed in six countries of Central and Eastern Europe. In two more years the remaining European state socialist regimes followed, including their birthplace and international fortress, the Soviet Union.

The "Annus Mirabilis" occurred two hundred years after the French Revolution, which destroyed European feudal regimes. The latter was symbolized by the collapse of the walls of the Bastille, which expressed the end of an oppressive feudal regime. The symbol of 1989 was the fall of the Berlin Wall, an emblem of a closed, oppressive, isolationist state socialist era and the division of Europe.

The revolutionary transformation, however, did not follow the classic scenario of the French Revolution. It began as a "negotiated revolution" in Poland when the two confronting parties had sat at a round table and, both having made compromises, agreed on a peaceful metamorphosis. It began as a reform from above in Hungary without any violent conflict when the old regime relinquished its remaining power to a new one. The revolutionary symphony of "Annus Mirabilis" began with two slow, but historically tense and powerful movements.

The first movement: the rise of an organized mass opposition, solidarity, confrontation, and collapse – Poland

The Polish workers continued their permanent struggle for a tolerable material existence. Reformist intellectuals became deeply disappointed after the promise and hope of the Polish October in 1956 and the rise and fall of Gomulka's "Polish road." Although an accidental spark was always enough to cause some explosion, the repeated heroic revolts and bloodshed did not lead anywhere. The seventies, however, brought a turning point.

Two years after the student revolt of 1968, an accidental spark caused a new explosion. Following an ill-timed announcement of significant price increases on December 14, 1970, in the midst of the pre-Christmas shopping, the dock workers of the ports of Gdansk, Gdynia, Elblag, and Szczecin spontaneously responded with a major strike.

Gomulka, who had attained power on the shoulders of the revolting Poznan workers, and in rejecting their condemnation had talked of "painful lessons," now accused them of being "anti-social" elements attempting to destroy People's Poland. The government used excessive force against the strikers and demonstrators. Street fights erupted throughout the ports, leaving forty-five people dead and over 1,000 wounded (Bromke, 1985, appendix). The same flood of worker dissatisfaction and rebellion which brought Gomulka to power in 1956 now washed him away: at the December session of the Central Committee he was forced to resign. A subsequent purge of about 100,000 party members led to a changing of the guard. Young technocrats took over under the leadership of the former miner and Katowice party chief Edward Gierek.

The new leadership had learned the Kádár lesson and sought to legitimize its power through economic prosperity. Based on an opening toward the West and taking huge Western loans, they initiated an overambitious investment program (Blazynski, 1987). They did so, however, without the essential economic reforms and the drastic reorientation and reconstruction of industry. The emerging world economic crisis after 1973 undermined the old-fashioned "modernization" efforts. Without industrial restructuring and adjustment, Poland declined into a tight indebtedness trap. In the Gierek decade of the 1970s, none of the basic problems of the Polish economy and society were solved (Glowacki, 1990). The old explosive problems accumulated again. This was the decade of the rise of a highly developed Polish non-violent intellectual democratic opposition movement. In 1976, it arrived at an entirely new stage in its development. The drama began in a traditional way: the government, running an ailing economy, announced new major price increases (of 30 percent to 100 percent for staple foodstuffs) on June 24, 1976. The next day workers' strikes and demonstrations erupted in major Polish cities. The revolt was centered in Ursus and Radom. The workers of the Ursus Tractor Factory left their work place, halted trains and destroyed tracks on June 25. The workers of the Ammunition Plant in Radom took to the streets to demonstrate. The agitated swarm confronted officials in front of party headquarters, attacked and nearly lynched one of them. The party building was occupied and burned. Street fights continued until midnight. The announced price increase was immediately withdrawn, but, as Jacek Kuron, the well-known dissident observed, "massive repression ha[d] begun against the participants in the demonstrations and the strikes" (Raina, 1987, p. 247). Cardinal Wyszynski protested against "the system of torture," beatings, arrests and prison sentences in his speech in Czestochowa in August.

On September 23, 1976, the opposition movement took the stage and founded the Committee for the Defense of the Workers (KOR), which, in a year, was renamed the Committee for Social Self-Defense (KSS-KDR) (Lipski, 1985). The opposition began to institutionalize the previously developed aim to separate a self-organizing civil society from the party-state. A standing bridge between the workers and the intellectual movements was erected. Its major architects were, among others, Jacek Kuron and Adam Michnik, the leading dissidents of the sixties and seventies. KOR activists founded a samizdat newspaper, *Robotnik* (The Worker), and mobilized workers by calling for the establishment of free unions. In 1978, a "Founding Committee of Free Trade Unions on the Coast" was formed. It became the basis of workers' mobilization.

In 1979 a third force joined the alliance: the church. "In June 1979," noted Timothy Garton Ash, "the Pope returned to his native land for the most fantastic pilgrimage in the history of contemporary Europe. . . . On the Blonia [in Krakow] . . . nearly two million people stood together, applauded together, sung their old hymns together. . . . For nine days the state virtually ceased to exist. . . . Everyone saw that Poland is not a communist country – just a communist state" (Garton Ash, 1985, pp. 28–9).

Those new dramatic events soon fed the burgeoning initiative of the democratic opposition. In the late seventies, domestic supplies had drastically deteriorated. Besides a permanent food shortage, firms and households were, from time to time, cut off from electricity. In this tense atmosphere, when the government announced certain price increases, history began to repeat itself. The workers of the Ursus tractor works and the Autosan car works in Sanok began to strike on July 1, 1980. Strikes spread like wildfire. Though the government immediately withdrew (the old pattern again), a new wave of strikes flooded the country on July 20, starting with a general strike in Lublin (Karpinski, 1982).

In August the shipyards and ports of Gdansk became the real center of the strike movement. Before dawn on August 14, a small gathering demanded the reinstatement of a popular worker of the firm, and a thousand *zloty* wage compensation. The multitude grew when the new shift arrived. A small man, an activist electrician of the shipyard, who had been dismissed four years before, climbed up on to an excavator and called for an occupation strike. A strike committee was founded, and the electrician, named Lech Walesa, was elected to head it. The demands went far beyond the price increase compensation, and gradually included the right of independent worker representation. On the next day the other shipyards and firms of Gdynia and Sopot followed and founded an Interfactory Strike Committee. By August 18, 156 firms had joined and formulated their requests in twenty-one points. The first and most important of them demanded the independence of the trade unions, and the freedom to strike and to publish. It was not a regular labor disturbance any longer: the focus was given to self-organization and democracy. On that day, the other industrial center on the coast, Szczecin, joined the organized strike. The coal mines and iron works of Silesia followed (Aschenrson, 1982).

The government was forced to send high-ranking officials to negotiate. The Interfactory Strike Committee of the coastal area was immediately assisted by opposition intellectuals. Sixty-four well-known intellectuals signed an "Appeal," and Tadeusz Mazowiecki and Bronislaw Geremek went to Gdansk. Walesa saw the urgent need for the help of experts in the talks with the government, and invited well-known Warsaw opposition intellectuals to join. Beside Mazowiecki and Geremek, Andrzej Wielowieyski, Waldemar Kuczynski, Tadeusz Kowalik, and Jadwiga Staniszkis formed an advisory body to prepare and assist the negotiations.

On August 23 the talks began. They were broadcast to the workers and families who gathered in the yard and before the gates. The agreements signed at the end of August and in early September accepted the existence of the new union as an "authentic representative of the working class." On the other hand, the workers approved "the leading role of the Party in the state" (i.e., not regarding the union) as well as Poland's international commitments.

A peaceful revolution emerged. Its talented leaders, religious workers, and former communists who long ago had became "dissident" intellectuals, were basically uncompromising, yet they knew their limitations. (As Geremek put it: the limitation is the movement of the Soviet tanks.) The permanent readiness of the Polish workers to struggle, and the matured political responsibility of their leaders to participate in a dialogue, built a new connection between opposition and government (Curry, 1980).

This Polish "self-limiting revolution," as Jadwiga Staniszkis called it, or the "evolutionary revolution," using Jacek Kuron's term, promised a peaceful transformation of the regime. By recognizing an independent union as the representative of the workers, the agreement, in spite of being a compromise, essentially ruined the monolithic political structures. Though most of the details remained unclear, a new form of political pluralism was discovered. "In my opinion the party will split up and a considerable segment of it will support the revolution," formulated Jacek Kuron in his scenario of a peaceful transformation. "Under these conditions ... the National Salvation Committee should be formed by people delegated to it by 'Solidarity,' the Church and the party . . . all other authorities and the government are suspended. . . . Simultaneously [the Committee] declares democratic elections" (Kuron, 1982, pp. 196–7).

On September 5 the party's Central Committee held a special session, and Edward Gierek, who had gained his post in the 1970 crisis and riots, was dismissed. At 2 a.m. Stanislaw Kania became the new party leader. The irony of postwar Polish history from the mid 1950s on, that each new leader was brought in by a new wave of workers' revolts and each one was swept away by yet another workers' uprising, was repeated for a third time. Changes in personnel, however, were of minor importance in the new situation.

It became much more important when the representatives of the new trade unions gathered in the Hotel Morski, Gdansk on September 17 and founded the united, nationwide organization of *Solidarnosc* (the name was suggested by one of the first dissidents, Karol Modzelewski). Lech Walesa was elected its chairman. Nearly 3 million people immediately left the "official" unions and joined. By some accounts, Solidarity had about 10 million members by the middle of 1981, and another 3 million people had joined its rural branch organization (Holzer, 1984).

Solidarity became the first and only organized opposition movement, "a civil crusade for national regeneration" (Ash, 1985, p. 78) in Central and Eastern Europe with the participation of the broad masses, combined with a highly developed intellectual opposition and assisted by the church, thus representing the majority of the nation. The monolithic ruling party was opposed by a monolithic opposition. Inside, however, Solidarity became a reservoir of rather different kinds of anti-regime forces, but, for the time being, it formed a united front.

In the tempestuous days of 1980–1, the new Polish government turned to long-required reforms. In feverish haste, the outline of an economic reform program was published in January 1981. The plan, which included the gradual abolition of centralized planning over the long run, contained, however, an inconsistent mix of wishful thinking, including certain central plan directives, centralized distribution of energy and raw materials, and state regulated prices. The most radical change in this program was the acceptance of worker self-management. The over-moderate reform plan was harshly criticized, especially after two other volunteer reform committees published their more radical programs.

The Association of Polish Economists worked out a proposal under the leadership of Jósef Pajestka. Here too, a key element of the reform suggestions was the introduction of a radical self-managerial system. Workers' councils would gain the right to "decide the development strategy, to accept the financial plans and balances of the firm . . . to share the profit and decide about the detailed principles of income policy" (*Reforma gospodarcza*, 1981).

A committee of young economists, headed by Leszek Balcerowicz, under the umbrella of the University of Planning and Statistics, presented the most radical and consistent reform program (though far from being without compromises) based on collective ownership and self-management (including a highest political representation as a second chamber of the parliament). The radical reform plans, however, were rejected.

But the revised official reform plan, which was accepted at the extraordinary party congress in July 1981, and the law on self-management were too little and too late. The economy was already in a downward spiral into chaos. Political events rushed even faster.

In October, Solidarity organized a one hour general strike as a warning, mobilizing the bulk of the population. The peasant wing of Solidarity was founded. The university students in Lodz had a victorious three-week strike in January–February 1981. In this agitated atmosphere, the uncertain party-state, which had lost its self-confidence, could not resist the demands: wages increased by more than 13 percent and 26 percent in 1980 and 1981 respectively and surpassed price increases. A "shortage-spiral" led to the total collapse of supply.

Rationing was introduced in April 1981, first for meat, then for butter, fat, margarine, sugar, sweets, cigarettes, soap, etc. Coal production, which was of central importance to Polish exports and energy supply, also collapsed and dropped by nearly 19 percent between 1979 and 1981. Coal exports, as a consequence, decreased by nearly 60 percent. A disastrous harvest decreased agricultural output by almost 18 percent. Since the gross value of foreign debt approached 18 billion dollars in 1979, and the national income dropped by 2, 6, and 12 percent in 1979, 1980, and 1981 respectively, and since hard currency income from exports declined by one-third in the single year of 1981, the country could not carry the burden of repayment any longer. First among the indebted Eastern countries, Poland asked for rescheduling.

Polish black-marketeers flooded West Berlin and other parts of Europe (as opposed to 0.6 million in 1979, almost 1.3 million Poles traveled to the West in 1981), while Czechoslovakia and East Germany closed their borders to the Poles. Crisis, decline, and chaos became unparalleled, deeper than anywhere and at any time in postwar Europe. The disintegration of the national economy and the chaotic situation became the arena for an ever-sharpening struggle for power. The rise of Solidarity alarmed the conservative wing of the ruling party and the secret police. An open confrontation became a distinct possibility.

The crisis exploded in March 1981. After unsuccessful negotiations in

Bydgoszcz, the local Solidarity organization occupied the council room. The police physically assaulted Solidarity representatives; their leader, Rulewski, was hospitalized. Solidarity stopped negotiating and announced a general strike for March 31. The party's Politburo declared that the "foundation of the socialist system is in danger." A Party forum of Katowice declared: "The Party . . . is penetrated by liberal-bourgeois, Trotskyist-Zionist concepts, nationalism, agrarism, clericalism and anti-Soviet views . . . generated by the Right" (Holzer, 1984, p. 226).

On March 6, 1981 the so-called Grunwald-organization was founded. It denounced the liberal wing of the party, using openly anti-Semitic rhetoric and equating the liberals with "Zionists." Several known liberals were expelled from the party. The hard-liner group of Olszowski, Moczar, Kociolek, and Grabski was strengthened within the party by intensified Soviet pressure. The Central Committee of the Soviet Communist Party sent an open letter to the Polish Central Committee and accused it of retreating in the face of "advancing counterrevolution," which is a "deadly danger for the revolutionary achievements," and declared: "We will not desert the brotherly socialist Poland in trouble" (*Życie Warszawy*, 1981).

A radicalization characterized Solidarity as well. The trend of peaceful pluralization of the regime by mutual compromises, the peaceful "self-limiting Polish revolution," had reached an impasse. While Walesa, Mazowiecki, Kuron, and Geremek wanted to follow the previous road, many others, including most of the local leaders, used stronger and stronger language during the preparation of Solidarity's congress, and the congress itself sent a message to the workers of the other Central and Eastern European countries encouraging them to establish their own independent unions. The Politburo accused Solidarity of endangering basic national interests. In October 1981 several spontaneous strikes engulfed the country, and the leadership of Solidarity, which struggled for control of the movement, organized a general warning strike. Walesa himself, in competition with the radicals, began to use stronger rhetoric and spoke of an "unavoidable confrontation." Bogdan Borusewicz gave a desperate insider's view in mid 1981 on developments: "The [Solidarity] movement was acquiring all the negative features of the [communist] system, intolerance against those who thought differently, suppression of criticism . . . Walesa . . . could not be criticised. . . . Liberal circles, based on the opposition, were gradually squeezed out of Solidarity by party propaganda on the one hand, by 'genuine Poles' on the other, and by the Church hierarchy" (Lopinski, Moskit, and Wilk, 1984). Adam Michnik, in a letter from prison, in December 1981, added: "The epoch between August and December demonstrated not only the vitality and talent of

Polish society but also revealed the dark nooks and crannies which reside in the collective unconscious . . . I now have the right to suggest that this movement should take a critical look at itself . . . about the lack of polemics, about ignoring . . . pluralism . . . individuals thirsting for greed for power" (Michnik, 1983, p. 28).

Meanwhile, in the deepening crisis and polarization in the Party, the military wing of the party leadership was strengthened: in February 1981 General Wojtech Jaruzelski, the Minister of Defense, became prime minister, and within a few months was also elevated to the post of secretary general of the party.

The General Secretary General Jaruzelski was a most atypical communist leader. Born to a family of gentry and educated in a Jesuit school, he spent part of his formative teens in Siberia during the war, where his family had been banished by the Soviets and where his father died. The young man at the age of 20, however, joined the Soviet-organized Polish army in 1943, and made his whole postwar career in it. He became the youngest general in 1956. At the age of thirty-seven he became chief political commissar, and five years later Chief of Staff. In 1968, he was appointed Minister of Defense.

The tall, bald man in his uniform, with a stiff back endowing him with an unbending appearance, dark glasses to protect his ailing eyes, and a hard-set, never smiling face, he later characterized himself, in his memoirs as a "child of Yalta." As he explained his actions, he could either go underground, prolong a hopeless civil war and bring enormous losses to the country, or, as he actually chose, adjust to reality, operate within the system, and try to improve it by expanding the area of sovereignty as much as possible.

His very personal decision to choose Miczeslav Rakowski, the editor of *Polytika* and leader of the party liberals, as his closest aide, first as deputy prime-minister, later as prime minister, definitely strengthened the validity of his later claim: he wanted to go further with reforms. He also recognized the possibilities that were offered by a certain polarization of Solidarity.

Walesa had gained only 55 percent of the votes at the Solidarity congress and became less and less able to control the radicalized movement. Moreover, with the introduction of self-management a new coordinating organization was founded, the *Siec* (Network), which sought to change the old *nomenclatura* and subordinate them to the enterprise councils. They achieved the passage of a new policy stipulating that the directors had to be elected by the workers' collective. The *Siec* prepared the foundation for a Polish Labor Party. Additionally, the founding of a Catholic Labor Party was also planned. All these plans reflected the initial disintegration of the monolithic opposition. In October, when Solidarity organized a one hour general warning strike, only 40 percent of the workers joined. On that basis, but mostly as a consequence of increased and unyielding Soviet pressure, General Jaruzelski began the preparation of a military takeover. As he later revealed, Mikhail Suslov, on behalf of the Soviet leadership, made the alternative clear: either the Polish army did it or the Soviet military would intervene. American intelligence, according to Brzezinski, also observed Soviet military movements (Ploss, 1986).

Deliberately or under severe pressure, Jaruzelski sent military "operational groups" to the villages and towns to prepare to take over the administration in November. On December 11–12, the National Committee of Solidarity gathered in Gdansk. Jaruzelski had already decided his plan of action: on December 13 the Polish army made its strange *coup d'état*, or, more precisely, the Communist Party, with the help of an obedient army, introduced martial law. Tanks occupied the center of Warsaw, and built road blocks to cut transportation between major cities. Civilian telephone and communication lines were cut as well. A curfew was introduced and all gatherings and organizations were banned. Internment camps were set up. Almost the entire Solidarity leadership and quite a few thousand activists were arrested in the early morning between 2 and 3 o'clock. Solidarity was outlawed. Thousands of firms were militarized, meaning that an army officer was appointed to oversee the concern under military rules and order. The whole country was placed under the control of the army. At 6 a.m. General Jaruzelski addressed the nation and declared a "state of war" against those who had brought the country to the "brink of an abyss." He announced a "socialist renewal" and appealed to Polish patriotism.

A spontaneous resistance engulfed the country. The leaderless Solidarity announced an immediate general strike. In the following two weeks several isolated strikes, occupations of the Piast and Wujek mines near Katowice, students' strikes and even the sit-in strike of the Polish Academy of Sciences, and the struggle against riot-police in Gdansk and Silesia, took place. There were a few locations, such as the Wujek coal mines in Katowice, where military action killed strikers. The total number of victims of the nation-wide military takeover was about twenty (Tymowski, 1982).

Strikes and confrontation, however, quickly evaporated. The well-prepared military action and the lack of information and communication worked. On Sunday December 13, Archbishop Glemp, in his broadcast sermon, declared that the action was dictated by a higher necessity, and it is "a choice of a lesser than a greater evil." He called on each Polish citizen to "subordinate himself to the new situation . . . [since] there is nothing of greater value than human life . . . I shall plead, even if I have to plead on my knees," added Glemp, "Do not start a fight of Pole against Pole" (Ash, 1985, p. 269).

The Jaruzelski *putsch*, however, was not the introduction of a "regular" military dictatorship. In his address to the nation on December 13, General Jaruzelski stressed that he was speaking as a soldier. "The army attempted to present itself as the arbiter between social forces . . . engaged in suicidal competition." It was, however, as Jacques Rupnik noted, "the party in uniform" (Rupnik, 1984, pp. 157–8).

The Party attempted to win some breathing space and, behind the shield of force, introduce major reforms and "consolidate" the country's economic and political situation. The ideal which Jaruzelski and the strongly reform-oriented Rakowski wanted to follow was that of János Kádár and the post-1956 Hungarian model (Rakowski, 1981a and 1981b).

The party-military government immediately declared its commitment to the social contract and to reforms. Having destroyed organized worker opposition, the military government introduced a major price reform and granted autonomy to most firms and enterprises on January 1, 1982. Energy prices, such as that of coal, increased by 3.4 times, the prices of industrial products by 1.5–2 times. Half of the consumer goods and three quarters of investment goods became available at free market prices. This was exactly the Hungarian reform model. The government was in a nervous rush. The National Bank was granted independence from the government, and investment and foreign trade were decentralized. Agriculture received incentives through increased prices. In July 1982 the government, for the first time in Central and Eastern Europe, opened the door to foreign companies, even assuring them tax-free status for three years. Private investment was initiated, and by 1986 already half a million private companies were functioning in the country. In 1983, again in a pioneering way, a law on retail trade declared equal status for state and private firms.

However, the belated Polish reforms could not work. The government, opposed by the bulk of society, isolated by a Western boycott, and arrested by an indebtedness trap, could only fail. János Kádár's "miracle" was not to be repeated.

To mention only some elements of the failure of the reform, suffice it to note that the government, constantly on the defensive and lacking legitimacy, decided to compensate for the price increases, and indeed declared on January 27, 1982 that compensations had to surpass the volume of price increases. A price–wage spiral generated a speedy inflation: from 6.7 percent in 1979, it jumped to 101.5 percent by 1982. Price controls were reintroduced. Several other steps counterbalanced the market-oriented reforms as well, the state distribution of energy and raw materials being one of them. The so-called "operational programs" for industry sought to assure domestic supplies and exports in fields of strategic importance. Initially there were fourteen central programs in 1982 but finally the entire Polish industry worked in the framework of central programs. The taxation system that was introduced led to the destruction of the firms' independence, since 75 percent of the firms' profits was channeled to the state budget. Labor and wage regulations remained centralized (Bożyk, 1989).

Old reflexes were also present, and Prime Minister Messner argued for a centralized system: "Large economic units . . . have greater opportunity and independence . . . can easier and better solve the problems of investment, exports and imports, and the practical implication of technological-scientific progress" (*Życie Gospodarcze*, 1985). Indeed, in 1984–5, under the umbrella of military control, sixty-five mines were centralized into nine huge units in the Katowice area, and all the mining-engineering companies were merged into one giant company. Private economy in non-agricultural spheres remained unimportant and offered only about 6 percent of the national product and less than one-third of services.

The Jaruzelski government achieved certain transitory results (Sanford, 1986), especially in agricultural prosperity and the pushing back of inflation to 15–17 percent annually by the mid 1980s. However, it could not create an efficient economic system and soon, in 1986, fell into a new economic crisis.

The soft military dictatorship, a desperate last ditch attempt at party-state rule, could not and did not intend to use naked terror, especially since the second half of the eighties was already characterized by the rejection of the Brezhnev doctrine and the introduction of *glastnost* and *perestroika* in the Soviet Union. Since the monolithic rule of the party-state based on military power was only justifiable because of the potential danger of a Soviet military intervention, the military regime lost its last "legitimization" (Johnson, 1983).

However, more than half of the Polish public, even retrospectively in 1992 (as polls documented), thought that the military takeover had been the only way to avoid a Soviet invasion and evaluated the introduction of martial law as a patriotic act of self-defense.

This view was strengthened by the later released fact of the defection of Colonel Kuklinski, one of Jaruzelski's closest aides. He presented the military plan for the introduction of martial law to the American government and escaped with his whole family to the United States in November, a few weeks before the action. The Reagan Administration, however, remained silent and did not even warn the Polish government or Solidarity. As Jaruzelski later explained, he interpreted this as silent American approval of his planned action.

Though the reform-oriented Jaruzelski leadership was one of the closest allies of the new enlightened ruler of the Kremlin, Gorbachev's opening of the system was the final blow to the Polish regime, which could no longer justify its rule even to its own elite. This led to a final phase of total demoralization and collapse. The assumed breathing space for the regime became the parting breath of Polish state socialism.

The events followed each other very fast. The Pope's second visit in 1983 helped the government to break out of international isolation, but strengthened the authority of the independent church and Walesa's status as the authentic representative of the Polish people. The partial, and then full amnesty in 1984 and 1986 brought about a sort of consolidation and normalization, but also stabilized a "political draw." (Michnik, 1985).

When a new wave of strikes began in May, then in August 1988, there was nothing else for the government to do but turn back to negotiations and bargaining. Solidarity gradually returned to the scene. Jaruzelski and Rakowski still hoped to retain some kind of shared power. The reemerging, but definitely weakened Solidarity – its weakness demonstrated by the moderate participation in the strikes – was ready for compromise. The possibility of a peaceful continuation of the "self-limiting revolution" was thus a real one. The party, even in the late summer of 1988, when General Kiszczak suggested the dialogue, waited for another half a year in the hope that Rakowski, the new prime minister with his radical, marked reforms, would be able to win the support of the population without the help of Solidarity.

When the government sat down at the round-table negotiations with Solidarity on February 6, 1989, it was not yet a total surrender. Kiszczak, addressing the fifty-seven participants as well as the entire populace (there was live TV and radio coverage), stressed that the talks are a "consistent continuation of the policy of 'socialist renewal' instituted in December 1981." He also announced the fixed "prerequisites" for an agreement, among them that "socialism would remain the system of government," but it should be socialism with "a clearly democratic and humanistic face." The "new political design," stated Kiszczak, introduced by constitutional amendments, would ensure greater representation while protecting the "inviolability" of the state's socialist foundations. Walesa, however, in answering Kiszczak emphasized that the reason for all the failures "was the fault of a bad system and a lack of freedom. . . . The time of political and social monopoly of one party over the people was coming to an end" (Radio Free Europe, 1989, pp. 3–5).

Jaruzelski himself, in the middle of the round-table discussions, clearly re-pronounced that Poland "shall not be pushed off the path of socialism. ... This is out of the question" (*Radio Free Europe*, 1989). Jaruzelski and his party, as Adam Michnik stated, thought "that it was not the communists who legitimized Solidarity, but it was Solidarity who legitimized the communists. ... An important role ... was played by General Jaruzelski," added Michnik, "as president ... he was completely loyal to the democratic process" (Michnik, 1993, p. 9). An uncertain Party still hoped for a kind of corporatist compromise. Toward this, therefore, it was ready to assure a certain parliamentary role for Solidarity.

The round-table talks led to a new compromise: the parties signed an agreement on April 5 for a semi-free election in June 1989, which allowed a free election for the less important upper house, and reserved 35 percent of the seats for independent candidates in the decision-making *Sejm*. The agreement, which guaranteed a communist majority and strong presidential power, seemed to be a good bargain for the government, which had been caught in the trap of a newly exploding inflation and a total collapse of the domestic market.

The "good bargain," however, proved to be the last miscalculation of the party-state, unable to halt the historical process of erosion. The June elections led to a landslide electoral victory for Solidarity, which gained 99 out of 100 seats in the Senate and all the independent seats of the *Sejm*. The humiliating defeat of the regime was completed. Small wonder that General Kiszczak, the designated prime minister, was unable to form a coalition government.

President Jaruzelski could do nothing but accept Solidarity's candidate, Tadeusz Mazowiecki, who, on August 24, 1989, became the first non-communist prime minister of the region since the communist seizure of power. Though the agreement specifically called for a coalition government, with a communist president and majority in the *Sejm*, a total Solidarity takeover was only a matter of time. The key governmental post of the transformation, the portfolio for finance, was filled by Leszek Balcerowicz, who represented a neo-liberal free market position and became the symbol of a most radical and rapid transformation, the so-called *shock therapy* (Balcerowicz, 1992).

The peaceful transformation of power took another two years: after the resignation of Jaruzelski, Lech Walesa, the legendary Solidarity leader, was elected as president of Poland. The process was crowned by the parliamentary elections in 1991.

The second movement: the "social-democratized" reform-from-within opposition; reform and collapse in Hungary

The same political landslide occurred in Hungary between 1988 and 1990. In Hungary, however, there was no strong, organized mass opposition from without. The small dissident groups played an important role in the emerging moral crisis and in influencing the younger generation and the intelligentsia toward further major reforms, but they could not destroy the regime. Opposition, nevertheless, was born as an international movement and represented an alternative to state socialism as such. The rise and success of Solidarity consequently had a direct impact on Hungary as well. The most evident connection was their influence in pushing the Hungarian reform wing toward a radicalized, social-democratized platform. They inspired the realization for the need for political reform and the importance of pluralism, which did not belong to the demands of the economic-reform oriented reformists.

The basic confrontation in this case, however, occurred within the party, between the centrist-conservatives and the "reform-from-within" opposition. The latter had a long and strong tradition. The reform group around Imre Nagy between 1953 and 1956 had been definitely the strongest in the region. Although defeated in 1956, a great many of them remained in the party and again played an important role from the mid sixties on. Others, who did not reenter the party, contributed from the outside as part of the reform intelligentsia.

The confronting two wings of the party represented two rather different concepts: the centrist-conservatives were classical communists of the post-Stalin era, while the reformists were gradually shifted towards "Eurocommunist," social democratic views.

Following a relatively successful period of reform from the mid sixties on, a conservative counter-reform of late 1973 emerged victorious, and the reform wing suffered a new devastating defeat. All their leading representatives, including Rezsö Nyers and Lajos Fehér, were dismissed from the Politburo and government. Needless to say, the emerging recentralization and restrengthened central planning could not improve the situation. Quite the contrary, this was the period when Hungary toppled into its own indebtedness trap.

At the end of the seventies a return to reform became unavoidable. The new confrontation between the two wings, however, occurred in a semi-hidden way. Secretary General Kádár and the center of the party turned back to reform. The new wave was heralded by the removal of some of the key figures of the counter-reform conservatives: Béla Biszku, number two in the party hierarchy, was forced to retire in April 1978. The Central Committee of the party criticized the price policy that had been followed since 1973 and confirmed the need for introducing a new price reform.

This was the beginning of a turning back toward reform. A new price reform was instituted in two stages, in July 1979 and in January 1980. Domestic prices were linked for the first time with world market prices. Price reform abolished a great part of subsidies. Goods sold at free market prices expanded from 37 percent of retail turnover in 1979 to 50 percent in 1980. In the meantime a uniform exchange rate was introduced instead of separate tourist and commercial rates.

Huge state owned companies were dismantled. A single electrical maintenance company (Gelka), which operated nationwide and ran 320 service depots in the country without competition, was decentralized: in January 1983 the huge monopoly organization was replaced by small council-owned companies and the smaller units were leased out. The strict limitations on agricultural cooperatives of the mid seventies, which destroyed their industrial side activities, were removed in 1978, leading to an upswing of industrial and service activity in the cooperatives. Firm independence was strengthened by granting and gradually extending export rights. The industrial branch ministries, the institutions of state command, were abolished. In December 1980 a single Ministry of Industry was established.

The most significant new reform step of the early eighties was the legalization of the "second economy," which was a moderate and partly hidden form of giving a green light for grass-roots privatization. The Politburo passed a resolution in September 1979. The growth of small private industry and retailing was triggered by a range of preferences and incentives. The number of private craftsmen, shopkeepers and caterers and their employees increased by 40 percent in the first half of the 1980s. The fully private sector, however, remained small and produced 7 percent of GNP.

Another form of hidden privatization: the private leasing of state-owned shops and restaurants, began in 1981, and in five years 12,000 were leased. "Civil-law companies" and so-called small cooperatives (essentially private firms) were allowed, and they began mushrooming in the early eighties: in the first year of existence 11,000 new small private companies were founded. A great variety of private businesses were allowed and started to flourish. Private taxi cabs flooded the streets. "The dynamic development of the private sector characterized the entire 1980s in Hungary. Privately owned firms produced 10 percent of GDP in 1980 and 20 percent in 1989" (Árvay, 1993, pp. 44–5).

The private or semi-private (state-owned but leased and privately run) "second economy" (in contrast to the state-run "first economy") became a dominant sector of the Hungarian economy and involved about three-quarters of active earners and altogether about half of the population. In the mid eighties about 80 percent of construction work, 60 percent of services, one-third of agricultural production, and 15 percent of industrial output was produced by private business, producing about one-third of the GNP (Berend, 1990).

The new wave of reforms continued in the eighties. In April 1984 a firm's autonomy was strengthened by introducing elected company councils and the election, rather than appointment, of top management. Simultaneously, a bank reform abolished the monopoly of the National Bank and introduced a two-level banking system. The National Bank returned to its classical role as the bank of issue, while a network of commercial banks took over the role of financing the economy. In 1987 Western-type value-added taxation of firms and a comprehensive, progressive personal income tax was introduced. The reforms were aimed at building a regulated mixed-market economy.

The reform breakthrough of the 1980s, in spite of its impressive progress, still could not create a flexible market economy. The Hungarian reforms remained the most radical half-measure. Additionally, in 1982–3, a grave liquidity crisis necessitated a high degree of direct control which extended to compulsory export assignments at the company level. The government, losing ground and experiencing mounting popular dissatisfaction, did not risk strongly unpopular measures. To avoid bankruptcies and unemployment, the government continuously subsidized permanently deficit-producing firms. On the other hand, almost 90 percent of profits earned by highly profitable companies were channeled to the state budget through direct intervention, leaving the good firms crippled. The party still wanted to maintain full employment and at least slow down the decline of living standards. New foreign loans, which sharply increased indebtedness, were used for the repayment of old debt, deficit financing and the subsidizing of consumption goods. The crisis was not solved, and the unavoidable measures were postponed (Révész, 1990).

Following the pattern of the 1960s, the reform wing of the party tried to convince János Kádár, gain his support, and make the reform official policy in this way. This succeeded, since he, indeed, was able to support the continuation of reform. There was, however, a high price to pay for this: too much compromise. Demands for a "reform of the reform" (thus, a radical completing and progressing) were rejected by Kádár: "We have heard opinions expressed that we should now reform the reform as well. Nothing could be further from our thoughts: we shall apply a socialist system of management which has been proven in practice . . . we will not replace this system . . . by anything radically different" (Kádár, 1983).

János Kádár, then in his seventies, was no longer flexible enough. He denied that the country was in crisis and angrily rejected any attempt to link economic reform with political changes. He became more and more sclerotic and closed, practically unable to continue a dialogue, and grotesquely repeated: "we should only work better." Kádár, a fanatical chess fan and amateur player, symptomatically enough, stopped playing with partners from the eighties on, and started to replay matches alone. His genuine conservatism became dominant.

The steep personal decline of Kádár, however, was rooted in the fact that he, as very many others among his opposition and even in the West, remained trapped in the old views and responses, neither realizing the dramatic change of the role and position of the Soviet Union, nor recognizing the opening of new possibilities.

The reform wing did not see this change until the late eighties. The militant reform intelligentsia, experts in the apparatus, and radical party reformers gained a new impetus and inspiration from the Gorbachev opening, by *glasnost* and *perestroika* in the second half of the eighties. They felt that the door at last was opening and the strongest obstacle to further reform was disappearing. It became more and more clear that it was not the previous external barrier but the former hope, the master of wise compromise, Secretary General Kádár and his old centrist-conservative guard, who were the real impediments to an efficient reform. Radical reform was possible not with but only against Kádár.

The reform wing, influenced by the opposition, by Eurocommunists, and European social democratic connections, gradually recognized this and began to emphasize the need for political changes. The transitory success of the counter-reform attack in the mid seventies offered the lesson: without an institutionalized change of the monolithic political structures, radical and continuous reform progress was impossible.

From 1982–3 on, the need for political reform towards a pluralistic democracy and a major revision of obsolete ideology was pronounced. The radicalization began. In 1986–7 a group of economists and sociologists of the Financial Research Institute (*Pénzügykutató Intézet*) worked out a study entitled "Change and Reform," in which they expounded a program linking the rational tasks of short-term macroeconomic stabilization with long-term economic and political reform, and the bringing about of the necessary freedom of the press, information, and society. The document, which was denounced by the conservatives as "oppositionist," was accepted by the reformists at a sub-committee of the

Central Committee of the Party. The program of a quasi-oppositional grouping became the basis of a party resolution which stressed the "imperative to develop socialist democracy and modernize . . . political institutions" (Allásfoglalás, 1987). This was already a first sign of an internal revolt against the party leadership. On the basis of a general dissatisfaction and moral decline, encouraged by the Gorbachev phenomenon, and at last recognizing the hopeless political impotence of an aged leadership, the reform wing became active and more aggressive.

Even more importantly, a new paradigm of complex reform emerged. In this view, effective economic reform would be impossible without major political reform and pluralization as a guarantee of radicalism and as a value in itself. Democracy rather than "democratization" of the old structures became a leading slogan, though not properly clarified in content. The social democratization of the party reformers made rapid progress.

Besides Rezsö Nyers, the living symbol of reform, an agile and ambitious new reform leader emerged, Imre Pozsgay, who was ready to cross the Rubicon between "democratization" and democracy. To create a new popular basis and find a new way, the Pozsgay group sought to secure an agreement with a strengthening opposition, which echoed the dissatisfaction of the majority of the population, expressed radical views, and offered a renewed basis from the outside to the opposition from within (Gati, 1990).

This was the reason for a meeting in remote Lakitelek on September 27, 1987, when representatives of different opposition trends met. The host Sándor Lezsák welcomed leading populists such as Sándor Csóori, István Csurka, the dissident liberal democrat writer György Konrád, and leading reform-communists from the Pozsgay group, Mihály Bihari and Zoltán Biró. The keynote speaker, Imre Pozsgay, stressed: "It is time to work out alternatives . . . of comprehensive and radical reform, including ownership relations, distribution and political relations . . . [reforms, up to now] remained actions of an enlightened absolutist power circle. . . . We have to go beyond this concept. . . . The basic field of the reform is not the economy . . . and the barriers have to be swept away first in the political arena." Pozsgay suggested a constitutional change by introducing an institutionalized democratic Rechtsstaat with a real legislative role for the parliament, with local self government, and with a referendum system on major national issues to create a new "national coalition" (Jegyzökönyv, 1991, I, pp. 39–40). As one of his closest aides, Mihály Bihari, put it: "Socialism is in crisis . . . a historically institutionalized dictatorial political regime pretends to be democratic . . . we have arrived at a crossroads" (II, p. 47).

The reform-from-within opposition in Hungary became one of the strongest opposition forces in the region. Naturally, they were not dissidents; they did not attack the regime from the outside but sought to reform and save it from within. One might therefore use the term collaborators instead of opposition. No doubt, reform communism was on the wane after 1968, and its disappointed adherents either made their compromises and obediently followed the party line, or split and declined into political apathy. Very few became dissidents and founders of emerging opposition movements. Indeed, the only country in the region where a reform-from-within movement survived and potentially flourished in the eighties was Hungary, uniquely governed by the Kádár regime, which was characterized in the early eighties by Konrád as an "enlightened, paternalistic authoritarianism, but measured with a willingness to undertake gradual liberal reforms" (Konrád, 1984, p. 128).

What was the basic difference between the Polish Solidarity or the Czechoslovak Charter 77 movements on the one side and the Hungarian reform-from-within trend on the other? Did the first two oppose the regime while the latter one collaborated? In fact, the line distinguishing them was not so marked. The powerful Polish Solidarity opposition at the height of its influence made major compromises with the regime, accepted the reality of Soviet domination, and was ready to share power with the communists. The dividing line between being the victim or supporter of the regime was not a Chinese wall. "This line," stated Václav Havel, "runs *de facto* through each person, for everyone in his or her own way is both a victim and a supporter of the system." Comparing his greengrocer's and the prime minister's situation, Havel adds: "Differing positions in the hierarchy merely establish differing degrees of involvement" (Havel, 1985, p. 37).

Although their program had a lot of similarities, especially regarding a mixed-market economy and a pluralistic, legal state and society, the democratic opposition deliberately sought to act outside the given framework of the regime, while the reform-opposition movement remained within. The latter was certainly less radical and had a different vision of the future.

Did the first two opposition movements seek to change the regime, while the latter was only interested in reform? Of course, to a certain degree, this is the case. On the other hand, to cite again Havel: "Is it possible to talk seriously about whether we want to change the system or merely reform it? . . . this is a pseudo-problem. . . . We are not even clear about where reform ends and change begins."

Although the Hungarian reformists collaborated and made more compromises than the much more steadfast Czechoslovak and Polish opposition, and although they sought to reform and ultimately save the regime by changing it, their position nevertheless manifested an uncertain and ever-evolving demarcation line between reforming and changing the regime. The hard core of the Hungarian reformists took pluralism and markets seriously, and aimed for *Rechtsstaat* and mixed ownership. The late eighties clearly showed that they were ready to go ahead with these goals. They, of course, did not sympathize with *laissez-faire* capitalism and dreamed about Western (often Scandinavian) welfare socialism. In fact, they had certain similarities at this point with the ideals of the populist opposition.

Who decided to join the opposition and attack from the outside, and who associated with the inner reform opposition? Those who lost their faith in reform after 1968 often denounced those who still tried to convince themselves of the possibility of reform. Several people in Hungary, however, thought that reform was more realistic since there was no alternative as long as the Soviet Union continued to exist. This was not only a reformist's self-deception, but a widely accepted view of Western analysts as well. After repeated uprisings and their suppression in a world order where the West never even attempted to risk confrontation, there was no alternative, remarked Rudolf Tokes, to "accepting gradual reforms as the only realistic strategy of political change in the shadow of the USSR" (Tokes, 1979, p. xviii). Psychological factors also played a role. Who remained in the reform camp? Those who were more cautious? Those who did not want to risk too much? Those who turned more easily toward compromise? Those whose characters were more compliant? All of these certainly contributed to such a decision.

The reform opposition made a permanent advance in the eighties in Hungary. In its struggle against the conservative wing it gained at a certain point a helping hand from a part of the party apparatus, which was demoralized and disappointed by the lack of leadership and by the delay of required and recognized action. The pressure and demand to hold an extraordinary party congress (two years before its regular time) became extremely strong toward the end of 1987.

The Politburo, split on the issue, could not resist: in May 1988 a nation-wide party conference was held, which swept away the entire "old guard," including János Kádár, the unchallenged Secretary General for a third of a century, and the majority of his Politburo. Leading reformers Rezsö Nyers and Imre Pozsgay replaced them in the Politburo, and one third of the Central Committee was changed, markedly strengthening the reform trend. The victory of the reform wing was not total, however: the key position of secretary general was filled by the pragmatic conservative Károly Grósz. Ambiguity and confusion was unavoidable. The party conference nevertheless announced a new program, and declared the need for a great leap forward: the goal of a mixed market economy and the requirement of radical political reform to create democratic political pluralism (though without clarifying its character) and a *Rechtsstaat*.

The historical process followed its own logic and led to a series of "minor turning points." The Secretary General *and* prime minister Grósz was replaced by a radical reform-oriented government led by Miklós Németh and a collective "quadriga" of party leaders (Nyers, Pozsgay, Németh, and Grósz). A major new breakthrough and total victory of the reform-opposition came in February 1989. Characteristically, it was connected with an evaluation of an historical event. In "normal" circumstances it would be debated among historians. In Hungary, it was the central taboo of the Kádár regime: the events of 1956.

The duality of the "official" concept of "counter-revolution" and popular memory and the term "revolution" as used by the population characterized the whole Kádár regime. As a part of the major victory of the reformists, a four member expert committee was appointed to reevaluate the history of Hungarian state socialism. The document, which was debated in January 1989, stated: "against the old solutions and reactions [of the regime] which seemed to be un-defeatable, a mass demonstration of elemental strength flooded the streets in October 23, [1956] and in the same evening the 'weapon of critique' was changed to the 'critique of weapons': a people's uprising emerged against the government and regime." Because of immediate Soviet military intervention, "the uprising became a fight for national independence. ... the democratic and national demand of the workers was clearly expressed by the mass movements in Budapest and in the countryside" (Berend, 1989b, p. 32).

The re-evaluation of 1956 as a genuine people's uprising and struggle for independence against Hungarian Stalinism and Soviet dominance, and not a counter-revolution, was debated by the Central Committee in February 1989. The acceptance of the concept, which previously was only asserted by the opposition, heralded a dramatic change. A main topic of the opposition's attacks had now became a resolution of the party. The re-evaluation was an open challenge to the Kádár regime, which defined itself as a safeguard against bourgeois counter-revolution. If the suppressed people's uprising fought for genuine democratic and national demands, then the Kádár regime was a conservative "counter-revolution."

The re-evaluation, therefore, was not an historical debate, but opened the door for the most radical transformation. Indeed, the same session which reassessed 1956, debated further steps toward a democratic transformation and, for the first time in Central and Eastern Europe, approved the concept of a multi-party system and free elections, and also declared its readiness to compete with other parties on an equal basis, without any kind of (Polish-type) pre-arrangement (Soós, 1993).

Opposition groupings, which had not been able to play a direct role, were now legalized and began to form dozens of new parties. The prewar Smallholder and Social Democratic parties were reorganized, the Hungarian Democratic Forum emerged from the Lakitelek gathering, liberal democrats, the hard nucleus of uncompromising dissident groupings, founded their Free Democrat Alliance, and the Federation of Young Democrats, which had the same political character but focused on the younger generation, also became a party. Though an alternative trade union organization, the Democratic League of Independent Trade Unions, was also founded in December 1988, it could not attract the masses who remained in the old unions. A civil society was in the making.

Following the Polish pattern, and owing to the increasing pressure of the opposition parties, the ruling party had to begin a dialogue with the opposition parties that began to play an important role from that time on. The round-table debate began in June 1989 with the participation of nine opposition parties and organizations, and ended on September 18. From that very date the opposition's impressive participation increased the momentum for further changes. This time, however, as was the case in Poland, even the strongest opposition groupings were ready to compromise. In Poland, "they use the labels 'us' and 'them,' in Hungary this deep split ... does not exist ... Sándor Csóori, a poet and founder of the country's largest opposition group, the Democratic Forum, [stated] '... we can work with men like Mr. Pozsgay. ... our idea is a sort of coalition'" (Echikson, 1992, p. 430).

The reform-from-within opposition, which practically took over the government and played a dominant role in the crisis ridden party, increased its activity. Expert committees began to work out a detailed plan for a three to four year transition toward a consistent market economy, based on mixed ownership, in 1988 – the first "transformation" plan in the region. The plan aimed at creating a liberalized import policy, free market prices, and the creation of markets for capital and labor in three years. Its implementation immediately began. The Németh government introduced major, radical reforms, with a breakthrough in privatization and subsequent marketization. New deregulation cleared the road for private enterprise: the limitation of employees in private businesses was abolished. Foreign investors were permitted to buy or own even 100 per cent of Hungarian firms (Brown, 1991a).

The peaceful demolition of the regime continued. In October the parliament enacted an amendment to the constitution, based on the round-table agreement. The Soviet type "people's republic" and its institutions were abolished. A constitutional court was established and a multi-party political system, and protection for public and private ownership and basic human rights, were declared. The freedom of the press was guaranteed and anyone was permitted to start his own newspaper (Horváth, 1992).

In the summer, the leader of the 1956 revolution, Imre Nagy, and his comrades executed with him in 1958, were reburied. "Three weeks later, on the very day that the Hungarian Supreme Court announced Imre Nagy's full legal rehabilitation," János Kádár died. "Shakespeare would not have risked such a crude tragic irony" – remarked Timothy Garton Ash (Ash, 1992, p. 439). The two burials closed a historical period. Kádár's Hungarian Socialist Workers Party (the ruling communist party) did not survive its founder for long: it deliberately abolished itself in October 1989, with its reform majority creating the Hungarian Socialist Party with a social democratic platform, which had already been the ideological orientation of party reformists for a long time.

The self-confident reformers played an impressive historical role, making courageous reform measures. They were rather popular in the country and highly valued in the West, and offered an attractive and realistic program. Instead of state socialism, they sought a democratic, pluralistic Western type of socialism, with a multi-party system, free elections, institutionalized human rights, and a social market economy based on mixed ownership, as well as an export-oriented economic policy adjusted to and integrated into the world market, but still one with a strong social orientation. Some of their leading figures, such as Pozsgay and Szürös, were coquetting with Hungarian nationalism. Pozsgay definitely counted on his alliance with the Democratic Forum, which, especially with its strong populist founding nucleus, shared quite a few of his aims and values. The first congress of the Forum in March 1989 expressed the goal of a "third road" between capitalism and socialism, and declared that "a strict market-based economy would only enrich a narrow group and impoverish the majority." Even the second congress in October 1989 "continued in the same ... direction as the ... first congress," concluded Radio Free Europe's analyst. "The Forum did not endorse total privatization, and by privatization it did not mean ownership by individual private citizens ... the entrepreneurs ... would not be individuals but groups" (Radio Free Europe, 1989b, pp. 23–4).

Pozsgay, the socialist nominee, was actually accepted by the Forum as the main presidential candidate in an early election in November 1989. A formation of this new coalition, however, was stopped by the liberal democratic opposition (SzDSz and Fidesz), which did not sign the round-table agreement. Instead the opposition initiated a referendum over the election of the president and was accompanied by harsh anti-communist attacks and strong criticism of the Forum's attempt to compromise. They achieved a victory in November 1989. Though the Democratic Forum declared a boycott, 58 percent of the people participated and, with an incredibly narrow margin of only 0.07 percent, the presidential election was postponed until after the parliamentary election.

An undisturbed free election was held in March 1990. The reform-from-within concept and the reform wing of the party, in contrast to its genuine aims, precipitated the collapse of socialism. A well-structured, rapidly strengthened opposition dominated the political arena, and a coalition of mid right parties formed the new government. The socialists, with fewer than 10 percent of the votes, joined the opposition in the newly elected parliament.

As one of the foreign observers remarked in 1989: "Hungary proceeds at break-neck speed with a quiet democratic revolution." The peaceful reform-revolution, or, as Timothy Garton Ash called it, the *refolution*, was completed in two years.

State socialism simply collapsed. The people were fed up with reform promises and the lack of improvement, and they wanted real change: a change in the system. The former ruling elite, demoralized and devoid of self-confidence, no longer believed in its "mission" or simply could not see a way out of the deepening crisis or a possibility for a socialist renewal; tired and frustrated, then simply gave up without resistance. As Jaruzelski answered the question as to whether the communists were fearful about giving up power: "No, I'd say it was done with a satisfaction, that we were discarding a burden we weren't able to carry anymore. . . . There came a moment when all the reserves of the old system became exhausted" (Jaruzelski, 1992). Although they did not intend to give up power but wanted instead to share and save it, they in the end accepted the historical reality.

The year was far from over. President George Bush noted that 1989 would be remembered as a year "when the human spirit was lifted and spurred on by the bold and courageous actions of two great peoples, the people of Poland and Hungary" (Radio Free Europe, 1989c, p. 20).

The third movement: the collapse of state socialism in four countries in six weeks

The Polish and Hungarian collapse had a penetrating impact all over Central and Eastern Europe. The regime was totally discredited, and there were no forces to save or revitalize it anymore. Both harsh military solutions (Polish martial law) and methodical, even partially successful reforms (in Hungary) failed to protect or correct the system. What kind of action and endeavor remained for the others to choose? Both directions led to dead-end roads. The regimes and their leading elites throughout the region lost hope and vigor.

Hardening the hard-line – self-destruction by non-action

A couple of rigid, non-reforming governments, however, were led by old routine and inertia. They suspiciously watched and angrily criticized the Polish–Hungarian trend and were shocked by Gorbachev's *perestroika*.

Albania and Romania emphasized their independent, separate roads and rejected "selling out socialism." They accused any kind of reform as "going back to capitalism." Enver Hoxha's line, repudiating reformism, continued. His view in the late sixties, when he said that Eastern Europe "undertook a series of 'reforms' which paved the way for the gradual degeneration of the socialist economic order and . . . [the beginning of] the wholesale restoration of Capitalism" (Hoxha, 1980, pp. 8, 10), remained valid in Albania. At the end of 1989, Ramiz Alia, the "more pragmatic" successor of Hoxha, also repeated with national pride: "Socialist Albania . . . has always been and is independent and sovereign in all things . . . Our socialist road was our own choice and was not imposed on us. . . . The crisis that is sweeping the countries of the East is the crisis of a definite community, but not the crisis of socialism. . . . Consequently," added Alia, "the events taking place over there have nothing to do with us" (Radio Free Europe, 1989d, pp. 1–2).

The non-reforming countries represented a horizontal chain consisting of East Germany, Czechoslovakia, Romania, Bulgaria, and Albania. They were also severely hit by a deepening economic crisis, political tension, and were challenged by the international changes ongoing from the mid seventies. They, however, rejected adjustment. Their response was a strengthened rigidity and pretended self-confidence.

In some cases during the late eighties, governments engaged in empty reform rhetoric and hesitant initiations of reform. The first reaction to towering economic difficulties and decline in these countries was a campaign for "strengthening work and plan discipline." As Romania's Nicolae Ceaușescu often remarked, shortcomings and mistakes originate in an improper implementation of plans. Albania's Enver Hoxha and later Ramiz Alia continually denounced bureaucratic practices both on the governmental and local levels.

The Husák regime in Czechoslovakia, which denounced the Prague Spring and the market-oriented economic reform of Ota Šik as an attempt to restore capitalism, proudly declared in April 1976: "After April 1969 the Marxist–Leninist principles of management were restored, particularly the leading role of the Party and . . . the state plan as the principal instrument of management" (Kaser, 1987, p. 216).

During the shocking structural economic crisis, the Czechoslovak party emphasized actions to "strengthen planning discipline." Gustav Husák, in his opening speech at the congress, repeated the old Stalinist view: "Most of the mistakes . . . originated in subjective factors . . . the main cause of the problems are the lack of discipline and a neglect of the interests of the society . . . The key factor [is] the improvement of the method of planning . . ." (Husák, 1979, pp. 246, 251–2).

The "Guidelines" for the 1976–80 plan, presented at the 11th Party Congress in Bulgaria, sought to improve planning by "raising the scientific level of social management" and giving prominence to "objective methods of planning and cybernetics" (Kaser, 1987, p. 221).

The train of state socialist economy was running full steam toward the abyss. Farsighted and enlightened political leaders and experts were seeking to change tracks, or even to halt the train and direct it "backward." But the conductors in charge (the Ceauşescu-type *Conducători* [leaders]) merely called for better maintenance and upkeep of the engine, or a more vigorous supply of coal for the burners.

When reform and restructuring became the official line of the Gorbachev-led Soviet Communist Party, the non-reforming Central and Eastern European countries reacted in two different ways. "We will never permit the weakening of the leading role of our Marxist–Leninist party," announced Albania's Ramiz Alia, "for the sake of the so-called pluralism handed out by the bourgeoisie" (Alia, 1989). In an article published in early 1989 in *România Liberă*, the separate road was strongly stressed: "It is the specific merit of the Romanian Communist Party . . . to have struggled decades ago against the dogmatic views of a 'common pattern' . . . for building socialism. As there are no patterns for building the new society, there can be no compulsory patterns or recipes for improving socialist construction . . . any tendencies to pose as 'judges' or 'teachers' that teach others or judge other country's policies is absolutely inadmissible" (Romania, 1989).

Ceauşescu, who established his stature by not joining Brezhnev's invasion against Czechoslovakia, two decades later, on August 19, 1989, according to the information of the *Gazeta Wyborcza*, hoped to escape by initiating a "united action of the members of the Warsaw Pact against Solidarity's moves to take over the Government in Poland" (*Gazeta Wyborcza*, 1989).

Bulgaria and Czechoslovakia followed a slightly different road. Zhivkov, who always leaned the way the wind was blowing from the Soviet Union, and Husák, whose regime was a product of the Soviet-led invasion and was entirely dependent on Moscow, could not flatly reject Gorbachev's *perestroika*, especially as there was Soviet pressure on the non-reforming allies. Hence, they pretended to follow. "Bulgarian *perestroika*" was announced at the party congress of 1986, and a so-called economic reform was urgently introduced in January 1987. A larger part of income, from that time, remained with the firms, which had to compete with each other for investment. The Central Committee gave some lip service to further reforms in July 1987 and December 1988. Bulgaria half-heartedly made her hesitant steps but, until the very last minute, did not implement even a fraction of her half-measures.

From 1987 on, the Bulgarian media began to follow Soviet *glasnost*. Courageous articles, such as a series in four parts in *Trud* ("Corruption Dressed in Power"), unmasked abuses of power. Moreover, the jamming of foreign radio broadcast ended. The party leadership, however, was clearly terrified of its own "*glasnost*": in March 1988 the Party's Central Control Committee called for the dismissal of the editor of *Trud* and the author of the incriminating article "for infringing the Leninist line of *glasnost*." In April, the editor-in-chief of the weekly *Literaturen Front* was dismissed, followed by the editor of *Narodna Kultura* in November. In the summer of 1988 two reformers of the party leadership – Stoyan Mihaylov and Chudomir Alekandrov – were expelled from the party. In January 1989, thirteen members of a dissenting human rights group were arrested.

The same pattern characterized the Czechoslovak policy. Husák changed his rhetoric in December 1986, and declared that "the present system of management and planning no longer corresponds to ... conditions," and a "restructuring of economic management ... is needed ... to bring the Czechoslovak economic mechanism closer to measures being adopted in the Soviet Union" (Mastny, 1988, p. 232). Husák's bogus "reform" was nothing other than an experiment with decentralization in a certain selected group of companies from January 1987 on. The reform document announced thirty-seven new principles, and the most "radical" proposal was a "drastic" cut in central administrative directives.

The party pronounced the need and its readiness for a "dialogue with the people," while leading a fierce attack against the opposition. In January 1989, playwright Václav Havel was arrested and imprisoned for the third time since 1968, and a new wave of arrests followed in February. The party openly criticized the "limitless ideological liberalism" of some of the neighboring countries. The party journal *Tribuna*, even in the early fall of 1989, stated that Czechoslovak [and German] conditions allowed for "gradual and continuous reforms, without any major de-stabilization." The opposition had no chance of instigating "a parliamentary revolution" (Radio Free Europe, 1989e, pp. 3–5). In fact, just the opposite happened: a major de-stabilization occurred without a real step in reform.

"If . . . [the Party would] recognize the institutional guarantees of economic plurality . . . " Václav Havel explained in 1987, "it would be acknowledging the legitimacy of something beyond its own claims to total power" (Havel, 1991, pp. 341–2). Self-destruction, however, became unavoidable. The rigid systems, which continued to follow the same path that had already proved to be a dead-end, suddenly collapsed. The "dominos" of the orthodox state socialist regimes fell one after another.

Revolutionary crescendo: four countries in six weeks

The effect of the Polish and Hungarian cases and the Russian reform-trend (the "crawling counter-revolution," as the Czech Fojtikova, wife of the newly appointed hard-liner chief ideologue, called it), left the conservative ruling elite shocked and paralyzed, and mobilized the intelligentsia and younger generations. The situation became exceedingly tense and dangerous. A spark could easily cause an explosion.

The spark was supplied by Hungary in the spring and summer of 1989. The Németh government announced in May that it was going to destroy and remove the Iron Curtain, the fortifications along her border with Austria, a symbol of oppression. For the Hungarians this action was mostly a metaphorical gesture, as everyone already had a passport and the freedom to travel to the West. The watch-towers and barbed wire fences were dismantled and resourceful entrepreneurs sold its pieces as souvenirs.

This historically significant step also had practical implications regarding the two Germanies: thousands of East German tourists who were not allowed to travel to the West and spent their vacations in Hungary and in the Balkans tried to escape to West Germany via Hungary. In the early summer months about six thousand Germans had illegally crossed the Hungarian–Austrian border, and thousands waited for West German passports in refugee camps in Hungary.

There had been a valid agreement between Hungary and East Germany since 1969 according to which Hungary guaranteed not to allow East German citizens to leave for a third country without a valid visa. Gyula Horn, the Minister of Foreign Affairs, went to Berlin and attempted to get a guarantee that if the refugees were sent back, the East German government would allow them to leave. Since East Germany was not ready for that, the Hungarian government decided to follow the United Nations decision to give the refugees free passage to a third country.

In ten days, on September 11, Hungary opened her border. Within a few hours 20,000 East Germans crossed the border towards West Germany.

The exodus of tens of thousands of East German citizens had begun. East Germans inundated Bonn's embassies in Prague and Warsaw, applying for permission to leave for West Germany. At the end of September, after his disastrous fiasco in Hungary, Honecker agreed that the 2,500 refugees at the West German embassy in Prague could leave freely. Moreover, the aged, ailing hard-liner, who had just recovered from an operation in mid-August, and was preparing the October 7 celebrations of the fortieth anniversary of the foundation of the German Democratic Republic, tried to demonstrate that these "traitors" were being "expelled," and decided that the trains carrying the refugees had to cross East Germany.

Masses in movement

Three trains, full of German refugees en route from Prague to West Germany, passed the railway station of Dresden on the night of October 4, 1989. A huge throng gathered and attempted to get on board, but the riot police attacked them. For two days they fought as people and sought to halt the trains by lying on the rails, attacking the trains, and clashing with the police force. More than 1,300 people were arrested.

At this moment the entire young generation of the country revolted, and even enlightened members of the elite joined in. Endless mass demonstrations engulfed Dresden; another series began in Leipzig on October 9, followed by Berlin. During the three weeks between October 16 and November 8, more than two hundred major demonstrations took place in the country with the participation of 1.3 million people. The obedient German *Untertan* (loyal subject) ceased to exist. After the celebration of the fortieth anniversary of its foundation, the German Democratic Republic disintegrated.

The exodus continued. Austrian, German, and Hungarian television had live broadcasts from the Hungarian–Austrian border. Euphoric young refugees were interviewed and were obviously in a celebratory mood. Radio Free Europe and Voice of America covered the event, and the people of East Germany, Czechoslovakia, and other bloc countries learned of the breathtaking mass exodus (Brubaker, 1990).

The East German government had to act. Paradoxically enough, the only way to stop the exodus was to open the Berlin Wall, which had been built to stop the exodus nearly three decades before. On November 9 Günter Schwabowski announced the opening of the wall and declared that each East German citizen could travel freely to West Germany. An excited young crowd from the East and West climbed to the top of the *Brandenburger Tor* and the wall, while others began to open new passages.

The Berlin Wall, the symbol of the separation of the two Germanies and Europe, collapsed. Virtually the entire world watched the event; history was in the making. In one single week about 5 million East Germans visited West Berlin. The exodus still continued and reached a monthly 50,000 to 60,000 in December and January. The German multitude was in permanent movement, and nobody could reject the idea that Germany must be a single, united fatherland, as the popular German slogan stated: *Deutschland, einig Vaterland.*

An aged and frightened Husák regime in Czechoslovakia, the closest ally of East Germany, and its perplexed population that now began to hope, watched the broadcasts of the collapse of Honecker's Germany. The deeply apathetic Czech masses, who had turned their backs on politics during the twenty years of the Husák regime and instead had tried to "cultivate their own garden," were suddenly mobilized. There were signs of change already in 1988 when a petition for greater religious freedom was signed by a half million people. At the anniversary of the foundation of independent Czechoslovakia, 10,000 people occupied the streets of Prague.

The real breakthrough of the Czechoslovak masses – after the collapse of the Berlin Wall – erupted on November 17. Nearly 15,000 young people gathered to commemorate the fiftieth anniversary of the martyr student, Jan Opletal, killed by the Germans. Some of the speakers at the meeting openly expressed their commitment to "actively support the ideals of freedom and truth." The demonstration, officially legalized outside the center of the city, began to move. The young demonstrators marched along the Vltava to the National Theater and then turned toward the heart of the city, the Wenceslas Square.

The throng more than doubled during the march, and reached between 30,000 and 50,000. Before they reached the square, special anti-terrorist riot forces surrounded the demonstrators and brutally attacked them. More than 500 people were wounded and 100 arrested.

The repression could not halt, but rather mobilized, the people. During the next two days student strike committees were founded, the theaters canceled their performances and opened debate sessions instead. On November 20, 200,000 people occupied the streets of the capital. On the next day the same multitude flooded the city and heard Václav Havel, who spoke to them on freedom and democracy from a balcony in Wenceslas Square. The following day, 100,000 people occupied the streets of Bratislava, the Slovak capital (Frankland, 1990).

The swarm was unstoppable: on November 23, 300,000 people participated at a mass rally where the Civic Forum, founded four days before, announced their demands for democracy and free elections. In Bratislava, on the same day 50,000 people gathered to hear Alexander Dubček, the leader of the Prague Spring, address the public for the first time in twenty years. A week later, he spoke to 300,000 people in the Wenceslas Square. A general strike was called for November 27 when four fifths of the population opposed the government and supported the new opposition party, the Civic Forum.

The non-revolting, quiet majority which, according to a bitter remark of Václav Havel, had been preoccupied and corrupted by consumerism from the 1970s on, occupied the streets of Prague, Bratislava, and Brno, demanded democracy and a "return to Europe," and re-conquered their own country.

The magic November days roused and mobilized the masses. The news arrived everywhere, even in countries which continued to control information. The ruling elite lost the remainder of its self-confidence and the hope of outside help. As people saw the masses in action they lost their fear and shared a euphoric collective experience of "living in the truth," the dream of Havel a decade before (Wheaton, 1992).

A real feeling of internationalism emerged. Czech and German, Hungarian, and Romanian intellectuals, students and workers – a rare episode in the history of the region – now believed that they were helping each other's struggle against a common enemy. In the euphoric November days the people of Central and Eastern Europe also felt and believed that they belonged to an international community and enjoyed the admiration and benevolent assistance of the Western world. People firmly believed that the West, which consistently inspired their struggle against communism and Soviet domination, would rush to help them.

The first Western reaction was jubilent and promising. In the miraculous month of November 1989, the West, indeed, rushed in with promises of help for those countries that had already begun their march toward transforming the system: the Italian government, joined by Austria, suggested regional cooperation with Yugoslavia and Hungary, and the ministers of foreign affairs of the four countries met in Budapest on November 11–12. In less than two weeks, the European Community's Executive Commission hosted a meeting of representatives from twenty-four leading industrial nations to coordinate aid for Poland and Hungary, and donor nations pledged some 6.5 billion dollars in economic aid and food. Three days later, on November 27, the foreign ministers of the European Community offered temporary new trade concessions, including an end to restrictions on the import of some farm goods and textile products. On the next day, President Bush signed a bill authorizing 938 million dollars in aid over three years for Poland and Hungary.

The doors at least seemingly opened toward the European Community and for major Western assistance. The people of Central and Eastern Europe hopefully watched Western enthusiasm and also realized that their actions, unlike in the past, would not generate Soviet repression. During these revolutionary days of November, Tadeusz Mazowiecki, Solidarity's Prime Minister, paid his first official visit to Moscow, and signed a joint statement on November 27. It repeated Prime Minister Ryzhkov's words: the Soviet Union "does not impose its recipes ... on anyone and respects the right of each nation to freedom of choice." Gorbachev, in his toast at the official banquet, proclaimed: "It might surprise some people that I wish you success" (Radio Free Europe, 1989f, pp. 14–15).

The revolutionary fire-ball continued. Agitated masses, encouraged by dramatic breakthroughs in the neighboring countries, forgot the fear which had paralyzed them for so long. Countries that had no revolutionary traditions, whose fate was always determined by great powers, suddenly began to create new traditions.

Five weeks after the collapse of the Berlin Wall, a month after the bloody Prague demonstration, and nearly three weeks after the Czechoslovak general strike, the people of Timişoara, a Transylvanian city of mixed ethnic Romanian and Hungarian population near the Hungarian border, said "no." The reason was an everyday incident: the ethnic Hungarian pastor, László Tökés, a critic of the regime who was courageous enough to resist administrative repression, including his bishop's command, refused to leave his congregation and church, and was ordered to evacuate by the police forces. A scared and brainwashed population had not reacted to such repression before; but not this time. On December 15, 1989, hundreds of determined Hungarian parishioners surrounded the home of Pastor Tökés to prevent the police from acting. In a country where nationalism was used to legitimize a most oppressive Ceauşescu regime, hundreds of Romanians joined in support of the Hungarian pastor.

A rising dissatisfaction led to a militant anti-government demonstration in the border city with a huge ethnic Hungarian minority, where the inhabitants regularly watched Hungarian television and thus were not cut off from information about mass demonstrations and collapsing state-socialism. *Securitate* forces opened fire on the crowd. Nearly one hundred people were killed, several hundreds wounded.

The old pattern, accusing the demonstrators of being fascist counter-revolutionaries led by imperialist and hostile Hungarian conspirators, did not work any longer. Since clashes continued in some Transylvanian cities, the self-confident dictator (who in the middle of the turmoil went on a two-day state visit to Iran) called a mass meeting in Republic Square, in the center of Bucharest, immediately after his return on December 21 to condemn the anti-socialist and anti-Romanian conspiracy and rebellion.

The multitude was expected to act as usual. Workers and employees were ordered to march, carry slogans and hear the *Conducător* [leader], who spoke from the balcony of the Central Committee building. But this time, the same obedient masses who formerly followed the ritual suddenly turned against the dictator. A small group of courageous people began to shout: "Down with Ceauşescu!" Others followed. The entire country watched the televised event as the dictator was forced to cut his speech short and retreated from the balcony. Riot police with tanks, tear-gas, and water cannons cleared the square (Brown, 1991).

Bucharest, Republic Square, December 21, 1989 was probably the most dramatic scene of the "Annus Mirabilis." At the beginning the masses obediently followed orders but the crowd of loyal servants metamorphosized into courageous revolutionaries ready to fight. A routine pro-government demonstration became the beginning of a revolution.

Students, intellectuals, and other citizens gathered at night in the center of the capital. A brutal secret police and its strong and well-equipped army began shooting in the darkness. Workers arrived from the suburbs. A state of emergency was declared and the army was ordered to act, but General Vasile Milea, the Minister of Defense, refused to fire on the people and was himself shot ("committed suicide," as the official report stated). A bloody revolution engulfed the center of Bucharest. Revolutionaries attacked public buildings and occupied the headquarters of the state television company, which became the center of a fully broadcast revolution. The 75,000 strong *Securitate* elite army clashed with armed people and the army units which joined the uprising. The area of the Central Committee building and the Royal Palace, the Ministry of Defense, and the television center became genuine battlefields. Several thousand people were killed, but the masses destroyed the hated regime (Fowkes, 1993).

Different views have been expressed on the beginning of the Romanian revolution: was it a genuine revolution or a *putsch*, organized by disillusioned former Ceauşescu aides? Even if it had began as a coup, the masses became the decisive forces of the events.[1]

The newly mobilized and excited masses became the main actors in the belated "imitative" Albanian revolution. The obedient and disciplined populace had been accustomed to participating in celebrations and parades. The effect of the news of the region-wide revolts was irresistable and inspiring as it spilled over borders. Young people excitedly watched what happened in the region from East Germany to Bulgaria and followed the same road. On December 8, 1990, demonstrations erupted at Tirana University. The next day, acting on old reflexes, the party responded by sending in the riot police. The masses continued their movement and pushed the party leadership into a corner. The first concessions by the government were followed by a new and more fervent wave of mass demonstrations: Kavajë, Shkoder, Durres, and other cities were engulfed by an impassioned swarm of people who demanded democracy and the resignation of the government. For a second time, police forces and heavily armed troops attacked the crowd.

The bloody scenes generated an even more resentful and powerful mass action: tens of thousands began to escape from the country. Within a few weeks at the end of the year fifteen thousand Albanians left for Greece. The exodus continued into January. In the port cities thousands attacked and occupied ships, and more than 20,000 people fled to Italy. There was a miners' strike in Valias and other industrial centers, and hunger strikes of students in Tirana. In the spring of 1991 the first multi-party elections were held in Albania.

Impotent potentates and powerless power

When the masses took control of events, the most frightening and seemingly stable powers, and leaders who had survived many decades of difficult power struggles and ruthlessly eliminated their rivals and enemies, were instantly transformed into political dwarfs and "paper-tigers." After decades of unquestioned rule, a stubborn, aged and ailing Erich Honecker, who did not hesitate to order his soldiers to fire at those who attempted to escape to West Germany, and who was still convinced of the successes of his regime, lost the battle in his own Politburo. Following a hard-line policy and using force, if needed, became impossible. The first reaction was an attempt to suppress demonstrations. But what

[1] The right-wing journal *Vremea*, stated: "It was a palace coup of the political apparat that was transfered to the Romanian people in December 1989. The Romanian people took to the streets ... demanded bread and dignity, while ... [those who prepared the coup] wanted revenge and their lost positions" (Ungheanu, 1992, pp. 1–3).

could the brutal 85,000 man special force of the Ministry of Interior do against the continued Dresden and Leipzig demonstrations of hundreds of thousands, or against the November 4 demonstration of 1 million people in East Berlin? The brutal use of police force at the very first stage of demonstrations on October 4 in Dresden, then on October 7 in Berlin, Leipzig, and Potsdam, did not halt but rather fueled the uprising. Force was no longer an option.

Honecker could no longer count on Soviet assistance. Günter Schwabowski, the party secretary in Berlin, and Egon Krenz, secretary for security affairs, and several other leading party officials still believed in traditional maneuvering and personal changes: at the special session of the Central Committee, Honecker resigned from all his posts "for health reasons," and was replaced by Krenz on October 18. The next day, at a party meeting in Dresden, Hans Modrow, the reform-oriented local party chief, spoke about the need for Gorbachev-type reforms.

This could not pacify the masses any longer: demonstrations endlessly continued. On November 8 the entire Politburo resigned, including reform-radicals such as Hans Modrow, who replaced Willi Stoph as prime minister on November 13. On December 3, the entire new Politburo resigned again, and Egon Krenz retired from all his party and state posts. Within a few days, Gregor Gysi was elected new party chairman.

Changes in leadership, the traditional reaction to political crises in one-party political structures, which herald "new courses" and open "new chapters," was the immediate response of the orthodox party-states under the pressure of the masses. Czechoslovakia and Bulgaria acted the same way.

Personnel changes, though in a rather awkward way, began in Czechoslovakia at the end of 1987. The dual power of Gustav Husák as party chief and head of state was broken; though he remained President of the Republic, party leadership was taken over by Milos Jakeš. This was a meaningless maneuver, a change without change. Personnel changes continued along the same lines in 1988. The most hawkish Vasil Bilak was replaced by the similarly hardliner, conservative Jan Fojtik as chief ideologue. The dismissal of Bilak was also counterbalanced by the resignation of Lubomir Strougal, the relatively more liberal prime minister who at least flirted with some kind of economic reforms.

More and more futile personnel changes followed the deep political crisis of November 17, 1989, when the use of a brutal police force turned out to be highly counterproductive: Husák was removed from the Politburo and Jakeš was replaced by a colorless local party leader, Karel Urbánek, on November 24. Two days later, at a Sunday session of the Central Committee, fifteen members of the twenty-four-member Politburo were dismissed. On the 29th, Alois Indra, another symbol of post-1968 hard-line policy, resigned from the Assembly's chairmanship. On December 4, Prime Minister Ladislav Adamec, who replaced Strougal in 1988, was succeeded by Marian Čalfa, his Slovak deputy.

A last effort was made to save power by sharing it in early December. On December 9 Husák resigned as president, and a new coalition government was formed that included such leading representatives of the opposition as Jan Čarnogursky and Jiři Dienstbier, and non-communist free market technocrats such as Vacláv Klaus and Vladimir Dlouhy. By the end of the month, this kind of maneuvering came to an end and the regime collapsed (Goldfarb, 1992).

Personnel changes had much more important significance in the case of the more traditional despotic regimes of the Balkans. In Romania and Bulgaria, the nearly Stalinist-type despotism of Nicolae Ceauşescu and Todor Zhivkov went unchallenged by mass movements. Personal rule, in both cases, was combined with a high-level of nepotism. Stalin's famous term, "Socialism in one country," was often paraphrased as "Socialism in one family," regarding Romania under the Ceauşescus. Thirty-six members of the Ceauşescu family held leading positions in the eighties, and even the 14th Party Congress in Bucharest in late November, 1989 – at a time when the Berlin wall had already collapsed and the Husák regime was practically in ruins – elected six Ceauşescus into the leading bodies of the party. The dictator, his wife, brothers and sons, relatives and their servants clearly dominated the party-state.

The ruthless and oppressive but still paternalistic Todor Zhivkov, who successfully expelled, killed, or "domesticated" (invited to his dinner table) all his adversaries, established and was able to maintain a clan-type rule completely unchallenged since 1954(!). Zhivkov's attempt to build a family-led regime, however, was much less successful than Ceauşescu. His most important partner was his daughter, Lyudmila Zhivkova, who became the "empress" of culture. Her husband ruled national television. The rather popular heir died in 1982, as a consequence of a car accident. Zhivkov's new effort to elevate his son, Vladimir, was much less successful. His appointment as head of the Central Committee's Commission for Culture was too late to be swallowed.

In the cases of Romania and Bulgaria, changing the old regime seemed to be achievable only by eliminating the intolerable personal rule of the aged despots, who had ruled the country for decades. Previous attempts to carry out a palace coup to get rid of Ceauşescu had failed. The paranoid dictator was suspicious and vigilant enough to remove anyone who posed a threat in time to prevent any successful endeavor. That happened to Generals Ion Ioniţa and Nicolae Militaru, and to Silviu Brucan, a leading diplomat and ideologue. Legendary party veterans such as Brucan, Gheorghe Apostol, the one-time secretary general, Corneliu Mănescu and Constantin Pârvulescu tried to mobilize the party to force the dictator's resignation in the spring of 1989. The open letter, though it had a strong echo in the West, led only to their house arrest. Since a dramatic personnel change was prevented, and the use of force became counterproductive, only the bloodiest revolution could clear the road towards a transformation in the agitated atmosphere of December 1989 (Behr, 1991).

In Bulgaria, however, a successful palace coup prevented later dramas. In the summer of 1988, Zhivkov was strong enough to launch a preventive blow and remove Chudomir Alexandrov and Stoyan Mihaylov, two conspirators against his personal rule, from party leadership. He was unable to repeat his success in the fall of 1989, when Petar Mladenov, his Minister of Foreign Affairs, together with Prime Minister Georgi Atanasov, economic chief Andrei Lukanov and, most of all, General Dobri Dzurov, the Minister of Defense, after three months' of preparation, won a majority of the Politburo and attacked Zhivkov. The palace revolution of the Mladenov-faction in the Politburo occurred without a major mass movement, and even more surprisingly, without the existence of a real reform-wing in the party. It happened in a proper and formal, but still quite unusual way: at the one-day Central Committee session on November 10, the seventy-eight-year-old Zhivkov resigned as Secretary General and President of the republic, and even asked to be released from the Politburo.

His fifty-three-year-old successor, Petar Mladenov, immediately declared in his first speech that he would implement *glasnost* and *perestroika*, and that the command system would be dismantled once and for all. Bulgaria was to be transformed into a modern democratic state based on the rule of law. The process, however, did not stop at this point. In December, the leading role of the party was nullified and the free elections of June 1990 declared. The removal of the old despot went hand in hand with the dismantling of the old regime.

Ramiz Alia was in a better situation in Albania since he took over only in the mid eighties after the death of his master, and had initiated a certain opening of the country and a changing of leadership style. He thought he might survive politically by sacrificing other top leaders. After the first students' riot and a counterproductive police intervention, he dismissed six members of his Politburo, including Foto Cami, the chief ideologue, and, as a most symbolic break with the past, removed the dead dictator's widow, Nexhmije Hoxha, from the chairmanship of the Democratic Front. These tactics, however, did not work for long. The regime was moving toward the abyss.

The stubborn, mostly aged potentates lost their strength; in the new situation they had hardly more than one chance to use police power, and in the resulting tempest proved to be totally powerless. The traditional tactic of taking the wind out of the opposition's sails by personnel changes no longer worked. The frightening regimes became fragile, and revolt, which had previously proved to be hopeless because of the Soviet presence, now offered an easy victory. There was almost nothing to lose and everything to gain. The silent countries of the region suddenly were rocked by ever strengthening tremors of a political earthquake.

Scenes of a revolution

The collapse of Central and Eastern European state socialism was accompanied by genuine revolutionary events. New, previously unknown revolutionary leaders emerged. In the overcrowded Wenceslas Square in the heart of Prague a euphoric crowd listened to the shy, informal playwright, with a boyish smile on his face: Václav Havel, the active leader of a passive, moral opposition, who did not have much faith in mass demonstrations and rebellions, speaks to the people from a balcony. A sports bag on his shoulder, he is on his way to have a dialogue with the prime minister.

In the heart of Bucharest, students, intellectuals, and workers gathered in the evening. The organizer and virtual leader of the throng was a young Bucharest actor, Mircea Diaconu, who organized "resistance points," convinced army units to join the rebels, and addressed the entire nation on television. Another self-appointed leader, the young rector of the Polytechnic, Petre Roman, spent the whole night with the crowd and also took command. The retired General Militaru addressed the army and directed military actions via television.

After the first major demonstration at Tirana University, a belated attempt to duplicate the neighboring countries' path in Albania brings the country to the brink of civil war. There was wild reaction to brutal police intervention. A twenty-eight-year-old philosophy student, Azem Hajdari, emerged as a revolutionary leader: on behalf of the revolting students, he presented to party chief Ramiz Alia on December 11 demands for the introduction of political pluralism and the free foundation of political parties. The acceptance of the demands was the first act of the party-state's withdrawal and the collapse of the regime (Biberaj, 1992).

Besides the emerging revolutionary leaders and the spontaneous and emotional speeches from balconies (the inseparable symbols of revolutions), the demolishing of statues and rescuing of fallen dictators also characterized the Central and Eastern European scenery.

The turning point of Albania's follow-up revolution in February 1991 was connected with the students' demand to remove the name of the former dictator Enver Hoxha from Tirana University. The official refusal to this was answered with a hunger strike of seven hundred students. On February 20, 100,000 agitated people gathered in the main square of Tirana and tore down the many times larger than life statue of the dead dictator Enver Hoxha. The regime was symbolically destroyed, and reality followed: the party-state accepted the demands for a free election.

The tragi-comic escape attempt of Louis XVI (in female dress), that well-known scene of the French Revolution, was repeated in a modern setting in Romania. The revolutionary masses, joined by army units, advanced on the building of the Central Committee. At this moment a helicopter emerged from the roof of the building, the dictator and his wife on board, together with some of their closest aides, one of them, because of the lack of room, sitting on the dictator's lap. They landed on an empty field and continued their route by car. After Hollywood-type helicopter and car chases, a showcase televised "trial" was held, death sentences promptly handed down, and the firing squad followed. The entire country watched these events on television, and had seen the dead bodies and glazed eyes of the despised couple. No longer were they posing for the cameras, but lay instead in the dirt before a bullet-ridden wall. The destruction of state socialism had been accomplished.

The fourth movement: funeral march for Yugoslavia

The collapse of the regime had a different scenario in Yugoslavia. At the end of World War II, communism had triumphantly emerged as the result of a heroic revolutionary resistance movement and a victorious civil war. State socialism in Yugoslavia was always, from its birth on, an independent national regime. Tito reunified a ruined Yugoslavia, which had been drained of blood in a bitter civil war. "Without communism," noted Ivo Banac, "there would not have been a postwar Yugoslav state" (Banac, 1992, p. 171). The national communist character of the Yugoslav regime became more emphasized when Tito successfully resisted Stalin. In the last period of his reign, Tito made a new effort to stabilize and protect his multi-ethnic country. He gave up centralizing attempts and shifted the country toward a federal system. The new constitution of 1974 guaranteed a high degree of independence for the six republics and two autonomous territories; moreover, it established a collective presidency of the eight leaders of the republics and provinces (after the death of Tito, the life-time president) with annual rotation of the eight leaders as president. The same pattern was introduced for the party leadership. The bodies operated on a consensual basis.

Nonetheless, three strong federal linkages existed: Tito himself, his communist party, and his federal army. The death of Tito in May 1980 destroyed the strongest pillar of a federal Yugoslavia. Although there was no struggle for succession, the collective leadership of the country and party, the lack of an authentic and respected central figure, became a factor in the further decline of federalism (Bilandzic, 1986).

The economic decline of the eighties became first and foremost the Achilles heel of the multi-national and multi-religious Yugoslav state. It is important to note that these economic difficulties had a special role and a much greater importance in Yugoslavia than in the other state socialist countries. The economic issues, in the special ethnic-religious structure of the country, were immediately transformed into political-national questions. It is thus unavoidable to note the growing economic predicament of the country. Living conditions continuously declined. In 1988, 400,000 workers participated in strikes. The situation significantly deteriorated in the first half of 1989: inflation reached 2,000 percent and unemployment hit a record of 20 percent, while 60 percent of the workers lived under the official minimum subsistence level.

The federal government of the talented Croat economist, Ante Marković, made a very successful attempt to stabilize the economy and accomplished a major reform breakthrough. His currency stabilization, combined with the introduction of the convertibility of the Yugoslav dinar on January 1, 1990, was a milestone on the road toward marketization, especially because it was accompanied by an entire set of prepared and enacted reform measures. All these might have led to a Hungarian-type of transformation. But that did not happen.

Economic difficulties in a country with a delicate ethnic-religious mix and enormous social-economic and cultural differences, where near Western standards and Third World characteristics co-existed in legally equal republics of one federal state, all quietly contributed to a total collapse and disintegration. There was no similar situation in a single country of Europe in which the most advanced part, Slovenia, and one of the most backward provinces, Kosovo, had 6:1 difference in per capita income. The Slovenian income level was three times closer to the German and French standards than to the Kosovo level. Listing the "lessons" of the Yugoslav collapse, Branka Magaš observed: "There is little doubt that uneven economic development has been the main motor of Yugoslavia's political disintegration. Throughout the country's history, Serbia has tried to compensate for its relative economic weakness by attempts . . . to dominate the central state apparatus" (Magaš, 1993, p. 334).

Struggling against the burden of the backward republics, one should add to the above arguments that the more advanced Western republics had always sought to strengthen their autonomy and independence. During the dramatic end of the eighties and in 1990–1, when the Central and Eastern European countries began to compete for Western recognition and the earliest (assumed) acceptance by the European Community, the more well-to-do republics of federal, multi-national states felt the attraction of being rid of the heavy load of their more backward and more severely crisis-ridden partner republics. It was a serious consideration in the Czech Republic as well as in Slovenia.

This westernmost Yugoslav republic with its long historical tradition as a province of Austria, which though representing only 8 percent of the population of the country, produced 20 percent of its gross national product and nearly one third of its exports, easily imagined a most promising future alone, as a future member of the European Community.

Economic differences and conflicting interests, of course, appeared in rather complex ways. They were automatically mixed with the national issue and surfaced as national conflicts. The striking disparity between the economic level of Slovenia and Kosovo, for example, appeared as an ethnic and religious conflict between Catholic Slovenes and Muslim Albanians. Long and painful traditions, as well as the memory and the unhealed wounds of the bloody civil war of the previous generation, proved to be very much alive. The late eighties became the scene of a reemerging and unfinished civil war.

It was also this time ignited by political manipulators in an attempt to gain or consolidate power. In this nationally and ethnically mixed, and economically imbalanced, country, it was always a tempting possibility for demagogues to channel people's dissatisfaction into a reservoir of aroused nationalism. Nationalism as a substitute for failed modernization has been commonplace in twentieth century Central and Eastern Europe. The failure of the eighties mobilized traditional reflexes: in post-Tito Yugoslavia, the road of Greater-Serbian nationalism was chosen by the new party leader of Serbia, Slobodan Milošević, who was elevated to his post in 1986. This popular demagogue, surrounded by Serbian nationalists, launched a new war in "protection of the Serbs."

The former Mayor of Belgrade, Bogdan Bogdanović, clearly realized and expressed the connections between economic failures and nationalism. In an interview in the fall of 1991, soon after the civil war began, he stated: "Serbia has lost this war . . . all our modern wars and our entire modern history. . . . A feeling of failure lies at the very heart of Serb nationalism, and with that came all the various justifications for this failure. . . . This history gambled away – this century and a half gambled away" (Magaš, 1993, p. 344).

A new nationalist campaign actually began in Kosovo after the death of Tito in the spring of 1981. A student protest against poor living conditions developed in a province-wide demonstration demanding the status of a republic in the federation. The rebellion in the Albanian populated province of Serbia was declared a counter-revolution. Martial law was introduced and heavily armed troops and special units clashed with rebels, killing more than a dozen and wounding 150 Kosovars. Permanent tension and violent confrontation, the arrest of more than three thousand Albanians in the following years, followed. Tens of thousands belonging to the Serbian minority of Kosovo left the region.

The Kosovo crisis reemerged as a consequence of strengthened Serb nationalism in the second half of the eighties and generated a complex political crisis. In September 1986 the Serbian Academy of Art and Sciences, at the initiative of a group close to Milošević, drafted a seventy-four page memorandum. After describing the serious economic and political crisis of the country, they harshly criticized Tito and other non-Serbian Yugoslav leaders, whom they blamed for a situation that could lead to social upheaval and even the disruption of the Yugoslav state. They declared the "loose confederation," created by the constitution of 1974, to be a conspiracy of the Croats, Slovenes, and other non-Serbs, which weakened the country, while at the same time denying equality for Serbs, the only true nationality in the country, who did not have the right to use their own language and (Cyrillic) alphabet when living in other republics of Yugoslavia. The Croats and Slovenes, they added, are the obstacles to Yugoslav unity, and such unity would be a prerequisite to solving the crisis. They also spoke of an anti-Serb and anti-Montenegran "genocide" in Kosovo, and denounced an assumed anti-Serb coalition of other nationalities.

The Serbian centralization concept, which stressed "Yugoslav interests" in contrast to selfish republican self-interests, met with the strongest opposition in other republics. But Milošević strengthened his national line, and the Serb National Assembly enacted an amendment to the constitution in February 1988 curtailing the autonomy of the Kosovo and Vojvodina provinces. This provoked a violent protest in Kosovo in March, which was brutally suppressed with the mobilization of 10,000 troops and the killing of twenty-four people. Former Kosovo party leader Azen Vllasi and others were arrested.

In the summer of that year, on the 600th anniversary of Serbia's defeat by the Ottoman Empire, at a memorial service at the ancient battlefield

Kosovo Polje, Milošević spoke of the struggle for a "re-unification of Serbia." Serbia is fighting again, he stated, and it might not exclude the possibility of a new armed war. In the summer and fall of 1988, ninety major pro-Milošević demonstrations were organized and 5 million (!) Serbs participated in countless nationalist rallies.

In this situation a bitter and open national confrontation began. The Kosovo events and the policy of Milošević mobilized Slovenia and Croatia, and the deeply rooted national conflict followed its own logic: the Slovenian and Croat Communist Parties, leading the fight against Serb domination and its aggressive representation in the Serb communist leader, Slobodan Milošević, turned against state socialist political structures and party rule, and toward advocating the right of self-determination. The Communist Parties of the different republics of Yugoslavia, though they formally belonged to the same League of Communists, a former pillar of Yugoslav federalism, now became the forerunners of local national interest.[2]

As a symbolic event, it pays to mention the mass meeting in Ljubljana in February 1989, when the Slovenian party leader, Milan Kucan, assured the Kosovo Albanians of his support and demanded free elections in Kosovo to determine the status of the area. The Slovenian Communist Party, however, went much further. In the fall of 1989 the Yugoslav crisis culminated with the adoption of a constitutional amendment by the Slovenian National Assembly, affirming the right of national self-determination and the right of secession (Hayden, 1992). Milan Kucan in the meantime suggested the introduction of a multi-party system and free elections in Slovenia. The Slovenian party thought of a coalition government after the elections of 1990. Political pluralism, a multi-party system and a market economy became the leading principles of the communist parties of the non-Serb republics in Yugoslavia.

In August 1989, the Central Committee of the Macedonian party made a radical decision in the same direction. The Croatian Communist Party followed in December 1989, and voted for the introduction of a multi-party system with a mixed market economy at their 11th Party Congress. National conflicts were thus combined with the controversy over the political structure and, ultimately, over changing the system as such.

Ivo Banac spoke of the "Yugoslav non-revolution of 1989–90,"

---

[2] While on a spring 1989 visit to the Serbian Academy of Sciences, this author held an informal talk with the leaders of the Academy about the Hungarian reform decisions to introduce the multi-party system. The President of the Serbian Academy jokingly remarked: "We had already introduced the multi-party system in Yugoslavia, and we have eight competing parties in the eight republics and provinces."

maintaining that since "Yugoslavia itself is the product of communist rule," an anti-communist revolution must be anti-Yugoslav as well, and "post-communism also means post-Yugoslavism" (Banac, 1992, p. 186). Paradoxically, in reality the process went the other way around. The communist parties of the republics turned against Yugoslavism, and in their struggle against Serbia were ready to introduce multi-party democracy. To fight successfully for their belated national revolution, they were inclined to abandon their monolithic power and give up state socialism. The 14th Congress of the Yugoslav Communist Party in January 1990 concluded the process and the party ceased to exist. There remained only one last stronghold of federalism, the Yugoslav army. But not for long.

Although Serbian nationalism was traditionally amalgamated with a Serbian-led aggressive Yugoslavism, in the sharpening confrontation of Serbs, Slovenes, Croats and Albanians, the tactics changed. In the session of the Serbian parliament on June 25, 1990, Milošević clearly declared that Serbia "connects its current administrative borders only with federally organized Yugoslavia. Should there be any changes in the organization of Yugoslavia . . . the question of Serbia's borders is an open political question" (Banac, 1992, pp. 181–2). The alternative to a federal Yugoslavia was an enlarged Serbia absorbing the areas where substantial Serb minorities live in Croatia and Bosnia-Herzegovina. The Greater Serbia concept stemmed from the fact that 40 percent of Serbs lived in the neighboring republics and represented 31 and 12 percent of the population of Bosnia-Herzegovina and Croatia respectively. The joint Slovene – Croat proposal of April 1991 to form a loose confederation of six independent states was thus rejected by Serbia.

The Croatian national ambition did not want to deal with the problem of the Serbian minority. As the Serbs sought to dominate the federal Yugoslav state, the Croats wanted to do the same with the Serb minority. After the April 1990 multi-party elections in Slovenia and Croatia when the national opposition gained the upper hand, the nationalist trend was strengthened. Franjo Tudjman, the President of Croatia, followed a similar nationalist policy to that of Milošević, and decreed the replacement of Cyrillic or biscriptual signs with Latin ones, purged Serbs from the state administration, and replaced the Serbian police force in the areas of the Serbian minority. The representatives of the latter initiated an agreement to guarantee cultural autonomy for the Serbs, including control of the schools in their settlements, but it was refused by Tudjman. Then the Serb minority sought to hold a referendum over their demand for political autonomy inside Croatia, but this was declared to be illegal.

Both Slovenia and Croatia rushed to finalize secession: in December

1990 the Slovenian government held a referendum on the declaration of independence which took place on June 26, 1991. A day before that the Croatian parliament voted for Croatian independence. Serbia, in competing with the rival republics, followed this pattern and held its first multi-party elections in December 1990. Milošević with his reorganized, now Socialist party, gained the absolute majority. His opponents, Vojislav Šešelj and his Serbian Radical Party and its paramilitary Chetnik organization, Mirko Jović's Serbian National Renewal Party and its military wing, the *Vitezovi*, and Vuk Drašković's Serbian Renewal Movement, were even more violently and extremely nationalist, and argued for the expulsion of the non-Serbs from Serbia and equally promoted the idea of Greater Serbia.

The Yugoslav political arena and the first free elections in each republic were dominated by the nationality question. Confrontation became unavoidable. A day after the declaration of Slovenian independence, the Serbian-led Yugoslav army launched an attack on Slovenia. This war was the last action of the Yugoslav army to keep federal Yugoslavia together by force. But it soon ended, and Serbia accepted the European Community's mediation and signed the Brioni Agreement on Slovenian independence. The strong Serb-dominated army from this time on gave up the Yugoslav ideal and became the executor of the Greater Serbia idea.

The vanguard of Greater Serbian nationalism, however, was the Serb minority in Croatia and Bosnia-Herzegovina itself. They began to organize their own paramilitary organizations and demanded the recognition of their right to self-determination and to join Serbia. Actually, they demanded nothing more than what the Slovenes and the Croats (and later the Bosnians) had already done. The nationalizing new independent states refused to accept this demand. As the chronicler of the disintegration of Yugoslavia phrased it, "the Krajina formula of 'self-determination' for every minority ... leads inexorably to the Lebanization of Yugoslavia. This means the collapse of all central authority and transfer of power into the hands of local warlords" (Magaš, 1993, p. 349).

The Serbs of Vojina Krajina did not meditate on the old "threshold principle," on how large a minority should be to earn the right of self-determination. This area was a traditional military borderland between the Ottoman and the Austrian empires, and the Serb population of the area are the successors of the liberated free military colonists, peasant-soldiers who grew up with weapons in their hands. They never turned to the authorities for justice, but made their own. These traditionally cruel fighters still carried the memory of the last civil war during World War II. Most families had somebody to mourn, since the main fronts and the bulk of the bloodiest atrocities of that civil war occurred precisely in this area, the real fault-line of Yugoslavia (Glenny, 1992). What actually began was the continuation of the unfinished civil war 1945. Mobilized memory, mutual suspicion, and misunderstanding became real factors of hatred and brutal revenge. On the morning of June 26, 1991, the Serbian guerilla army, the so-called *Martićevći*, launched an attack against the Croat police station in Glina. Thus began the civil war which soon spread into Bosnia-Herzegovina.

Yugoslav state socialism was destroyed together with Yugoslavia herself (Cohen, 1992). Following strong traditions, the federation and the state socialist system ended in a violent, dramatic civil war, which shocked the whole world in the early 1990s. The Yugoslav case heralded an emerging major danger: the collapse of Central and East European communism has the potential of unleashing partly hidden and long-repressed national sentiments and hatreds in the "belt of mixed populations," which, in a difficult economic and political crisis, could engulf the region in national conflicts and civil wars. The reality of this immense but so far not unavoidable danger depends greatly on the success of the transition, on the successful or failed march toward Europe.

Part III

Back to Europe? Post-1989 transformation and pathways to the future

After its mid twentieth-century detour, its revolt against the West, Central and Eastern Europe has settled down to a post-communist transformation characterized by a return to Western values and the parliamentary democracies' road to an export-led modernization (integration into the world market with an emphasis on exports), both of which it had abandoned at the beginning of the century.

Privatization, the transition to a market economy, and the *laissez-faire*, anti-isolationist policies of the early post-communist years, have caused dramatic economic and social set-backs. Is Central and Eastern Europe a worthy candidate at this point for full and equal membership in the European Union, for successful integration into the world market and the community of civic societies?

Can the poor peripheries follow the road of the rich core with any degree of success, or will corrective measures be necessary? Can the peripheral nations ever "enter Europe," or are they doomed to remain on the outside, in the backyard of the European Union or an all-powerful Germany? Will market democracies prevail or will autocratic nationalisms lead to new uprisings? In other words, does history move forward or in a circle?

Not only did each of these prospects seem possible at various points in the early transition years; they are still indicative of possible, greatly divergent futures for Central and Eastern Europe's countries or sub-regions.

8   Building a parliamentary market system

At this historical point (1989) the story of state socialism came to an end. Was it the end of Central and Eastern Europe's detour in its twentieth-century revolt against the West, having rejected Western values and institutions, and having tried to break out from its peripheral status by moving to the right, and then to the left? The countries of the region now hope to return to Europe and the world system and catch up with the West. They are rushing to copy Western institutions, knocking at the door of the European Community, attempting to attract foreign capital. Has the story of the detour really ended?

This question is not yet answerable. The political roads toward the European Community are open. The East could thus become a part of the West if the requirements of joining are satisfied. As several Western and Eastern politicians have suggested, it is only a question of time.

It is not out of the question, however, that, as Adam Przeworski phrased it, the "East" may become the "South" (Przeworski, 1991). Using another oft-mentioned metaphor, the region, instead of joining Europe, might march out of Europe straight to the Third World. Central and Eastern Europe is in flux. What will happen? Something new is definitely in the making. The historian cannot predict the future, but can offer an analysis of the emerging new developments *in statu nascendi*, to discover the imminent trends, the choices and determinants, in their historical context.

Building a parliamentary-market system

"Let us teach ourselves and others that politics can be not only the art of the possible . . . but that it can even be the art of the impossible, namely the art of improving ourselves and the world," declared Václav Havel, newly elected president of Czechoslovakia in his New Year's Day speech in 1990. Concluded Havel: "I dream of a republic independent, free and democratic, of a republic economically prosperous and yet socially just, in short, of a humane republic which serves the individual. . . . People, your government has returned to you!" (Havel, 1991, pp. 395–6).

The year 1990 was a year of great dreams and expectations. The countries of the region opened new chapters in their history. They prepared for their first free elections. Every one shared the vision that Havel expressed. Every one hoped that the Western world would rush to help and that Europe would open its doors to them. Central and Eastern Europe was full of hope and anticipation: the watchwords of the year in the region were "Europe" and "Democracy."

Some uncertainty was expressed as well, in the form of warnings regarding the legacy of the ruined economy and of two or three difficult years ahead, and on the decayed moral environment. A dawn of new values and new customs, however, had arrived. The new is always laden with promises, but is invariably frightening as well. A new tension emerged in 1990, but it stemmed mostly from the strain of great expectations. In the spring and summer of that year, the free parliamentary elections established a new political setting for the region (Tismaneanu, 1992).

Elections and parties; parliamentary democracy in the making

Three different types of electorial results and, consequently, three distinct political arrangements characterized the region. The first type of elections were concluded in a well-structured political arena with the presence of most European political features, and offered representation for various social-political groupings. This case, after 1990, was embodied solely by Hungary. The second type of elections led to the overwhelming victory of a monolithic opposition, which incorporated rather different political views into one single party. This was the case in Poland and Czechoslovakia. The third type, distinguished in the Balkan countries, was characterized by the victory and absolute majority of the former communist parties, now reformed as socialists.

On March 25, 1990, more than four million Hungarians, 63 percent of the eligible voters, participated in multi-party elections in Hungary, and opted for a change of the system: the Hungarian Democratic Forum (*Magyar Demokrata Forum*, MDF) won a landslide victory. More than 42 percent of the votes went to this center-right, populist-national-conservative-Christian democratic party. This made it easy to form a right-of-center conservative coalition, together with the Smallholders and the Christian Democratic parties. The coalition had together 60 percent of the seats in the neo-gothic house of parliament.

On the other side of the house, three opposition parties took their places: the Free Democratic Alliance (SzDSz), formed by former leading dissidents, a pronounced anti-communist, social-liberal party; the Alliance of Young Democrats (Fidesz), which shared classical liberal values; and the Hungarian Socialist Party (MSzP), founded by the reform wing of the former ruling party in October 1989 on a Western socialist platform.

The Hungarian political setting was thus relatively well structured, with representation from all major center-right and center-left European political wings. The country successfully avoided fragmentation and chaos in the political arena. Dozens of scattered small parties, including the re-established former ruling Hungarian Socialist Workers Party, among almost sixty others, could not achieve the required 4 percent minimum of votes to gain seats in the parliament.

Normal political life and the working ability of the parliament was assured. It was strengthened by an early political pact between the MDF and SzDSz. The strongest opposition party accepted a reduction in the number of parliamentary decisions that required a two-thirds majority, which the MDF paid for with its acceptance of the presidential candidate from the SzDSz, Árpád Göncz, a playwright who was given a life sentence after 1956 and freed by the general amnesty in the early sixties. His election by parliament created a healthier balance of power. The new setting thus assured a steady political framework for the difficult process of transformation.

The situation was rather different in the Czechoslovak elections of early June, 1990. Although old and new parties were formed, they could not establish themselves and mobilize supporters. The dominating force in the political arena was unquestionably the Charter 77 opposition, the moral victor of the previous decade and the hero of the November days of 1989, as well as the Civic Forum Party and its Slovak equivalent, the Public Against Violence, established by Charter activists during the turbulent November days.

The early summer elections thus brought about a landslide victory for a monolithic, triumphant opposition, especially in the Czech lands, where the Civic Forum gained more than 53 percent of the votes and 67 percent of the seats in the republic's assembly. In Slovakia, the vote was much more divided. The Public Against Violence became the strongest single party with 40 percent of the seats, but the conservative Christian Democratic Movement, led by the Slovak dissident, Jan Čarnogursky, also acquired a strong political position (22 percent of the seats).

Besides the massive majority for the former opposition, there were virtually no competitors on the political stage. The only significant political force in both parliaments was the reorganized Communist Party, which in both cases won nearly 14 percent of the votes and 15–16 percent of the seats. The Czechoslovak elections were thus similar to the (semi-free) Polish elections of 1989, when the monolithic party-state lost to the monolithic opposition. Hence the political scene was yet to be structured in both Poland and Czechoslovakia.

The massive majority of the former opposition, in spite of their unquestioned rule, was fragile: they were united only in opposing state socialism, and represented rather diverse ideas and visions about the future. A combination of contrasting conservative, populist, liberal free-market, and social democratic wings were amalgamated in one party. After the elections centripetal forces stopped working and unity began to disintegrate. The lack of a well-structured political scene, of course, did not hinder an immediate start towards the institutionalization of democracy and the preparation of a market transformation, but the first governments had to face strong criticism and opposition from within their own parties. Large masses of people realized that they were not being represented. Internal struggles and the splitting of the leading political parties followed.

The Polish, Hungarian, and Czechoslovak elections led to the victory of centrist and right-center parties and coalitions. Although several changes occurred during the very first years of transformation, this basic character had not changed by the end of 1993.

A third type of electoral result characterized the Balkans. Without a real opposition movement in these countries, the few intellectual dissidents, writers, and scholars were severely isolated. The Balkan countries remained more rural than the other countries of the region. Urban inhabitants hardly surpassed one-third to one-half of the population. The Soviet type of modernization had much greater relative results here compared to the more developed countries of the region, and the communist parties followed a markedly nationalist course.

After a completely unexpected revolutionary transformation, the Balkan opposition forces found themselves totally unprepared. Although the free formation of parties was guaranteed and began almost immediately, the process of transition remained in the hands of the only existing political force, the Communist Party. Most of the compromised old leadership was removed, and the parties changed their names and reorganized themselves on a social democratic basis.

The new leaders, who played an important role in all these transformations, enjoyed a certain popularity, and the first free elections thus led to their overwhelming victory. The reorganized former communist parties won an absolute majority in all the Balkan countries in the 1990–1 parliamentary elections. In Bulgaria, where the traditional Agrarian party could not attract more than 8 percent of the voters, and the newly formed European-oriented Union of Democratic Forces received 36 percent of the seats, the absolute winner was the Bulgarian Socialist (former Communist) Party, with over 53 percent of the parliamentary seats.

In Romania in 1990, the National Salvation Front, which emerged in the political vacuum following the collapse of Ceauşescu's dictatorship, and was led by communists who had been pushed aside (after having initially been favored) by Ceauşescu, won 67 percent of the votes, and its leader and presidential candidate Ion Iliescu captured 85 percent. "Historical" parties, such as the National Peasant-Christian Democratic Party and National Liberal Party, were reestablished by their emigrant leaders who had spent most of the postwar decades abroad. But they had a difficult time establishing themselves, and suffered devastating defeats: the Liberals won less than 11 percent and the Peasants hardly more than 4 percent of the vote. The Hungarian party became the second largest party in the parliament with a 7 percent share.

The Serbian republic and Montenegro reflected the same Balkan phenomenon of decisive communist electoral victories in 1990. At the end of December the Serbian Socialist (former Communist) Party captured 194 seats of the republic's 250 seat parliament, while its major opponent, the Serbian Renewal Movement, gained only nineteen seats. Slobodan Milošević was elected president by more than 65 percent of the vote. Milošević, in the midst of a cruel nationalist crusade in Bosnia-Herzegovina, was able to repeat his victory and win an absolute majority at the end of 1992.

All the other republics, including the more Western Slovenia and Croatia, but also the typical Balkan republics of Bosnia-Herzegovina and Macedonia, produced rather different results. The central question of the 1990 elections in Yugoslavia was not so much the question of democratic transformation but that of nationalism. As the country fell apart, its republics basically voted according to their assumed national interests.

In Croatia, Slovenia, Bosnia-Herzegovina, and Macedonia during their respective elections of April, May, November, and December 1990, the former communists were defeated, and a recently established, ethnically comprised separatist opposition won the elections. It should be noted that in Slovenia, where the parliamentary elections were won by the united democratic opposition, the victor of the presidential elections was Milan Kućan, head of the Communist Party of Slovenia from 1986 on, because voters saw him as "the biggest protector of Slovenian interests and the founder of Slovene statehood" (*Borba*, 1990). Kućan also repeated his victory at the end of 1992. The national issue, indeed, played the central role in Yugoslav elections.

In November 1990, the Macedonian and Bosnian elections were clearly dominated by the national issue: the two leading and victorious opposition parties, the Internal Macedonian Revolutionary Organization (IMRD) and the Bosnian Muslim Party for Democratic Action, were both ethnically based. In the Bosnian case, the reformed communist party ended in fourth place behind three ethnically based parties. At the end of the year, Alija Izetbegovic, a militant Muslim who was twice imprisoned under Tito for his "pan-Islamic activity" and his "Islamic Declaration," was elected president of the republic. In the Macedonian case the highly nationalist, traditional IMRO appealed to Macedonian sentiment at the expense of the republic's Serb and Albanian population and succeeded.

As Petar Gosev noted in early 1991, a "new totalitarianism in the form of nationalism" threatened Macedonia, which was "increasingly becoming a post-communist society, [but] this did not mean that it had also become democratic" (Andrejevich, 1991, p. 29).

The first free elections in Albania followed the typical Balkan pattern. The Communist Party, based on its rural constituency, received almost 65 percent of the votes. The democratic opposition, the Albanian Democratic Party, established three months earlier, benefitted from the urban vote and mustered only 27 percent.

New elections and a better structured political arena

Although the first elections resulted in three different types of governments, they did not last for long. It is small wonder that only one parliament and government, that of Hungary, proved to be stable enough to complete its term. All the others were undermined by internal conflicts or external attacks. The general political development and the emergence of a better structured political system with the participation of various political wings and parties created early political crises in all of the countries.

Within a few months after the first elections a gradually developing opposition began to exploit the disappointment of the population and led a successful campaign against the reform communist governments of the Balkans.

Although successfully securing an absolute majority, these parties could not stabilize their power. On the contrary, as the Los Angeles Times reported in the fall of 1991, "distress over the hardships inflicted by reform has already exploded into anti-government rioting in Bulgaria, Albania and Romania, all of which ousted elected leaderships over the past year" (Williams, 1991).

Indeed, Petre Roman's government in Romania was forced to resign as a result of a violent miners' revolt against it in the fall of 1991, a year and a half after it took office. On September 25, a few thousand miners stormed the capital from the Jiu Valley, the "Ethiopia of Romania," and angrily attacked government buildings and clashed with riot police, leaving three dead and 455 injured during two days of street fighting. The next day, the government resigned.

In the second parliamentary and presidential election in the fall of 1992, the government still emerged victorious. Although the ruling socialists lost substantial ground, they remained relatively the strongest party (with over 25 percent), and Iliescu himself was reelected with 60 percent of the votes.

The Albanian government suffered a defeat only three months after its impressive electoral victory in March 1991. A bloody rebellion in Shkoder and Shengjin, a strike in the chrome mines in April and May, additional attempts of large numbers to escape to Italy, and a partly successful general strike in May (with the participation of nearly half the country's work force), all contributed to paralyzing the economy. In June, the government resigned and the first coalition government was established. But the revolts continued. In the summer, 10,000 Albanians escaped to Italy. In the ports of Vlore and Durres, twelve people were killed when the crowd attempted to board ships and leave the country. In Tirana, 25,000 people demonstrated to demand the resignation of Ramiz Alia, the former communist party chief and newly elected president. In mid September 100,000 people called for his ouster. A new election in March 22, 1992 led to the total defeat of the former Communist Party, which lost 40 percent of its supporters in one year and received less than 26 percent of the vote. At the same time, the leading right-of-center Democratic Party increased its support from 39 to 62 percent. The party's head, Sali Berisha, was elected president. Alexander Meksi formed the first non-communist government, and declared a radical program of marketization and privatization.

In Bulgaria, the democratically elected president was forced to step down in July 1990 respectively, only one month after the elections, and was followed by the government in November. A second election led to the narrow victory by the opposition in October 1991. The Union of Democratic Forces received more than 34 percent of the votes compared with 33 percent for the socialist party. Only one other party, the ethnically-based Turkish Movement for Rights and Freedoms, passed the 4 percent hurdle (receiving almost 8 percent). The former communists, the unchallenged victors of the 1990 elections, lost the second elections. The center-right conservative, *laissez-faire* political forces became dominant in almost the entire region.

The second round of parliamentary elections in 1991–2 brought quite the opposite results to those of the first in Poland, and in Czechoslovakia as well. They went hand in hand with the split or fragmentation of the former united opposition. Two years after its historic landslide victory in

1989, the first entirely free election in Poland in October 1991 ended with the defeat of a badly broken Solidarity. However, no clear winner emerged. Among the thirty parties and groupings that gained parliamentary representation, the two largest, Mazowiecki's Democratic Union (*Unia Demokratyczna*, UD), with the legendary Jacek Kuron and Bronislaw Geremek in the leadership, and the Alliance of Democratic Left (SLD), based on the former, now reformed Communist Party, both received about 12 percent of the votes. Only a coalition of at least five parties could attain a majority in the 460-seat *Sejm*. Among the parliamentary parties, only nine received more than 5 percent of the votes.

One of the most striking changes was the resounding defeat of the Solidarity Trade Union, which ran independently in the election but received only 5 percent of the votes. The seriously flawed electoral system, without a minimum percent hurdle, led to an extreme fragmentation of political forces and brought roughly twenty small parties into the parliament. "Embarrassingly low voter turn-out resulted in a parliament handicapped ... by the lack of the possibility of creating a stable coalition." Poland's fate, noted Jerzy Boniecki, "is doubtful and unknown" (Boniecki, 1992, p. 48).

In the greatest political surprise of all, the minority government failed, and the third parliamentary elections in Poland in September 1993 led to a devastating defeat of all the parties related to Solidarity, President Walesa, and the Catholic Church. Hardly more than four years after the landslide victory of Solidarity, the Democratic Left Alliance and the Polish Peasants' Party, successors of the former communists, gained 64 percent of the seats in the *Sejm*, while the new party of the formerly legendary Lech Walesa gained a mere 5.4 percent, and the liberal remnants of Solidarity, the Democratic Union, 10.5 percent. Equally sensational was the fact that none of the Catholic parties was able to gain a single parliamentary seat.

In Czechoslovakia, the various political trends had a different impact in the two parts of the federal republic. The monolithic former opposition ruling parties began to disintegrate a year and a half after their great electoral victories in 1990. From the very beginning at least two highly distinctive wings existed within the government party. One comprised the center-left opposition and former reform-communists of 1968 led by Milos Hajek, which founded their Club for Socialist Restructuring and developed social democratic concepts. Two other groupings, the Left Alternative and the Club of Social Democrats, with Petr Uhl and the weekly *Tvorba*, united those who played a pioneering role in the formation of the Charter 77 movement.

From October 1990 on, however, an accentuated right-center force was in the making. The Interparliamentary Club of the Democratic Right was established, calling in its first statement for radical privatization. In place of its former leadership, the Forum elected the conservative advocate of market capitalism, Vacláv Klaus, as its chairman. He sought to reorganize the Forum from a rather loose agglomeration into a strong party with a concise vision and political philosophy. His first action was an attempt to expel the *Obrada* and Left Alternative from the Forum. A definite shift to the right began.

The disintegration of the Slovak Public Against Violence occurred simultaneously. As early as April 1990 a mass demonstration in Bratislava demanded Slovak independence and formed a National Council for the Liberation of Slovakia.

The separatists did not seem to represent a real danger of disintegration, since the polls, even at the end of the year, revealed that only a minuscule 5 percent of Slovaks wanted an independent Slovakia. Still, a nationalist elite continued its struggle. In March 1991, Vladimir Mečiar, the prime minister of Slovakia after the electoral victory of the Public Against Violence, left the party and premiership in opposition to federal policy, arguing that it was no longer suitable for Slovakia. This caused the united opposition and government coalition of Civic Forum and Public Against Violence to break apart. Within a few months, the new elections of June 1992 clarified the situation. In the Czech lands three parties replaced the Forum: Vacláv Klaus' Civic Democratic Party, Jiři Dienstbier's Civic Movement and the Civic Democratic Alliance; in Slovakia the leading party split into two, Vladimir Mečiar's Movement for a Democratic Slovakia and the Civic Democratic Union.

No longer could a single party gain a majority. More than one third of the votes were given to Klaus' and Mečiar's parties in the two republics respectively, while nearly 15 percent went to the former Czech and Slovak communists. The other parties were rather small. The most striking novelty of the second election was the virtual disappearance of the former genuine Civic Forum type of parties. Klaus' orthodox, conservative market liberalism and Mečiar's emphatic Slovak nationalism combined with leftist-populist economics did not leave a place for the heroes of the former opposition and the November days of 1989. Dienstbier's party gained less than 5 percent of the vote.

Thus, the structuring and restructuring of the newly emerging party system, splits and merges, the founding of new and the disappearance of "old" parties, all belong to this process. Tectonic political forces were still at work and might have led to a well-structured party system with adequate representation of divergent social interest groups, but they could also generate important yet unstable and fragile policy changes.

Several signs in 1993–4, such as the result of the Polish parliamentary elections, reflected a strengthening of the shift from the center-right to the left-of-center. The most striking change was expressed by the Hungarian elections of May 1994, when the Socialist Party won an absolute majority of 54 percent. The Central and Eastern European experiences of the early 1990s generated a strong backlash and pushed the countries toward this path. What has appeared in Central and Eastern Europe is by no means a revival of communism but a sign of a more pragmatic and socially more sensitive direction. The various socialist parties were mostly founded not by former old guard communists, but in most cases by reformist groups of the previous leading parties that adopted a social democratic ideology. They share the basic Western values such as parliamentary democracy and private-market economy, but advocate a much stronger social sensitivity. They are definitely more "statist," have closer connections with the unions, and oppose *laissez faire* ideology. The political revolving door is moving rather fast in Central and Eastern Europe.

Rising nationalism has had an increasing impact on party formation and policy orientation, and plays an important role in some crisis-ridden areas. The December 1993 elections in Serbia were a clear manifestation of competing nationalism. Milošević, who had established himself as an ardent Greater Serbian nationalist, was challenged with a non-confidence vote, but the third parliamentary elections ended with an even more convincing victory of Milošević's Socialist Party, which won almost half of the seats. The focal point of the elections, however, was not a political or social orientation, nor a transformation policy, but Greater Serbian nationalism. The competitors were also extreme nationalists.

Although the political arena is highly unsettled in Central and Eastern Europe, a multi-party, parliamentary system is clearly in the making. The first four to five years of tempestuous transition actually represented a consistent approach toward institutionalized democracy. A parliamentary legislature, new constitutions and constitutional amendments, a series of newly enacted laws and institutional changes all served the introduction of a Western type of political structure.

The classic principle of modern democracies, the separation of legislative and executive power and the independence of the courts, was immediately institutionalized. Political pluralism was introduced along with a multi-party system, modern property rights, human rights, guaranteed freedom of the press and association, freedom of travel, and an unhindered development of a heretofore non-existent civil society. With the adoption of amendments to the penal code that eliminated such infamous "political crimes" as disseminating anti-state and anti-party propaganda, as well as the notorious paragraphs on economic sabotage for not fulfilling centrally determined quotas and compulsory deliveries, the "legal" basis of terror was destroyed and crucial preconditions for the building of democracy were fulfilled.

The new governments prepared and parliaments debated and enacted a series of new laws and amendments. After the first free elections in March 1990, the Hungarian parliament enacted 134 new laws and 128 amendments, thus nearly nine laws per month, during the thirty-six months between May 1990 and December 1992. The extensive law-making covered almost all spheres of life. Most of the laws, however, increasingly regulated seven major fields such as social insurance (thirty-one laws), privatization (twenty-six laws), taxation (twenty-six laws), budget and state household (twenty-one laws), courts (twenty laws), local governments (nineteen laws), and land, including cooperative farms (seventeen laws). Constitutional courts were established in quite a few countries to safeguard the fledgling and fragile democracies. Most of the countries reorganized their legal systems.

This new political development in Central and Eastern Europe, however, may cause a feeling of historical *déjà vu*. Since the end of the 1870s this is the third time that the countries of the region have adopted Western constitutions and institutions. The first time was after regaining independence from the Ottoman Turks, Russians, and Austrians at the end of the nineteenth and the beginning of the twentieth century. The second time was during the short-lived democracies after World War II. Most of those cases created a strange duality: a Western-type constitutional-legal-institutional system was laden with clientist, autocratic, and corrupt elements; democratic parliaments were replaced with bogus ones; and parliamentary parties were counterbalanced by the army, the mobilized mob, and, at times, paramilitary terrorist organizations. Institutionalized human rights went hand in hand with the widespread practice of ethnic and religious hatred and oppression; freedom of press with the blackmailing and even killing of journalists; working parliaments with the murder of its representatives – all these "peacefully" coexisting in the stormy history of the region, reflecting typical characteristics of "peripheral" political structures and realities, and rendering constitutional rights quite meaningless. The experiences of adopting but never realizing the Belgian constitution in independent Romania, or introducing the most advanced Western-type constitution but then carrying out a military takeover in independent Poland, represents a tradition that belongs to the late nineteenth and early twentieth-century history, and to a political culture throughout the region. Professor Ewa Letowska, the renowned Polish human rights activist, warned in 1992: "Poland is not a state of law

[*Rechtsstaat*] and it will not be for a very long time. The law is still treated in an expedient way, as a tool of the existing politics or policies ... The subordination of law to politics still exists although it has been oficially rejected" (Wolicki, 1992, p. 39).

The first years of the transition thus represented a breakthrough toward democracy, the first battle was resoundingly won; but the war for democracy is far from over.

Social transformation, the new political elite and leaders

During the first years of transformation, significant social restructuring began. The number of blue-collar workers notably decreased. As a consequence of a severe industrial decline of roughly 40 percent of output, what was once a most numerous class of blue-collar industrial employees has drastically shrunk. In addition to the 10–14 percent of these temporarily unemployed, a great many permanently left their previous field of occupation. In Hungary, for example, at the end of 1993, while unemployment reached 13 percent, the number of industrial employees was only 60 percent of the 1988 level. Although the figures vary, the trend is basically the same across the entire region. There has been a marked shift toward the service sectors and self-employment. Many members of the oversized industrial work force have shifted into the previously backward service sector.

Another important social transformation characterizes the rural population. Except in Poland and Yugoslavia, a collectivized agriculture employed a homogenized peasantry, the owner-employees of the collective farms. In the new situation the land was practically reprivatized in most of the countries, and a new independent farmer-peasant layer began to emerge.

For several years, however, the bulk of the members of former collective farms, remained in the collectives. As Brooks and Meurs revealed, surveys made in 1991 and 1992 showed that 62 percent of Romanian and 46 percent of Bulgarian rural dwellers preferred to remain in cooperatives instead of reestablishing private farms (Brooks and Meurs, 1994). The majority of Hungarian farmers, in spite of a political-ideological crusade against cooperative agriculture, remained in the collectives even in 1993. Since the entire transformation is taking place at a time of deep agricultural crisis and severe decline of output, a new exodus has marked the countryside. In Hungary, during the four years since 1989, half of the farming population has left agriculture.

In contrast, the heretofore barely or non-existing entrepreneurial class began to rise. Grassroots privatization, the foundation of family businesses, and various kinds of small-scale enterprises led to the emergence of 1–2 million small businesses in each of the countries. A new phenomenon of a rising entrepreneurial class, comprising 5–10 percent of the population, became one of the most important social changes in the region.

Surprisingly, the most visible and spectacular element of social transformation was the transmutation of the political class. Most of the old elite was replaced almost immediately after the first free elections. Primarily early retirements and a return to professional fields, and, in some cases (to use Pierre Bourdieu's terms), the change from "political capital" to "financial capital" going to private business, were the main exit roads for the old guard.

The change of guard offered a tremendous opportunity to fill the political vacuum. The birth of a new regime always does so for various oppressed and marginalized people. It is also unavoidable that dubious personalities would exploit the fluid, unsettled situation.

The December 1993 elections and the Zhirinovsky phenomenon in Russia warned the international community of this danger. Desperation directed every fourth voter to support a party of adventurers and irresponsible demagogues. The Zhirinovsky syndrome was less ominous in Central and Eastern Europe. Similar characters and demagogues naturally appeared in the rank and file of the new political elite. Zeljko Raznatović ("Arkan"), wanted by the Interpol for bank robbery and manslaughter, would become a political factor and a member of the parliament in Serbia. Miroslav Sladek, a former censor in the Husák regime, became the leader of the far-right, racist, expansionist Republican Party in Czechoslovakia. Marian Munteanu, a sinister political chameleon, became an actor on the Romanian political stage. The former communist youth leader emerged as an internationally recognized hero and a symbol of democratic opposition to the "half-communist" Iliescu government in the summer of 1990, when he led a student demonstration and hunger strike. In December 1991, Munteanu founded a fascist-type party, a follower of Codreanu's infamous Iron Guard. The celebrated Budapest playwright of the 1970s to 1980s, István Csurka, who signed an agreement to report to the secret police in 1957, became a leading figure and one of the vice presidents of the Hungarian Democratic Forum in 1989, and then established his own extreme right, neo-fascist party, Hungarian Truth and Life, an advocate of anti-Semitism, aggressive nationalism and authoritarian power in 1993 (Held, 1993).

The list of these types of dubious characters, sometimes criminals or pathological cases, is quite long. Most of them fortunately remained at the periphery of the political arena, and some soon disappeared from public life. Some, however, are potential contenders and in the case of continuous economic decay could become dangerous.

The new political class was basically recruited from three main social-political sources. The most obvious source was the rank and file of the former opposition or dissidents. They had struggled against the communist regime, were permanently harassed, and even arrested; they were the ones that history had now proven to have been right. Their prominent role, together with free elections, endowed the newly arranged systems with self-evident legitimacy.

The second source of the new political elite was the former non-party intellectuals, experts, lawyers, professors, teachers, even lower-level government technocrats from different fields. They had not risked their positions by joining the opposition, but quietly worked on the sidelines. In some cases they did not want to get involved and deliberately avoided politics. Quite a few, however, had simply been unable to attain a more successful career because of limited ability. In most cases they only wanted to do their best, and therefore collaborated with the *ancien régime*; but they stayed out of the limelight and tried to improve what they could in their narrow environment. They worked as fellows at the research institutes of the National Academy of Sciences, as private attorneys, as editors in publishing houses, as academic people or department chiefs at ministries. Now they climbed to greater heights, and quite a few have proved to be much better than their previous political appointee predecessors. Several others took advantage of the massive personnel changes and rose to positions far beyond their competence.

The third main source of the emerging political elite was a part of the old elite that had been able to survive either because it had previously belonged to the reformist party opposition or to the party intelligentsia struggling for reforms, and had played an important role in implementing those reforms, or, most particularly, because they were technocrats who offered their much-needed expertise to the former opposition now in power. Others simply abandoned the sinking ship and changed their colors, becoming nationalist demagogues, agitating populists, and enthusiastic neophytes in the service of the new power. Some of them subsequently remained on the left, joined and led the reformed communist parties, and became socialist members of the parliaments and new governments.

New political leaders emerged from this rising new elite, some as genuine protagonists and charismatic leaders of the historical transformation of their countries, others as instinctively skillful political tacticians. They came from each of the three groups mentioned above. The Polish Walesa, the Czech Havel, and the Bulgarian Zhelev emerged from the opposition, the Hungarian Antall and the Czech Klaus from the non-party intelligentsia, while the Romanian Iliescu, the Serb Milošević and the Slovenian Kučan from the old party elite. Others were somewhere in between: Mečiar, a former boxer and fervent Slovak nationalist leader, began his career as a party cadre, but was expelled from the party after 1968 and became a non-communist intellectual; Sali Berisha, the first Albanian president elected after the electoral defeat of the post-communist regime, joined the Communist Party in 1971 at the age of twenty-eight, and remained in it to make a professional career as a cardiologist. The leaders had rather different family and educational backgrounds. Their names, however, became linked with the historical transition of Central and Eastern Europe.

Lech Walesa, the legendary Solidarity leader, was an electrician of the Gdansk shipyards, an embodiment of the postwar generation of Polish workers. He completed his education before reaching the secondary level, and instead learned a trade. Deeply religious, self-conscious, self-confident, and militant, Walesa was ready to fight for his rights and for the interests of his entire class. He was dismissed from the shipyard because his speech mobilized the workers in 1970, and became the central figure of the 1980 struggle.

As much as he was a typical representative of the Polish workers, however, he was also a unique personality, a genuine, instinctive political talent. He emerged in 1980 at the age of thirty-seven as the paramount founder and leader of Solidarity, and he became a symbol of resistance in the eighties. His charisma unified not only the opposition, but an entire nation in the struggle for a free, independent Poland in 1988–9. His role in the difficult and risky encounter with the regime, which entailed both confrontation and compromise, was outstanding and, as J.F. Brown pointed out, Walesa appeared wiser, politically mellow and even showed "a touch of greatness. ... [H]is contribution to Poland was almost unimaginable, and his place in the Polish pantheon of heroes already assured" (Brown, 1991b, pp. 89, 98).

At the age of forty-seven, Walesa became the president of his country, a difficult new situation for a former opposition union leader. It is a well-known dilemma of history, the national hero in opposition faced with the danger of losing his charisma as a politician of the establishment. The short history of these years has already produced quite a few paradoxical situations. The union leader Walesa, the renowned organizer of strikes and uncrowned advocate of workers' interests, was replaced by President Walesa, who denounced the workers' strikes as destructive actions and agreed to the dismissal of militant strikers. Walesa, the fabled master of a unified opposition, was supplanted by presidential candidate Walesa, who repeatedly attacked his closest allies, who shamefully alluded to the alleged Jewish origins of the former Catholic opposition leader, his friend and now rival Tadeusz Mazowiecki. His one-time close advisor, Adam Michnik, remarked in the summer of 1990 "You are slowly changing into a Caesar," and predicted that Walesa might introduce the first Peronist-style government in Central and Eastern Europe (*Time Magazine*, 1990a, 1990b). Copying Pilsudski's notorious pattern, Walesa founded a new party, with a similar name to that chosen by Pilsudski in the thirties, the party of Non-Party Bloc (BBWR). "When the time comes to introduce a dictatorship," announced Walesa in early 1994, "the people will force me to accept this role and I shall not refuse. Most likely that is where we are heading" (*New York Times*, 1994). Lech Walesa, the congenial opposition leader, lost his charisma and popularity, hitting bottom in mid 1994 with (according to the polls) 5 percent of the vote.

Václav Havel's portrait shows some similar traits, though he was born to a well-to-do family and grew to be a self-educated playwright and political thinker. Havel embodied the Czech intelligentsia. A committed democrat, an advocate of the multi-party system in 1968, and a self-sacrificing defender of human rights and freedom, Havel patiently suffered harassment by the authorities, worked in a brewery, was arrested and imprisoned three times, developed a philosophy of peaceful, passive resistance, and became the central figure of the Charter 77 opposition.

Exceedingly informal and idealistic, indeed, politically naive, Havel, though initially not attracted to but stirred by power, soon emerged as a symbol of a true and democratic Czechoslovakia. At the age of fifty-three he became the genuine leader of the stormy November days in Prague. His personality endowed the emerging new system with an internal and external legitimacy. His masterful addresses to the people, his broadcasts and "fireside chats," his widely published, brilliant political essays and his official visits abroad all served to endear him to audiences with openness, profound virtuosity, and personal charm.

As president, however, Havel soon lost ground to hard-nosed and ambitious pragmatists, who rejected his initiatives one after the other. His hand-picked candidates and political allies were voted down, and he was forced to sign several laws that he had openly opposed. In 1992 the most celebrated leader of the historical transition of Central and Eastern Europe was pushed out of politics. But he returned to the scene by accepting a position of "powerless power" from the hands of Vacláv Klaus, who recognized the advantage of retaining him as a figurehead. Although Havel stated a year earlier that he had no desire to be a mere figurehead, he became attracted to this role and accepted it after the disintegration of Czechoslovakia.[1]

Needless to say, Havel became a symbol of the noble goals and ideals of the transformation and expressed basic moral questions; on the other hand, his position had eroded, and he was no longer able to influence historical events. Having wanted to be a powerful president, he settled for the role of a Western European style head of state. It is certainly part of the transformation process in the region.

József Antall had a rather different background. He played no role in the Hungarian opposition and was unknown before 1989. He neither represented the working masses nor the high-level charismatic type of intellectual. His involved, monotonous style, endless sentences and dreary speeches could hardly attract the people. Antall worked as a high school teacher and then as the director of the Museum and Library of the History of Medicine as a typical non-party intellectual and second-rank pundit of the cultural establishment of the Kádár regime.

At the age of fifty-eight, however, he suddenly found himself in the middle of a political upheaval when his family background became a source of strength. His father had been a high official in the Ministry of Interior of the Horthy regime, and in that capacity had helped to save refugee Polish officers who escaped after Poland's surrender to Hitler in 1939. He also helped a few hundred Jews to evade deportation to Nazi death camps, and after the war joined the leading Smallholders' Party. In the years of Stalinism he was isolated but never prosecuted. This family background representing the politically tolerant minority of the Christian-gentry political elite of the Horthy regime, coupled with his sober-minded, tranquil personality and unique ability to unite different political wings and negotiate with the powers-that-be (at the round table debates), gave him the prestige to elevate him to the top of the Hungarian Democratic Forum, which had lacked a recognized leader. Its populist founders, mostly writers, invited him as the representative of a moderately conservative party, the symbol of a "tranquil force." He became a kind of embodiment of continuity with the country's non-communist past and, indeed, led his new party to an impressive victory to become the first prime minister of post-communist Hungary.

Respectful and instinctively talented in behind-the-scenes maneuvering,

---

[1] In an interview Havel maintained that it was not an absolute certainty that he would be elected the first president of the independent Czech republic. He made it clear that he "enjoys the work. I got to know some 72 different states, many prime ministers . . . kings and queens. . . . Now I have many friends among [them] . . . and this was quite a pleasant experience. . . . I don't want to disappear from public life" (Kamm, 1992, p. A3).

Antall retained his position in the center of his party. Although he did not distance himself from the party's extreme right-wing populism, he avoided fraternizing with its ideas for three years and successfully isolated it at the beginning of the fourth year of his government. However, his government sought a monopoly of the media, and executed a takeover of the broadcasting media. The ruthless media-war, as Western newspapers rightly reported, "undermined the image earlier enjoyed by Hungary as the most stable and promising of the emerging democracies" (Williams, 1993).

Antall showed an impressive personal strength in struggling with a terminal illness during his entire premiership and remained in office until the very last weeks of his life. Certainly the least colorful prime minister in the region, Antall was the only one among those elected in the first free elections in 1990 who retained his position through 1993. He never gained popularity and was constantly ranked in the bottom third in the popularity polls, in contrast to his permanent rival and the most popular politician of the country, President Árpád Göncz. When Antall died a few days before Christmas 1993, nearly a quarter of a million people bowed before his coffin expressing respect for his contribution to the stability of the country.

Slobodan Milošević represented a rather different type of new leader, as one who emerged in communist Yugoslavia as a party technocrat. Educated and fluent in English, Milošević worked as a banker and simultaneously rose in the party hierarchy. In 1986, a few years after the death of Tito, he was elevated to the top Serbian party leadership as a representative of the new and educated professional generation of postwar Yugoslavia, and as an ardent representative of Serbian interests.

Milošević was flexible enough to understand the need for continuing reforms toward a more consistent mixed market economy and political pluralism. He did not go into decline with the eroding system in the late eighties, but instinctively turned towards deeply rooted Serb nationalism. A passionate demagogue and forceful speaker capable of mobilizing the masses, he acquired a well-based popularity. From the summer of 1988 to the spring of 1989, he was able to mobilize roughly 100 protest rallies with 5 million participants demanding the guarantee of endangered Serbian national interests. He easily won Serbia's three free elections with his reformed former communist party. In conflicts ranging from a confrontation with Kosovo Albanians to a clash with the gradually distancing and ultimately secessionist Slovenes and Croats, Milošević in 1990 was transformed at the age of forty-nine from communist party chief to genuine, steadfast Greater Serbian nationalist leader.

The names of Walesa, Havel, Antall, and Milošević are closely connected to the historical transition of their countries. Recognized, celebrated and even admired, these new politicians, remaining at the helm of their countries' governments during the most difficult of times, soon found themselves in very hot water.

The transition towards a private market economy

The new governments of Eastern-Central Europe inherited a declining, bankrupt economy. The situation was characterized by stagnation spanning a decade and a half, a decline in GNP and a deterioration in the standard of living, inflation, indebtedness, and insolvency, and most of all, a hopeless structural crisis and lack of adjustment.

The task of the freely elected governments was enormous. Together with the democratic transformation, a complex economic metamorphosis was needed. Its content was at least three-fold. First of all, macroeconomic stabilization had to stop a galloping and, in the case of Yugoslavia, hyper-inflation. To achieve this the governments had to cope with the legacy of a shortage economy and radically improve supplies to the population. The stabilization of state budgets compelled the governments to curb huge budget deficits and halt an ever increasing debt crisis by achieving a surplus in foreign trade and an equilibrium in the balance of payments. Hence, stabilizing the economy had been and still remains a rather difficult program.

Nevertheless, a second layer of economic tasks emerged: the beginning of marketization and privatization of the formerly state-owned economies. This required both complex deregulation to abolish all the restrictive regulations, and vast legislative work to create the legal and institutional framework of a market economy. Price and import liberalization required a total reorientation of state socialist economies that had operated with an artificial fixed price system in an isolated and protected market. The entire price system, ownership structure, taxation, state subsidized production and services, and protectionist economic policy with its tariff system, had to change dramatically. Marketization and privatization were handled as a medium-term goal which would be achievable in four to five years.

The third, and certainly most difficult long-term task of the three-fold economic transformation project was a restructuring of the entire economy to follow and adjust to the modern world economy. A new infrastructure based on a modern communications system, a renewed transportation and economic energy system, an enlarged service sector, technologically up-to-date industry and agriculture, and new competitive export sectors, were badly needed.

The three elements of economic transformation were closely connected and had to start simultaneously in order to be carried out. Such a demanding and dramatic transformation had hardly ever happened before; there were no adequate international experiences to learn from. Moreover, short- and long-term goals sometimes confronted each other. There was no alternative to beginning the reorganization and transition. The legitimacy of freely elected governments, the newly emerging hopes and promises of being integrated into Europe and acquiring foreign assistance, and the anticipated foreign investments and domestic entre-preneurial incentives, all offered a unique possibility for the undertaking of drastic operations. The economies were still in the dark but the governments, experts, foreign advisors, and even the various peoples assumed that they were about to see the light at the end of the tunnel.

Although their basic goals were rather similar, each country had a very different background and starting point. Different approaches were applied to achieve the goals of economic transformation. One of them was the Hungarian (and for a short while Yugoslav) "gradualist road," in contrast to the Polish "shock treatment" of "overnight" transformation, while gradualist practice was mixed with "shockist" rhetoric in Czechos-lovakia (Ehrlich, 1994). The Balkan countries, for a very short period, flirted with a sort of "third road" to combine certain elements of the old regime with market capitalism.

Hungary, Yugoslavia, and Poland were the only countries in the region where previous reforms had already laid the foundations for full marketization, and where a substantial privatization had occurred before the multi-party elections.

Because of the peaceful "refolution," Hungary was the only country to enter into the new era with prepared plans for an economic transformation. In the summer of 1988 a large network of six expert committees began to work out detailed long-term plans for a new economic strategy. The preparation of a transition towards a mixed market economy was led by the legendary reformist and "father" of the economic reforms of the sixties, Rezsö Nyers, minister of state in the first post-Kádár government. Working Committee No.1 was responsible for presenting a complex short-term program of transition between 1990 and 1992. The 162 page plan, which, in the words of the head of the Committee, was "not partial, weakened by compromises, or over-gradualist in that it does not touch the foundation of the economic system, and not moderately corrective . . . but a complex, consistent reform which radically transforms the basis of the economic system" (Berend, 1989, p. 11), was on the government's desk in the early spring of 1989. The plan proposed "an immediate start to widespread privatization of property and a long-term leasing of state property, assisted by low interest credits" (Berend, 1989, p. 160), the "attraction of foreign capital," the foundation of a Stock exchange, and a whole set of deregulating measures. A three-year plan of import liberalization (of about 80 percent of imports) was also part of the program. The last reformist government of Miklós Németh adopted and began to implement the transition plan. The new government inherited an advanced process of transformation.

The government received a "present" of another transformation plan, completed by a joint Hungarian-International "Blue Ribbon Commission," initiated by Professor Paul Marer of Indiana University, after the round table agreement in the summer of 1989. Its deliberate goal was to present a program of transition for the newly elected government (Hungary, 1990).

The strategy of continuing what was already a long-established reform process was not questioned in Hungary. "Shock therapy" had no advocates in the country, since there was no uncontrolled inflation and it was evident that, based on the previous results of the reforms and the major changes of 1988–9, a transition in certain basic spheres might be gradually completed in three to four years.

Consequently, within two years, a market price system was practically completed and subsidies were mostly abolished for industrial and agricultural products and were substantially decreased for services. Marketization was established with import liberalization between 1989 and 1991: respectively 36, 60, and then 86 percent of imports were liberalized during these years. Because of its gradual nature, the transition was not coupled with intolerable inflationary pressures. Although the rate of inflation substantially increased in 1990 and 1991, reaching 25 percent and 35 percent respectively, it was brought under control but remained relatively high at about 25 percent.

The retreat by the state and the advance of the market was closely connected to the development of a modern monetary system. The monopoly of the National Bank as the single creditor had already been eliminated in 1987, and thirty-six commercial banks were functioning in the country by the end of 1991. The 1991 law covering the National Bank continued "de-statization" by reestablishing the bank's autonomy from the government. The role of middle- and small-scale banks increased rapidly.

The most radical change in the Hungarian reform program and one of the key elements of the transformation occurred with the privatization of what was basically a state-owned economy. The change to the system led to a rewriting of the privatization plans. The freely elected Hungarian parliament rejected re-privatization, i.e., restoring properties and firms to their genuine owners (or to their heirs), and instead pledged to pay a moderate amount of compensation. Exceptions were made for forcibly collectivized land, schools, and church property, which would be given back to their former owners unless they derived from the former landed estates. Property rights and the legal framework for unrestricted private enterprise, including unlimited foreign ownership of entire companies, were already granted in 1988–9. One should differentiate among three levels of privatization: "grassroots" privatization, meaning the foundation of new, mostly small- and medium-scale private enterprises; "small-privatization," i.e., selling small state-owned firms, mostly single units of retail trade and service companies; and "big privatization" of the huge, mostly monopolistic state-owned industrial and banking companies. The first two proved to be easier but the last was rather difficult to realize.

Since private capital accumulation already had a decade-long history in Hungary, grassroots privatization and the foundation of new small- and medium-scale firms gained momentum from 1989 on. More than 77,000 large and 87,000 medium-size private firms were established, and the number of small family companies rose to 663,000 between the end of 1988 and early 1993.

The so-called small privatization was also very successful. The privatization of retail trade chains, shops and restaurants in Hungary, with more than 10,000 units sold, was nearly finished at the end of 1993. Private firms, according to several evaluations, produced about 55 percent of the country's GDP and employed more than 40 percent of the working population in 1993. Forty percent of private business is now engaged in trade, less than one quarter in manufacturing, and nearly 40 percent in services.

The number of foreign companies and joint ventures were more than 13,000 (compared with 1,332 in 1989), and invested capital totalled $5.5 billion at the end of 1993. According to the Research Institute of Privatization, the share of foreign ownership in Hungarian firms is more than 10 percent, a clear sign of foreign interest. With its earlier start, relative stability and more advanced market relations, Hungary attracted more than half of Western investments into Central and Eastern Europe. The government, however, expected 25–30 percent foreign participation, which has not appeared. Except for a few big multinationals such as General Motors, General Electric, Audi, Suzuki, and one of the biggest foreign landmark investments in Central and Eastern Europe made by an American-German consortium (Ameritech Corporation and *Deutsche Bundespost Telekom*), most of the investments were small. In 1989–90, 90 percent of investments with foreign participation represented less than $130,000 each.

The most difficult part of privatization is the selling of big state-owned companies. Hungary decided to follow a gradual privatization and sell the companies piece by piece. The supervision of privatization is conducted by the State Property Agency (*Állami Vagyonügynökség*), which was already established in February 1989. State firms were first transformed into shareholding companies. To initiate a domestic capital market, the stock exchange was reopened. Though still in a rather embryonic state, it has nonetheless created a necessary institutional background. Most of these firms, however, remained in the hands of the state. In March 1992, over 86 percent of the assets transformed to joint-stock companies remained in the hands of the State Property Agency, and only 2.5 percent belonged to private Hungarian investors; another 8 percent was purchased by foreign investors.

Through the end of 1993 only about 14 percent of big state-owned firms were privatized and, as Paul Marer rightly noted, "the most desirable ones have already been acquired" (Marer, 1993, p. 12). Thus for the time being industrial privatization has hit a dead-end. An important part of investments was channeled into real estate and retail trade chains, fields that do not contribute directly to the creation of a competitive economy.

In the first four years of transition very little happened in terms of restructuring and, except for a newly emerging automobile industry (practically the only field to receive substantial investments from big conglomerates), there are very few signs of the creation of new leading export sectors in Hungary. The automobile industry, however, has emerged as a symbol of change. General Motors' "greenfield" investment in Szentgotthard and cooperation with Rába led to the beginning of car production in Hungary: in March 1992, the first Opel Astra rolled off the assembly line; fifteen thousand followed annually. Although only the assembly and painting is done in Hungary, involving fewer than 500 workers, and though all its parts are delivered from GM's other European plants, the enterprise still embodied a promising message. Even more so was the launching of *Magyar Suzuki* in August 1992, producing 60,000 cars per annum in its newly built factory in Esztergom, and employing 1,500 workers. Initially 40 percent of the components in the Swift cars will be Hungarian-made, but the number might increase to 60 percent. With an estimated total of 100,000 cars to be built, the *Magyar Suzuki* plant would cover the demand of the domestic market.

Although itself not an investment in new potential export sectors, the acquisition of a 30 percent share of the Hungarian state telephone company for $875 million by the *Ameritech-Deutsche Bundespost* consortium is, as *The New York Times* reported on December 20, 1993, "one of the biggest privatization deals in Eastern Europe" (Perlez, 1993). The modernization of the communication system, first of all the backward telephone network, is a prerequisite for the creation of a modern technological infrastructure and new competitive export sectors.

Still, in spite of its important results, the privatization process was rather slow. It happened partly because the new political elite wanted to block the road toward spontaneous "self-privatization" in order to prevent the former managerial elite from exploiting their position to become a part of the new entrepreneurial class. In 1990–1, 70 percent of privatization cases were initiated by the companies and their managers searching for foreign partners. In some cases, this type of privatization was accompanied by corruption, with the old managers selling the state company at an unrealistically low price to a private firm he or she co-owned or to a foreign company in exchange for the position of top manager. In 1990, the government abruptly dismissed the director of the successful *Hungaroton* company, a record and compact disc producer, who adroitly prepared the firm's "self-privatization," with investments from EMI, the leading British company in the field. The deal collapsed and the case became a milestone in the process of banning "self-privatization."

Another reason for halting the process was the recognition of the political self-interest of the new governing party in utilizing state assets in order to build a new clientalism and strengthen its position of power. As Éva Ehrlich noted, the government had "nationalized the privatization." According to a report at the end of 1993, the government "slowed the transfer of state property to private ownership" in order to keep state control and retain its monopoly (*Los Angeles Times*, 1993).

The original plan of the government to privatize half of the state-owned companies in four to five years failed. A partly privatized banking system was re-nationalized by increased state participation in 1993–4. The MDF-led coalition government announced its new program, according to which the state's share by the end of the 1990s would decline to 25 percent for banking and 20 percent generally. However, quoting Paul Marer, "Many . . . doubt whether the current government is truly committed to significant bank privatization, or is only paying lip service to it" (Marer, 1993, p. 6). Still the main reason for slow progress, and a general characteristic of privatization in the entire region, is the lack of sufficient internal capital accumulation and investment, and also of foreign participation.

The economic transition plans revealed certain similarities to Yugoslavia, also a former pioneer of market-oriented economic reforms. Based on previous partial reforms, the government of Ante Marković planned to radicalize the reforms in order to bring about real change. The Croatian reform economist proposed a program of "new socialism" in January 1989, which sought to combine workers' self-management with a proper market environment. Having witnessed the collapse of socialism in neighboring countries, Marković radicalized the plan further and presented the program in December 1989 with the promise of building "a new economic and political system." The Federal Assembly passed seventeen laws from a package of twenty-four suggested by Marković. The new reform was thus introduced and linked with a radical stabilization of the currency. In December 1989 the inflation rate reached 2,600 percent. The new dinar (which was equal to 10,000 old ones) was introduced on January 1, 1990, with the aim of decreasing inflation to 13 percent by the end of the year. For the first time in Central and Eastern Europe, the stabilized currency was made convertible by firmly tying it to the West German mark (1 DM = 7 YD), and it served to push marketization even further by automatically implementing the world price system. At the same time domestic price controls were also removed on almost 85 percent of all commodities. Only the prices of certain basic services, raw materials, and energy sources remained under state control. Wages were temporarily frozen. Marketization was intended to be combined with a "pluralism of ownership," i.e., a mixed ownership structure which would include private, public and mixed property as well as a uniform, modern taxation system.

Serbian president Milošević, however, opposed the Marković government, and the Slovenian Assembly also resisted against any kind of centralized economic policy. Yugoslavia was soon engulfed in civil war, and the continuation of a promising peaceful transformation was halted.

The transition followed a different pattern in Poland. The catastrophic Polish economic situation, with a hyper-inflation of 740 percent in 1989, an inability to repay foreign credits, and a severe shortage of food and consumer goods, required desperate measures: the new Solidarity government, which took office in September 1989, rejected the previously accepted Electoral Platform of the Citizen's Committee "Solidarity," a continuation of the Round Table contract (Kowalik, 1989–90), and decided to adopt the most drastic transformation, the so-called shock treatment. The government took advantage of its strongly based legitimacy, and was courageous enough to implement painful measures.

The "Balcerowicz Plan," named after its initiator and deputy prime minister of the Mazowiecki government, with the help and advice of the Harvard economist Jeffrey Sachs, hurriedly prepared a combined macro-stabilization and marketization plan that the International Monetary Fund received with the greatest enthusiasm. Western governments and journals praised the shock therapy as the most appropriate measure and clear proof of the regime's determination. The advocates of the policy became international celebrities virtually overnight.

The plan was implemented by January 1, 1990. Subsidies of basic food, housing, and energy, which totalled more than 30 percent of budgetary expenditures in 1989, were drastically cut to 15 percent. Expenditures on health and education were reduced. A strict wage control allowing wage increases of only 20–60 percent of the inflation rate of the previous month, with a 200–500 percent penalty tax on wage increases above the limit, was combined with total price liberalization. Consumption declined by almost 35 percent.

The austerity policy was combined with monetary stabilization (Błażyca, 1991). The Polish *zloty* was tied to a number of convertible currencies and the exchange rate was kept relatively stable. The Polish currency was made partially convertible, enabling enterprises and individuals to buy and sell currency on the domestic market, and causing the "black" exchange rate to disappear. Inflation was curbed, and the increase in retail prices dropped to 250 percent in 1990 and to 70 percent in 1991. Inflation further decreased to about 60 percent in 1993.

Privatization also gained impressive momentum with over 51,000 new private companies established. The number of non-agricultural private firms reached 1.8 million in the spring of 1994. Besides already existing private agriculture, private industrial sales comprised 22 percent of the total, private construction 44 percent and transportation more than 16 percent already by the end of 1991. Most of the private firms (80 percent of them) dealt with trade, especially imports and services.

The privatization of state-owned retailing networks (by open bidding) was rather rapid: at the end of 1991 more than 85 percent of them became privately owned. The decisive question, however, was the privatization of large state-owned industrial firms, which produced about 70 percent of the industrial GNP as late as 1992. The interest in buying these firms was practically non-existent. Altogether, twenty-six large state firms were sold in the first two years of privatization, and 566 former state-owned companies (from 7,000) became private at the end of the third year. Certain surveys reported that only an additional 3–4 percent of the assets of the state companies may have found domestic buyers (Connor, 1992). In mid 1994, 5.3 million people, or 60 percent of the labor force, was employed in private firms that produced 55 percent of the GDP.

Foreign investment also remained disappointingly limited. The first year was rather promising: the number of joint ventures jumped from fifty-five (in 1988) to 2,480 (in 1990). The number of foreign owned companies and joint ventures continued to increase to over 5,000 by 1991, but the amount of invested capital reached only $670 million in

1991, which was less than a third of foreign investment in Hungary.

There were a few major investments, such as Unilever's decision to buy 80 percent of the shares of *Pollena Bydgoszcz*, the leading Polish detergent producer. As part of the multi-national empire, the renamed company, *Lever Polska*, doubled its production with a 4 million dollar investment. In addition, Pepsi-Cola announced a new 60 million dollar investment in Poland. Fiat, Ameritech International and France Telecom were also major foreign investors. At the end of 1993, news agencies reported that General Motors would buy a part of the FSO car factory near Warsaw in a $25 million investment and assemble 30,000 Opel Astra cars annually.

But two-thirds of foreign or joint companies' investments were in the range of $50,000-60,000 and only 0.5 percent of investments were above $3 million. Thus privatization, assisted by foreign participation, hit a dead-end, and further development promised to be very slow.

A special barrier to privatization in Poland is the unique power of the workers' councils, which have rather broad self-managerial rights and mostly oppose privatization, especially those with foreign capital involvement. "The idea that state property ... would be delivered dirt-cheap into the hands of foreign capital or ... those [Polish people] who have been able to amass capital," argued Zbigniew Romaszewski, "while perhaps effective from the economic point of view, is most assuredly not acceptable from the social point of view" (Romaszewski, 1990, p. 41). "The most dangerous ... [risk] involves the sale of enterprises to foreigners," argued Stanislaw Polaczek, because it "could cause the loss of national property for the benefit of foreign interests" (Polaczek, 1993, p. 41). Several major financial scandals created a strong anti-privatization political atmosphere in the country.

To accelerate the process, the government in June 1991 proclaimed the adoption of shock treatment for the privatization strategy as well. In the framework of a mass privatization program, the government announced the distribution of vouchers or investment certificates to all adult citizens. At the same time the government announced that it would set up a national investment fund to manage the privatized firms.

Each state-owned company selected for privatization by the government would allocate 60 percent of its shares to the funds, and in this way to the public at large. An additional 15 percent of the shares would be distributed among the company's employees, and 30 percent was to remain under state ownership. The plan envisioned a two-year period of implementation, with shares being made available only in 1994. At the end of 1993, in the fifth year of the Polish transformation, only about 13 percent of previously state-owned large industry was privatized.

Although the term shock-therapy was linked to the Polish transition, the Czechoslovak government announced that it would follow an even more consistent strategy of a "Big Bang," especially in its privatization drive. On January 1, 1991, after a year of preparation, Vacláv Klaus, the Minister of Finance and free market ideologue, introduced a radical marketization by liberalizing prices and imports. The first shocking effect was a price increase of almost 50 percent in January and again in February, which slowed to 2–5 percent during the spring. Consumption immediately declined by 37 percent. The privatization schedule was even more radical. In October 1990 the Federal Assembly passed a law on restitution. Unlike those adopted in other countries of the region, the law guaranteed that private properties confiscated between 1955 and 1961 (about 70,000 units) would be returned to their former owners.

In the same month another law implemented the so-called small privatization, which stipulated that 100,000 state-owned stores, hotels, and restaurants be auctioned off to private bidders starting in January 1991. The calculated value of small businesses on sale was about $6.5 billion. By the end of 1993, more than 21,400 small firms were sold and the entire process was nearly concluded. Grassroots privatization was highly successful as well, for by June 1992 there were 1.2 million newly founded private firms in the country. In November 1990, the government also approved a draft law on large-scale privatization for about 3,000 state-owned companies, which were transformed into joint-stock companies. Their privatization was to be based on a voucher scheme. Accordingly, each adult citizen was offered investment vouchers worth 1,000 points for a nominal fee equal to $80, which authorized citizens to buy thirty shares (since initially every share was priced at the same number of points) of state companies at the stock exchange, which had opened in 1991.

In the first round of voucher-privatization in early 1992, the shares of 1,400 firms were put on sale, and auctions of assets with a net value of $9.3 billion began. More than 8.5 million Czech and Slovaks participated, and nearly 1,000 state companies and 56 percent of the offered shares were allocated. "Almost overnight," reported the World Bank's bulletin, "Czechoslovakia will boast the biggest private sector in Eastern Europe" (*Transition*, 1992, p. 3). Indeed, at the end of 1993, nearly 60 percent of the Czech economy was already privatized. The shares, however, were transformed to investment funds, and 5.7 million people opted to sell their voucher-booklets, resulting in the accumulation of two thirds of total voucher points in the hands of 420 private investment funds. The second round of voucher-privatization began in early 1994 and attracted 5.6 million citizens, who planned to buy about 770 state-owned companies.

In mid 1994, half of the gainfully occupied population worked in the private sector that produced 65 percent of the country's GDP.

Although foreign investment was not a central factor in Czechoslovak privatization, some landmark investments may have significant long-term impact. Between 1900 and 1993, about $2 billion in foreign investment was channeled into the country, much less than that in Hungary and Poland. Nearly one quarter of this was channeled into the tobacco industry, and another quarter to automobile production.

In November 1990, 40 percent of the famous *Sklo Union*, the state-owned glass company and an important exporter, was bought by the Japanese-controlled Belgian *Glaverbel*. One of the biggest foreign investors in the Czech Republic is Philip Morris, which bought the Czech *Tabak Kutna Hora*, a state monopoly. The American firm increased its market share to 75 percent of the Czech and 62 percent of the entire Czech and Slovak cigarette market.

The single biggest deal was signed in 1991 with the German Volkswagen company, which bought 31 percent of the shares of the most important Czech industrial firm, *Skoda*, for $333 million. According to the agreement, Volkswagen would invest $6.3 billion into *Skoda* over seven years, acquiring 70–75 percent of the shares. The transaction, if fully realized, would be the biggest cross-border investment in European history. Within two years, in September 1993, however, as Reuters reported, Volkswagen canceled the biggest chunk of its investment program and would not build the planned engine producing plant, but instead only an assembly plant, in Mlada Boleslav. The investment project was cut to nearly half the original one.

Although following different roads, the three pioneering countries in transition – Hungary, Poland, and the Czech Republic – achieved important results in the transformation towards a private market economy.

The Balkan countries, partly because of their later start and partly because of a different political environment, followed a slower and more cautious road during the first period of transformation (Altmann, 1994). However, in 1991–2 most of the Balkan countries adopted the same course that the pioneering ones followed. Their advance, however, still lagged behind. The National Salvation Front in Romania initially had a "Third Road" concept. One of the leading ideologists of the front in the immediate post-revolutionary period, Silviu Brucan, argued in the summer of 1990 that "Romania has a lot to learn from the example [of South Korea] if it wants to avoid becoming an exhausted half-colony of the West." This strategy, he argued, offers both "a great opening to Western investors and joint ventures, while maintaining a strong state sector and thus efficient control over development." He also advocated the combination of the South Korean with the Austrian model, especially the "social policy of Austria" (Ionescu, 1990, p. 28).

According to the government program of May 1990, a price liberalization was implemented in three stages in two years and was completed by 1992. Subsidies were gradually cut. In September 1992 prices of staple foods doubled. As with the marketization process all over the region, the Romanian price liberalization led to a 228 percent price increase between June 1991 and June 1992. The process continued and inflation remained at a high level of about 200 percent in 1993.

In the summer of 1991 the government implemented a partial privatization of both the agricultural and non-agricultural sectors of the economy. Unlike the Polish, Czech, and Hungarian programs, this was based on the idea of creating a mixed economy. The government intended to privatize 53 percent of the state's assets, about 6,000 so-called commercial companies, while retaining the remaining 47 percent, the so-called strategic sectors such as mining, transportation, armaments, and communications, in a framework of reorganized, autonomous state-owned companies. The plan called for privatizing the "commercial" companies within seven years, partly by distributing "property certificates" or vouchers among adult citizens. The voucher would comprise 30 percent of the assets, while the remaining 70 percent was to be sold on the market (at least 10 percent of them annually) by the newly established State Property Fund. By the end of 1992, privatization had hardly begun, and 90 percent of the industrial output was produced by the almost intact state sector. In October of that year, the government decided to privatize more than 3,000 small firms and 2,500 medium-size companies, mostly shops, restaurants, hotels, and service units, and had sold more than 2,000 units by the middle of 1993. Privatization on a larger scale began in 1993 on an experimental basis by privatizing thirty-two companies during the year. The first landmarks were the privatization of the Ursus Brewery in Cluj and the Petromin Shipping Company. The latter, with its 100 ships, was privatized in a $355 million investment by a Greek company purchasing 51 percent of the shares and guaranteeing nearly another $300 million further investment. The American Purolite International chemical firm bought a 60 percent share of Viromet SA for $39 million.

The slow progress of privatization is partly connected to the lack of foreign interest. In the first four years of the Romanian transformation, foreign investment in the country totaled only roughly $700 million.

An over cautious policy and various strict limitations also slowed down the transformation. Even grassroots privatization had heavy ideological restrictions placed on it, which was unique in the region. The number of employees in private firms was limited to twenty, and most of the newly established firms set up during the first one and a half years, 115,000 out of 145,000, were one-man or family businesses. Privatization, however, gained momentum. Private firms employed 1.5 million of the 4 million workforce, produced roughly one-third of the gross domestic product, and accounted for more than half of the retail trade, while 27 percent of total exports came from private firms in mid 1994.

In Bulgaria, after an overcautious, slow start, a radical reform package was accepted in February 1991. Prices were liberalized for everything except energy products, and the exchange rate was standardized and floated on the free market. Liberalization of foreign trade also contributed to a speedier marketization process, together with the elimination of the state monopoly on foreign trade. Persistent price adjustments to the world market resulted in a high inflation rate, generating a 120 percent increase in the month of February alone. The total price increase for 1991 was 334 percent, accelerating to 500 percent in 1992 and decreasing to 100 percent in 1993. The inflation rate since the beginning of the economic reform totaled more than 1,400 percent.

A number of new laws were enacted accelerating privatization. Reluctantly, Bulgaria embraced radical measures: a restitution law guaranteed the return to their previous owners of residential, industrial, commercial, and landed properties that were nationalized or confiscated after 1947. This uniquely radical step was the most important element of Bulgarian privatization: by June 1992 3,600 shops, 2,600 houses and apartments, 600 industrial sites, and 130 restaurants were returned to their former owners, as well as 85 percent of all eligible land. The grassroots privatization of establishing new private firms by the end of 1992 led to the registration of nearly 180,000 new small business, mostly in trade and services. In June 1991 the government completed the first auction of state-owned shops and gasoline stations. Another 1,500 units were immediately prepared for a second round of small-firm privatizations.

In 1993, a sort of voucher-privatization plan was accepted as well to sell 500 companies to citizens above the age of twenty who were eligible to receive state credit and join one of the ten State Investment Funds. As a result of the privatization rush of the Lyuben Berov government, the percentage share of the private sector in the Bulgarian economy had reached 40 percent by mid 1994, mostly the result of reprivatization, and grassroots and small privatization.

Big-privatization has been rather slow partly because of the lack of foreign capital inflow. During the four years of transformation, though 1,200 joint ventures were established, the $20 million investment of the Belgian Amylum company, which bought 80 percent of the Carevcsni

Produkti corn processing factory in Raz Grad, was regarded as a landmark investment. There was altogether only $220 million in direct private capital investment in Bulgaria between 1990 and end of 1993.

In the summer of 1991, the transition began even in such a latecomer as Albania when the new post-communist government of Prime Minister Fatos Nano announced a reform program. All the well-known measures of marketization and privatization appeared in moderate form in the program, which planned to introduce a two stage price reform and gradual privatization, beginning with the cottage industry and retail trade, but foreseeing the long-term existence of a state-owned sector working in a market environment.

In some of the war-ridden former Yugoslav republics, a slow advance toward privatization also began. The Slovenian parliament enacted a privatization law in November 1992, but the new government of Joseph Drnovsek proposed new amendments that promised to privatize 400 firms in 1993. Slovenia preferred the method of self-privatization, and established regulations limiting foreign participation to 40 percent of the shares. Croatia enacted a restitution law for all properties in private ownership before May 15, 1945. On this basis applications for 53 percent of the land and 1,805 companies were submitted. By the middle of 1993, 1,567 companies were prepared for privatization and transformed to joint stock companies, but only half of them were actually privatized.

Privatization, price, and import liberalization, the foundation of a capital and labor market, and the opening of the economies to foreign goods and investment, were only the first steps in a long march that should prepare the road for economic modernization.

The role of foreign assistance

When the old regimes in Central and Eastern Europe began to collapse in 1988–9, a euphoric West immediately reacted and declared itself ready to assist in building up the new order. This generated exaggerated hopes in the region. Most of the expectations were unrealistic and naive. Members of an emerging new political elite spoke of the West's moral and political responsibility to finance the stabilization of currencies, cope with the indebtedness, and assist the transition toward a market economy. People fervently hoped that their countries would be accepted by the European Community. Calls were often heard for a new version of the Marshall Plan. In the post-World War II period, the United States sacrificed about 1 percent of her GNP annually for four and half years and paved the road for both a successful European reconstruction and, in connection with it, her own unparalleled prosperity. If the advanced Western world followed the same path today and sacrificed only 0.5 percent of its aggregate 20 trillion dollar GNP, it would assure 100 billion dollars annually for the countries of the region.

The initial Marshall Plan provided aid of only 3–5 percent of the GNP of the recipient countries, which guaranteed an import surplus equal to 3–5 percent of their GNP to assist in reconstruction, investment in new sectors, and the importing of new technology. Based on that experience, as new Marshall Plan advocates argued, $10–15 billion annually could help finance the transition in Central and Eastern Europe, a region of about 125 million people with an average $2,500 per capita income. Counting an additional $30 billion for the successor states of the former Soviet Union, a total of $45 billion would provide effective international assistance, which is hardly more than 0.25 percent of the GNP of the advanced world.

Jeffrey Sachs used a different comparison: "The amount [of $15 and $30 billion] seems to be large, but let's compare it," he suggested, "with the annual budget of NATO, which is now $250 billion (to defend the West) . . . with the military threat ending, the aid would finance itself, since it would make it possible to cut defense expenditures the same amount or even more" (Sachs, 1992, p. 17).

The opponents of organized Western assistance maintained that nothing on the scale of the Marshall Plan was needed. The International Monetary Fund, the World Bank, and most particularly private sources would be able to cover the necessary investments.

Indeed, throughout November 1989, the crucial month of the collapse of state socialism, an enthusiastic readiness in the West to help was clearly expressed: the European Community's Executive Commission hosted a meeting of representatives of twenty-four leading industrial nations and pledged $6.5 billion in economic aid for Poland and Hungary. Three days later, the foreign ministers of the European Community offered temporary trade concessions, including an end to restrictions on certain imports. The following day, President Bush signed a bill authorizing nearly $1 billion in aid for Poland and Hungary.

The impressive rush to support the region culminated in a pledge by the so-called G-24 block, the most advanced countries of the world, of $27 billion over three years (between 1989 and 1991) for economic stabilization and restructuring in the three "first-comers," Hungary, Poland, and Czechoslovakia. According to certain estimates, the G-24 block together pledged $45 billion to all of the Central and Eastern European countries over three years, and $62.5 billion over five years (G-24, 1995). The required $10–15 billion per annum was thus spontaneously committed. One should not forget that this happened at the beginning of the process, when the initial Western reaction still followed the old reflexes of the Cold War, and when it seemed to be a vital interest of the West to contribute to the disintegration of the Soviet bloc and provide incentives for the destruction of state socialism throughout the region. In other words, as it did when the Cold War began in 1947, a Marshall Plan strategy reappeared when the Cold War ended in 1989.

But once state socialism collapsed and the Cold War was over, Western enthusiasm (though its rhetoric continued) was replaced with doubts and revulsion. Consequently, a tremendous gap was created between the amount of aid promised and what was actually disbursed. In the summer of 1991, the European Commission revealed that only 11 percent of the amount committed to Poland, Hungary, Czechoslovakia, Romania, and Bulgaria was actually sent. During the first four years less than $11 billion was disbursed for six countries of the region. With Polish debt reduction included, the disbursed amount reached $19.1 billion (Ners, 1995, p. 34). Some of the bilateral assistance was spent in the donor country: 60 percent of the 4 billion schilling Austrian credit for Eastern Europe actually benefitted the Vienna construction industry by guaranteeing credits for Vienna-based companies and their Austrian-made businesses in Eastern Europe. Other sources maintained that 70 percent of Austria's East European assistance was spent in Austria, for example for constructing the highway between Vienna and the Hungarian border. In other words, the region had received only a fragment of the required amount, which could not make a real difference in its transition.

Regarding private investments, which was to be responsible for financing a greater part of the transformation, there was roughly $13–15 billion invested in the region as a whole by the end of 1993.[2] This represented nearly 1 percent of the total amount of international investments between 1989 and 1993. Foreign investments, moreover, did not represent an increasing trend. According to the New York based *East European Investment Magazine*, the total value of deals with the former Soviet bloc, including the successor states of the Soviet Union, was $28 billion in 1992. Fully a third of this, however, was to go to Kazakhstan, the new "oil-sheikdom," exactly the same amount as the total given to the twelve countries of Central and Eastern Europe. The main attraction was oil and mining. Deals connected to these sectors comprised 60 percent of planned investments in 1992.

This traditional, peripheral type of investment does not offer much promise for the region's economies in transition. It had represented only between 1 percent (Czech Republic) and 0.08 percent (Romania) of the countries' real GNP. In contrast, the investment funds of the world with their roughly $14,000 billion, have a rather different orientation. The

---

[2] According to Krzysztof Ners' calculations, direct foreign investments to the six countries of the region "barely surpassed $10 billion" (Ners, 1995, p. 39).

Latin American periphery, much better known to American investors, was more attractive: Brazil and Mexico offered 22 percent and 18 percent interest respectively in guaranteed state bonds, and has attracted nearly five to six times more investments totalling $60 billion in 18 months since mid-1991 than the Central and Eastern European countries. Tiny Singapore alone attracted 50 percent more investments than the six transforming Central and Eastern European countries combined during the early 1990s.

Thus, the amount of Western assistance actually disbursed in the countries of transition, including private investment, may altogether total roughly $20–35 billion between 1989 and 1993 – a figure which remained below the minimal requirements (if one accepts the concept of the Marshall Plan that credits should amount to 3–5 percent of the GDP of the recipient countries for at least four to five years). The per capita average assistance amounted to $30 in the six countries of the region in 1993, compared with the Irish $262 and Portuguese $173 annual average inflow from the European Union between 1989 and 1993, let alone the East German $5,900 average annual per capita capital inflow from the Western *Bundesländern*. Foreign assistance, therefore, did not reach the critical mass and could not play a determinant role in abetting a smooth transition.

Moreover, counting the huge capital outflow from the region in the form of payments of interest and principal, the outflow of profits not being reinvested, capital withdrawals, and illegal transactions,[3] one certainly cannot speak of a net capital inflow to the region in the first three to four years of transition.

Hungary, the primary recipient of foreign investment through 1993, received more than $2.5 billion in IMF and World Bank credits and nearly $7 billion in direct private investments, but has had a repayment burden of $2.4–3.5 billion annually, which she has managed to meet. Considering the total balance of payments, the net capital outflow from Hungary totaled $1.6 billion annually during the four years of transformation. "It means that Hungary since 1990 ... paid as much to the advanced countries," summed up Pongrác Nagy, using calculations based on reports of the Hungarian National Bank and the World Debt Tables of the World Bank, "as the economic great power, the United States, offered recently to help Russia" (Nagy, 1993).

Thus Hungary paid roughly $6 billion more to the West than she gained from Western credits and investment. Illegal transactions, and the

---

[3] One of the most successful entrepreneurs told me in Budapest in early 1993: "I sold my share in one of the joint ventures for half a million dollars. Since I am not certain about the future of the country, I am looking for a good investment opportunity in the West."

criminalization of the economy may have caused even bigger losses. (According to several esitmates, illegal capital outflow from Russia, where criminal activity has reached shocking levels, may total $150 billion, many times more than the pledged $28 billions Western assistance. Capital flight from the crises-ridden peripheries is a widespread phenomenon.[4]

Concerning the other pillar of Western assistance, the promise of integration into the European Community or, using Jacques Attali's term, the creation of a Continental Common Market in Europe, very little actual progress has occurred. After 1989, the G-24 countries decided to liberalize the access of Central and Eastern European countries to Western markets. The Generalized System of Preferences was extended to Poland and Hungary in 1990, and to Czechoslovakia in 1991. Specific quantitative restrictions on trade were lifted as well. EFTA agreed to eliminate tariffs on most manufactured goods. The agreements with the European Community contained a gradual elimination of restrictions against industrial products over ten years. Moreover, the agreements guaranteed an asymmetric tariff reduction, with the Western countries consenting to lower tariffs twice as fast as the Eastern countries. As a gesture, the Community decided to abolish certain tariff barriers for industrial products such as cars by the end of 1994.

The European Community, however, maintains high protective tariffs and quotas on the most important export products from the region, i.e., those that would have a comparative advantage in Western markets. Agriculture, steel, chemical, textile, clothing and shoe industries remain highly protected. The Community continues to introduce special measures and restrictions against Eastern imports if needed. Different export quotas and other measures defending Western markets are strong enough to compensate for the moderate concessions made regarding trade liberalization. For agricultural subsidies alone, the industrialized West spends $250 billion annually, five times more than that for foreign assistance.

As a consequence, during the first four years of transformation, the Western countries gained much more from trade liberalization than did the Eastern ones. While Austria's total exports declined by nearly 6 percent in 1993, her exports to the East increased by more than 4 percent. Moreover, Austria achieved an impressive export surplus since her imports from the Eastern countries declined by nearly 5 percent. The

---

[4] "The external position of debtor countries has been severely aggravated by private-sector capital outflows. Capital flight is estimated at around $50 billion for Latin America during 1978–83. A significant part of the debt increase throughout the period accounted for unrecorded capital outflows from Argentina. Capital flight was as much as two times as great as the increase in gross external debt for Indonesia" (Reisen, 1985, pp. 115–16).

European Community, until 1990, had a mostly negative balance in its trade with Eastern Europe. In 1992, compared with 1988, the Community's exports increased by 30 percent while its Eastern imports declined by nearly 20 percent. In 1992 the European Community doubled its trade surplus with the East in one year, accumulating a $3.1 billion surplus. Between 1989 and 1993 Central and Eastern Europe's share of imports into the European Union increased from 2.7 to 4.2 percent. However, its share in exports from the European Union increased from 2.8 to 5.3 percent (*Euro-East*, 1994).

The November 1992 episode of a "tariff-war" and restrictions against the expansion of Eastern steel products to the European markets is rather telling: four countries of the region, Czechoslovakia, Hungary, Poland, and Croatia (the first three having signed an agreement with the Community on decreasing trade barriers) more than doubled their share in the European steel-pipe market during the last five years (from 7.8 to 18 percent). The Community immediately introduced a special dumping-tariff: 30, 22, 17, and 11 percent in the case of the Czech, Hungarian, Croat, and Polish products respectively. The incident clearly demonstrated the veracity of a statement made by the then president of the European Bank of Reconstruction and Development in the fall of 1992: "The limited measures of the European Community did not lead to results until now. Western Europe, in reality, is building up a new kind of a Maginot Line (Atalli, 1992)." One should add that this Maginot Line might very well prove to be more defensible than the original one was.

Opening the doors of the European Community to the three most advanced and more rapidly transforming Central and Eastern European countries will take, in the best estimate, at least a decade, while the others cannot even foresee such a development. The opportunity of joining Europe, in fact, is rather limited and doubtful because of strong opposition from the Southern newcomers and French agricultural interests, as well as a growing trend toward consolidating and deepening rather than broadening the Community. Additionally, there are other newcomers as well, such as Austria and Sweden, whose healthier economies have a strong claim to Community resources. Moreover, the European Community is more and more preoccupied with its own internal problems. Integration in Europe, a *par excellence* prerequisite of transformation, is thus delayed until the next century.

From a potential "Marshall Plan strategy," the Western world turned to a "Münchhausen-strategy." Freiherr Münchhausen, the eighteenth century soldier, adventurer, and liar, rescued himself from a trap in one of his stories by using his own hair. This is now the task of the Central and Eastern European countries. One of *The New York Times* editorials aptly noted that "no country – including West Germany after World War II and, more recently, Mexico – has successfully undergone economic transformation without substantial external help" (*The New York Times*, 1993). And substantial help is clearly not on the horizon for this "forgotten region," as Charles Gati once labeled it. "Eastern Europe," added Ivan Volgyes in 1991, "is of secondary importance to the West, and is more so as the Soviet Union is disintegrating" (Volgyes, 1991).

9   Economic decline – political challenge – rising nationalism

---

"Annus Mirabilis" followed by "Anni Miserabiles": transition and severe economic decline

Closing down obsolete, uncompetitive sectors, ending subsidies or dismissing a part of the work force were important steps of the transformation. A negative side effect of this, however, is the resulting decline in production and increase in unemployment. Adjusting to world market prices and liberalizing imports creates competition for the heretofore protected and isolated Central and Eastern European economies, and this was also a prerequisite for market adjustment. On the other hand, it has caused a decline in output. In an age of major technological change and structural crisis, adjustment inevitably generates what Josef Schumpeter described as "creative destruction."

Lacking or losing popular support, state socialist regimes sought to avoid destruction by resisting substantial reform. But by defending the existing structures they also destroyed the prerequisites of a creative adjustment.

The impact of the lack of adjustment became stronger after 1989, since new governments, which were seeking to adjust to the world market, were opening their economies and were unable to create market protection.

New and unfavorable external economic factors have contributed to the difficulties. The collapse of the Soviet Union and the former Comecon market, a mini Gulf-oil-crisis in early 1991, and a severe recession in the Western world in 1991–3 had negative repercussions and created additional barriers on the road to Central and Eastern European transformation.

Hence the exaggerated expectations and overoptimistic forecasts inevitably collided with harsh realities. The deterioration of the economy was much deeper and lasted much longer than originally anticipated. The former Solidarity advisor Tadeusz Kowalik presented a dramatic picture on the Polish situation: "Over the first year alone (1990) the national income declined not by the forecasted 3 percent but by 13 percent, distributed income declined by as much as 18 percent, and industrial production declined not by the forecasted 5 percent, but by 23 percent. Real wages were lower by about one third" (Kowalik, 1992, pp. 5–6). The Polish situation worsened in 1991. While the government had predicted a 3.5 percent increase in GDP, industrial output and GDP continued to decrease by more than 7 percent, and the electro-mechanical and chemical industries fell by 29.1 percent and 14.3 percent respectively in 1991. In the spring of 1992 the decline reached its nadir with a nearly 20 percent decrease in GDP and a 40 percent decline in industrial output. According to government figures, state-owned firms accumulated roughly $18–20 billion in debts to each other and were unable to repay them. More than 40 percent of the firms were practically bankrupt.

Unemployment, which was 6 percent at the end of 1990, reached its zenith in 1993 at more than 16 percent. The destruction was hardly linked with any kind of "creative" impact: "Productivity is going down and production cost per unit is going up," summarized a Polish analyst, "further undermining the competitiveness of Polish products. The percentage of costs in the total revenues of enterprises increased from 78.9 percent to 87.1 percent in the first half of 1991.... It is clearly evident that continuation of the 'shock treatment' policies enhances further the cost-driven inflation by increasing the cost of capital and further reducing demand" (Koźmiński, 1992, pp. 324–5).

In Czechoslovakia, the consequences of transformation were similar: instead of the planned decline of 5–10 percent, the GDP fell by 16 percent and industrial output dropped by 23 percent in 1991. At the end of 1992 their decline surpassed 20 and 36 percent respectively. Many companies, between 30 percent and 50 percent according to certain estimates, were near bankruptcy. Unemployment, however, still hardly surpassed 3 percent because of continued state subsidies – in spite of a *laissez faire* rhetoric.

In the analysis of several Polish economists, the reason for the unstoppable decline was the failure of ideological shock therapy. "It would be difficult to deny," stated Kowalik, "that the depth of crises was the result of shock therapy" (Kowalik, 1992, p. 6).

This argument, however, is somewhat contradicted by the fact that a rather similar decline occurred in the barely reforming Romania. Alin Theodor Ciocarlie's description in the summer of 1991 of the Romanian economy was as dramatic as was Kowalik's of Poland: "A highly alarming situation is the spectacular decline in primary economic resources . . . 26 percent in net coal . . . 34.7 percent in petroleum . . . As a direct consequence, industrial output is only 83 percent of the output of the same period last year . . . Industrial decline has affected services, too, which have gone down by 14 percent . . . the wholesale sale of goods has gone down by 30 percent" (Ciocarlie, 1991, pp. 1–2).

In "gradualist" Hungary industrial output also dropped by nearly 40 percent and GDP decreased by roughly 30 percent between 1989 and 1992. A great number of companies accumulated a total of $6–8 million of debt and were unable to repay it by the fall of 1993. More than 1,500 financially bankrupt companies were liquidated.

After a slow start, unemployment (from 0 percent) also jumped to over 13 percent at the end of 1993, with almost every fourth worker unemployed in certain regions, such as the northeastern base of "heavy industry." There is also a striking decline in the formerly successful agricultural sector, a leading export sector. Internationally, Hungary has ranked among the top five countries for per capita grain and meat production. Agricultural production declined by 10 percent both in 1990 and 1991, but in 1992 it fell by a dramatic 23 percent. The use of artificial fertilizers dropped drastically to one fifth of its previous level. The so-called side activities of the cooperative farms, such as food processing and different kinds of industrial and service ventures, virtually disappeared. Investments declined by 70 percent.

The state subsidized the slaughtering of animals. As a consequence only 440,000 people continued to be employed in agriculture in 1992, just half of those who worked in the sector a decade before. In 1992, 25 percent of collective farms went bankrupt. In an analysis debated by the presidium of the Hungarian Academy of Sciences in early 1993, the authors maintained that "there is a danger of a total disintegration of Hungarian agriculture" (Sipos, 1993, pp. 123, 127). The first years of transition have thus caused more destruction to Hungarian agriculture than did the notorious forced collectivization of the Stalinist period.

Several factors contributed to the latter phenomenon. Most important was the legacy of a hidden agricultural crisis in the 1980s. The relatively high cost of production did not cause perceptible consequences at the time, since export markets were available and agriculture was heavily subsidized. After 1989, the hidden crisis became manifest from one year to the next. A re-privatization program to reconstruct the old ownership structure had caused serious uncertainties. Before the forced collectivization, 56 percent of gainfully occupied people worked in agriculture in Hungary; in 1990, only about 12–13 percent did. In these circumstances, re-privatization could not provide an incentive for the return to peasant farming: by the end of 1992, more than 800,000 applications were registered reclaiming nearly one third of the arable land of the country, but only 20 percent of the applicants were seeking to cultivate their own land.

The most devastating effect, however, was the elimination of subsidies. Budgetary restrictions, international requirements, and an exaggerated free-market ideology encouraged the government to eliminate subsidies and open the domestic market. Direct subsidies for producers dropped from $2.6 billion in 1987 to $265 million in 1992, while subsidies for consumers of agricultural produce declined from $1.4 billion to $200 million. Hungary subsidized only 8 percent of the value of agricultural output, while the average subsidies to agriculture in G-24 countries reached nearly 44 percent, and in the European Community countries 49 percent. The Community has an import tariff of 250 percent for beef; Hungary has one of only 15 percent. Small wonder that food imports to Hungary from the European Community had increased by 32 percent in 1991, while Hungarian food exports, in the transition years, declined by 50 percent. The first half of 1993 itself resulted a 36 percent decline compared with the previous year.

A successful reorientation of Hungarian agricultural exports from the Comecon area to Western Europe was a major economic achievement, though there has been a high price to pay for it: "these exports are viable only at such a low price that it cannot entirely cover the cost of production" (Sipos, 1993, p. 122).

The same phenomenon battered Polish agriculture, where long-standing private farms had to face devastating competition from highly productive Western farms. "The dairy cases of Poland's grocery stores," reported Joel Havemann from Kaczewo in the summer of 1992, "are stocked high with butter from Germany and the Netherlands, so high that native son Brunon Wardecki cannot profitably sell butter even to his local market. . . . When the Warsaw government engineered Poland's overnight transition to a free-market economy on January 1, 1990, it virtually abolished tariffs on farm imports, making the country's agricultural market one of the most open in the world" (Haveman, 1992).

Reprivatization of agriculture also created a chaotic situation in the Bulgarian countryside, with the dramatic decline in technology and livestock. In 1992, nearly 1.9 million sheep, half a million pigs, and a quarter of a million cattle were slaughtered because private farms could not maintain them. The most devastating consequences could be found the formerly successful sectors and the leading export sector of Bulgarian agriculture, tobacco production and processing. In the 1980s, Bulgaria was the biggest tobacco producer in Europe, supplying nearly one fifth of the European market. *Bulgarotabac* was the biggest cigarette and second biggest tobacco exporter in the world. These two items accounted for half of the country's exports in food processing. By the end of 1992, tobacco production dropped by 50 percent and its percentage share in the

European market halved. The American companies rushed to occupy the former markets of the Bulgarian cigarette companies, which were working at only 60 percent capacity.

Severe economic decline has been the most common characteristic of Central and Eastern Europe in the early 1990s. Beside shock-treated Poland and gradualist Hungary, "the most dramatic output losses – measured output has fallen by more than *half* – have been in Albania . . . and the successor states of the former Yugoslavia," summarized two World Bank experts. "These extreme cases are attributable to special circumstances – in Albania, the disruptive disintegration of an unusually closed regime . . . and in Yugoslavia the civil war" (Blejer, 1992, p. 2). Underemployment reached new heights in Bulgaria (18.5 percent), Romania (18 percent), and Slovakia (17.5 percent) in 1994 (CEER, 1994).

Civil war notwithstanding, the Yugoslav economy was already on the verge of a collapse by the summer of 1991. Industrial production fell by 30 percent and GNP by 20 percent, tourism plummeted from 8 million visitors to the country in 1990 to a few thousand in 1991, which alone led to a loss of about $4 billion, and the unemployment rate soared to a catastrophic 20 percent.

The GDP of the other five countries of the region declined by an average of 25–30 percent, and industrial output fell by 30–40 percent. Although statistical reports are not accurate and cannot properly measure the results of the new small-scale private sector, the margin of error may not drastically change the picture. The year 1989, the "Annus Mirabilis," was followed by several "Anni Miserabiles" in the early 1990s.

Eroding welfare system and lost security

The severe decline of the economy has strongly affected the majority of the population. After the decade-long stagnation, living conditions have dramatically deteriorated. Although it is difficult to draw up a balance sheet of the spectacularly improved supplies and the end of the many hours of queuing on the one hand, and the skyrocketing prices and deteriorating social welfare on the other, it is clear that the peoples of the region have definitely lost their accustomed security.

Because of its ideological underpinnings, state socialism built up a welfare system that included free medical and education services, a low retirement age and long, partially paid maternity leaves. Moreover, staple food products, rents, children's clothing, and cultural services were highly subsidized. State socialism combined a very low, virtually non-European income level with a premature complex welfare system.

The deepening economic crisis of the 1980s already undermined this welfare system. Its basic institutions, however, did not change until 1990. From that time on the decline was startling. This was partly a natural consequence of marketization. The expensive welfare system, which created an unbearable burden on the state budget and was one of the sources of the malfunctioning economy, had been inefficiently run and offered increasingly diminishing services. The system was ripe for change. Its gradual erosion, however, was taking place without the replacement of a new social safety-net, often mentioned in the government's programs.

IMF and World Bank credits were strictly conditioned, and the governments of the countries were forced to keep the budgetary deficit under 5 percent of GDP and cut social expenditures in a drastic way. In the fall of 1992, the newly appointed prime minister of Poland, Hanna Suchocka, was faced with a difficult dilemma when the IMF suspended credit to the country because of its high budgetary deficit. She attempted to save a part of the required money on pensions, and had to confront the opposition in parliament. Decreasing the deficit from 7.5 to 5.5 percent of GDP, in accordance with the conditions of the IMF, pushed Polish governmental policy toward harsh social conflicts in the summer and early fall of 1992.

Soical security and welfare were dismantled in Central and Eastern Europe. The reforming governments, including the socialist governments of Poland and Hungary in the mid-1990s, as well as international institutions, all maintained that it was an unavoidable price to pay for market reforms.

In a period of rocketing unemployment, the Minister of Labor in Solidarity's new government, Jacek Kuron, the former initiator of the "Workers' Self Defense," now followed a non-interventionist policy. Retraining and job creation was left to local initiatives. Unemployment benefits, which previously had no time limits, were now regulated to the effect that the period of eligibility was reduced.

Budget difficulties were accompanied by a lack of social sensitivity. As deputy minister Piotr Mierzewski stated in early 1990: "Society . . . cannot be permitted to go bankrupt because of health expenditures" (*Rzeczpospolita*, 1990). The policy of supplying certain prescription medicines for free was halted in September 1991. In 1991 and 1992, drug consumption in Hungary also declined by 22 percent and 33 percent respectively.

In late 1990, fully 90,000 pre-school places were eliminated and kindergartens were closed, mostly in the Polish countryside, since various companies and state farms were no longer subsidized to run them. A large network of kindergartens, which educated about two thirds to three quarters of pre-school children in the region, were gradually collapsing.

"The recent cuts and restrictions in the state budget," stated Julia Szalai, a former opposition analyst of Hungarian social policy, in 1992, "have been 'successfully' shifted . . . onto pensions, child care allowances, sick benefits, etc. which are not inflation-proof" (Deacon, 1992, p. 157). The erosion of these welfare institutions was dramatic in a period of a galloping 20–30 percent annual inflation. Much more serious cuts were introduced by the socialist government in early 1995.

What was stated about Poland was true of the entire region: "As a consequence of decreasing budget incomes . . . social services are taking further considerable cuts. In recent years the gap between Poland and Western Europe in education, health care, culture, etc. has considerably increased" (Koźmiński, 1992, pp. 21–2). Without a macro-social "safety net," Julia Szalai expressed, "Hungarian society will fall apart. Serious symptoms of social disintegration indicate that the danger of a 'Third World' splitting of the social structure could be its fate in the near future . . . " This road might not lead to Europe but "out of it" (Deacon, 1992, pp. 158–9).

The government in Czechoslovakia declared that the country intends to return to the prewar health insurance system. The Western media reported that "wary Czechoslovaks prepared to give up free health care" (Simons, 1993).

In certain fields the cancellation of subsidies has already led to the total collapse of certain services. This is the case with cultural "services," which suffered virtually everywhere in the region as a result of marketization. High subsidies for books, theater, and movie tickets naturally disappeared. Since income levels had in the meantime decreased, prices for books and cultural entertainment became prohibitively expensive for the bulk of the population. Publications, newspapers, magazines, and theater programs, previously limited and censored for political consider-ations, are now under the "censorship" of a limited market.

All these transformations should be counted as elements of reestablishing a "normal" market economy. One should not forget, however, that in Central and Eastern Europe an artificially low income level was counterbalanced by a welfare system of free or inexpensive services. But the latter has collapsed or rapidly eroded, while the low income level has further declined. A significant decrease in income and the standard of living, caused by high inflation and increasing unemployment, characterized the early 1990s.

After a relatively successful shock treatment against hyper-inflation, the inflation rate remained high in Poland after having reached 40 to 70 percent between 1991 and 1993; in Hungary, inflation apparently peaked at 35 percent in 1991, and dropped to a more moderate 23–24 percent in 1992 and 1993. Inflation was unavoidable in countries opening what were heretofore closed economies: Albania suffered a 30 percent inflation rate in 1991, while Romania was battered by levels as high as 200 percent, and Bulgaria entered a staggering hyper-inflation in the winter and early spring of 1991, when the monthly inflation rate peaked at 123 percent. In the summer, however, it slowed down to about 6 percent per month, but it was still high enough to severely erode incomes and salaries.

Price increases were only partially compensated and always a year afterwards, leading to a dramatic decline in the standard of living. The situation was exacerbated by an abruptly increasing unemployment rate of 10–14 percent in the region. Wages and pensions, not indexed, consequently eroded to a significant degree. Real wages decreased by 15–20 percent in Hungary within two years, but this trend was almost halted in 1992. Certain social groups, including a large number of retired people (representing 22 percent of the population), were sliding into poverty. Pensions, in real value, declined in a single year (1992) by 15 percent, at a time when the decline of real wages in general was almost terminated. According to Rudolf Andorka's calculations, the percentage share of the Hungarian population having an income below subsistence level increased by three times – from 10 percent to 30 percent – between 1980 and 1994. (Andorka, 1996) People living in poverty – measuring the poverty line between 35 to 45 percent of the average wage level of 1989 in the various countries – strikingly increased: from 4 percent to 25 percent in the Czech Republic, from 25 percent to 44 percent in Poland, from 34 percent to 52 percent in Romania, and from 6 percent to 34 percent in Slovakia, according to UNICEF figures. Children living in poverty reached 50 percent to 60 percent of the child population in most of the countries.

All these phenomena signal the reappearance of an early capitalistic class society in Central and Eastern Europe. A dramatic change of social fabric that may become an important obstacle to modernization. An increasing poor lower class may supply cheap labor for peripheral industries, but not the educated labor for modern sectors.

The severity of the situation is illustrated by the increasing poverty in Yugoslavia. In the summer of 1991, before the armed conflict broke out, 5.5 million people, more than one quarter of the population, lived below the poverty line. Poverty reached tragic proportions during the years of the civil war: more than half of the Serbian population lived below the subsistence level in the winter of 1993–4. According to the World Bank's calculations, Yugoslavia belonged to the medium level of development in 1989 with a $3,060 per capita GDP. It dropped to a level comparable to some of the poorest African countries, such as Zambia, Zaire, and Uganda.

All of this is going hand in hand with a growing polarization of society. The dynamic development of the new private businesses has led to the emergence of a class of *nouveau riche*, narcissistically flaunting its wealth by driving luxury Mercedes and Rolls Royce cars. Quite a few of them have skillfully avoided their share of taxes, and their presence underlines the striking and conspicuous disparities in society after decades of relative egalitarianism.

"The impression of general impoverishment is generated by the fact," noted Rudolf Andorka, a sociologist-statistician, "that the real income of half of the Hungarian society really decreased, while in contrast, the real income of roughly 20 percent of the population increased, and for half of the latter group quite strikingly. These two divergent trends explain the noticeable signs of both impoverishment and enrichment" (Andorka, 1993).

The causes of decay and the question of the model of transformation

What was the reason for the extremely sharp and unexpected economic decline? There are different schools of thought and various possible answers to this question. One of the most widespread explanations of the dramatic decline is a historical coincidence of several factors. First was the collapse of the Comecon market which absorbed 40 percent to 75 percent of the foreign trade of the countries of Central and Eastern Europe. The Comecon market, furthermore, was a protected, non-competitive market where second-rate products were exchanged for other kinds of second-rate merchandise, and which used barter trade to avoid hard currency payments. After four decades of trading within Comecon, all of a sudden in 1990 the countries of the region had to reorientate their exports and imports. Reorientation was not merely geographic, i.e., to find Western markets for goods which were previously sold on the Eastern markets. The real problem was competitiveness in quality and in the cost of production, packing, and advertising; in other words, adjusting to the much higher requirements of the Western markets. The task was gigantic. In 1992, the main trading partner of all of the Central and Eastern European countries was the West. The destructive side-effects of this transformation, however, were significant.

Another factor was the recession in the West in the early 1990s. It had a combined negative impact on the East. It made Eastern exports to Western markets much more difficult and Western protective measures more severe. Altogether it sharpened competition in the world market in the very period when trade in the former communist countries was being reoriented.

Moreover, recession made most Western countries more introverted. The possibility of foreign aid and assistance markedly deteriorated. It certainly contributed to the unexpectedly low capital inflow to the region. Other negative accidental factors, such as the Gulf War with its accompanying temporary oil price increases at the very beginning of the transformation, also had a short-term effect. The Yugoslav civil war, beginning in the summer of 1991, caused severe losses. The United Nations boycott against Serbia caused the loss of billions of dollars in trade and transportation for Bulgaria, Romania, Hungary, and practically all of the countries of the region. Moreover, it made several investors and businessmen rather cautious in investing in the region. The losses in trade and capital inflow were therefore serious. These historical factors contributing to decline were furthermore combined with the unavoidable negative side effects of the transformation from a planned and protectionist to a free–trade market economy.

A second school of thought stresses the role of the unavoidable transitory sacrifices that have to be made to secure the future. Both of Ralf Dahrendorf's phrases, that "things get worse before they get better," and that the peoples of Central and Eastern Europe have to march through the "Vale of Tears" to arrive at market prosperity, have often been quoted. They imply that there is an unavoidable negative side effect of market transformation, but that it will be followed by prosperity in the future. János Kornai, one of the leading experts of the state socialist economy, shared this view when he stated in December 1992: "The severe decrease of production is a painful side effect of the healthy process of changing the system. Whereas . . . economic decline seems on the surface to be similar to other cyclical phenomena and structural transformations . . . this is something rather different . . . [I]ts cause is the transition from socialism to capitalism. . . . To end the decline one should . . . accomplish even faster the tasks still remaining" (Kornai, 1992b).

The "transformational recession," as Kornai called the economic decline in Central and Eastern Europe, has a multi-causal explanation. He speaks about six main factors being behind it: a "shift from a sellers' to a buyers' market; contraction of investment; a shift in the composition of output; a shift in the composition of foreign trade; disruption of coordination; enforcement of financial discipline" (Kornai, 1993, p. 2).

In this interpretation even the "disruption of coordination" and the "enforcement of financial discipline" are strong reasons for decline since, once the command economy was abolished, a market economy could not automatically start to function because a coordination void developed. This was the main reason for the dramatic decline and economic chaos in Bulgaria and Albania, where the elimination of the old regime was not immediatelly followed by consistent reforms.

In Michael Mandelbaum's interpretation, it is only a question of time and patience: "The . . . ultimate success will depend . . . on how long and how consistently the policies can be sustained. . . . Free markets will work. . . . So if the people . . . can endure the hardship that the policies of stabilization, liberalization, and institution building inflict, they will emerge at the other end . . . of the valley of tears, into the sunlight of Western freedom and prosperity" (Islam, 1993, pp. 11, 15).

Those with more complex analyses, however, were not satisfied with the above arguments, and searched for additional factors to explain the decline. A third school of thought maintained that besides "transformational decline" and unfavorable international circumstances, the most important contributions to economic disaster were severe policy mistakes. The root of the crisis, according to some analysts, was the mistake of attempting to transform state socialist economies overnight. The critics of shock treatment argued that sharp decline was most of all a consequence of mistaken shock therapy.

Criticisms of shock therapy, often heard in 1991 and early 1992, were muted afterwards. This happened partly because severe economic decline characterized not only the countries that applied shock treatment, but also those that followed even overcautious approaches. Furthermore, the decline in income and output in Poland stopped in the summer of 1992, and growth followed. In 1994, Poland with a 5 percent growth rate was not only the best example of a transforming country in Central and Eastern Europe, but was ranked first in growth in Europe. Shock therapy was celebrated as the most efficient and successful method.

New doubts emerged in 1993, partly because an unstoppable decline continued in most of the region's countries, and partly (especially in the fall and winter of the year) as a consequence of the Polish elections of September and the Russian political crisis. In Russia, the revolt of the old parliament and the armed "solution" to the crisis in October was followed by the December elections and the clear danger of mass dissatisfaction, with every fourth voter voting for the extreme right-wing, fascist-type party Vladimir Zhirinovsky.

The experts who denounced the "fast transition" and maintained that capitalism in the West was never "introduced" by a "Big Bang" gained ground. As Shafiqul Islam suggested, a more "evolutionary model – a growth oriented, sector-sensitive, and . . . gradualist approach – [is needed which] has a much better chance at controlling inflation, promoting recovery, and putting the transitional economies on a sustainable path toward capitalism than the 'creationist model' being tried currently" (Islam, 1993, p. 211).

Paul Marer sought to challenge the overall validity of the celebrated shock treatment and reestablish the genuine concept of shock therapy as a cure for "large macro-economic disequilibrium," which is required only in certain situations and certain countries, while others "had no need for shock therapy" (Marer, 1993b).

Michigan economist Thomas Weisskopf argued that "shock therapy is extremely unpopular . . . [and the Russian government should search far and wide for an alternative strategy of transition that would not impose such huge immediate costs on so many people" (Weisskopf, 1993). The Columbia University economist Padma Desai stated: "The IMF has to relax its insistence on rapid, sweeping market reforms . . . Russia must introduce, step by step, a package of feasible measures . . . The shock of sharp cutbacks . . . hasn't worked – and won't" (Desai, 1993b). The Western media also began to question the region's too rapid transformation because of its social costs and political consequences.

A fourth school of thought describes policy mistakes in a rather different way. It does not stop at the problem of the timing and rapidity of the transformation and goes beyond accusing shock therapy per se. It sees a much more general and widespread series of policy mistakes in all of the countries of the region. Richard Portes argued that there was a "serious macro-economic policy error in both Poland and Czechoslovakia: initial excessive devaluation of the currency . . . a move to convertibility must be accompanied by a sensible exchange rate policy: do not devaluate excessively; peg initially: then go to a crawling peg. The opening to trade with the West – with convertibility, low tariffs, and few quantitative restrictions – was too abrupt . . . many important industrial branches became vulnerable" (Portes, 1993).

The drastic deterioration of general economic conditions, Domenico Nuti observed, "is not [a] necessary concomitant of transition, nor a consequence of shock therapy . . . but the unnecessary consequence of policy failures" (Nuti, 1993). Nuti lists several policy failures, such as the dearth of liquidation and bankruptcy procedures, which had long encouraged firms to accumulate debt. But the primary focus of his criticism is "the failure in government management of the state sector."

Indeed, in most of the countries, the state sector was handled as if it was an instantaneously disappearing group of companies. State-owned big industry was written off, and served only as a source of state income. In most of the countries, state companies were and are overtaxed, unable to invest in themselves. They utilized their last reserves and began to concentrate on exporting to the West but, renounced by their respective governments and unable to adjust to the rapidly changing situation, they were for the most part doomed to dependence on the government and outside sources. This "betrayed," ailing state sector, however, still represents the bulk of the economy, manufacturing 50 to 70 percent of domestic production, but there is little interest in revitalizing the viable parts of it.

The list of policy mistakes is quite long. Sándor Kopátsy added a few more items: "It is fashionable to explain the decline of the economy as a necessary sacrifice of transformation. In reality it is not true. During the past five years, financial requirements for Hungarian firms were so mistaken that they could destroy the big industrial sector of each country of the world" (Kopátsy, 1993). Kopátsy mentioned, among other reasons, the abolition of subsidies without any kind of compensation, the mistaken taxation of inflationary profits, the lack of, then the poor implementation of, the bankruptcy law, a too high interest rate which channeled industrial profits to the state-owned banks, and an exchange rate policy which overvalued the currency and made imports more expensive and exports less profitable.

These mistakes undoubtedly contributed to an unexpectedly deep and long economic decline in the transforming economies. Some of the mistakes were certainly unavoidable because of the lack of experience in directing a process that was unprecedented in history. On closer analysis, however, it becomes clear that most of the above listed policy mistakes were not only the consequences of an understandable lack of experience. An important source of policy mistakes and economic turmoil in Central and Eastern Europe was an ideological approach to the practical problems of transformation. Several policy makers of the region were "new believers" who were convinced that there was only one single "design," an imagined ideal *laissez faire* capitalism without state ownership and intervention, and who rejected all other options.

The new governments enthusiastically copied "Thatcherism" and "Reaganomics." The highly redistributive Scandinavian model was considered too statist and socialist. In the place of Austrian *Sozialpartnerschaft*, the regimes seek to crush the trade unions, which they view as being either "Red" or anachronistic to the changing times, and they frown upon union organizing as potentially undermining the democratic order. The half century triumph of West European mixed economies in

France, Italy, and Austria, with 20–50 percent state-owned economies, was counterbalanced by a pronounced trend toward privatization in the eighties. The successful road of the East Asian countries, which in several cases combined market-oriented modernization with strong state interventionism, was not even considered in Central and Eastern Europe (Berend, 1994).

This ideological approach was also the source of other serious mistakes. Since the neo-liberal paradigm is based on the assumption of an ideal equilibrium and a perfect market and market mechanism, the followers imagined the possibility of "introducing" this type of market which would automatically solve everything.

Alec Nove critically cited Marek Dąmbrowski and Vaclav Klaus as those resisting "interventionist pressures" and "the demand for a kind of government investment policy." As Nove pointed out, any kind of allocation for restructuring, any "state influence on the branch structure of the economy," or any "priority in government (economic) policy" over the market mechanism was rigidly opposed. "No industrial policy, no energy policy, no investment strategy. All will come about by itself if and when macro-economic stabilization is achieved" (Nove, 1995, p. 233).

David Stark strongly criticized the ideological approach of Central and Eastern European transformation and rejected "design capitalism." Stark argues that "transformation schemes that rely on a single coordinating mechanism [i.e., the market] do not so much emulate capitalism, as echo the implementation of state socialism." He added: "A policy of all-encompassing marketization across all sectors would therefore pose a new obstacle to international competitiveness. Markets are but one of many coexisting coordinating mechanisms [such as "networks," "alliances," "inter-firm agreements," etc.] in modern capitalism."

Why did an ideological *laissez faire* policy prevail? In Michael Mandelbaum's explanation it was because of the Western example: "the West supports the creation of Western-style politics and economics ... simply by the example that it sets. Many of the people who lived under communism wish to remake their countries in the image of the West ... Western prosperity can be seen on television ... by everyone from Berlin to Vladivostok" (Islam, 1993, p. 13).

Alec Nove went further when he passionately remarked: "Extremist neo-conservative think-tanks send missionaries to expound the gospel: Roll back the state, do not copy Western Europe ... *laissez faire* is seen as the answer" (Nove, 1995, p. 220). Jeffrey Sachs, Anders Åslund, Stanislaw Gomulka, and many other Western advisors have indeed "expounded the gospel" of *laissez faire*.

The attractive Western blueprint and the inticing advice to copy it initiated and mobilized the new elite to adopt the model, even if it was difficult and painful. They thought that it was a rational price, an "entrance fee" for joining Europe. "I understood the difficulties that we faced because of the Balcerowicz Plan," stated Bronislaw Geremek, one of the most influential Solidarity leaders, "but at the same time I knew that this was the only way that we could secure the chances for Poland of getting a place in the European economic order. In other words: without ... a very painful renunciation ... we had no chance to overcome the distance separating us from the threshold allowing us to start the process of integration. I was also aware that we must move very quickly ... because Europe had frankly no intention of waiting for us." As Andrzej Olechowski, a close aidé to Walesa and member of several Polish cabinets, added, "even a unilateral opening of the economy to the world is advantageous. ... Liberalization may be harmful ... Nevertheless, the overall prosperity will increase" (Kowalik, 1994, p. 122). Geremek, Olechowski, and many others were convinced that a bold policy to introduce a Western *laissez faire* system would result in a great leap to European standards.

The role of the international financial institutions effectively fostered the realization of these concepts. Most of the countries of the region were handicapped by an indebtedness trap and needed foreign assistance for their macroeconomic stabilization. All were highly dependent on Western trade markets and, above all, the acceptance of the European Community. In other words, they had no other choice but to follow the "advice" of the so-called G-7 governments, the IMF, and World Bank, which were often accompanied with strict conditions on credits and trade concessions.

As Mira Muc, head of the Slovenian privatization office stated in the early summer of 1993: "We gave our word to the World Bank to privatize 400 firms in 12 months ... without which there are no credits" (Muc, 1993). The Commission of the European Communities, as it was reported in 1989, was given the authority to manage and control assistance to Eastern Europe by the EC members. As a prerequisite to receiving assistance from the EC members, recipients were required "to make rapid movement toward free market economies ... and furthermore, 60 percent of its lending is earmarked for private sector projects, directing capital away from the hands of the state. Conditions like these favor the radical over gradualist model of transition" (Crawford, 1993).

"The West is imposing strict and damaging conditions on the new democracies," noted Misha Glenny, "in order to influence their socio-economic development ... along lines preferred by the West" (Glenny, 1990, pp. 194, 197). "The actual economic programs of the governments," stated Federigo Argentieri, an Italian expert of the Central and Eastern

European transformation, "are dictated more by the International Monetary Fund than by anybody else, leaving not very much room for maneuvering, except for nationalist and populist demagoguery" (Argentieri, 1992).

Moreover, the newly established parties and freely elected governments began to compete with each other in demonstrating their determination to follow the Western world. The applause in the West that immediately followed was encouraging. Shock therapy was definitely the best propaganda for the former state socialist countries. The West rewarded Poland with a unique and unparalleled gesture: it wrote off 50 percent of Poland's official debt in April 1991, while the American administration took the spectacular step of reducing Poland's American debt by 70 percent. The remnants were written off in 1993. Václav Klaus used the most extreme shock-therapy rhetoric to "sell his policy in the West and attempted to hide pragmatic state interventionist steps."

In competing for foreign aid and for easy access to the European Community, which was seen as a realistic possibility in 1989, Central and Eastern European governments became free traders and anti-state-interventionists to a degree surpassing the countries that were classic adherents of that policy. The new elite thus became the world's most ardent advocates of free trade ideology, and they followed it with neophyte bigotry. Anyone who questioned this policy fell under suspicion and was arbitrarily accused of harboring nostalgia for the collapsed regime or of attempting to preserve certain elements of it.

A *laissez faire* market economy without state interference, protectionism, and public ownership became a religious commitment in the 1990s. The conservatives' attitude was superbly characterized by Guy Molyneux: "today's conservatives . . . [have an] unquestioning faith in markets. . . . Expanding markets and cutting taxes is the answer to every – not just some, but every – social problem. . . . If problems remain, that is only because we still haven't gone far enough – the response of all true ideologues" (Molyneux, 1993).

Moreover, this unquestioning faith did not remain the monopoly of certain conservative groups but became a sort of *Zeitgeist*. Most of the European countries and all of the successful Asian modernizing economies followed a state interventionist policy, and several had mixed ownership, in the unparalleled growth period after World War II. When the new structural crisis emerged after 1973, previously triumphant Keynesism was defeated by a jubilant Chicago School version of free market ideology. "Reaganomics" successfully promoted *laissez-faire* ideology and free market policies, and offered the spectacular American upswing in the early to mid eighties as an example to be emulated. Reaganomics was presented as a simple and quick solution to the world's complex economic ills. Similarly, "Thatcherism" offered a "vaccination" against the *Sozialpartnerschaft* and social-democracy, and initiated instant privatization in Britain. The relatively successful adjustment of the advanced core countries to the new technological and structural requirements of the eighties thus led to a triumphant vindication of free market ideology.

Indeed, the entire world was on a spectacular march towards a *laissez-faire* system. From Great Britain and France to Latin America, countries which had turned towards strong state interventionism, built a huge public sector, and instituted planning during the postwar period, now dramatically revised their policy and introduced privatization. Marketization became a leading trend through deregulation and elimination of obstacles to free trade set up during the postwar decades (Berend, 1994).

The blueprint of Central and Eastern Europe's private market economy, which was in the making in the early 1990s, was thus the model of a self-regulating free market economy. Karl Polanyi defined the model as "an economic system controlled, regulated, and directed by markets alone," and added: "No measures or policy must be countenanced that would influence the action of these markets. . . . Only such policies and measures are in order which help to ensure the self-regulation of the market by creating conditions which made the market the only organizing power in the economic sphere" (Polanyi, 1964, pp. 68–9).

This model had a relatively short history from the end of the eighteenth century in Britain, followed by the core countries in Europe and later the United States. The model, however, was highly challenged in the 1920s and even more in the 1930s to the 1950s. The self-regulated market was, however, successfully restored after World War II by the United States and some of the core countries of Western Europe, but was effectively applied only in a handful of the most advanced countries of the world.

The application of the self-regulating free market model in the transforming Central and Eastern European countries was certainly a historical mistake. A pragmatic approach to the tasks of economic transformation in the region would rightly recognize the need for "tariffs at a significant level" along with a "transitional wage subsidy"; and "all this," asserted Richard Portes, "argues for an active policy, for the kind of industrial restructuring that cannot be left to the market" (Portes, 1993, p. 46). Shafiqul Islam also urged "temporary protective walls of tariffs, as well as *direct* budgetary subsidies." The philosophy of "the survival of the fittest should be persued first at the national level, and the survivors should then be gradually exposed to foreign competition." Islam denounced the Polish non-tariff policy ("incredibly . . . [the] average tariff rate in

Poland [9 percent] was only slightly higher than in the United states [5 percent], and while Washington maintained quantitative restrictions on almost forty food and agricultural items . . . quotas and other non-tariff barriers are virtually non-existent in Poland"), and called for "a strong state with a coherent plan, [since this] is precisely what [the] command economy needs to free itself from the strangling grip of the state. . . . The creationist model of laissez faire capitalism is an appealing but abstract ideology" (Islam, 1993, pp. 209–12).

State intervention, industrial, structural, and investment policies are especially needed to make significant advances in restructuring the economy. The central goal of marketization and privatization is the creation of the prerequisites for an efficient, reactive economy. In the first years of transition, however, because of a quasi-religious "de-stateization," economic restructuring and attempts to generate adequate responses to the challenges of the world economy were "temporarily" pushed aside.

Any kind of source allocation for restructuring, any interference to structural transformation, or any governmental action over the market mechanism was rigidly opposed.

The Schumpeterian term "creative destruction" was certainly never used more often than in these years in Central and Eastern Europe. By 1992–3, however, destruction was so unexpectedly striking, and economic decline so sharp, that the creative part of the transition is still being delayed. "The fall in output," stated two World Bank experts, "does not seem to have been accompanied by the radical economic restructuring that many expected as part of the reform process" (Bleyer and Gelb, 1992, pp. 2–3). Richard Portes added: "Industrial restructuring . . . has made little progress. Privatization will not cure that" (Portes, 1993, p. 41).

The core issue of the structural crisis, the need for a structural-technological adjustment, is thus yet to be addressed. Structural changes, including macro-economic sectoral changes, the branch composition of industry, and micro-economic changes on the enterprise and product level, represent the essence of economic adjustment. From this respect, the short history of transformation has had a rather mixed record. The most impressive positive change characterized the previously neglected service sector. Services, in contrast to the decline of industrial and agricultural output, increased by 5–7 percent in Hungary in the early 1990s, and trade, transportation, and non-material services increased their share in Hungary's Gross Value Added from nearly 47 percent to 62 percent between 1989 and 1993. In Poland, the Czech Republic, and Bulgaria, the share of services increased from 36 percent, 32 percent, and 30 percent to 53 percent, 50 percent, and 47 percent respectively during the same period (Ehrlich 1996; Ordnung, 1996). A backward telephone system received the largest foreign investments in Poland and Hungary, and started to be modernized.

A passive and defensive restructuring caused important structural changes in ill-structured industries. The oversized and obsolete "heavy industries" dramatically declined. Entire factories and branches were closed. Some noticeable attempts were also made to create new competitive industries. The latter was connected with a few isolated large-scale investment projects of several Western conglomerates, mostly car makers such as Volkswagen, General Motors, General Electric, Audi, Unilever, and Suzuki, that established some new modern industries and infant export branches. A definite drive emerged to create a modern car industry in Central and Eastern Europe. Others, such as Ameritech International and German Bundespost, will contribute to the creation of a modern communication infrastructure, which is a major basis of restructuring as well. But very few multi-nationals have shown genuine interest in the area, and those who have mostly did so at the beginning of the transition. Some other Western giants preferred to build profitable Pizza Hut and Kentucky Fried Chicken chains and to monopolize the cigarette market. Needless to say, however, Pepsico and Philip Morris cannot possibly generate a major structural change.

A silent micro-economic restructuring was forced by the drastic change of trade orientation. The shift of exports from Comecon to Western markets, and the liberalized import competition encouraged and even mandated the improvement of several export items. Industrial consumer goods exports, for example, turned out to be competitive because of positive changes in quality and cost of production.

The positive signs, however, are mostly accompanied and even counterbalanced by long-term structural deterioration.

The severe industrial decline hit the various branches of industry unevenly. Paradoxically, the branches at a lower development level, those which produce relatively basic products using a high degree of energy and raw materials such as iron, steel, and textiles, are more competitive on the world market than the more sophisticated processing branches. Cheap exports thus helped to keep production at a relatively higher level in the more traditional branches of industry than in the more modern sectors. Engineering, electronics, transportation, communication technology, and pharmaceuticals, those which are responsible for technological development and higher value-added, suffered the most. According to the analysis of the Ministry of Industry and Commerce, there was a negative structural change in Hungarian industry, an opposite trend to that of the advanced industrial nations. While the energy sector's output (including mining) increased from 25 to 36 percent, the output of engineering declined by nearly two thirds in four years and its percentage share dropped from 30 to 22 percent between 1988 and 1992. Some well-established industrial cultures such as radio, TV, and communication equipment, and the production of medical, precision, and optical instruments, lost 67–72 percent of its work force (Ehrlich, 1996). The export of machinery, transport equipment, and other capital goods dropped to less than half of their 1989 volume, while the export of fuel and electric energy increased by 26 percent in Hungary in 1993. The machinery and equipment represented 55 percent of Czechoslovak exports before 1989, and their share declined to 25–6 percent during the early 1990s. The export of raw materials, fuels, food, and products classified chiefly by material, on the other hand, increased from 31 to 61 percent. "On the whole," concluded Nikolaj Ordnung, "the structure of Czech exports moved closer to that of the developing countries" (Ordnung, 1996).

Although four to five years is too short a period to foresee the various adjustment processes of the twelve countries, historical parallels provide a warning of things to come. What is emerging in Central and Eastern Europe now is rather similar to the region's response to two previous challenges of similar structural crises. In the 1870s and in the 1930s, major structural crises were generated by changes in the old technological regime. A whole set of changes required dramatic adjustments by shutting obsolete sectors and establishing rapidly developing new ones. Central and Eastern Europe could not successfully accommodate the changes, and responded by attempting to save and protect the obsolete sectors of its economy. Grain production remained dominant and grain continued to be the leading export item of Russia, Romania, and Hungary. The latter succeeded in building a high protective tariff around the Austro-Hungarian empire, and compensated the lost Western markets with the huge imperial one.

During the Great Depression, almost the entire region "escaped" from economic adjustment and preserved the obsolete structure of its economy by accepting Hitler's offer to take refuge in the German *Grossraumwirtschaft*, a protected, isolated regional agreement system (based on bilateral trade agreement with Germany). The countries of the region, after signing the agreements in 1934–35, escaped from the depression, recovered from the serious decline, and reached, or even surpassed, the pre-depression level of GDP and output. They could not adjust, however, to the technological-structural transformation of the so-called "fourth industrial revolution." They remained agricultural countries, and the gap between them and the advanced world continued to broaden (Berend and Borchardt, 1986).

The essence of the transformation of the 1990s is to create the prerequisites of economic adjustment, and to accommodate it through a dramatic technological-structural modernization. A marketization and privatization program is definitely the most important prerequisite for catching up. Marketization and privatization themselves, however, do not mean structural and technological adjustment, and do not automatically lead to it. One may not forget that the peripheral private market economies of pre-World War I and II Central and Eastern Europe were unable to provide an adequate response to the world market challenges of that time. The heart of the matter is not just to stop further decline and generate a new growth process. This has already begun. Most of the countries that have already hit rock bottom, such as Poland, successfully halted decline in mid 1992. Poland became the fastest growing country of depression-ridden Europe in 1993, with its move than 4 percent growth. Albania also stopped its decline in output and income and accomplished positive growth results. The Czech Republic and Hungary had a 2.6 and 2.0 growth rate respectively in 1994. Industrial output has already increased. All the countries of the region are inching toward the 1989 level of their GDP, and reached 80–97 percent of it in 1995 (*Annual Report*, 1995). To stop further deterioration and achieve growth was crucially important. One should not forget, however, an important limitation of possible recovery. Reconstruction might happen on the old technological and structural basis as, again, it occurred in both post-world war reconstruction periods in this century. Rising output and GDP is thus a good sign but does not yet signal a real success in transformation. It may not be successful without a breakthrough in economic adjustment to the world economy.

The gap between the further advancing core and the unsuccessful peripheries is growing consistently and considerably. Growth rates vary significantly, exhibiting a sharp divergence in performance. In 1913, the intercountry income spread was 10:1, in 1950, 26:1, and in 1989, 39:1, between the core and the peripheries. (Maddison, 1994). Central and Eastern Europe, in spite of its various attempts to catch up with the Western core, reflects a somewhat similar trend. In 1820 and 1870, the countries of the region reached roughly 58 percent and 49 percent of the West European core's per capita GDP level respectively. In 1913, as a consequence of their failure, or rather partial modernization, they declined to 42 pecent of the Western standards. This level hardly changed during the next quarter-of-a century, and stood at 44 percent in 1938. After the slight improvement until the mid-1970s, a dramatic decline followed: the gap between 1973 and 1993 increased from its 1:2 level to 1:4. This position is far worse than the one at the beginning of the nineteenth century (Maddison, 1995). Andrew Tylecote categorically stated in 1992: "Europe is tending to polarize into a dynamic *core* and a less dynamic *periphery*, the core being characterized by a tendency to rapid product innovation and low inflation, and the periphery by the opposite. This structural imbalance will be exacerbated by further economic integration ... the ex-command economies are taking their place, inevitably, as a new periphery" (Tylecote, 1992, p. 249). As Scott Eddie maintains, the history of the area "suggests a highly pessimistic outlook both short-term and long-term ... [These countries] have to depend on their own resources for growth for a long time to come ... There seems little chance of escape from the vicious circle" (Eddie, 1994, pp. 127–8).

Short-lived enthusiasm accompanying the transformation of 1989 definitely disappeared from Central and Eastern Europe. In the spring of 1992 Václav Havel poignantly expressed the general atmosphere of the region. In his essay, "Paradise Lost," Havel presented a gloomy list of "serious and dangerous symptoms" characterizing the political arena and penetrating a part of society: "hatred among nationalities, suspicion, racism, even signs of fascism; vicious demagogy ... a hunger for power ... fanaticism of every imaginable kind; new and unprecedented varieties of robbery, the rise of different mafias; the general lack of tolerance, understanding, taste, moderation, reason. ... Citizens are becoming more and more clearly disgusted with all this" (Havel, 1992, p. 6).

What were indeed exaggerated expectations have been replaced by pessimism and hopelessness. The landslide victory of the Polish socialists (former reform communists) who, with their Agrarian colleagues, won roughly two thirds of the seats of parliament in the September 1993 elections, and the disastrous defeat of Solidarity and the parties related to the Catholic Church, was the strongest expression of the change of the political landscape. The Hungarian elections reflected an even more pronounced breakthrough of the socialists, who gained 54 percent of the parliamentary seats at the May 1994 elections. With the left-center liberal Free Democrats they formed a coalition with a 74 percent majority. The former ruling coalition suffered a devastating defeat. Socialists have also won elections in Bulgaria.

In the winter of 1995, the legendary solidarity leader Lech Walesa was defeated by a young former communist in the Polish presidential elections. At the same time, the barely reformed Russian Communist Party won the largest number of votes in the Russsian parliamentary elections, followed by the nationalist-adventurist Party of Zhironovski.

Four years after the Annus Mirabilis, hopes have evaporated and dissatisfaction and even nostalgia for the lost societal security has emerged among the great mass of the population. People are suspicious, impatient, and intolerant; many are feeling that they are being cheated again. Are we confronted here with the old Biblical syndrome, when the ancient Hebrews, newly liberated from Egyptian servitude and wandering through the desert towards the Promised Land, began a rebellion against Moses out of a desire to return to their secure "flesh-pots" in Egypt? Or do the peoples of the region no longer believe in the promised miracles and have thus begun to doubt that they are heading toward Canaan?

Emerging but marginal xenophobia and right-wing extremism

The lost security and dissatisfaction is a fertile soil for demands of "law and order," for a strong and attentive power, and for the rise of hatred against "others," especially stigmatized minorities. One must not forget its deep roots in the history of the region. Oppression of minorities and aggressive anti-Semitism has characterized the entire modern history of Central and Eastern Europe. "Recycled" ideas are reappearing in the periphery of Central and Eastern European society. The phenomenon was highly visible and often sensational. A few skinheads, statements of certain politicians, and fascist-type journals have generated worldwide suspicions and scandal. What is the real extent of various kinds of extremism in Central and Eastern Europe in the early 1990s?

According to the polls and the electoral successes of extremist parties and politicians, the best estimate of the support that extremist elements have so far commanded is no more than 5–10 percent of the region's populace. The most well-known, and in a certain period most dangerous, anti-Semitic right-wing populist, István Csurka, who held the post of the vice-president of the Hungarian Democratic Forum, and who headed his own independent party, could muster only 1.5 percent of the votes in May 1994. These marginal political forces are able to exploit the situation as was clearly shown by the December 1993 elections in Russia. The ugly face of hatred and violence, though marginal, has become a part of the political scene.

A highly visible and, for a great many people, rather disgusting and frightening sign of the rebirth of right-wing extremism was an attempt to rehabilitate notorious right-wing national leaders of the past, among them fascists or fascist sympathizers and allies of Hitler and Mussolini from the 1930s and 1940s. As professor Ion Pompiliu Caliu stated in December 1993: "From the gallery of the great Romanian patriots of our contemporary history, Marshal Ion Antonescu must be honored and venerated as a national hero" (Caliu, 1993). The whitewashing of the roles of Marshal Antonescu of Romania, Admiral Horthy of Hungary, and President Monsignor Tiso in Slovakia, the reactivation of fascist Ustasha symbols in Croatia and the revival of the Chetnik organization in Serbia, the celebration of March 15, the day of the declaration of the "independent" fascist Slovak state, are a permanent cause of political concern.

Atrocities against Gypsies, Asian guest workers, and African students have become an everyday phenomenon in the region. The "otherness" of a huge Gypsy population[1] provides a basis for hatred and violence. A revival of open anti-Semitism, however, is equally present even in countries where Jewish communities hardly exist any longer. In April 1990, a local war broke out between Gypsies and a group of skinheads in the Czechoslovak town of Plzen, and a month later some 200 skinheads attacked Gypsies and Vietnamese in the center of Prague.

The right-wing Republican Party-Association for the Republic, which was established in December 1989, advocated the expulsion of 35,000 Vietnamese and nearly 10,000 other, mostly Cuban, guest workers from Czechoslovakia, and proposed drastic measures against the half-million strong Gypsy population. Miroslav Sladek, the thirty-five-year-old former engineer and party leader, organized a series of demonstrations between March and June to protest against both German capital investment, allegedly designed to transform the Czech and Slovak people into "guest workers" in their own country, and the Czechoslovak government, which was accused of being "still ruled by communists." The 1990 elections revealed a public support of less than 1 percent for the Republicans, but in the summer of 1992 they became the fourth strongest party, though with only 6.5 percent of the votes.

In the spring of 1991, the International Helsinki Federation for Human Rights reported widespread "pogroms against Gypsies in Romania." In less than a year violence broke out against Gypsies in twenty-four villages, in which houses were burned and Gypsies expelled from the area. Particularly serious incidents were reported in the villages of Mihail Kogălniceanu and Bolintin Deal, where every house belonging to a Gypsy was burned to the ground. The ultra-nationalist magazine, *România Mare*, described Gypsy villages as "vipers' nests," and praised Romania's wartime fascist dictator, Marshal Antonescu, for deporting the Gypsies to Transnistria.

There are not only frightening statements but continuously bloody

---

[1] Gypsy populations number roughly 800,000 in Bulgaria, 500,000 in Romania, 400,000 in Hungary and several hundred thousand in the successor states of Yugoslavia, Slovakia, and Poland.

actions: "Charred remains of houses burned to the ground line the Transylvanian road between Tîrgu Mureş and Cluj," the remnants of a serious atrocity on September 20, 1993, when three Gypsies were lynched and about 750 ethnic Romanians and Hungarians sprayed the houses of Gypsies with gasoline and set them aflame. "No one has been arrested for the killings, arson and destruction in Hadareni. . . . [A]lmost the whole village participated in the crimes," said the investigating prosecutor, Petru Dan (Kamm, 1993a). Officials of various levels often share the anti-Gypsy views. Prime Minister Vladimir Mečiar, in a speech on September 3, 1993, called the Gypsies, nearly one tenth of the population of Slovakia, "socially unadaptable" and denounced their high birthrate for producing children who constitute a "socially and mentally poorly adaptable [population] . . . who are a great burden on this society" (Kamm, 1993b).

In addition, Nazi-type anti-Semitism also openly appeared in the region. One quarter of those surveyed stated that Jews exercised an unduly large influence in Slovakia in the spring of 1991. Fedor Gál, head of the leading party in Slovakia, Public Against Violence, was harshly attacked and forced to leave the country because extreme nationalists "threatened him with lynching and accused him of 'not speaking Slovak but Hebrew'" (Ulc, 1993, p. 97).

România Mare [Greater Romania] and the magazine *Europa* became leading anti-semitic, xenophobic forums in Romania from early 1990 on. Communism was declared to have been brought to Romania by Hungarians and Jews. Former communist officials, including Elena Ceauşescu, were retroactively "Judaized." Lucian Radu Stanciu declared in *Europa* that the Jews were responsible for anti-Semitism because they maintained that they are the race chosen to dominate, "while the others are simply smeared as 'goyim,' to be used only as slaves" (Stanciu, 1991). Radu Theodoru went even further when he stated: the Jews "are attempting a third invasion of Romania under the protection of the second generation of Cominternists transformed into champions of capitalist liberty, investors, and merchants" (Theodoru, 1993).

In the spring of 1991, *România Mare* declared that "out of 20,000, there are still 5,000 [Jews] who occupy all commanding points in the country" (*România Mare*, 1991). In February 1990 another extreme nationalist and right-wing organization emerged, *Vatră Românească* [Romanian Cradle]. Violent atrocities culminated on March 19–20: *Vatră* mobilized 1,000 peasants from nearby villages, transported them to Tîrgu-Mureş, and attacked the headquarters of the Hungarian Democratic Union with clubs and axes. Two days of bloody violence left eight people dead and 300 injured.

One of the most paradoxical of phenomena has been the emergence of the Movement for Romania *Mișcarea* in December 1991. This organization deliberately molds itself after the infamous interwar populist-fascist Iron Guard Movement of Codreanu. Mișcarea introduced the uniform of the white-shirt with badges containing a variation of the cross. The organization advocates genuine "Romanianism" combined with Greek Orthodox Christianity (a marked characteristic of Codreanu's Iron Guard).

In 1991–2, attacks against African students, Gypsies, and Vietnamese were regularly reported in Hungary as well. The populist founders of the ruling Hungarian Democratic Forum utilized anti-Semitic rhetoric from the very beginning. At first they linked the Jews with communism, rehashing the Nazi concept of "Judeo-Bolshevism": the Forum's semi-official journal, *Hitel*, published articles interpreting the four decades of communist rule in Hungary as "Jewish revenge for the Holocaust." Causing widespread international consternation in the summer of 1992, István Csurka, one of the founders of the Hungarian Democratic Forum, denounced what he described as an international anti-Hungarian conspiracy of "communists, reform-communists, liberals . . . and related people in Paris, New York and Tel Aviv," who are giving direct orders to Hungarian president Árpád Göncz (Csurka, 1992). Within a few days, Gyula Zacsek, a member of the presidium of the Democratic Forum and also of the parliament, published the harshest Nazi-type anti-Semitic attack in the Democratic Forum's journal, *Magyar Fórum*, which he entitled "Termites devouring the nation." He had spoken on a Jewish-Communist-American conspiracy – regarding the "Soros-empire" – against the Hungarian nation that sought to "rescue and preserve their joint power" (Zacsek, 1992).

This phenomenon was quite widespread. As Adam Michnik noted, "This is the conspiracy theory. A vision of a Jewish, Freemason or Bolshevik conspiracy which governs the world. . . . They seek an embodiment of the devil, who is responsible for all the difficulties" (Michnik, 1992, p. 23). Though right-wing extremism has clearly appeared and represents a potential danger in the difficult years of transition, it has been unable to advance without an advantageous international environment, and remains on the periphery of Central and Eastern European societies and politics. The various peoples of the region have so far reacted in a politically mature way and have rejected extremism; up till now there is not a single country in the region where the Right has achieved a breakthrough.

Rising nationalism as the new-old leading force

The most powerful form of extremism, ever more prevalent in some of the countries in post-1989 Central and Eastern Europe, is nationalism. The strength and virulence of the new wave of nationalist revival and separatism is clearly shown by the fact that in the entire area of Central and Eastern Europe, including the former Soviet Union, where eight states had existed before 1989, there are now twenty-six states. Governments and peoples are ready to fight for national goals; bloody civil wars have erupted in the former Yugoslavia and on the periphery of the former Soviet Union.

Nationalism is the strongest political force and the most severe danger to the region. Although the facts are known, explanations for the rise of nationalism are rather confusing. Is nationalism a "natural" final stage of communism? In the summer of 1988, when Zbigniew Brzezinski had already predicted the collapse of communism, he spoke of nationalism, as "the most likely evolution." He stated that "the nationalist authoritarian phase of post-communist transition may be viewed, perhaps in the majority of cases, as an unavoidable stage in the progressive dismantling of the Marxist–Leninist systems" (Brzezinski, 1989, pp. 254–5). Adam Michnik also used this expression and remarked that nationalism is the last stage of communism. According to Otto Ulc, "the majority of the Czechs are inclined to view [Slovak] nationalism as the last stage of communism and as an expression of a "collective inferiority complex" (Ulc, 1993, p. 95). The Croatian government has the same view of Serbian nationalism, and has equated it with traditional Bolshevism.

In contrast to this widespread recent view, André Malraux and Karl Popper – based on earlier experiences – maintained that nationalist authoritarianism or fascism is not a last stage but a reaction to failed communism (and vice versa) (Popper, 1950). This concept is quite similar to recent explanations that Central and Eastern Europe is facing a sort of pendulum effect and a sudden, transitory resurgence of a previously suppressed ideal. Nationalism was thus a political trend that exploded because it had been swept under the rug and suppressed for almost half a century. Others are also promoting nationalist ideology as something which can easily fill the vacuum left behind after the collapse of communist values.

In reality, nationalism in Central and Eastern Europe has neither appeared as a last stage of communism nor replaced it, but has been continually present in the region since the early nineteenth century. It became the most decisive driving force in the first half of the twentieth century and, in most cases, successfully merged with state socialism.

Moreover, as the Czech dissident political thinker, Milan Simečka, stated a few weeks before the collapse of the regime, "behind the facade of the Marxist–Leninist jargon a reactionary populism was firmly embedded, characterized by class egotism, primitive consumerism, nationalism, anti-intellectualism, and anti-Semitism" (Ulc, 1993, p. 91).

"Reactionary populism" with its nationalistic course characterized the Stalinist version of state socialism from its birth, and became dominant in several countries of Central and Eastern Europe after World War II, particularly by the 1960s. The "facade" collapsed after 1989, and new-old nationalism, a consequence of "unfinished nation building" in peripheral Central and Eastern Europe, became visible, unmasked and open.

"New" nationalism, however, is not only connected with the past, but can also be seen as a reaction to the emerging future, to the "new" individualistic capitalism that is developing in Central and Eastern Europe. Nationalism is, in a way, a spontaneous reaction of populists, which is a well-known pattern in the history of the region. A striking similarity exists between the nineteenth and the late twentieth century nationalist movements. Eric Hobsbawm has pointed out that early nationalism subjectively appeared as a defensive reaction against the threat of social transformation, rather than against one that had already taken place. This defensive reaction, as he convincingly argued, was generated by a rising liberal capitalism, which destroyed traditional forms of solidarity and communal bonds while replacing them with nothing but the pursuit of self-interest. Certain elements that were unable to benefit as individuals in the new society passionately fought against it (Hobsbawm, 1990).

The late nineteenth century populist, völkisch, narodnik anti-Western nationalist reaction was now, *mutatis mutandis*, reappearing, with the familiar laments regarding the "selling out of the country to foreigners," the "dirty money" of speculators, the "Jewish international financial circles," and the "triumphant cosmopolitan old-new nomenclature."

Though a populist-nationalist reaction spontaneously reappeared in this dramatic transition period, this does not exclude the possibility of a deliberate and sinister attempt to provoke this phenomenon. Nothing is easier than fomenting nationalist emotions. Inflaming nationalist emotions is the cheapest political substitute for a successful blueprint for transition, and the most promising "wonder weapon" for an emerging political elite to both attain and preserve power.

Slobodan Milošević mobilized millions of Serbs to demonstrate and line-up behind him. But ambitious competitors have been just as successful in playing this game. New political leaders at times hypocritically exploit national emotions, but they also frankly believe in their national mission.

József Antall, a moderate right-of-center politician, stressed in his first statement after the 1990 elections that he was the Prime Minister of 15 million Hungarians, though only 10 million were living in Hungary. This motivation was even stronger in the right-wing faction of the Hungarian Democratic Forum at the end of the summer of 1992, when István Csurka proposed a new, radical nationalist program for the 1994 elections. The pillar of the new program is militant nationalism – "There is no other sacrosanct value but national interest" – which was to include plans for a new geopolitical arrangement: "In 1995 the Yalta agreement expires [sic]. ... The new century opens new possibilities ... for the Hungarians. The key question is whether a new generation ... will be able to exploit these opportunities to bring about new Hungarian living-space" (Csurka, 1992). The Hungarian term he used was a direct translation of its notorious German equivalent: *Lebensraum*. An aggressive nationalism, however, did not become the official policy of the Hungarian government.

Most of the parties and governments in the region were only "playing" with fire. Nationalist parties in Romania are urging reunification with the former Soviet republic and now independent country, Moldova. Certain Albanian nationalist circles and extremist parties are speaking of a "Greater Albania," and propagating the concept of a merger with Kosovo and even with certain parts of Montenegro. "In early 1990 the infamous IMRO (Inter-Macedonian Revolutionary Organization) was reestablished in Bulgaria with the program of reunification of Macedonia. The Bulgarian National Radical party proposed to unite Bulgaria with Macedonia and Thrace" (Troxel, 1993, p. 197). The party, however, in coalition with another extreme nationalist party, gained only 1.8 percent of the votes in the 1991 elections. The potential of nationalist policy was clearly shown by the results of a Gallup poll in October 1991, where 65 percent of the Bulgarian respondents considered Macedonians to be Bulgarians, and nearly one third would support unification.

In some cases, however, the wild fire of nationalism is already burning. The disintegration of Czechoslovakia, while remaining a peaceful confrontation without a barbaric civil war, was one of the most spectacular outcomes of it. Neither the Czechs nor the Slovaks were agitated. The bulk of the Slovak population was not enthusiastic about an independent Slovakia at all. According to polls taken in July 1992, six months before the separation, only 16 percent of Slovaks sought complete independence; more than twice as many were for federation. No mass movements emerged for separation, and the idea of "loose federation" or confederation became popular in Slovakia. The new political elite of the Czech and the Slovak republics, however, passionately promoted separation. It was a significant and rather loud force. In March 1991 five nationalist groups issued the first Declaration of Slovak Sovereignty. They characterized "Czechoslovakism [as] a monstrous fascist, genocidal theory aimed at the extermination of the Slovak nation" (Ulc, 1993, p. 96). The Mayor of Zilina, Jan Slota, threatened the public lynching of any Slovak who sought to preserve Czechoslovakia. In March 1991, Prime Minister Mečiar was forced to resign and leave the Public Against Violence because of his nationalist views. He then founded his own party, the Slovak Democratic Movement, which won the election in Slovakia in 1992 and pursued the road of confrontation.

Václav Klaus, his Czech counterpart and the most ardent advocate of *laissez faire* policies (Nelson, 1995, p. 13), was not prepared to make compromises, especially in terms of the rapid pace of transition. His strategy of "all or nothing" precluded any sort of agreement. One of his associates, Vladimir Dlouhy, the Federal Minister of Economics, stated in an interview on April 21, 1992, that he preferred a split rather than slowing down reform. Klaus and his government were convinced that the more developed Czech Republic, without the less developed Slovakia, might be more successful in the transformation and be accepted into the European Community at an earlier date. Klaus certainly believed that cutting off ties with Slovakia would "shift" the Czech Republic toward the West, and he emphasized that his country does not belong to the Central European, and especially not to the Eastern European region, but to the West.

Mečiar and the Slovak nationalists provoked the Czechs in order to gain semi-independent status in a loose federation or confederation. Klaus exploited the situation and rigidly refused any kind of compromise, thus pushing the country to separation. The two hard-nosed, uncompromising leaders, while often declaring an opposite intention, moved the country towards disintegration. A powerless President Havel tried to halt separation by advocating a referendum which, according to the polls, would have kept the country together. He was, however, reluctant to exploit his tremendous popularity, and thus suffered a new defeat as a result of his moral, non-aggressive attitude. In July 1992, he decided to resign so as not to preside over the disintegration of the country.

On August 26, 1992 the two prime ministers, Klaus and Mečiar, met in Brno. With the impossibility of compromise quite obvious, the two politicians agreed that the federation should split into two separate states by January 1, 1993. On August 31, 1992, Slovakia enacted her new constitution. With the exception of World War II, the Czechoslovak republic existed for three quarters of a century. She died peacefully, without devastating emotions, her destiny determined around conference tables and not on battlefields. She was the victim of politicians working within a proper legal framework, and not warriors, but her end was definitely against the will of the majority of her population.

The seeds of new national conflicts were automatically sown by the separation. If the Slovaks have the right of self-determination inside Czechoslovakia, why not grant the more than 600,000 Hungarians, a significant minority in a Slovakia of 5.5 million people, the same right or at least some autonomy within Slovakia? If the post-World War I and World War II peace treaties and arrangements are not valid any longer for the Slovaks, why should they be valid for Hungarian nationalists in Slovakia or Hungary who seek a revision of the clearly unjust treaty of Trianon? A Hungarian movement in Slovakia is seeking autonomy, which the Slovak authorities view as unconstitutional. The conflict may be explosive, especially since the bulk of the Hungarian minority is living next to the Hungarian border.

Civil war in Yugoslavia

The most dramatic eruption of extremist nationalism has led to a suicidal civil war in the disintegrated former Yugoslavia. The collapse of state socialism in the Yugoslav case was a side effect of the breakdown of a federal Yugoslavia. The first free elections were followed by the declaration of Slovenian and Croatian independence. The founding of independent republics was succeeded by war. As resurgent Greater Serbian nationalism and Slovenian and Croatian separatism were the main driving forces leading to the collapse of state socialism in Yugoslavia, the same forces shifted the country into a murderous civil war in the summer of 1991.

The first act of the civil war began two days after the declaration of Slovenian independence. The Serb dominated Yugoslav army, still guided by the concept of Yugoslavism, declared its intention to safeguard Yugoslav borders and launched an attack against the western republic on June 27, 1991. An instant European Community mediation, however, lead to the Brioni Accord in which the Serbs recognized Slovenian independence. After ten days, the war against Slovenia ended with the victory of the latter.

The declaration of Croatian independence had a much bloodier aftermath. The drive of the Tudjman administration collided head on with the interests of Greater Serbia. Milošević's Serbia was ready to accept the secession of the ethnically homogeneous Slovenian Republic, but demanded the territories of Croatia inhabited by Serbs.

Moreover, the real vanguard of Greater Serbianism was the Serbian minority itself in Croatia. Unlike the highly assimilated urban Serbs of Zagreb, Vukovar, and other Croatian cities, who were often called *hrbi* [contraction of *hrvativ* = Croats and *srbi* = Serbs] the rural Serb communities in the Krajina region highly opposed the nationalizing attitude of the Croatian state. These Serbs, who had demanded cultural autonomy in August 1990 in the Yugoslav federation and had already stated in May 1991 that in the case of the declaration of Croatian independence they would join Serbia, now began their own war. Their paramilitary units, the so-called *Martićevći*, launched the first attack against a Croat police station on June 26. The new atrocities led to an outright war by September. It has became one of the most cruel and horrifying wars of the second half of the century (Glenny, 1993).

The area of civil war was soon enlarged and reached its most tragic momentum in the Bosnia-Herzegovina crisis. After the *fait accompli* of Slovenian and Croatian independence and the beginning of an aggressive Serbian drive for the creation of a Greater Serbia, the other republics of Yugoslavia had to face a difficult historical decision. In March 1992, the small republic of Montenegro voted to remain together with Serbia in a shrunken Yugoslavia. Macedonia, meanwhile, declared her independence.

President Alija Izetbegović made a desperate attempt to prevent the violent disintegration of Yugoslavia and find a compromise in the spring of 1991. When this experiment failed to win the other republics approval, there remained no viable alternatives for Bosnia-Herzegovina. Both the Muslim and Croat nationalities, two thirds of the 4.4 million inhabitants of the republic, refused the first alternative of remaining under a Serbian led small Yugoslavia. The 41 percent Muslim population did not accept the second alternative, the March 1991 agreement of Serbia and Croatia, initiated by president Franjo Tudjman, that partitioned Bosnia-Her-zegovina between the two countries.

A third alternative was realized: in October 1991, the Muslim Party for Democratic Action and the Croatian Democratic Community approved a memorandum on Bosnian independence. The Serb Party, representing nearly a third of the population, vehemently protested since, according to the agreement of December 1990, all draft legislation required a three party consensus. The Bosnian Serbs countered the actions of the Bosnian Muslims and Croats by declaring their right of self-determination and founding the first Serb Autonomous Region. They also declared that if

Bosnia-Herzegovina broke away from a federal Yugoslavia, the Serbian autonomous regions would secede from Bosnia.

All the alternatives were thus dead-end roads. And each decision had to lead to war. The war, indeed, erupted after the referendum and declaration of Bosnian independence in March 1992. The civil war in Bosnia-Herzegovina became a strange mixture of a national fight for independence of Serbo-Croat Muslims, Serbs and Croats, combined with a religious war between Orthodox and Catholics and between Christians and Muslims. It turned into the most cruel kind of warfare, failing to differentiate between soldiers and civilians, using torture, rape, and facial mutilation against the fallen enemy, dynamiting homes, shelling people standing in line for bread, and regularly breaking truces. "After reporting for more than a year on the reborn Chetnik movements in Serbia," noted a British reporter, "I have found its most striking characteristic to be its obsession with violence. Its members apparently take pleasure in torturing and mutilating civilians and military opponents alike" (Glenny, 1992b, p. 30). John Kifner, the reporter of *The New York Times*, revealed the emergence of "gangster elements as the front-line fighters for the Serbian, Croatian and Muslim communities" (Kifner, 1993).

All this happened among people who had lived as peaceful neighbors, and had intermarried for decades. This war led to the killing of roughly 250,000 people, the forced migration or emigration of 500,000, and the dislocation of two million persons.

The progress of a belated nation-building proved the validity of the comments of the mid nineteenth-century Austrian poet, Franz Grillparzer, who had warned, regarding his time of nation-building in the Habsburg empire in 1849, that this development might mean the progress *"von Humanität durch Nazionalität zur Bestialität"* [from humanism through nationalism to bestiality].

There are various biased and one-sided interpretations of the tragic Yugoslav events. Serbs and Croats blame each other. "Croatian officials say," noted Misha Glenny, the British chronicler of the drama, "that this is not a nationalist war but a struggle between a Bolshevik administration in Belgrade, and their own free-market democracy – a claim as misleading," added Glenny, "as the Serbian view of the conflict as a war of liberation against a revived fascist [Croatian] state" (Glenny, 1992b, p. 31).

According to Branka Magaš, the "Milošević's regime [is a] a racially based, proto-fascist formation" (Magaš, 1993, p. xx) that "destroyed [Yugoslavia] for the cause of a Greater Serbia . . . [while] the whole nation was seemingly united behind the counter-revolutionary project" (Ibid., p. xiv). Although most of the accusations have targeted Milošević's

Greater Serbian nationalism, other views, such as those of Sir Alfred Sherman, a former advisor of Prime Minister Thatcher, blamed Bosnia's attempt to create an Islamic state or even an Islamic bridgehead in Europe. The Bosnian Serb leader, Radovan Karadzić, faulted the resurgent anti-Serb Croat and Muslim coalition and spoke about a war of Serbian self-defense: "We are fighting to protect ourselves from becoming vulnerable to the same kind of genocide that this coalition waged upon us in World War II, when 700,000 Serbs were killed. We will never again be history's fools" (Karadzić, 1992). Although historically there are several true elements in all of these arguments, one should not merely accuse certain main actors and parties. The reasons are much more deeply rooted and historically based.

The heart of the matter is the attempt to build an ethnically based nation in an area where the population is highly mixed, and where ethnic-national homogenization did not occur during the early modern centuries. The multinational South-Slavic experiment of Yugoslavia, both in its centralized and (after 1974) federalized versions, became a victim of a passionate national endeavor to create independent ethnic-territorial national units. Misha Glenny spoke about the "central truth of the Balkans," which, according to him, is the fact that "once the area begins to destabilize, a significant element in each national group in the region radicalizes in the hope of transforming a historical myth of nationhood into the reality of a nation-state" (Glenny, 1993).

The different parties wanted to realize the right of self-determination, a well-known principle after World War I. In contrast to the post-World War I situation when, as Eric Hobsbawm noted, a kind of silently accepted though never exactly clarified "threshold principle" existed in creating relatively larger independent states, this time this "threshold principle" had evaporated (Hobsbawm, 1990). Each small ethnic and religious group was ready to fight for its own independent state. Two million Slovenes, fewer than two million Bosnian Muslims, and fewer than one-and-a-half million Bosnian Serbs all demanded the same right, while the "nationalizing" majority nationalities, the Croats in Croatia, the Muslims in Bosnia, and the Serbs in Serbia denied the same right for Serbs in Croatia, Kosovars and Hungarians in Serbia, and Serbs in Bosnia.

Some of the demands were accepted by the international community as just while others were labeled as destructive attempts to "Lebanize" the region. The European Community, pushed by Germany, rushed to recognize independent Croatia, Slovenia, and Bosnia-Herzegovina in January and March 1992 respectively. They did so without setting any kinds of conditions regarding national minorities living in those countries.

On the other hand, the same attempts of the Serbian minorities in the Krajina regions of Croatia and Bosnia-Herzegovina were often considered unjustified. "The Krajina formula of 'self-determination' for every minority," stated Branka Magaš, "leads inexorably to the Lebanization of Yugoslavia. This means the collapse of all central authority and transfer of power into the hands of local warlords" (Magaš, 1993, p. 349).

But the above statement is rather reasonable, well illustrating the fact that the right of self-determination is inapplicable in an area where various ethnic-religious enclaves are inserted into other ethnic-religious enclaves. The relatively homogeneous Serbian communities living in Croatia and Bosnia-Herzegovina are partly separated from each other by Croatian and Muslim communities, and partly mixed with them. The territories of the Serbian ethnic enclaves inhabited by Serbs are only as much as 60–70 percent Serbian. It means that the right of self-determination in the form of independent territorial-ethnic-administrative national units is simply impossible in most of the South Slavic areas (Drakulic, 1993).

The realization of this principle automatically leads to an attempt at "*rascistiti teren*," as the Serbs call it, meaning territorial but most often translated as ethnic cleansing, a most inhuman method of nation building. Serbian military and paramilitary units made broad use of this method by launching the most cruel attacks against civilians, including a deliberate campaign of raping women (*Helsinki Watch*, 1992), to force the Croatian or Muslim population to escape from coveted territories. Although the majority of the atrocities were committed by Serbs, the method itself was used by all sides. According to the Zagreb office of the Helsinki Watch organization, the Tudjman government acknowledged the destruction of 7,000 houses of Croatian Serbs. "Altogether about 280,000 Croatian Serbs have fled the country as a result of the dynamite campaign and other measures" (Binder, 1993).

Indeed, the creation of independent nation states in the past was always accompanied by violence and forced homogenization of the population of certain countries, consisting of various ethnic, linguistic, and religious minorities. The introduction of standardized official languages went hand in hand with the oppression of others, and territories of several nation states were united or enlarged by bloody wars. To repeat earlier historical developments centuries later in an entirely changed value system and international environment makes the process even more difficult.

The ruthless civil war, generated by the belated new South-Slavic nation-building attempts, had other historical determinants besides the failure to apply the right of self-determination. The devastating conflict of the early 1990s were as much the consequences of a new confrontation of real or imagined national interests as it was the laceration of old wounds. In 1991, the Yugoslav civil war of 1941–4, which ended without a real end in 1945, renewed itself. Old hatreds, biases, and suspicions were instantly revitalized.

The mobilized memory of the past became a vital and real factor of confrontation. The declaration of Croatian independence recalled for the Serb the bloody episode of "independent" wartime fascist Croatia, founded by Hitler and run by the *Ustashi*. The reintroduction of the old Croatian national symbols such as the *Sahovica*, the red and white chequered shield, used by the fascist *Ustashi*, recalled the memory of the horror of the most cruel anti-Serb terror of the *Ustashi*. The terrible incidents of Glina, one of the first scenes of the new confrontation, where Croat fascists slaughtered 1,800 Serbs in a church and on the outskirts of the township in 1941, and the Kozara operation of the *Ustasha* army which captured and killed 10,000 Serb partisans and peasants, including about 4,000 children, re-emerged from history and, all of a sudden, became a part of the present. The most notorious *Ustasha* concentration camp of Jesenovac, where – according to the revised and more moderate new calculations – at least 200,000 people were exterminated, including Jews, Gypsies, anti-fascist Croats, and, most of all, Serbs, became a mobilizing factor and a source of continuous revenge. One should not forget that nearly 1 million of the 1.7 million Yugoslav victims of World War II, including the civil war during the war years, were slaughtered by other Yugoslavs.

Almost every family in Yugoslavia had something to recall. Misha Glenny, in his striking book on *The Fall of Yugoslavia*, listed several telling examples. Among them is the story of General Ratko Mladić, commander of the Krajina Serb paramilitary units, a Bosnian Serb whose father was killed in the fight with Croat *Ustashi*. The entire family of General Blogoje Adžić, a Serb from Croatia and operational commander of the Yugoslav army, was killed by Croatian fascists during the war. "The most hawkish member of the Serbian government," Glenny continued his list, "Budomir Košutić, advocated a crusade of retribution against Croats. As a child in Croatia, Košutić watched how his father was told to divide his children into two groups, one group would be shot, the other allowed to live" (Glenny, 1992, p. 122).

There was a great deal for the Croats to avenge as well. The Croatian prisoners of war, the remnants of the *Ustasha* army, escaped to the West and surrendered to the American army, but were transported back to Yugoslavia in early 1945 and machine gunned by Tito's mostly Serbian communist partisan army. The brutal postwar Serbian revenge, tortures and killing of fascists and collaborators (real and alleged alike) in Croatia, Bosnia-Herzegovina, and Vojvodina without careful investigation, and the use of a rather broad interpretation of collaboration (such as continuously running a business under German occupation or fascist Ustashi rule), caused severe and innumerable wounds to be reopened.

Moreover, not only did an unfinished civil war continue after a half century "armistice," but century-old reflexes began to work. One should not forget that the bloodiest front-lines are in exactly the same places and that most of the harshest atrocities of the recent Yugoslav civil war occurred in the same areas, on the same historical fault-lines where Muslims and Christians, Serbs, and others confronted each other for centuries. The Krajina regions were the so-called military borderlands between the Habsburg and Ottoman empires where military colonists and free soldier-peasants were settled, exchanging military service for freedom and land. Their permanent preparedness to fight, their natural attitude to use the weapons they grew up with, turned them into warriors. They learned for centuries not to rely on the authorities who were alien, corrupt, and brutal but to make their own justice. Revenge and vendetta became the natural way to settle disputes. Extreme brutality including facial mutilation belonged to this tradition.

For the Krajina Serbs fighting and war were natural. Nándor Major of Novisad was thus partially right when he stated that Milošević "used armed Croatian Serbs to attack Croatia ... [and] Bosnian Serbs to generate 'civil war' in Bosnia-Herzegovina" (Major, 1993). Milošević could certainly use the Serbian minorities of the other Yugoslav republics to promote his Greater Serbian goal, but the rural Serbian communities of the Krajina under extremist warlords were willing to fight, and began to do so independently. History is a heavy burden on contemporary Yugoslavia and helps us to understand the rationale of its irrationality.

"[I]n Yugoslavia today," stated Ivo Banac, "one can see only the apocalyptic beasts of hate and anger. Luckier observers, living in post-Yugoslav times, will be able to study the fruits of strength and movement" (Banac, 1992, p. 187). The wording of the above statement, an echo of the words of the Croatian writer Ivo Andrić, is used as a telling motto by Banac. It has a promising message: "It happens from time to time in human societies," wrote Banac, citing the words of Andrić, "that hate and anger burst their banks, that they destroy everything, overshadow reason, and silence all better human instinct. . . . But a deeper and better considered view shows that . . . hate and anger do not destroy life – they only transform it. . . . Only hate and anger can erase the frontiers of rotten empires . . . and bring down wrongs. . . . Afterward, hate quenches and anger abates, but the fruits of strength and movement remain" (Banac, 1992, p. 168).

The "fruits of strength and movement" might be some new, settled, and prosperous nation states and a peaceful "cantonized" Bosnia-Herzegovina. The material and moral destruction of the Yugoslav civil war might, however, yield poisoned fruits, continuously destructive strength and dangerous movements. Forces which may destabilize an entire region and incite further local conflicts may undermine a genuinely long and difficult transformation process, and endanger the possibility of catching up with the West and joining Europe.

Conclusion

Resurgent extremist nationalism is the most frightening danger in a Central and Eastern Europe in flux. Several potential hot spots of ethnic–national conflicts exist in the area. Among them, Kosovo and Macedonia are the ones most often mentioned. The Greater Albania concept, realized during World War II, and the explosive Albanian national movement in the Kosovo region, which is, as the cradle of Serbia and the scene of the historic defeat by the Ottoman army that destroyed independent Serbia for centuries, sacrosanct for Serb nationalists, might be, as it actually was for more than a decade, a new center of national confrontation. Serbia's repressive policy in Kosovo may provoke an armed Albanian resistance as Adem Demaqi, the radical leader of Kosavars, already urges.

Macedonia, with its Albanian and Serbian minorities in its Western and Northern areas, and the highly explosive international situation between Albania, Greece, Bulgaria, and Serbia, may be potential battlefields as well. Greece refused the recognition of Macedonia and Bulgaria, maintaining that the Macedonians are Bulgarians. According to certain apocalyptic forecasts, "if Macedonia becomes the Southern Balkan battlefield, the opening gun will be fired in Kosovo. A war in Kosovo would spread southward to Macedonia because . . . western Macedonia would destabilize the already delicate relations between Albanians and Macedonians. If fighting broke out in Macedonia, the Albanian, Serb and Bulgarian militaries would be under great pressure to cross the border in defense of their minorities. . . . That would amount to a full-scale Balkan war" (Glenny, 1993).

Minority questions might generate ethnic-national conflicts in the Danube Basin as well among Hungarians, Slovaks and Romanians. Géza Entz, deputy minister of the Hungarian government responsible for minorities abroad, said in 1993: "the choice was between autonomy and civil strife. . . . The longer the Romanians and Slovaks and others are unreceptive to this, the deeper the political crisis will grow." "I see a certain strategy to create a precedent in Slovakia," answered Frantisek Miklosko, a senior member of the opposition Christian Democratic Party of Slovakia, "that precedent would be autonomy, and this is impossible" (Engelberg, 1993).

The leading former Czechoslovak dissident and Charter 77 (later Civic Forum) representative Jan Urban pessimistically forecast: "After the split of Czechoslovakia, the democratic parties of Hungary will be soon defeated. The chauvinistic campaign 'of the holy struggle for the rights of the oppressed brothers' . . . will elevate the nationalist movement to power" (Urban, 1992, p. 17). Jan Urban was certainly not objective. But he is far from alone in predicting the dangers. James F. Brown, an American expert on Central and Eastern Europe, stated in a more general way in the summer of 1991: "old national issues have already come back on the agenda. The integrity of Czechoslovakia . . . Greater Albania – the reunion with Kosovo; the Bessarabian question. If these have returned, then why not the Macedonian question and a few years down the road, Transylvania and the whole Trianon cluster?" (Brown, 1991b, p. 35). "Does the obvious appeal of nationalism, whether minority-based or state-based," asked another American expert in 1991, "mean that the European Continent will again see an upsurge in interstate conflict or even warfare? Is modern Europe doomed to repeat the fate of the most nearly analogous period, that between the two World Wars?" (Linden, 1991, p. 33).

These questions are already partially answered by history. The gloomy forecasts and hidden predictions, however, have yet to be proven true.

Although valid or semi-valid arguments may justify a myriad of national claims, the prospect of resurgent nationalism in Central and Eastern Europe is potentially one of the most perilous political pitfalls of the coming years, and may lead the countries to inescapable quagmires, sucking them into the all too familiar trap of authoritarian nationalist regimes.

Confrontation or cooperation, nationalist dictatorship or parliamentary democracy and a gradually developing civil society will determine not only the political future of Central and Eastern Europe, but also its ultimate road of economic-social transformation. Indeed, the opposite is also true: the future success or failure of economic transformation will determine the political destiny of the region. The interrelationship between the two is extremely strong.

The key to the situation, however, is rapid economic recovery and the beginning of, at least, mild prosperity. Though the first years of transformation have had considerable impact, and though some processes are already irreversible, it is quite possible that we will see several new upturns, and downturns, before the century is over.

Economic, social, and political constraints may lead the countries to search for different solutions. The forgotten alternative of post-World War II Western Europe, or more precisely, the mixed economies of France, Italy and Austria, with their successful attempts at building a *Sozialpartnershaft* out of the postwar recovery, might reemerge. Dirigist, populist regimes, and/or social democratic roads, or a combination of both, were practically excluded during the first years of transition in the region. Now all these alternatives may rise to the surface and become part of the political reality. The *laissez-faire* model of economic transformation may be corrected in several countries, and the model of a regulated market economy might be combined with a more aggressive structural policy and adjustment.

By the mid 1990s the bulk of the countries of the region will certainly end their economic decay, and a new sustained growth will improve the crisis ridden economies. The main question is, however, what type of prosperity will emerge: a prosperity based on adequate technological-structural changes, and new, competitive export sectors, resulting in a catching up process gradually leading toward Europe; or prosperity and growth in the region, but only as a backyard of the European Community or Germany, without proper restructuring, and with a continuously increasing gap between the Western and Eastern halves of the continent.

The historical question is whether Central and Eastern Europe will be an equal part of the new Europe, or only a peripheral part of it, as it has been in its entire early modern and modern history. Which road will triumphantly emerge in the region? Which countries will be more successful at integrating themselves into Europe? One certainly cannot predict a single common road. Differing historical factors may play a determinant role in causing increasing disparities. Major differences have always existed. The Western rim of the region, after long periods of belonging to the East, was "shifted" toward and became a part of the West as a result of favorable internal and international circumstances from the Middle Ages on.

Endre Ady, the early twentieth century poet and passionate advocate of modernization, bitterly spoke of Hungary as a "Ferryboat-country" sailing towards the West, and then returning back to the East (Ady, 1905, pp. 45–7). Today, history offers a new opportunity to set sail. The relatively small countries of the Western rim of Central and Eastern Europe are undoubtedly in a better position for both departing and arriving than the others. Five-six countries on the eastern border of Austria and Germany (and the European Union), mostly relatively small nations with five to ten million inhabitants, but, together with Poland, not larger than sixty to seventy million people, may have the opportunity of being accepted into the European Union. In this case, they would get access to both Western markets and assistance, and might repeat the "miracle" of the Mediterranean countries. This acceptance, though a major economic burden, is still a vital political and security interest of the West. A relatively declining, humiliated, and chaotic East and South East Europe, with its explosive ethnic and minority conflicts, and its emerging nationalist-populist extremism, might represent a permanent danger for the West, especially for neighboring Germany, and prompt a response to safeguard the eastern border of the European Union by creating a *cordon sanitère* between itself and the crisis-ridden East, especially Russia. If security interests demanded it, the western rim of Central and Eastern Europe, which had made the best advance toward adjusting to the West and has a tradition of being a backyard of German-speaking Central Europe, might be consolidated and restructured by the Western powers as a part of an enlarged European Union.

As for the others, it may very well be the case that a successful transformation and a catching up process will remain a dream. Russian, Romanian, Serbian and Albanian responses to the historical challenge will certainly be different from the Czech, Slovene, Hungarian, and Polish ones. Several countries will continue their historical detour and remain in the periphery of Europe. The "longue durée" of history is clearly forecasting this destiny. Favorable internal and external circumstances, including sound policies and alliances, however, may promote auspicious change. Ultimately, history represents an unlimited combination of continuity and change.

Bibliography

Aaman, Anders, 1992. *Architecture and Ideology in Eastern Europe During the Stalin Era. An Aspect of Cold War History*. Cambridge, Mass.: MIT Press.

Aczél, Tamás (ed.), 1966. *Ten Years After: The Hungarian Revolution in the Perspective of History*. New York: Holt, Rinehart and Winston.

Ady, Endre, 1905. "Morituri" in *Helyünk Európában. Nézetek és koncepciók a 20. századi Magyarországon*. Vol. I. (Iván T. Berend and Éva Ring, eds.). Budapest: Magvető Kiadó.

Alia, Ramiz, 1989. *Zeri i Popullit*. September 29 (Translated by Radio Free Europe).

Allásfoglalás . . . 1987. "A MSzMP KB álláfoglalása" in *Népszabadság*. July 14.

Altmann, Franz-Lothar, 1994. "Market Transformation: A Case Study on the Balkans" in Ivan T. Berend (ed.), *Transition to a Market Economy at the End of the 20th Century*. Munich: Südosteuropa-Gesellschaft.

Alton, Thad P., 1990. *Agricultural Output, Expenses and Depreciation, Gross Product, and Net Product in Eastern Europe, 1975-1989*. New York: L.W. International Financial Research.

Alton, Thad P. *et al.*, 1990. *Selected Charts of Economic Performance in Eastern Europe*. New York: L.W. International Finance Research, Inc.

Andorka, Rudolf, 1993. "Növekvö társadalmi különbségek?" in *Napi Gazdaság*. Budapest, December 4.

Andorka, Rudolf, 1996. "The Emergence of Poverty During the Transformation in Hungary," in I.T. Berend (ed.) *Long-term Structural Changes in Transforming Central and Eastern Europe*. Munich: Sudosteuropa-Gesellschaft, (forthcoming).

Andrejevich, M., 1991. "Resurgent Nationalism in Macedonia. A Challenge to Pluralism" in *Radio Free Europe. Report on Eastern Europe*. Vol. 12. No. 20. May 17.

Annual Bulletin of Housing Building Statistics for Europe 1961-1991. 1991. New York: UN/ECE.

Annual Bulletin of Transport Statistics for Europe, 1961-1990. 1990. New York: UN/ECE.

Annual Fertilizer Review 1975. 1976. Rome: FAO.

Annual Report of the European Bank of Reconstrction and Development, 1995. London: EBRD

Antonian, Armen, 1987. *Toward a Theory of Eurocommunism. The Relationship of Eurocommunism to Eurosocialism*. Westport, Conn.: Greenwood.

Arendt, Hannah, 1951. *The Origin of Totalitarianism.* New York: Harcourt, Brace and Co.

Argentieri, Federigo, 1992. "Hosszú, gyötrelmes út" in *Népszabadság.* Budapest, August 8.

Aron, Raymond, 1966. "The Meaning of Destiny" in Tamás Aczél (ed.), *Ten Years After: The Hungarian Revolution in the Perspective of History.* New York: Holt, Rinehart and Winston.

Ash, Timothy Garton, 1985. *The Polish Revolution. Solidarity.* New York: Vintage Books.

1992. "Budapest: The Last Funeral" in L.H. Legters (compiled), *Transformation and Revolution 1945-1991. Documents and Analyses.* Lexington: D.C. Heath.

Árvay, János-Vértes András, 1993. *A tulajdonosi szerkezet változása Magyarországon 1980-92 között.* Budapest: GKI.

Ascherson, Neal, 1982. *The Polish August. The Self-Limiting Revolution.* New York: Viking Press.

Attali, Jacques, 1992. "Egy Kontinentális Közös Piac felé" in *Népszabadság,* Budapest, September 26.

Ausch, Sándor, 1972. *Theory and Practice of CMEA Cooperation.* Budapest: Akadémiai Kiadó.

Authy, Phyllis, 1974. *Tito. A Biography.* Harmondsworth: Penguin.

Balcerowicz, Leszek, 1992. *Leszek Balcerowicz – 800 dni – szok kontrolowany.* Warszawa: Polska Oficyna wydawnicza "BWG."

Balogh, Sándor (ed.), 1986. *Nehéz Esztendök Krónikája, 1949-1953. Dokumentumok.* Budapest: Gondolat Kiadó.

Balogh. Sándor *et al.*, 1985. *Magyarország a XX. században.* Budapest: Kossuth Kiadó.

Banac, Ivo (ed.), 1992. *Eastern Europe in Revolution.* Ithaca, NY: Cornell University Press.

Batt, Judy, 1988. *Economic Reform and Political Change in Eastern Europe. A Comparison of the Czechoslovak and Hungarian Experiences.* New York: St. Martin Press.

Bauer, Tamás, 1981. *Tervgazdasági Beruházások, Ciklusok.* Budapest: Közgazdasági és Jogi Kiadó.

Behr, Edward, 1991. *Kiss the Hand you Cannot Bite. The Rise and Fall of the Ceausescus.* New York: Villard Books.

Belmustakov, L. 1951. in George Radó (ed.), *Irodalom és képzömüvészet a mai Bulgáriában.* Budapest.

Bence, György and János Kiss, 1978. *Az elszakadás után.* Budapest-Paris: Magyar Füzetek, No. 2.

Bence, György, János Kiss, and János Kenedi, 1979. *Nyilt levél a Charta 77 aláíróihoz. 1979. Október 26.* Paris: Magya Füzetek. No. 5.

Berend, Ivan T., 1964. *Gazdaságpolitika az elsö ötéves terv megindításakor 1948-50.* Budapest: Közgazdasági és Jogi Kiadó.

1979. *A Szocialista Gazdaság Fejlödése Magyarországon, 1945-1975.* Budapest: Kossuth Kiadó. 3rd edition.

1983. *Gazdasági Útkeresés, 1956-1965.* Budapest: Magvetö Kiadó.

1986. *The Crisis Zone of Europe.* Cambridge: Cambridge University Press.

384   Bibliography

1990. *The Hungarian Economic Reforms 1953-1988*. Cambridge: Cambridge University Press.

1994. "End of Century Global Transition to a Market Economy: Laissez-Faire in the Peripheries?" in Ivan T. Berend (ed.), *Transition to a Market Economy at the End of the 20th Century*. Munich: Süosteuropa-Gesellschaft.

Berend, Ivan T. (ed.), 1989. *A Gazdasági Reformbizottság Programjavaslata 1990-1992*. Budapest: Közgazdasági és Jogi Kiadó.

Berend, Ivan T. and Knut Borchardt, 1986. *The Impact of the Depression of the 1930s and its Relevance for the Contemporary World*. A/5 Session, 9th International Congress. Bern: International Economic History Association.

Berend, Ivan T. *et al.*, 1989. "Történelmi útunk. A munkabizottság állásfoglalása" in *Társadalmi Szemle*. XLIV. evf. Különszám. March.

Berend, Ivan T. and György Ránki, 1982. *The European Periphery and Industrialization 1780-1914*. Cambridge: Cambridge University Press.

1985. *The Hungarian Economy in the Twentieth Century*. London, Sydney: Croom Helm.

Bernstein, Barton J. and Allan J. Matusow (eds.), 1968. *The Truman Administration A Documentary History*. New York: Harper & Row.

Biberaj, Elez, 1986. *Albania and China. A Study of an Unequal Alliance*. Boulder: Westview Press.

1992, "The Last Domino" in Ivo Banac (ed.), *Eastern Europe in Revolution*. Ithaca: Cornell University Press.

Bilak, Vasil, 1980. *Vybrane Projevy a Stati*. Vol. I. Prague: Svoboda.

Bilandzic, Dusan, 1986. *Jugoslavija Poslije Tita, 1980-1985*. Zagreb: Globus.

Binder, R., 1993. "Croatia is Said to Oust Many" in the *New York Times*, NY. December 8.

Biszku, Béla, 1975. "A munkásosztály vezetö szerepe, a szocialista demokrácia" in *Társadalmi Szemle*, No. 4.

Blażyca, George and Ryszard Rapacki (eds.), *Poland Into the 1990s. Economy and Society in Transition*. London: Pinter.

Blażynski, George, 1987. *Towarzysze zeznaja: z tajnych archiwow Komitetu Centralnego: dekada Giereka, 1970-1980 w tzw. Komisji Grabskiego*. London: Polska Fundacja Kulturalna.

Blejer, M.I. and A. Gelb, 1992. "Persistent Economic Decline in Central and Eastern Europe. What are the Lessons?" in *Transition. The Newsletter About Reforming Economies*. The World Bank, Vol. 3, No. 7. July-August.

Bobbio, Norberto, 1990. *L'utopia capavolta*. Turin: La Stampa.

1994. *Destra e sinistra. Ragioni e significanti di una distinzione politica*. Romea: Donzelli.

Boniecki, Jerzy, 1992. "Niesamowity rok 1991" *Kultura*. 3. Warsaw.

Borba, 1990. Belgrade, April 10 (Translated by Radio Free Europe).

Bowers, Stephen R., 1984. "Stalinism in Albania. Domestic Affairs Under Enver Hoxha." *East European Quarterly*. No. 4.

Bożyk, Pawet, 1989. *Marzenia i Rzeczywistość. Czy Gospodarskę Polska Mogżna Zreformować*. Vol. I. Warsaw: Panstwowy Instytut Wydawniczy.

Bożyk, Pawet (ed.), 1988. *Global Challenges and East European Responses*. Warsaw: PWN, Polish Scientific Publishers.

Brahm, Heinz, 1970. *Der Kreml und die CSSR, 1968-1969*. Stuttgart, Berlin, Cologne, Mainz: Kohlhammer.

Bromke, Adam, 1985. *Eastern Europe in the Aftermath of Solidarity*. Boulder: East European Monographs; New York: Distributed by Columbia University Press.

Brooks, Karen and Mieke Meurs, 1994. "Romanian Land Reform 1991-93" in *Comparative Economic Studies*. Vol. 36. No. 2. Summer.

Brown, James F., 1991a. *Surge to Freedom. The End of Communist Rule in Eastern Europe*. Durham and London: Duke University Press.

1991b. "The Resurgence of Nationalism" in *Radio Free Europe. Reports on Eastern Europe*. No. 2, No. 24. June 14.

Brubaker, Rogers, 1990. "Távozás, tiltakozás és lojalitás Kelet-Németországban." *Társadalmi Szemle*. No. 4.

Brezezinski, Zbigniew K., 1961. *The Soviet Bloc, Unity and Conflict*. New York: Praeger.

1990. *The Grand Failure. The Birth and Death of Communism in the Twentieth Century*. London: Macdonald.

Bugajski, Janusz, 1987. *Czechoslovakia, Charter 77's Decade of Dissent*. New York: Praeger.

Bugajski, Janusz and Maxine Pollack, 1989. *East European Fault Lines. Dissent, Opposition, and Social Activism*. Boulder: Westview Press.

Bulletin of Atomic Scientists. 1946. May 1.

Caliu, Ion Pompiliu, 1993. Interview in *Europa*. Bucharest, Vol. IV. No. 155. December 7-15.

Carlton, David, 1981. *Anthony Eden, a Biography*. London: Allen Lane.

Carroll, Lewis, 1976. *Alice's Adventures in Wonderland* and *Through the Looking Glass*. Harmondsworth: Puffin Books.

Ceaușescu, Nicolae, 1968. *Cuvîntare la adunarea generale a scriitorilor, 16 noembrie 1968*. Bucharest: Editura Politică.

1969. *România pe drumul desavirșirii construcției socialiste. Rapoarte, cuvîntari, articole. Ianuarie 1968-martie 1969*. Bucharest: Editura Politică.

1981. *Socialist Democracy in Romania*. Bucharest: Meridiane Pub. House.

CEER, 1994. *Central European Economic Review*. Wall Street Journal Europe Publication. Vol. 2. No. 3. Summer.

Chapman, Colin, 1968. *August 21st, The Rape of Czechoslovakia. With on the Spot Reports from Prague by Murray Sayle*. Philadelphia: Lippincott.

Checinski, Michael, 1982. *Poland, Communism, Nationalism, Anti-Semitism*. New York: Karz-Cohl Publishers.

Chervenkov, Vlko, 1954. Report at the party congress in *Shesti kongress na Blgarskata komunisticheska partija*. Sofia.

Churchill, Winston, 1948-53. *The Second World War*. Boston: Houghton Mifflin. Vol. VI.

1974. *Winston S. Churchill. His Complete Speeches, 1897-1963*. Ed. by Robert Rhodes James. New York: Chelsea House. Vol. VII. 1943-9.

Ciocarlie, Alin Theodor, 1991. "Starea economiei risca sa compromita privatizarea" in *Adevarul*. Bucharest, Vol. I. No. 470. August 22.

Cohen, Lenard J., 1992. *Regime Transition in a Disintegrating Yugoslavia. The*

Law-of-Rule vs. the Rule-of-Law. Pittsburgh: University of Pittsburgh, Center for Russian and East European Studies.

Congress, 1970. *American Congress' Joint Economic Committee Papers*. Washington, DC.

Connor, Walter D., 1979. *Socialism, Politics, and Equality. Hierarchy and Change in Eastern Europe and the USSR*. New York: Columbia University Press.

Connor, Walter and Piotr Ploszajski with Alex Inkeles and Wlodzimierz Weselowski (eds.), 1992. *The Polish Road from Socialism. The Economics, Sociology and Politics of Transition*. Armonk: M.E. Sharpe.

Cornea, Doina, 1991. *Scisori deschise și alte texte*. Bucharest: Humanitas.

Crawford, Beverley, 1993. *Market, States, and Democracy. The Transformation of Communist Regimes in Eastern Europe and the Former Soviet Union*. Working Paper. Berkeley: Center for German and European Studies.

Crocker, David A., 1983. *Praxis and Democratic Socialism: The Critical Social Theory of Marković and Stojanović*. New Jersey: Humanities Press.

Curry, Jane Leftwich, 1980. *The Polish Crisis of 1980 and the Politics of Survival*. Santa Monica: Rand Corporation.

Curry, Jane Leftwich (ed.), 1983. *Dissent in Eastern Europe*. New York: Praeger.

Csurka, István, 1992. in *Magyar Fórum*. Budapest, August 20.

Czerwinski, Edwards and Jaroslaw Piekalkiewicz (eds.), 1972. *The Soviet Invasion of Czechoslovakia. Its Effects on Eastern Europe*. New York: Praeger.

Daniels, Robert V. (ed.), 1962. *A Documentary History of Communism*. Vol. II. Vintage Press.

Davies, Norman, 1986. *Heart of Europe. A Short History of Poland*. Oxford, New York: Oxford University Press.

Dawisha, Karen, 1988. *Eastern Europe, Gorbachev, and Reform. The Great Challenge*. Cambridge, New York: Cambridge University Press.

Deacon, Bob et al., 1992. *The New Eastern Europe. Social Policy Past, Present and Future*. London, Newbury Park: Sage Publications.

Demographic Yearbook. 1950-90. New York: United Nations.

Desai, P., 1993. in the *New York Times*. December 10.

Deutscher, Isaac, 1967. *Stalin. A Political Biography*. London, New York: Oxford University Press.

Dewavrin, André, 1947. *2e Bureau Londres par Colonel Passy*. Monte Carlo: Raoul Solar.

The Dialogues of Plato. 1897. New York: Scribner's. Vol. II.

Djilas, Aleksa, 1991. *The Contested Country. Yugoslav Unity and Communist Revolution, 1919-1953*. Cambridge, Mass.: Harvard University Press, Russian Research Center Studies, No. 85.

Djilas, Milovan, 1962. *Conversations with Stalin*. New York: Harcourt Brace Jovanovich.

1980. *Tito. The Story from Inside*. New York: Harcourt Brace Jovanovich.

1983. *The New Class. An Analysis of the Communist System*. San Diego: Harcourt Brace Jovanovich.

1984. "Hungary and Yugoslavia" in Béla Király et al. (eds.), *The First War Between Socialist States: The Hungarian Revolution of 1956 and Its Impact*.

New York: Brooklyn College Press. Distributed by Columbia University Press.

Dodic, Lazar, 1970. *Historischer Rückblick auf die Stellung Albaniens im Weltkommunismus 1941-1968.* Trittau/Holst.: Scherbarth.

Donáth, Ferenc, 1980. *Reform and Revolution. Transformation of Hungary's Agriculture, 1945-1970.* Budapest: Akadémiai Kiadó.

Drakulic, Slavenka, 1993. *Balkan Express. Fragments from the Other Side of War.* New York: W.W. Norton & Co.

Dubček, Alexander, 1968. "Nadále pujdeme cestu nastoupenou po lednu" in *Rudé Právo.* July 19.

Dudás, József, 1956. Statement in *Magyar Függetlenség.* Budapest, November 1.

Dybowski, S. 1953. *Problemy rewolucji kulturnej w Polsce Ludowej.* Warsaw.

Echikson, William, 1992. "Bloc Buster" in L.H. Legters (compiled), *Eastern Europe. Transformation and Revolution, 1945-91. Documents and Analyses.* Lexington: D.C. Heath.

Economic Survey of Europe in 1991-1992. 1992. New York: United Nations.

Eddie, Scott M., 1994. "The Transition to Market Economies. Lessons from Hungary and the Case for Pessimism" in David Good (ed.), *Economic Transformations in East and Central Europe.* London, New York: Routledge.

Ehrlich, Éva and Gábor Révész, 1991. *Összeomlás és rendszerváltás Kelet-Közép-Európában.* Budapest: Institute of World Economics. Manuscript.

——— 1994. "Economic Difficulties and Pitfalls of Transformation: A Case Study on the Czech, Slovak, Polish, and Hungarian Republics" in Ivan T. Berend (ed.), *Transition to a Market Economy at the End of the 20th Century.* Munich: Süosteuropa-Gesellschaft.

Enrlich, Éva and Gábor Révész, 1996. "Structural Change in Hungarian Economy in the Frist Phase of Transition, 1989–1993," in: I.T. Berend (ed.) *Long-term Structural Changes in Transforming Central and Eastern Europe.* Munich: Sudosteuropa-Gesellschaft (forthcoming).

Engelberg, S. and J. Ingram, 1993. "Now Hungary Adds Its Voice to the Ethnic Tumult" in the *New York Times.* January 25.

Eötvös, József, 1978. "Diary" in *Történelmi Szemle.* Budapest, No. 2.

Euro-East, 1994. Brussels: European Information Service, No. 25. September 19.

European Marketing Data and Statistics. 1990. London: Euromonitor.

Fehér, Ferenc and Ágnes Heller, 1983. *Hungary 1956 Revisited. The Message of a Revolution – A Quarter of a Century After.* London, Boston: Allen & Unwin.

Fenyö, E.A., 1950. "Lengyelországi beszámoló" in *Szabad Müvészet.* Budapest, No. 3-4.

Fertilizer Yearbook 1986, 1987, 1990. Rome: FAO.

Ferge, Zsuzsa, 1996. "Is the World Falling Apart? A View from the East of Europe," in: I.T. Berend (ed.) *Long-term Structural Changes in Transforming Central and Eastern Europe.* Munich: Sudosteuropa-Gesellschaft (forthcoming).

Fischer, Mary Ellen, 1989. *Nicolae Ceausescu. A Study in Political Leadership.* Boulder: L. Rienner Publishers.

Fischer-Galati, Stephen A., 1967. *The New Rumania. From People's Democracy to Socialist Republic.* Cambridge, Mass: MIT Press.

388   Bibliography

1970. "The Socialist Republic of Rumania" in Peter A. Toma (ed.), *The Changing Face of Communism in Eastern Europe*. Tucson: University of Arizona Press.

Fishlow, Albert, 1986. "The East European Debt Crisis in the Latin American Mirror" in Ellen Comisso and Laura D'Andrea Tyson (eds.), *Power, Purpose, and Collective Choice. Economic Strategy in Socialist States*. Ithaca, NY: Cornell University Press.

Fleischman, Janet, 1989. *Destroying Ethnic Identity. The Hungarians of Romania*. New York: Helsinki Watch Committee, Human Rights Watch.

Földes, István, 1973. "Fogadatlan prókátorok" in *Népszabadság*. December 24.

Fontaine, André, 1968-9. *History of the Cold War*. New York: Pantheon Books.

Food Consumption Statistics 1964-78. Geneva: ILO.

Fowkes, Ben, 1993. *The Rise and Fall of Communism in Eastern Europe*. Basingstoke: Macmillan; New York: St. Martin's Press.

Frankland, Mark, 1990. *The Patriots' Revolution. How East Europe Won its Freedom*. London: Sinclair-Stevenson.

Frunza, Victor, 1990. *Istoria Stalinismului în România*. Bucharest: Humanitas.

G-24, 1995. *G-24 Scoreboard of Assistance*. Commitments to the CEEC 1990-4. Brussels.

Gati, Charles, 1990. *The Bloc that Failed. Soviet-East European Relations in Transition*. Bloomington: Indiana University Press.

Gazeta, 1989. *Gazeta Wyborcza*. September 29.

Georgescu, Vlad (ed.), 1985. *Romania. 40 Years (1944-1984)*. New York: Praeger.

Gerö, Ernö, 1952. *A vas acél és gépek országáért*. Budapest: Szikra Kiadó.

Gheorghiu-Dej, Gheorge, 1953. in *Elöre*. Cluj, August 25.

Gibney, Frank, 1959. *The Frozen Revolution. Poland: A Study in Communist Decay*. New York: Farra, Straus and Cudahy.

Gierek, Edward, 1980. Raport na *VII. Zjazd PZPR. 11-15 lutego 1980. Podstawowe dokumenty i materialy*. Warsaw.

Glenny, Misha, 1990. *The Rebirth of History. Eastern Europe in the Age of Democracy*. Harmondsworth: Penguin.

1992a. *The Fall of Yugoslavia. The Third Balkan War*. London, New York: Penguin.

1992b. "The Massacre of Yugoslavia" in *The New York Review of Books*. January 30.

1993. "Is Macedonia Next?" in *The New York Times*. July 30.

Goldfarb, Jeffrey, C., 1992. *After the Fall. The Pursuit of Democracy in Central-Europe*. New York: Basic Books.

Goldstucker, Eduard, 1979. Interview in George R. Urban (ed.), *Communist Reformation. Nationalism, Internationalism, and Change in the World Communist Movement*. New York: St. Martin's Press.

Gomulka i inni, 1987. *Dokumenty z Archiwum KC 1948-82*. London: Aneks.

Gottwald, Klement, 1954. *Selected Speeches and Articles, 1929-1953*. Prague: Orbis.

1981. *K vojenské politice KSC*. Prague: Nase Vojsko.

Greenhous, S., 1993. "IMF May Loosen Conditions for Aid to Russia. Call for a Social System" in the *New York Times*. December 22.

Gtowacki, Andrzej, 1990. *Kryzys polityczny 1970 roku*. Warsaw: Instytut

Wydawniczy Zwiazkow Zawodowych.

Hacker, J. 1983. *Der Ostblock. Entstehung, Entwicklung und Struktur 1949-1980.* Baden-Baden: Nomos Verlag.

Hahn, Frank V., 1993. "Incomplete Market Economies" in *Proceedings of the British Academy. 1991 Lectures and Memoirs.* London: Oxford University Press.

Hammond, Thomas T., 1982. *Witnesses to the Origins of the Cold War.* Seattle: University of Washington Press.

Hassner, Pierre, 1976. "Postwar Western Europe: The Cradle of Eurocommunism?" in Rudolf L. Tokes (ed.), *Eurocommunism and Détente.* New York: New York University Press.

Háy, Gyula, 1956. "Az emberi méltóság diadala" in *Irodalmi Ujság.* Budapest, May 5.

Hayden, Robert M., 1992. *The Beginning of the End of Federal Yugoslavia. The Slovenian Amendment Crisis of 1989.* Pittsburgh: The Center for Russian & East European Studies, University of Pittsburgh.

Havel, Václav, 1985. *The Power of the Powerless. Citizens Against the State in Central and Eastern Europe.* Ed. by J. Keane. London, Melbourne, Sydney, Auckland, Johannesburg: Hutchinson.

1991. *Open Letter. Selected Writings 1964-1990.* Selected and edited by Paul Wilson. New York: Knopf.

1992. "Paradise Lost" in *The New York Review of Books.* April 9.

Haveman, J., 1992. "Silver Curtain: Economies Decaying" in *Los Angeles Times.* August 11.

Hegedüs, András, 1988. *A történelem és a hatalom igézetében.* Budapest: Kossuth Kiadó.

Held, Joseph (ed.), 1993. *Democracy and Right-Wing Politics in Eastern Europe in the 1990s.* Boulder: East European Monographs.

Helsinki Watch, 1992. *War Crimes in Bosnia-Hercegovina.* New York: Human Rights Watch.

Hendrych, Jiři, 1960. in *Vytvárné umeny,* Prague, No. 10.

Hiányzó lapok 1956 tötenetéböl. Dokumentumok a volt SzKP KB levéltárából. 1993. Budapest: Móra Ferenc Kiadó.

Hobsbawm, Eric, 1990. *Nation and Nationalism Since 1780. Programme, Myth, Reality.* Cambridge: Cambridge University Press.

Hodos, George H., 1987. *Show Trials. Stalinist Purges in Eastern Europe, 1948-1954.* New York: Praeger.

Hoffman, Eva, 1993. *Exit into History. A Journey Through the New Eastern Europe.* New York: Viking.

Holzer, Jerzy, 1984. "*Solidarność,*" *1980-1981 – geneza i historia.* Paris: Instytut Literacki.

Horowitz, Irving Louis, 1986. "The Jews and Modern Communism. The Sombart Thesis Reconsidered" *Modern Judaism.* No. 1.

Horváth, Ágnes and Árpád Szakolczai, 1992. *The Dissolution of Communist Power. The Case of Hungary.* London, New York: Routledge.

Hoxha, Enver, 1980. *Speeches, Conversations, and Articles 1969-70.* Tirana.

1986. *The Artful Albania. Memoirs of Enver Hoxha.* Edited by Jon Halliday. London: Chatto & Windus.

Hungary in Transformation to Freedom and Prosperity. Economic Program Proposal of the Joint Hungarian-International Blue Ribbon Commission. 1990. Indianapolis: Hudson Institute.

Husák, Gustáv, 1977. *Revolucni odborové hnuti a Unor 1948.* Prague: Prace.

1979. *Válogatott beszédek, cikkek.* Budapest: Kossuth Kiadó.

1981. "Prednesená generálnim UV KSC soudruhem Gustávem Husákem na XVI. Sjezdu KSC dne 6. dubna 1981" in *Zpráva o cinnosti strany a vyvoji spolecnosti od XV. sjezdu KSC a dalsi ukoly strany.* n.p.: Svoboda.

Iglesias, Enrique V., 1985. "Latin America: Crisis and Development Options" in Colin I. Bradford, Jr. (ed.), *Europe and Latin America in the World Economy.* New Haven: Yale University, CIAS.

Industrial Statistics Yearbook, 1990. Vol. II. (and *Yearbook of Industrial Statistics.* Vol. II. 1969, 1981.) New York: United Nations.

Institute of Jewish Affairs, 1986. *The Use of Antisemitism Against Czechoslovakia. Facts, Documents, Press Reports.* London: World Jewish Congress.

Ionescu, D. 1990. "Quest of a Model: Development Strategies Under Discussion" in *Radio Free Europe. Report on Eastern Europe.* Vol. 1. No. 39. September 28.

Ionescu, Ghita, 1964. *Communism in Rumania, 1944-1962.* London, New York: Oxford University Press.

Irodalmi Ujság, Budapest, 1955. December 10.

Islam, Shafiqul and Michael Mandelbaum (eds.), 1993. *Making Markets. Economic Transformation in Eastern Europe and the Post-Soviet States.* New York: Council on Foreign Relations Press.

Isusov, Mito, 1990. *Poslednata Godina na Traicho Kostov.* Sofiia: Izd-vo "Khristo Botev."

Jaruzelski, Wojciech, 1992. "Jaruzelski, defending record, says his rule saved Poland" in *The New York Times,* May 20.

Jaszi, Oszkar, 1961. *The Dissolution of the Habsburg Monarchy.* Chicago: University of Chicago Press.

Jegyzökönyv ... 1991. "A lakitelki tanácskozas jegyzökönyve." Part I. and II. in *Társadalmi Szemle.* Budapest, No. 2. February; No. 3. March.

Jezierski, Andrzej, 1971. *Historia gospodarcza Polski Ludowej 1944-68.* Warsaw: PWN.

Kádár, János, 1983. "Folytatjuk a bizalomra épült nyilt és öszinte politikát." in *Népszabadság,* Budapest, April 30.

Kamm, H., 1992. "Nation Split, Havel Aspires to a New Political Life." in *The New York Times,* September 30.

1993a. "To the Gypsies Death is a Neighbor and so is this Implacable Hatred" in *The New York Times,* October 27.

1993b. in *The New York Times,* November 17.

Kaplan, Karel, 1978. *Dans Les Archives du Comite Central. Trente ans de Secrets du Bloc Sovietique.* Paris: A. Michel.

1986. *Die Politischen Prozesse in der Tschechoslowakei 1948-1954.* Munich: Oldenbourg.

1990. *Report on the Murder of the General Secretary.* Columbus: Ohio State University Press.

Karadzić, Radovan, 1992. Interview in *Los Angeles Times,* August 30.

Karpinski, Jakub, 1982. *Countdown. The Polish Upheavals of 1956, 1968, 1970, 1976, 1980.* New York: Karz-Cohl.

Karta, 1977. "Karta praw i obowiazków rzemiseslnika" in *Prazolnicza gospodarska nieuspoleczniona. Wydzial Geografii i Studiów Regionalnych.* Warsaw: UW.

Kaser, Michael, 1965. *Comecon. Integration Problems of the Planned Economies.* London: Oxford University Press.

Kaser, Michael C. (ed.), 1987. *The Economic History of Eastern Europe 1919-1975.* Vol. III: Institutional Change Within a Planned Economy. New York: Oxford University Press.

Kaser, Michael C. and Janusz G. Zielinski, 1970. *Planning in Eastern Europe. Industrial Management by the State.* London: Bodley Head.

Kaufman, Michael T. 1987. *Mad Dreams, Saving Graces. Poland. A Nation in Conspiracy.* New York: Random House.

Kecskeméti, Paul, 1961. *The Unexpected Revolution. Social Forces in the Hungarian Uprising.* Stanford: Stanford University Press.

Kéthly, Anna, 1956. "Szociáldemokraták vagyunk!" in *Népszava*, Budapest, November 1.

Kifner, J., 1993. "An Outlaw in the Balkans is Basking in the Spotlight" in the *New York Times*, November 23.

Kimball, Warren F. (ed.), 1984. *Churchill & Roosevelt. The Complete Correspondence.* Princeton: Princeton University Press.

Király, Béla, Barbara Lotze, and Nándor F. Dreisziger (eds.), 1984. *The First War Between Socialist States. The Hungarian Revolution of 1956 and its Impact.* New York: Brooklyn College Press.

Koestler, Arthur, 1941. *Darkness at Noon.* London: Macmillan.

Komócsin, Zoltán, 1974. "Változatlan politikával" in *Népszabadság*, Budapest, March 23.

Konrád, George, 1984. *Antipolitics.* London: Harcourt Brace Jovanovich.

Konrád, George and Ivan Szelenyi, 1979. *The Intellectuals on the Road to Class Power.* New York: Harcourt Brace Jovanovich.

Kopátsy, Sándor, 1993. "Gazdaságpolitikai úttévesztés" in *Napi Gazdaság*, Budapest, November 17.

Kopecky, Václav, 1950. in *Vytvárné umeny*, Prague, No. 1.

Korbonski, Andrzej, 1965. *Politics of Socialist Agriculture in Poland, 1945-1960.* New York: Columbia University Press.

Kornai, János, 1959. *Overcentralization in Economic Administration.* Oxford: Oxford University Press.

1980. *Economics of Shortage.* Amsterdam, New York: North-Holland.

1992a. *The Socialist System. The Political Economy of Communism.* Princeton: Princeton University Press.

1992b. in *Magya Hírlap*, Budapest, December 24.

1993. "Anti-Depression Cure for Ailing Postcommunist Economies" in *Transition. The Newsletter About Reforming Economies.* The World Bank, Vol. 4, No. 1. February.

Kousoulas, George D., 1965. *Revolution and Defeat. The Story of the Greek Communist Party.* London: Oxford University Press.

Kovács, Béla, 1956. Statement in *Kis Ujság*, Budapest, November 1.

Kovács, István (ed.), 1985. *Az Európai Népi Demokráciak Alkotmányai*. Budapest: Közgazdasági és Jogi Kiadó.

Kowalik, Tadeusz, 1989-90. "Toward a Mixed Socialist Economy" *International Journal of Political Economy*. No. 4.

1992. *Creating Economic Foundation for Democracy*. Paper, presented at UCLA, manuscript.

1994. "The 'Big Bang' as a Political and Historical Phenomenon: A Case Study on Poland" in Ivan T. Berend (ed.), *Transition to a Market Economy at the End of the 20th Century*. Munich: Südosteuropa-Gesellschaft.

Koźmiński, Andrzej K., 1992. "Transition from Planned to Market Economy: Hungary and Poland Compared" in *Studies in Comparative Communism*. Vol. 25. No. 4. December.

Krajowa, 1978. *Krajowa konferencja PZPR. Podstawowe dokumenty i materialy*. Warsaw.

Kuczynski, W., 1990 *Po wielkim skoku*. Warsaw: PWE.

Kuroń, Jacek, 1978. *Zasady ideowe*. Paris: Instytut Literacki.

1982. *Polityka i odpowiedzialnosc*. London: Aneks.

Kusin, Vladimir V., 1971. *The Intellectual Origin of the Prague Spring. The Development of Reformist Ideas in Czechoslovakia, 1956-1967*. Cambridge: Cambridge University Press.

Lange, Oscar, 1958. *The Political Economy of Socialism*. The Hague: Van Keulen.

Lazar, D., 1956. "In pragul unei etape noi" in *Arta plastica*. No. 1. Bucharest.

Legters, Lyman H., 1992. *Transformation and Revolution, 1945-1991. Documents and Analyses*. Lexington: D.C. Heath.

Lenárt, Jozef, 1980. *Vybrane prejavy a state*. Vol. I. (1949-72), Bratislava: Nakladatel'stvo Pravda.

Lendvai, Paul, 1969. *Eagles in Cobwebs. Nationalism and Communism in the Balkans*. New York.

1988. *Hungary. The Art of Survival*. London: I.B. Tauris.

Lewis, Paul G. 1984. "Legitimation and Political Crisis: East European Developments in the Post-Stalin Period" in Paul G. Lewis (ed.), *Eastern Europe: Political Crisis and Legitimization*. London: Croom Helm.

Lewis, Paul G., (ed.), 1984b. *Eastern Europe. Political Crisis and Legitimation*. London: Croom Helm.

Linden, Ronald, 1991. "The Appeal of Nationalism" in *Radio Free Europe. Reports on Eastern Europe*. Vol. 2, No. 24. June 14.

Lipset, Seymour Martin. 1960. *Political Man. The Social Bases of Politics*. Garden City: Doubleday.

Lipski, Jan Józef. 1985. *KOR. A History of the Workers' Defense Committee in Poland, 1976-1981*. Berkeley: University of California Press.

Loebl, Eugen, 1976. *My Mind on Trial*. New York: Harcourt Brace Jovanovich.

Logoreci, A., 1977. *The Albanians*. London: Victor Gollancz.

Lomax, Bill, 1976. *Hungary 1956*. New York: St. Martin's Press.

Lomax, Bill, 1984. "The Quest for Legitimacy" in Pual G. Lewis (ed.), *Eastern Europe: Political Crisis and Legitimization*. London: Croom Helm.

Lomax, Bill, (ed.), 1980. *Eye-witness in Hungary. The Soviet Invasion of 1956*. Nottingham: Spokesman.

Lopinski, Maciej-Marcin and Wilk Moskit-Mariusz, 1984. *Konspira*. Paris: Editions Spotkania.

Los Angeles Times, 1993. December 6.

Losonczi, Agnes, 1974. *Zene – Ifjúság, Mozgalom*. Budapest.

Lovas, István-K. Anderson, 1984. "State Terrorism in Hungary: The Case of Friendly Repression" in Paul G. Lewis (ed.), *Eastern Europe: Political Crisis and Legitimization*. London: Croom Helm.

Lovenduski, Joni and Joan Woodall, 1987. *Politics and Society in Eastern Europe*. Bloomington: Indiana University Press.

Luard, Evan (ed.), 1964. *The Cold War, a Re-appraisal*. London: Thames and Hudson.

Lukacs, John, 1961. *A History of the Cold War*. Garden City: Doubleday.

Maddison, Angus, 1989. *The World Economy in the 20th Century*. Paris: OECD.

Maddison, Angus, 1994. "Explaining the Economic Performance of Nations, 1820-1989" in W. Baumol, R. Nelson, and E. Wolff (eds.), *Convergence of Productivity. Cross-National Studies and Historical Evidence*. Oxford: Oxford University Press.

1995. *Monitoring the World Economy 1820-1992*. Paris: OECD.

Magaš, Branka, 1993. *The Destruction of Yugoslavia. Tracking the Break-Up 1980-92*. London, New York: Verso.

Major, Nándor, 1993. "Volt e jobb megoldás Jugosláviában?" in *Népszabadság*, Budapest, July 28.

Marer, Paul. 1993a. "The Economy of Hungary: Retrospective and Prospective," Bloomington, Indiana. Manuscript.

Marer, Paul, 1993b. "Economic Transformation in Central and Eastern Europe" in *Making Markets. Economic Transformation in Eastern Europe and the Post-Soviet States*. Ed. by S. Islam and M. Mandelbaum, New York: Council on Foreign Relations Press.

Marer, Paul et al., 1991. *Historically Planned Economies. A Guide to the Data*. Washington, DC: The World Bank.

Marx, Karl, 1966. *Critique of the Gotha Programme*. Moscow: Progress.

Marx, Karl and Friedrich Engels, 1970. *The German Ideology*. New York: International Publishers.

Mason, David S., 1992. *Revolution in East-Central Europe. The Rise and Fall of Communism and the Cold War*. Boulder: Westview Press.

Mastny, V. (ed.), 1988. *Soviet-East European Survey, 1986-87. Selected Research and Analysis from Radio Free Europe/Radio Liberty*. Boulder: Westview Press.

Mienecke, Friedrich, 1922. *Weltbürgertum und Nationalstaat. Studien zur Genesis des deutschen Nationalstaates*. Munich: Oldenbourg.

Michnik, Adam, 1983. "List z Mokotowa – grudniowe rekolekcje" in *Krytyka. Kwartalnik Polityczny*, 16.

1985. *Takie czasy – rzecz o kompromisie*. London: Aneks.

1993. "Ja jestem polskim inteligentem. An interview with A. Michnik by Adam Krzeminski and Wieslaw Wladyka." *Polityka*. No. 6.

Mikolajczuk, Stanislaw, 1948. *The Rape of Poland. Pattern of Soviet Aggression*. New York: Whittlesey House.

Minc, Alain, 1992. *The Great European Illusion. Business in the Wider Community.* Oxford: Blackwell.

Mlynař, Zdenek, 1980. *Nightfrost in Prague. The End of Humane Socialism.* New York: Karz Publishers.

Moeller van den Bruck, Arthur, 1931. *Das dritte Reich.* 3rd edn. Hamburg: Hanseatische Verlagsanstalt.

Molyneux, Guy, 1993. "Conservatives: Are They Now Softheaded?" in *Los Angeles Times*, October 17.

Monticone, Ronald C., 1986. *The Catholic Church in Communist Poland, 1945-1985. Forty Years of Church-State Relations.* New York: East European Monographs.

More, Thomas, 1975. *Utopia.* Cambridge: Cambridge University Press.

Muc, Mira, 1993. Interview, in *Napi Gazdaság*, Budapest, June 5.

Muller, Jerry Z., 1982. "Communism, Anti-Semitism and the Jews." *Commentary.* No. 2.

Nagy, Imre, 1957. *On Communism. In Defence of the New Course.* London: Thames and Hudson.

Nagy, Pongrác. 1993. "Van-e forráskiáramlás Magyarországrol?" in *Napi Gazdaság.* Budapest, July 9.

Narkiewicz, Olga A., 1990 *Patrification and Progress. Communist Leaders in Eastern Europe, 1956-1988.* London: Harvester Wheatsheaf.

National Accounts Statistics: Main Aggregates and Detailed Tables 1988, 1990. New York: United Nations.

Nelson, Daniel N., 1995. "Syndromes of Public Withdrawal in Postcommunism." *Transition. The Newsletter about Reforming Economies.* Washington, DC: The World Bank. Vol. 6, No. 1-2. January-February.

Németh, László, 1956. "Emelkedö nemzet" in *Irodalmi Ujság.* Budapest, November 2.

Ners, Krzysztof J. and Ingrid T. Buxell, 1995. *Assistance to Transition Survey.* Warsaw: Pecat.

New York Times, 1946. September 18.

1993. "The Urgency of Aiding Russia" Editorial, January 27.

1994. July 6.

Nitze, Paul H., 1989. *From Hiroshima to Glasnost. At the Center of Decision - A Memoir.* New York: Grove Weidenfeld.

Nove, Alec, 1995. "Economics of Transition: Some Gaps and Illusions" in B. Crawford (ed.), *Markets, States, and Democracy.* Boulder: Westview Press.

Nuti, Domenico M., 1993. "How to Contain Economic Inertia in the Transitional Economies?" in *Transition. The Newsletter About Reforming Economies.* The World Bank. Vol. 3, No. 11. December 1992-January 1993.

Nyers, Rezsö, 1968. *Gazdaságpolitikánk és a Gazdasági Mechanizmus Reformja.* Budapest: Kossuth Kiadó.

Ordung, Nikoloaj, 1996. "Structural Changes in a Tranforming Economy: The Case of the Czech Republic," in: I.T. Berend (ed.) *Long-term Structural Changes in Transforming Central and Eastern Europe.* Munich: Sudosteuropa-Gesellschaft (forthcoming).

Palairet, Michael, 1994. "The Rise and Fall of Yugoslav Socialism. A Case Study of the Yugo Automobile Enterprise 1954-92" in *Economic Transformations in East and Central Europe. Legacies from the Past and Policies for the Future.* Ed. by David F. Good, London-New York: Routledge.

Pasic, Najdan, 1987. *The Political Articulation and Aggregation of Plural Interests in Self-Management Systems. The Case of Yugoslavia.* Washington: East European Program, European Institute, Wilson Center.

Pelikan, Jiři, 1971. *The Secret Vysokany Congress. Proceedings and Documents of the Extraordinary Fourteenth Congress of the Communist Party of Czechoslovakia, 22 August 1968.* London: Allen Lane.

1976. *Socialist Opposition in Eastern Europe. The Czechoslovak Example.* New York: St. Martin's Press.

Perlez, J., 1993. "Western Ventures Helping East's Phones to Ring" in the *New York Times*, December 21.

Ploss, Sidney I., 1986. *Moscow and the Polish Crisis. An Interpretation of Soviet Policies and Intentions.* Boulder: Westview Press.

Polaczek, Stanistaw, 1993. "Polityka pieniezna panstwa w latach 1989-92" in *Kultura*, 5.

Polanyi, Karl, 1964. *The Great Transformation. The Political and Economic Origins of our Time.* Beacon Hill, Boston: Beacon Press.

Polanyi, Mihael, 1969. "The Message of the Hungarian Revolution" in *Knowing and Being. Essays.* Ed. by Marjorie Grene. Chicago: University of Chicago Press.

Popper, Karl R., 1950. *The Open Society and its Enemies.* Princeton: Princeton University Press.

Portes, Richard, 1993. "From Central Planning to a Market Economy" in *Making Markets. Economic Transformation in Eastern Europe and the Post-Soviet States.* Ed. by S. Islam and M. Mandelbaum, New York: Council on the Foreign Relations Press.

Poznanski, Kazimierz Z, 1986. "Economic Adjustment and Political Forces: Poland since 1970." in E. Comisso and L. D'Andrea Tyson (eds.), *Power, Purpose, and Collective Choice. Economic Strategy in Socialist States.* Ithaca, NY: Cornell University Press.

Poznanski, Kazimierz Z. (ed.), 1993. *Stabilization and Privatization in Poland. An Economic Evaluation of the Shock Therapy Program.* Boston: Kluwer Academic Publishers.

Pravda, Alex (ed.), 1992. *The End of the Outer Empire. Soviet-East European Relations in Transition, 1985-1990.* London, Newbury Park, Calif.: Sage Publications.

Pravda, Alex and Blair A. Ruble, 1986. *Trade Unions in Communist States.* Winchester: Allen & Unwin.

Pravda, 1947. June 16.

Pravda, 1948. Editorial. January 28.

Pravda, 1956. July 22.

Productivity Yearbook, 1949-90. Rome: FAO.

Provoláni, 1968. "Provoláni Cs. predstavitelu vsemu ceskoslovenskému lidu!" in *Rudé Právo*, September 11.

Průcha, Vaclav a kolektiv, 1977. *Hospodárské dejiny evropskych socialistickych zemí.* Prague: Svoboda.

Pryor, Frederic L., 1985. *A Guidebook to the Comparative Study of Economic Systems.* Englewood Cliffs, NJ: Prentice Hall.

Przeworski, Adam, 1986. In *Transition from Authoritarian Rule. Comparative Perspectives.* ed. by Guillermo O'Donell, Philippe C. Schnitter, Laurence Whitehead. Baltimore: Johns Hopkins University Press.

1991. *Democracy and the Market: Political and Economic Reforms in Eastern Europe and Latin America.* Cambridge: Cambridge University Press.

Radio Free Europe, 1989a. The broadcast of Radio Warsaw, February 6, 1989. In *Radio Free Europe Research.* Vol. 14. No. 9. March 3. Part IV. of 4 parts.

1989b. *Radio Free Europe Research.* Vol. 14. No. 48. December 1. Part IV. of 4 parts.

1989c. *Radio Free Europe Research.* Vol. 14. No. 50. December 15. Part I. of 3 parts.

1989d. *Radio Free Europe.* Vol. 14. No. 51. December 22. Part II. of 2 parts. Background report/229.

1989e. *Radio Free Europe.* Vol. 14. No. 40. October 6. Part IV. of 4 parts.

1989f. *Radio Free Europe.* Vol. 14. No. 50. December 15.

Radnóti, Sándor, 1979. "*A szamizdat jó dolog, de . . . Részlet egy Kenedi Jánoshoz irott levélböl.*" Paris: Magyar Füzetek, No. 3.

Raina, Peter, 1969. *Wladyslaw Gomulka: zyciorys polityczny.* London: Polonia Book Fund.

1978. *Political Opposition in Poland 1954-1977.* London: Poets and Painters Press.

Rákosi, Mátyás, 1949. Speech at the Budapest Party Activ, *Szabad Nép,* Budapest, October 1.

Rakovski, Marc (Gy. Bence and J. Kiss), 1978. *A szovjet tipusú társadalom.* Paris: Magyar Füzetek. No. 2.

Rakowski, Mieczystaw F., 1981a. *Przesilenie Grudniowe. Przycznek do Dziejów Najnowszych.* Warsaw: Panstwowy Instytut Wydawniczy.

1981b. *Rzeczpospolita na progu lat osiemdziesiatych.* Warsaw: Państowy Instytut Wydawniczy.

Rechowicz, Henryk, 1977. *Boleslaw Bierut, 1892-1956.* Warsaw: Panstwowe Wydawnictwo Naukowe.

Reforma, 1981. *Reforma gospodarcza: Główne kierunki i sposób realizacji.* Warsaw: Polskie Towarzystwo Ekonomistów.

Reisen, Helmut, 1985. "Disequilibrium Prices and External Debt: An Empirical Analysis for 1978-1984" in Colin I. Bradford, Jr. (ed.), *Europe and Latin America in the World Economy,* New Haven: Yale University, CIAS.

Report, 1952a. On the Slansky trial. In *Rudé Právo,* November 20.

1952b. On the Slansky trial. In *Rudé Právo,* November 24.

Resolution, 1956a. "Az MDP KV határozata, 1956 junius 3." In *Szabad Nép,* Budapest, July 1.

1956b. "Az MDP KV határozata, 1956 július 18-21." In *Szabad Nép,* Budapest, July 23.

Révai, József, 1952. *Kulturális forradalmunk kérdései.* Budapest: Szikra Könyvkiadó.

Rogers, Everett M., 1986. *Communication Technology. The New Media in Society.* New York: Free Press, London: Collier Macmillan.

Romania, 1989. *România Liberă*, Bucharest, January 17.

1991. *România Mare*, Bucharest, May 31.

Romazewski, Zbigniew, 1990. "Trudne drogi demokracji" in *Kultura*, Warsaw, 9.

Rothschild, Joseph, 1989. *Return to Diversity. A Political History of East Central Europe Since World War II*, New York: Oxford University Press.

Rousseau, Jean-Jacques, 1983. *On the Social Contract: Discourse on the Origin of Inequality; Discourse on Political Economy.* Indianapolis: Hackett Publishing Co.

Rudé Právo, 1968, April 10.

Rumler, Miroslav, 1968. "Aktualnost nemarxistickych modelu rustu" in *Rudé Právo*, Prague, July 11.

Rupnik, J., 1984. "The Military and 'Normalization' in Paul G. Lewis, (ed.), Poland" in *Eastern Europe. Political Crisis and Legitimation.* London: Croom Helm.

Rykowski, Zbystaw and Wiestaw Wtadyka, 1989. *Polska Próba-Paxdziernik '56.* Kraków: Wydawn. Literackie.

Rzeczpospolita. 1990. Warsaw, February 22.

Sachs, Jeffrey D., 1992. "Honnan jöhetnek a százmilliárdok. Eszrevételek Berend T. Iván tanulmányához" in *Népszabadság*, Budapest, January 11.

Sanford, George, 1986. *Military Rule in Poland. The Rebuilding of Communist Power, 1981-1983.* New York: St. Martin's Press.

Sartori, Giovanni, 1991. "Rethinking Democracy: bad polity and bad politics" in *International Social Science Journal.* No. 129. August. Blackwell Journals UNESCO.

Schatz, Jaff, 1991. *The Generation. The Rise and Fall of the Jewish Communists of Poland.* Berkeley: University of California Press.

Schönfelder, Bruno, 1987. *Sozialpolitik in den sozialistischen Ländern.* Munich: G. Olzog.

Schumpeter, Joseph A., 1961. *Konjunkturzyklen. Eine theoretische, historische und statistische Analyse des kapitalistischen Prozesses.* Göttingen: Van der Hoeck & Ruprecht.

1976. *Capitalism, Socialism, and Democracy.* London: Allan and Unwin.

Seton-Watson, Hugh, 1952. *The East European Revolution.* 2nd edn. London: Methuen.

Shafir, Michael, 1985. *Romania. Politics, Economics and Society. Political Stagnation and Simulated Change.* London: Pinter.

Shawcross, William, 1990. *Dubcek and Czechoslovakia, 1968-1990.* London: Hogarth Press.

Šik, Ota, 1968. *Plan a trh za socializmu.* Prague: Academia.

Simecka, Milan, 1984. *The Restoration of Order. The Normalization of Czechoslovakia, 1969-1976.* London: New York, Verso.

Simons, M., 1993. "Wary Czechoslovaks Prepare to Give Up Free Health Care" in the *New York Times*, December 17.

Sipos, Aladár and Halmai Pál, 1993. "Jelenkori agrárproblémák" in *Magyar Tudomány*, Budapest, No. 2.

398   Bibliography

Široký, Viliam, 1953. in *Plánované Hospodarstvi*, Prague, No. 9-10.
Skilling, H. Gordon, 1966. *The Governments of Communist East Europe*. New York: Crowell.
1976. *Czechoslovakia's Interrupted Revolution*. Princeton: Princeton University Press.
Skvorecky, Josef, 1968. *Nachrichten aus der CSSR. Dokumentation der Wochenzeitung "Literarni Listy" des Tschechoslowakischen Schriftstellerverbandes Prag, Februar-August 1968*. Frankfurt am Main: Suhrkamp.
Slingova, Marian, 1968. *Truth Will Prevail*. London: Merlin.
Social Indication of Development, 1989. Washington, DC: IBRD.
Sokorski, W., 1952. "Zadania wspotczesnej plastyki" in *Przegląd Artystyczny*, Warsaw, No. 1.
Soós, Károly Attila, 1986. *Terv, kampány, pénz*. Budapest: Közgazdasági és Jogi Kiadó.
Soós, László (ed.), *As MSzMP KB 1989-évi jegyzökönyvei*. Budapest: Magyar Országos Levéltár. Vol. I.-II.
Soska, K., 1966. "Dve Koncepce Rozvoje Ceskoslovensko Ekonomiky." *Hospodarske Noviny*, Prague, No. 26.
Staar, Richard Felix, 1988. *Communist Regimes in Eastern Europe*. 5th edn. Stanford: Hoover Institution Press.
Stalin, Joseph V., 1947. *Problems of Leninism*. Moscow: Foreign Languages Press.
Stanciu, Radu Lucian, 1991. in *Europa*, Bucharest, Vol. II. No. 33. July.
Stark, David, 1992. "Can Designer Capitalism Work in Central and Eastern Europe?" in *Transition. The Newsletter About Reforming Economies*. The World Bank, Vol. 3, No. 5. May.
Statistical Yearbook, 1973-89. Paris: UNESCO.
Statistical Yearbook 1987, 1990. New York: United Nations.
Statisticheskoj ezhegodnik stran-chlenov SEV, 1990. Moscow: Sekretariat SEV.
Stokes, Gail (ed.), 1991. *From Stalinism to Pluralism. A Documentary History of Eastern Europe Since 1945*. New York: Oxford University Press.
Suedosteuropa in Weltpolitik und Weltwirtschaft der Achtziger Jahre, 1983. Herausg. von Roland Schoenfeld. Munich: R. Oldenbourg Verlag.
Suny, Ronald Grigor, 1987. "Second-Guessing Stalin. International Communism and the Origin of the Cold War." *Radical History Review*.
Svitak, Ivan, 1990. *The Unbearable Burden of History. The Sovietization of Czechoslovakia*. Prague: Academia.
Syrop, Konrád, 1957. *Spring in October. The Polish Revolution of 1956*. London: Weidenfeld and Nicolson.
Szabad Müvészet, 1952. Budapest, No. 7.
Szabad Nép, 1956. Budapest, October 7.
Szajkowski, Bogdan, 1983. *Next to God-Poland. Politics and Religion in Contemporary Poland*. London: Frances Pinter.
Szász, Béla, 1979. *Minden Kényszer nélkül. Egy müper kórtörténete*. 2. kiadás. Munich: Griff.
Szegi, P., 1950. "A müfajok gazdagsága" *Szabad Müvészet*, Budapest, No. 9.
Szelenyi, Ivan, 1983. *Urban Inequalities under State Socialism*. Oxford: Oxford University Press.

Szentiványi, József, 1973. "Interview" in *Társadalmi Szemle*, No. 1, Budapest.

Szücs, Jenö, 1985. *Les Trois Europes*. Paris: Editions l'Harmattan.

Taras, Raymond (ed.), 1992. *The Road to Disillusion. From Critical Marxism to Post-Communism in Eastern Europe*. Armonk: M.E. Sharpe.

Tardos, Tibor, 1956. "Önálló kommunista gondolkodást!" in *Irodalmi Ujság*, Budapest, April 7.

Teichova, Alice, 1988. *The Czechoslovak Economy, 1918-1980*. London, New York: Routledge.

Terziiski, Petur, 1984. *Sotsialiticheska Bulgariia v Dati i Subitiia, 1944-1984. Khronika*. Sofia: Nauka i izkustvo.

Theodoru, Radu, 1993. "Sinteze" in *Europa*, Bucharrest, Vol. IV. No. 156. December 14-20.

Timár, Mátyás, 1975. *Reflections on the Economic Development of Hungary, 1967-73*. Leyden: A.W. Sijthoff.

Time Magazine. 1990a June 18.

Tismaneanu, Vladimir, 1992. *Reinventing Politics. Eastern Europe from Stalin to Havel*. New York: Free Press, Toronto: Maxwell Macmillan Canada, New York: Maxwell Macmillan International.

Tokes, Rudolf L. (ed.), 1978. *Eurocommunism and Détente*. New York: New York University Press.

1979. *Opposition in Eastern Europe*. London: Macmillan.

Tomaszewski, Jerzy, 1989. *The Socialist Regimes of East Central Europe. Their Establishment and Consolidation, 1944-67*. London, New York: Routledge.

Torańska, Teresa, 1987. *Oni*. New York: Harper & Row.

Tossiza, Evangelos Averoff, 1978. *By Fire and Axe. The Communist Party and the Civil War in Greece 1944-49*. New York: Caratzas Brothers.

Transition, 1992. *Transition. The Newsletter about Reforming economies*. The World Bank, Vol. 3. No. 5. May.

Trojanowicz, Zofia (ed.), 1981. *Poznański czerwiec 1956*. Poznań: Wydawnictwo Poznanskie.

Troxel, L., 1993. "The Political Spectrum in Post-Communist Bulgaria" in *Democracy and Right-Wing Politics in Eastern Europe in the 1990s*. Ed. by J. Held, Boulder: East European Monographs.

Truman, Harry S., 1955-6. *Memoirs*. Garden City: Doubleday. Vols. I-II.

Tylecote, Andrew, 1992. "Core-Periphery Inequalities in European Integration, East and West" in Wolfgang Blaas and John Foster (eds.), *Mixed Economies in Europe. An Evolutionary Perspective on their Emergence, Transition and Regulation*. Aldershot, Brookfield, Ve.: Edward Elgar.

Tymowski, Andrzej (ed.), 1982. *Solidarity under Siege*. New Haven: D.H. Back Press.

Tyson, Laura D'Andrea, 1980. *The Yugoslav Economic System and Its Performance in the 1970s*. Berkeley: University of California Press.

Ulc, O., 1993. "The Role of the Political Right in Post-Communist Czech-Slovakia" in *Democracy and Right-Wing Politics in Eastern Europe in the 1990s*. Ed. by J. Held, Boulder: East European Monographs.

Ungheanu, Mihail, 1992. "Pirateria Istoriografică" in *Vremea*. Bucharest, Anul I. No. 83. December 10.

Urban, J. 1992. " A süketek vaksága" in *Népszagadság*. Budapest, August 1.

Vallin, Jacques and Alan Lopez (eds.), 1985. *La Lutte Contre la Mort. Influence des politiques sociales et des politiques de santé sur l'evolution de la mortalité*. Paris: Presses Universitaires de France.

Vámos, Tibor, 1991. *Alámerült alépítmény*. Budapest, manuscript.

Verdery, Katherine, 1991. *National Ideology Under Socialism, Identity and Cultural Politics in Ceausescu's Romania*. Berkeley and Los Angeles: University of California Press.

Volgyes, Ivan, 1991. "Hirek, hiedelmek, vélemények" in *Népszabadság*. November 16.

Vucinich, Wayne S. (ed.), 1982. *At the Brink of War and Peace. The Tito-Stalin Split in a Historic Perspective*. Boulder: Social Science Monograph, Brooklyn College Press.

Weber, Max, 1978. *Economy and Society. An Outline of Interpretive Sociology*. Ed. by G. Roth and C. Wittich. Vol. I. Berkeley: University of California Press.

Weisskopf, T., 1993. "Letter to the Editor" in the *New York Times*. December 6.

Wheaton, Bernard and Zdenek Kavan, 1992. *The Velvet Revolution. Czechoslovakia, 1988-1991*. Boulder: Westview Press.

Williams, C.J., 1991. "Turmoil in Leadership Traps. Balkans in a Vicious Cycle. *Los Angeles Times*. November 12.

Williams, C.J., 1993. "Hungary's Premier Antall Hangs On" in *Los Angeles Times*. December 6.

Wojciechowski, A., 1957. "Ostrożnie-świeżo malowane!" *Przeglad Artystyczny*. No. 2. Warsaw.

Wolicki, Krzysztof, 1992. "Rozmowa z Professor Ewą Letowską" in *Kultura*. Warsaw, 3.

World Tables 1984-90, 1990. Washington, DC: The World Bank.

Yugoslavia's Way. The Program of the League of the Communists of Yugoslavia. 1958, New York: All Nations Press.

Xydis, Stephen G., 1963. *Greece and the Great Powers 1944-47*. Salonikia: Institute for Balkan Studies.

Zacsek, Gyula, 1992. "Termeszek rágják a nemzetet, avagy gondolatok a Soros kurzusról és a Soros-birodalomrol" in *Magyar Fórum*. Budapest, September 3.

Zhdanov, A.A., 1952. *A müvészet és filozófia kérdéseiröl*. Budapest: Szikra Könyvkiadó.

Zinner, Paul E., 1956. *National Communism and Popular Revolt in Eastern Europe. A Selection of Documents on Events in Poland and Hungary, February-November, 1956*. New York: Columbia University Press.

Zinner, Tibor, 1991. "Törvénytelen szocializmus. A Tényfeltáró Bizottság Jelentése" *Uj Magyarország*. Budapest, May 30-June 17.

Zivot Strany. 1989. Prague. No. 9.

Zycie, 1985. *Zycie Gospodarcze*. Warsaw. No. 23.

Zycie Warszawy. 1981. June 11.

Names index

Subject index

abortions 204
Afghanistan 238
agriculture 207
  Bulgaria 344
  central planning 77–8
  employment 184–5, 190, 193
  Hungary 102, 149, 343–4
  investment 162, 193
  isolated market 195
  labor productivity 195
  modernization 193–4
  output 194–5
  Poland 115–16, 161, 344
  production structure 195
  restructuring 314
  Yugoslavia 98, 161
  see also collectivisation; food
Albania 65
  anti-government riots 308–9
  bloody revolution 287
  civil war 16
  communist takeover 15–16
  constitution 50–1
  economic decline 345
  elections 308
  national Stalinism 95, 174
  New Course 105
  non-reforming 278
  privatization 334
  rejects anti-Stalinization 127–9
anti-Semitism 67–71, 366–9
  Czechoslovakia 68–9, 175–6
  Hungary 368–9
  Poland 69–70, 175–6, 241–2, 260
  Romania 368
  see also Jews
architecture 88
arms race 233, 234
atomic bomb 29–31
Austria 106
automobile industry 224–5, 325, 358

Balkan federation 59, 64

banking system 73–4, 269, 323, 326
Belgium 27
Berlin blockade 35
birth rates 201–2
Bolshevism 40
  see also Marxism
Bosnia
  elections 307–8
  independence 375
  see also Yugoslavia
Bulgaria 4
  agriculture 344
  anti-government riots 308–9
  bogus reform 280
  Bulgarization 175
  constitution 50–2
  cultural policy 89–90
  democratic coalitions 19
  dissidents 247
  foreign investment 333–4
  leadership changes 289–90
  nepotism 289
  New Course 104
  non-reforming 278, 279–80
  political parties 306–7
  privatization 333–4
  social policy 166–7
  Soviet intervention 22–3
  tobacco 344–5
  transition 333–4
  Writers' Union 104

cars *see* automobile industry; consumption
central planning 41–3, 74–9
  abolished 161
  agriculture 77–8
  deviation punished 56
  and foreign trade 77–8
  incentives 76–7
  production index and indicators 76
  target bargaining 75
China 128, 131
class *see* society

Lightning Source UK Ltd.
Milton Keynes UK
UKOW02n0725241116

288399UK00006B/52/P

9 780521 550666